The Generation of Plays

The *Generation of Plays*

Yorùbá Popular Life in Theater

Karin Barber

Indiana University Press
BLOOMINGTON & INDIANAPOLIS

Publication of this book is made possible in part with the assistance of
a Challenge Grant from the National Endowment for the Humanities,
a federal agency that supports research, education, and public
programming in the humanities.

This book is a publication of
Indiana University Press
601 North Morton Street
Bloomington, IN 47404-3797 USA

http://www.indiana.edu/~iupress

Telephone orders 800-842-6796
Fax orders 812-855-7931
Orders by e-mail iuporder@indiana.edu

© 2000 by Karin Barber

All rights reserved

*No part of this book may be reproduced or utilized in any form or by any means,
electronic or mechanical, including photocopying and recording, or by any information
storage and retrieval system, without permission in writing from the publisher. The
Association of American University Presses' Resolution on Permissions constitutes the
only exception to this prohibition.*

*The paper used in this publication meets the minimum requirements of American
National Standard for Information Sciences — Permanence of Paper for
Printed Library Materials, ANSI Z39.48-1984.*

Manufactured in the United States of America

Library of Congress Cataloging-in-Publication Data

Barber, Karin.
　The generation of plays : Yorùbá popular life in theater / Karin Barber.
　　p.　cm.
　Includes bibliographical references and index.
　ISBN 978-0-253-21617-5
　　1. Theater—Nigeria.　2. Traveling theater—Nigeria.　3. Oyin Adéjọbí
Theater Company (Nigeria)—History.　4. Yorùbá drama—History and
criticism.　5. Yorùbá (African people)—Social life and customs.　I. Title.

PN2993.4 .B37 2000
792'.089'96333'0669—dc21

00-040740

1　2　3　4　5　　05　04　03　02　01　00

For Barbara and Charles Barber

CONTENTS

Acknowledgments   ix
A Note on Orthography   xi

1 Introduction:
   Yorùbá Popular Theater from the Ground Up   1
2 The History of a Founder, a Genre, and a Public   18
3 The Actors   62
4 Getting a Show on the Road   93
5 The Generation of Plays   131
6 Filling Out a Play   172
7 Audiences   204
8 Television, Film, and Video   240
9 The World of the Work: Place, Gender, and Politics   265
10 Literacy, "Enlightenment," and "Tradition"   306
11 Work, Destiny, and Self-Making   348
12 Language and the Moral Public   399
13 Conclusion: The Lessons of Example   422

Appendix 1: Synopses   435
Appendix 2: Yorùbá Text of a
Scene from *Taking Care of Kúnlé*   443
Notes   447
Bibliography   463
Index   475

ACKNOWLEDGMENTS

This book has taken so long to write that its subject matter has become historical more or less by default. This was a good thing in a way, because it encouraged me to take a long view of a subject I had originally envisaged as a very immediate, in-depth immersion in a contemporary genre. I began doing fieldwork with the Oyin Adéjọbí Company in 1981, assisted by a research grant from the University of Ifẹ̀ (now Ọbáfẹ́mi Awólọ́wọ̀ University), which I acknowledge most gratefully. But the project really began earlier. My original reason for choosing to study in Nigeria was the fame of Yorùbá theater of all kinds—masquerades, literary theater, popular theater. When I got there, however, I changed my dissertation topic to Yorùbá oral poetry, since it was so clear that genres such as *oríkì* were the bedrock of all the modern popular forms. So by the time I started working with Mr. Oyin Adéjọbí and the Adéjọbí Theater Company I had already finished my doctoral dissertation and was working as a lecturer in the Department of African Languages and Literatures at the University of Ifẹ̀. The climate of Yorùbá scholarship there—conducted in Yorùbá and addressed to a Yorùbá readership—provided an indispensable context and an enduring inspiration for my work. Conversations with colleagues at Ifẹ̀ were formative, and I thank Ọlábíyìí Yai, Akínwùmí Ìṣọ̀lá, Ọlásopé Oyèláràn, and 'Bíọ́dún Jéyìífò in particular. I am especially indebted to Báyọ̀ Ògúndíjọ, who worked with me as transcriber, went on some theater trips with me, and over a period of nearly 20 years talked with me about the plays and his interpretations of them in a most illuminating fashion. Other people who helped me at various times included Josy Ajéìígbé Faramádé, Andrew Apter, Délé Láyíwọlá, and the whole Láyíwọlá family. Elio Montanari threw himself into the life of the theater with great panache in order to take the photographs.

Of course my biggest thanks go to the members of the Oyin Adéjọbí Theater Company themselves. Their unfailing generosity, kindness, and hospitality and their good humor through thick and thin made this research project one that gave me almost unalloyed pleasure from start to finish. Oyin Adéjọbí, Grace Adéjọbí, and Emily Adéjọbí in particular were the souls of kindness, and Alhaji Kàrímù Adépọ̀jù and John Adéwuni were unforgettable traveling companions.

The original fieldwork took three years (1981–1984), supplemented by several shorter spells after that. When it came to writing about it, however, the material was so voluminous—and so interesting in itself, quite apart from anything I might want to say about it—that I didn't know where to start. There was the additional question of how to write about plays which most of one's readers have never seen and never will see. What I decided to do was to publish, with Mr Adéjọbí's kind permission and with Báyọ̀ Ògúndíjọ's help, an edition of three of the theater company's plays, transcribed from recordings of live performances and published in Yorùbá with an accompanying English translation. Only after that did I begin to grapple with the question of how to bring audiences, actors, plays, sedimented history, and the archaeological layers of the repertoire into one picture. In 1993–1994, when I spent a year at the Institute for Advanced Study and Research in the African Humanities at Northwestern University, conversations with Catherine Burns, Keith Breckenridge, Catherine Cole, and Stephan Miescher helped me to form an approach. Five years later, when I had a manuscript more or less in hand, I was invited back to teach at Northwestern for a quarter; I took the opportunity of inflicting great chunks of it on my graduate class. To David Donkor, Erin Haney, Erica Immucci, Siri Lange, Christina Nystrom, and Kristin Swenson, my thanks.

Jane Guyer was especially crucial to the development of my thinking, and I can never thank her enough for her perceptive, imaginative, and inspiring suggestions. Stephanie Newell was also a huge help. I am grateful to John Peel and Tom McCaskie for vital guidance at strategic moments. Paulo Farias helped me continually, in ways too numerous to mention.

At Indiana University Press, Dee Mortensen and Kate Babbitt combined impeccable editorial skills with unfailing good humor and sympathy.

Finally, my lifelong enjoyment of all kinds of theater I owe to my parents, Charles and Barbara. This book is dedicated to them with my love.

A NOTE ON ORTHOGRAPHY

In this text I have followed Yorùbá scholarly "best practice" by using full diacritics (tone marks and subdots) on all Yorùbá words, whether these appear as quoted Yorùbá-language texts or as isolated words in the body of the argument.

The exception I have made is in the case of names of cited authors whose works appear in the bibliography. Here I have followed the common practice of marking subdots but not tone marks. This system has been adopted so that bibliographic references will correspond to the form in which they are usually found in databases, library catalogues, and other bibliographies.

When quoting Yorùbá printed texts (e.g., church programs) I have reproduced the original orthography, which usually means omitting many of the tone marks although not the subdots. This is also true of book titles in Yorùbá.

In the English translations of Yorùbá-language interviews and other texts, I have used **bold type** to indicate that the word was in English in the original text; for example, the translation of the sentence "Ó fún mi ní experience" will be rendered "It gave me **experience**."

The Generation of Plays

Oyin Adéjọbí. ©Elio Montanari

1 Introduction: Yorùbá Popular Theater from the Ground Up

Long before the play proper begins, its advent is announced and expectations begin to mount. First there is the "parade" around town, the pink lorry blaring out its announcements over a hand-held megaphone; then the long and insistent sequences of drumming that waft out of the hall while would-be spectators are still hanging around outside making up their minds whether or not to buy tickets; then the long wait while the hall slowly fills up and excitement increases with the density of the crowd; and finally the opening glee. The opening glee is heralded by a pause, darkness as the hall lights are turned off, the slow opening of the curtains, the sight of Adéjobí already seated center stage, often illuminated only with a single spot, and the entry of his chorus, who appear like fluorescent ghosts in the blue light. As they enter, Adéjobí's magnificent voice rises over the hubbub to lead the first song.

Adéjobí then addresses the audience directly, welcoming them, thanking them for coming, sometimes complaining about their small number or congratulating them on turning out in force. He tells them the title of the play. The audience usually responds to his greetings with murmurs or excited shouts. Adéjobí and the chorus then sing four or five more songs, some of which may be greeted by the audience with applause and signs of recognition.

The flimsy curtains, made of many yards of flowery cotton cloth, are drawn again and there is a long pause. Jùjú music comes over the sound system. The audience talks and laughs in the dark. The jùjú music stops. The curtains open, and a world is inaugurated.

POPULAR PRODUCTION

More than 100 professional, popular Yorùbá theater companies plied the roads of western Nigeria in the decade spanning the mid-1970s to the mid-

1980s (Jeyifo 1984). Each of these companies employed a dozen or more paid performers; each had its own repertoire of improvised but carefully planned plays.

This exuberant proliferation of dramatic activity was lifted on the swell of petro-naira in the 1970s. People had cash for entertainment, and in town halls, hotels, community centers, and schools they congregated in large numbers—usually late at night—to participate in the theater companies' activities. The programs were extremely varied. Some companies specialized in mythological dramas, others in moral thrillers set in the contemporary underworld; some were loose-jointed comedies, others were plotted with meticulous logic. Some made extensive use of traditional drumming, dance, and costume; others consisted entirely of contemporary naturalistic dialogue. But they had several things in common. They all represented an extended, worked-out narrative entirely through the actions of dramatic characters put on stage to establish themselves through their own speech, not through the voice of a storyteller. This was a form unknown in Yorùbá culture before the missionary and colonial interventions of the nineteenth century. They all shared an aesthetic of intense impact, achieved by incorporating and juxtaposing dense, concentrated chunks or sequences of dramatic action and display. They all purported to edify their audiences through the demonstration of a "moral lesson." And finally, they all shared a love affair with the Yorùbá language. "*Inú eré lèdèé kù sí*" [It's in the plays that the language survives], said one spectator, and he meant the language in its fullest sense—its idioms, archaisms, innovations, slang, dialectal peculiarities, and its sacred and secret registers.

The people who produced the Yorùbá popular theater did not belong to the social and educational elite. The great majority of the performers, though they had been to school, had not gone far enough to achieve white-collar occupations. They could read and write in Yorùbá but were usually not fluent in English. They were typical of the mobile, entrepreneurial, urban-oriented, aspiring strata which, for want of a better term, have been called the Nigerian "intermediate classes"—usually evoked not by structural definitions but by lists of occupations: tailors, bricklayers, clerks, shoeshine boys, petty traders, taxi drivers. It is a category that is defined by what it is not: not illiterate farmers, on the one hand; not salaried professionals, on the other. These "in-between" people typically went from primary or modern school to apprenticeships in skilled manual trades and then entered the fluid and competitive world of small-scale artisanal production and trade which dominates the economy of Yorùbá cities and towns.

The audiences who went to see their plays were drawn from a wider social range than the performers. The traveling companies would perform in remote rural villages if invited to do so, but they also greatly prized the occasional opportunity to give command performances for elite social clubs and civic associations. Oral and vernacular in medium, this theater was equally accessible to both illiterate and educated people. Some theater groups were so successful that their leaders became stars with a following drawn from the entire population of western Nigeria and beyond. Preeminent among these was Hubert Ògúnǹdé [Ogunde], who became a recognized cultural ambassador abroad and was entrusted at home with the task of establishing a multicultural pan-Nigerian national dance troupe. The theater's attraction for people of all social categories lends credence to the claim that this theater played to "'the people as a whole', rather than to exclusive, partial groupings or strata of the population, as is the case with the modern English-language, literary theatre" (Jeyifo 1984, 2).

But in practice the popular theater's largest and most dependable audience was drawn from the same intermediate section of the population as the performers and was predominantly youthful, poor, and male. The intellectual avant-garde might make an exception for famous troupes such as Ògúnǹdé's, but on the whole it despised the popular theater for its vulgarity and lack of social or political radicalism.[1] Though modern, this theater had little in common with the "art" theater of the universities, which was usually scripted and in English. Though orally improvised, it did not belong to the world of treasured, long-standing indigenous traditions either. Like its producers, it occupied a cultural space defined by what it was not—it fit neither the model of "modern literature" (i.e., written texts in European languages) nor the model of "traditional heritage." For this reason it received little official recognition or support even at the time of its greatest efflorescence. Cultural forms in this unclassifiable zone, despite their stupendous scale and impact, have tended to slip from view in the polarized purview of many scholarly discussions of African culture (see Fabian 1998; Barber 1997c).

This theater was oriented toward the ethos of school, church, progress, and literacy and was dedicated to the transmission of "lessons." But its educative thrust was very far removed from that of conscientization and development theater, which has come to dominate discussions of popular theater in Africa. Pioneered in Latin America but widely adopted as an African theater movement in the 1970s and 1980s (Desai 1990; Kerr 1995; Mda 1993; Mlama 1991), conscientization theater was spearheaded by a radical university-based intelligentsia, and its claims to credibility rest on the degree to which it is able to "involve" and "engage" the peasant participants whose outlook on the world it seeks to transform. The Yorùbá traveling theater did not have this point of departure. Its output would be described by conscientization theorists as "people's" rather than "truly popular" culture: that is, as culture which emanates "in a spontaneous and natural way" from the people (see Etherton 1982, 321) without reflecting their true interests and without opening their eyes to their real historical situation. It could be accused of being politically conservative and often misogynistic.

All the same, this was the theater that people went to in vast numbers across western Nigeria. It spoke of things that concerned them in genres and language of their own choosing. Though not usually politically radical, it was certainly associated with a resilient will to self-betterment. It had an affinity with the vigorous activities of local communities which founded town improvement unions, opened schools, and built roads and bridges without the support (let alone the instigation) of central government throughout the twentieth century. Like other commercial "people's" theater genres in Africa,[2] it drew its ideas from close rapport with its audiences, yet was at times capable of going beyond what they expected.

The popular theater was part of a great Yorùbá-language cultural efflorescence in colonial and post-colonial western Nigeria. Alongside the theater, there was an extraordinary flowering of popular music—*jùjú* from the 1940s to the 1980s, then *fújì*—which influenced the entire continent and reached international audiences (Collins 1985; Waterman 1990a; Barber and Waterman 1995). Popular Yorùbá-language writing, both newspapers and novels, began to find a mass audience as primary education expanded (Ogunṣina 1992), and by the 1970s there was an extensive literary field which encompassed fiction, poetry, and written drama, attracting readers not only in schools but also among the public at large (Iṣọla 1988, 1992; Babalọla 1985). New genres of neo-traditional poetry—broadcast, performed live, and published in books and magazines—became immensely popular in the 1960s and 1970s. The producers of all these genres were drawn from the same "intermediate" strata as the theater. Entrepreneurial, mobile and innovative, they were formed by a dual experience of school and apprenticeship which prepared them for clerkly occupations associated with literacy on the one hand and artisanal, manual work on the other. This dual orientation shaped the production of almost all the new popular Yorùbá cultural forms of the twentieth century. It gave rise to a ferment of productive activity which used the methods and techniques of other small-scale artisanal businesses in the informal sector but which was also imprinted through and through with an aspiration to "enlightenment" and which adopted the speaking position of a preacher or teacher from which to edify the audience.

As artisans, these cultural producers participated in the vigorous small-scale production which proliferated in every Yorùbá town in the colonial period and expanded uncontrollably in the years of the oil boom. They regarded themselves as practical producers who worked with familiar materials to make something that could be sold on the open market. The theater company members always stressed that though what they produced was a *play*, nonetheless what produced it was *work*. The orientation toward production was indeed so powerful that audiences too regarded themselves as producers: their self-appointed task being to actively extract from the dramas the lessons which they could then apply to their own lives.

This scene of intense, proliferating, small-scale productivity is not best approached through consumption-oriented theories of contemporary culture. Especially incongruous to popular culture in West Africa are those theories that assume a radical separation between production (by cosmopolitan technocratic elites) and consumption (by local masses), and which imagine these masses being unilaterally transformed by their exposure to the flow of internationally generated images. Local, small-scale West African producers are socially and physically close to their consumers, sharing much the same social experience and outlook. Indeed, consumption and production themselves are often almost indistinguishable. While active audiences see themselves as *producing* personally applicable lessons, locally produced genres may, conversely, be seen as a *mode of consumption* of other genres, both endogenous and exogenous. Hausa writers "consume" and render locally consumable Hindi musical films by producing romantic novelettes that develop their themes in Hausa (Larkin 1997), while Jímọ̀ Àlíyù's massively popular Yorùbá TV serial *Arélù* "consumed" and rendered consumable esoteric traditional verbal genres such as *ọfọ̀* (incantations) that had never before been so blatantly and extensively exposed in a public arena. In West Africa, then, people continually produce new forms in order to come to grips with the massive transformations of modernity.

The flow of images brought into West Africa by transnational media has certainly been significant in the way people imagine themselves and others and visualize future possibilities and alternatives, in ways suggested by Appadurai's fascinating discussion (1996). But in western Nigeria at least, in the period under study in this book, people's overwhelming preoccupation was with social transformations that were perceived as locally rooted and were actually experienced on the ground—the long-term and far-reaching transformations unleashed by cash-crop farming, urbanization, wage labor, the breakup of the old lineage-based residential compounds, Western education, and conversion to world religions. Such changes were well understood to issue from global power relations—the first half of the twentieth century was nicknamed the era when *ayé dayé òyìnbó*: the world became the world of Europeans. But people still saw these social transformations as being *their* concern and being rooted in *their* own lived experience. It was these locally experienced transformations that set the terms in which images of other lives and other cultures were appropriated—in different ways at different historical moments. And it was these transformations which remained the mesmerizing focus of popular commentary, and which all the new popular genres of the twentieth century— the Yorùbá novel, drama, neo-traditional poetry, visual art, popular music—were created to grapple with. In western Nigeria, as elsewhere in Africa and beyond, it was vernacular genres, representing local experiences, that held people's attention.[3] What popular television audiences gathered in crowds to watch was not *Dallas* but Yorùbá-language drama (see Ẹsan 1994, 252)—drama which drew not only on the conventions of imported forms such as the sitcom but also, extensively, on old oral arts such as praise poetry and incantations, "consuming" both in new acts of production.

If the popular theater companies used artisanal modes of production, they were also working with materials which allowed them greater scope for innovation and experiment than in most artisanal trades. Ideas, narratives, and linguistic extravaganzas could balloon out and shrink away again with extreme rapidity. The theater as a genre underwent rapid expansion, diversification, and transformation and then a sudden and unexpected demise. This vitality and changeableness has been adduced as a characteristic of African popular culture in general (Fabian 1978). The Yorùbá popular theater exploded into life in the 1940s, established its fullest range of generic forms in the 1960s and 1970s, and by the late 1980s had begun to wither away, crushed by the economic collapse and superseded by film and video. This study is therefore able to chart the whole life span of a live theater company over a period of fifty years. While 'Biọdun Jeyifo's study, undertaken at the height of the Yorùbá traveling theater's efflorescence, brilliantly charts the rise and spread of the movement as a whole, the present study focuses on a single company—the Oyin Adéjọbí Theatre. Because the Yorùbá popular theater was so diverse, the Oyin Adéjọbí Theatre cannot be taken as *representative* of the whole movement; but it can be taken as an *example* of it—sharing many features with other groups while deliberately developing its own special characteristics.

THE GENERATION OF PLAYS

Like many popular West African cultural forms, Yorùbá popular theater was open and incorporative in mode, and this made it hospitable to foreign elements.

In the three years during which I worked most concentratedly with the Oyin Adéjọbí Theatre (1981–1984), I was a foreign element myself and was incorporated into the plays not so much for my acting ability as for my novelty value. I was given small parts in numerous stage plays and a larger role in the popular television series *Ilé-ìwòsàn* (*Hospital:* western Nigeria's answer to *Casualty*). By hanging around the company headquarters in Òṣogbo for days at a time, waiting for things to happen; traveling to distant venues with them over car-destroying roads; sleeping on town hall floors and being there when emergencies erupted behind the scenes, I got an impression of how their methods of production actually worked. By seeing and appearing in the same plays over and over, for several years, I began to form a sense of how these plays were changing, where their inner pulse was, what their growing points were: in short, how they were generated.

This method of investigation enabled me to put into practice an approach in the sociology of literature which has been imagined in the past but never, as far as I know, fully implemented. You could call it generative materialism.

Almost all sociology of the arts, by the very nature of its subject matter, starts from the finished "work" and then proceeds to contextualize it. The contextualization may be strongly explanatory, as in the great early Marxist tradition represented by Georg Lukács and Lucien Goldmann and continued in different ways by Pierre Macherey and Terry Eagleton, in which the economic, social, and cultural levels of production are dialectically interrelated in such a way as to explain or interpret the ideological properties of texts.

More recently, there have been essays in contextualization which renounce causal explanations and even the separation, for analytical purposes, of levels of social reality. This is true of the cultural materialism and new historicism of the 1980s and 1990s, which, though in some sense the heir to Marxist sociology of literature, undertook "a radical contextualizing of literature which eliminates the old divisions between literature and its 'background', text and context" (Dollimore and Sinfield 1985, 4), refusing to privilege the literary text above other cultural texts,[4] let alone "explain" one in terms of the other. Even though the field of "text" has here been radically expanded to include laundry lists as well as the first folio, however, the starting point is still completed textual objects.

But Yorùbá popular theater—because it is a living, contemporary, collectively improvised, and continually emergent form—gives one the chance to start from the other end. Instead of taking a finished text and seeking to contextualize it, one can ask how people's lives, practices, and knowledge give rise to certain kinds of texts. One can start from production and inquire how what is produced *comes out of* existing repertoires, procedures, and habits. These include the social formation of the actors themselves, whose experience was the basic material out of which the theatrical work was produced; the artisanal methods of production which the theater shared with other small business concerns in western Nigeria; the textual and ideational materials with which they worked to assemble their dramas—a vast, open-ended repertoire of narratives, themes, and verbal genres, including the resources of written Yorùbá literature and the plays of other theater companies; the presence of an active audience whose responses and interpretations fed the gradually emerging and growing text; and the shared horizons of audience and performers which made possible the projection of certain kinds of persons, certain modes of address, within emergent western Nigerian social strata.

Thus what the plays say, and what they do, can be tracked through multiple inputs into the generative process and can be understood from the ground up, as they come into being.

A generative approach rather like this was proposed by Henri Lefebvre, in *A Critique of Everyday Life*. He suggested that within the general framework of Marxism there are two ways of approaching cultural works. Both seek "the link which exists between what men think, desire, say and believe for themselves and what they are, what they do" (1991 [1947], 145). The more familiar way is to "proceed from ideas to men, from consciousness to being—that is, toward practical, everyday reality—bringing the two into confrontation and thereby achieving *criticism of ideas by action and realities*." But one could also take the opposite course and start by "taking real life as the point of departure in an investigation of how the ideas which express it and the forms of consciousness which reflect it emerge," leading to a "*criticism of life by ideas* which in a sense extends and completes the first procedure" (1991, 145). By grasping and reconstituting the everyday life of a period, Lefebvre seeks to understand how the people who led that life could subscribe to certain forms of consciousness, certain ideologies, which did not necessarily correspond to their own actual experience. Though his quarry is the dubious and treacherous one of "false consciousness," he does not accept the easy explanation that these forms of consciousness were imposed from above by the ruling class. Rather, he asks "How did those illusions which were formulated into ideas by official spokesmen *take shape in the depths of the social sediments and 'strata', in the heart of the 'masses'*? How and why did they accept them?" (1991, 146, my italics). In other words, Lefebvre engages with the popular views which many Marxist critics have been content to dismiss as an imposed false consciousness serving the interests of the dominant class.

As Lefebvre himself pointed out, the "criticism of life by ideas"—the ground-up approach—is complementary to the "criticism of ideas by life"—the approach that starts from completed texts; indeed, it is obvious that in a sense they are interdependent, for the ground-up approach must always have some idea of the "texts" it wishes to illuminate, otherwise one would have no idea of which aspects of "life" to start from. But this complementarity does not mean that generative materialism is simply an elaborately inverted way of doing what sociology of literature has always done. On the contrary, it yields distinctive insights—insights which would not come one's way if one started from the transcribed text of an improvised popular play and set out to "contextualize" it after the event.

Generative materialism focuses on potentiality. When the performers start to devise a new play, infinite possibilities stretch in front of them, suggested rather than constrained by the genre within which they work. What shapes their production is not a consciously mastered set of rules or conventions but a disposition or habituation, a common sense formed through experience and example that tells them that certain things will come off while others won't—always fueled by the responses of the live audience and continually adjusted in their light. Not only is the theater not canonical, it is also consciously actuated by the quest for innovation. It continually goes beyond the permutation of known elements. No rendition of a play or a theme is wholly predictable, for though it will recycle much existing material it will also always exceed it in one way or another.

The improvised Yorùbá theater thus makes exceptionally visible what is true of all forms of cultural production, even those that adhere to much more precisely defined generic conventions. All the extant symphonies of Mozart could be analyzed and the analysis fed into a computer program which would enable one to generate a "new" Mozart symphony which would sound exactly like Mozart. But that computer symphony would lack the one thing that marks all Mozart's real symphonies: the increment. Each one *extends,* however minutely, the range of features we think of as "typical" of Mozart's work. The computer symphony would be drawn from within the existing range and would not extend it; the meristem—the living growth point—would not be there. To assert this is not to cleave to an inappropriate model of "originality" or "genius," but to argue that all models of textual or cultural production which base themselves on the idea of permutations of existing, given elements (formalism and structuralism are the two best known in African Studies) miss the thing that makes these performances and texts worth listening to: the sense that in some way, however slight, they might surprise you. Something might break through the carapace of known form; new historical experience might be struggling to find expression (Medvedev and Bakhtin 1978, 136).

The creatively emergent is not confined to big, long-lasting innovations such as the rise of the novel or the introduction of the picture-frame stage. Critical and creative metalinguistic consciousness is at work even in the briefest and most mundane of everyday utterances (Hanks 1996, 193). Croce goes so far as to argue that the linguistic process is inherently aesthetic, every linguistic act potentially a work of art: "An epigram belongs with art: why not a simple word? A novel belongs with art: why not a brief news item in a newspaper?" (Croce 1992, 14–15). This perspective seems particularly appropriate to Yorùbá textual production, where the "smallest" verbal genres—the proverb and the epithet—are regarded not only as the seeds of all the great literary genres but also as their summation (see Barber 1999).

In the generation of popular Yorùbá plays, every moment and every level of production is a site of creative potentiality. Stories are drawn from available repertoires but are reshaped; characters are excavated from the repositories of the actors' personal experience, which is always incrementally growing; speech emerges from moment to moment, infused with what is current in the streets, adapted in the light of the audience's reactions, adjusted to the speech of the other characters in the scene, and fed by the actor's own inspiration as well as the manager's continually updated instructions. New characters might be added on the spur of the moment if a new performer unexpectedly becomes available; a new speech in one part of the play might instigate inspired echoes in another part. Collective improvisation based on a strong individualism—the desire of each actor to expand and realize the potential of his or her part—gives rise to continual pervasive emergence of novelty in every dimension of performance. A non-generative approach might collect several performances of the same play and analyze the differences as examples of "variation"—as if there were a norm from which the variations deviate. A generative approach envisages a productive field of potentialities, from which multiple performances emerge. At every point, creators of these plays are expanding and concretizing one potentiality and in the process bypassing others.

All Yorùbá performance, formal and informal, is improvisation: which, as Margaret Thompson Drewal puts it in her study of Yorùbá ritual, is "moment-to-moment manoeuvring," where "each move is contingent on a previous move and in some measure influences the one that follows" (1992, 7). Drewal suggests, I think rightly, that Yorùbá philosophical views give a central place to the as yet undecided, the emergent and contingent character of human experience, conceiving of human beings as endowed with generative agency that molds and even instigates that which emerges. If this is so, then the popular theater is a central, highly condensed and vital instantiation of this deep-rooted and pervasive cultural orientation. Maybe this helps to explain why the theater, at its height, enjoyed such extraordinary popular success, while scripted theater never did.

This approach enables us, ultimately, to get at the question of how Yorùbá dramaturgy works: how, out of a diversity of suggestions and possibilities, habits and alternatives, in the shifting, apparently formless, apparently chaotic scene of postcolonial urban Nigeria, clear and complex works do crystallize; the producers do get it together, the show does get on the road. Rather than tracing the strategies of the popular in evasion, irony, and subversion of official institutions, as in Certeau (1984), what seems to be called for in western Nigeria is a way of understanding how ordinary people succeed in establishing and institutionalizing their own unofficial modes of operation and making them work despite the absence of a consistently functioning centralized structure. The creative organizational forms that make possible the rapid assemblage and orchestration of a huge funeral ceremony, the functioning of complex networks of commerce (Guyer 1997), or multi-layered systems of patronage (Barnes 1986) are also what make possible the operations of the theater.

A generative approach not only brings into view the repertoires or fields of argument out of which a play emerges and re-emerges. It also engages with the "traditions of invention" by which such repertoires and fields are continually replenished. For cultural production such as the Yorùbá popular theater is multiplicative and proliferative; it is set up to generate variety and difference, "not only reproducing a finite set of known roles and functions with respect to a 'system of thought' but also endorsing a constant and volatile engagement on its boundless frontiers" (Guyer 1996, 1).

This in turn brings to the fore the importance of genre, which could be understood as an accumulated knowledge of how to generate cultural forms: rules of thumb, dispositions, a sense of what goes with what, what is appropriate in what context. A disappointing feature of Lefebvre's critique of everyday life is that it does not deal with any of the actual genres or cultural works through which ideas are given form. "Ideologies" and "consciousness" float in midair, as if accessible without an understanding of specific conventions of registration and embodiment. But to grasp the meaning of "attitudes," "beliefs," "cultural expressions," and the like, it is crucial to understand *how* things are said, in what words or images, drawing on what repertoires, in response to what conventions. What is required is attention to just how textual forms *work:* a feeling for words and how they are put together, a sense of form, of how action is bodied forth upon the stage, and how the bits of a story cohere. Contrary to what some anthropologists' use of them suggests, fictional and other worked-upon texts are not a kind of raw material from which one can extract data about cosmology or consciousness by penetrating or bypassing their distractingly "literary" features. On the contrary, it is precisely those features—generated in accordance with the conventions of a specific genre—that enable things to be said and enable the listener to interpret them.

Genre conventions function as a guide to cultural producers feeling their way around a field of possibilities. Indeed, they may suggest clumps of possibilities in the first place. (Your first thought might be "I want to stage a play" rather than "I want to demonstrate the consequences of treachery.") Genre suggests, as well as organizes, options. But genre also takes shape through the multiple choices of the artists and is constantly subject to revision. A sense of genre is formed through familiarity with numerous, different examples, and each new work adds another example to the range. If a sense of genre is fundamental to the interpretation of texts—and I believe that it is—a ground-up generative approach puts one in a position to sense the continual incremental transformation of genre, its perpetual openness, which derives from the fact that it is not a set of laws but an accumulated way of doing things that gets changed in the doing (Fowler 1982).

A generative approach makes possible a real "science of the concrete," one which focuses on the concrete itself rather than taking the purpose of analysis to be to map all cultural outputs onto the same deep structures of the mind. A generative approach directs our attention to the detail of the plays, the precise ways in which possibilities are followed through and the "lessons" are concretized. But it does not lead us into a bottomless swamp of ethnographic minutiae, for the questions that animate the inquiry are "What is the detail *for*? How and why is the text set up *like that*?" And this takes us back to general and comparative questions.

A ground-up approach of this type is not a demonstration of method for its own sake, and its aim is not merely to furnish further evidence for the claim that performance is emergent, fluid "repetition with difference." That has already been amply demonstrated by other studies. Rather, its aim is to get at what is significant about these plays, to their performers and to their audiences and therefore to cultural historians—and why it is significant. My assumption is that *what* they signify is inseparable from *how* they signify, and that *how* they signify can only be understood through the process of production. A generative approach, above all, attempts to grasp the phenomenon whole. It attempts to seize all at once the conditions, processes, and outcomes of cultural production, keeping in view the innumerable dialectical links running between them. It avoids compartmentalizing "text" and segregating it from the experiences and productive operations from which it arises and in which it is embedded. Throughout this book, I have tried to attend to the continuities between plays and lives, texts and experiences—and to develop in the process a holistic approach which goes beyond reductive or reflectionist assumptions about the relationship between "art" and "life" without dissolving all social productivity into one all-embracing metaphorical text.

THE EMERGENCE OF PUBLICS AND PERSONS

The history of the theater company and its work illuminates the larger history of the formation of colonial and post-colonial public arenas and ideas about the person. The popular theater was both a product of this history and a key factor in its unfolding. The institutions of colonial culture—schools, churches, organized sports, printed publications, the media—provided the models and the expectations which underpinned the modern popular theater and its characteristic use of time and space. In their mode of address, the popular theater groups participated in the constitution of a new kind of audience, imagined and addressed as a "public," anonymous and of boundless extent. The presence of new kinds of entertainment-seeking crowds in colonial Nigerian cities galvanized the early amateur theater groups into turning themselves into professional, commercial organizations. Traveling theaters in turn, tirelessly seeking fresh customers in every town and village of the Yorùbá-speaking area and beyond, created a mass theater-going audience with well-formed preferences, loyalties, and expectations. Performing in a version of "standard Yorùbá" and giving preference to those themes and oral arts held in common by all the culturally distinct "Yorùbá sub-groups," they contributed to the "cultural work of Yorùbá ethnogenesis" (Peel 1989), that is, to the emergence of a pan-Yorùbá consciousness not known before the rise of cultural nationalism in the colonial era (see also Waterman 1990b).

Perhaps even more important than pan-Yorùbá identity, however, was the fact that this new public was addressed above all as a moral domain. All commentary and all critique was ultimately moral in tenor, and politics was always a sub-category of common morality that applied to everyone. It was in this way that the public's highly heterogeneous components—Muslim, Christian, traditional; salaried, self-employed, unemployed—were aggregated, and non-Yorùbás were implicitly included, even if their lack of the language usually prevented them from participating fully. The moral purview was inclusive, appealing to common sense and to basic human decency. Thus the theater, though exclusively in Yorùbá, considered itself to represent values common to all Nigerians, all Africans, and indeed to all human beings.

The popular theater, in common with the popular Yorùbá novel and popular art, introduced wholly new representational forms into the public domain. These genres projected detailed evocations of lifelike ordinary individuals into everyday, recognizable space, endowing them with a verisimilitude that at first glance looks like European realism—suggesting new inflections of the concept of the person. In their explorations of the consequences of moral action, the Adéjọbí Company's plays undertook extended and repeated investigations into the nature of individual success and failure, into the sources of self-realization. A close look at the texts of these plays enables us to explore what kind "modern self" is in fact projected, and how individuality, autonomy, and agency are conceptualized. The picture they suggest corroborates recent arguments that "modernity" is "a multidirectional, open-ended process" (Breckenridge and Appadurai 1988, 1), "inescapably plural" (Kaviraj 1997, 113). "Everywhere, at every national/cultural site, modernity is not one but many; modernity is not new, but old and familiar; modernity is incomplete and necessarily so" (Gaonkar 1999). The bipolar before-and-after narrative of modernity that traces the emergence of the universal, individualistic, autonomous, post-Enlightenment "modern self" from its particularistic, communalistic, tradition-bound antecedents is called into question by these representations.

"Enlightenment" was indeed a central concept in the self-making of the aspiring intermediate and elite classes in Nigeria. But it did not exactly mean what Kant meant by it. In a field of radical disjunctions, oppositions, and doubling, it involved the attempt to recuperate valued elements from the very ideological repertoires that were being rejected. In the name of civilization, it edited the habitus from within—but as if from an external vantage point—conceptualizing "tradition" as a field while still inhabiting it. "Enlightenment" and its opposition to a previous state of "ignorance" was always an unstable and Janus-faced concept in Yorùbáland. From its earliest recorded uses in the nineteenth century, it had the potential to flip over and stand for its own obverse—the cultural degradation following from the abandonment of traditional ways, as opposed to the benefits of progress and literacy. The editorial project of selection, rejection, and recuperation, then, always contained the potential for a wholesale repudiation of its own goals. At different historical moments in the theater company's work, different readings of the concept of enlightenment came to the fore.

The history of publics and persons emerges from many angles in the course of this study, both in the theater company's mode of engagement with its audiences and in the arguments of its plays. The primary organizing principle of the book is to track, from the ground up, the generation of plays, seeking at every step to retain the continuity between what people "think, desire, say and believe for themselves and what they are, what they do" (Lefebvre 1991, 145). Each chapter also, however, points outward to different dimensions of the larger social and historical environment.

The study starts from a contextualizing historical introduction in Chapter 2 which sets out the parameters within which the theater company, as I met them in 1981, were working and the history which they brought with them. The next five chapters then trace the production of plays, starting in Chapter 3 with the actors themselves and moving through the material and organizational dimensions of the theater company's operation (Chapter 4) to the stages by which a play was created and "filled out" by improvisation and interaction with audiences (Chapters 5, 6, and 7). Chapter 8 shows how the media expanded the theater company's range of address and how the theater company handled this interface with the official and technocratic world. The following three Chapters, 9, 10, and 11, show how various dimensions of the performers' concrete experience were worked through, worked in, and worked out in the content of the plays themselves: Chapter 9 deals with the dramatic use of common experiences of place, gender, authority, and political power; Chapter 10 with the theater company's orientation toward literacy and "enlightenment"; and Chapter 11 with self-fashioning and self-realization. Finally, in Chapter 12 I look at what I personally see as this theater company's greatest achievement, its extraordinary collective and creative control of the Yorùbá language and the ways in which this drew upon and fed into the constitution of a popular moral public arena.

The argument of the book is embedded in very detailed empirical material. But it invites a broadening of the scope of its enquiry through comparison with other cases, parallel or divergent. Such comparative or higher-level analysis could develop in two theoretical dimensions. One is the inquiry into the modes of cultural generation. If what the texts of African popular culture say is interesting; if what they say is inseparable from how they say it; if this in turn is shaped by how these genres are produced, then a comparative approach to African popular culture that merely juxtaposes "texts" is leaving out much that is vital. One could instead begin from the conditions and methods of production, the life situations of the producers, and the audiences to which they address themselves. One could ask, for example, how far artisanal entrepreneurial strata in different countries and contexts adopt similar compositional and improvisatory methods and whether this gives rise to similar conceptions of performance, text, and message.

The second dimension is the historical inquiry into the constitution of a public arena and associated new forms of representation or projection of the person. Were new public arenas constituted in the same way all across Africa—in places where media transmission came much later than it did in Nigeria, in places without an oil boom, in places where people were dispossessed of their means of production and turned into a much more classical waged-labor force than ever happened in coastal West Africa? What are the key parameters in the construction and emergence of new kinds of public space, new kinds of being together in public, new forms of address, new representations of the individual? Is the apparent "realism" and the portrayal of everyday life, found right across the continent in the colonial era in visual and verbal arts, a unified phenomenon or do different situations produce different "realisms"? The present study could thus supply one component in a broader picture of the constitution of modern African public life.

Comparison in a field such as this can only be partial and piecemeal; doing without the assumption that there are discrete, stable entities for comparison; and using tracking rather than mapping procedures—as does the present study itself. In the final chapter I draw together three of the key terms which have proved most useful in tracing the generation of plays—the concepts of experience, example, and potentiality—in the hope that their configurations may have some resonance for other studies too.

Because this book is about the generation of texts out of lives, I have represented the actors' and audiences' views and experiences through extensive quotation of their actual words and in the discussion of the plays have returned incessantly to the transcripts of recordings of actual performances. This means that the book is full of texts. This heavy loading of the discussion with example serves another purpose too. The formerly exuberantly vital Yorùbá popular theater is now all but dead, dormant, or departed into other forms such as video drama. It is sad that it was so inadequately documented before its unpredictable and untimely end. The recordings I made, though a mere drop in the vast ocean of Yorùbá popular theater, probably represent the single largest corpus collected from any theater company's repertoire. I recorded numerous versions of ten of the Adéjọbí Company's live stage plays, having acted in five of them; I saw several others and made notes on them without recording them; I found detailed representations of several more in the "photoplay" magazine *Atọ́ka;* I had access to printed texts for two of the early native air operas staged by the company in the 1950s and early 1960s; and I also made notes on, copied, or purchased recordings of numerous episodes of two television series and several video dramas produced by Adéjọbí or by his manager Alhaji Kàrímù Adépòjù. In addition, I recorded and transcribed a number of interviews with actors and audience members, mostly in Yorùbá.

In order to give a sense of the possibilities and (provisional) limits of the genre, I have had to draw on a wide range of examples throughout the discussion—for genre conventions by definition can only be grasped through exposure to a range of instantiations. One problem with many studies of African popular and oral genres is the over-reliance on a single instance, from which large conclusions are sometimes drawn. My approach, by contrast, depends on being able to form a sense not only of the genre and its conventions, but also of the even larger field of materials, narratives, and arguments that the genre draws upon to constitute itself. Such an array of plots, characters, and scenarios may be bewildering at first. Plot summaries have been provided in an appendix as a guide to the forest of narratives. My hope is that this profusion of text will be entertaining rather than daunting. The material does, at any rate, constitute an archive of sorts, bearing testimony to the efflorescence of a remarkable cultural form in Nigeria's recent past.

When quoting from plays, I have given the text first in Yorùbá (transcribed from recordings) and then in English translation, for my hope is that at least some of my readers will want to get closer to the linguistic creativity of the theater than reliance on a translation alone would allow. Rather regretfully, and purely to lighten the textual freight, I have decided to represent other texts—interviews, oral autobiographies—only in English translation. Much of the colloquial speech of the actors and audiences was peppered with English expressions, which I have indicated in the translation by the use of **bold type.** When the actors and audience members chose to speak in English, this is indicated at the end of the quotation.

This book, then, is mainly about what people said, either directly, in conversation, or indirectly, through the highly worked-upon artifice of lengthy, speech-dominated dramas. When I began this project I had a residual prejudice in favor of "overhearing" rather than "interviewing"; I felt that what people said to each other or said to me in spontaneous and unsolicited conversation would be more valuable than what they said in a formal recorded testimony. I thought immersion in the daily life and activities of the company would tell me more than controlled and demarcated interview sessions. I sat around a lot and did have some very entertaining hours chatting about everything from the servant problem in England to the nature of life after death. But it was only when I made appointments for structured interviews that people began to pour out their life histories and their personal philosophies, vividly and artfully told. I found that in daily talk as in the plays, it was premeditated spontaneity, worked-upon improvisation, framed in accordance with well-established narrative and dramatic genre conventions that enabled people to produce interpretations of experience that satisfied their own requirements. Thus I found out what I should have known already, that just as people's lives infuse their narrative drama, so narrative drama infuses their lives.

2 The History of a Founder, a Genre, and a Public

The history of any Yorùbá popular theater company is told by its founder-proprietor, and follows his life: each company is thought of as having been created by the initiative of one person—almost always a man[1]—and as subsequently belonging to him, embodying his identity and constituting his self-realization as a successful social being. He is seen as a pioneer who took the initiative to convene performers, hold them together through the hard times, and generate the theatrical ideas upon which they exercise their talents. The Oyin Adéjọbí Theatre Company's history could not have been told by anyone except Oyin Adéjọbí himself, and the core of the account that follows is drawn from a long autobiographical narrative he told me soon after I first attached myself to the company. As recounted by him, it is a story of the fulfillment of personal potential in the face of enormous obstacles. For Oyin Adéjọbí was the victim of childhood polio and had entirely lost the use of one leg.

Two other histories, however, unfold pari passu with Oyin Adéjọbí's theatrical life story. One is the history of the genre, which can be at least partially reconstructed from early texts, from the theater company members' memories, and from the survival of elements of earlier styles in some of the plays in the contemporary repertoire. The genre of popular theater Adéjọbí adopted and contributed to had its own internal history of stylistic transformation. Changes in form and content were undoubtedly precipitated by changing social conditions, changing popular preoccupations, and audience demand for novelty; but the range of possibilities open to the theater company at any given point was set by what they and others had been doing before. Conventions could be modified, added to, and even inverted, but not wholly escaped from. In its 40-year history, the Adéjọbí Company moved from a stylized musical theater on Biblical themes in which the entire text was sung—much of it chorally—to an apparently naturalistic theater on themes of everyday life in which the entire text was composed of improvised, lifelike speech. The steps by which this transformation was achieved constitute a history to which the theater company members themselves often alluded and which they would explain, justify, and take pride in or sometimes mildly regret.

The third history is that of the milieu in which Adéjọbí worked and from which he drew his actors and his audiences. The circumscribed civil society of Lagos and Òṣogbo which floated the early theater companies and "inspired" the theater leaders with its enthusiastic support was vastly expanded and diluted following the opening up of primary school education in the mid-1950s and the flow of oil wealth in the late 1960s and the 1970s. Droves of primary school leavers* left home for bigger urban centers, hustled or labored for money while seeking salaried employment, and sought entertainment—and in some cases work—in public halls, hotels, stadiums, and cinemas. The changing composition of their public presented the theater companies with an expanded range of opportunities as well as daunting challenges. The theater, having begun as the amateur creation of a public-spirited Christian elite, became a form of professional mass entertainment plying the roads and colonizing the airwaves of western Nigeria in a ceaseless quest for fresh audiences.

The interactions of these three histories—of the founder, the genre, and the public—were mediated by the emergence of what could be called the sphere of popular cultural production (on analogy—though not a very close one—with Bourdieu's "sphere of literary production"[2]). In the middle to late colonial period a recognizable category of professional popular "artists" became visible—writers, musicians, theater and film workers, and visual artists. Aware of each others' activities and in keen competition for the same audiences (see Jeyifo 1984, 4), they actively cultivated sections of the public, responding to popular taste but also seeking to shape it. This emergent, self-conscious category of producers clustered around charismatic stars (the theater and band leaders, pioneering popular writers and visual artists) who strove to make their own work distinctive. Competition thus fostered diversity and specialization (see Collins 1989) but also encouraged the repetition of successful models, thus consolidating prevailing trends and establishing certain innovations as recognized genres.

The intertwined histories of the Adéjọbí Theatre Company can usefully be divided into three broad phases: a foundational phase (1948–1962) during which the company was created and led by Oyin Adéjọbí as a church-based amateur group performing choral Bible stories to elite Christian audiences; the period of the company's greatest efflorescence (1963–

---

*The term "school leavers" refers to pupils who have attended school for some time and then left—with or without qualifications—to enter the job market. It can be applied to pupils who have left school at any level of primary or secondary education. This usage is well established in Nigeria and has entered academic discourse (see, for example, Callaway 1960).

1988) in which Adéjọbí collaborated with his manager, Alhaji Kàrímù Adépòjù, to run a commercial, professional, traveling theater staging plays on secular, folkloric, and topical themes to vastly expanded, ecumenical audiences; and a period (1988 onward) during which Adéjọbí and Adépòjù parted company as the live theater declined and was replaced by video drama consumed by fragmented and religiously polarized audiences.

FOUNDATIONAL PHASE, 1948–1962

EARLY YEARS IN ÒṢOGBO

Oyin Adéjọbí was born in Òṣogbo in the late 1920s, at a time of intense social transformation. In the span of his father's lifetime can be seen extremes of social experience thrown up by the imposition of colonial rule and the spread of its institutions into the Yorùbá hinterland. The first Church Missionary Society missionaries arrived in Òṣogbo in 1900; the railway, which heralded a commercial revolution in the area, followed in 1905, together with postal services and telegraph; major foreign firms began setting up branches there from 1908 onward; and Òṣogbo became a dynamic commercial center attracting numerous immigrants. Cocoa farming and other cash-crop production—kola, yams, maize, and cassava—were established in the Òṣun area, and because of its location on the railway the town became a major collection center for these cash crops. Cash crop production, wage labor, and the introduction of other new forms of paid employment transformed not only the local economy but also relations between family members, precipitating the breakup of large patriarchal compounds into smaller units headed by self-supporting younger men.[3] In the 1930s, Christian and Islamic conversion accelerated and the availability of formal schooling widened. New economic and social classes emerged, defined by trade and produce buying, by education and white-collar employment, and by new artisanal occupations which, by the 1940s, were practiced by a substantial and organized section of the Òṣogbo population (Schwab 1952, 79).

Old structures of political authority also changed. The Atáọja, the Ọba of Òṣogbo, became the chairman of the town and district council; he shared some of his authority with an elected district councillor and was supported by a stipend from the colonial government rather than exclusively from tribute, taxes, gifts, and fines from his subjects. His chiefs, palace staff, court clerks, and messengers were also paid by the government, so that the old circuits of patronage—by which wealth and power were invested in Ọbas by the people and at least partially redeployed for their benefit—were replaced by an externally supported one-way authority system whose ultimate backing was the colonial police and army.

Adéjọbí's father was a member of the royal lineage of Òṣogbo. According to Adéjọbí, he was a direct descendant of Lárò-oyè, the legendary founder of the town, and he lived up to his status. He had many wives and children, he lent money to people and received many *iwòfà* (pawns or bondsmen) in return, and he had extensive farmlands where these *iwòfà* and other dependants worked. His house was constantly overflowing with visitors; every Friday the Ọba sent his royal drummers to play for him. When a prominent fellow citizen held a festival, Adéjọbí senior would ride out on horseback to greet him. "Every day was like a festival in the house of Adéjọbí," as Oyin Adéjọbí put it. All this evokes a big man of the old style; a man whose greatness depends on "having people" in the form of descendants, dependants, clients, and well-wishers. But Adéjọbí senior was also one of the first converts to Christianity in Òsogbo. He belonged to the exclusive band of the "enlightened" who saw themselves as collaborating, in the face of ignorance and superstition, for the progress of the town. He also moved into the cash crop economy, becoming a leading cocoa grower and subsequently a successful produce buyer for G. B. Ollivant.[4]

His first son, Oyin's oldest half-brother Adéléke Adéjọbí, moved even farther away from the old order. He was a key figure in the Independent church known as the Church of the Lord Aládùúrà, eventually becoming its primate. Adéléke Adéjọbí lived and worked in Lagos for several years and then began extensive missionization trips to Sierra Leone, Ghana, and the Gambia. He was monogamous—married to a "charming young Yoruba wife, who had received a good secondary education and had worked in a Government office in Lagos" (Turner 1967, I:120). He not only traveled to the United Kingdom for training but also envisaged the United Kingdom and the United States as part of a mission field that was potentially global in scope.

Oyin Adéjọbí was thus born into a family where the lives of his father and senior brother straddled the world of the great old compounds headed by patriarchs and the world of the educated, monogamous, mobile new elite; the world of "wealth in people" and the world of "enlightenment"; a world where the Ọba was the unquestioned magnetic center of the social universe and a world where civil servants and churchmen constituted parallel and alternative centers of authority and the Ọba became a symbol of "tradition."[5]

Because he could not walk easily, Oyin's parents at first did not want him to have to struggle to go to school. Instead they apprenticed him to a nearby goldsmith, where he spent three years learning the trade. But by then an aunt—his father's younger sister—had observed Oyin's intelligence and urged his father to send him to school at all costs. Adéjọbí senior was eventually persuaded, and Oyin began to attend All Saints' Primary School, led there on horseback every day by his father's Hausa ostler. He did spectacularly well, progressed rapidly through the classes, and obtained high marks in his Standard VI final examination. He wanted to become a schoolmaster. "After Standard VI in those days a person could become a teacher, and that was to become an important person. It was to become a big man." But when he sought a teaching job he was turned down on the grounds that his infirmity would prevent him from standing at the blackboard. He abandoned the idea of teaching and did not pursue the possibility of continuing at school, even though his older brother Adélékè offered to pay the fees for any grammar school or college of education he chose. Instead he went to live with Adélékè in Lagos; this must have been about 1945 or 1946. Oyin, still in his teens, went to the glamorous capital: "Lagos! The magic name" where "the night spots never shut" (Ekwensi 1961, 167–168).

LAGOS, C. 1945–1953

Lagos in the 1940s was a fertile ground for cultural innovation. Here not only the Yorùbá popular theater but other immensely influential performance genres such as *jùjú* music had their inception. Lagos was the strongest magnet in Nigeria for migrants at that time, and between 1931 and 1950 its population almost doubled (Baker 1974, 33). The resulting population density was intensified by the physical position of Lagos, an island in a lagoon. When Oyin Adéjọbí arrived there, the huge expansion of the settlement onto the mainland was well under way. Ebute Metta, where Adélékè Adéjọbí first settled and founded his first Lagosian church before moving onto the island, was densely populated, and settlements were creeping up the road and railway line into Yaba, Mushin, Ikeja, and Agege. But the center of gravity of Lagos was still the island,[6] and there was consequently a massive concentration of people in a small space, all within reach of the principal central venue for cultural performances. There was no need to take shows to the people, for the people were already there on the doorstep.

This population was highly heterogeneous. Lagos culture had been hierarchically segmented since the nineteenth century, when an Anglicized elite of repatriated Yorùbá slaves made their way back from Sierra Leone, where they had been deposited. These "Saros" constituted an exclusive, highly educated, professional, and mostly Christian elite. At a somewhat lower level were the "Brazilians" or Aguda, repatriated slaves from Brazil and Cuba, who were mainly Catholics and practiced artisanal trades—builders and carpenters who were responsible for some of the most striking architecture in Lagos. These two elites were imposed upon an indigenous pagan population of fishermen and traders, who by the late nineteenth century were becoming predominantly Muslim rather than Christian.[7] From 1920 onward, there was an acceleration in the in-migration of people from other West African countries (especially Ghana) and other parts of Nigeria (especially the Yorùbá hinterland and eastern Nigeria). By 1931 the migrants already outnumbered the resident population. Oyin Adéjọbí was one of hundreds of thousands of young men with primary school qualifications drawn by the commercial opportunities, the educational facilities, and the availability of waged employment in the metropolis. This history of social layering produced a population that was both stratified and exceptionally diverse in terms of religion, class, occupation, and ethnicity. Not only did these people bring in and support a wide variety of specialized performance styles, they also favored the development of new, mixed genres. Furthermore, this population contained an exceptionally high proportion of waged or salaried workers whose routine released them after office or laboring hours into a period of "leisure" and whose pay packets provided them with the means to pay for entertainment.

Lagos was not only the main port but also the colonial government headquarters. Like most capital cities along the West African coast, it was thus the nub of a double articulation, economic and political, between the colonizing country and the hinterland. The population of Lagos was overwhelmingly involved either in administration (as churchmen, and as government workers whose occupations ranged from railwaymen to clerks) or in commerce (ranging from petty traders to major importers, from transporters to accountants). In Lagos primary produce was collected for export and imports were debulked for further distribution. People in Lagos were more attuned than those in the hinterland to the idea of money as the universal solvent and to cultural innovation, including—but not confined to—the arrival of new things from overseas. Lagos was the focal point where new models and new materials for cultural production were first seen.

From the mid-nineteenth century onward, government and commerce needed literate employees and people desired clerical jobs. This impetus drove and sustained educational expansion in Lagos and resulted in the highest concentration of government and missionary school places per head in Nigeria. Since incoming migrants also tended to have at least primary school qualifications, the result was the highest literacy rate in the country (48 percent in 1950: see Baker 1974, 81). The voracious demand for qualifications was not satisfied by official provision, however, and innumerable private institutes, evening classes, and typing schools sprang up to fill the gap. As an advertisement for one such school put it in 1948: "Colony Evening Classes . . . offers grand opportunities to all who can't gain admission into day secondary school" (*Nigerian Daily Times*, January 12, 1948). Oyin Adéjọbí attended two private institutes of this type, arranged through his brother before he arrived in Lagos. One, owned by Mr. Ayọ̀ Oyèésíkù, in Broad Street, taught stenography and accounting. The other was a private music school in Corsair Lane run by a Ghanaian, Kobina Creppy, where Oyin learned to play the piano and organ. Though it was the music lessons that had the greatest consequence in Oyin's life, as his narrative will show, the clerical training allowed him to get his first salaried job. Through a friend of his brother, he obtained a post as a storekeeper and accountant with the international trading concern SCOA.

In the 1940s, Lagosian commerce, though rapidly expanding in volume and international in scale, still had a human face and was still intertwined with older forms of local production. For though growing explosively, Lagos was not yet the vast, dysfunctional conurbation it was later to become—the huge anomic industrial estates at Ikeja and Agege were phenomena of the 1950s and 1960s (see Peace 1979). Such industrial production as there was tended to be old-fashioned and artisanal, and commerce could still be understood as the result of individual enterprise. The expectant population could learn from the newspapers which steamer would arrive on which day. Personal announcements welcomed sons of Lagos who had gone abroad for training and come back as doctors or lawyers, and advertisements announced specific goods that had "just arrived," or had been "just unpacked" or "just opened from bales."

Oyin Adéjọbí's description of his second job in Lagos—also obtained through personal contacts in the church—shows how commerce could be linked to local ingenuity and productivity. One of the biggest markets for imported goods in Lagos was for patent medicines and remedies—Eno's Fruit Salts, Horlicks, Beecham's Pills ("the laxative for the liverish") and innumerable other cures for every condition. Adéjọbí was employed by the founder and proprietor of Broadway Chemists: an artisanal pharmaceutical factory and retail outlet right in the heart of Lagos, which, apparently stimulated by the success of the innumerable importers, provided homemade remedies which were able to satisfy local wants.

> He made me the Factory Superintendent. Because we had a very extensive factory.... They made APECS powder. They made **Worm Expeller.** And what was that medicine for pregnant women called? **ASP.** No—**AST.**[8] There were a lot of ladies working there, and young men. So, my table would be here, as I'm sitting, and the factory reached out to about there [indicates the distance]. Tables here, tables there. They would give each of us different kinds of work, some would be wrapping **APECS Powder,** others would be pouring the **AST** into bottles, others would be decanting the **Worm Expeller.** As some were pouring it, others would be sticking on the labels saying **"Broadway Chemists."** And such like. People would be quickly packing them. At that time.

The proprietor of this cottage industry was a kindly patron and paternalist who took a liking to Oyin, providing him with a "room and parlor" in his own compound in Broad Street when Adéléke Adéjọbí left Lagos to carry out his missionary work abroad. So, like traditional craft production in Nigeria, Broadway Chemists took charge of the entire process of production, including packaging, advertising, and retailing, and it took at least some personal interest in its employees; but its stimulus was imported products, with which it successfully competed to meet old wants in a new way.

CULTURAL PRODUCTION IN LAGOS

If the presence of a crowded, waged, educated, and heterogeneous population at the hub of Nigeria's commerce stimulated cultural production in the Lagos of the 1940s, it also gave it a specific form. Entertainments—records, films, musical instruments, troupes of artistes—were among the most eagerly awaited imports from Europe in 1940s Lagos. But people did not merely consume what was brought to them in the merchant steamships. Innumerable amateur and a few professional local groups were formed whose activities included the staging of theatrical and musical shows of their own. Broad swathes of Lagos's highly segmented society participated in one way or another. Many of their productions incorporated novelties from overseas or were stimulated by imported forms, but they voiced the concerns and aspirations of the local population. Many of them, furthermore, drew inspiration from, and contributed to, the rising tide of Nigerian and ethnic cultural nationalism that characterized the politics of the 1940s.

The high levels of literacy and the high value placed on education by the Lagos population made possible a broad consensus built around the notion of "enlightenment." Education was not only a means to getting salaried and waged work; it was also prized as a moral and civilizing asset, a source of refinement regarded as indispensable both for personal advancement among the elite and for the progress of the future self-governing nation. Young men joined "Reading Circles" and "Literary Societies," some associated with schools, some with occupational groups or Muslim and Christian organizations, and some of nationalist orientation. They staged debates and lectures of a high moral and social tone (e.g., "Doctors are more useful to this country than teachers"; "High Life and Its Fruits"; "The Future of Muslim Youths"). Though Jagua Nana, in Cyprian Ekwensi's novel of the same name, is deeply bored by the lecture her young man takes her to, Freddie regards it as an important means of self-edification (Ekwensi 1961). The goal was explicit: as an advertisement for one literary society in *The Comet* put it, "The Sonian Reading Circle caters for youths eager for self-improvement through Reading."[9]

"Enlightenment," bound up as it was with Western-type schooling, had long been the preserve of the Saro elite. In Victorian Lagos (Echeruo 1977; Leonard 1967) the Saro maintained their cultural distinction by staging English-language revues based on English music hall traditions (but with the class signifiers reversed) and excluded the Lagos indigenes by the high price of admission. From the 1880s onward, however, a more radical wing of the Saro elite espoused Yorùbá cultural nationalism, and this drew them both to the indigenous, longstanding performance genres such as proverbs, oríkì, and Ifá poetry, which they collected and transcribed, and also to the new Christian but popular forms of expression being generated by the African churches, who, fed up with white control, had from 1891 started to break away to run themselves. From the early years of the twentieth century these churches had begun to stage Yorùbá-language dramas and develop a style of choral singing more congenial to Yorùbá musical traditions than the Anglican hymns (see Leonard 1967; Adedeji 1971). This effort was greatly reinforced from the 1930s onward by the rise of the Aládùúrà churches—independent churches which went much further than the African churches in indigenizing both form and content of Christian worship.

In the 1940s, Lagos culture and society was still residually under the patronage of the Saro oligarchy and the colonial government officials. The Lagos town council still only had three elected representatives, the franchise was still tightly restricted by a property qualification, and those elected were still all Saro. But the huge numbers of immigrants from the hinterland—many of them educated and radical in outlook—had breathed a new pan-Nigerian anti-colonial air into the old oppositional-cum-collaborative nationalism of the Saro. A new popular press, founded by Azikiwe, and new forms of mobilization and address anticipated and hastened the formation of new political parties, the attainment of universal adult franchise, and elections to a regional self-governing council—all of which had been achieved by 1951. When Oyin Adéjobí was in Lagos, then, the city was on the very brink of far-reaching transformation.

In the field of cultural production, the result was a consensus built around the ideals originally embodied in the Saro elite, but now rendered more open, available, and popular. If the Saro still retained a certain superiority and exclusiveness, other segments of the population now participated vigorously in the public culture of enlightenment. In addition to the African and Aládùúrà churches, these now included the modernizing wing of the Lagosian Muslims; occupational groups such as the railway workers and police; and many "tribal unions," especially from the east of Nigeria, and especially their women's sections. A new culture was forming which, if not yet really "popular," was at any rate ecumenical, active, public-spirited, and anxious to include as wide a constituency as possible. Túndé King, the father of Yorùbá jùjú music, can be taken as a sign of the times. A Saro—but from a Muslim family—who worked as a clerk at the United Africa Company but hung around in his leisure hours with the local "area boys," he began by playing his syncretic, hymn-highlife-ragtime blend for the "parlor parties" of elite ladies and gentlemen and ended up with a vast patronage network and a popular following who bought his records, listened to his broadcasts on subscription radio, and attended his live performances (Waterman 1990a, 55–81). The parlor door was no longer shut against the multitudes; nor were the parlor performances any longer wholly distinct from the hybrid popular shows being staged by a variegated coalition of religious, ethnic, and occupational groups.

Announcements and reports in the press of the 1940s suggest a proliferation of public performances undertaken by a wide array of groups. What is most striking, however, is the things they had in common. In the first place, they shared, to a very large extent, the same actual public space: the venue almost all groups usually chose was the Glover Memorial Hall—in preference, for instance, to the school or church halls which were the home ground of some of the groups. (The only frequent exception to this was the staging of "tribal dances," which, though they did sometimes take place in the Glover Hall, more often took place in the grounds of people's houses, in sports stadiums, and in tennis courts.) Thus the same physical space, at different times, was host to such varied spectacles as a "Sacred Native Air Service of Songs" by the augmented Choir of Jehovah Shalom Church Lagos;[10] an Islamic Native Air Opera featuring "The Life of Gbajabiamila" in aid of the Education Fund of the Young Ansar-ud-Deen Society;[11] a three-act operetta entitled "A Royal Jester" performed by the Lagos Progressive Literary Society;[12] "Outward Bound" performed by the Lagos Players (apparently a largely expatriate group);[13] a "Nigeria Police Concert" written, produced, and performed by African members of the police force;[14] and "a grand Yoruba Variety Entertainment and Magical Display" in aid of the Zamratul Islamiyyah Education Fund.[15]

The Glover Memorial Hall was also the place where some professional local or itinerant entertainers staged their shows: the most famous of these being Cassandra and Bobby [Benson], who specialized in an Americanized music-and-dance concert featuring ragtime and Negro spirituals, and Hubert Ògúnǹdé, who shifted his troupe from amateur to professional standing early in 1946; both before and after this date he staged most of his musical dramas in the Glover Hall. Though many other professional groups—especially those based around a dance band—preferred to play at nightclubs, the Glover Memorial Hall was the one space in which all currents of amateur and professional popular entertainment could conceivably cross.

The second thing shared by the entertainments staged by voluntary bodies was a public commitment to social causes. All these shows charged admission, and almost all announced the object for which the money was being raised: Christian, Islamic, and Hometown Union[16] education funds; benevolent funds for ex-servicemen and for prisoners of war; funds to support Police Sports and the Women's Guild Auxiliary; the Nigerian War Relief Fund; the New Mosque Building Fund; the Cathedral Harvest Fund.

Third, they also clearly shared a range of performance idioms. It is notable that the Young Ansar-ud-Deen Society, the organization of modernizing Muslims, should take over the "native air opera" format devised by the African and Aládùúrà churches, and that the CMS church St John's (Aroloya) should have a concert party group which announced a "wonderful Variety featuring MARTYRDOM OF ST CYRIL AND FAITHFUL AL-HAJI."[17] It is perhaps even more impressive that Qur'anic schools, which were *not* part of the modernizing movement oriented toward Western-style education but on the contrary were devoted exclusively to Qur'anic studies conducted in Arabic in the traditional manner, should still have felt the urge to enter the common public space to demonstrate the achievements of their pupils through a shared performance format. The Fortunate Arabic and Quran School staged a "Grand Native and Arabic Entertainment" at the Glover Hall in 1942, and *The Comet* reported that

> The Hall was taxed to its utmost capacity by a surging crowd of spectators. The performance commenced with an open glee ASALATU by the pupils. Other items on the programme such as drill play, recitations and Songs in Arabic were well rendered and the conversation in Arabic and other Arabic songs were well enjoyed. The audience was [so] fascinated by the Arabic songs rendered by five girls, that presents were given to the performers.[18]

At one end of the spectrum of theatrical formats lay scripted drawing-room comedies, melodramas, or light opera in English; at the other end lay indigenous traditional dances and masquerades. The performances at the English end of the spectrum were by no means the exclusive preserve of the expatriate Lagos Players. There were several other groups which put on English-language plays, ranging from *Twelfth Night* to *At The Mercy of Tiberius*, the synopsis of which suggests an extraordinarily convoluted melodrama. The cast list of the latter production, which was staged by the Christ Church Cathedral Youngmen's Club ("assisted by well-known ladies") shows that almost all the performers were from prominent Saro families.[19] The performances at the indigenous end of the spectrum—the "tribal dances," also referred to as "folk dances," "magical dances," and "variety dances"—were staged primarily by Hometown Unions (mainly from the east) toward the end of the 1940s when ethnicity was becoming a defining feature of political mobilization. They were often performed by real dancers, masqueraders, acrobats, and musicians from the association's home base, brought in for the occasion. The Ibibio States Association, for example, announced that their Ofiok Udino drama would be "using expert actors from the Ibibio country," while the Issele Union, Lagos Branch, urged its sympathizers to "Come and hear the thrilling voices and display of newly imported ladies from home."

In the middle ground between these two extremes lay what was surely the most versatile and popular format, the concert party or variety show that was favored by all groups except the Aládùúrà churches. One of the strengths of concert party was its flexibility and incorporative capacity, which enabled it to mediate between divergent tastes and tendencies. Composed of a string of self-contained, unrelated turns and set pieces, and relying for its effects on contrast, it was capable of absorbing almost any style of cultural performance that came to hand and adapting to new fads at short notice. Thus the Police Concert in 1946 was able to include two items that belong to the "tribal dance" end of the spectrum—the Onitsha "Dance of the Guinea Fowls" and "The enthralling 'Black Magic' act of the Yorubas called 'Agemo'" in which "the large mat just kept on sending out smaller ones until we saw a very small one hardly two feet high" (*Nigerian Daily Times*, January 14, 1946). But it also included a very popular African American genre, "Songs from the Plantations," as well as sketches with "lady impersonators" reminiscent of Ghanaian concert party.[20] Other concerts included large items from the English end of the spectrum: for example the Ansar-ud-Deen Girls' Association advertised "a grand concert entitled 'Bishop's Candlesticks', interspersed with African airs, dialogues and recitations."[21]

Operating on the compositional principle of *assemblage* rather than *organic unity*, concert was able to take advantage of available talent without having to depend on any one performer. This also enabled it to cross the boundaries between amateur and professional entertainers with great ease, assisting the emergence of new categories of professional performers. Amateur concerts could include professional or semi-professional spots: in the Nigerian Railway Christmas Concert in 1945, Hubert Ògúnǹdé and his company contributed several "native airs" and extracts from three of his most popular plays at a point when he was in the very act of shifting his company from amateur to professional, commercial status. Professional concerts, conversely, could give a temporary slot to a well-known amateur performer. And voluntary associations of all kinds could "sponsor" professional shows by undertaking all the arrangements and expenses, advertising the event, and paying the performers a fee, after which they were entitled to keep any profits for the good cause they represented.

But if the concert party or variety show was the mainstream format of the time, dramatic forms developed by the churches had a more direct and consequential impact on the development of the Yorùbá popular theater— so much so that these church dramas have sometimes been treated, misleadingly, as the "source" or "origin" of the whole Yorùbá popular theater movement. One of these church drama forms was the commemorative pageant, re-enacting the historical establishment of the mission churches— much in evidence in the 1940s and 1950s, when a lot of centenaries were being celebrated around the country.²² Pageants were re-enactments of actual events conceptualized as belonging to a fixed, dated past—which had left its material traces—as opposed to the revivification of the eternally relevant narratives of the Bible. Some years later, as we shall see, Adéjọbí tried his hand at a commemorative drama of this type, and though he did not repeat the experiment, it may have played some part in the development of his "realist" style.

But by far the most important genres of church drama were the "native air" forms of the African and Aládùúrà churches. It was these forms which most immediately involved Oyin Adéjọbí in Lagos and which launched his career. In the 1940s, three variants of the Yorùbá sacred music performance could be distinguished: services of songs, cantatas, and native air operas. All were based on the style of composition known as native airs: original compositions with Yorùbá lyrics and tunes which followed the tonal contours of the words but which added a melody and harmony reminiscent of African and Aládùúrà church hymns. The themes were always moral and could be either Biblical or topical in theme. The form and the name were of long standing, having been mentioned in CMS correspondence as early as 1857 (Ajayi 1965, 225). CMS churches continued to compose them for special occasions and they also featured in "concerts" by secular organizations. However, it was the African and Aládùúrà churches that saw their potential for expansion. A service of songs was a complete program purely of native airs that were performed on stage by a choir with suitable choreographed movements. Cantatas and native air operas involved more ambitious narrative and theatrical effects. A religious theme or a story from the Bible was dramatized and distributed between several characters, with the rest of the choir as chorus. The use of terminology varied, but generally it seems that "cantatas" meant choral sung texts with less plot and characterization than "native air operas": a cantata could be on a theme such as "Jubilee Thanksgiving" or "Calvary," but native air operas tended to be on meaty subjects such as the Fall of Man, King Solomon, and Nebuchadnezzar (a favorite staged by numerous groups).²³

By the time Adéjọbí arrived in Lagos, a number of composer-dramatists had already become well established in the genre. A. B. David and G. T. Onímọlẹ̀ were already famous for their native air operas in the 1930s, and Ògúnǹdé had started his career as a dramatist by staging no less than five very popular ones in two years (1944–1946). Ògúnǹdé is credited with breathing dramatic animation into the form—hitherto a rather static choral affair—and for creating impressive visual effects with costumes and scenery. In the 1940s, native air operas were often staged in the Glover Memorial Hall rather than in the church hall, and in many cases they seem to have attracted audiences and brought their performers fame which went well beyond their own congregations. They became a form of public self-announcement on the part of the church as well as an activity creating solidarity among their own members.

Services of songs, cantatas and native air operas were different from the variety format in three ways: their medium was exclusively Yorùbá, rather than a mixture of Yorùbá, English, and pidgin; they were thematically homogeneous and/or narratively coherent, rather than being made up of an assemblage of diverse and unrelated star turns and party pieces; and their subject matter was predominantly sacred and usually drawn from the Bible.

The Church of the Lord, under whose auspices Adéjọbí produced his first public shows, provided a particular microcosm of enlightened civic culture in Lagos. The membership, like that of other Aládùúrà churches, was not elite, but drew predominantly from a population of "small traders and farmers, clerks, artisans, drivers, the unemployed and many women" (Turner 1967, II:19). Most of the members (about two-thirds) had primary education, and about half of these also had some secondary education. Almost all had already been Christians before they joined the Church of the Lord and many were the children of Christian parents. Many were migrants, and many were socially as well as geographically mobile. The social sphere which Adéjọbí inhabited through the Church of the Lord was a modest one, but one which nonetheless knew itself to be a cultural instigator and capable of a long reach, out to other groups and up through several social layers to the patrons of enlightenment. The congregations included some influential people who exerted themselves on behalf of their brethren—as Adéjọbí's first two employers, friends of his brother, did for him. African and Aládùúrà churches—like all the other voluntary associations discussed above—made a point of announcing the expected presence of distinguished patrons at their performances—sometimes generic ("supported by some prominent ladies and gentlemen") and inclusive ("supported by the Elite [European, Syrian and African] of the Community"), and sometimes individual: "Mr Ayo Lijadu, Editor of the *Nigerian Daily Times* and secretary general of the Press Association of Nigeria presiding," "under the chairmanship of His Worship the Magistrate O. Jibowu."[24]

If it sought the patronage of the elite, it was also active, self-reliant, and confident of its ability to articulate the ideals of its own lower-class membership. The public performances of services of songs, cantatas, and native air operas were only the most spectacular and public manifestation of a vigorous, critical, and sociable religious life which was also conducted through more frequent or continuous activities such as choir practice; Bible study and discussion groups; the production and dissemination of a flourishing print culture of tracts, pamphlets, and books; and the regular meetings of an array of auxiliary church associations convened on the basis of age, gender, or special interests and tasks. In its orientation to literacy, its preference for monogamy, and its insistence on individual self-direction, the Church of the Lord could be seen as an agent for the popular articulation of "progressive" ideas, originally associated with the elite, among a much broader popular stratum. But it was more than this. The Church of the Lord, like the other Aládùúrà churches, was a radical movement which insisted on hard and absolute choices that were not derived from the received wisdom of the Anglicized elite and that involved a critical process of rejection and recuperation of prevalent values. Their cultural productivity was founded on this fundamental sense that its individual members were active, thinking beings seeking to reshape their lives in accordance with strong moral precepts.

Oyin Adéjọbí's theater, and other parallel theater groups, thus had their inception in a unique conjunction of forces. The civic culture of Lagos, with its proliferation of diverse participating groups coalescing around a common understanding of social progress, provided a larger context in which the lower-class, active, and edification-oriented Aládùúrà congregations had their place. Performance traditions nurtured predominantly within the African and Aládùúrà churches shared public space with alternative but parallel traditions carried on by Anglican, Ansar-ud-Deen, trade union, and ethnic associations. Despite incipient cleavages, all at that time could be understood to be participating in a common public culture.

Several features of this situation proved to have a lasting resonance for the traveling popular theater groups that subsequently emerged, among them the Oyin Adéjọbí Theatre Company. Though the 1940s coalition of voluntary public-spirited interest groups dissolved in subsequent years, the popular theater strongly retained both the central ideal of enlightenment as an ecumenical public good and the notion that theatrical performance was a contribution to such enlightenment. The popular theater groups continued to address a "public" which was defined not in class or religious terms but rather by its assumed shared commitment to self-edification. The fluid relationship between amateur and professional performance, such that each could co-opt the other—and such that amateurs always charged admission while professionals always claimed to be doing a public service—remained characteristic of the popular traveling theater up to its decline in the 1980s. The popular theater throve on the proliferation of alternative formal theatrical models available at the moment of its inception. It drew some of its defining features from the Aládùúrà native air opera: the exclusive use of Yorùbá as medium of expression, an emphasis on thematic consistency and narrative linearity and coherence, and the use of song as a form of dramatic speech rather than as a set piece or "turn" included in a variety program. But it also drew on the possibilities of the compositional mode of assemblage characteristic of the concert party. It retained the possibility of incorporating "turns" when talent became available—and dropping them when necessary; in its opening glee (a term taken from the concert party) it preserved a slot for the variety format of discrete items of entertainment; and within the bounds of narrative coherence and quasi-realist characterization, it exploited the opportunistic, presentational mode of address to the audience. It also nodded in the direction of the type of scripted English play put on by the Lagos Players, for though the Yorùbá popular theater was almost wholly improvised, there is a real sense in which both directors and actors referred mentally to a kind of virtual script (see Chapter 10). And it drew from the great success of indigenous displays of "folk dance" the encouragement to incorporate chunks of Yorùbá traditional performance arts—a tendency which emerged early on in Ògúnǹdé's use of traditional dancing in the 1940s, reached its apogee in 1963 in Ládiípọ̀'s *Ọba Kò So* (assembled almost entirely out of existing Yorùbá performance arts), and enjoyed a resurgence in some of the new video dramas the theater companies began making in the 1990s.

THE ADÉJỌBÍ SINGING PARTY

From the moment he began learning music, Oyin Adéjọbí became wholly engrossed, and he rapidly discovered his own gifts.

> When I went to that organ place, it absorbed me totally, so that once I'd learned **how to type,** once I'd **become a typist,** you see, I just concentrated entirely on music, until I could play really well. I learnt both piano and organ, and could play both. The method was Smallwood, Smallwood Musical Notes, that's what we used, and I learned from it on and on, until I could play in all kinds of keys, in fact, I learned it **to the point where** I was leading the choir of the church. The Church of the Lord Aládùúrà. I was leading that church choir at that time.

Very soon, he began to compose his own native airs for the choir. Encouraged by his choristers' response, he began to find a larger stage:

> You see, what happened was that when I began to teach songs to the choir, there were a lot of people in that choir, both men and women, which was very inspiring and encouraging.[25] That was how I came to get the idea of putting together my own program of songs on interesting and entertaining subjects, and on events that had impressed me, that I could teach to the choir . . . I would compose the songs, and teach them to the choir. Songs about Christianity and about things that were interesting. For example, at that period I remember there was a woman who stole a baby in the hospital. She stole a baby. I composed a song about it at that time.

And all kinds of things that happened in Lagos at that time that were interesting. I made up songs about them.

Adéjọbí composed a whole service of songs, taught them to his choir, printed the songs as a pamphlet ("they were many!"), and organized a public performance at the Glover Memorial Hall.

The performance was lively. Accompanied by drums and piano, the choir danced as they sang. "The singers described [enacted, expressed] their meaning with their hands, with their eyes, with their mouths, with their feet, when we were doing that service of songs." The audience was large and highly appreciative:

> You see, that effort of ours—the crowds were enormous in Glover Hall, and this inspired me: what with the way they flocked in, the way they applauded and cheered when they heard the songs we sang. When they saw how the performers were dancing to the music, and **demonstrating** the meaning, it excited people so much.

The immediate outcome was that representatives of Radio Nigeria, who had attended the performance, came back the next day to ask Adéjọbí and his group to perform for radio.[26] They were given a half-hour slot, which was repeated frequently. Adéjọbí reconstituted the church choir, incorporating other music enthusiasts, as an autonomous association called the Adéjọbí Singing Party. "Salaried workers were among them, teachers were among them, government clerks and artisans were there." This group met after work in the yard of the house where Adéjọbí lodged. Each week they learned new songs—sometimes as many as four, five, or even six—which Adéjọbí had composed for that week's program. But this extremely intense creative activity was not the end of it. "You see, as we went on singing all those songs, and all that work was going forward, our name began to be known, our fame began to spread. The people of Lagos began to love me— so much that all kinds of churches began to invite me to come and teach them songs, to come here, to go there, to come and do a service of songs for them." So in addition to preparing the radio programs, Adéjọbí was acting as a freelance composer-director all over Lagos. Under his direction, the various church groups would mount programs of songs, invite audiences, appoint chairpeople to preside, and use the occasion to raise money for the church, paying Adéjọbí a token amount for his trouble.

This ferment of activity generated a new project. "One day, a thought occurred to me—that I should take a story and set it to music [lit. *fi ìtàn kọ orin:* take story to sing song]. And the first story that I composed in song was a Bible story, it was about Adam and Eve." The story, however, does not seem to have been taken only from the Bible. It opened with a scene in which God calls on his angels to go to earth and fetch clay for the creation of human beings. The hotheaded angel who agrees to go turns out to be Death, "and that was the reason why human beings have to die, that's the way we shaped the story." It ended with a similar motif: after God had driven Adam and Eve out of the Garden, "then, we finished the story with a scene where God is very upset with the World because it was plunged in the darkness (of ignorance and wrongdoing). So he calls his angels again and asks them to go and set the world to rights. But the angels say they won't go. But one particular angel stands up and that is the one that the story tells us was Jesus Christ, and he said he would go to the World, and he came to earth via Maria's womb." The theme of God's disillusionment and his command to a messenger to go to earth may have come from the medieval morality play *Everyman*. In any event it was evidently a very popular scene: it recurs in Dúró Ládiípọ̀'s *Ẹ̀dá* and in Adéjọbí's own *The Gospel Fruit in Oshogbo*.[27]

Adéjọbí saw this play as a definitive breakthrough into drama. Whereas the service of songs had been dramatic and expressive, in *Paradise Lost* "we didn't just add expression to a program of singing: we used the songs to do a real play. We actually made it into a play." Though several other dramatists had staged native air operas quite recently in Lagos, Adéjọbí said he did not consciously model his drama on theirs. He saw it more as being precipitated from out of the highly dramatic and expressive style of song which he had been composing feverishly for his group. Certainly it seems to have been distinctively his own style from early on. A comparison of two texts which survive—Ògúnǹdé's *King Solomon* and Adéjọbí's *Hannah's Trial and Triumph*—suggests that Ògúnǹdé was given to splendid, stately effects, with much praise singing and many repeated choruses, while Adéjọbí had a gift for comedy and for the economical, effective evocation of personality through speech-like verbal nuances.

On the other hand, the success of this first attempt by Adéjọbí at a native air opera did bring him into friendly contact with Ògúnǹdé. Ògúnǹdé and A. B. David came together to the first performance, and after it was over they came to Adéjọbí and shook him very warmly by the hand. "This caused me to begin moving with Ògúnǹdé, so that I'd go to watch his rehearsals—not that I performed with him, but I would just go and be there at his rehearsals, and as things developed I began to borrow his scenery after he had finished a production. There was nothing that I would ask him for at that time that he wouldn't give me." Adéjọbí's gifts had evidently attracted another "helper," one of those crucial agents in every successful person's life story, whose advent is often unpredictable though predestined.[28]

Paradise Lost was so successful that Adéjọbí was inspired to go on to compose many other plays. Unlike Ògúnǹdé, who was already staging folkloric and topical stories, Adéjọbí at that time had only one source: "All those different plays were from the Bible, because, as far as I was concerned, at that time, I didn't think that there could be anything apart from the Bible—that there could be a story which surpassed those of the Bible. If I picked up the Bible—all the more so as I was an Aládùúrà, and liked to read the Bible—I would always **come across** a story that was **interesting** in the Bible, and I would turn it into a play."

As before, his creative productivity was stimulated by a voracious demand. "All the Christian churches in Lagos and its surrounding areas would use us to raise money: they would pay us, we would perform for them, they would invite people, they would raise money from it, and so on." By popular demand, then, the Adéjọbí Singing Party was becoming an itinerant drama group.

The churches that hosted these performances often built the drama into a larger program of social, celebratory, or commemorative events, including speeches by the chairperson, donations, hymn-singing, and so on. They distributed printed programs giving the order of events, the names of the principal participants, and a synopsis of the play. Sometimes, instead of a synopsis, there would be an entire text. One such text survives from an early Bible opera of the Adéjọbí company, *Hannah's Trial and Triumph*. The performance for which it was printed took place in 1953, in Òṣogbo, after Adéjọbí had moved back home and begun another life. But this production was a resurrection of a play first performed in Lagos soon after *Paradise Lost*. It is the earliest text of any play by the Adéjọbí company that I have been able to find.[29] Though it does not show everything that was done in performance, it gives a good idea of the distinctive style of one of Adéjọbí's earliest plays.

Hannah's Trial and Triumph was taken from the first book of Samuel, and follows the Biblical text closely. The text of the opera was entirely sung, with more solo passages than choral. The variety-show format of the opening glee which precedes the play proper is adapted to serve the purposes of a coherent overall narrative and thematic structure. It anticipates the events of the story and highlights the moral that can be learned from them. The text of play itself is distributed between five main characters, two of whom are women: Elkana, his first wife Hannah, his second wife Peninna, the priest Eli, and the young Samuel. There are also several smaller parts for Eli's sons Finihasi and Hofini (Phinehas and Hophni) and for the armies of the Israelites and Philistines. From the beginning, then, Adéjọbí avoided a charismatic actor-manager's temptation to structure the entire action around one central character. The distribution of parts between a core of five to seven equally balanced actors—including strong female parts—remained a feature of his productions throughout his career.

Hannah's trial is her childlessness, and the opening glee, anticipating and encapsulating the moral of the story, presents her as an example of someone who endures her trial with fortitude and is rewarded. In the discursive mode of the opening glee, the message can be encapsulated in a brief, though expansible, formulaic statement. In the drama, it has to be demonstrated through a sequence of events. Even the bald printed text reveals that the enactment of these events was animated by a lively and expressive style of individual characterization. Though the text follows the Bible closely—at times word for word—the characters also seem to speak in a lifelike way through the sung dialogue. When Elkana, the loving husband, mildly remonstrates with Peninna for tormenting her childless co-wife, she turns on him a blast of compounded self-righteousness, spite, and menace:

> Elkana o gbọ, ṣora o
> Ma fa jọngbọn lese
> Jọwọ ṣora o gidigidi
> Emi ki isẹgbẹ Hannah ninu ohun gbogbo
> Ara mi ẹ gbọ
> Mo ji mo ki ẹ ku owurọ . . . iyẹn irẹlẹ
> O pe mi mo ndaun—pe ki lo fẹ
> O ran mi niṣẹ mo si ranmọ rẹ
> Ki lo ku niwa ara mi o ẹ sọ fun mi
> Ijọngbọn lo nfẹ a o jọ ṣe ni—Ijọngbọn
> Ijọngbọn o—eṣu a bẹ o.

> Elkana listen, you be careful
> Don't provoke trouble
> Please be very very careful
> I am not Hannah's age-mate in anything
> My people, listen
> When I get up I greet her good morning, humbly
> When she calls me I answer, saying what do you want?
> She sends me on errands and I send your child
> What more remains for me to do, you tell me
> If it's trouble you want, we'll make it together—trouble
> Trouble—Èṣù will run riot.

In the middle of this, Elkana interjects "Just listen to that!" But he then appears to lose his nerve: as the text eloquently states at the end of the passage, "ELKANA ESCAPED!"

This text also reveals that Adéjọbí's taste for neat, well-structured plots shaped his work from the beginning. Though *Hannah's Trial and Triumph* may seem to have been carved rather awkwardly out of a longer narrative, the opening glee and closing song show that Adéjọbí managed to draw from it a compact double structure—a figure of eight. The first part shows the consequences of good behavior—Hannah's patient endurance is rewarded by the birth of a son. The second part shows the consequences of bad behavior—the priest Eli's neglect of the moral education of his sons is punished by their death in a battle against the Philistines. In the opening glee, the universal desirability of having children is affirmed (*Eni bi ko ni ku lagbara Edumare / Eni ko ibi a f'owo sosun laipe jojo:* Those who have given birth will not die, by the power of God; Those who have not yet given birth will very soon be dipping their hands in camwood [i.e., caring for a baby]). In the final song, childbirth is seen as only the start, and the importance of good upbringing is stressed (*Mo bi — mo bi — ki i somo / Ka bimo o — ko dabi kiko / Ka k'omo o, ko dabi ko gbon o:* "I have given birth—I have given birth"—that is not a child / To give birth is one thing, to educate the child is another / Educating a child is one thing, the child being wise is another). Thus the two complementary halves of the play are knit together.

And while the plot sticks fairly closely to the book of Samuel, there are embellishments which show that the story is being recreated for the edification of a contemporary local audience. Thus Peninna tells her assembled children that they are going to Silo to be baptized, be given names, and become full Christians. She then tests her son Ejide on the Lord's Prayer!

ÒSOGBO IN 1953

In 1953 Adéjọbí returned to Òsogbo. Lagos, with all its intensity and dynamism, was thought to be too dangerous for a young man left on his own. With Adéléké now absent on a permanent missionary expedition, his family wanted Oyin to come home: "They believed that if a young man grows up in Lagos without anyone around to guide him, it will not be long before he goes off the rails. Especially in matters to do with women."

When he returned he set about getting a job. He started as a clerk-typist with a private company called Dada Transport Service, and then, within two years, passed a civil service exam with top marks and thus secured a job as council clerk. He also involved himself in All Saints' Church, the Anglican church in Òsogbo—according to Turner the retention of affiliation to an established mission church was common among Church of the Lord devotees—and soon after his return married one of the church choristers, Grace Ọwọadé Látònà.

Provincial life—as the Lagos press patronizingly called it—was much quieter than that of the metropolis. Òsogbo was heavily Muslim, the first grammar school for the whole Òsun area had been opened only in 1949, and the educated (largely Christian) elite was small. But the commercial and manufacturing dynamism that had characterized the town since the opening of the railway in 1905 continued to attract immigrants and enterprises of all kinds. Major international trading firms including Paterson Zochonis, John Holt, G. B. Ollivant, the United Africa Company, the Société Commerciale de L'Ouest Africain (SCOA), and the Compagnie Française de l'Afrique Occidentale (CFAO) all began to operate branches in the town from 1908 onward (Schwab 1952; Awẹ and Albert 1995). Settlers were attracted from neighboring areas, and between 1911 and 1952 the population increased from less than 60,000 to nearly 165,000 (Egunjọbi 1995, 16).[30] In the new commercial quarter along the main road, most of the 240 shops noted by Schwab were owned or rented by immigrant Yorùbá (Schwab 1952, 15). Near the railway depot there was a foreign quarter, the home of "Government and European concern employees, of clerks, and teachers who are stationed temporarily in Oshogbo" and there was also a Hausa quarter on the outskirts of the town (Schwab 1952, 16).

This influx of commercial and administrative personnel was paralleled by internal developments in the town, notably the increasing influence of the small but articulate educated elite, and the expansion and collective organization of new categories of artisans. The educated elite were not formally recognized in local government until 1950, just before Adéjọbí's return, when provision was made for the first time for elected members to sit on the town and district councils alongside the traditional chiefs. But they had already shown themselves as a force to be reckoned with. Most of the chiefs were illiterate and depended heavily on the literate council and court clerks to guide them in their administrative business. In 1936, the wealthy and educated townspeople founded the Oshogbo Progressive Union, whose first president also became the first elected councillor, and who were active in promoting modernizing projects. They had the patronage of the Ọba. Both Adénlé I (on the throne when Adéjọbí returned) and his predecessor Látọ̀nà II (who reigned 1933–1946) were literate. Adénlé I, formerly a primary school headmaster, was the author of several edifying literary pamphlets in Yorùbá. According to Ulli Beier, he was an "educated, enlightened ruler" who actively sought the advice of the educated elements in town, while still remaining "interested and knowledgeable about its ancient traditions" (Beier 1960, 99).

> Gradually in the years between 1940 to 1950 the voice of this segment of the population was heard more and more as they began to oppose the unrestricted power of the chiefs. They represent only a very small percentage of the population, but due to the fact that they are both vocal and literate, they exert a political power that is disproportionate to their size. (Schwab 1952, 78)

Artisanal activity intensified in the period after 1910, and established crafts such as smithing, weaving, and dyeing (for which Òṣogbo was famous) were rapidly outnumbered by the proliferation of small colonial-era enterprises concerned with road transport, tailoring, carpentry, motor repair, bread-making, printing, catering, shoe repair, radio repair, and so on. The practitioners of these new artisanal trades were as conscious as the elite of representing a new social force. Many new associations for specific occupations and lines of business were established in the 1930s and 1940s, and in 1944 a larger organization, the Oshogbo Artisan and Workers Union, successfully protested against tax extortion by the traditional chiefs.

The situation, as viewed by Schwab in 1952, was one that gave radical progressive potential to new social forces; the old order had weakened enough "to allow such new groups as the artisans, wealthy traders, literate clerks and school teachers to throw off the yoke of tradition and speak out against the chiefs for a new regime that they are earnestly desiring to create" (Schwab 1952, 79).

In the two decades following Adéjọbí's return (1953–1972), the population nearly doubled again (Egunjọbi 1995, 16). Artisanal production enterprises as well as commerce continued to expand[31]—and this booming activity later led to the selection of Òṣogbo as a site for federal-led industrial development and the consequent establishment there of a steel-rolling mill and a machine-tool production factory. The elite of the 1950s were buoyed up by an expanding commercial horizon and sense of increasing prosperity.

As in Lagos, the educated elite did its best to promote enlightenment. It is noteworthy that the grammar school was built not by missionaries but as a result of concerted fund-raising efforts and planning over several years by community leaders of Òṣogbo, Ìkìrun, Ẹdẹ, and Òkukù (Bamisaiye 1995, 56). The Oshogbo Progressive Union had a Study Circle which held meetings at the Progressive Hall, and a Reading Room was opened in 1947. All Saints' School—the oldest and most prestigious primary school—put on plays and songs, and had long been capable of producing its own programs of native airs.[32] The combination of commercial vigor, thriving artisanal production, and an active, articulate elite were favorable to new cultural developments. Òṣogbo was in fact about to become the scene of an impressive cultural efflorescence, a major center for the visual arts and the third capital for theater after Lagos and Ìbàdàn, in which three of the top theater managers converged: Kọ́lá Ògúnmọ́lá, Dúró Ladiípọ̀, and Oyin Adéjọbí himself. In 1960, Ulli Beier commented on the "colourful vitality" of the town and "a certain generous 'laissez-faire' attitude to life and people that strikes one as urban," in contrast to other similar-sized towns which may "give one the feel of overgrown villages" (Beier 1960, 95, 99).

THE AMATEUR THEATRE GROUP, 1953–1962

On his return from Lagos, Adéjọbí did not expect his theatrical activities to continue. He was going back to a large, highly respected and prosperous family, a family of royal blood where, as he was told, "you don't drum for other people—other people drum for you." He was going back because it was time for him to get married and become the respected head of a household himself.

His fame, however, had spread from Lagos—carried by the radio as well as by word of mouth—and almost immediately he was approached by All Saints' Church to stage a fund-raising play for them. "When they approached me, I was delighted. I was very happy—extremely happy! Because I realized then that another path had opened for me to use the gift that God had given me. Whatever work I do, I do it wholeheartedly and successfully—whether it's typing, or secretarial work—but all the time, composing songs, drumming, and acting were my real passion."

He asked for people to work with, and the church representatives immediately obliged:

> So they took me to their car, and drove me to—it's called—they had founded a high school in Òṣogbo, the Anglican Girls' School. They told them all to line up, and the schoolmasters and mistresses as well, they lined up, then they said I should point to anyone I thought would be useful. A lot of those ladies were waving to me, and jumping about in their eagerness. Well, we collected about forty women that day.

He then proceeded to do the same at the boys' secondary school, and thus he assembled the cast of his first play in Òṣogbo, a repeat of *Hannah's Trial and Triumph*. History repeated itself in other ways too. As in Lagos, the success of his first production was so great that he was immediately overwhelmed by requests from other churches and associations to do the same for them. Instead of going from church to church, devising and rehearsing new plays each time, he decided to revive the idea of a permanent, amateur group which could perform its own plays for any organization that invited them. This new group he called the Òròkí Royal Theatre Party, in honor of his town (Òròkí is the *oríkì* of Òṣogbo) and his family's royal ancestry.

The membership was strong:

> In those days, we were many, because it was something prestigious. Anyone who managed to get into that kind of association, ah! it would be accepted that they must be cleverer than other people. At that time, we had about seventeen men and twenty women. Anyway there were really a lot of us. The whole house would be in uproar, the noise would spread far and wide, when we were doing our stuff. The house wasn't big enough to hold us, so we would go into the backyard, and people would peer in over the wall and we'd have to drive them away. So that our fame spread far and wide.

Grace Látọ̀nà, soon to become Oyin Adéjọbí's first wife, joined his first Òṣogbo group as soon as he started it in 1953. Like Adéjọbí, she stresses the prestigious and voluntary character of membership in those days and the high status of many of the participants. She remembers that

> We were many. We were many, with many substantial people among us. . . . Educated people who did it out of interest, not because of money, they were the kind of people who formed the group in those days. . . . People who liked it, who were interested, they were the ones who would come then. When there was no payment involved, it was for love, because people enjoyed it. If people left the group, it was because they were going away for further education, they would go away to do exams. That's how it was then.

She added that far from making money out of it, "those big, important salaried people . . . they would contribute to the upkeep of the theater group out of their salaries."

Their first production in Òṣogbo, the re-staging of *Hannah's Trial and Triumph*, was in aid of the All Saints' Church building fund. By 1961 the fund had served its purpose and a new church had been built. To celebrate this event, Adéjọbí and the Òròkí Royal Party presented a drama very much in the CMS commemorative mode, but with Adéjọbí's distinctive sharp characterization, humor, and realism. The play was entitled *The Gospel Fruit in Oshogbo*, and re-enacted the arrival of the first Christian missionary in Òṣogbo, Rev. John Mackay, in 1900, through a sequence of alternately comic and impassioned vignettes: Mackay's first conversation (through an interpreter) with the Atáoja, Ọba of Òṣogbo, whom he meets in the midst of the Òṣun festival; the conversion of an Erinlẹ̀ worshipper who wants to secure waged work on the church building program; further scenes in which the converts seek to convert others in the name of enlightenment and progress and in which Mackay tends the sick and disarms the predatory Ṣàngó cult; and Mackay's exhortation to the chiefs to send their children to school, followed by a charming schoolroom scene in which the children chant the alphabet. Finally, we are shown the building of the first church, with a closing song exhorting the people *Olọkọ mọkọ, ah! iṣẹ ya . . . kenikeni maṣe ṣọlẹ o* [Owner of the hoe, take up your hoe, it's time to work . . . let no one be lazy].

Except for *Orogún Adédigba (Adédigba's Co-wife)*, his first secular play which told the story of events in his own childhood, Adéjọbí did not further develop the idea of a drama based on historical documentary or re-enactment of recent past events. But thematically, if not formally, *The Gospel Fruit in Oshogbo* is germinal to subsequent developments. In a very clear form, one can see some of the central contradictions and tensions surrounding the idea of "enlightenment" and the problems of reconciling a cultural nationalist affirmation of traditional culture with a Christian di-

Grace Adéjọbí. ©Karin Barber

chotomous model of light and dark, Christian and pagan, modern and outmoded. The play will be discussed more fully from this point of view in Chapter 10.

According to Adéjọbí, it was after he moved to Òṣogbo that he began gradually to include spoken dialogue in his plays. "It would be sung, but little by little we would insert speech into it." The text then was made up of two parts: "The spoken part is the part where we just give them the idea, but the part that we want them to sing, I will have composed it in advance, so that that's what they will sing." He explained further how the actors handled the spoken part:

> At that time, we didn't usually write a script, no one wrote a script for a play at that time. What usually happened was that we would write down **sketches:** "Scene 1, So-and-so will go out, so-and-so will come in," and so on, what do you call it? **Synopsis** is what they call it now, but in those days we didn't know that term. . . . So, when

we had explained to the people who were learning the play, they would just **improvise** the words. If we told them the story, for example, "Your wife arrives, she flies into a rage with her husband, and says Why did you have to do this, and this, and this . . . ?" We'd say, "All right, do that! You are the wife, you are the husband."

The program of *The Gospel Fruit in Oshogbo* certainly suggests extensive passages of improvised speech. Whereas the printed text of *Hannah's Trial and Triumph* is made up entirely of sung verses, much of the printed text of *The Gospel Fruit in Oshogbo* consists of stage directions or synopses of action, which must have been improvised. The only speeches to be printed are the sung verses, but it is clear that there was much other dialogue that was not sung. It was probably not included in the printed text because it was not fixed and not learned by heart. It is as if the lively talent for colloquial speech, already shining through in the sung verses of *Hannah's Trial and Triumph*, was now breaking into a less constraining form. With it seemed to come a heightened sense of comedy and an unsentimental depiction of everyday problems—such as the Erinlẹ worshipper's money difficulties vis à vis his in-laws, which led to his becoming one of the first, exemplary converts in Òṣogbo.

By the late 1950s and early 1960s, Òṣogbo was becoming a center of theatrical and other cultural activity. Kọ́lá Ògúnmọ́lá, a teacher who had already been staging Bible operas in his previous posting in Èkìtì (Beier 1981), moved to Òṣogbo in 1955, where he began by running an amateur *jùjú* band but soon resumed the staging of plays, sacred and secular. Dúró Ládiípọ̀, a native of Òṣogbo who had been working as a teacher in Kaduna, returned in 1959 and after staging a Christmas cantata in 1961 moved into musical mythological-historical drama with *Ọbá Mọ́rọ̀* in 1962 (Ogunbiyi 1981). Commentators have always stressed the striking differences between the theaters of Dúró Ládiípọ̀, Kọ́lá Ògúnmọ́lá, and Hubert Ògúnǹdé and have paid tribute to the uniqueness of each (Beier 1954, 1967, 1981; Jeyifo 1984; Ogunbiyi 1981). Adéjọbí's was an equally distinctive and original mode. Thus theatrical activity in Òṣogbo was not only intense at this period, but it was also throwing up an array of new, alternative, and contrasting forms.

As in Lagos, even when dramas were tied to specific church occasions, they would often take place in secular public spaces. *The Gospel Fruit*, though part of an All Saints' Church event, was put on at the Recreation Club Garden in Òṣogbo, and other native air operas were staged at the Billiard Room.[33] This suggests that there may already have been a paying audience outside the ambit of the church congregation. The enthusiastic support of this potentially enormous public was the incentive for the next step, which Adéjọbí took in 1963.

The Efflorescence of the Theater, 1963–1988

THE PROFESSIONAL COMPANY, 1963–1972

In the years after Independence in 1960, western Nigeria as a whole saw a great multiplication and increased activity of small business concerns. The expansion of the civil service and teaching professions, and the Nigerianization of both, had provided many individuals with the capital to launch their own manufacturing or trading concerns, while the flood of primary school leavers produced by the Universal Primary Education scheme from 1961 onward[34] filled the cities with job-seeking potential employees and apprentices to work for them (Lloyd 1974, 75–76; Callaway 1960, 1973). Much of this feverish business activity was directed toward "import substitution," and small manufacturers struggled to compete with cheap mass-produced goods from abroad. For cultural producers, however, conditions were more favorable. In the field of culture, people often preferred local products. Yorùbá theaters, authors, and artists were boosted by the post-Independence mood of self-reliance and confidence, summed up by the phrase "*tiwa n tiwa*" [our own is our own].

In this atmosphere of cultural and commercial vitality, Adéjọbí took a bold step. On December 31st, 1962, he hosted his usual New Year's party for his group. When the company was assembled, he called them around him and said to them, "Now, there's an important improvement I want to make in this theatre, and I've written it down." Then he took out his written announcement and read to them: "From January 1st, 1963, I want only people who are prepared to drop their other work—if they're teachers, they'll resign, or if they work for the court—because I want full-time actors and actresses. Therefore, by January 1st, when you assemble [for rehearsal], I expect to see only those who are prepared to leave their other work and to take on this work [the theater] as their profession."

The next day, very few people turned up. Others explained to him later that they could not possibly abandon their jobs to join a professional theater company. Those people who did turn up became the core of a new organization, a paid company whose salaries started at £5 a month. The kind of people who joined were those whose previous work paid less well even than this: "people who got occasional work as bricklayers, for instance, or casual laborers, that kind of thing—those were the permanent members, especially women—women outnumbered men." At this point, then, the theater company very decisively lost social status. Formerly a voluntary activity patronized by the public-spirited Christian elite, it suddenly became a collection of runaway apprentices, manual laborers, and the otherwise unemployed. Once they started to perform for a living, public perceptions of them plummeted. They became a crew of *alágbe*—"beggars"—"people who drum and dance while others are working," pot-smokers, drinkers, and womanizers. This, as we shall see, was an image they struggled against for the rest of the history of their theater.

Nonetheless, for Adéjọbí the professionalization of the company was definitely a positive move, to be understood as a pioneering venture by an astute and gifted cultural entrepreneur. The company became an organization of true specialists, pursuing their métier in an economic niche discovered and defined by themselves—the hallmark of Yorùbá business success.[35] A hobby became a productive, thriving business, whose profitability vouched both for the value of what it produced and for the charisma of its patron-owner.

Adéjọbí himself did not yet resign from his post as council clerk. He had recently passed an examination which brought him accelerated promotion, and he planned to use part of his salary to support the activities of his theater group. "If I had resigned from my job at that time—how much did we [the theater] bring in at that time? We had no lorry. We had nothing. That meant that my salary was contributing to the progress of the theater work, that's why I couldn't resign." In this, he was adopting a common strategy among would-be entrepreneurs of the region, who would run a "private venture" artisanal business such as tailoring, carpentry, or shoemaking after their return from a day's work at the office (Callaway 1967, 163), thus combining the security of a regular wage with the deep satisfaction of self-employment.

True to local business practice, too, was his method of keeping his options open by retaining and adapting the old voluntary basis of recruitment alongside the new basis of contractual paid employment. He continued to involve amateur enthusiasts—the teachers and other professionals who had not given up their jobs to join his company—as occasional "guest artists," a policy which he retained throughout the life of his theater company.

The professionalization of the company ushered in an era of even more intense theatrical activity.

> We did very many new plays. Because my brain was working like a clock. To the point that you could never meet me socially. **Anywhere** that you met me at that time, you'd see that I was **busy writing something. I must be busy writing something. Either composing a song, or writing out an idea on a play.** I was inspired to bring out a new play **every month.**

Instead of playing only in Òṣogbo unless invited to other towns by church groups, the company now became a traveling theater, hiring a lorry and arranging itineraries for itself. When Adéjọbí was on leave, he traveled

Alhaji Kàrímù Adépòjù.

with them to towns all over the Yorùbá-speaking area. They would also be invited by an increasing number of secular associations such as town progressive societies, and social clubs "like the Inland Club of Adó-Èkìtì." When Adéjọbí was not on leave, the company still went on tour, led by a succession of managers responsible to Adéjọbí. "Some were good, others were not good. They took the company off on tour, and when they arrived they would report everything that happened." The uncertainties arising from this kind of delegation were permanently resolved in 1964, however, when Adéjọbí promoted one of his actors, Kàrímù Adépòjù, to the post of manager. Extremely efficient and reliable, devoted to Adéjọbí and the welfare of the group, Adépòjù was and is also a theatrical genius—a brilliant comic actor, but also a brilliant playwright, director, and stage manager. He remained with the Adéjọbí Company until the late 1980s, to its immense benefit and enrichment.

The first play this new professional company staged was neither a Bible play nor an episode of church history. The company, now called the Adéjọbí Musical Party, appropriately enough began with a play based on Adéjọbí's own life. *Adédigba's Co-wife* showed "how I became a man who walks with a stick." Adédigba stood for Adéjọbí's mother Esther, and the co-wife was the person who, driven by unprovoked hatred, used witchcraft to strike Oyin with the illness that crippled him.

Like the Biblical and church history plays, *Adédigba's Co-wife* was largely sung. According to Grace Adéjọbí:

> It was songs from Scene 1 to the end. Whatever you wanted to say, you would sing it. There was no speech—it was all song. Here's an example [sings]:

> Hmm, hmm, hmm, our husband
> Our husband, listen now
> We would never betray anyone
> We would never do evil.
> Don't punish us for something that's already over and done with
> Please
> We could never be treacherous
> We could never do evil.

> You can see that this is very different from saying, "Look, please, husband, we wouldn't do anything bad. Please. Don't beat us! You're punishing us for nothing!" Because in those days, unless you had a brain you couldn't do this work—people would run away from it, because there were too many songs to learn. The opening glee was made up of songs, the closing glee was songs. And when we began the play, from beginning to end it was also songs.

However, the trend toward inserting spoken dialogue, already (according to Adéjọbí himself) under way, was greatly reinforced by the success of this play, because it led to the theater company's immediately being taken up by television.

Television had been introduced in western Nigeria in 1959 (Mackay 1964, 61). The Western Nigeria Television Service at Ìbàdàn was the first television station in sub-Saharan Africa, and it was notable for its principled and innovative commitment, right from the beginning, to airing Yorùbá-language programs. This was made easier by the huge ferment of verbal, musical, and theatrical creativity all around it, which offered abundant material for documentaries, serials, and feature films.

In 1962 Adéjọbí composed a marriage anthem for an influential acquaintance who was so delighted with the composition that he soon afterward brought a representative of WNTS to discuss the possibility of the group's performing for television. They showed him *Adédigba's Co-wife* and "he was so much impressed that he immediately gave us a date." There were no recording facilities at WNTV at that time, so the performance was broadcast live:

You only have to go into the studio and start the performance and you are thrown open to the viewers, right like that; so that immediately after the performance that night, I came out of the studio to see great numbers of people waiting to congratulate me. They so much liked the play that ... many people made present to me in cash and all the rest of it. Since then—and that was in 1963—I have been on with the television. (English)

Among their subsequent television projects was the comedy series *Kóòtù Aṣípa (Magistrate's Court)*, which ran from the late 1960s onward. Several of their stage plays—including *Kúyẹ̀*, *Lániyọnu* and *Èkùrọ́ Olọ́jà* [*The Royal Palm-nut*]—were made into TV dramas, and they also did one-hour dramas specially for television.

To Adéjọbí, Grace, Kàrímù Adépọ̀jù and others with whom I discussed it, the importance of television was primarily publicity. It made them better known and thus attracted larger crowds to their stage plays, over which they had more control and from which they made more money. However, Adéjọbí also acknowledged that even though the television stations were unreliable and stingy in their payments, the lump sums he received for the group's plays and serials did enable him to equip the company once it went professional. In the early days, Grace recalls, the company had no vehicle. They would sometimes "charter" a lorry for the day but on other occasions would have to travel by public transport. "If we went somewhere like Ìkìrun, then we would have to go the rest of the way to Ìrágbìjí on foot, carrying the loads on our heads. We'd have to walk to Ìrágbìjí. When we got there, we would still have to rent a vehicle to do the **parade** in." By 1964, Adéjọbí was able to buy a small lorry for the company to travel in, greatly enhancing the well-being of the group and the success of their tours. Money from television also enabled Adéjọbí to invest in improved scenery, lighting, and sound equipment and later in a small generator.

Their involvement in television impinged on the form of their drama as well as its viability as a business. Grace thought it was the influence of TV which led the company to use spoken instead of sung dialogue:

You see, we wouldn't have used spoken dialogue, except that when we began this play [*Adédigba's Co-wife*] they said they wanted us to talk, not to sing all of it. That was what **stopped** us from singing ... we really got used to it to the point where it affected our stage performances.

Attention to the time a performance took—measured in hours and minutes—also became habitual, partly as a result of involvement in television. Adéjọbí recalled that his earliest Bible plays just went on as long as it took to get to the end of them. If audience reactions slowed it down so much that it took twice as long as it had in rehearsal, no one thought anything of it:

> In those days, it would take just however long it took. [Laughs] It went on until we got to the end—I mean to say that sometimes it might take an hour and a half, but another time it might still be going on after three hours. We just kept going. Especially when the audience was enjoying it and applauding and cheering—we just kept going.

Television required a stricter temporal budgeting which also began to affect the way the stage plays were structured. By the 1970s, when a stage play got "too long" as a result of elaborations and accretions, it would be cut back. Three hours was by then considered to be the limit. But—as will be shown in Chapter 8—the interaction between television and stage was not a one-way traffic. The stage plays also invaded the TV medium, importing their own techniques of improvisation, populist morality, and penchant for the occult. The result was an extremely dynamic and popular TV culture which attracted audiences greatly in excess of the number of families who actually owned TV sets. This in turn fed into the appetite for film and video drama, which eventually contributed to the demise of the live theater.

In the 1960s, then, Adéjọbí turned his amateur theater group into a paid, professional traveling theater. His output of plays accelerated and his resources increased with his success, both on television and on stage. Strategies for commercial success included advertising, diversification, and the rapid response to audiences' tastes. This was the period in which the parade and the poster, as well as radio announcements, became key elements in the company's public self-projection. Like all small businesses in the region, they were assiduous in keeping more than one iron in the fire, composing a palette of activities which supplemented and reinforced each other. They added not only television shows but also a regular radio serial to their repertoire, and when the opportunity arose, had their plays serialized in the popular photoplay magazine *Atọka*, in which stage plays were represented in photographs with bubble captions added. They became highly attuned to topical themes and to emerging audience preferences.

When he staged *The Gospel Fruit in Oshogbo* for the All Saints' Church, the audience and performers were well known to each other. Many of those present in the audience were members of church committees involved in organizing the event. Adéjọbí himself was a former member of the Building Committee, and one of his leading performers, Gabriel Adébáyọ̀ Ayọ̀délé, was on the Parochial Committee. Many other committee members had sons or daughters singing in the opening glee. All present, then, had a vested interest in the success of the occasion.

When the theater became a traveling company, they could no longer rely on this kind of automatic support and goodwill from a known, established audience. As Jeyifo observes, the decisive change for all the theater companies making the transition to professional status was that the audience now "had to be cultivated, it had to be fought for, and it had to be taken into account at every level of practice" (Jeyifo 1984, 40–41). They had to find out by trial and error "what our public wants," and they had to devise shows which would appeal to the widest constituency possible. Changes in the Adéjọbí Company's repertoire and style both tested, and attempted to shape, their audiences' tastes.

During this period the style of plays gradually moved in the direction of greater naturalism as the sung text was progressively shed in favor of spoken dialogue. Several of the plays originally created in the 1960s that still survive in the company's repertoire today retain strong traces of an intermediate style, halfway between the Biblical "opera" and the contemporary quasi-realistic domestic comedy. In *Kúyẹ̀* (first produced c. 1964), *Láníyọnu* (c. 1967), and *The Royal Palm-nut* (c. 1968), there are long passages of solo and choral singing: to set the scene, to convey moments of intense emotion, and—interestingly—to lay out contextual narratives essential to the development of the plot. Although recordings made in the 1980s can only serve as traces and clues to what the original style of the 1960s might have been, they are still noticeably different from the texts composed for the first time in the 1980s. It is as if the repertoire were a palimpsest of superscribed layers, always being effaced and reconstituted but nonetheless distinct enough to give a clear impression of the history of a changing form.

The Royal Palm-nut, as recorded in 1988, is a good example of the fluid amalgam of sung and spoken text characteristic of the plays originating in the 1960s. In the first scene, the town chiefs meet under the chairmanship of the head divination priest, the Àràbà, to find a successor to the late king who died almost ten years ago. There are large stretches of sung text, led by the Àràbà, who orchestrates the whole scene, supported by all the other characters as chorus. This sung text is discursive and expository, supplying much information essential to the unfolding of the plot not given in the speech-like dialogue. For example, Àràbà and the chorus sing an explanation of the "royal palm nut":

ÀRÀBÀ: Ẹnikẹ́ni tó wù tí 'óò joyè yìí o
    Níláti wékùrọ́ ọlọ́jà
ẸGBÈ: Olè ló jàà
    Tó kólé awo lọ
    Èkùrọ́ ọlọ́jà ìí parun láàfin.
    Káláyé tóó wàjà, a wálé a wánà

A wá gbogbo ìlú poo, a ò ri i.
Ẹnikẹ́ni tí 'óò jọba Àròbájọ
Kó múra gidi ló tọ́ o.
Èkùrọ́ ọlọ́jà a-wọ́n-bí-ojú
Látigbó dégbó a lè má ri
Látijù déjù a lè má kò ó
Ẹnìkan ṣáá tí ò mọ̀lòo rẹ̀
Ó lè ri he lórí ebè
Kó pọkọ́ rẹ̀ pọ̀ lólú-igbó
Ẹnikẹ́ni tí 'óò jọba Àròbájọ
Kó múra gidi ló tọ́ o.

ÀRÀBÀ: Whoever is to be ọba
Must find the royal palm nut
CHORUS: A thief stole it
When he robbed the sacred meeting-house
This royal palm nut disappeared from the palace.
Before the late Ọba died, we searched high and low
We searched the whole town, we didn't find it
Anyone who wants to become king of Àròbájọ
Must make a great effort
The royal palm nut is as precious as eyes
You can search entire forests and not find it
You can travel entire plains and not meet it
But someone who didn't know its value
Could just happen on it in a yam field
He could strike it with his hoe in the thickest forest
Anyone who wants to become king of Àròbájọ
Must be prepared for an arduous search.

It is only in the song that we learn that the original royal palm nut was stolen by thieves before the late king's death. We learn from the song the true extent of the royal palm nut's rarity and are given a hint about events that will later take place in the narrative—when a farmer picks up a royal palm nut in his farm without knowing its value. And it is through the song that Àràbà and the chiefs command the two candidates to depart on their quest, setting the rest of the play's action in motion.

But the sung set pieces are washed over by a torrent of fluid, colloquial, repetitive speech, animated by an intense and combative engagement between the speakers—who constantly interrupt and contradict each other, each apparently striving to expand his or her own space of utterance. Here they are suggesting solutions to the awkward fact that Ifá, instead of selecting one candidate from the five who are in the running, has pronounced two of them to be equally eligible:

JAGUN: Hain, Àràbà—
ÀRÀBÀ: Ẹ̀n-ẹ́n?
JAGUN: N óò bá ní nígbà tí Ifá ti mú àwọn méjì un, ká wáá kó wọn lọ sí ọjà Ọba, ká laago pé tòọ̀, ẹ̀yin ará ìlú o, àwọn méjì tÍfá mú rèé o. A á fi wọ́n sórí oyè bí o.
(Ìyálóde dìde fùù, ó fẹ́ẹ́ sọ̀rọ̀.)
ÀRÀBÀ: Ẹn, wá o. Ìyálóde pẹ̀lẹ́pẹ̀lẹ́ o, pẹ̀lẹ́pẹ̀lẹ́ o. Pẹ̀lẹ́pẹ̀lẹ́ o, Ìyálóde.
ÌYÁLÓDE: O ò ní í gbọ́, ògidi wèrè ni ọ́. Ká maa lé ọn sílẹ̀ bí ẹní lé iṣu! Ṣé ọ̀rọ̀ nù-un?
ÀRÀBÀ: Ìyálóde . . . Ìyálóde . . . Ní sùúrù.
ÀRÓ: Jagun, ọ̀rọ̀ burúkú ni ìwọ náà sọ. Ọ̀rọ̀ tí ò dáa lo sọ. Áà! O wáá sọ ọ́n di iṣu, ká maa lé wọn sáàrin-injà. Àwa tó jẹ́ pé àbájáde ìpàdée wa làwọn ará ìlú ń retí. Ṣe ìlú ló yẹ ó yàn fún wa ni àbí àwa ló yẹ ká yàn fúnlùú?
JAGUN: Àró, àbá ni wọ́n ní á mú wá o.

JAGUN: Er, Àràbà—
ÀRÀBÀ: Yes?
JAGUN: I want to suggest that since Ifá has picked both of those candidates, we should take them both to the Ọba's market, ring a bell, and announce to the townspeople that these are the two candidates that Ifá has chosen. So we are going to install both of them.
(Ìyálóde jumps up in outrage)
ÀRÀBÀ: Wait, wait. Ìyálóde, calm down. Calm down, calm down, Ìyálóde.
ÌYÁLÓDE: You are crazy. You want to pile them up one on top of the other like yams?
ÀRÀBÀ: Ìyálóde, Ìyálóde, be patient.
ÀRÓ: Jagun, what you said is very bad, it is not good at all. Ah! You want to turn them into yams, to be piled up in the middle of the market. When the townspeople are waiting for our decision. Do you think it's right that the townspeople should decide for us, or that we should decide for the townspeople?
JAGUN: Àró, we were asked to make suggestions.

Though this flow of words sounds unpremeditated, the improvised speech is actually planted with proverbs and prepared jokes, and its sequences are structured. The foolish suggestion that both candidates should be made Ọba at once, for example, is one step in a longer series of fantastic and implausible proposals which the chiefs take turns to put forward. The overall texture of the play depends on the structured alternation between melodious, orderly, discursive, collective sung speech—speech which carries authority—and ebullient, variable, flowing, individualistic, often apparently disorderly and unpredictable spoken dialogue.

During the 1960s the range of themes and sources also expanded dramatically. Adéjobí no longer limited himself to Bible stories and episodes of church history. He began to gather inspiration from all sides: from events in his own babyhood and childhood, from published Yorùbá novels, from stories he had heard his father and other people tell, from well-known Yorùbá myths, and from popular contemporary anecdote. As Adéjobí's range of interests expanded, he sometimes simply added to and adapted existing plots, producing extraordinarily eloquent and poignant hybrids—just as he had added new methods of recruitment and organization without abandoning the existing ones.

THE RISE OF PROFESSIONAL THEATER

In the 1970s, the decade of the oil boom, there was a remarkable expansion and diversification of popular traveling theater in western Nigeria. Until 1960, there were at most a dozen professional and amateur companies in operation (Jeyifo 1984, 36). In the 1960s many new groups were founded. But it was between 1970 and 1980 that the professionalization of the theater took off, and by 1980 there were nearly 120 self-supporting commercial touring companies (Jeyifo 1984, 68). Ranging from hugely profitable commercial and artistic successes such as the theaters of Hubert Ògúnǹdé and Moses Ọláìyá (Bàbáa Sàlá) to poor groups struggling to raise the money to buy basic equipment, these theaters plied the roads of western Nigeria in a constant quest for fresh audiences. Theater trucks joined the buzzing ferment of road transport, whose expansion and extension was a spectacular feature of the second half of the 1970s when the oil boom was at its height. The theaters visited the smallest and most remote towns; they toured the north, where Yorùbá-speaking enclaves turned out in their thousands to see them; they colonized the prestigious National Theatre building in Lagos—built for the FESTAC 1977[36] celebrations. They drew student crowds in university theater buildings, filled cultural centers with well-to-do people when they did benefit performances for elite social clubs, and attracted masses of school-children, workers, farmers, traders, and artisans whenever they went on tour.

This buoyancy was made possible by the great expansion of a potential entertainment-seeking public. Young people in particular who had money to spend and whose consumption habits had been shaped by the proliferation of available cultural goods—popular jùjú and fújì bands, cassettes, records, magazines, cinema, fiction, sport, television—were potentially prepared to pay for an evening's drama. Both imported and homemade cultural goods flooded the market. Live audiences for the popular theater—the physical crowds that packed the halls and hotels—increased in size and number, and very popular theater leaders could even fill a sports stadium (Jeyifo 1984, 115). As the theater expanded its thematic range, it became more appealing and more accessible to lower-class youth, and as the availability of education increased, so did the numbers of young people who developed a taste for drama at school. And a second, invisible theater audience addressed by television ballooned far beyond the live ones: a dispersed, anonymous public which nonetheless disclosed itself in continual small signs of public recognition—as when people in the street would hail the actors by their television characters' names.

As the field of theatrical production expanded with unregulated exuberance, the professional theater companies became sharply competitive. Each cherished its own repertoire and bitterly resented any suspicion that other companies were "stealing" its plays, ideas, or personnel. Successful companies established a house style and capitalized on the particular attributes of their own stars. This in part explains the huge diversification of theme and style to be found in the theater of the 1970s and 1980s, stemming from continual innovation and the refinement of specialisms. There were mythological plays drawing heavily on older oral traditions, reminiscent of Dúró Ládiípò's style; thrillers set in the criminal underworld; morality plays set in the folkloric world of traditional chieftaincy; and loose-jointed comic extravaganzas revolving around a popular star and a fresh haul of gimmicks—this being a specialty of Bàbáa Sàlá. At the same time, however, the expansion of the supply of shows meant that audiences developed well-defined expectations and could be intolerant of shows which did not match them. Competition meant that all the companies felt under pressure to supply "value for money" in the shape of a mixed bill incorporating a range of known successful elements. Almost all, for example, would precede the play proper with a variety-style curtain raiser, the opening glee, which could be made up of songs, comic monologues, duets, sketches, dances, or displays of traditional orature. The play proper would always be an extensive and usually coherent narrative lasting two hours or more. Most groups would inject a certain amount of buffoonery and horseplay into it, coin catchphrases for the audience to repeat, add displays of chanting, incantations and magical battles, or stunts, turns, and comic business wherever possible—and, above all, provide messages the audiences would want to hear. All the successful theaters achieved striking linguistic effects and vivid visual coups; they shared an aesthetic of intense impact attained through suspense, surprise, and the juxtaposition of unlike elements. Thus the expansion of the field of theatrical production, and the intense competition within it, had the effect of promoting diversity on the one hand and of stabilizing the theater form as a recognizable genre on the other.

Though these groups were in competition, they also recognized each other as fellow professionals. An Association of Theatre Practitioners of

Nigeria was established, with Hubert Ògúnǹdé as president. In 1981 Oyin Adéjọbí was the secretary, reflecting the prestige of his group and its status as one of the earliest theater companies to be established. All the professional theater companies registered, paid dues, met annually, and occasionally organized cooperative ventures such as theater festivals or mass gatherings for the funerals of prominent members. As Jeyifo has pointed out, the theater companies had a strong sense of corporate group identity and vocational distinctiveness (1984, 7) and a strong commitment to improving their professional skills and standing (1984, 84–86). The Association represented this commitment and demanded recognition for it.

THE OYIN ADÉJỌBÍ COMPANY, 1972–1988

In December 1972, ten years after launching his professional theater company, Oyin Adéjọbí took voluntary retirement from his employment as council clerk.

> I didn't just take voluntary retirement for no good reason. I wouldn't have done it if I hadn't realized that that employment was hampering me just when everything was going so well with the theater. The theater work was progressing, when we performed on television our fame spread, when we performed on the radio, our fame mounted, everything was going splendidly—I would sometimes be in the office when a new idea would occur to me—but someone would put a **file** on my desk and I had no choice but to attend to it. . . . That's what led me to resign.

He resigned with no savings and only a small pension, but the theater company did so well that within six months of his resignation he had earned enough to buy a car. In the following years he married several more wives. All of them became actresses, but only after their marriage to him. Unlike Ògúnǹdé, he did not make a habit of marrying existing actresses in order to keep them in the company; rather, he made a habit of utilizing whatever resources were available for his drama, and these included wives and children as well as "guest artists" and anything else that came to hand.

He added many new plays to his repertoire. Increasingly, these were contemporary in theme and "naturalistic" in style. Old plays like *Kúyẹ̀, Ìpadàbọ̀ Odùduwà* [*The Return of Odùduwà*], and *The Royal Palm-nut* were kept in the repertoire and gradually adapted, but new ones were constantly added. The newer plays of the late 1970s and early 1980s dealt mainly with three issues: insubordinate women, legitimate and illegitimate acquisition of wealth, and the misuse of power.

The newest plays were carried almost entirely through lifelike speech and usually used songs only where they were dramatically realistic. Thus in

Mo Ráwọ̀ [*External Appearances*], the only singing in the play is provided by the worshippers at an Aládùúrà church where Bísí, the heroine, goes for help with her boyfriend problems, while *Ọ̀nà Ọlà* [*The Road to Riches*] includes a birthday party scene in which the guests, led by a super-fashionable M.C., sing comic versions of recent pop songs. Alhaji Kàrímù Adépọ̀jù put this increasing "naturalism" down to the march of progress: he said that plays like *Kúyẹ̀* and *The Royal Palm-nut* used to have more songs in them, but "*bígbà ṣe ń lọ síwájú náà ni ojú ń là*" [as time went forward, enlightenment increased].

As the text of these plays became increasingly composed of spoken dialogue, the opening glee became more separate from the rest of the show. It remained the one repository of Adéjọbí's personal genius, his gift for musical composition. Usually taking between twenty minutes and half an hour at the beginning of the show, it consisted of a medley of songs, composed and sung by Adéjọbí in his wonderfully mellifluous voice, accompanied by a singing and dancing chorus made up of the women of the company, dressed in a uniform which was changed from time to time and which ranged from trouser suits to Hawaiian grass skirts. In the early days—as we saw in the case of *Hannah's Trial and Triumph*—the opening glee anticipated and commented on the theme of the play: each play had its own opening glee specially composed for it. By the early 1980s, however, the opening glee songs were of a general nature, reflecting on moral and philosophical issues or commenting on topical social trends. Adéjọbí selected five or six songs each night from a larger, enduring repertoire. They usually had some general relevance to the play, since they emerged from the same concerns and drew on the same field of images and idioms, but they did not refer specifically to it.

Throughout the 1970s, then, the theater company consolidated itself and expanded its field of operations. By the early 1980s, as well as managing a repertoire of some 20 live plays, which it constantly added to and adapted, it was producing two television serials and a radio serial and was frequently featured in *Atọ́ka*.

The Adéjọbís' only remaining ambition was to make a film, which after the phenomenal success of Hubert Ògúnǹdé's *Aiyé* (1979) and *Jáiyésinmi* (1983) had become the focus of every theater company's dreams. The public, whose voracious appetite for stage drama had floated the traveling theater in the 1940s and carried it on an ever-increasing tide of enthusiasm right up to the 1980s, now demanded Yorùbá films. The richest companies managed to go into film production while keeping a live company in operation at the same time. The films, when made, would be taken on tour just like live plays—no copies of the film would be released on general distribution, for the companies needed to keep close control over the sale of tick-

Emily and Adédùnmọ́lá singing the opening glee. ©Elio Montanari

ets. These groups continued to travel, but instead of getting up on stage and performing every night, they could now sit back and watch themselves on the screen.

There was a brief but prolific boom in Yorùbá-language films in the early 1980s, suggesting that a real popular indigenous cinema was about to be born. If the films lacked the extraordinary vitality of the live shows, fed as these were by the constant collaborative interventions of the audience, they did enable the theaters to explore other dimensions of creativity. Many films entered the realms of fantasy and myth, emboldened by the visual possibilities of cinema. Others attempted (as the stage plays rarely did) to enter satirically into the domain of the well-to-do educated middle classes—the world of politicians, businesspeople, and professionals. This world could be evoked visually, by shots of glamorous offices, tower blocks, yachts, well-guarded mansions, and so on, even when middle-class behavior and mentality was beyond the experience of most of the actors. Oyin Adéjọbí and Alhaji planned several film projects, even commissioning professional screenplays. But their assiduous efforts to raise the capital from well-

Ọyin Adéjọbí singing the opening glee. ©Elio Montanari

wishers and wealthy patrons came to nothing. By the late 1980s the live theater was in decline but the new film boom appeared to be beyond their reach.

DECLINE OF THE LIVE THEATER, 1988–

ECONOMIC COLLAPSE

In the late 1980s the Nigerian oil-boom economy collapsed. The naira went into free fall; imports became astronomically expensive; lack of spare parts gradually strangled the informal transport system; surplus cash dried up in people's pockets. It became much harder to keep a theater company on the road. Large popular audiences dwindled—people had no money for entertainment, and anyway they feared to go out in the increasingly dangerous night-time streets. In 1988 when I went to Ìbàdàn for six weeks to try to broaden my knowledge of the live popular theater, I kept showing up at community halls and cultural centers to see theater companies whose live performances had been advertised in the papers and on posters—only to find that the show had been canceled or replaced with a film screening.

It also became almost impossible to raise capital for film projects. Only the very rich companies could now hope to make films. The better-known actors in other companies were signed up to perform with them on a film-by-film basis. Cinema thus convened a new kind of super-company, featuring stars from numerous smaller groups—a co-operation that was virtually unheard of before the advent of film-making. Once again, the theater groups showed their ability to adapt existing organizational modes to a new situation.

Companies which could not afford to make films turned to video instead. They began to make video dramas for sale directly to the VCR-owning public—a smaller and more middle-class public than the one that had attended the live theater, but nonetheless a substantial one. Battered cassettes—often copies of copies—were on sale in motor-parks, supermarkets, and record shops (see Lawuyi 1997; Haynes 1995, 1997). The videos, however, usually made with a single camera and the least possible outlay, did not extend the dramatists' imaginative range as much as the cinema films did. The videos have been described as the equivalent of junk food, quickly and cheaply produced, quickly consumed, and quickly forgotten (see Haynes 1995). Nonetheless, they are symptoms of cultural and religious change which cannot be ignored.

In 1988 Alhaji separated from the company he had worked in for so long to set up a video-production organization of his own. In this he was remarkably successful, producing several secular and religious dramas which received high praise from the normally disparaging Nigerian press. Adéjọbí also produced several video dramas with members of his company and a great variety of "guest stars." The themes and modes of representation in the video dramas produced by both men suggest public anxiety and an incipient moral dislocation or disaggregation. This will be discussed further in Chapters 8 and 10.

INTERSECTING HISTORIES

Adéjọbí's narration of his life highlighted several themes that he clearly felt deeply about. Shaping his whole narrative was the familiar theme of early hard work and suffering eventually rewarded by great success. He also laid emphasis on the theme of the cultural pioneer and originator, evoking with extraordinary intensity and vividness the excitement of being in full creative spate, "thinking of one song after another . . . so many ideas would be coming into my head." His own role as creator was always in relation to the people his gifts attracted—his choir, his theater company, his audiences, eminent colleagues, and producers from radio and television. His creativity attracted these people's love and admiration; but their love and admiration also "inspired" his creativity.

The demand for his creations, right from the beginning, was in part the hunger of the media. Radio Nigeria, then WNTS, and later OYO-TV and other new television stations, had slots to fill, and Adéjọbí was approached by the producers without—in his account—any solicitation from himself whatsoever. The media were what made him more "publicly known" and increased the demand for his productions. Thus the technological agents of modernity played their part in constituting the deeply personal rapport he felt existed between himself and his audiences, from the very inception of his career.

As the story of an individual, then—a charismatic founder and convener—this history dwells on the theme of self-realization through dialogue, the inspiration imparted by the devotion of a steadily widening public. As the story of a company, what we can see is two ironically parallel trajectories: as the company professionalized it became more expert, more experienced and more successful; but at the same time, as it moved away from the world of the active, self-confident, educated, amateur Christian elite, it lost status and social esteem. Much of the actors' self-positioning revolved around an attempt to affirm their professionalism while denying and denouncing the disparagement that in the public eye went with it. These changes in personnel and public attitudes were aspects of large-scale, gradual changes in the theater's social milieu: the great expansion of an entertainment-seeking public, the proliferation of cultural goods available for them to consume, and the increasing projection to dispersed, anonymous media publics.

And as the story of a genre, what we see is a transition, accomplished over many years and with several long-lasting intermediate stages, from wholly scripted, stylized, sung text to wholly improvised, informal, spoken text. The effect was of increasing "realism." The requirements of television contributed to this shift but do not wholly explain it. As I shall suggest later, it was rather part of a much wider shift in popular forms of representation, seen in novels, visual art, and urban oral traditions throughout the Yorùbá-speaking area and far beyond.

The great live traveling theater movement which seemed set to flourish for another fifty years when I worked with the Adéjọbís in the early 1980s seems now to be almost over. It is impossible to believe, however, that the vast reserves of talent, imagination, and dedication can simply have evaporated. New genres may even now be in formation.

# The Actors

When Adéjọbí put his company on a paid, professional basis in 1963, it immediately lost status. As we have seen, the teachers and civil servants who had participated as amateurs left, to be replaced by applicants who were jobless or daily paid manual workers. But the "lumpen" character of the new membership, alluded to by Adéjọbí in his autobiographical narrative, was modified as the company became more successful and more prosperous. By the time I joined them in 1981, it had settled into a definite and distinctive social layer, a particular strand of the "intermediate" strata of western Nigeria. This chapter discusses the composition of the company and the social formation of the actors.

RECRUITMENT

The actors arrived in the company by a variety of routes and remained part of it with varying degrees of commitment. The company was structured in rings, with the longest-serving and most deeply committed members at the center. At the heart of the company were three people who had been involved from the early days of its history: Oyin Adéjọbí himself; his first wife Grace Ọwọ́adé Látọ̀nà, who had participated since the amateur group began its activities in 1953; and Alhaji Kàrímù Adépọ̀jù, who had joined in the year that the amateur group became a professional one, in 1963.

Grace Ọwọ́adé Adéjọbí was the senior wife and undisputed "Mama" of the company, with a grown-up son working in Ìbàdàn, a daughter finishing her secondary education, and younger children who usually accompanied the group on its trips. She was 47 when I joined them in 1981. Humorous, mild, and self-deprecating, she was treated with affection as well as respect by all the company. She was a native of Ọ̀sogbo, related to the royal family through her father's mother. Her father was a well-to-do building contractor who traveled from town to town according to the requirements of his trade. Grace's mother was the second of three wives. Trouble with her co-wives led to her leaving for Ghana in 1948, when Grace was fourteen. She did not take Grace with her. She remained away for 20 years, pursuing a profitable trade in provisions in Elmina. She sent money to maintain Grace and pay her school fees. Grace attended primary school up to Standard V, but then made a mistake which put an end to her education:

> You see, it's not good for people to pursue the vanities of fashion. I had some younger relatives, they were Muslim girls. They didn't go to school at all, they were getting married. So it happened ... my mother had sent my money for school fees to me. Then those girls bought cloth for *Iléyá*, the Muslim festival, and I took the money that I'd been sent and I bought some cloth too. I too bought that cloth, I spent my school fees on cloth. I wanted to be fashionable too. Then I wrote to my mother saying that the money she sent for school, I'd spent it on cloth. And my mother didn't send any more money.
>
> And our principal in those days liked me because I was very good at running—on Empire Day I would run in the Senior Girls' races, in the Junior Girls, I was champion in the Lime and Spoon Race, Threading the Needle, Catching the Train, everything ... Hundred yards, Junior Girls, Senior Girls. There was nothing [I didn't excel at]. If only it had been like in Ghana, because one of my junior siblings ... if they could have given me a scholarship for running, if there had been something like that in Òsogbo.... So that principal really liked me, so much that she would help me by not expelling me when everyone else was being expelled [for nonpayment of fees], because I ran for them. But when there was really no solution any more, I had to leave.

On leaving school, Grace trained as a sewing mistress (i.e., a seamstress), having formed a liking for sewing in school handiwork lessons. Before she completed the training, in 1953, at the age of 19, she joined the Adéjobí Musical Party. She had known about Adéjobí and his musical activities while she was still at school and he was still in Lagos; but when he returned, she heard more about him. Mrs. Clegg's house, where she went for her sewing lessons, was next door to the Adéjobí family house. One of her senior male relatives, Mr. Adéníyì, was Mr. Adéjobí's close friend, and it was he who told Grace that they were forming a singing and drama group at Adéjobí's house and introduced her to him. She was also a chorister at All Saints' Church, where Mr. Adéjobí came to serve as choirmaster. Through these various threads of connection, she came to join Adéjobí's group and then to marry him.

Alhaji Kàrímù Adépòjù was Mr. Adéjobí's employee in the sense that he was paid a salary to do his job. But in every aspect of the theater company's affairs, he was Adéjọbí's partner and collaborator and was indispensable to its artistic output. His genius for dramatization and his brilliant comic acting were vital elements in its success. Alhaji was an austere man with a dry sense of humor, given to sarcasm. He had a thoughtful, inquiring mind and would often engage me in long philosophical discussions. Unlike any of the others, he enjoyed talking English, and his quoted words in this chapter are not translations but what he actually said.

About 10 years younger than Grace, he was nevertheless still of the generation whose parents, in this area of Yorùbáland, tended to migrate to Ghana for long periods.[1] His father was a trader, and Adépọ̀jù was actually born in Ghana during one of his parents' spells of migration. When he was two, they returned to Nigeria for a short time, but then went back to Ghana, where they stayed long enough for him to begin Qur'anic school there. When they finally returned to Òṣogbo, he attended an Ansar-ud-Deen Primary School and, having completed Primary 6, went to a modern school in the Mid-West, where he stayed with a "brother" (a senior male relative of his own generation). Modern schools were then a relatively new institution, having been started in 1955 as a cheaper and more accessible alternative to grammar schools. One of the functions of the 3-year modern school program was to prepare pupils for teacher training college, in order to meet the huge requirement for primary teachers which followed the inauguration of the Universal Primary Education scheme the same year. They were distinctly less prestigious than grammar schools, whose 5-year program led to the WASC/WAEC exam which was a prerequisite for admission to the university.[2] But Kàrímù Adépọ̀jù did not proceed to a training college on completion of Modern III. His brother in the Mid-West was a tailor, and Adépọ̀jù also learned tailoring after school hours by helping him in his work. When he left school, he returned to Òṣogbo. He had long since formed an interest in theater:

> When I was in primary school, I am highly interested in drama because in our school— primary school—we usually do festival in our school which our master Mr. Oyin Adéjọbí used to come here to teach us drama. In our school, during the festival we used to collect ourselves to come to Oyin Adéjọbí house. He teaches a drama—a play—and we go back to our school and display it.

On his return to Òṣogbo, a friend asked him to go with him to see Dúró Ládiípọ̀, who had recently become a "dramatist popularly known," and they joined Ládiípọ̀'s theater company together in 1962. A year later, after he had been let down by the more senior members of the company, he left Ládiípọ̀ and approached Oyin Adéjọbí. Adéjọbí had just converted his company to a paid professional organization, and he was looking for actors; but at first he refused to take Adépọ̀jù on, fearing that Ládiípọ̀ would accuse him of poaching. Adépọ̀jù persisted, coming to the house every day until at last Adéjọbí relented and hired him, starting on a salary of three pounds a month. After the departure of the two earliest leaders of the group—the first manager Lérè Pàímọ́ and the first director Mr. Ayẹni—and that of their successor Mr. Akinadé, who combined both roles in one, Adépọ̀jù became the manager, a position he has filled ever since. Unlike most of the members of the company, he was able to pursue his ambition with little opposition, because "my father had already died before I joined the group, and I have only a mother who did not oppose me in anything I'm doing." He was an extremely popular actor, well known for his role as Bàbáa Wándé on television, and well paid. This, he said, went a long way toward overcoming the stigma attached to actors. He said that although in general no parent wants their daughter to marry an actor, his own parents-in-law had been very happy, because "Before I marry her, I had become a popular actor."

Around this core of founder-members, there was an inner circle of actors and actresses distinguished by their "long stay" and loyalty to the company and by their acting skills, born of experience as well as innate talent. Three of them were Adéjọbí's second, third, and fourth wives: Margaret (Ìyáa Gbádébọ̀[3]), who married Adéjọbí in 1964; Deborah (Ìyáa Jọkẹ́); and Emily (Ìyá Ají), who married Adéjọbí in 1969. At the end of 1981 a quarrel precipitated the departure of both Margaret and Deborah. Margaret had returned by 1986, but Deborah had not. In 1982 Adéjọbí married another much younger woman, Yẹmisí. Grace and Emily then were the two stable figures in the group. Both were highly experienced and talented actresses, capable of playing all the female parts between them. Emily, though a mature woman by the early 1980s, was delightful and convincing in ingénue parts and was also very good at playing deceitful, manipulative, and domineering women. Grace—who had been a great beauty herself in her youth—excelled at strong-minded and talkative old women. There had been other actresses in the past who were unmarried or married to men outside the company, but they had not stayed. The prejudice against actresses was so strong that it was almost impossible to keep girls, let alone other men's wives, for long. Their parents or husbands would turn up, create a scene, and take them away. Adéjọbí—whatever his religious convictions regarding polygamy—was more or less obliged to marry women if he wanted actresses.

Emily certainly married Adéjọbí with a view toward going on stage. She had left modern school without finishing when her father fell sick, and after his recovery she went to stay with a senior female relative in Òsogbo, where she got a job as a "ward maid" in a private maternity hospital. She met Adéjọbí when he came to discuss the possibility of renting premises in her aunt's neighborhood. I asked if she was already interested in theater before she got married, and she replied: "It was that very work, in fact, that I was interested in. When he said he wanted to marry me, I said, well, as long as I can join in this work, and not tell my parents yet that I am going to marry you, and he agreed." But eventually they had to break it to her parents, and her father flew into a rage:

> He said he wasn't happy about it. He said if it was because of my having to leave school, if I wanted to go back, I should hurry up and write to all the schools saying I wanted to come back. And if it was because I didn't like the work I was doing [as ward maid], then it would be better for me to go back to the farm and carry logs, that would please him more than if I begin dancing all about the place.

It was only years later, after the birth of two children and persistent conciliatory messages, that her parents accepted either her marriage or her profession.

Margaret, on the other hand, stressed that she married Adéjọbí without any intention of becoming an actress. She too had gone to modern school but left after the first year when her father died. She then got a job as a clerk to a medicine seller, which she did for about two years before following her mother's younger sibling to Iléṣà, where she again sought work as a clerk for a while, before coming back to Òṣogbo. Asked how she met Mr. Adéjọbí, she replied "People who don't know any better think that it was in order to join the theater that I came here and that we got married. But it wasn't like that." She went on to explain that she had met Adéjọbí when she came to the house to look for Grace, who was working as a sewing mistress, to ask her to do a job for her, and their relationship developed from there.

Although rehearsals and meetings were going on all around her, it was only after the birth of her first child, Gbádébọ̀, that she was persuaded to take part in a play, and then only to save the situation in an emergency. It was in 1964, soon after the company had been reconstituted on a professional footing, and the play they were doing was a Biblical one, *Samson Alágbára* [*Samson the Strong*]. They had been invited by a certain social club to perform in the Fákúnlé Hall in Òṣogbo. On the day of the performance the leading actress, Esther, could not be found. "So, Alhaji, Bàbáa Wándé [Kàrímù Adépòjù] came to me and said look, something's happened, one of their actors has disappeared, what about it? Could I do the part for them? And that's how I first stepped onto the stage, in that Fákúnlé Hall." Her performance was such a success that she continued playing parts whenever there was a performance in Òṣogbo, and when Gbádébọ̀ got bigger, she began to go on tour with them too. But while she was proud of her success, Margaret did not give the impression that theater was her entire life. She said she was hoping that in future Mr. Adéjọbí would build a shop for her where she could sell soft drinks and snacks.

Yẹ́mísí, the newest of Adéjọbí's wives, had not become part of the inner circle of the company when I talked to her a year or so after her arrival. Her father was a soldier who was constantly moved around the country. She was brought up by her grandmother in Ọyọ́, where she went to primary school. Then the grandmother returned to her native town, Òṣogbo, and Yẹmisí came with her and went to modern school there. Her examination grades were not good enough to get her admission to any further education, so she decided to try acting instead. She already knew Adéjọbí's daughter Adédùnmọ́lá from church—both belonged to the Church of the Lord and they became friends through the Bible study group—but she was introduced to Adéjọbí by a man who lived in the same house as her and was a member of the company at the time. This man continued to act as a go-between, until "I wrote an application. And he [Adéjọbí] asked Well? Where was I from? I said I was a native of Òṣogbo. He asked about my parents, and I explained to him. And then he took me on." From the start, negotiations for her to enter the company and solicitation of her hand in marriage seem to have gone hand in hand. When her relatives heard about it they refused to allow it. They came and took her away to live with an uncle in Lagos. But eventually "God softened their hearts" and they accepted both her marriage and her work.

In addition to Margaret and Emily, the inner circle also contained some younger men, the most important of whom were John Adéwuni and Dayọ̀ Akínpẹ̀lú. **Dayọ̀ Akínpẹ̀lú,** popularly known by the name of his TV character "Àlàbí Yellow," chosen because of his light complexion, had been with Adéjọbí for a number of years and had become one of the company's most popular stars when he suddenly defected from the company in dramatic circumstances the night before we were due to start filming a new television serial (see Chapter 8). His aim was to establish a theater company of his own, but this apparently was not a great success. Years later he returned to Adéjọbí and moved heaven and earth to get him to take him back. He resumed his leading position in the company for a while. But by this time, the company was already beginning to sink into inactivity as funds for film-making failed to materialize.

John Adéwuni arrived later than Akínpẹ̀lú, in 1977, but his unshakable reliability and loyalty—as well as his coarse but effective acting style—had made him indispensable by the early 1980s. He was one of the actors motivated by a real passion for the theater. A native of Ẹdẹ, he was the son of a farmer and went to primary school "in the grass [i.e., bush] of Ẹdẹ, in other words our farm," but then went on to do modern school years 1 and 2 in Odẹ-Òmu, and to Ẹdẹ town itself to complete Modern 3. He had discovered his interest in performance through school drama:

> When I was at school, I was extremely keen on anything to do with singing or acting. I was extremely keen on drumming. If a drama

> group came to perform for us, I would always be the first to go and find out what kind of show it was going to be. And when we did end-of-year plays, it would be me who would be on the drums, drumming. I would usually play the largest part in any school play. From that time onward, I knew in my heart that if I didn't become a singer, then I would become an actor as I am today.

When he completed Modern 3, therefore, John looked for opportunities to get involved in theater. There was a small theater group in Ẹdẹ which was advertising for actors, and he would have joined this one if he had not met a woman member of the Adéjọbí Theatre who was married to an Ẹdẹ man. This woman told him that Adéjọbí was also looking for performers, and a few days later she took him to meet Adéjọbí in Òṣogbo. He met Adéjọbí, Alhaji, Grace, and the other wives, and "they welcomed me very warmly. . . . When I explained how much I loved theater, they were very pleased." He began to rehearse with them, traveling every morning from Ẹdẹ until, after two months, he decided to move to Òṣogbo permanently.

However, predictably, he met with opposition to his choice of profession.

> After I had moved here, my parents began to give me trouble, saying that I had left school and didn't want to go any further with my education, that I'd taken up theater instead, that they weren't happy about it, and so on, until the person born immediately after my mother, that person took me away, and took me to Ilóbùú. I went to learn the business of "home doctor" there, after I'd spent a year here [in Òṣogbo]. But when I realized that this work that I was learning . . . my heart was still with the work that I had left, I mean theater work, that's where my heart lay, so after I'd spent about nine months learning this other work, I came back to the theater here in order to take it up again.

He did not say goodbye to his master in Ilóbùú and told no one where he had gone: "They were looking for me all over, thinking maybe I'd gone to Lagos, I'd run away to Lagos—they had no idea that I'd gone back to the work I was doing before. Only when they saw me on television did they realize that this was where I was." However, after he had achieved fame and modest wealth through acting, his family became reconciled to it. The theater company itself, he said, was also like a family to him, and he never wanted to leave it.

The inner circle of key actors was surrounded by another circle of people who were relatively permanent fixtures in the company but who had not become main-part players. One devoted member in this category, notable for his loyalty and "long stay," was **Fẹ́mi Adéníjì** (also known as Fẹ́mi

Dayọ̀ Akínpẹ̀lú and John Adéwuni. ©Elio Montanari

Ìlá because he came from Ìlá-Ọ̀ràngún), nicknamed "Sálánkó." His story gives a particularly vivid insight into the lives of the people in this strand of the intermediate classes.

Fẹmi's father was a carpenter, his mother a washerwoman. Fẹmi went to a Seventh-Day Adventist primary school in Ìlá and, after completing Primary 6, was apprenticed as a mechanic. Four years into his apprenticeship, before he had "freed," he had a serious accident. Petrol that had splashed onto his clothes when he was servicing a car caught fire and he suffered terrible burns. His mother and aunt rushed him to the local dispensary (there was as yet no hospital in the area) where prompt treatment saved his life. It was six months before he came out. He never regained his full strength, and he was not able to continue as a mechanic, since he "could no longer push cars about." So he went to stay with his older sister, who was married to a man in Ìnísà, and learned the work of metal trunk-making. He completed the apprenticeship and "freed" after four years, then returned to Ìlá and set up as a trunk-maker in his home. However, this did not pay, and he moved to Jebba on the banks of the Niger to work as a laborer in the paper mill there. That was where his association with Oyin Adéjọbí began. In 1975 the theater company came to Jebba on tour and performed *Adédigba's Co-wife*. Fẹ́mi had loved drama since he was a small child, and he was a particular fan of the Adéjọbí Theatre Company. He had watched them when they came to perform in Ìníṣà and at Ìlá Grammar School. On this occasion, in Jebba, he made up his mind to join them:

> When they finished the play, I was elated, and I went and prostrated to them and said I wanted to join their company right away. They said I was too small. I said I would go with them.

Fẹ́mi was 22 at the time, and he managed to persuade Mr. Adéjọbí that he was old enough to travel with them. They were in the middle of a long tour, and he went with them to Òmù-Àrán, Ìlọrin, Káínjí, Ìkọ́lé, Ìjerò, Arámọkọ, Ìyìn, Ìgèdè, Ìkàrẹ́, Àkókó, and Ògbàgì—all small towns in the northeastern part of Yorùbáland (except for Ìlọrin and Káínjí)—before they went back to Òṣogbo.

When he first joined, he waited a few days to see what would happen. Then they asked him if he could travel ahead and stick up the posters. He said "Ah, there isn't anywhere I can't go." So they gave him posters to stick up in the Èkìtì towns they were going to tour. They gave him money for his fare, money for meals, and money to find overnight accommodation. They did not pay him a salary straight away: "They were watching me to see whether I would stay or whether I would run away." Once he had convinced them that he would stay, they began to pay him a monthly salary. However, the following year, when they were not making much money, he did run away and joined with a younger relative to found a new troupe, the Adéògún Theatre, made up of "very small actors." After seven months, however, he left them and returned to Adéjọbí, where he has stayed ever since. He said he was satisfied with the life. He liked running errands, reporting on what he had done, and knowing that the boss was pleased with him. Whatever the boss asked him to do, he would gladly do it. He was satisfied with his pay and was grateful that he had managed to marry on it. His wife was Ṣọlá, an actress already on the fringes of the company before he married her. He loved acting and had been given a number of small parts, including one of the two false friends in *Láníyọnu* (see Barber and Ògúndíjọ 1994) and a chief in *Fọlájiyọ̀* [*The Overreacher*]. It was clear that he was not destined to be given big roles. Alhaji observed that his "real work" was the posters, and even in an emergency, when a leading actor suddenly became unavailable, it was not Fẹ́mi who was asked to step in. His loyalty and dependability, however, made him a relatively significant figure in the company.

Another Fẹ́mi, **Fẹ́mi Bámidélé,** was better educated and a better actor than Fẹ́mi Ìlá. He joined the company after modern school in 1979, at the age of 23 (his education had been interrupted by a queuing system whereby he worked on his father's farm after Primary 6 until his older brother had finished grammar school, for his father could not afford school fees for two at once). Because he had loved drama at school, and because he had seen the Adéjọbí Company on television and in *Atọ́ka* magazine, he wanted to join them the moment he finished school. He remembers vividly how he gained admission to the company:

> I took my **application** to them. On that evening as I was taking it to them, I met their manager, the one they call Bàbáa Wándé. He was on a motorbike. And he asked where I was going, and I said I wanted to see the Bàbá, and he said that's him sitting down over there. He said is anything the matter? I said it's an **application** I've brought, because it was evening by then, I and my friend from Bendel had gone together. . . . When I went over to him [Adéjọbí], he said I should come back in the morning. So we went again the next morning. He asked all kinds of questions. He asked where I'd had my education and I said I'd been to modern school. Then he said I should come back the next day. I asked him to give me time to go back to school to get my testimonial. He said I could. So in the late afternoon, I came. And two or three days after I joined them, we went to perform *Ọláníyọnu*, in the army barracks at Ẹdẹ, and he gave me the part of one of the two friends. . . . He wanted to try me out, to see whether I could do it, he was testing me.

Fẹ́mi Bámidélé, like many of the others, left briefly after he had joined the company but returned and continued to play small but colorful roles both on stage and in television serials.

The outermost fringes of the company were made up of the very new and untested arrivals, drivers (some of whom also aspired to act), "daily paid" performers, and "guest artists." These were all people nobody counted on but who were always needed and used when they were available. There was a constant turnover of drivers, and Mr. Adéjọbí often expressed doubt and dissatisfaction about their competence and reliability. When I took a census of the company in 1983, there were three drivers (to handle the car, "staff bus," and truck). Hamed Akínwálé joined the organization in 1982, left, and returned in 1983. He was from Modákẹ́kẹ́, had gone up to Primary 5 before lack of money put an end to his education, and had then been apprenticed for four years as a mechanic and had "freed," after which he had learned to drive trucks and tippers. He was introduced to the theater company by Fẹ́mi Ìlá. Abíọ́dún Ọdéjìnmí completed primary school in Òṣogbo and then trained as a welder, but changed to driving after a year and a half of his apprenticeship. He had a strong link with the company, for his mother was the full younger sister of Grace Adéjọbí. He was also friends with Dayọ̀ Akínpẹlú and John Adéwuni. He said that he often acted in the plays as well as driving, but he made a clear distinction between "Company" and "àwa tá a wà under Company" ("the [Theatre] Company" and "we who are under the [Theatre] Company"). Moses Joseph, a native of Ìlá-Ọ̀ràngún, came to work for Adéjọbí in 1983, attracted by the plays which he had seen on television and in *Atóka* magazine. He too had been to school up to Primary 6, and he had then been apprenticed as a welder. He freed after three and a half years and went to Oǹdó to work. However, from his schooldays he had always wanted to work in a theater group. He had undertaken the apprenticeship just to occupy himself until he was old enough to join a theater company, for he knew that "actors are usually fairly old, so, when I thought I had reached the right 'gauge' [level], and could do that work, I decided I wanted to work in a theater." He was hanging around at the time I talked to him, hoping for a part in one of the new plays. The plays they were currently taking on tour were all old plays and all the parts were filled.

Isiaka, the son of an Ìbàdàn butcher, was a newcomer who was luckier; he had joined the company for a short time once before, in 1976, and returned in 1983. He had been educated up to Modern 3, then began to train as a welder but did not like it and left to join the theater. After leaving Adéjọbí the first time, he worked in an electronic company in Ọ̀sogbo, having learned electrical work from his older brother on weekends. On his return to the theater company, he was given good parts, such as the comic houseboy in *The Royal Palm-nut,* and was put in charge of the lighting and sound systems after Dayọ̀—formerly the electrician of the company—defected.

Another newcomer with the potential of becoming "long stay," was **Morádékẹ́,** a young woman who joined in 1982 and was "married" to John Adéwuni, without any ceremony having yet been performed. After Primary 6, she learned sewing for three years and also worked as a clerk for a woman provisions trader before a relative introduced her to Mr. Adéjọbí. Despite opposition from other members of the family, she began to work in the company dancing in the opening glee and playing small parts.

Another very new arrival in 1983 was **Sunday Fágbáyììmú,** a self-educated man whose ambition was to have an "*ewì* business," that is, a business composing, performing, recording, and selling the neo-traditional topical and moral poetry called *ewì,* a style popularized by Láńrewájú Adépọ̀jù for whom Sunday had previously worked. He was employed by Adéjọbí, but he also gave the impression of being a kind of guest artist, one who would grace the company with his special talents for a while without being committed to it in the long term.

A true guest artist of impressive talent was **Lásún Ọláììtán,** a headmaster who had been with Adéjọbí in 1963 at the time of transition from an amateur to a professional company. His grandfather was a hunter and an expert *ìjálá* singer. His father was a policeman who knew nothing of oral poetry. However, in Mr. Ọláìítán's view the talent was reborn in himself and as a gift from God he had to use it, despite his father's furious opposition. Mr. Ọláìítán only performed occasionally; parts in which he could display his poetic chanting were created for him on the spot when he presented himself. He was paid an amount agreed with Mr. Adéjọbí beforehand, but friendship and the memory of the early days in the theater company also seemed to play a part in his involvement.

A "daily paid" performer was the *dùndún* drummer, a professional from one of the drumming lineages of Òṣogbo who was hired by the day whenever they did a play that had a talking drum in it but who was free to pursue his profession in the normal way otherwise.

Finally, there were the bit-part players who had a permanent link with Adéjọbí but only an intermittent availability: his children. Adédìran, his first son, worked in Ìbàdàn but occasionally came and helped out. Adédùnmọ́lá, his oldest daughter, was a grammar school girl hoping for admission to the university. She danced in the opening glee whenever she was at home. Her ambition was to do a degree in music or theater arts and then get a job in television or film production. Some of the younger children traveled with the company when it went on tour and played small parts as required. One of them was even born in the middle of the show. Emily described it:

> We finished singing the opening songs and I went offstage to change into the costume for Kúyẹ̀'s wife that day. That's when I went into labor, and told them that that was the end of the play for that day as far as I was concerned. I couldn't perform any more. They said they would take me to Ìjerò. We were performing at Kówo that day. I said I won't be able to go a single kilometer before I give birth, so it would be better if they just left me in that hall. Then Màmá (Grace) begged me to get into the vehicle, so I went quietly and took refuge in the vehicle. The Bàbá who was our driver at that time, when he was about to start the engine, I said, "Bàbá, don't bother, just hang on a minute." So that Bàbá stopped. That's where I had the baby. When I'd had the baby, that Bàbá rushed into the hall shouting that the person he'd been told to take to hospital had already given birth inside the vehicle! All the audience came out and crowded round saying "What, is this the woman who finished dancing only a minute ago, ha, these actors!"

MOBILITY

It was striking how many of the actors were brought up by a succession of relatives other than their parents and how many had moved from one town to another, sometimes repeatedly, before they had grown up. Multiple mi-

Adédìran Adéjọbí and John Adéwuni. ©Elio Montanari

Emily Adéjọbí with Kingsley, a "short-stay" member of the company. ©Elio Montanari

Adédùnmólá, Adéjọbí's daughter. ©Elio Montanari

gratory journeys are of course the norm in western Nigeria (Peil 1981; Peil, Ekpenyong, and Oyenẹyẹ 1988; Adepọju 1976). According to Lloyd, "It seems likely that one-quarter of the population of Yorùbá country is living away from home—in neighbouring provincial towns, in other areas of Nigeria or in the cities" (Lloyd 1974, 78). Fostering, furthermore, is positively viewed and very common, especially among close relatives (Peil, Ekpenyong, and Oyenẹyẹ 1988). Nonetheless, the wanderings of the theater company members did seem more frequent than most people's. The men in the company had all moved around and lived in different towns during their schooldays and after. John Adéwuni, Alhaji Kàrímù Adépòjù, and Fẹ́mi Bámidélé all went to another town to attend modern school. After his accident, Fẹ́mi Adéníjì went from Ìlá to Ìnísà to live with an older sister and then to Jebba. Several of the young temporary men employed as drivers and odd-job men had similar histories. The women seemed to have been passed around from relative to relative even more frequently. None of them had parents who lived together or stayed in one place throughout their children's schooldays. Grace's father, the building contractor, was constantly away: "He worked in Ìbàdàn, in Lálupọn. He went all over the place, he wasn't confined to one area. Because he would be called to different places to work." Her mother, as we saw, spent 20 years away in Ghana, leaving Grace to be brought up by co-wives and aunts. Margaret went to school both in her father's town, Òṣogbo, and her mother's town, Abẹ̀òkúta. After her father's death she worked in Òṣogbo, and then "I followed the person born immediately after my mother, that person was in Ilésà, so, I **boarded** with him/her.... After I'd done that for quite a time, I came back to Òṣogbo." Emily's parents came from Ìrẹsì, but she grew up in Ifẹ̀, where her father had made a cocoa farm. On leaving Primary 6, she went with an older sibling to Ìbàdàn, where she began modern school. She left after two years to look after her father, who was sick in U.C.H. hospital in Ìbàdàn. When he recovered, they returned to Ifẹ̀. She then left Ifẹ̀ and went with her "aunt" to Òṣogbo, where she worked as a ward maid until she married Adéjọbí. Yẹ́misí, the youngest wife, moved about too. Her father was an Òṣogbo man, but she never lived with him because he was a soldier, constantly on the move. Her mother was from Ìrẹsì. But it was with her mother's mother that she lived, first in Ọ̀yọ́ (where she was born), then in Òṣogbo, which she said her grandmother returned to after she, Yẹ́misí, had finished primary school in Ọ̀yọ́. Morádékẹ́'s story was even more complicated. She explained it to me as follows:

> KARIN: Are you a native of Òṣogbo?
> MORÁDÉKẹ́: I'm a native of Ilésà.
> KARIN: Were you born at Ilésà?
> MORÁDÉKẹ́: Yes, Ilésà was where I was born.
> KARIN: What was your father's work?
> MORÁDÉKẹ́: Policeman.
> KARIN: What about your mother?
> MORÁDÉKẹ́: She was a food-seller.
> KARIN: How did you come to be at Òṣogbo?
> MORÁDÉKẹ́: How I came to be at Òṣogbo was, I was working as a seamstress in Abẹ̀òkúta, at my mother's house.
> KARIN: Let's begin from the beginning. You were born in Ilésà?
> MORÁDÉKẹ́: Yes.
> KARIN: Did you go to school there?
> MORÁDÉKẹ́: I went to school in Abẹ̀òkúta.
> KARIN: Did you move to Abẹ̀òkúta when you were very small?
> MORÁDÉKẹ́: When I was small, they took me to Àkúrẹ́ in Oǹdó State.
> KARIN: So your mother didn't live at Ilésà for long?
> MORÁDÉKẹ́: She didn't live at Ilésà for long.
> KARIN: What about your father?

MORÁDÉKẸ́: The same thing, he didn't live long at Iléṣà either. They first took us to Àkúrẹ́, we went to school there. The C.A.C. [Christ Apostolic Church], at Òkè-Àró. Then after a long time, we left there and came to Abẹ́òkúta.
KARIN: Did your father go too?
MORÁDÉKẸ́: When we were in Àkúrẹ́, and father was there too, he then left Àkúrẹ́ and went to Igbó—that place in the Ìjẹ̀bú area. And then after some time he died. And we came home. When the funeral was over, we went back to Abẹ́òkúta. [She finished primary school there and did three years' apprenticeship to a sewing mistress, after which she freed.] After I'd **freed,** I went to Iléṣà, to stay with my older brother's family. I was working as a clerk for a woman who sold provisions. My aunt who was here in Òṣogbo then said to me that that work wasn't profitable, and also that without proper supervision I would probably go off with some man. So she brought me to Òṣogbo.... I lived with her. But she's gone to Iléṣà now.

The mobility of the modern popular traveling theater, then, could be seen as consonant with the earlier lives of its performers, almost all of whom learned to shift for themselves in a succession of partial and temporary homes and to look for work and contacts in new places. It is perhaps no accident that so many of the major theater leaders initially had jobs that involved "posting," that is, being sent to a succession of strange towns in the course of duty. Ògúnǹdé was a policeman and a teacher before becoming a professional theater impresario; Ládiípọ̀ and Ògúnmọ́lá were also teachers. Their association with the church reinforced this propensity, for the church was the first public institution deliberately to send its agents out into "foreign" fields, so that an Ẹ̀gbá pastor such as Charles Phillips could spend the best part of his life in Òǹdó.

The membership of the Oyin Adéjọbí Company, then, was not recruited through systematic advertising and auditions. People approached, were tried out, hung around, drifted off, or stayed to move gradually toward the center of the company, where they had regular pay, more responsibilities, and better parts. The main requirement for would-be actors, at least in the early stages, was endurance: the sheer ability to stick to the company until they began to be accepted and given things to do. Fẹ́mi Ìlá's persistence, even when Adéjọbí had told him he was too young to join, was a well-known strategy used by would-be apprentices in other trades too, for example boys who insinuated themselves into the transport business by hanging around motor-parks (Otudeko 1977, 105–106). Actors were not recruited with a view to filling particular roles or even types of roles; rather, a company was assembled around the patron-convener in order to include a wide variety of potential skills. The "need to cultivate diversity" of which Guyer speaks in the context of a Yorùbá village economy (1997, 38) was clearly no less crucial in the theater company. The potential talents of the recruits were then explored by trying them out in a series of parts; both the actors and the parts were gradually adapted until they fit, and space was made for the display of any special skill that became available.

Keeping the company together was always a preoccupation of Adéjọbí, and even "long stay" members could depart without notice—to found their own group, as Dayọ̀ tried to do; to further their education, like Fẹ́mi Bámidélé; or simply to try to find some better-paying job when times were hard. Permanent actresses were secured mainly through courtship and marriage. Permanent actors were held most strongly, perhaps, by feelings of loyalty to a quasi-family and also by public recognition which associated them permanently with particular roles—usually in a television series—that they could only play under the auspices of the company. Most of the members had no prior connection with the company but had conceived an ambition to join after seeing its plays on stage or (especially among the younger ones) on television or in the pages of *Atóka*. Some, however, such as Yẹmisí and Abíọ́dún, had prior links of kinship or friendship to established members; and others, such as Morádékẹ́ and Ṣọlá, entered into an informal marriage with a member of the company before or after joining. Some of the members came from Òṣogbo—Grace, Alhaji, Yẹmisí—but others moved to Òṣogbo in order to be with the company: among them Fẹ́mi Ìlá, John, and Sunday. Many went to school and then lived and worked in a succession of places and only came into contact with the company after some other cause had brought them to Òṣogbo. Among these were Margaret, who was working as a clerk for a provisions merchant when she met Adéjọbí; Emily, who came to stay with a senior female relative and got a job in a local hospital; and Fẹ́mi Bámidélé, who was in Òṣogbo to finish his secondary school course, which he had started in Ilóbùú. Most were Christians, but some—including Alhaji, Isiaka, and Hamed, the driver—were Muslim.

Despite this variable and opportunistic mode of recruitment, however, the people they ended up with, both men and women, were remarkably homogeneous in terms of social class. All had much the same level and type of schooling, and most had been apprenticed to learn an artisanal occupation before joining the company.

SCHOOL

All the members of the Adéjọbí Company had been to school, but only one—Adéjọbí's own daughter, who was not a full-time member—had been to grammar school and aspired to a university education. Among the more central and permanent members of the company, the norm was six years of primary education followed by one, two, or three years at modern school. Alhaji, John Adéwuni, Fẹ́mi Bámidélé, Isiaka, and Yẹ́misí, Adéjọbí's youngest wife, all completed the 3-year modern school program. Emily, the next-to-youngest wife, and Margaret, the second wife, both began modern school but had to leave for family reasons after two years and one year respectively. Grace, the first wife, went up to Standard V (two years of infants' and five years of primary education, under the old system: Standard VI was commonly regarded as equivalent to, if not better than, Modern III). The more peripheral members and those who played only small parts tended to be the ones with less schooling. Fẹ́mi Ìlá, Morádéké (John Adéwuni's second wife), and the drivers Abíọ́dún Ọdéjìnmí and Moses Joseph all had six years of primary education; Hamed Akínwálé, another driver, had only five.

School played an ambiguous but powerful role in the formation of the actors' aspirations and self-understandings. In Adéjọbí's youth, and even when the longer-established members of the company such as Alhaji and Grace were young, schooling translated directly into status and prestigious jobs. The ideal was to complete Standard VI and then proceed to grammar school or, failing that, to a teacher training college. This would open the door to a civil service job or even to scholarships abroad. When modern schools were inaugurated in 1955, the intention was that they would be preparatory to further training, if not for teaching then for some commercial or technical occupation. But no member of the theater company managed to go beyond Modern III, and they remarked on this with regret. Grace spoke with nostalgia of all school activities—sports, needlework, drama—as if they were inseparable and represented a good life that she had thrown away by her foolish misuse of the school fees. Adéjọbí himself evoked most powerfully a sense of lost opportunities, a road not taken, a block which appeared to have been placed by himself in his own path. It was evident that he was very proud of his rapid progress through the primary school. He completed the 3-year infants' program in one year,[4] and later he was promoted from Standard II straight to Standard IV because he had done so well. He thus finished the 9-year program up to Standard VI in only six years. He was a star pupil:

> I remember something that happened to me when I was in Standard IV. In those days, there would be an end-of-year exam. They called it "ODCC," that is, Òsogbo District Church Council, it was they who set that exam for the Standard IV pupils. All the Standard IV classes in Òsogbo, and in the whole Òsogbo area, would do that exam together. Well, I came top. It was marked out of 400, I got

366. The person who came second got 298. And that's just one example.

So, having finished Standard VI with flying colors, he was well placed to go on to grammar school—and you will remember that his older brother Adéléké (the Church of the Lord leader) was keen to assist him. He sent Oyin a list of possible grammar schools and colleges and told him to pick whichever one he wanted to go to. But—inexplicably even to himself—Oyin did not take up this glittering offer.

> I don't know what it was, I just didn't feel like going to school any more, maybe I didn't understand things well enough then. Because if I had wanted to go, I had someone who would definitely have helped me, and I would have gone really far [in schooling]. But for some reason I just didn't want to go at all.

Instead, he tried to go straight into teaching, but, as we saw in the last chapter, found his path blocked by his physical disability. That was when he went to Lagos to live with Adéléké, study in private institutes, and begin his career as a composer. This story is partly about how Oyin came to find the path in life which brought him to such satisfaction and such fame. It was partly because he didn't "go far" in schooling that the theater became his life's work and field of self-realization. But his autobiographical narrative also echoes with a sense of loss and waste, for he knew he had extraordinary academic gifts. After his return to Òṣogbo in 1953, he entered a competitive examination for a post as local government clerk. His account of this suggests the continued centrality of examinations and academic success in his scheme of things:

> When I applied, they called 75 of us for **written tests,** out of the 75 that they called, do you know, I came first. Because the type of question they asked at that time, I realized that it was something I had already come across at school, they called it **general—general knowledge** or something like that. They might ask "What is the thing that people go in, that travels in the air and carries you to England, what is it called?" We would write the answer down. They asked all kinds of things like that. It didn't take me long to finish my paper that year. The surprising thing that happened, that I **remarked,** was that the master who was running the exam for us—and there were 75 of us!—an elderly gentleman with white hair, he was there, and when I finished it, and put down my pen, that master seemed to think that I hadn't been able to answer, he didn't know that I had finished it. So he came up to me GRA GRA GRA, and when he reached me he said "Aren't you doing it any more, then?" I said I'd already finished it! So he opened my answer book

and read it. Then he closed it, and took it away, and called his colleagues who were moderating the exam with him. They all went into a huddle outside and looked at my answer book, all of them were peering at me through the window to see the man who . . . then they came to me and said if I wanted to have a breath of air I could go outside. **Meanwhile,** the other candidates didn't know what had **happened.** They probably thought "Ha! This old man doesn't know what to write, they've sent him out," and so on. **So,** when it was all over, and they'd marked it, I got virtually full marks! I got virtually full marks! Hmm. That's how I came to be employed by the council.

This episode is one of the high points of his long and detailed rendition of his life story, showing how much his examination success still meant to him even after he had become a famous and sought-after church composer.

The relationship between school and theater was both genetic and oppositional. Many of the company members saw drama as something that essentially emanated from the school system. Most of them said they developed their interest in drama from participation in end-of-year school plays and from watching the traveling companies when they visited the schools. And in Alhaji's case, as he explained, there was an even more direct link between his primary school and the Adéjọbí Company, for Mr. Adéjọbí himself organized the (Muslim) pupils of this Ansar-ud-Deen primary school to put on their own plays.

At the same time, however, there was a sense in which continuing at school was clearly seen as an alternative and opposed trajectory to joining a theater company, and in some ways a more desirable or prestigious one. Many of the actors went out of their way to explain the block that prevented them from continuing in school. Grace wasted her school fees on clothes. Emily gave up school to look after her sick father. Her parents saw the theater as a starkly undesirable alternative to school and told her that if she was joining the company out of resentment at having her education cut short she should apply immediately to go back and do Modern III. Margaret said she could not go beyond Modern I because her father died. Hamed, one of the drivers who was hoping to act, said he could not even finish primary school because of lack of money. Yẹmisí finished Modern III and only decided to join the company because her examination grades were not good enough for her to gain admission into further education. Fẹ́mi Bámidélé pieced his modern school education together in stages, in danger of being blocked at every step. First he waited three years after finishing primary school so that his older brother could finish grammar school. Then he went to Ilóbùú and attended St Paul's Modern School for two years. Lack of money forced him to leave before finishing the course, and he tried to fill the gap with evening classes in Òṣogbo. But when it emerged that the government had not approved the school running the classes, he left. Two years later he got admission to an Ansar-ud-Deen modern school in Òṣogbo, and there he finally completed Modern III. Later he left the company to try to join another evening class, but he did not get far before he returned.

Some of the actors felt that the theater and the school were in competition and that people had to choose which route to take. Yẹmisí said that any future child of hers would make up its own mind: "If he/she likes, he/she can turn in the direction of drama, and if he/she likes, he/she can turn in the direction of school." When I asked Emily if her little boy Ajíbọ́lá would become an actor, she confirmed this expectation with the words "*Ajíbọ́lá ò tiẹ̀ féẹ́ lọlé-ìwé rárá*" [In fact Ajíbọ́lá doesn't want to go to school at all]. She had had to send him away to stay with a relative so that he would at least complete primary school before becoming an actor. Where adult members of the company were concerned, Emily saw schooling as a drain on the company's workforce. She said that it was hard to keep the company together, because "If you assemble a theater company today, by tomorrow the parents of some of them will be saying that Grade II [teacher training college] has opened, they're going back to school, they're going to do something or other."

John Adéwuni championed the choice of the theater alternative, arguing that he had done as well out of acting as some of his contemporaries had out of further schooling:

> Someone who goes on with school does it to get money [in future], we too who didn't go on with school, I don't think that those who are highly educated . . . I don't think they're doing any better than those who didn't go beyond the eight years [*sic*] that modern school pupils do. I don't think they're doing any better than me. What they've achieved, I too have achieved. Now, in this line of work that I'm in, God has been good to me, I've married, I've got a child . . . he's getting on for two years old.

Sunday Fágbáyìímú was only a temporary and minor member of the company, but his career sheds much light on the powerful, competing but intertwined desires for schooling and for the theatrical limelight. He was born in a village called Ikiyìnwá near Iléṣà and went to primary school there. "Due to [the fact] that my parents were so poor, and by that time I came from a polygamous family, therefore my parents didn't have time for me to go further with my education." His father was a farmer, and for a while, after finishing Primary 6, he worked for him on the farm. He was then sent to Ìbàdàn to stay with his older brother to learn trading. "We call that trade 'fancy.' . . . It may have another name, we usually call it 'fancy.' It is something like underwears, singlet, pants, brassiere, and something like that. Wearing by both men and women." His brother had a shop, but after he had learned the trade Sunday decided to set up on his own: "I have no money to establish a shop, then I have to walk around to 'go slow' [traffic jams]. When there is 'go slow' I will walk around the place." In this he was so successful that from a starting capital of fifteen shillings he had made £35 within a month.

> So, when I get that money, I buy cloths, rent a room. Rent at Ìbàdàn then, starting from one naira per month. I have a room. I bought a single bed, and Gambari-made mattress. I think you know that type of mattress. It's not original one. Locally made. So I have it. Spend about 15 pounds to furnish my room. So, the little amount remain, I am still hawking. I hawk till six or seven months, before I get a kiosk. (English.)

However, his business later failed and he returned to his village to seek help from his parents to re-establish it. When no help was forthcoming, he decided to pursue a lifelong ambition to become a writer and performer of neo-traditional chanted poetry of a type popularized by Túnbọ̀sún Ọládàpọ̀ and Lánrewájú Adépọ̀jù.

> When I see that they can't do anything to re-establish, I decided to come back to Ìbàdàn again. I went to one *ewì* exponent, Lánrewájú Adépọ̀jù. But before that in my village, I develop my talent through reading Yorùbá book published by Lánrewájú Adépọ̀jù, Adébáyọ̀ Fálétí, Túnbọ̀sún Ọládàpọ̀, and so on. By reading those books, I develop *ewì* talent. So I start to like *ewì*. So, there's one ceremony in our village by that time: "send-off party" for our catechist. I went there and sing *ewì*, so that's why everybody knows that I have the talent. And they advised me not to sit at the village and go to town to spread my talent around. (English.)

His method of composing *ewì* was as follows:

> I wrote it down. I wrote it down. After I wrote it, I memorize it, if I . . . at times, I read, I sing it through reading in the book. . . . I learn it through reading book published by superior seniors in the exponent like Lánrewájú Adépọ̀jù, Adébáyọ̀ Fálétí, Túnbọ̀sún Ọládàpọ̀. . . . I listen to their performance on radio and television and at times watch them 'live play'. That's why I get the idea.

To him, then, the literacy learned at school fed directly into his ambitions for self-development as a performer. In 1975 he went back to Ìbàdàn and approached Lánrewájú Adépòjù, who gave him a job in his small theater company, the Akéwì Theatre. He worked as an actor but also occasionally had the opportunity to perform *ewì* at public functions when Lánrewájú was unable to go. He would sometimes perform Lánrewájú's compositions, sometimes his own. Though still wishing to re-establish his "fancy" trade, he stayed with Lánrewájú for three years and then moved to the Adéjọbí company. Though his main aim was really to accumulate enough capital to re-launch his trade, he was also determined to "re-establish my *ewì* business, maybe to go to radio or television very soon, or something like that. So, I can't leave *ewì* as that. I will do it for life." His longer-term ambitions were "to become a film star" and "to be a famous writer like James Hadley Chase."

> I will go back to my trade because when I settle down, if I have a group right now and some children maybe I can put the trade on their lap. So, I'll face writing in my future. I believe that I'll become famous writer. That is my great ambition. (English.)

So Sunday had strong aspirations to a world informed by literacy and literary art. He learned and composed *ewì*—a performance art—through the solitary study of books in his village, and he was also a reader of novels in English and Yorùbá. He had actually written a novel in Yorùbá; he kept the typescript in his box. In this novel, the hero is prevented by poverty and his father's polygamy from getting an education as a child. As an adult, he learns to read and write as a result of the patronage of a rich businessman and marriage to this patron's daughter. But he only achieves independence and full self-realization when he is driven out by them and makes his own way to fame and fortune through boxing. The alternative life, however—scholarship rather than showmanship—is represented throughout the novel in the form of his beloved younger sister, to whom he is devoted. With his support, she goes to grammar school and then to university.

Sunday, like Alhaji, enjoyed speaking English on formal occasions such as recorded interviews. As the quotations above show, he was remarkably fluent for a primary school leaver. He explained that

> After leaving school I don't happy that I stopped at primary school, but I told you before, my parents have no means to help me go further, so I went evening classes, in Ìbàdàn. So there I read up to the level of secondary class three there. Even I take correspondence examination from London. (English.)

To Sunday, theater did not seem to be simply an alternative to schooling; rather, it was part of a multi-faceted project of self-improvement, in which literacy, performance, and entrepreneurship were intertwined.

APPRENTICESHIP

The consistency of the educational level achieved by the majority of the theater company members was paralleled by the homogeneity of the type of alternative or previous jobs they held. None came to the theater after being farmers; with the exception of Sunday Fágbáyìímú, none had been traders either. Given the limitations of their education, none except Oyin Adéjobí himself had had the opportunity to be civil servants or teachers. Rather, all had a background in artisanal or low-level secretarial or service occupations. Almost all the men in the company, and some of the women, had been apprenticed to a master craftsman to learn a manual skill.

Adéjobí was apprenticed to a goldsmith for three years. Alhaji learned tailoring, and kept a small tailor's business going intermittently even after becoming Adéjobí's manager (see Aluko, Oguntoye, and Afonja 1972, 322). Grace and Morádéké learned "sewing" (i.e., sewing by women, which usually excluded the larger and more prestigious men's garments such as embroidered *agbádá*). Fémi Adéníjì trained as a mechanic and then as a metal trunk-maker before working in a paper mill. John Adéwuni was sent to learn "home medicine" before he rebelled. Isiaka, Abíódún Odéjìnmí, and Moses Joseph all learned welding. Isiaka also learned electrical work informally from his older brother. Hamed Akínwálé trained as a mechanic and driver. Some of the women got low-level jobs in the service sector which did not require apprenticeship: Margaret worked as a clerk to a trader, Morádéké as clerk to a provisions merchant, Emily as a cleaner and general factotum in a private hospital. Only Yémisí and Fémi Bámidélé joined the theater straight after Modern III without learning any other work (although Fémi had worked for some years on his father's farm while waiting for his turn to go to school).

Apprenticeship was a formal and binding arrangement, in which the parents of the apprentice paid the master an agreed fee and the apprentice "served" the master until he completed the training, going to his workshop every day and doing odd jobs as well as basic elements of the work process. At the end of this period, when the master decided the apprentice was competent—and often after pressure from the apprentice and his or her family—the apprentice would "free" in a formal ceremony which marked his or her transition to the status of independent worker. In some cases a certificate was provided, and the freed apprentice would become a member of the relevant craftsmen's guild or association. This system operated for those members of the company who learned tailoring, sewing, car repair, welding, and metal trunk-making. Fémi Ìlá was proud of the fact that he not only completed four years' apprenticeship in metal trunk making but also "got a certificate to prove it." Grace said that she not only freed in her trade of sewing but that she even had apprentices of her own who themselves completed the training and freed.

Driving instruction was quicker and could be arranged by individuals who would make a deal with an experienced driver. Thus Abíọ́dún Ọdẹ́jìnmí, after spending a year and a half learning welding and giving it up without completing the training, went to a man who was a driver with the Ministry of Health and made a contract to pay him N35 to teach him to drive. Abíọ́dún agreed to wash the vehicle in which the man taught him, but he did no other work for him. Unfortunately, the man was transferred to Ìkàrẹ́ before the driving lessons were complete and did not refund any of the money. But the training enabled Abíọ́dún to pick up lorry driving—to which he then turned—in a short space of time, and "when I knew that I was expert enough to get a driving license, I went to do the test and got my license on March 10, 1977," at the age of 20. Hamed Akínwálé, after spending four years learning to be a mechanic and "freeing," spent another three learning to drive a trailer.

Several members of the company had learned an occupation informally, by living with and assisting a relative in the evenings and weekends. This was how Alhaji learned tailoring and Isiaka learned electrical repairs.

The actors' participation in the world of manual trades is not surprising, since by far the commonest step after Primary 6 was apprenticeship. Apprentices in the Western Region in the 1960s and 1970s greatly outnumbered secondary school pupils (Fafunwa 1974; Koll 1969; Oyeneye 1979). Artisans or craftsmen were fairly low in the social hierarchy, both in popular estimation and in the actual options open to them. They were less highly esteemed, and had fewer options, than moderately prosperous farmers, moderately successful traders, or low-grade white-collar workers, let alone literate professionals such as doctors and lawyers and successful businessmen such as produce buyers and lorry owners (Koll 1969). But, as Koll pointed out in 1969—and this observation has only become more true in subsequent years—artisans were certainly not the bottom of the heap. They were better off and more highly regarded than poor farmers, agricultural laborers, or other laborers (what Mr. Adéjọbí referred to as "daily paid workers") or the swelling army of the unemployed school leavers. Most primary school leavers, if they could not squeeze their way into grammar or modern school, preferred apprenticeship to working on their fathers' farms or working for someone else as a waged laborer or servant. Though not everyone who completed an apprenticeship succeeded in practicing the craft they had learned, the training at least gave them skills and the chance of setting up their own business. The independence of a master craftsman compensated to some extent for low income, for there is a strong and almost universal preference in western Nigeria for autonomy in work—no one wants to work for someone else, whether it is an individual employer or a gigantic firm (Peil, Ekpenyong, and Oyeneye 1988, 574; Lloyd 1974, 154). Moreover, the educational level of many of the theater company members was above average for artisans at that time,[5] enhancing their prospects further.

The practice of the theater can be understood as an amalgam of "clerkly" and "artisanal" modes, springing from the twin bases of the social identities of the members: their (limited) schooling and their apprenticeship in skilled manual trades. As we have seen, the theater company trained its members in much the same way as other artisanal enterprises. Theater apprentices were taken on, given menial jobs to do for little or no pay, tried out in small roles, and only gradually incorporated into the company if they were reliable and showed ability in a succession of increasingly demanding tasks. As in many artisanal trades, the "apprentices" became part of the household. The headquarters of the enterprise was Mr. Adéjọbí's family house in Gbáẹ̀mú Street; it was here that the actors congregated, chatted, idled, rehearsed, ate, and sometimes—after a late return from a long journey—slept. Inside, the house was divided down the middle by a corridor which widened, behind the two front parlors, into a large social space. Sometimes we rehearsed in this space—which was also where Alhaji parked his motorcycle at night—and sometimes in the back yard, a spacious enclosed area with washhouse and toilet and kitchen, where people also washed their clothes. The boss's household, then, was the primary work space.

Like apprentices to artisanal trades, too, actors learned their skills not by formal instruction—let alone written courses—but by participating in the production process, at first in easy or unimportant tasks and gradually in more difficult and bigger ones. Apprentices in manual trades learn holistically, gradually familiarizing themselves with every part of the production process. As they are learning they work alongside other more expert people so that they see the entire process going on from the beginning of their training. In many artisanal trades, moreover, the process is not confined to manufacturing an object, such as a metal trunk, a garment, or a chair. It also involves cultivating both suppliers and specialists in related, complementary trades; selecting, pricing, and bargaining for supplies; advertising the workshop or the product, usually through personal contacts; building up a clientele; and selling the finished product (Berry 1985, 147–148; Callaway 1967, 164; Oyeneye 1979, 138–145; Adam 1995, 61–62). Similarly, neophyte actors were involved from the start—often from the very first day—in the performance of real public shows. In addition to appearing on stage, they were expected to help with numerous other tasks, effectively participating in the whole theatrical production process (see Chapter 4). Even though particular actors became known for particular parts, each was expected to take over another actor's part at a moment's notice if necessary. And the theater company as an organization was responsible not only for the creation and performance of plays but also for purchasing and maintaining equipment, designing costumes and getting them made up, identifying potential audiences, cultivating "sponsors," organizing itineraries, designing and distributing posters, and responding to feedback. The skills that theater practitioners and artisanal apprentices learned on the job included not only how to do things themselves but also how to tap into other people's skills, establishing productive links with suppliers, customers, and the occupants of other specialist "niches" (compare Guyer 1997, 223, 229). Members of the theater company had to be able to get a printer to print the posters on time and at a reasonable price; they had to be able to book a hall and make sure it was unlocked at the right time; they had to be able to negotiate with television studio managers, school principals, hotel proprietors, petrol station attendants, vulcanizers (i.e., tire repairers), mechanics, electricians, seamstresses, and traditional drummers and orchestrate inputs from all of them. The ability to gain access, to convene, and to co-ordinate—playing it by ear and adapting to the peculiar rhythm of each specialist who is brought in—is the key to all artisanal enterprises in western Nigeria, very markedly so in the case of a large, complex, and multifaceted operation such as a traveling theater.

On the other hand, this artisanal practice was overlaid with procedures borrowed from the civil service. Actors wrote "applications" and were "interviewed." When they were taken on, their names were inscribed in a register by Mr. Adéjọbí, together with their starting date and their agreed salary. Salaries were paid monthly and were graduated, so that actors could expect regular increments, as in the civil service. The payments would be made formally, and the actors would write receipts for the management: as John Adéwuni explained, with some pride:

> And we have a way of distributing the money, and we have something that everyone will write, saying that I have received my money this month. We have a **receipt** thing. If baba arrives now, everyone will sign in front of him that "I've received my money, I've received mine." If they pay the salary today and it happens that there's someone who hasn't time to come until tomorrow, he'll get his money tomorrow and he'll acknowledge then that "I've received my salary."

Similarly, the rehearsal schedule imitated the timetable of office work. It was important to the actors to be seen to be working at a regular and respectable profession. They would be required to assemble at the Adéjọbí house every day at 9:00 A.M. even when no rehearsal was planned. As John Adéwuni put it:

You see, now, when we who aren't natives of this town, who are not natives of Òṣogbo, when we're in the house, those of us who are living together in the house, each one will say he/she is going to his/her place of work, and if you don't say you too are going to your place of work, won't they despise you for that? [laughs] Every day, at nine o'clock, we have to be here.

Non-natives of a town, people who live as tenants, are often people who have been posted there as teachers, police, local government workers, or other civil servants and who observe formal-sector hours and discipline.[6] As these remarks of John's indicate, there was more at stake than just the usefulness of literacy and bureaucratic regimens in the company's operations. What was at stake was assimilation into a distinctive social sphere, access to which was normally determined by level of education.

But, important as these procedures were in defining and affirming the theater company's status as a "clerkly," formal-sector organization, they did not displace or subsume the pattern of personal relationships, which was like that of other small artisanal enterprises in being modeled on the patriarchal family. Such organizations could be called "business families," perhaps, rather than "family businesses." Instead of business profits being sacrificed to the well-being of the owner's family (a criticism made of other Yorùbá small businesses: see Callaway 1973, 45), the family was subsumed into a larger project of self-realization, of which the company's business success was the visible proof. Recruitment was a form of assemblage in which actors were taken on not for specific tasks but as whole persons bringing with them a trail of potentially helpful or harmful family connections, experiences, and habits. After Yẹmisí had written her letter of application, Mr. Adéjọbí asked her where she came from; on hearing that she was a native of Òṣogbo, he asked which family she belonged to, and then he took her on. "Applicants" who smoked, drank, or let it be known that they were there against their parents' will would be sent away. Though Mr. Adéjọbí would sometimes advise an aspiring actor to wait a while and come back when older—as he did with Fẹ́mi Ìlá—at other times he would take in very young aspirants and care for them like his own children. Samuel Babátúndé, who attached himself to the theater company as a prospective screenplay writer when Mr. Adéjọbí was trying to raise the capital to make a film in 1983, told me he had been with the company much earlier in his career, when he was still a schoolboy. In 1971, when he was 15,

There was a complete breakup in my house, that is, we had a fight in my house, my mother and my father. I had to leave school because my father had another wife that made them to fight. So, my father rejected my mother and her children. I was one of them. I had to leave the school, came here.... I went with my uncle to meet the manager, Alhaji Kàrímù Adépòjù. So we had a talk and I told him that I would like to join the theater. So, I was taken immediately without any hitch. So, on the fifth day, I came straight to Gbáẹ̀mú here on my own and I joined the group.... I used to sleep [at Ìsàlẹ̀ Ìjẹbú, Adéjọbí's old house]. I was staying with him, and when he's gone to office, I used to come here to join the theater, it's around nine o'clock in the morning every day. (English.)

When the quarrel between his parents was settled, however, they came to take him back home to finish his WAEC, even though "I never wanted to go back. I was forced to go back by my parents. I was already enjoying the theater life."

The bureaucratic norms by which the company's business relations were ideally regulated did not always hold. There were many months when salaries were late or held over to the following month. Actors who remained loyal were sometimes compensated by the distribution of bonuses in good months. No real sanctions could be applied to actors who came late or were often absent, apart from getting rid of them altogether. Such selfish behavior was deplored by other actors, but discipline clearly depended on good will and a spirit of loyalty rather than on any regulatory mechanisms that Adéjọbí or Alhaji could apply.

The management treated the company members as more than mere employees. Fringe members not yet on full salary could go to the boss for a loan if they were hard up. John Adéwuni was shocked when I asked if an actor's pay would be stopped if he was off sick:

> Certainly not. Everyone is sick sometime or other. Human bodies are not wood or stone! If someone is sick, well, the man who is our father, who is our real boss [i.e. Adéjọbí] . . . if one of us is seriously ill, he'll arrange for him or her to be taken to hospital to a doctor who's a friend of his, and he will take care of him/her.

Fellowship and the sense of belonging were among Hamed Akínwálé's reasons for wanting to work as a driver for the theater company rather than for some other employer:

> The reason why I like it is just that "Let's walk together and be many," well, "that's what befits people." So, and being with my "daddy" as well, I like to be able to say I'm with him, we're working together, we're doing the plays together. And it's also helpful to him if I'm with him. I just like it.

Some of the actors' reflections on the nature of the theater as a collective enterprise added a suggestion of a religious fellowship to the basic model of a business family. Abíọ́dún Ọdẹ̀jìnmí, a member of the First Baptist Church in Òṣogbo, saw co-operation and "love" as the key to successful productions:

> What is good is if we all love each other, in this Company of ours, because where there is love, I don't think we can attempt any project and fail. Once there's love, and we like each other.

The clerkly and artisanal models, derived from the actors' own experiences as pupils and as apprentices, were fundamental to the self-conception of the theater. But it is also important to recognize the ways in which the theater was—and was seen and experienced as—something unique, sui generis, impossible to assimilate to any other trade or occupation. Most apprentices were bound over to a master by their parents (Oyeneye 1979, 105–106). The parents paid a fee, and at the end of the training the apprentice freed and was able to set up business on his or her own. In the theater, the process was the reverse. Many of the young applicants ran away from the apprenticeship their parents had put them into in order to join the theater. The theater was always their own choice, and it was often made in the teeth of concerted parental opposition. As John put it, "So I began, I came to work here, because I love this work, it's not that anyone brought me here to learn the trade, I liked it and that's why I came here to do it." His problems arose not from the work or the personal and professional relationships governing it, but from the relatives he had tried to escape from: "The only difficulty that I have experienced was the pressure and harassment I got from my people, who were saying 'Leave that place! It's only motor-park touts who join theaters,' that's the problem I can say I faced at the beginning." And just as he freely chose the theater company and made it his alternative, optative family, so the theater company chose him and freely took him as one of them: "Because the way they took me into this theater, it was the way full brothers take each other, it was as if they were my real parents, that's how they took me in."

To become a member of Adéjọbí's extended household, they often had to sever their ties, at least temporarily, with their own household. Running away, defying one's father, recurred frequently in their stories. And conversely, once they had apprenticed themselves to the theater, they were expected to stay there. When they matured they did not free: rather, they became all the more deeply embedded in the company as they moved toward its center and became more indispensable to its operations. Although the ultimate goal of the more successful young male actors was often to leave and found their own company, Adéjọbí and Alhaji did not see this as a normal and expected development. When actors left they were bitterly criticized, and if they returned they would have to apologize abjectly and strain every nerve to prove their loyalty before they would be taken on again.

Though civil service procedures had a great deal of symbolic as well as practical significance in the theater's operations, it was also quite clear that the theater's essential mode of being could not be contained within a bureaucratic framework. Mr. Adéjọbí himself highlighted this when he explained his reason for resigning from his post as council clerk in 1972: creative ideas were occurring to him thick and fast and demanding to be developed, and written down, immediately. And then "someone would put a file on my desk and I had no choice but to attend to it." The inspirational, improvisatory, intense, and erratic processes of play creation were incompatible with the routines of the town council office. People did not join the theater mainly for a secure job, an incremental salary, and a pension. They joined the theater because they felt an overpowering attraction to it and the responsive stirring of their own gifts.

4 Getting a Show on the Road

The material assets of the theater company—equipment and persons—defined the character of the shows it produced. The basic equipment (scenery, lights, and amplifiers) marked the temporal and spatial parameters of the show, differentiating it from other spectacular forms such as festival drama and masquerade shows. The organization of the actors, all of whom were artisanal all-rounders with aspirations to be recognized as specialist "stars," involved division of labor in the management of the equipment as well as in the distribution of parts. The nature of their production can only be understood if we start from its concrete, practical, and logistical base: how they got a show on the road, how they kept the company going.

DIVISION OF LABOR

Apart from one or two of the drivers, all the people employed by Adéjọbí had a chance to perform parts—though sometimes only very small ones—on stage. Conversely, all the actors were expected to do other jobs as well. These jobs included booking venues and advertising a tour; packing, unpacking, setting up, operating, and maintaining the company's equipment; selling tickets and controlling the admission of the public; and selling snacks and sweets to the public before the show.

The division of labor among the members will be clearer after an inventory of the company's equipment. In 1981 they had three vehicles: a truck, for carrying the scenery, costumes, props, household equipment (including a bed and several mattresses, cooking pots, mats, etc.), and the younger and newer of the company members; a mini-bus, known as the "staff bus," for the more senior actors; and Adéjọbí's Peugeot station wagon, in which he traveled with Emily and other select members of the company or visitors. The truck usually set off to the evening's venue well in advance of the bus and car, partly because it was slower, and partly so that those actors responsible for unloading the heavy equipment and setting it up would have plenty of time.

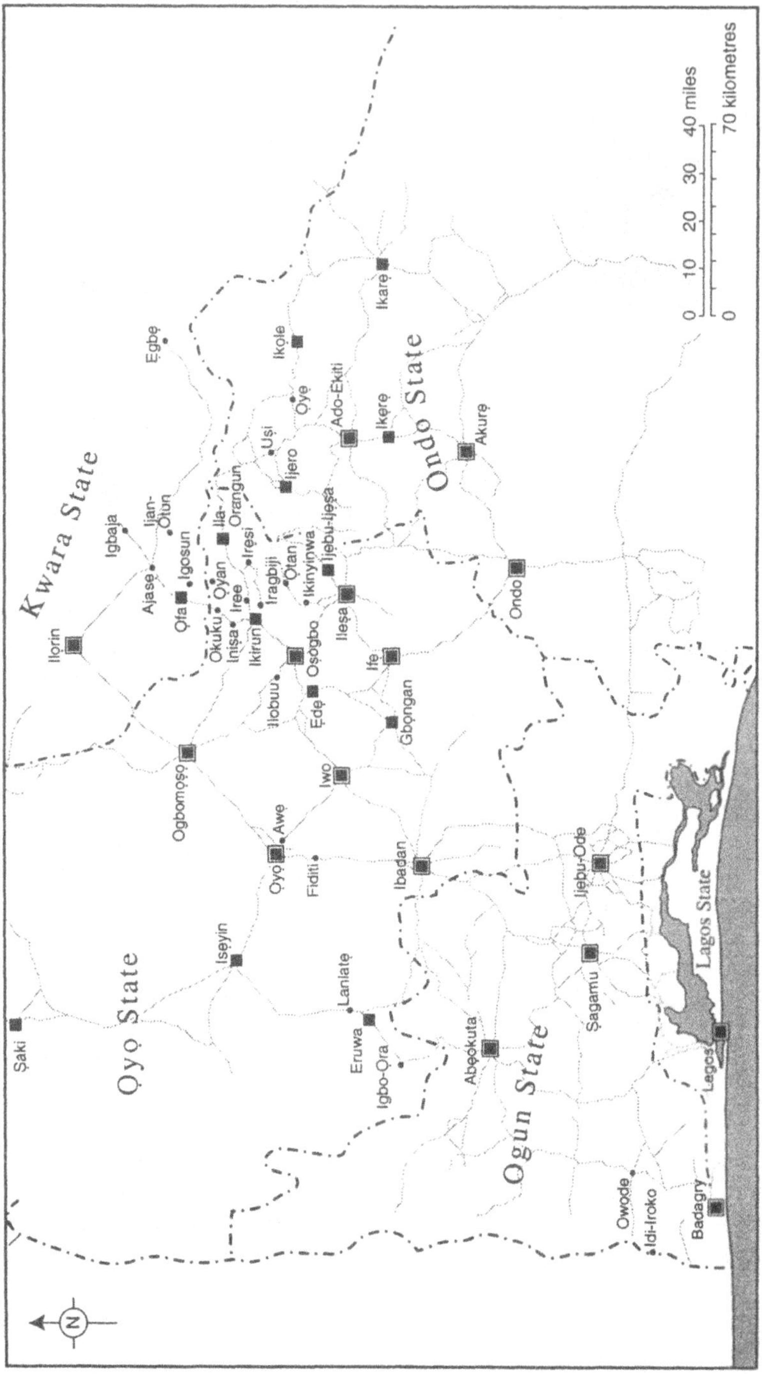

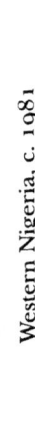

Western Nigeria, c. 1981

Emily in the "staff bus." ©Elio Montanari

The stage equipment consisted of a curtain, made of many yards of flowery cotton material; a backcloth, made of similar material but in a different color and pattern, suspended from iron rods fastened across the tops of four heavy iron stands; four sets of heavy three-leaved folding screens, two with a window, one with a door, and one without any aperture; a pair of larger two-leaved folding screens; two microphones on stands, which could also be removed and held by hand; a very large amplifier; a spotlight and a bundle of fluorescent tubes which were laid horizontally along the front of the stage; a portable generator; a large cassette player, used to broadcast popular music before the show and during scene changes; a set of four standing conga drums; and assorted pieces of furniture. Supplementary items such as chairs and small tables were usually borrowed from the hall in which the performance was taking place. The same backcloth and folding screens were used for every play. Unlike some theater companies, who went in for eye-catching and artistic backcloths designed specially for particular plays, the Adéjọbí Company treated the set

The company acquires a new instrument. ©Elio Montanari

as a purely functional backdrop for the action. From time to time the curtain and backcloth were changed and the screens were repainted. This was part of an overall process of refurbishment—akin to periodically changing the costumes the women wore for the opening glee—rather than an attempt to make the scenery match the content of the play. Although "realistic" to a limited extent—indoor scenes were indicated by the screens with windows and doors, forest scenes by removing the screens and dimming the lights—most of the work was done by the audience's imagination. The scenery was, however, extremely versatile. They made it work equally well in the National Theatre, with its vast, deep, wide stage, and in hotels and community halls where the acting space was so small that the actors had to stand almost on top of each other. They found ways of rigging up the curtain even in halls where there was no proscenium arch and nothing to fix the string to.

Although non-specific and neutral, the scenery was considered essential to the performance of a play. Performing in the round was unthinkable. This is what happened once: we had set up all the scenery in the church hall where we had expected to perform, in Ìjàn-Òtún, a small town in Kwara State far to the north of Òṣogbo. It had been a tricky business, and the younger stage hands had been baffled by the problem of how to make the curtain stay up in the absence of anything to fasten it to. Alhaji worked out

A church hall venue in the small town of Ìjàn-Òtún. ©Elio Montanari

a solution, and was congratulating himself on having got it all finished, when a policeman arrived and informed Adéjọbí that fire regulations made it impossible for the performance to take place in the hall. For some reason, Adéjọbí was unable to fix this. We had to move out and find another venue. But there was no other hall in that small town. The best they could offer was a playing field outside the primary school. We proceeded to carry everything back to the lorry; we borrowed all the benches and chairs from the church hall and carried them to the field, too. Alhaji and his assistants then spent several hours erecting a platform out of boxes and planks, fixing uprights and rigging up the curtains. By the time they had finished night had fallen. When the audience arrived, the auditorium was ready for them, with rows of chairs and benches facing forward toward the illuminated stage, which was separated from the auditorium by a gap and by its raised height. It seemed out of the question to perform on the grass, in the midst of the audience, in daylight: "Our public would not like it."

The sound system was also considered essential. The audiences were

Loading the lorry. ©Elio Montanari

An open air set improvised at Ijàn-Ọ̀tún after the church hall venue fell through. ©Elio Montanari

often large and usually exuberant. Audiences of schoolchildren in particular were very boisterous. The acoustics in most halls were poor, and without a microphone to quell them an actor stood little chance of holding his own against their uproar. The plays were therefore choreographed around the microphones: actors would come up to a standing mike when it was their turn to speak, deliver a speech, and then fall back to allow someone else to have a turn. This worked well for the "set pieces" which stud the plays (see Chapter 5). More fluid interaction could be achieved by removing the mikes from the stands and holding them like stage props.

The theater company's adherence to particular demarcations of time and space—the front-facing auditorium, the picture-like stage, the determinate time slot announced on the posters—and to a particular mode of projection, involving the choreographed use of microphones, were fundamental to their conception of drama. It was through these means that they constituted the spectators as a new kind of audience, as will be shown in Chapter 7.

The lighting was minimal. They usually relied on the existing lighting in the hall, supplementing it with the spotlight and fluorescent tubes. Nocturnal, supernatural, and sylvan scenes were usually played in almost total darkness, and even the brightest scenes were dimly lit. According to Alhaji, "This is what our public wants." Sometimes, however, lighting was used for effect: notably, climaxes were marked—not always at the end of a scene—by total blackout. Colored gels were used when the company could get them, to produce a reddish or bluish light for evil characters and spirits.

Costumes included the matching outfits of the women who danced in the opening glee; several sumptuous men's outfits of the prestigious handwoven cloth *aṣọ òfì* for kings and chiefs; the skeleton costume for the spirit in *Kúyẹ̀* (also used in *The Royal Palm-nut*) and a velvet robe for the water deity in *Láníyọnu;* various uniforms—for example, for the nurse in *Ìtọ́júu Kúnlé* [*Taking Care of Kúnlé*] and the fake soldier in *Àkọ́bí Olóògbé* [*The Heir*]. Even when actors wore their own clothes to play certain parts, it was considered important to keep them separate from their ordinary wear. What was seen on stage was supposed to be a "surprise" for the audience.

This, then, was the equipment that the actors managed and operated. The only real specialists were Fẹ́mi Ìlá and Dayọ̀ Akínpẹ̀lú. Fẹ́mi's main work, as we have seen, was to book venues and put up posters in the towns to be visited before a tour began. It took up most of his time and was described as his main job; the acting he did was regarded as secondary. Dayọ̀ Akínpẹ̀lú, who had trained as an electrician before joining the company, was in charge of the generator, stage lights, and sound system. When he left, this job was taken over by Isiaka, who had learned electrical work from his brother before becoming a permanent member of the company. Isiaka said that it was his main job, since he remained at the switchboard the whole time except when he was needed on stage.

The lighting system.
©Elio Montanari

All the other jobs were shared more or less informally among the actors. According to Alhaji, "Everybody knows how to drum." Only the talking drum was the province of a specialist. Margaret, however, qualified this statement, explaining that "Some of them can't even beat an ordinary gong-bell," and only those who knew how to do it would "face the drums." Girls as well as boys could take their turn at the congas: Adédùnmọ́lá, Adéjọbí's eldest daughter, said she liked drumming as well as singing and dancing in the opening glee. All of the young men were also expected to help set up the stage scenery. John Adéwuni's experience showed that there was a hierarchy of seniority in this work:

> What happened is that when I first arrived, we would be assigned to different jobs; some would set the stage after we'd unloaded the lorry ... some had the job of arranging the chairs in the hall. ... At that time, my job was to set up the scenery, once we'd arrived at a place. But now that we've got more people, and now that I'm beginning to be a bit more senior in the company, all I do is supervise the others in the work, because sometimes we will go ahead to

Dayọ̀ fixing the sound system.
©Elio Montanari

a place. Before the boss arrives, I'm the person next in command after the manager [Alhaji] who supervises the others in their tasks.... I'll make sure they get on with it, so that the audience can come in quickly. And when we've finished the stage, if it's a town performance, if we go around drumming, I'll go with them to drum for them. We'll play the drums, starting from here and going all round the town. To say that "We've arrived, come and watch the play this evening."

Fẹ́mi Bámidélé helped to organize the more junior members when they were setting up the stage. He was also put in charge of the costumes:

When they shared out the jobs, they made me the costume manager, which meant that if a costume went missing, I would be responsible. When we are about to begin a play, I'm the one who distributes the costumes to each of the actors. The part of policeman, I allocate his costume to him; this part, this costume, that part, that costume, I'm the one who allocates them to them.

Starting a "parade." ©Elio Montanari

The women sometimes helped out with jobs such as arranging the chairs, but their main responsibility was selling the tickets—a job that seemed to be entrusted only to Adéjọbí's wives—and collecting them from the audience at the door. They also sold soft drinks and sweets to the children outside the door (*Pẹpẹminti lẹ́nu gẹ́ẹ̀tì* [peppermints at the gate], said Yẹmisí dismissively). They were also in charge of domestic life behind the scenes: establishing a comfortable base, feeding the children, strolling down to the market to buy cooked food, attending to Adéjọbí's needs. It was common to see a real encampment behind the stage: children sleeping on mats; women combing and plaiting each other's hair, crocheting, and knitting; and people eating and gossiping. The first performance I did with them was in the Olúbàdàn Stadium in Ìbàdàn, where the stage was a platform erected in the middle of the field. Before the show began, I saw the women and children camping underneath the stage, resting, eating, and attending to the babies. A friend who went with me commented "They are like the *egúngún òjẹ̀*, who can take their position anywhere."

SOME TRIPS (FROM MY DIARY)

FRIDAY 17TH APRIL 1981

It was slow getting off the campus. The Modákẹ́kẹ́-Ifẹ̀ fighting meant a slow and thorough check of every vehicle at the gate,

Deborah Adéjọbí encamped behind the scenes.
©Elio Montanari

and there was quite a queue. When I got out at last, I took the Sékọ̀nà road because I had heard there were immense hold-ups all along the Ìbàdàn road. It was slow and uncomfortable, crawling over great potholes all the way, and wondering if any of the villages were actually hideouts for armed men.

I arrived at Adéjọbí's house at three instead of two. The lorry had gone since morning; Adéjọbí, Emily and Adédùn were still at home. Adéjọbí had a visitor, a drama student doing an M.A. at Ìbàdàn University, who had come to get some "materials." Fairly soon we set off for Ìlá. I took a newcomer called Ṣọlá who said he knew Lagos but not Òṣogbo, and we picked up Alhaji from his house on the way. We turned off at Ìkìrun and after that there was a very bad one and a half hours of rutted and ridged laterite road, through Ọ̀tan, Iree, Ọbagun. How could a great town like Ìlá have such poor access roads? The whole car shook as if it was going to disintegrate on the spot. By early evening we reached Ìlá and parked in a yard next to the Cooperative Association Hall, where the lorry already was. We got out, stretching, looking at the red dust that covered the car. "Ẹ kú iwájú, ẹ kúùrìn . . . " ["Greetings for getting here first. Greetings for the journey."] Ìyáa Mosún [Maggie] and Ìyá Adé [Grace] had taken up their positions at the back of the stage, mats, bundles, and paraffin stoves arranged. "Ìyáa Jọkẹ́ ńkọ́?" "Ó lọojà." ["What about Ìyáa Jọkẹ́?" "She's gone to the market."] The hall was small, almost square, with pillars between the floor and the acting area, which was not a built up stage, just the end of the hall. There were about 50 rusty standard iron chairs and a few benches. It was a bit dingy. The screens and curtains were already set up, and also the lights.

Emily, Ìyá Adé, and I went for a walk round the market, which was close by. We met Ìyáa Jọkẹ́ [Deborah] coming back as we set off; she had bought yams. Emily bought some peanuts, that was all; we walked through and went back. "Kí lo óò je?" ["What will you eat?"] If there had been a food-stall I would have stopped and eaten, but we decided on ẹkọ and àkàrà [cornstarch and beancakes] and sent Fémi, the man with the damaged throat who was a son of Ìlá but who worked for the company. Before he had set off, Emily brought me ẹkọ and ẹ̀fọ́ [spinach sauce] and cold water instead. "Sùgbọ́n kò léran," everybody explained. "Good Friday ni, a à gbọdọ̀ jẹran" ["But it's without meat. . . . It's Good Friday, we are not allowed to eat meat"].

Then I sat in the passenger seat of my car, with the door open; Alhaji sat on a chair between the two cars; Adédùn sat inside the Peugeot 504. We talked at great length. We talked about cats. John, who was also in the 504, said there was a cat at the Blind Centre somewhere that was as big as this—(like a goat). "Ṣé òun náàá fójú?" ["Is it also blind?"] I asked facetiously, which amused John a lot. He quoted it again later, chuckling reminiscently. Alhaji wanted to know why I didn't have a servant living in my house to do all my odd jobs for me "like other salaried people do." I began to talk about British attitudes and how nowadays we felt uneasy about having servants: "Bí ẹrú, bí ìwọ̀fà ló jọ lójúu wa" ["It seems reminiscent of servitude to us"]. Alhaji pointed out that even if the British wanted servants, where would they get them? "Kò sẹ́ni tí yóó ṣe é. Gbogboo wọn ti kàwé tí wọ́n ti ń dá iṣẹ́ ṣe fúnraa wọn" ["There's no one who would do it. All of them have gone to school and are employed in their own right/working for themselves"]. But here, he persisted, I ought to have someone, like a young girl from Òkukù, so that it's not just me alone in the house. It's not good to live all by yourself like that. . . . What would happen if he came to visit me? Who would get food ready for him? Who would open the door if I happened to be out at work? He wouldn't like to be my visitor. . . . I saw he had a point, so I said, "Nítoríi tiyín, Aláájì, màá gba ọmọ-ọ̀dọ̀. Ṣùgbọ́n ẹyọ kan kò tó láti ṣe irú èyin lálejò. Màá gba márùn-ún" ["Because of you, Alhaji, I'll employ a housegirl. But a solitary one wouldn't be enough to do the honours for someone like you. I'll employ five"]. Alhaji gave one of his rare laughs. Now we got onto the subject of lectures. The whole idea of a lecture—material which you prepare beforehand, which you write down, which you then read through, but which you deliver as if talking spontaneously—was quite strange to them and they questioned me closely till they had got it all laid out step by step. Then degrees—if I had already got the last degree of all, what was I doing this for? Why didn't I buy a bigger car, like a 504?

I went to join Ìyá Adé at the gate. It was getting dark. No one bought any tickets, but a lot of children and youths came to ask the price, to find out if there was a student discount, and to hang around generally. After a while I went back to the car. Someone asked "Ṣérò ti ń dé?" and someone answered "Ẹyọ kan péré kò ìtíì dé" ["Have the crowds begun to arrive?" "Not a single person has arrived yet"]. They remembered that the last time they came to Ìlá the same thing had happened. No one came till eleven. But then, when they came, the hall was packed and people were hanging on the windowsills.

Later I decided to take up my position in the hall so that I could sit right at the front to record. The front row was actually already full by the time I went there, but they were obliging enough to let me bring another chair and insert it into the middle. The audience so far was all young men and schoolboys. When the hall filled up and I looked again later, I saw only two women and a few older men; otherwise all were youths.

The play, *Àjàgbé Ejò* (a joking praise-name for an articulated lorry, or tractor-trailer), was advertised as a new one. It had a small cast, and the plot was clear and coherent. Ìyáa Bùnmi makes advances to Àlàbí, a young co-tenant in a rented house, while her husband is away; Àlàbí turns her down; she is furious and prevents him from telling her husband by getting her own false accusation in first. Àlàbí comes under suspicion of having tried to kill the husband by *jùjú*, but is saved by the landlord who thinks up a scheme to get at the truth.

Later when they were discussing the idea of fitting a part for me into it, John said that Bàbáa Fàtáì (the dopey friend of the husband) hadn't been there in the original version; it had been added. When I looked at it, I could see that the whole play was made up of layers added one on top of the other, corresponding to the importance or centrality of the actors. Each component was a polished vignette, with its own point or centre of gravity, and the dialogue seemed to have been carefully orchestrated. You got the impression of a series of coherent sequences, each leading up to its own climax, and often resting on the contrast between the characters. The landlord was large, stately, benign, and pompous while his wife was thin, snappy, and wiry and kept darting in and out. Alhaji's truck driver—the husband of Ìyáa Bùnmi—was bluff, gruff, and sardonic, while his wife was manipulative and subtle. Emily gave a marvellous portrayal of a thoroughly reprehensible woman—charming, appealing, vulgar, childishly gleeful when she's got what she wants, ruthless, unscrupulous. She made it seem so easy, being so nice on the surface and so nasty underneath.

But maybe it was the opening glee that attracted me most. The drab hall, the listless cast, were suddenly transformed. Ìyá Ajíbọ́lá [Emily], Adédùn, Ìyáa Jọkẹ́ [Deborah], Ìyáa Mosún [Maggie], in their blue embroidered trouser suits glowing in the ultraviolet light, suddenly came to life. "Orere ọkọọ̀ mi . . . " they sang, each one's face transfigured with mischief and vivacity.

Afterwards we slept in the hall. I laid my four chair cushions out, put the blanket on top, and lay down, in the same place where all the women were except Ìyá Ají [Emily]. It was a dreadful night, oppressively hot, infested with mosquitoes, the lights kept full on, the blanket tickling . . . I hardly slept. In the morning the next-door house kindly allowed us to use its outdoor bathroom, and after washing from a bucket I felt better. Without eating or drinking, I followed the other vehicles out of Ìlá. Adédùn rode with me to keep me company.

SATURDAY 18TH

I spent the day in Òkukù [the site of my Ph.D. fieldwork several years before]. At 6.30 in the evening the 504 arrived to take me to Òyán, where they were doing *Articulated Lorry* again. We called on the Ọlóyàn-án when we got there. He was as charming and friendly as ever, though he looked thinner and more frail than in the days when I went there to celebrate the Agbaa festival. Then we went to the hall. I think it was St Peter's Anglican

Church Hall. It was an odd-shaped open-air courtyard with a raised stage at one end.

It was getting dark, and I sat down on one of the iron chairs and waited. People eventually began to come in in ones and twos. We waited and waited for the Oba's wife, who said she was coming once she had left the wedding (the Olóyàn-án's son was marrying). She didn't come, but some young girls of the family did, and sat next to me and we chatted.

This was another free-lance performance, not sponsored by any association. There were interesting differences from last night's show. Everything was staged the other way round, starting from the opening glee where the two pairs of women were the same but stood at the other side of *Bàbá* from yesterday. The calculation of the 16 rooms' rent was much more protracted, more definite and funny, with the Akòwé doing long multiplication in the air and "cancelling" everything with great panache. But they made much less of Ìyáa Bùnmi's instructions to Bàbáa Fàtaì about how to catch up with Àjàgbé to get his lift. Yesterday she described how he would "yí biri" [spin round] at the roundabout, and he enacted this, spinning round and saying "Tá a bá yí biri biri báun ta ló mọ ibi tí a óò dárí sí?" [If one spins round and round like that, who knows where we'll end up?] Today he just said he couldn't do all that and might just as well go home.

[Afterward they took me back to Òkukù, where I stayed the night while they went on to Òṣogbo.]

FRIDAY 12 JUNE

When I arrived in Òṣogbo again after such a long gap (having seen Adéjọbí when he called in his car, with Emily and a new driver, last week) he seemed delighted to see me, vindicated in his belief that I would come. We were to go to Ilésà to do *Articulated Lorry*. This time I was to have a part, which Alhaji told me about before we set off. I wrote it down in my diary. I was to be a tenant in the same house where Bàbáa Wándé and Àlàbí Yellow were living and I was to speak in response to the landlord's new rules about living in the house, saying that I was only a stranger and "tí àlejò kò bá fẹ́ ìjòngbọ̀n lọ́dọ̀ Baálé, ohunkóhun tí Baálé bá fẹ́ ni ó gbọdọ̀ bá a fẹ́ ni" [If a visitor doesn't want trouble with his landlord, he has to want whatever the landlord wants]. Later, when Àlàbí Yellow is falsely accused of using *jùjú*, and comes to the landlord for help, I was to be seated at his right hand and advise him thus: "Ohun tí èmi féẹ́ dábàá ni pé, tí a bá fi sùúrù wádìí ọ̀rọ̀ yìí a á mọ eni tó ń purọ́ nínú àwọn méjèèjì" [What I want to suggest is that if we take pains to investigate this matter, we'll be able to find out which of the two of them is lying]. Finally I was supposed to remark "Àṣé mo ní ká fi sùúrù wádìí ọ̀rọ̀ yìí—ṣé ẹ ródodo báyìí?" [Didn't I say that we should take pains to investigate this matter—now you see that the truth has come out], when the whole thing was cleared up. In composing these lines, Alhaji tried out several versions before he settled on the one he liked. After that he and Adéjọbí tested me once or twice in the car on the way there. My car was left in the garage. I asked after Bàbá Sáídì. Apparently he had not come back since the last time I was with them, when he had been preparing his baby's *ikómọjáde* ["outing" or naming ceremony]. The new driver, Burọ̀dá Àkànmú, was a large quiet man like a boxer.

The performance was in Iléṣà Training College in a large dirty hall with gym equipment (rope ladders, etc.) at the back. I was happy that I didn't have to wear the heavy Ọtún Ìyálóde costume [which I'd worn in *The Overreacher*] but felt occasional flickers of fright at saying lines that were so exposed in the structure of the play. (At the same time I knew I would do it.) I went over the words in my head as we sat behind the scenes.

I noticed again the changes in some lines and the general flexibility about staging. Just before we were due to go on I asked Alhaji "Will there be enough chairs for all the tenants?" He looked and saw that there wouldn't be, and made someone carry an extra chair on. But I realised that if they had been a chair short it wouldn't have mattered at all—someone would just have gone and fetched one in an entirely natural and unobtrusive manner. Sèlìá took on a basket instead of a metal tray to collect the anticipated rent from the new house; the food that Bàbáa Wándé offered Bàbáa Fàtáì as a present from Hausaland was different. I didn't get the impression that they were making do with substitutes because they couldn't lay their hands on the "right" prop: it seemed more as if the actors were operationally tuned to produce the required effect from a range of possible materials, just as there was a range of acceptable degrees of elaboration in the dialogue, so that sometimes one bit would be amplified and sometimes another.

On the way back there was a heavy rainstorm. The windscreen wipers weren't working (Adéjọbí told Boọ̀dá Àkànmú in irritable tones that he ought to notice this kind of thing in time;

Alhaji Kàrímù Adépòjù behind the scenes. ©Elio Montanari

Àkànmú said he did notice, it happened just as we were leaving Iléṣà.) But if we stopped, the ignition would get waterlogged and we wouldn't be able to start again. So Àkànmú drove the whole way along that bad narrow road with his head and shoulders out of the window in the rain, peering out to the side of the road.

Eventually we made it and sat around for a while deciding who was to sleep where. They pressed me to take a bed, even though there weren't enough to go round. Eventually I accepted Emily's, because she said she would sleep "nínúu yàrá" (in Adéjọbí's room) anyway. Alhaji was perched on his motorbike in the corridor. "Àbí oríi machine lẹ ẹ ti maa sùn, Alhaji?" [Or are you going to sleep on the motorbike, Alhaji?] I asked. All the girls laughed and repeated the question to him. "Ẹ sì kú oríi re, Alhaji, tí machine fi pé méjì nílé yìí. Tí ìkan kò bá tẹ́ yín lọ́rùn, ẹ lè bọ́ sórí èkejì" [And you're lucky that there are two motorbikes in this house. If one doesn't suit you, you can transfer to the other]. Alhaji assumed his famous put-upon look, which almost sent the girls into hysterics. That night I slept comfortably till about six, when Kàmárù (Adéjọbí's mother's sister's son) started coming in and out every five minutes to root under the bed for pots and pans and food supplies. "Àṣé yàrá Ìyá Ají, Central Stores ni!" [This room of Ìyá Ají's is the Central Stores!]

[We spent the day rehearsing for the TV hospital series, discussed in Chapter 8.]

TUESDAY 16TH JUNE

I got to Òṣogbo just on 3.30 and half an hour later we left for Lagos. We were going to do a play called *Taking Care of Kúnlé*. On the way Alhaji told me what part I would play—someone who commiserates with the household of a woman presumed dead—and Adéjọbí said we would rehearse tomorrow afternoon. Tonight was just for getting there. We did get there, in the dark, after being stopped several times by police checks, and went to Olówónílará Hotel, just opposite the mansion of Bello, the manager of another theatre company, Òjó Ládiípọ̀'s. Most of the company, it turned out, were to sleep in Bello's house. Adéjọbí was to have a room in the hotel; so was Alhaji. Adéjọbí then succeeded in negotiating an extra room for me, which I shared with Adédùn—and later Màmá Adé brought her little boy Ṣolá there to sleep too.

We went in the car to the National Theatre—what for I don't know. Bello introduced me to the Director or Chairman of the Nigerian Council for Culture and the Arts, the semi-government body which had invited us. Emily, Adédùn and I went into the theatre, stopped by arrogant liveried men at the door. A play was going on which we saw from behind the stage. Then we came out and went back in again with Alhaji, Bello and the Director, and watched a bit of the play from the auditorium. It was in Hausa. It seemed stylised and polished, offering a glimpse of an alien culture where people's faces are expressive and mobile in a different way. In the car going back Adéjọbí asked me what I thought of it. "I was just sorry I don't understand Hausa, because it was obviously a good production," I said. He laughed patronisingly and disbelievingly. Alhaji made fun of the audience. "Altogether eight people," he said. It was true the audience was small. Adédùn and Ìyá Adé had laughed continuously to encourage them, then left ostentatiously. Alhaji, Bello and I had watched for a bit longer.

We got back to the hotel and stood around talking to some women belonging to Bello's company. Then I was offered food with Adéjọbí (courtesy of Bello) and having eaten it—*àmàlà* and a soup full of different things—I went to bed. A while later Adédùn joined me on the single bed and tossed and turned until morning. We'd been told we'd leave for the theatre at five. Adédùn got up and put the light on at three. I got up at 5.30. But when it came to it, we didn't leave until 9.30, because Adéjọbí remembered that the technicians probably wouldn't be there till then.

There followed a long day of doing absolutely nothing. We watched as the boys put up the set. The miles of blue front curtain were not used in the National Theatre. There was no front curtain at all, and Adéjọbí had to be wheeled on and off under cover of ordinary theatre darkness which wasn't quite dark enough.

Wandering around the theatre.... There was a Russian sputniks exhibition where there were some friendly girls giving out badges of Lenin and spaceships. Visiting the Ladies: the impeccable changing rooms with pink lavatory paper in every cubicle. Having lunch and dinner at the Cultural people's expense, served by unfriendly ladies from giant thermos containers. Toward evening things got more jovial. Bàbáa Fàtái collected all our orders for drinks. "Champagne," I said. "Thank you," he said, deeply gratified. "That is the sort of order I want. Here is your champagne." He gave me a Tom-Tom sweet....

The play, like *Articulated Lorry*, was a tight, fast comedy, extremely well constructed, stylish and funny. The dialogue interlocked, forming repeated crescendoes, each leading smoothly to the next. It was the story of a woman who goes missing after a boat accident and is presumed drowned; immediately, her good friend starts making up to the bereaved husband and eventually seduces him with the aid of *jùjú*. Alhaji was the husband, and his delivery was very finely judged. He came across as a decent, respectable working man who—despite having unknowingly eaten a love potion—is still sufficiently in command of himself to be morally responsible for his actions and terribly ashamed of them at the end. He isn't just a victim of the unscrupulous woman, he is somehow to blame for letting her get to him. His timing—and especially his use of silences—were impeccable.

We eventually left at about ten the next morning, and branched several times to make visits in Lagos and Ìbàdàn, so we didn't get back to Òṣogbo till after three. (The lorry had been back since eleven.) I drove straight to Ifẹ̀, knowing I'd have to be back at Òṣogbo early the next morning for a television serial rehearsal and recording.

9TH SEPTEMBER

A little later than the appointed time, as usual, I was hurrying along the same old road to Òṣogbo, remembering the trip when that little lateness had made me almost miss them, and wondering if it was that type of appointed time or the usual one where you get there all hasty and sit and wait for three hours. It was the usual one. While I sat in my usual place on the maroon plastic settee, Adéjọbí, seated at his table in the corner, broke off what he was writing to tell me that three sets of people had invited the company to take part in films. First there was Adé Love, located at Ṣàgámù, who asked the whole company to come on September 15th. But they decided they couldn't, so only Ìyá Adé is to go, to play the old woman in the film. Then Bàbáa Sàlá is beginning one in October. "Is it a comedy?" "That's what we are all asking ourselves," he said, and told me the story: an incredibly rich man employs a houseboy who steals a large sum of money and runs away—but the rich man doesn't notice, he's so rich. One day the houseboy comes back and performs the "money-doubling" trick on his former master, cleaning him out of his entire fortune. The master staggers off, a broken man, into the forest, is enriched again, impoverished again, and decides to die. The rest of the story is his journey into supernatural realms in quest of death, which is ended when he finally succeeds in drowning himself. "Doesn't sound like a comedy to me." "It ends sadly, but it has funny bits in it." Then, after that, Ògúnǹdé was starting a new film. The two would overlap. Adéjọbí explained that Ògúnǹdé claimed that Bàbáa Sàlá hadn't told him about his own proposal, and as President of their Association he didn't see why he should shift his own programme to accommodate him. Nevertheless it was clear that he would lose if he didn't, because all the best actors would be involved with Bàbáa Sàlá when Ògúnǹdé wanted to start. Adéjọbí, as secretary, was trying to resolve the quarrel amicably. He had known about Bàbáa Sàlá's plans for more than a year. "Was there a quarrel between them before?" "There was, actually, but long long ago. It wasn't fifteen years ago and it wasn't twenty five years ago.

Both of them said it was all forgotten and finished." If Adéjọbí was going to be in both films, would he have time to do stage performances as well? "Thank you. They *say* we have to be on location throughout, that they don't want us to go anywhere. But that's not possible. We already have some invitations . . . " He mentioned two, one in October, one in November. "It wouldn't be good for us to be out of circulation for too long at a time."

We talked for hours. It turned out that we were waiting for Alhaji. He had gone to Lagos with Adé and Elúwọlé (the Manager of Ìṣọ́lá Ògúnṣọlá's company) to get his new car, bought for him by Adéjọbí. It was a Beetle. Eventually Adé and Elúwọlé came back, saying they had left Alhaji in Lagos and that he would bring the car and meet us in Ìwó. After a long afternoon of sitting around, we were suddenly galvanised by Adéjọbí's "Ṣíra, ó yá!," and bundled into the cars to go to Ìwó. Adé came with me to show me the way.

The road through Ẹdẹ, Awó, and other places like Bada, Ogbaagba, and Labulabu was terrible, and I arrived two hours later feeling dead beat. We were to perform in a hotel on the outskirts of Ìwó—Ewé Ńlá Hotel—a rather sleazy place, but with a walled front court to park our cars in. The acting place was a hall with big square pillars and a small bar at one end, a couple of anterooms at the other. Adéjọbí said that they normally played in the Town Hall when they came to Ìwó because it is much bigger. This hotel hall had only about a hundred chairs set up in it. But they had pulled down the Town Hall to rebuild it—something wrong with the foundations. The people who came in the lorry had already gone round on parade, but not many posters had been put up and someone was being blamed for it—when I asked, Adéjọbí said something about "**man** yẹn" ["that man"], and I began to think that hanging around behind the scenes doesn't necessarily provide a richer view of what is going on than a formal interview.

I had a part in this performance [of *Taking Care of Kúnlé*]. I was to be one of the patients at the clinic where the lost wife turns up half-drowned and is restored to health. It didn't really matter what was wrong with each of the preceding patients— they just had to have a little story, when they were called by the nurse, to set the scene before Wúrà came in. I was going to have a twisted ankle. I thought up a story about rabbits. Rabbits and guinea pigs had been a new thing in Òkukù not long before. Enterprising people tried to breed them for food, but not very successfully. So I said my uncle had decided to breed rabbits, and then he went away on a trip and asked me to look after them for him. As I opened the cage to put the food in, a rabbit jumped out. When I turned round to catch it, another one jumped out. I began to run after them. They ran all the way up the main street and into the *sùnábọlẹ̀* [the untarred bush road], and there was a place where they were connecting NEPA [the Nigerian Electric Power Authority: i.e., electricity] to a new house on the outskirts of town. Well, I didn't know that they were already connecting NEPA to that house, and that they had dug a deep trench for the cables. Five foot deep. I was running so fast that it just looked like a shadow on the road. So I ran into that trench, but the rabbits jumped over it and disappeared into the bush. And that is why I have a twisted ankle. Mr. Adéjọbí liked this story when I tried it out on him and told me to include it.

We weren't ready to start, and Ìyá Adé, always thoughtful and concerned, urged me to go and rest. She showed me where the bed had been set up invitingly in one of the anterooms, and I went and lay down in the dark for an hour or so. When I got up, about nine, there was no sign of action and Alhaji still hadn't arrived. I said to Adédùn, "But we can't start without Alhaji, can we?" "Oh, we'll start." "Who'll play Alhaji's part?" "One of the others." She told me that all the men watch how to do all the male parts, and all the women do the same for women's parts. All can do anything. Even so, their attitude seemed (to me) astonishingly casual. Adédùn said "Perhaps Alhaji will arrive before the Opening Glee finishes." But he didn't. We started a bit before ten, and the Opening Glee was over, Adéjọbí back in his place, before I asked him "Who's going to play Bàbáa Kúnlé?" He looked as if the question hadn't previously occurred to him. "Thank you," he said in his thoughtful rumbling way. "Er—call Dayọ̀ for me" (this to Adédùn). Dayọ̀ came, but by that time Adéjọbí was already talking to Elúwọlé, Ògúnṣọlá's Manager (who'd come with us to watch) about something else. Eventually, in a leisurely way, he turned to Dayọ̀. "Now, Dayọ̀, who's going to play Bàbáa Kúnlé?" "We thought that I should." "You? No, no, that's not a good idea at all. That will never do. No, look, John will play Bàbáa Kúnlé. Then we'll ask Manager to take John's part." Manager Elúwọlé agreed, even though he didn't belong to the company and had probably never seen the play before. The play was starting, the Ìyá Enídìrí and Emily were already on stage. Meanwhile Adédùn was rapidly explaining to Manager what he would have to do. She went on explaining right up to the moment when he had to go on in the second scene, with Adéjọbí as Baálé and Dayọ̀ as his fellow comic elder.

It was a coarse audience. Not many, people kept commenting—maybe about a hundred. They were all young, predominantly men, though there was a sprinkling of girls and a handful of children.

The difference between this performance and the one I saw in the National Theatre seemed so great that you would have thought it was a different company—yet the differences were all small: questions of timing and expression. The Lagos performance was a polished, scintillating farce. Everything fitted, nothing was excessive, every component was well defined. This one was coarse. John did all the basic moves required of Bàbáa Kúnlé, but he lacked the repressed force and accuracy of Alhaji, who just has to walk on stage with a particular expression on his face to bring the house down. John was more diffuse and blustering. The polished set pieces which worked so well in Lagos were blurred here, only partly because Manager Elúwọlé didn't really know what he was supposed to be doing.

Just before I was due to go on, Adéjọbí called me in his confidential, cosy way. "Do everything exactly as you did it when you were showing it to me earlier. Don't leave anything out, and take your time to say it slowly. It's so funny, it's really good." So I limped painfully on (and was met by real, though puzzled, concern from the audience, who presumably thought I'd strayed into the building by mistake in my distress!), and told the long story about how Bàbá Ghana had asked me to look after his rabbits. I told it slowly and even added some extra details. The audience liked it—though, as throughout the performance, they were rowdy and inattentive in places. The bits they were really rivetted by—the noise reached yelling-pitch—were when Bàbáa Kúnlé ate the medicine (tonight they shouted "Eat it!"; in Lagos they'd said "Don't eat it!"), the fight, and the send-off of Àṣàbí. They also liked the lovers' rapture scene where they dance suggestively and feed each other rice.

Afterwards the wives generously insisted that I sleep on the bed, even though I'd brought my cushions, and I did sleep very well. Next morning, without washing, eating, or drinking, I set off back over that dreadful road to Ẹdẹ and from there to Ifẹ̀.

Ifẹ̀ seemed very quiet. Endless rain, power cut all evening. Back on the road tomorrow!

* * *

SEPTEMBER 1983

The group had had a bad summer because of the elections. Adéjọbí said they didn't perform on stage at all. Because of this—and because the Ọ̀yọ́ T.V. who owed them money hadn't paid—they hadn't had enough money to launch a tour. Launching a tour requires money for posters, which cost 50k each to produce, money for Fẹ́mi Adéníjì to go to all the places in advance and book them, money to get the vehicles in order. Adéjọbí said it would all cost at least N300. However, when some money came through, at the end of the summer, they at once began planning the tour. There was already a performance long since booked and paid for at the KS Motel in Ìbàdàn. There was also a tentative plan to go to Ẹgbẹ̀ on Thursday 27th October and work up a tour in that area before coming down to Ìbàdàn. The Ẹgbẹ̀ people had already been given this date but until the money came through the company was talking of cancelling it. On Thursday afternoon Sunday Fágbáyìímú came to give me the programme they had arranged. It was neatly typed:

DATE	MONTH	TOWNS
SATHURDAY 29th	OCTOBER	EGBE
SUNDAY 30th	OCTOBER	IGOSUN
MONDAY 31th	OCTOBER	OFFA
TUESDAY 1st	NOVEMBER	ILORIN
WEDNESDAY 2nd	NOVEMBER	LANLATE
THURSDAY 3rd	NOVEMBER	LANLATE
FRIDAY 4th	NOVEMBER	IBADAN
SATHURDAY 5th	NOVEMBER	OYO

Sunday explained that the Saturday 5th November fixture was not yet definite but the others were. I prepared to leave on the morning of Saturday 29th. However, on the Saturday morning I opened my flat door to find a note from Sunday saying "Baba send me to inform you that our tours arrangements have been changed. We don't go to Egbe today again, but we will be there tommorow by the grace of God. Unexpectedly NTA Ilọrin Crew came on Thursday evening to start a recording of two lenght plays which we expect to finish today thats why we cancel and prosphone Ẹgbẹ date to tommorow instead of today."

On Sunday, therefore, at a quarter to two I set off for Ẹgbẹ̀, knowing only that it was beyond Àjàsẹ́. I branched at the Adéjọbí house in Òṣogbo and was told they'd already gone, about an hour before. Adédùn was at home because her class started the next day. Beyond Àjàsẹ́ I began to ask the way to Ẹgbẹ̀. Everybody said "Maa lọ tààrà, sòsé. Ó wà níwájú . . ." [Keep going straight ahead. It's far ahead]. I reached Òmù Àrán and it was still *wájú wájú* [far ahead]. I gave a woman a lift to Obbo. She took me to her house for a soft drink and I basked in the friendliness radiating from her, her husband, and two guests in her beer parlour who said (their smiles making their meaning clear) "You are very grateful to be with us, indeed." They said it was about 20 km to Obbo (pronounced Òbo), straight, *sòsé*. The road was good. The landscape had become the open, semi-savannah with steep hills and massive outcrops of rounded black granite, so exhilarating after the flat spongy vegetation of central Yorùbáland. Eventually Ẹgbẹ̀ lay before me, a pretty town lodged in a valley and up the hillside. It was a quarter past six. I drove in without seeing the pink lorry or bus, so conspicuous wherever they go. But I saw Alhaji's blue beetle in front of me and followed it, sounding my horn intermittently without attracting his attention. Only when the bystanders' cries of "Òyìnbó" got loud enough did he look round, stop, jump out, and meet me, who had also got out, in the middle of the steep sandy road. We greeted, re-embarked, I followed him back to the hall which, it turned out, I had missed on my way in, since it was right on the outskirts of the town before I'd even begun to look. It was the Mẹkùn Cinema Hall, attached to the Àjíkẹ́ Nursery School. The lorry and the bus were there. Bàbá was installed on the side of the high concrete stage, behind the scenery which was already up, surrounded as usual by bundles, suitcases, mats, cooking equipment, etc. Emily and Yẹmisí both had stocks of sweets, chinchin, and hardboiled eggs to sell at the gate when the audience began to come in.

The play was *Ọkọ Ìyàwó* [*Besotted Bridegroom*]. I wanted to record it because I had been told that it had changed and improved since I last saw it. The cinema hall was a big open square with a gallery at the back and a high concrete stage, about four feet high with two sets of concrete steps cut into it at the back on each side. When the scenery was set up on it the maximum size of the acting area was about 16 ft. by 6 ft. The chairs for the audience were set well back, leaving a gap between the stage and the front row of about 27 ft.

The audience was small but polite and appreciative. I was already sitting in the auditorium waiting to record when Sunday and Fẹ́mi came and said "Ṣó ò ní í act? Wọ́n mà ti múra part kan fún ọ" [Aren't you going to act? They've made up a part for you]. I went to see Alhaji and he described where I would appear and gave me some lines. He was unhappy that I didn't have another costume to change into. "Everybody has seen that one, it's too common. When you go on stage you have to wear something different, to surprise them. Haven't you got a native dress?" "But would native dress be appropriate for a contractor?" "It would be funny." But I didn't have it with me and we were about to start. "Go and rehearse with Papa," he instructed me, which meant go and tell Adéjọbí what he had decided I should say. Adéjọbí was already getting into his costume. So all I could do was give him a bald summary. He assimilated this new element immediately, and in Scene 2 made the most of elaborately addressing the contractor through Mosún, gesturing to her to sit down as if she couldn't understand "Jókòó" and expressing great astonishment at her presence. Yẹ́misí as Sẹlia too rose to the occasion, giving the contractor an amazed look and greeting her with trepidation.

Adéjọbí and Alhaji were highly pleased with this new addition. "It's very nice. It fits. You must come when we are performing in the KS Motel, it's very important you should be there. People will so much like this new part."

The next morning Fẹ́mi was sent to tell me that contrary to their earlier decision, we would now be leaving immediately. Before, Adéjọbí had said that he would like to rest and look around the town and that we wouldn't leave until about eleven. I hastily assembled myself for departure because, not knowing the venue in Ọ̀fà, I had to follow them. We left soon after eight.

The Ọ̀fà performance was at the Ìyẹ̀rú Ọ̀kín Cinema Hall, rather similar in design to the Ẹgbè one except that there was no gallery. It was painted a glorious pink outside and had a poster for a porn movie to be shown the next night. The audience was again small and well-behaved. Comments included "A à rína" [We can't see] when they put on the dreadful fluorescent footlight which shines more in the eyes of the audience than onto the actors, screening them from us with a greenish-yellow glare. Alhaji would have preferred to use the single big spotlight, but explained that the generator was not strong enough to carry the spotlight as well as the microphones. The microphones would stop working. And in fact the mikes were giving

Before the show at Ọ̀fà. ©Elio Montanari

a lot of trouble in this performance, one of them going off and on and making a scratchy sound, the other emitting a screeching hum.

On Tuesday they went to Ìlọrin and performed *External Appearances* in the Niger Hotel. On Wednesday they went to Làǹlátẹ̀ via Ìsẹ́yìn. The road was terrible, the journey arduous. The bus had two flat tyres and they didn't get to Làǹlátẹ̀ until 5.30, having left Ìlọrin around nine in the morning. In Làǹlátẹ̀ they performed in the College of Education.

On Thursday they went to investigate the already-mooted possibility of performing in Èrúwà Teachers' College, but as no definite booking had been arranged with the college, it wasn't possible. The date was instead fixed for 18th November. They didn't put up any posters, as they chose the venue so late. They performed in the Scorpio Hotel and very few people turned up. On Friday they came from Èrúwà to Ìbàdàn, but branched to visit someone on the way and didn't arrive till 2.30. The performance at the KS Motel was scheduled for 4.30 and they wanted to start even earlier because there was a film show at 6.00. So they whipped up the set in record time and within an hour of their arrival the opening glee ladies were hastily combing out their hair, powdering their faces and getting ready to go on. The play was over by six and I left them packing up to go on to Ọ̀yọ́ that evening. Ọ̀yọ́ was the last day of their trip, at the Federal Government Girls' School.

THURSDAY 17TH NOVEMBER

I made an effort to leave Ifẹ̀ at 7.00 A.M. as requested, but actually left just at eight. Entering Abẹ́òkúta two and a half hours later I spied the pink lorry parked at a filling station and pulled in to be met by the cheerful salutations of Sunday and the new driver whose name I still don't know. It turned out they had been sent to meet me. They conducted me to where the company had stayed the night—far on the other side of Abẹ́òkúta, a complicated journey through a very big, confusing city. Alhaji commented "Anywhere I go once, I know my way through it—except Abẹ́òkúta. I've been twice and still don't know the way." The company was packing, almost ready to leave, Adéjọbí already installed in his place in the car. A brief prayer meeting was held, standing in front of the lorry, which all attended except Alhaji and me and Adéjọbí, who remained in the car. Then we set off for Igbó-Ọ̀rà.

There was nothing there that reminded me of my visits ten years ago, when I stayed in the rural health centre with chronic diarrhoea, and took the Baálẹ̀'s son there to treat his guineaworm. The town hall was an impressive stone-faced structure next to the police station. On the other side, there were crowds of people around a table—FEDECO [Federal Electoral Commission] workers who had come to be paid their fees. We hung around a while waiting for the man to bring the key. The bus went on a quick parade with Yẹmisí doing the talking: "Ẹ kú déédéé iwòyí. Ẹ wáá weré Oyin Adéjọbí ní Town Hall lálẹ́ òní, eré tí orúkọọ rẹ̀ jẹ́ *Ọkọ ìyàwó*, ẹ fojú fórojú, ẹ fójú lónjẹ ayọ̀ lóníí, ní Town Hall." [Greetings for this time. Come and watch the play of Oyin Adéjọbí in the Town Hall this evening, the play entitled *Besotted Bridegroom*, come and feast your eyes with joy today, in the Town Hall.] When the door of the hall was opened, we saw that the whole of one corner was stacked with waste paper. Closer inspection showed them to be used ballotpapers and unused FEDECO envelopes. It was a mountain. Most of the papers that I saw had the thumbprint against UPN, but NPN got in in all Ìbàràpá. A brief debate and Alhaji decided simply to pitch the scenery in front of this huge heap. There was no stage—we were on ground level. Everything was set up

Waiting for the audience. ©Elio Montanari

and then people drifted off here and there to amuse themselves for the rest of the afternoon. Around four thirty they did another parade with both the lorry and the bus, going in different directions to penetrate the whole town. I talked to Adéjobí, then interviewed Emily and again interviewed Adéjobí. As it got dark, Sunday began to sell tickets. People began to drift up, cluster, and chat. The recorded music began to waft out of the hall, and then the drums. The company was gearing up for another show.

PROFIT AND LOSS

Over a period of three years, from 1981 to 1984, I gathered information about the business arrangements of the company by documenting, with greater or lesser degrees of thoroughness, the way 64 performances were set up and carried out. These should be seen as a mere sample of a much fuller program of tours. For the first two years my record-keeping was patchy. I did not obtain a list of all their performances during this time; I missed many, especially in 1982 when I was away for six months; and I watched and even acted in quite a number of performances without keeping any written notes about them. Only for three months, from October 30, 1983 to February 2, 1984, did I obtain a complete inventory of the company's tours, their expenses, and their income.

Of the 64 shows that I recorded information on, 30 were performed in "town" venues, 32 in schools and colleges, one in the Olúbàdàn Stadium, Ìbàdàn, and one in the National Theatre, Lagos. The "town" venues included co-operative halls, church halls, cinema halls, town halls, community halls, privately owned halls, and hotels. Most of them had a platform stage and all had a large square or rectangular auditorium with chairs and benches. Some—such as the hall in Igbó-Orà described above—had no stage. The company simply rigged up its scenery across one end of the hall and performed as if on a platform stage. The educational institutions they went to were mainly teacher training colleges (20 out of 32) and secondary schools (8 out of 32); the others were the University of Ifẹ̀, Abẹ́òkúta Polytechnic, the University of Ìlọrin, and Ọ̀tùn Technical College. Most of the educational venues had an all-purpose assembly hall with a platform or stage; a few had curtains and lighting. Only two venues in the whole list—Odùduwà Hall, at the University of Ifẹ̀, and the National Theatre in Lagos—had fully equipped modern stages with built-in facilities for lighting, sound, and curtains.

The company began its arrangements for a tour by booking a series of halls in a string of towns: usually one hall for one night in each town, though they would sometimes stay two nights, performing once in a boarding school or residential college for the students and once in a "town" venue for the general public. To have a hall—a space, preferably indoors, in which an acting area could be defined, the scenery could be set up, and the audience could be arranged in rows that were spatially separated from the actors—was the sine qua non of performance. The halls varied greatly. Some were enormous bare concrete shells with low ceilings and fluorescent lighting; some were old plastered buildings with pillars, wooden rafters, and backstage anterooms. Once or twice the company performed in a hotel courtyard—an enclosed but roofless space—and once, failing to secure their usual venue, they booked a disused warehouse, but canceled the performance because the place still smelled too strongly of fish.

The most valuable form of booking was a "sponsored" performance. This was a performance that was undertaken in response to an invitation from a social club or religious or progressive association. The association would negotiate well in advance for a particular play that would be performed on a date and in a venue chosen by them for an agreed-upon lump sum. Of the 64 shows I have some record of, only seven were sponsored: two by church groups, one by a Muslim association, two by social clubs, and two by official national organizations (the Nigerian Association for Physical Health Education and the Nigerian Council for Culture and the Arts). In the two cases of sponsored performances that I got more details about, an advance was paid when the date of the performance was fixed and the balance was handed over at the performance itself. The association (the Muslim Graduates Association in one case, the Fìdítì Social Club in the other) made all the arrangements, booked the hall, did the advertising with radio announcements and posters, and sold the tickets. They kept the whole take from the performance; if it exceeded the original lump sum, they made a profit.

The advantage to the theater company of a sponsored performance was, first, that the lump sum was usually greater than the average take for a normal college or public performance. The Muslim Graduates Association paid N800 for *Besotted Bridegroom;* Fìdítì Social Club paid N500 for the same play. The take for unsponsored performances during the three months that I kept detailed financial records ranged from N41 to N500 (averaging N197) for a "town" show and from N73 to N678 (averaging N242) for a "college" show. Second, the take from an unsponsored show had to cover the expense of booking and hiring a hall, advertising with posters and radio announcements, and—intermittently—paying an "entertainment tax" of 30 percent to the police, who would be sent to collect it on the spot. All this was covered by the sponsor in a sponsored performance. Third, the sponsor usually took the trouble to book a high-class venue and make sure that well-to-do members of the association turned up in large numbers. Thus, the company was assured a substantial, punctual, and appreciative audience in a good hall, all of which made their job easier. Finally, the sponsoring institution would sometimes also play host: at the KS Motel, the Muslim Graduates Association arranged overnight accommodation for the company; at Fìdítì, according to Mr. Adéjọbí, the Fìdítì Social Club gave them "a great reception"; and another sponsoring group, the Trumpet of God church group, fed the whole company *àmàlà* and chicken before the show when they went to perform for them at Gbòngán.

The great majority of performances were not sponsored. There were nonetheless great variations among them from the point of view of profitability and convenience. Many of the college performances and some of the town ones were "invited" even though they were not sponsored. This meant that a school, college, or town association asked the company to come, negotiated the date and the venue, and perhaps helped with some of the arrangements, in return receiving a small share of the take: either a percentage (typically 5–10 percent) or a fee. College performances tended to be the best in this respect. The students were keen to have the theater company visit and were helpful about putting up posters, arranging the chairs, and so on. They usually provided a large and punctual audience, especially in residential colleges where there was nothing else to do in the evening. The helpers were often also satisfied with a very small "dash" in compensation. They used their collective bargaining power, however, to beat down the price of the tickets. Tickets in schools were normally less than in town performances anyway; but whereas Adéjọbí would have liked to sell them for N1 (and town tickets for N2–3), on several occasions the students got them reduced to as little as 50 kọbọ. Sometimes even college audiences were a disappointment: the students sometimes failed to advertise properly or failed to get permission for the performance to take place.

Most town performances and many college ones were organized by the company without any invitation. In that case, they would book the halls themselves—usually using ones they had been to before—and would bargain about the price with the proprietor or the institution concerned. Some charged a fixed sum, others a percentage. Odùduwà Hall at Ifẹ̀ was the most expensive, the manager wanting to split the take 50–50 with the company, but after some bargaining agreeing to accept N278 out of a total of N678. Other less splendid halls were more modest in their demands, but their cut still reduced the company's profits. On one occasion, the manager of the Niger Hotel at Ìlọrin initially asked for N150; Adéjọbí was expecting to pay about N70, depending on how well they did that night; in the end, they sold N270 worth of tickets and gave the manager N50. The proprietor of the Mẹkùn Cinema Hall at Ẹgbẹ̀ asked for a third of the takings and thus received more than N30 out of the miserable N108 they took at the gate that night. The Scorpio Hotel in Èrúwà got N20 out of their take of N97. Colleges and town halls were better: Ṣakí Teachers' College, for instance, asked for 10 percent but in the end took only N30 out of a take of N450; Awẹ́ High School wanted 10 percent but accepted N5 out of a take of N140; and a number of schools and colleges charged nothing at all.

Adéjọbí, Alhaji, and others would decide which towns to go to. Sometimes they built a short tour around an existing "invited" or sponsored performance. In January 1984 they arranged a blitz of Èkìtì, going to Ìjerò, Ìdó, Òró, and Ẹkàn Ńlá in one tour, to Ọyẹ́, Ọ̀tùn, Usi, and Ẹ̀fọ̀n-Àlàyè on the next, and to Oǹdó, Ìgósùn, Ìgbàjà, Oǹdó again, Ìkẹ̀rẹ́, Adó-Èkìtì, and Òkè-igbó on the third, all in rapid succession. They went only once to Lagos, once to Abẹ̀òkúta, and once to Ìjẹ̀bú-Òde. The larger towns which they returned to on two or three separate trips during the period I was with them were mainly in the northern and central Yorùbá areas: they included Ìlá, Ìlọrin, Iléṣà, Ifẹ̀, Ọ̀yó, Ọ̀fà, and Ọ̀yán. They performed twice in Òṣogbo, but said they did not like it, despite the convenience, because they were obliged to let in all their friends from other theater companies for nothing. The general principle was to take each new play once to each major urban center, sometimes also doing a college show in the same city. If they were invited back to the same place, they would take care to stage a different play that people had not seen recently. Once I was present when they arranged a tour to a previously unexplored area, the southwest coast of Yorùbáland. The planning went like this:

12TH NOVEMBER 1983

It was a long time since they had been down Ìjẹ̀bú way. Most of the northern towns had seen both their new plays (*Besotted Bridegroom* and *External Appearances*)—some, like Ìlọrin, more than once. Ìjẹ̀bú was not considered good for public performances, but there were many colleges and polytechnics there. Somebody suggested Badagry. "A á tà dáadáa ní Badagry. Wọ́n léníyàn ń wòran gidi níbẹ̀" [We'll sell well in Badagry. They say people are great show-goers down there]. Adéjọbí hit on the idea of a tour taking in Badagry, Owódé, Ìdí-Ìrókò, and then Lagos (Mushin and Agege). "Have you been to Badagry recently?" I asked. "I have never been there in my life. Even Ìdí-Ìrókò, I've been there only once, and not to perform. We went to take part in Ògúndé's film *Aiyé*. There were two locations, that was one of them. There was a hotel there, Frontier Hotel, where we could perform." "Why did you decide to go to Badagry after all this time?" "Well, we have been pressed so much by students asking us to come. And then my people say that it is good." Sunday said that this new tour should be at the end of the month, and that those performances that fell just after payday should not be school ones but public ones. In this way a new tour was planned in five minutes of discussion.

After an itinerary had been drawn up and typed out by the clerk, Fẹ́mi Ìlá or some other functionary would be sent to book the halls and put up posters. This cost money, but much depended on it. Fẹ́mi's transport money had to be paid, and according to Adéjọbí it cost a lot: "To fix the last tour, he took N65; to fix the new one, he took N35 but lost it in Ìbàdàn and had to come back for more. These illiterates!" Posters cost 50 kọbọ each to print; they would show the name of the company and the title of the play but leave blanks for time and place which the fixer would fill in by hand before he put them up. Alhaji explained that the number they used varied: "As big as the town is—according to its size—we can't use more than 100 poster or 80 poster. We pay in advance—thousand, two thousand each poster." They sometimes also used handbills which they distributed immediately before a play. Before the visit to Abẹ́òkúta, Adéjọbí decided to distribute handbills throughout the town and to make the Polytechnic performance open to the public. Sunday drafted the handbill on the spot, and the printer was sent for: "He lives nearby." On the other hand, a tour could be held up while the company waited for the posters to be made, for they could not start without them.

When the audience and the take was small, poor bookings and insufficient advertising were blamed. In the week's tour from Ẹgbẹ̀ to Ọ̀yọ́, described in the diary extract above, the sponsored performance at the KS Motel in Ìbàdàn was the only booking that was made well in advance and regarded as unchangeable. The first port of call, Ẹgbẹ̀, was by invitation. A date had been fixed but was changed at the last minute when the Ìlọrin television crew arrived unexpectedly to record the two "full-length plays" they had earlier commissioned. Mr. Adéjọbí said the reason they went to Ẹgbẹ̀, a very distant and small town, was that "many students who saw us 13 years ago have been to press me to come again"; but in the event, he said, the change in date, from the 27th to the 30th of October, without notice, meant there was "no audience" (between 40 and 50 people paid for tickets). As a result of this change, the planned performance at Ìgósùn had to be dropped, involving a waste of posters and Fẹ́mi's travel money. The performance in Ọ̀fà took place as scheduled, but they sold only 60–80 tickets. At the Niger Hotel at Ìlọrin the next day, about 70 tickets were sold; the cost of advertising on the radio (N26)—something they only did in the larger cities—and the cost of the hall (N50) was offset by the higher ticket price of N4. The next day they drove to Làǹlátẹ̀. The Làǹlátẹ̀ College of Education had invited them and the trip had been arranged some time before. The students had put up the posters themselves, and expected a 15 percent share of the take. About 100 people bought tickets. Mr. Adéjọbí explained that they would have made more except that "the college is not residential, and is in the middle of the bush." The next venue, Èrúwà, was not included in their original itinerary. "Èrúwà was terrible," Mr. Adéjọbí said. They had been hoping to perform in the Èrúwà Divisional Teachers College but had not been there in advance to arrange it, and it turned out that the college could not have them until some two weeks later, on November 18th. So they had performed in the Scorpio Hotel instead, but "as we had not advertised with posters, very few people came." The performance at the KS Motel the next day was a welcome contrast, with a large and appreciative audience, and the balance of the lump sum assured (the advance had of course long been spent).

Audience sizes certainly varied dramatically. At St Helen's Teachers College, Oǹdó, more than 500 people bought tickets at 50 kọbọ each. At Ṣakí Teachers College 450 people paid for tickets; at Ìséyìn Town Hall the next day only 33 did, and "the tax people came, but when they saw there was no audience, they went away." My impression, however, was that the number of people watching the play exceeded the number of people who actually paid for their tickets. I do not remember ever seeing an audience of only 40 people. On the contrary, I remember packed halls, bursting at the seams with spectators. One reason for this impression may have been the sheer exuberant volubility of the audiences, who could generate a lot of noise and excitement even when they were relatively few. But it also seems likely that many people got in without paying—either because they were friends of the organizers or of members of the company, or because they gave the gatekeepers the slip. Once in the middle of *Kúyẹ̀*, as I was sitting beside Adéjọbí in my role as royal wife number two, he started gazing up at the rafters. Thinking this was a new dramatic effect, I gazed with him: he then whispered to me "Look at all those people trying to get in." There was a hole in the roof and through it were gazing a cluster of eager spectators, watching the show from above.

Whenever possible, the company would return to sleep in Òṣogbo after a performance. This involved late-night driving, since the play did not usually finish till after midnight, and the scenery then had to be dismantled and the equipment packed into the lorry. Driving at night was considered very dangerous by most people in western Nigeria at that time because of the increase in armed highway robbery. However, the Adéjọbí Company members had hardened themselves to such fears, saying that as long as they stayed in convoy nothing would happen, especially as they were well known and loved by everybody. When they were too far away from Òṣogbo to return the same day, or when they were on a tour of towns which were all close to each other so that going back each night to Òṣogbo would waste petrol and make no sense logistically, they would usually sleep in the hall itself. Only rarely did they take hotel rooms, because the cost was so high that it cut dramatically into their income. For example, at the Niger Hotel on December 26th, 1983, they took three rooms at N18 per room, and this had to be paid for out of a total take of about N160. At the Ọ̀yọ́ Wayside Hotel they had to pay N20 for their accommodation out of a take of about N100, though at this venue they were not charged anything for the use of the hall. At Ọ̀fà on October 31st, 1983, Mr. Adéjọbí was exhausted and unwell. They went to the Queen's Inn Hotel, owned by the Olófà of Ọ̀fà, which was the one Adéjọbí normally patronized:

> We went in to look: a single room was N10, a double N14. Each had a wide mattress on a shaky black metal four-poster bed, neat check gingham bed covers, and a fan. The bathroom, to be used by all, had a bath filled with yellowish water; a toilet whose cistern was brimming and dripping on the floor but whose flush was unable to dislodge the huge turd floating in the bowl; and a washbasin, very dirty. Adéjọbí then revealed that he was going to spend the whole day here resting in the hotel. He was very tired. The room they had given him at the Ẹgbẹ̀ Cinema Hall [the night before] had turned out to be dreadful. They hadn't gone to bed till after two last night because they were packing the set up and discussing changes and improvements that could

be made. Adéjọbí had also been suffering from a recurrent illness. By the time we got back to the hall everybody was asleep, stretched out on mats. John was suffering from fever. . . .

. . . The next day they were planning ways to scrape enough money together for petrol for the lorry and bus to go to Ìlọrin. They had put N5-worth into each yesterday, and "ìyẹn la fi *parade* lánàá, a *parade* lẹ́ẹ̀méjì lánàá" [that's what we used to do the **parade; we paraded** twice yesterday]. Ìyá Adé had annoyed them by dashing off to Òṣogbo to see her children first thing in the morning, taking the money from last night with her. Alhaji was suggesting that Fẹ́mi Ìlá should collect whatever amount Yẹ́misí and Emily had on them and hope it would be enough for the petrol. . . . Another hint of financial tightness was Adéjọbí's unease at staying in a double hotel room. He had said "Shouldn't I rather take a N10 room and save four naira?" He also felt embarrassed to be living more luxuriously than the rest of the company, despite the special claims of his age, disability, illness and exhaustion. The company drew water from the hotel bathroom and some of them slept in the big front parlour on mats.

As this diary extract shows, touring was very arduous. In the past, the group had undertaken extensive itineraries, going as far as northern Nigeria (where they played mainly to the Yorùbá-speaking trading diaspora) and staying away months at a time. Now, however, most tours did not last more than a week without the break of a day or two at home in Òṣogbo. But the company was usually busy. When they were in Òṣogbo, they were often rehearsing and recording episodes for their two TV serials or their radio serial or preparing "full-length plays" for one or another television station. They would often rehearse all day and then go off in the evening to a not-too-distant town to perform, returning in the early hours of the morning, only to get up and begin rehearsing again at nine the next day. The pattern from October 27th, 1983 to February 2nd, 1984 was as follows: 3 days' television recording, followed immediately by 7 days' touring; a week at home; 5 days' touring; 2 days at home; 6 days' touring; 5 days at home; 6 days' touring; 12 days at home; 9 days' touring; 16 days at home; 5 days' touring; 1 day at home; 10 days' touring. They gave a total of 43 stage performances in this period of 99 days. In addition, there were 5 shows that were planned and then canceled: one because of a riot in Ọ̀yọ́ College of Education; one, at Ìkẹ̀rẹ̀ Èkìtì Teachers' College, because a master died and the company spent the evening condoling with the family and staff instead; one in Ìgbàjà, because the road was so bad they could not get there; one because of the fishy smell in Ìlá; and one, in Ẹkàn Ńlá, on December 30th, because not a single person turned up, perhaps because of rumors of the impending military coup.

The total money from tickets sold at these 43 shows, after the cost of hiring the hall and paying a share to whoever invited them had been deducted, was N8,893. Adéjọbí paid each member on a tour N2 per day for food money, and the total bill for this over the period must have been about N2,060. Salaries, he said, cost between N2,500 and N2,600 a month, depending on the current strength of the company, so about N7,800 must have been needed in the three-month period in question. In addition, there was money for petrol, vehicle repairs, advertising, and the fixer's transport fares to be found. As Adéjọbí said, "Each time, we either have nothing left after a tour, or about N20." Indeed, these figures seem to suggest that touring alone could not support the company. They must have depended on the irregular but large sums that they could get from television companies for serials and full-length plays. Alhaji complained that the TV stations did not pay on time and sometimes failed to pay at all. However, when they did, the company could expect a financial boost. Ìlọrin Television, for example, paid them N3,600 for the two full-length plays they recorded on October 28th–30th. They also had a regular income from the long-running television and radio serial *Magistrate's Court*. Television and radio did not pay individual actors, and the members of the company did not expect a share of these payments, except insofar as they enabled Adéjọbí to pay their monthly salaries on time.

There were times when the company was flush—when Adéjọbí bought a VW Beetle for Alhaji in 1981, for example, or when he decided to change the curtains and backcloths and the opening glee costumes to give the shows a new look. Prosperous periods seem to have alternated with financially precarious ones when salaries were held over for several months and new tours could not be launched for lack of funds. The actors said they were always eventually paid their salaries in full, but that there could be periods of serious hardship while they waited. This alternation of fat and lean seems to have gone back many years. Fẹ́mi Ìlá, for instance, left the company he had so passionately desired to join only a year after Adéjọbí had taken him on in 1975 because he could no longer endure the lean patch they were going through at the time.

But the relatively modest scale of the rewards reaped by actors must be seen in the context of other informal sector employment at the time. In the early 1980s, N100 a month was the target in the campaign for a legal minimum wage, and it was regarded by skeptics as an impossibly high figure. Many daily paid people earned much less than this. The company members were paid less than N100 when they were first taken on, but the system of regular increments meant that after a few years they would be getting between N100 and N200 or even more. It seemed to be enough for the young men to marry on—the most important milestone in their journey to self-realization as social beings—and several of them expressed deep satisfaction with their conditions of employment.

The company, then, was more than a business. It was an *ẹgbẹ́*—an association—"a key concept in all domains of social life" (Guyer 1997, 40), characterized by a solidarity deriving from the common interests which brought the members together, by its occupational distinctiveness, and by its internal division of labor. The *ẹgbẹ́* was convened around the material assets—their vehicles, instruments, and equipment—which they jointly managed. Its layered structure, assembled around the magnetic center of the patron-boss in rings according to the actors' degree of dependability and "long stay" made it highly adaptable with regard to personnel: it could cope when people unexpectedly dropped out—as when Alhaji was unable to make it to Ìwó—and make the most of it when new people suddenly became available. In a similar way, the habitually irregular rhythms of work—the bursts of activity alternating with long periods of waiting around and the switches between travel, recording, and rehearsal—gave the company great flexibility in its orchestration of performing opportunities. They could make the most of payday every month and Christmas every year; they could always accept sponsored invitations no matter what else was on the agenda; they could cope with the unpredictability of television stations; and if some of the members were invited to go and perform in another group's film, even this could be accommodated. This flexibility sprang from the self-conception all the performers had of themselves as members of an *ẹgbẹ́* engaged in a collective enterprise rather than as employees in a firm. Although relationships among the members were hierarchically layered and Adéjọbí and Alhaji always had the last word, all the members could contribute not only to the creation of the plays themselves but also to the planning and management of the company's practical affairs. When a tour was being planned their knowledge of particular towns and halls could be rapidly assimilated into the management's calculations; when a practical problem arose with the scenery or lighting, the junior members could try to solve it before they called in a more senior person. The company was an assembly of all-rounders who all prided themselves at the same time on their special skills. The art of running the company, from a practical point of view, was the art of assembling, fostering, orchestrating, and exploiting the possibilities of those diverse aptitudes.

5 The Generation of Plays

Plays were generated out of the people and ideas available. Narratives were drawn from a wide range of written and oral sources and freely adapted. Dramatic plots were constructed to match the composition of the company. Characters were excavated from the experience of the actors. In the generation of a play, the theater company "made do" as well as "made up," improvising not only the dialogue—which will be discussed in the next chapter—but also the larger structures of the drama: the layout of the scenes, the interaction of the characters, and the linkage of action and its consequences that made up the plot. This artisanal approach to the acquisition and deployment of material fused with a clerkly orientation to literacy and to the idea of a written script. The result was a distinctive style, controlled and yet exuberant, constantly burgeoning and constantly held in check, comprehensively envisaged and directed by Alhaji, and yet always sprouting in different directions under the influence of audience response.

"GETTING AN IDEA"

The creation of a new play began when Mr. Adéjọbí or Alhaji "got an idea" for a story. The kernel of the story could be extracted from a variety of sources. At least two plays in the repertoire were based on myths of Yorùbá gods and heroes: *The Return of Odùduwà*, about the legendary founder of the Yorùbá nation, and *Morèmi*, about the heroine who saved Ifẹ̀ from destruction at the hands of the Igbo.[1] These mythical themes were felt to be more "weighty" than other stories; according to Mr. Adéjọbí, they involved doing "research" among the old people who knew the true stories, and Adéjọbí would charge more for them if invited to do a sponsored performance. It was *The Return of Odùduwà* that he wanted to use as a basis for his first film once he had raised the capital: it was generally felt that the prestigious and expensive medium of film deserved the most valuable kind of story.

However, traditional myths were not the mainstay of the company's repertoire. Some plots did have a folkloric quality, but they were not usually drawn direct from Yorùbá folktales. *The Royal Palm-nut,* for example, opens with the town chiefs sending two rival candidates to the throne out on a quest: an initial setup that seems to promise a typical folktale structure in which two characters pursue parallel courses, one doing everything wrong, the other doing everything right and winning the prize. This story, as Adéjobí explained, was indeed derived from an oral source in the person of Adéjobí's father, who used to tell stories "when matter happened," that is when issues arose which could be illuminated or expounded by a narrative analogy. But, as we shall see, Adéjobí's dramatized version of the story did not follow the folktale plot structure through; only one side of the double, parallel narrative was developed, and this was increasingly hijacked by the mesmerizing figure of the manipulative and adulterous wife of one of the candidates. *Kúyẹ̀,* which also had a "folkloric" atmosphere, being situated in a realm of traditional ọbas, wrestlers, and forest spirits, was actually based on a picaresque novel by J. F. Odúnjọ. Over the years it became progressively re-oralized and boiled down to its essential plot elements (see Chapter 11).

Popular Yorùbá-language literature, especially texts that were used in the school curriculum, provided a fertile source of ideas. *Taking Care of Kúnlé* owed its plot to another J. F. Odúnjọ novel, *Ọmọ Òkú Ọ̀run,* though only part of the narrative was used and many other elements were added. The Adéjọbís' *Gbangbá D'Ekùn* was a popularized version of Olú Daramọ́lá's written literary drama *Ilé tí a fi itọ́ mọ.*

Other plots, according to Alhaji, were about "what is actually going on":

"We get our themes from our own experience, or from what people tell me has happened in their experience. There was one play we did called *Dálé Moṣú.* 'Dálé moṣú' means a married lady who leaves her husband and comes back to live in her father's house, which is not what is supposed to happen. I have a brother in Lagos who told me this story. A certain woman had two men friends. One was a Muslim, the other a Christian. And each one didn't know about the other one. Well, she had a child for both of them."

"Do you mean she didn't know who was the father?"

"Yes. So she told both of them she had a child for him. So on the naming ceremony day, the Christian man brought Wòlíì. The Muslim brought Alfáà. To do the ceremony. Well, the woman asked the Christian to come in the morning and the Muslim to come in the evening. So they wouldn't know. But they met there. But each one thought the other was helping—maybe he was the wife's brother or something. Until the two of them realized. Then they get annoyed and both of them leave. The woman is left alone. So she goes back to her father's house."

"What about the baby?"

"Ah well," said Alhaji, spreading his hands. The baby's fate was not part of the story. "So we made it into the form of play. And we performed it in *Atóka.*"

"Real experience" is narratized and circulates in the form of anecdotes, while existing stories become the templates by which real experience is apprehended. This story—which has all the hallmarks of a well-formed popular tale—is recounted by Alhaji as something that actually happened, not to him but to someone his brother knew in another city. In this cycle, written texts may participate on the same footing as the anecdotes of experience. Many plays seem to have been an amalgam of hearsay, anecdote, folktale, and written fiction.

When tales, anecdotes, and written fiction were exploited for their potential "ideas," the theater companies were selective, doing work to discard the elements that did not suit their theater and to generate additional elements to give the stories substance and theatrical presence. Indeed, one good way of forming a sense of the limits and possibilities of the genre as a whole is to look precisely at the "entry requirements" for imported materials and at the mutations they undergo in being adapted for the stage. The Adéjọbí Company's rendition of the published literary drama *Ilé tí a fi itọ́ mọ*, for example, though apparently sticking fairly closely to the original,[2] made selective and strategic changes which altered the whole tenor of the play. In the literary drama, the focus is on the relationship of a monogamous middle-class couple and the threat to it posed by the husband's affair with his secretary. The husband eventually realizes his mistake (helped, it must be said, by Ifá divination) and returns to monogamous contentment, a sadder and wiser man. In the Adéjọbí play, the husband is brought to his senses not only by reflecting on the value of his partnership with his wife, but also by catching the secretary in full-blown flirtation with another boyfriend. The focus is thus shifted from a middle-class concern with the nature of a good relationship to the popular contrast between good wife and bad gold-digging "harlot."

It is important to note, however, that generic boundaries were always flexible. Taking literary drama on board could result in an extension to a theater company's range. It did so in this case, for despite the stereotyping, the Adéjọbí Company broke new ground in its conceptualization of female roles. And this was a possibility within the Yorùbá popular theater genre as a whole, with its pervasive adaptability and willingness to experiment: another example is the Ìṣọ̀lá Ògúnṣọlá company's version of the published poetic drama *Efúnṣetán Aníwúrà* (see Jeyifo 1984, 140–158), which led to a kind of historical purism as well as the use of a fixed script that was rare in the popular theater.

Thematic borrowing and re-assemblage was easier when ideas had already been converted and tried out as theatrical spectacle. But recognizable borrowing from the repertoires of other popular theater companies was frowned upon. Theater companies had no copyright. They had to protect their own creative resources as best they could by stamping them with their own distinctive house style and by angrily denouncing other companies whose plays seemed too similar. As a result, what was most often apparent was waves of thematic excitement, where numerous theater companies could be seen staging plays on similar subjects but so ingeniously varied and differentiated that every possibility seemed to be exploited and no exact copying was visible. The theme of magic wealth or counterfeit money, for example, treated in *Láníyonu* and *The Road to Riches,* was staged over and over again in innumerable variants by different theater companies. The theme of the Aládùúrà preacher, prominent in *External Appearances,* taps into the success of this motif in the output of several other theaters, including Lérè Pàímọ́'s *The Secret Is Out* (see Barber, Collins, and Ricard 1997), and the Òrànmíyàn Theatre's *Ìyá Aládùúrà [Woman Aládùúrà Preacher]*. The popularity of plots culminating in magical battles between good and evil forces was given a great boost by the sensational success of Jímọ̀ Alíù's theatrical repertoire, and particularly by his TV serial *Àrélù* in the 1980s, where almost every episode showed the heroine Òrìṣàábùnmi confronting the villain Fádèyí with streams of highly charged incantations. The Adéjọbí company's use of this element is to be seen in *Kúyẹ̀* and in later versions of *Besotted Bridegroom.* The rate and scale of borrowing and recycling was so huge as to amount to the constitution of an almost open field of theatrical intertextuality; but each theater worked so hard to mark and differentiate its own output that mere repetition of a theme or plot almost never seemed to occur.

Within the Adéjọbís' own repertoire, plot elements and thematic ideas were continually being recycled. One can see different stories being mapped onto the same plot structures several times over. *External Appearances,* for example, is the story of a fast young city woman who wants to find a husband but plays off one suitor against another until the two principal ones find out about each other and abandon her. This is a transmutation of the underlying structure of *Dálé Moṣú,* as recounted by Alhaji above: the core of both stories is the woman who tries to keep two men and loses both. However, the elements are transposed. In *External Appearances* the Aládùúrà prophet is not an adjunct but the pivotal character who advises her on her choice of husband; the baby is not hers but her prolific cousin's, who arrives at the end to awake the heroine to a sense of her missed opportunities; and she doesn't return to her father's home at the end, though the values of home are nonetheless affirmed in the person of the cousin.

Láníyọnu shares with *The Royal Palm-nut* its central situation: a town without an Ọba, in which a divination priest and an unruly group of town chiefs consult Ifá and argue over the succession. In *Lániyọnu,* the problem is eventually solved not by a quest, as in *The Royal Palm-nut,* but by the arrival of the eponymous hero. *Lániyọnu,* furthermore, appears to be assembled from materials drawn from two different repertoires of plot elements, one half being similar to the *Kúyẹ̀* story of a dispossessed, mistreated outcast stumbling as if accidentally on great good fortune, the other resembling the narrative setup of *The Road To Riches,* in which the exemplary character is a prosperous trader-contractor who made his way in the world by prudence, hard work, and a head for business. The play is assembled by suturing these two halves together by means of a radical transformation scene. In all three plays—*Kúyẹ̀, Lániyọnu,* and *The Road To Riches*—the same basic plot elements are recycled and re-assembled to address the same question about the nature of human self-realization: but each proposes a significantly different answer.

When they decided to put on a new play, then, they began by "getting an idea" from the sea of possibilities surrounding them in popular narrative, personal anecdote, print fiction, traditional legend, and the plays of other theater companies, as well as their own past successes. Mr. Adéjọbí's description of "getting an idea" suggests that it could be a slow process of gestation or accumulation rather than a sudden brainwave:

> It might take quite a long time—it's no question of a month—because I am not easily satisfied. So, when I put down an idea, I will read over and over again, and I put it away for some time, and I start to think on it, perhaps I could get some idea. And if I like, as a friend, I will call you, you will not even know that I'm trying to put on a play. I will ask of you, suppose that this and that happen, how do we solve the problem? And you will tell me. And it may happen that sometimes when I go around I could see something very much like an idea, in the play, then I will get hold of that too. (English.)

The core plots, then, did not come ready-made. They were assembled out of components collected from different sources and carefully fitted together; and the resulting narrative was still only a starting point, on which Mr. Adéjọbí then proceeded to work with thought, imagination, and the inputs derived from consultation with friends.

"WRITING OUT THE PLAY"

After "getting an idea," the next step, according to Adéjọbí, was for him to "write out the final play." The process began with his solitary reflection upon the kernel of the story. In the case of *The Royal Palm-nut,* he said:

> The story was first told by my late father. I was then still going to school. Because my father used to tell stories—especially when

matter happens—that dealt with the necessity for somebody to be loyal, to be sincere, to be truthful. When my father was addressing people generally, or his children, he first told me—told us—told the story, not told me or any other person—he first told the story and I listened well to that story, what he was saying. Then, I never thought I would become somebody who would be writing plays at all. But the story interested me so much, and I was thinking all the time about it. "So, it is possible for a man to think of something that does not belong to him or her! Á-à-á!" So, but it occurred to me that I should write a play, about twenty years ago [c. 1968] then I kept off myself from the house, I went somewhere, I sat down, I took my paper and biro [pen], and I first wrote up the story. It was the story I wrote down I started to read over and over and over again. So, after—when I got the play, I assembled my people and told them the story, I told them that I would plan it out. I planned it out, and I presented what I planned out to them. (English.)

The emphasis in Adéjọbí's account is on writing. His father originally told the story orally, and Adéjọbí's creative process culminated in his re-telling the story orally to his company: but he lays much stress on the intervening stage, when he closeted himself, alone, with "paper and biro," and subjected the story to intensive writing, reading over, and ratiocination. What he seems actually to have written down, most often, was a synopsis of the story—a practice encouraged, if not instigated, by television managers, who insisted on vetting every episode of their television comedies in advance. Adéjọbí would refer to the written synopsis when he initially "told his people the story," but thereafter it would be consigned to his files.

Alhaji said, "Baba gives me the story, and I turn it into a play." This involved, first of all, breaking it into chunks of action which could be represented as unified scenes. As Adéjọbí put it:

> We write it in form of story first, then we will break it into what I will call parts. When I say parts, I mean for instance you have the part where the Àràbà [in *The Royal Palm-nut*] addressed the other kingmakers, OK. It may end there, and sometimes it may not end there. We may have another scene when the chiefs will come to meet Àràbà one by one at his private residence trying to win him to their side. So after breaking the play up like that, we start choosing the cast, the actors and actresses. (English.)

It was Alhaji who broke the narrative up into dramatic sequences, determined the shape of each scene, and mapped out the principal stretches of dialogue. I asked him how he did this, for I had been impressed by the way he seemed to have an inner vision of the entire complex sequence of action and dialogue that made up a three-hour drama. Alhaji's first response was "I cannot explain that much because I can say it's God's gift." However, he went on to talk about the way he saw the process:

> Let's say I have got an idea now, and let's say baba writes the play, he tells me the story, immediately he's telling me the story I started to read it in my head, and I was seeing it, the way how to direct it. (English.)

Alhaji thus combines, with perfect harmony, ideas of telling and ideas of writing. He uses the words synonymously. Baba (Adéjọbí) "writes the play," which is to say he "tells me the story"; as he tells him the story, Alhaji starts to "read it in my head," which enables him to "see it, the way how to direct it." He then thinks over what he has been told, working on it in his mind:

> This is the way I did it. Let's say I was told the story, and I left that place immediately. On my way to anywhere I'm going, I started to remember, think over, "How can we do this?" Before I go round and come back I should have collected the way we can do it and how we can do it, that it should be publicly well. (English.)

Like Adéjọbí, Alhaji talks of "collecting" the elements that make up the play; but in his case he seems to be alluding more to an internal creative process than to the harvesting of existing narrative resources. His bodily progression from place to place as he "goes round" the town and "comes back"—he seems to suggest—mirrors or induces his mental progression around the places of the imagination. And he suggests that this process of "collecting" results in a comprehensive scheme of dramatic dialogue and action which he works out on his own, before he begins imparting it to the company.

When he took the actors through the play in rehearsal, he certainly seemed to be referring to a complete mental script. When the actors were experienced, he would give them key lines and organize the order in which they were to make their points; but when they were inexperienced, he would sometimes painstakingly teach them what to say line by line. During actual performances, I would sometimes see him walking up and down behind the scenery, correcting actors and giving them cues in a penetrating undertone.

The actors themselves used the language of instruction and correction to describe how Alhaji "taught" them their parts. Abíọ́dún Ọdéjìnmí, a small-part actor on the fringes of the company, explained that when the company is assembled by the manager, "each person has to correct his/her mistakes" and the right thing is to "accept gladly without arguing." Emily Adéjọbí, by then an actress of fourteen years' standing, spoke in terms even more strongly redolent of the schoolroom:

> Before we go to the town where we're going to perform, we'll first assemble on the premises [Adéjọbí's house] in Òṣogbo, the boss will tell us which play we're going to do. The manager will teach each of us. If he teaches us in the morning, from about nine o'clock to twelve, anybody who still doesn't know his own [part], they'll tell us to meet at five o'clock in the evening. We could still be there till seven or eight, they won't let us go until we know it.

Even the most experienced actors and actresses stressed that it was their duty to accept correction from Alhaji or Adéjọbí when their mistakes were pointed out.

But instruction was not necessarily, or exclusively, coaching in how to perform one particular part. It was more like a process of being seasoned; of absorbing, through constant exposure, a repertoire of possible ways of meeting the moment-to-moment requirements of the play as it moved along. Many of the actors spoke of the importance of "experience," using the English word. Experience was the fruit of "long stay" and "endurance," and it was what eventually enabled actors to generate their own text within the general guidelines provided by Alhaji.

In my own experience of being inserted into plays, the "teaching" at first involved detailed instruction in dialogue and movements. I was told where to stand and what to say word for word—as when Alhaji coached me in the three sentences he had given me in *Articulated Lorry*. But later, after more exposure to the company, the plays, and the audiences, it became a matter of Alhaji and Adéjọbí selecting and emphasizing points in a text that I generated myself—as when I made up the story of the escaped rabbits in *Taking Care of Kúnlé* (see Chapter 4). Judging from the actors' reminiscences, this was how they learned, too. They were "told" what to do beforehand, but actually learned on the job, absorbing a multiplicity of skills simultaneously.

Alhaji was not particularly complimentary about his actors' contributions to the conceptualization of a play. When I asked him if he invited their suggestions, he said "I try to ask them so as to have with them experience, I used to ask them, but if they didn't say anything, I will have to tell them, do this." Nonetheless, those actors who had stayed with the company long enough to acquire a repertoire of roles, sequences, and lines became part of the company's textual patrimony. Their departure represented not just the loss of a performer, but the loss of a component in the generation of the text. According to Emily, one of the worst hardships in theater life was the turnover of actors. Each time an actor leaves, "It causes problems. We have to start all over again with someone else, teach him and teach him until he too knows how to do it."

Their talents—despite Alhaji's disparaging remarks—helped to constitute the actual content of the play. For a brief period in 1982 the company employed a young man, Kingsley, who, though Yorùbá, had lived in contact with Hausa traders and had perfected the art of speaking Yorùbá with a heavy Hausa accent, replacing open vowels with closed and distorting the tones. When the company were putting together their new play *The Road to Riches*, the opening scene was built around this talent. It showed the birthday party of a rich, successful man Ọláòṣebìkan (see Barber and Ògúndíjọ, 1994) and its function was simply to introduce the characters and the idea that Ọláòṣebìkan was wise as well as rich. The backbone of the scene was speech-making: first, Dayọ̀ Akínpèlú's introductory remarks as the M. C., made in an affected Lagosian accent; then prayers by a mallam, made in a heavy Hausa accent; and finally Ọláòṣebìkan's own matchless eloquence as he distributes tokens of his wisdom to the guests. The role of the mallam was not indispensable to the plot. Had the play continued to be performed after Kingsley's departure (in actual fact the play was a flop and was discontinued after only a few performances), another character would have been concocted to take his place, in a manner to be discussed more fully in a moment. Nonetheless, the presence of the Hausa mimic at the time when the plot was initially being worked out clearly fed into the construction of that scene, perhaps even suggesting the whole idea of opening with a sequence of public speeches and prayers.

Whether they made overt "suggestions" to Alhaji or not, the more senior actors always had a large share in the generation of dialogue and character. They felt that only people with certain reservoirs of personality could undertake certain kinds of part: "You have to be strong to play the Ìyálóde; she's a tough character, not just anyone can do it," said Grace of her part in *The Overreacher*. This sense of their individual capacities to generate particular types of stage personae existed in tension with pride in their versatility. They were unanimous in their insistence that they could play any part and that no actor would ever claim any part as exclusively his or her own. When I asked Emily which part she liked best, she responded,

> I wouldn't reject any of them. There's no part that they assign you to [that you don't do]—because no one is **permanent** in any part. Now, this part that I'm playing now, someone else did it before, and when she was no longer available I took it over. Maybe tomorrow, someone else will play the part I'm doing, and I'll do someone else's. No one can say they only want to do one part. We do whatever we're assigned to.

Or, as Margaret put it, "Actors must not say that they prefer one part to another. Any part I'm assigned to, I'll do it **quite all right.**"

But when actors replaced each other, especially in the bigger roles, the play might be transformed. So much of the text and the feel of the play arose from the actors' own resources that a change of cast could almost generate a new play. I saw *The Heir* first in January 1982. The protagonist, an impostor who arrives to claim the inheritance of a missing first son, was played by Dayọ̀ Akínpẹ̀lú. In November of the same year I saw the play again. By then Dayọ̀ had left the company and Alhaji had taken over the part. These were the notes I made at the time:

> Alhaji played the part quite differently. Àlàbí [Dayọ̀] emphasised throughout the lightness, glibness, and dexterity of Láńre; his hollowness, the flimsiness and speciousness of his boasts and lies. Thus in the cloth-selling scene [where he sells a cloth-dealer a box full of rags, having convinced her that it is lace] he keeps up a constant stream of patter about his travelling, how he left Mọ́s-kò, went from there to Tòró-ń-tò, and from there to New York; he sidesteps awkward questions with even more elaborate smokescreens of verbiage. When the cloth-seller (played brilliantly by Margaret) asks him where he lives, so that she can come and thank him for the good turn he has done her, he replies airily that he lives in the Reservation up over there, and that everybody knows him by the name of "Traveller." When accounting for his long absence to the Baálé, he weaves a fantastic story about being stolen by *gbọ́mọgbọ́mọ* [childstealers], who took his blood from his arm to make medicine. "You can still see the scar . . . " he says, showing the Baálé his forearm, but then whipping it away at once with "Oh, it's faded." The tightrope walking, flirting with discovery and thus daringly reinforcing his claims, was done with great bravado by Àlàbí.
>
> Alhaji came across as a much more solid rogue, less eager to dazzle, but exuding an air of quite plausible cheap wealth—the jazzy white waistcoat, the dark glasses, the spiv-like manner, understated but nevertheless almost outrageous, so smug and wellgreased. In the cloth-selling scene he didn't dazzle the woman by flourishing samples of the laces, as Dayọ̀ did, giving exact details of each one and how many yards there were of it, and where it came from. He just stood there impassively telling her if she didn't want it there were others who would because this was a chance to make N12,000. In the deceiving-of-the-household scenes, he relied mainly on the claim that he had had a dream in which Bámgbádé appeared to him and informed him of what was going on (information he had actually got from an earlier call on Tàfá in his town).... Every time he was asked a question he would confirm his inheritance rights by adding "Yes, quite right, that's what Bámgbádé did say in the dream; I was only testing you." The dream legitimised everything.... Alhaji's Láńre, unlike Àlàbí's, really succeeded in passing himself off as an ex-driver made good. His lies

Dayọ̀ Akínpẹlú as Láńre in *The Heir*. The impostor spins a tale.

to Tàfá (who knew him when he was Bámgbádé's driver) are outrageous. He is now the manager of Julius Berger for all Nigeria; he owns a fleet of cars in the U.S.; he has four private planes ... he gives Tàfá a ticket to come and visit him in the U.S. After he leaves, Tàfá goes into a monologue on how people can change. The world transforms people almost miraculously. Who would have thought that somebody's driver, who used to pick up extra *kọ́bọ̀* selling second-hand tyres, could have become such a big man as this? (Later, when Láńre is about to be unmasked, Tàfá has another set piece, a long description of his sufferings when he tried to use his ticket at the airport!) The theme of baseless overnight fortunes seemed to come out much more strongly in this version because Alhaji's Láńre projected the image of the overnight wealthy man much more solidly.

Clearly, Alhaji not only played the part differently but also created a different part, with different dialogue and actions, to suit his own conception of

Alhaji Kàrímù Adépòjù as Lánre in *The Heir*.
©Karin Barber

the character—and this in turn affected the whole tenor of the play's message. Lesser actors in lesser roles would not have as much scope to do this, but the plays were conceived and constructed in such a way that such processes of re-generation were always possible.

Although they claimed that actors cannot choose their parts, many of the actors did have preferences. John's favorite part was the Ọba in *The Overreacher*—not surprisingly, since it was the central role and full of opportunities for the kind of comic bluster he excelled at. Fẹ́mi Bámidélé liked the part of the money collector in *Taking Care of Kúnlé*. Isiaka said that though there was no part he couldn't play, he was usually given characters like "scoundrels, thieves, hooligans, and that kind of thing" to play. Fẹ́mi Ìlá commented shyly that what he liked best of all was playing the *jàǹdùkú* (thug) in the TV serial *Ìgbà lódé* [*Modern Times*], because "I might be getting out of a taxi and I might jump down suddenly. The travelers would scatter in terror. They'd say 'The thug has arrived!'"

Indeed, recognition by the public both onstage and offstage exerted a powerful influence that counteracted the actors' versatility and interchangeability. The audiences knew the actors by the names of their most popular characters—usually from the TV series *Magistrate's Court*—and would hail them loudly by these names when they walked onstage, no matter what part they were playing. Alhaji was recognized by everyone as "Bàbáa Wándé," John as "Tàfá Olóyèdé." They called each other by these names offstage. Sometimes this recognition spilled over into the actual creation of characters in new plays. In both *The Road to Riches* and *The Heir* John's character is called Tàfá, even though the two are quite different, both from each other and also from the Tàfá in the TV serial. Alhaji was addressed and referred to in the opening scene of *The Road to Riches* as "Bàbáa Wándé," even though the character's name was Oláòṣebìkan. Audience recognition—which of course the actors sought and welcomed—thus exerted a homogenizing influence, promoting the emergence of a kind of flexible composite identity which operated both onstage and offstage and which could accommodate a wide variety of roles without losing a certain underlying continuity.

It must be stressed, however, that this tendency toward homogenization was very far from approximating to the fixed, specialized characterization of the commedia dell'arte (Lea 1962; Duchartre 1966), or even the somewhat more fluid permutations of character in Ghanaian concert party (see Barber, Collins, and Ricard 1997). There were no stable recurrent figures such as Harlequin or Opia, returning with all essential features intact in play after play; and no actors who only played one type of character. Perhaps the most versatile of them all was Alhaji, who was also the most acclaimed as a star. In *Kúyè*, Alhaji played an innocent deaf and dumb boy—a young lad—who generates a lot of mirth by his naive mimicry of everyone else's actions. In *Besotted Bridegroom* he played Bùárí, a crippled, one-eyed, irascible old man. In *Taking Care of Kúnlé* he played a sensible, progressive, modestly successful man who falls prey to the schemes of a seductress. In *Articulated Lorry* he played an uneducated heavy-drinking lorry driver with an unfaithful wife. In *The Overreacher*, he played Gbajúmò, the Oba's messenger, an ambiguous character, sly and subservient at one moment, plain-speaking and bluff the next. None of these characters was a fixed "type"; they were all very different from each other; and Alhaji played them differently. The continuity lay in things like his impeccable comic timing, a certain professional surface, his use of silence, not in recognizable traits of characterization.

The actors saw their success as arising from a combination of innate gifts, specialized talents, experience deriving from "long stay," knowledge deriving from instruction by the senior members (especially Alhaji and Adéjobí), and their own intelligence. Thus Margaret took great pride in her natural ability as a performer: she recounted how when she replaced a missing actress in a leading role at short notice, she was instantly "perfect": so much so that when Akin Ògúngbè, the manager of another company, saw her, he said, "This person who has never acted before gets up on stage and knows how to do it better even than myself!" But she also commented that in order to succeed, an actor has to know what he or she is good at and concentrate on developing that talent. Commenting on experience, she said "Above all, an actor needs endurance"; others spoke of how acting was hard at first, until "I got used to it." Finally, active intelligence is required if an actor is to respond quickly and accurately to instruction. As Yẹ́misí said, "If you are given a part, and if you're capable of thinking properly, you will quickly 'catch up.' Someone who doesn't catch on quickly will say that acting is hard. But there's nothing all that hard about it."

The one thing they never suggested was that acting involved observation and mimicry. Characterization was drawn out from within them, from their innate talent and their accumulated repositories of social experience. In this sense their performances are not best thought of as *representations*—they are not pictures of observed reality—so much as the *activation of potential* within them, potential whose gradual augmentation was social and unconscious, the deposit of daily life rather than the outcome of deliberate study.

SLOTS AND SET PIECES

Some of the plays in the Adéjọbí repertoire were structured around large numbers of actors and would have been difficult to perform with a smaller company. The "folkloric" plays usually needed more actors than the "modern comedies." The story of *Kúyẹ̀*, for example, could not be told with less than 17 people, and in fact more were actually involved in the performances I saw. Although there were only seven big parts, there were many smaller ones which could not be dispensed with: an Ọba must have an entourage, a wrestling match must have competitors, a forest of spirits must have denizens. Messengers, family elders, and an itinerant peddler played crucial roles in linking the different sequences and sites of action. *The Royal Palm-nut* and *Lániyọnu*, and to a lesser extent *The Overreacher* (which, though a new play in 1981, was set in a world that had much in common with the older "folkloric" style), were structured around a similar array of characters. In each, the core of the plot was carried by half a dozen key players—the inner circle of the theater company—but large numbers of smaller people were needed to move the story forward in crucial ways.

The "modern comedies" which became the mainstay of the repertoire in the 1980s also involved a division of labor between core members and peripheral ones, but the structure of the plays tended to be arrived at in a different way. There would be a central plot that could be carried by a small number of actors with very demanding roles; then side plots and extra episodes would be attached to add variety and substance to the drama and to

The Generation of Plays 145

The royal court in *Kúyẹ̀*. ©Ello Montanari

give the available actors something to do. The structure of the play can be envisaged as a solar system, with rings of planets of decreasing size and importance circling round a central core. Many of the characters and episodes in the outer rings of this system were not essential to the narrative in the sense that they could have been replaced by alternative characters or episodes, or removed altogether, without upsetting the logic of the plot.

Articulated Lorry illustrates this principle very clearly. Let me recapitulate the outlines of the plot:

> Among the tenants in a landlord's house are a young educated single man, Àlàbí, and a married couple, Bàbáa Wándé and Ìyáa Bùnmi. Bàbáa Wándé is a lorry driver. Ìyáa Bùnmi is better educated than her husband and also resents his absences on long-distance transport jobs. During one such absence, she makes advances to Àlàbí, who rejects them, at first politely but then, when she persists, with contempt. When Bàbáa Wándé returns, Àlàbí

tries to tell him about her behavior, but she does not allow him to be heard. She then attempts falsely to incriminate Àlàbí by accusing him of using medicines against her husband—medicines which she herself has laid out on the floor. A big furor erupts involving the landlord and other tenants, who all believe Ìyáa Bùnmi's accusations. To make sure, however, the landlord devises a test. He tells Àlàbí to beg Ìyáa Bùnmi's forgiveness and then to arrange an assignation with her. Bàbáa Wándé is to pretend to go off on another trip. They do this. Ìyáa Bùnmi accepts Àlàbí's pleas and apologies, comes to his room at the appointed hour and makes love to him, where she is caught red-handed by her husband. Àlàbí's name is cleared and the deceitfulness of women confirmed.

This plot is carried by three central characters—the young man, the husband, and the wife—with a fourth, the landlord, playing a smaller but structurally crucial role. Onto this core structure are added "extenders"—characters and episodes which add something extra without being indispensable to the unfolding of the central plot.

Some "extender" characters/episodes do enrich the context of action, even though they could be removed and replaced by an alternative. One such is the part of Àlàbí's mother, who comes on a visit to tell him that she has found him a wife, Wúlè, a beancake seller who is the daughter of a dear friend of hers. Àlàbí holds out against this plan because he wants to go on to higher education and does not want to burden himself at the outset of his career with the expense of a wife and children. There is a drawn-out comic confrontation between the two of them that is full of misunderstandings, as Àlàbí cannot help lapsing into English while his mother is given to speaking in oblique and proverbial Yorùbá. Though Àlàbí's mother could be omitted without altering the course of narrated events, her scene adds substance to the thematic contrast, developed throughout the play, between "educated" "enlightened" values and "uneducated" ordinary beliefs and behavior. And, coming early in the play, it highlights key aspects of Àlàbí's persona which are relevant to grasping the point of his subsequent behavior—notably, the fact that he is a young man capable of self-denial in the interests of his long-term project of educational self-betterment.

There are other satellite characters who are less entwined with the central themes of the play. One such is Bàbáa Fàtàí, a fellow tenant played by John. As I noted in my diary, John told me that "Bàbáa Fàtàí hadn't been there in the original version; it had been added." Bàbáa Fàtàí is a shopkeeper and a bit of a sap. He regards himself as Bàbáa Wándé's friend but is mistreated by him. This offers the opportunity for comic byplay—for instance in the episode when he discovers that Bàbáa Wándé, who offered him a lift in his lorry, has left without waiting for him. He tries to find out from Ìyáa Bùnmi how to get to the motor-park to catch up with him. Her complicated directions, involving roundabouts and multiple turns, leave him completely baffled. The character of Bàbáa Fàtàí also adds substance to the scenes in which Àlàbí is wrongfully accused and later vindicated. By loudly voicing his opinion that Àlàbí is guilty and then almost howling in outrage when the culprit is shown to be Ìyáa Bùnmi, he adds greatly to the dramatic tension and its resolution. John's ebullient blustering manner and ear-splitting voice did a lot to increase the impact of the guilty wife's exposure.

Another such character, who makes an appearance in the first scene and then disappears, is the party secretary. The landlord has just been made chairman of the local branch of a political party, and the secretary comes to negotiate the hire of the landlord's new house for the party's offices. Fẹ́mi Bámidélé made much of this little part, doing elaborate calculations of the rent on 16 rooms, multiplying and "canceling" with great zest.

In this play, in fact, the core plot was so compact that a large proportion of stage time was spent on the added-on episodes. The whole of the lengthy first scene could have been removed and replaced with an alternative without damaging the logic of the narration. This scene is an extended introduction to the landlord, his household, and his tenants. It opens with the landlord reading an article in the newspaper—a report that he has been made "chairman" of a party—and exulting in the grandeur of this appointment. He boasts to his wife that he is now so powerful as to be more or less above the law—a claim which she pooh-poohs. The party secretary then calls on him and they enter into protracted negotiations over the rent for the new house before the landlord tells him he will let the party have the house for nothing. The landlord then decides to make some changes in the household to reflect his new status. He summons the tenants and in a long speech issues a number of decrees: no one can support any other party while under his roof; no one must leave rubbish lying around the floor; no one must use wood fires for cooking any more; the walls should be kept spotless, not wiped with oily hands after a meal. This gives the opportunity for a series of comic responses by the tenants. Àlàbí treats them to a disquisition on how membership of political parties is handled in Britain. Bàbáa Wándé says that if there is mess in his part of the house, it is Ìyáa Bùnmi's fault. Bàbáa Fàtàí reproaches him for mentioning such things in front of everyone and then asserts that he will never join any political party. The characters thus present themselves one by one, but their discussion imparts very little information essential to the plot. Indeed, many of the elements apparently established in this scene are dropped later on. The theme of political party membership, for example, is not developed in the rest of the play. The egregiously self-important demeanor of the landlord and the implicit criticism of his involvement in politics is left behind. By the end of the play, he has become a wise and benign authority figure who solves the problems caused by Ìyáa Bùnmi's sexual rapacity. The more diffuse and pervasive theme of "progress" and "enlightenment"—evoked in Àlàbí's depiction of an imaginary political and social rationality and in the landlord's insistence on household cleanliness—does persist throughout the play and is perhaps its main source of thematic unity as well as its greatest point of interest; but this theme could obviously have been introduced in numerous other, similar, quasi-autonomous episodes, for there is no inherent or essential relationship between the landlord's political activities or rules of housekeeping and the rest of the action.

In the older "folkloric"-style plays, then, it was a matter of finding people to play all the parts—recruiting drivers, odd-job men, and hangers-on when necessary. In the domestic comedies that made up the bulk of their new plays in the 1980s, it was a matter of finding parts to give all the people—adding epicycles to the central characters' narrative orbits as the occasion arose. Whichever kind of plot they mounted, however, the company's mode of theatrical generation was such as to produce a kind of pervasive modularity.[3] Situations were set up containing slots which could be multiplied or reduced in number, according to the availability of actors. And the text moved forward by means of set pieces, each of which could be expanded or contracted, depending on how well it went down with the audience. Slots and set pieces characterized all the plays, whether folkloric or domestic.

The system of slots became apparent to me early on, as Alhaji and Mr. Adéjọbí kept effortlessly proposing parts to me—often mentioning them only as we were actually on our way to a performance or even just as we were about to start the play. Such parts were easy to tack on because they added to an existing series. The first play in which I was given a part was *The Overreacher*, a "folkloric" play in which the council of chiefs provided a natural and indefinitely extensible series. In the opening scene the power-crazy Ọba interrogates, threatens, and dismisses each of the chiefs in turn: each is required to explain his or her special role in the town and is then subjected to a barrage of tailor-made insults. *The Royal Palm-nut* and *Láníyọnu*—also "folkloric" plays—offered similar slots in the scenes where the chiefs meet to discuss the town's problems.

The domestic satires offered a wider range of slots. In *Articulated Lorry*, the landlord-and-tenants situation lent itself to multiplication, and I became another tenant. Each tenant was allocated his or her own spot, in which they were given scope to present their contrastive personalities. The only requirement was that I should add a further contrast (not difficult in the circumstances). In *Taking Care of Kúnlé* a similar set of slots occurred in

And another time, I played the nurse. The clinic scene with Grace as a patient in *Taking Care of Kúnlé* at Ijàn-Ọ̀tún.
©Elio Montanari

the clinic scene, where a series of patients appear one by one with comic or peculiar complaints before the main character, the half-drowned Wúrà, makes her entry. In the opening scene of *External Appearances,* a series of devotees in an Aládùúrà church are given assignments of fasting and prayer by the preacher in order to solve specific problems; this is a preparation for the arrival of the anti-heroine, Bísí, who comes with her complaint that though men pursue her they don't want to marry her. In one performance, when Mr. Lásún Ọláìítán—our "guest artist" extraordinaire—joined us for the evening, a special slot was opened for him in this series. He was cast as the old pagan father of one of the members of the congregation. The church member introduces the old man to the preacher with the idea of having him received into the Christian faith. A conversation at cross-purposes between the old man and the preacher follows, in which each systematically misunderstands the other's use of terms. The preacher tries to teach the old man Christian hymns, and the old man responds with *ijálá* chanting and incantations. It is possible that the entire sequence was lifted from some other play in which Mr. Ọláìítán had appeared in his earlier association with the company; but as far as I know, Ọláììtán, John, Alhaji, and Adéjọbí simply worked it out half an hour before the show, and the two actors performed it without rehearsal. In this case, then, the slot was so expanded that it became an entire additional episode, hooked on at a moment's notice to make the most of a temporarily available talent. (For a text of this passage and further discussion, see Chapter 10.)

There was a sense in which existing small parts could also be seen as slots available for a new occupant to take over and expand. This became apparent in a performance of *Besotted Bridegroom*, when Mr. Ọláììtán—the same week that he did the extra episode in *External Appearances*—took over the part of the *babaláwo*, usually played by a peripheral member of the company. His specialty was traditional oral poetry, and he greatly expanded the chanting of *ẹsẹ Ifá*, giving a performance in his resonant, musical voice which was much appreciated by the audience. All the plays, then, have sequences featuring a series of equivalent but contrasting characters, allowing the addition of extra slots for visiting performers; and all are constructed in such a way that existing small parts can be expanded to display new talent. This process of expansion can best be understood in the light of the pervasive use of set pieces.

All the plays feature monologues or carefully orchestrated dialogues in which the characters take a theme and elaborate it. Like a jazz solo (see Berliner 1994, 368–386), these set pieces spring from the ongoing thematic exposition of the play and serve ultimately to develop it; but they do so with an effect of "surplus," of entertainment for its own sake. A performer delivering a solo set piece will usually stand at one of the two microphones and direct his or her speech outward. She or he will be allowed to continue until completion is signaled, often by concluding a narrative sequence. Set piece speeches are key components in the generation of the text of all the plays. There are long monologues in which characters lay down the law (*The Overreacher*), tell stories about other people (*Taking Care of Kúnlé*), or invent personal experiences in order to deceive (*The Heir*). In *The Road to Riches*, the wife of the foolish, lazy, and greedy protagonist Tàfá becomes convinced that they will soon become rich by means of money magic. She conveys her hopes and delusions by narrating a dream:

ÌYÁ ṢÈYÍ: Ọ̀rọ̀ kan tí mo tiẹ̀ ránti, ǹ bá ti sọ fún ọ, kó tóó di pé o jíṣẹ́ ń mi. Mo mà láláà kan lóníì.
TÀFÁ: Álá kí ni?
ÌYÁ ṢÈYÍ: Ọ̀rọ̀ ǹ bá rò, ma ròfọ́, bí mo dé ma tami 'ápẹ. Ǹ bá ni . . . ǹ bá ń lọ lójúran o, nì ń lọ sàá sàá sàá sàá. Ṣé ẹ ri bí ǹ ṣe ń lọ, ńwòkè tí n óò wòkè báyìí, mo bá rí òpópó un ló lọ salaluu. Háhàà, irú àlá èwo ha nìín? Mo wáá dúó ńbo ni n yà sí? Òpópó èyí abàmì ni. Gbà tí n óò wáá wò, mo wáá rí arákùnrin kan, ní

ń bá ń bọ̀. Wò ó, ṣó o mọ léèsì eńyindin-yindin un tí ọn ń lò láyéèsìn-ín un, kòǹpílíìtì rẹ ló wọ̀. Ló bá fi alágbàáà'Jẹ̀sà lée lé e.

TÀFÁ: Íí ṣe rí?

ÌYÁ ṢÈYÍ: O ò mọhun tí ọn ń pè bẹ́ẹ̀? Dàkírọ́ọ̀nù olówó ńlá ní í jẹ́ báun.

TÀFÁ: N lẹ́ẹ́ pè lálágbàáà'Jẹ̀sà!

ÌYÁ ṢÈYÍ: Ṣó o rí i, ló bá tún e lé e, àwé, ní ń bá ń bọ̀. Háhà, mo bá dúó báyìí, mo ní kọ́mọkùnrin ní ìgbésẹ̀ fàájì báyìí! Nì ń bá ń wòran. Mo bá ní tó bá tiẹ̀ rííyàn níìsiíín, ó lè máa ròròkurò, èmi náàa bá pèìndà èmi bá ń lọ. Èyiùn lójú oorun o. Lílọ tí ǹ ń wá ń lọ, ni ń bá ń gbọ́, 'Ìyá Ṣèyí, Ìyá Ṣèyí, Ìyá Ṣèyí'. Gbà tí n óò bojú wèìn, ló bá di Baba -

TÀFÁ: - Ṣèyí!

ÌYÁ ṢÈYÍ: - Ṣèyí! Yéééè. Olódùmarè oò.

TÀFÁ: Àpẹẹrẹ re nù, àpẹẹrẹ re nù-un-ùn.

ÌYÁ ṢÈYÍ: Máa gbọ́ọ̀. Pípẹ tí ń pè mí tànmáàa yóò wáá bá mi ni, bìrí tó yà báyìí wíwò tí n óò wò, mo wáá rí pẹ̀tẹ́ẹ̀sì kan, gílásì ni wọ́n fi pẹ̀tẹ́ẹ̀sì ọ̀hún kọ́. Ńgbà mo kà á léní, èjì, ó jẹ́ méjìlélógún, fúláàtì. Ṣé ẹ rí àkàsọ̀ kììnní tí Baba Ṣèyí, tó o kọ́kọ́ gùn báyìí, kí n tóó bojú wẹ̀hìn, o ti dórí-òkè. Lo wáá káwọ́ lérí 'áárèní' báyìí, lò ń pé, 'Ìyá Ṣèyí, èyin kí ǹ ń pè ni?' Lẹ ní n máa bọ̀. Ibi àlá wáá gọ̀ sí rèé oo, ṣó o mọ bàtà àwọn ọmọ sùkúù tó rí kóbikòbi un, lójú oorun, n mo bá ko wọsẹ̀, témi èé wọ̀ lójú ayé télẹ̀. Wò ó, nì ń bá ń ṣe báyìí: Ikàá . . . ikòó . . . ikàá . . . ikòó . . . ìkòó . . . ikàá.

ÌYÁ ṢÈYÍ: I've just remembered something, I would have told you earlier, before you told me your story. I had a dream last night.

TÀFÁ: What kind of dream?

ÌYÁ ṢÈYÍ: "I would have said something important, instead I made vegetable sauce. When I get home, I'll put water in the pot."[4] I was going to tell you, as I was going along, in my dream, I was going ṣàá ṣàá ṣàá ṣàá. . . . So you see, as I was going along, when I looked up, I saw this road stretching ahead as wide as can be. Gosh, what kind of dream was that? I stood still, wondering which way to go. This road was really strange. And as I looked at it, I saw a young man coming toward me. Look, do you know that shiny lace that everyone's wearing now, well he had a 'complete' made of it.[5] And it was finished off with alágbàáà Ìjẹ̀sà[6] brocade.

TÀFÁ: What's that?

ÌYÁ ṢÈYÍ: You don't know what they call alágbàáà Ìjẹ̀sà? It's a very expensive kind of Dacron.

TÀFÁ: That's what you call *alágbàáà Ìjẹ̀sà!*
ÌYÁ ṢÈYÍ: So you see, he had this on top, and he was coming toward me. I stood still and said to myself—To think that a young man should be as well turned out as that! I was just gazing at him. But then I thought if he saw me now, he might get the wrong idea, so I turned my back and went on my way. All this was in my dream. So as I was going, I heard a voice saying, "Ìyáa Ṣèyí, Ìyáa Ṣèyí, Ìyáa Ṣèyí." When I turned round again to look, who should it turn out to be but Bàbáa . . .
TÀFÁ: Ṣèyí!
ÌYÁ ṢÈYÍ: Ṣèyí! Oh, God!
TÀFÁ: It's an auspicious sign. It's an auspicious sign.
ÌYÁ ṢÈYÍ: Now listen. The way he was calling me was as if he was going to come and join me, as he spun round like this and I was watching, I suddenly saw a skyscraper, and it was built of glass. When I counted the floors, there were 22 apartments. You see, Bàbáa Ṣèyí stepped onto the bottom flight of stairs and before I could turn round you'd reached the top! Then you leaned on the iron [railing] like this and called "Ìyáa Ṣèyí, isn't it you I'm calling? Or are you going to say you haven't seen me? Isn't it you I'm calling?" And you told me to come up. This is how stupid dreams can be—you know the shoes the schoolgirls are all wearing, with platform soles—in the dream, I was wearing them—which I've never ever worn in real life! And you see, I was going like this: *Ikàá . . . Ikòó. . . . Ikàá . . . Ikòó. . . . Ikòó . . . Ikàá . . .*

This speech luxuriates in its own extensivity. Ìyáa Ṣèyí (played by Deborah) spins it out, putting in all kinds of details—the sound of her footsteps, the slang name for the exact kind of cloth Tàfá [Bàbáa Ṣèyí] was wearing, the exact number of floors in the skyscraper, the kind of shoes she had on—to create a surreal image of fashion and wealth. In set pieces like this, the other characters are adept at stoking the fires. John, playing Tàfá, adroitly fed her questions and responses at appropriate moments—giving her the opportunity to explain the slang *alágbàáà Ìjẹ̀sà* and adding punch to her climactic revelation that the dream figure was Tàfá himself by anticipating what she is going to say a split second before she says it. This performative module is a kind of "turn," reminiscent of the concert party mode. It is created and sustained by the actress's bravura performance: the set piece is a space which the actor is licensed to expand through elaborations and variations on a theme. The prevalence of set pieces in these plays is testimony to Biọdun Jeyifo's observation that this is an actor's theater (Jeyifo

1984, 20–21). The growing points of the drama are essentially the sites where particularly gifted actors exploit the potential of their allocated set piece.

But the exploitation of individual actors' potential, by means of set pieces, is always in tension with the play's overall design. The expansivity of each module is checked not only by pressure from other actors' adjacent modules but also by Alhaji's architectural plan. Thus the oral improvisatory generative mode interacts with the manager's imagined script, sometimes producing extraordinary effects.

In some plays, this feeling of taut yet burgeoning modularity is pervasive—it is as if every component could be slotted in, unhooked, extended, or substituted. Within the tense horizon of Alhaji's design, the result is not indeterminacy but high definition and glitter, as sequences of "turns" slot together, each expanding to fill the space available and pushing its edges tightly against the adjacent ones. One such play was *Taking Care of Kúnlé*. On good nights, *Taking Care of Kúnlé* seemed to be composed of polished scales, presenting a hard, shiny but flexible surface. A remarkable exemplar of this style is the scene where the two family elders, Adéwálé and Owólabí, break the news of Wúrà's supposed death to her husband Ọ̀ṣọ́. This is an extended, carefully planned sequence for three, containing within it spaces for several solo set pieces. In the National Theatre performance, it went like clockwork—but clockwork powered by an explosive vitality, deriving from the expansive pressures of each set piece pushing against the linear requirement of the sequence—to get the bad news delivered. I will present the translation of the whole episode here, because it so clearly reveals the possibilities of modular composition. The Yorùbá text is presented in Appendix 2.

(Kúnlé, the couple's young son, is playing imaginary football by himself in the parlor)

KÚNLÉ: Hey . . . hey . . . hey . . . I've scored. I've scored. "A goal." I've scored. "A goal."

(Ọ̀ṣọ́ comes in)

ỌṢỌ́: Hey, is this the National Stadium? You're going to get into trouble today! . . . Hello, hunter. Have you been to wash the plates your mother told you to wash?

KÚNLÉ: Not yet.

ỌṢỌ́: She'll beat you within an inch of your life if she comes back in the night [and finds them still not done]. You naughty boy, you play football in the house when there's a field for you outside. Bandy-legged creature.

(Adéwálé and Owólabí arrive)

ADÉWÁLÉ: Hello to the householder.

Ọṣọ́: Who's that?
OwÓLABÍ: Hello to the householder. My dear Ọṣọ́. Er, Adéwálé, Adéwálé ...
ADÉWÁLÉ: Er, Ọṣọ́, Ọṣọ́ ...
Ọṣọ́: Do come in. Have a seat. Where are you coming from? Kúnlé! Kúnlé!
KÚNLÉ: Sir!
Ọṣọ́: So what's up?
OwÓLABÍ: Well ... er ...
Ọṣọ́: Or should I make some tea for you?
OwÓLABÍ: Oh, no, we're not going to be able to eat anything.
ADÉWÁLÉ: We're not going to be able to eat anything. We're not going to be able to eat anything.
Ọṣọ́ (TO KÚNLÉ): Go and buy some pemmican [hard hide strips chewed as a snack] for them.
OwÓLABÍ: No, really, you mustn't treat us as strangers ...
Ọṣọ́: What about something to drink?
ADÉWÁLÉ: We won't drink anything.
Ọṣọ́: I hope it's not because of some problem that you've come?
ADÉWÁLÉ AND OwÓLABÍ: Oh, no problem, no problem.
ADÉWÁLÉ: It was just that Owólabí said he wanted to see you.
OwÓLABÍ: Yes, but there's no problem. You see, Ọṣọ́ ... er ... may the king's hoe not cut your foot.
Ọṣọ́: Amen.
OwÓLABÍ: We meet the mountain at a height, a height. We meet the moon up on high. May the pole of your hunter's trap always fall forward [i.e., may you always make progress].
Ọṣọ́: Amen.
OwÓLABÍ: Er ... a younger relative of mine has come back from abroad, and he's gone and lost his job. So I said to him, well, you can't just sit doing nothing, you're going to have to find something to do. Ọṣọ́, please, could you find him a job where you work?
Ọṣọ́: How far did he go in school?
OwÓLABÍ: Oh, he went far. He went far. He has a lot of education.
Ọṣọ́: How many years?
OwÓLABÍ: He's studied a lot. He did ten years, ten years of European, twenty years of Yorùbá.
Ọṣọ́: Has he got a certificate?
OwÓLABÍ: Do you mean a *sabuketi* [certificate]?
Ọṣọ́: Yes.
OwÓLABÍ: O yes, he has. He has.
Ọṣọ́: Well, baba, it's exactly those kind of people with certificates

that we want in our place of work. But something happened there recently, otherwise I'd say you should bring him along tomorrow and he'd have been able to start straight away.

ADÉWÁLÉ: I hope it was nothing bad?

Ọṣọ́: It was.

OWÓLABÍ: Oh dear.

Ọṣọ́: It was something really bad. It was our European, Mister Wúù [Wood], that it happened to.

ADÉWÁLÉ: What, did his mother die or something?

Ọṣọ́: No. But you know the machine they use for cutting iron . . . well, to cut a long story short, that machine uses NEPA [electricity]. As the machine began work in the morning four days ago, to cut a long story short, the electricity was shut off. Our Europeans have their own electricity supply. If the NEPA is taken away, they pull this lever and their own supply starts. Do you follow me? So you see, the machine that was cutting iron. . . The European wanted to go past where it was. Just as he was passing the spot, NEPA brought the electricity back. The engine suddenly began to roll, and the piece of iron that was being fed in caught his arm, and—heeey!

ADÉWÁLÉ AND OWÓLABÍ: Hey! Ha!

Ọṣọ́: Someone came running and grabbed hold of the severed arm as it was flying off . . . do you follow me . . . and he said he should weld it back on, because you know if they hold something hot against that arm, it might fuse back on when they re-attach it. So he got some paper and tied it up with string so that they could take him to the hospital straight away. To cut a long story short, you see, the person who first put the arm back had been trembling so much that he had put it on back to front. So they had to pull it off again and put it back the right way round. So, in a word, they've taken him back to his country now, and no one knows whether his arm will join back on or not. And his replacement hasn't yet arrived. That's the reason why I can't promise that your relative can start work right now.

ADÉWÁLÉ: Ha, accidents can happen to anyone. May God not let us suffer losses!

Ọṣọ́ AND OWÓLABÍ: Amen. Amen.

ADÉWÁLÉ: May the Almighty not let us suffer losses!

Ọṣọ́ AND OWÓLABÍ: Amen. Amen. Amen.

ADÉWÁLÉ: Ah, the European who worked and worked and then had his arm cut off by a machine! May the Almighty not let us suffer losses. The European that woke up and arose from his mat, who greeted his children and his wife, "Good-bye. . . . I'm going to work to earn our daily bread," where he was expecting to find plentiful sustenance, but where the thing that was going to eat *him* met him on the road! May the Almighty not let us suffer losses.

Ọṣọ́ AND OWÓLABÍ: Amen.

ADÉWÁLÉ: You see, in our Europeans' workplaces . . . if a European is going to work, he'll work wholeheartedly . . .

OWÓLABÍ: You have to hand it to them.

ADÉWÁLÉ: They'll put on shorts and a skimpy shirt, and they'll be smoking their cigarettes . . .

OWÓLABÍ: . . . puffing away . . .

ADÉWÁLÉ: They give it everything they've got [lit. "If they use the head they also use the neck to do it"]. But look at us Africans . . .

Ọṣọ́: It doesn't bear thinking about.

ADÉWÁLÉ: We're useless. The work they give us to do, we don't do it.

OWÓLABÍ: We're no good.

ADÉWÁLÉ: And the money they give us, we use to collect fleets of cars, like someone gathering parcels of *ẹ̀kọ* . . .

Ọṣọ́: Don't go on, it doesn't bear talking about!

ADÉWÁLÉ: When we employ people we don't pay them, we look down our noses at them—"Have you finished? Have you solved the whole problem?"

OWÓLABÍ: We're no good.

ADÉWÁLÉ: The European who worked and worked and got his arm cut off by a machine! May the Almighty not let us suffer losses.

Ọṣọ́ AND OWÓLABÍ: Amen.

ADÉWÁLÉ: May God not allow us to meet misfortune on the way.

OWÓLABÍ: Amen. Er, greetings, Ọṣọ́, er, and how's Kúnlé?

Ọṣọ́: Kúnlé!

ADÉWÁLÉ: Ah, Kúnlé . . .

KÚNLÉ (ENTERING): Sir.

Ọṣọ́: Come here, come here. These gentlemen [fathers] want to say hello to you. Come over here.

OWÓLABÍ: Er, Kúnlé, may God watch over you.

Ọṣọ́ AND KÚNLÉ: Amen, amen.

OWÓLABÍ: May God watch over you.

Ọṣọ́ AND KÚNLÉ: Amen, amen.

OWÓLABÍ: May the Almighty watch over you.

Ọṣọ́ AND KÚNLÉ: Amen, amen.

ADÉWÁLÉ: He and his father are as like as two peas. Er, Ọṣọ́, it's up to you, it's your responsibility.

OWÓLABÍ: It's your responsibility.

ADÉWÁLÉ: It's up to you. This is your mirror. It will not break before your eyes.
Ọ̀SỌ́: Amen, amen, amen.
ADÉWÁLÉ: This is your photograph, it will not get torn.
Ọ̀SỌ́: Amen.
ADÉWÁLÉ: By the grace of God, the money that you need to send this child **overseas,** God will provide it.
Ọ̀SỌ́: Amen, amen.
ADÉWÁLÉ: His mother's Destiny too will support you.
OWÓLABÍ: His mother's Destiny too will support you.
Ọ̀SỌ́: Amen.
ADÉWÁLÉ: Er . . . and where is his mother?
Ọ̀SỌ́: She went to the farm market.
OWÓLABÍ: Oh, she went to the farm market. I see.
ADÉWÁLÉ: May she return in peace.
OWÓLABÍ: May she return in peace.
ADÉWÁLÉ: May God not let us suffer losses.
Ọ̀SỌ́: Amen, amen.
OWÓLABÍ: Er, Ọ̀sọ́, Adéwálé . . .
Ọ̀SỌ́ AND ADÉWÁLÉ: Yes?
OWÓLABÍ: Er, bad things are happening in our family that we didn't expect.
ADÉWÁLÉ: It's terrible.
Ọ̀SỌ́: Whatever's happened now?
OWÓLABÍ: Ọ̀sọ́, a lot has happened in our house that we didn't expect. Yes.
Ọ̀SỌ́: What is it?
OWÓLABÍ: It's all because of the truck-drivers of today . . .
Ọ̀SỌ́: What have they done?
OWÓLABÍ: Ha, bad driving is rife. Even though our elders and betters never cease warning them . . .
ADÉWÁLÉ: They never cease . . .
OWÓLABÍ: They keep saying, if you drink don't drive.
ADÉWÁLÉ: But they don't listen. Ha, may God not let us suffer losses!
Ọ̀SỌ́: So what new thing has happened?
OWÓLABÍ: It was only yesterday, Adéwálé and I were coming back from the farm. When we got to the edge of the market, there were people buying and selling right and left. And you see, there was an articulated lorry, carrying cattle . . . and you see, the speed at which that vehicle was coming was impossible . . .
Ọ̀SỌ́: It's not their fault. Those tires are like cows themselves! [i.e. are huge]
OWÓLABÍ: Ọ̀sọ́, the speed that lorry was coming, just before it

reached the crowds in the market, the **brake,** you know, when he tried to **brake,** the brake failed. In a word, this lorry crashed into the middle of the market and killed people in droves!

Òṣó: It killed people!

Owólabí: It killed people! It killed people! It killed people! There were more than sixty people killed that day.

Òṣó: An articulated lorry! What is the world coming to!

Adéwálé: Er, Òṣó, I want you to know that on that day, when the relatives of all those people who died went there, they were saying things like "Ha, don't grieve, let us accept it as the will of God, let's accept it as the will of God." They were saying they should accept it as the will of God. I was looking at them and thinking, when a person actually dies, and they say it's in the hands of God . . . But then I thought about it myself and in the end I realized that whatever happens to a person in life, he should trust in God. He should leave it in God's hands and accept his fate.

Òṣó: The relatives . . .

Adéwálé: Yes. They should accept their fate. They should say, well, the water is spilled but the calabash is not broken.

Òṣó: Yes, well, if they wanted to complain, what court could they go to? That's why they have to leave it to God.

Owólabí: Òṣó, let me say something to you. Among those who died, there was a certain woman . . .

Adéwálé: There was a certain woman among them who . . . who . . .

Òṣó: What is it?

Owólabí: This woman was a really good person . . .

Òṣó: She was a good person?

Adéwálé: She was a good person.

Òṣó: Where was she from?

Owólabí: She was from this very village. From a house that shall remain nameless . . .

Adéwálé: Ah, it was Odòjé's compound, it was called Odòjé's compound in the old days, I don't know what they call it now.

Owólabí: And look, that woman, I can see her as clearly as if she were standing before us, she was as fair-complexioned as anything.

Adéwálé: She was dark.

Owólabí: Oh yes, she was dark, and she didn't have marks. She was dark-complexioned.

Adéwálé: When we got to their house, when Owólabí and I got to their house, we began to weep. We wept. And they said don't

weep any more, let's accept it as Fate. Let's accept that that's what God decreed. Everything that happens to a person in life, we should accept as the will of God. We should accept our destiny.
OWÓLABÍ: Er, Ọ̀ṣọ́, may Wúràọlá arrive home safely.
Ọ̀ṣọ́: Amen.
ADÉWÁLÉ: When she gets back, say to her, Wúràọlá, please, next time you go to the farm market, don't sit at the side of the boat.
Ọ̀ṣọ́: Father, believe me, that's exactly what I said before she left.
ADÉWÁLÉ: Good for you. It's yesterday evening I'm talking about. This boat was going ... this boat was going ...
Ọ̀ṣọ́: What boat are you talking about now?
ADÉWÁLÉ: Er, Owólabí, tell him the rest for me.
OWÓLABÍ: So this boat was going ... this boat was going ... er, 'Wálé, tell him the rest.
ADÉWÁLÉ: It went gẹ̀ẹ́, gẹ̀ẹ́, gẹ̀ẹ́ ... it went gẹ̀ẹ́, gẹ̀ẹ́, gẹ̀ẹ́ ... it went gẹ̀ẹ́, gẹ̀ẹ́, gẹ̀ẹ́ ... Owólabí, finish it for me.
OWÓLABÍ: It went round and round. It went up and down. It went up and down. And then it went spinning, until—wòòòò.
Ọ̀ṣọ́: What did?
ADÉWÁLÉ AND OWÓLABÍ: The boat.
Ọ̀ṣọ́: Which boat?
ADÉWÁLÉ AND OWÓLABÍ: Wúrà's boat.
Ọ̀ṣọ́: Which Wúrà?
ADÉWÁLÉ AND OWÓLABÍ: Your wife.
Ọ̀ṣọ́: What happened to her?
ADÉWÁLÉ AND OWÓLABÍ: The river carried her off.
Ọ̀ṣọ́: I am dead. [*Wails:*] Yààyààyàá!

The scene ends with Ọ̀ṣọ́ calling his son to break the news to him, and then the entry of noisy sympathizers, among them Wúrà's friend Àṣàbí, who sets about appropriating Ọ̀ṣọ́ for herself on the spot.

In the sequence quoted above, Adéwálé and Owólabí, the two comic elders, have a thankless and risky assignment. Breaking the news of a death can cause injury, even suicide, if wrongly handled. Their strategy is to work toward the news they are going to break through a series of sideways steps, luring Ọ̀ṣọ́ to the point where his mind has been opened to thoughts of bereavement and filled with reminders about the proper way to handle grief before they actually tell him how the subject concerns him. But they are intensely nervous, and much of the humor of the scene comes from their double act, as each tries to shift the responsibility onto the other. Adéwálé does it first, saying that it was Owólabí who wanted to see Ọ̀ṣọ́. But Owólabí puts off the evil moment by pretending to have come about a job

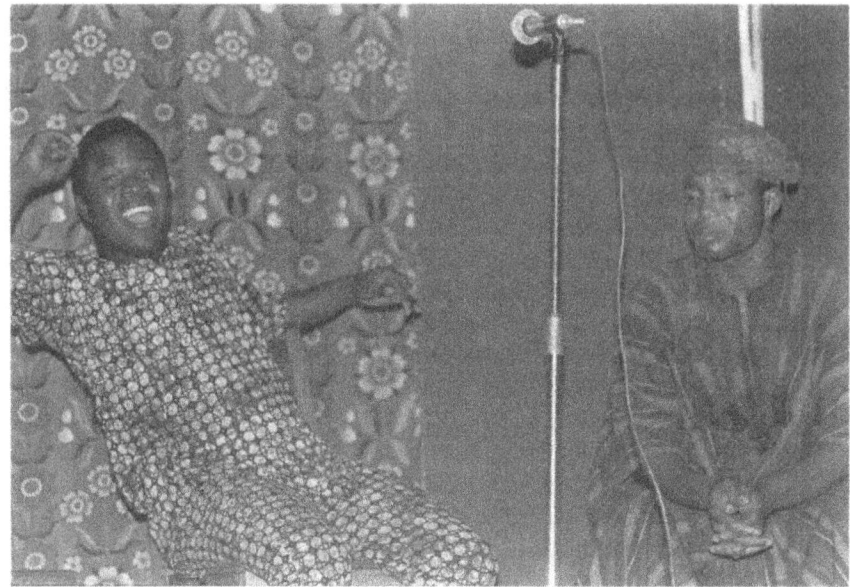

Alhaji as Ọ̀ṣọ́ and Dayọ̀ as Adéwálé in *Taking Care of Kúnlé*. ©Elio Montanari

for a younger relative. Unexpectedly, Ọ̀ṣọ́ plays into their hands by responding with a set piece of his own: a long narrative of a gruesome yet funny disaster that happened at work. This gives Adéwálé a chance to bring the conversation back to their purpose, by generalizing that "losses can happen to anyone." However, he seems unable to move from that to Ọ̀ṣọ́'s own specific loss: instead, he veers away again into ruminations about the European who lost his arm, and how hard these Europeans work. The monologue turns into a type of commentary, very popular in Nigeria, where a group criticizes itself by comparing itself to other groups, whose (often imaginary) virtues it extols.[7] Owólabí then takes the initiative to turn the conversation to the son, Kúnlé, and Adéwálé provides Ọ̀ṣọ́ some consolation in advance (he has a successor to replace him when he dies) as well as using this opportunity to mention Wúrà for the first time: "His mother's destiny will support you."

Next it is Owólabí's turn to edge the conversation one step closer to the bad news: "Ọ̀ṣọ́, bad things are happening in our family that we didn't expect." But the story he goes on to tell, in graphic detail, is again a postponement. He describes an accident with an articulated lorry in which 60 people were killed, including someone from their own village . . . a woman whose identity is deliberately left vague. In this narration, he takes the opportunity to stress to Ọ̀ṣọ́ the importance of accepting God's will. Ọ̀ṣọ́, not yet alert to the danger he is in, replies cynically that they have no option but to accept God's will, since there is no court of appeal where they could get the death rescinded. This story is a harbinger of the real story—it involves accident, deaths, including the death of a "good woman" not unknown to the speakers. When Owólabí describes this woman as "fair-complexioned," Adéwálé nudges the story an inch closer to home by correcting him: "She was dark"—like Wúrà. Owólabí at once seizes the point and develops it: "Oh yes, she was dark. And she had no marks." (Neither did Wúrà.) Now they have reached the last step. They mention Wúrà's journey. They mention the dangers of boat crossings. And then Adéwálé suddenly comes out with the truth, as if out of the blue: "It's yesterday evening I'm talking about. This boat was going . . . this boat was going . . . " Each elder throws the ball back into the other's court: "Finish it for me," "Finish it for me." And they end up finishing it together, answering Òṣó's by now desperate questions in unison.

There are four narratives embedded in this scene: the preliminary narrative of Owólabí's younger relative who has allegedly returned from overseas with high qualifications and has lost his job; the narrative Òṣó tells in response, of Mr. Wood's accident, and Adéwálé's elaboration of it; the probably fictional narrative of the lorry accident; and the true narrative of Wúrà's shipwreck. All these narratives are filled out with details, and all except the last are the sole responsibility of the teller. The teller sets the pace, elaborates, and expands at will, while the others respond and prompt him occasionally. Only the last narrative is told collaboratively, as Òṣó's questions drag monosyllabic components of an answer one by one out of the pair of elders. Thus the scene can be viewed as a sequence of highly choreographed set pieces linked by bridging passages of more fluid dialogue. But what makes them so effective in this particular context is that modularity is here given a dramatic motive. The set pieces are moves in a game; substitution and the production of parallels or series has a dramatic purpose, that of simultaneously preparing for and postponing the breaking of the tragic news. To me, this is the highest realization of the art of the Adéjobí Company. Òṣó's reaction, when he finally receives the truth, is electrifying. He leaps vertically up several feet and is caught by the two elders, where he remains, frozen in a crouched rictus in mid-air as the neighbors' wailing begins. This extreme climax is entirely appropriate, so effective was the slow inexorable buildup toward it.

The modularity achieved through slots and set pieces is an adaptation to the existing composition of the company, with its inner core of permanent actors (and even they are not always available) and its outer rings of newer and less dependable ones. The structure of the plays mimics the structure of the company and is perfectly adapted to make the most of its possibilities. Modular composition not only makes the most of existing

The aftershock. In another performance of *Taking Care of Kúnlé*, Alhaji as Òṣó falls to the ground after receiving the bad news from the two elders (Dayọ̀ and John). ©Elio Montanari

resources, it is also able to exploit the potential of any new element that may come along—a new actor with a special gimmick, a "guest artist" available only for a few days.

"FILLING OUT" AND CUTTING BACK

The play's imagined script requires the performers to traverse a complex, tightly articulated 3-hour narrative in a determinate sequence of steps. The serial slot structures and the sequences of set pieces provide landmarks and oases on this journey. But they also afford the actors scope to alter, elaborate, and amplify their parts in ways which may eventually change the whole balance and structure of the dramatic narrative. In this process, the presence of the audience is a crucial dimension, for audience response can foster the expansion of some parts of the play while inhibiting others.

At the beginning of *The Overreacher*, a newly installed and tyrannical Ọba summons his chiefs one by one to ask them their functions in the town. Each explains his or her particular role, and the Ọba then abuses, threatens, and drives them out on the flimsiest of grounds. In a performance I recorded in 1981, there were five chiefs: Jagun, Òtún Ìyálóde, Àró Ìlú, Ìyá Awo, and Ìyálóde. In 1988, when I recorded the play again, there were three chiefs: Jagun, Akọgun, and Ìyálóde, but the structure was the same one of serial repetition of modular episodes. In the seven years between the two recordings, each actor had gradually consolidated and filled out his or her part within the expansible framework of the plot. In the earlier version, each chief's speech was relatively short and unadorned. By 1988, their speeches were highly elaborate and much more differentiated from each other. This is a text and translation of chief Jagun's dialogue with the Ọba in the earlier recording:

OBA: Ìwọ tó ò ń wò ràngàndàn, tó o ṣojú bíi . . . bí ojúu kọ̀nkọ̀—oyèe kí n tìẹ?
JAGUN: Káábíèsí o o . . . kádé ó pẹ́ lórí o, kí bàtà ó pẹ́ lẹ́sẹ̀. Èmi tẹ́ ẹ̀ ń wò yìí ni Jagun o.
OBA: Ja—gun—un!
JAGUN: Èmi ni Jagun-ùn-lúu wa yìí.
OBA: Oyè wo ni ọ́n ń pè ń Jagun?
JAGUN: Hàà, tóguun bá déé, àwa làá jààà! Èmi tí wọn òó kọ́kọ́ tì ṣáájú nì-ín, tógun bá ṣelẹ̀ ńlùúu wa yìí.
OBA: Ìwọ lọ̀ ọ́ jagun-un?
JAGUN: Bẹ́ẹ̀ ni, Káábíyèsí . . . Ọkùnin làdáà! Tógun bá dé, ó ti yáà!
(Oba gbá Jagun mú, ó fẹ́ẹ́ tì í.)
OBA: Ẹ wo Jagun-ùnlú o. Ẹ wo Jagun-ùnlúù mi o. Jagun rèé o, Jagun n mo fẹ́ẹ́ lù, tó ṣubú un o o! Jagun-ùnlú nù-un o o. Wò ó, látòní e lọ, bí mo bá gbọ́ pé wọ́n pè ẹ́ ń Jagun, o dáràn. Bí mo bá gbọ́ọ́ Jáá—Wón pè ó ń Jagun, o jẹ̀gbèsè. O ò tiẹ̀ ní í loọlée yín mọ́. O òò wà láàfin-ìn mi, tó o òó jẹ́kan nínú àwọn èèyàn tó wà láàfin, tẹ́ ẹ ẹ̀ẹ̀ maa pa kóóko fẹ́sin. Ó yá, ẹ mu wọlé, ẹ mu wọlé.

OBA: You who are staring about so foolishly, with eyes like . . . like a bullfrog's, what is your title?
JAGUN: Your majesty, may your crown remain long on your head, may your shoes remain long on your feet. It is I, Jagun, that you see before you.
OBA: Jagun!
JAGUN: I'm the Jagun of this town.
OBA: What kind of title is Jagun?
JAGUN: Ha, if war comes, I am the one who will fight, I'm the one who will lead the fighters, if war breaks out in this town.
OBA: You are the one who will fight . . . ?
JAGUN: Yes, your majesty. A cutlass is male! If war arrives, I'll be ready.
OBA *(he grabs Jagun and pushes him over):* Look at the Jagun of the town, look at the Jagun of my town. This is Jagun. This Jagun, I only had to raise my hand and he fell down. That's the Jagun of this town. Look, from today onward, if I hear that anyone is

still calling you Jagun, you'll be in trouble. If I hear so much as "Ja—"! If anyone calls you Jagun, you will be in debt. And I'm not letting you go back to your house. You'll stay at my palace, and you'll be one of the people who live at the palace and cut grass for my horses. Go on! Take him inside! Take him inside!

Seven years later, the Jagun had considerably expanded his part. Rather than a bare formulaic exchange, there is a more fluid interaction, involving the other chiefs:

JAGUN *(ikọ́):* Kùhù.
ỌBA: Ikọ́ tó o hú un, ní ọ́ pa ọ́.
ÌJỌYÈ: Àmín, àmín.
ỌBA: Ṣe ara àwọn Olóyè nìín? Oyè kín loyè tiẹ?
JAGUN: Àfíyèsí, Jagun ni.
ỌBA: Kí niṣẹ́ẹ̀ rẹ láàrin ìlú?
JAGUN: Ìran babaà mi, Jagun ni, torí pé nígbà ogun kábá àọn babaà mi ni ọ́n jagun.
ÌYÁLÓDE: Bẹ́ẹ̀ ni.
JAGUN: Nígbà ogun Àgbádáìgì, àọn babaà mi ni wọ́n wà ń jagun, níjọ́ ọjọ́ náà lọ́hùn-ún, wọ́n jagun, wọ́n ṣégun. Ǹgbà babaà mí sì ṣílẹ̀ wò, wọ́n lémi nì ń ó gorí àléfà babaà mi.
ÌYÁLÓDE: Kábíyèsí o, ìran babaà rẹ ní í jọba.
ỌBA: O ṣe é aláwìyé. Ó wá dogun mélòó tíwọ gan-an jà?
JAGUN: Háà, Kábíyèsí, háà, lẹ́nu ìgbà tí mo mo gorí ìtẹ́ babaà mi, tí mo dolóyè Jagun yìí, ogun kan ò tíì wá, sùgbọ́n tí ogun bá wáyé, Àfíyèsí, ẹ ẹ́ gbà wí pé ọkùnrin làdá.
ỌBA: Ṣé wí péwọ yìí le jagun?
JAGUN: Emi ní ń ṣe mí? Há-hà! Emi ní ń ṣe mí láwọ̀ tí n ò ní le jagun? Héè, Àfíèsí o, ìjà àbí aáwọ̀?
ỌBA: Hóóòòò. Hóóóòòò. Ọ dáràn.
JAGUN: Àfíyèsí.
ỌBA: Ọ dáràn. Ikú pa ọ́.
JAGUN: Kábíyèsí.
ỌBA: Hèé, kí ló ṣe ọ́? Tí mọ bá tún gbọ́ Jagun, ikú pa ọ́. Tí mọ bá gbọ́ Jagun, sánmáńtì àti gaàrí ni n ó pò fún ọ. Fún irọ́ tọ́ ọ wá pa, ẹ wo Jagun ìlú, mo fọọ́ kàn án ló ṣubú wógẹ́.
JAGUN: N ò purọ́-ọ̀.
ỌBA: Ọ ò lọ ilée yín mọ́. Ọ ó wà láàfin mi tọ́ ọ ó maa pa kóóko fẹ́sin.
JAGUN: Haà, mo níyàwó ńlé, mo lọ́mọ.
ỌBA: Igbó lo ó kùú sí.

JAGUN: Haà, mọ dáràn.
ỌBA: Àtìwọ àtàwọn ìyàwóò rẹ tẹ́ ẹ lẹ́ ẹ ní.
JAGUN: N ò sọ pé mọ lọ́mọ.
(Wọ́n lé e lọ sínú ààfin.)

JAGUN *(coughs):* Hu-hu.
ỌBA: May that cough kill you.
CHIEFS: Amen, amen.
ỌBA: Are you one of the chiefs? What is your title?
JAGUN: Your Majesty, it is Jagun.
ỌBA: What is your function in the town?
JAGUN: It's a hereditary position, is Jagun, because at the time of the Kábá war, my forefathers were warriors.
ÌYÁLÓDE: That's true.
JAGUN: At the time of the Àgbádáìgì war, my forefathers were war leaders, in those far-off days. They made war, they were victorious. And when my father passed away, they said I was to inherit his position.
ÌYÁLÓDE: Your Majesty, just as your family inherits the position of Ọba.
ỌBA *(sarcastically):* Thanks for the explanation. And how many wars have you yourself fought in?
JAGUN: Ha, Your Majesty, ha, in the time since I ascended to my father's place, and became chief Jagun, there hasn't been any war. But if a war did break out, Your Majesty, you'll see that a cutlass is male!
ỌBA: Are you saying you wouldn't be able to fight?
JAGUN: Is there anything the matter with me? Ha! What is there to prevent me from fighting? Ha, Your Majesty, is it a fight or a dispute [i.e., I'm ready for any kind of battle]?
ỌBA: Ho! Ho! You are in trouble.
JAGUN: Your Majesty.
ỌBA: You're in trouble. May death strike you down.
JAGUN: Your Majesty.
ỌBA: Well, what's the matter with you? If I hear the name "Jagun" again, death will strike you down. If I hear "Jagun," I'll give you cassava meal mixed with cement to eat. To punish you for the lies you told . . . *(pushes him over)* Look at the Jagun of the town, I just touched him and he fell flat on his face!
JAGUN: I didn't tell any lies.
ỌBA: You're not going back to your house. You'll stay at my palace and cut grass for my horses.
JAGUN: Oh, but I have a wife at home, I have children.

ỌBA: You'll die in the bush.
JAGUN: Oh, I'm in trouble.
ỌBA: Both you, and the wives and children you say you have.
JAGUN *(terrified):* I didn't say I had any children.
(He is driven into the palace chamber)

In this more garrulous rendering, the Ọba has become more ferocious, emitting death-dealing curses, and Jagun has become more of a figure of fun. The structure of the episode is the same—it begins with the Ọba asking the chief to identify himself and ends with the chief being threatened and driven out of the room—but each actor has expanded his or her own part by elaborating and embellishing a handful of core statements.

The play, the actors say, becomes "fuller" in performance. Additions and revisions happened in two ways. One was by conscious decision of Alhaji and Adéjọbí, based on their own observations of how different sequences went down or in response to explicit advice and comments from individual members of the audience. As Alhaji put it:

> Let's say we compose a play now and we give a performance one day. Through the audience reaction, or some of them will tell us suggestions, or through their reaction, whether the play is good or it's not good enough, that will give us—to improve the idea or the acting.... Immediately I got the idea I will call them, "You did it this way before, we don't want it that way. Do it another way." And I will tell him the way, or tell her the way, he will do it. That is how we do our play. (English.)

Second, there is also a continuous, small-scale adjustment to audience response by the actors as they go along. Sequences that evoke audience hilarity will gradually be expanded, while dull sections will dwindle away. Over a long period, the combination of deliberate managerial decisions and small but cumulative changes by the actors can result in an overall large-scale change in dramatic shape. An example is *The Royal Palm-nut,* already well established in the repertoire by 1975 and enjoying a vigorous revival in 1988.

This is a summary of the original plot of *The Royal Palm-nut,* as told to me by Mr. Adéjọbí:

> There is a town whose Ọba has died and a successor has to be found within ten years of his death or misfortune will befall the townspeople. The chiefs have met and have consulted Ifá, but the oracle selects two of the five candidates, Làágbé and Tòkunbọ̀, without specifying which of the two should be chosen. The chiefs then remember that a special kind of palm nut is needed to install an Ọba, and that the one they used to use disappeared from the

palace during the confusion following the late king's death. So they decide to send the two rival candidates off on a quest to find another royal palm nut, which, like a four-leafed clover, is very rare but does occur in nature. The candidates are summoned and sent off on their quest.

One of the two candidates, Làágbé, has a good friend, Tóògùn, who promises to do everything he can to help him. However, one day Tóògùn goes to recruit the support of an acquaintance, Aṣaásan, at the very moment that Aṣaásan is being caught by his wife in an act of adultery with Làágbé's wife, Díẹ̀kọ́lá. In accordance with the pact of friendship he has with Làágbé, Tóògùn goes the next morning to tell his friend what he saw, but meets only Díẹ̀kọ́lá at home. She gets him to admit that he has come to expose her, and when pleading fails, she turns the tables on him and pre-empts his story by telling Làágbé, the minute he comes back, a dramatic story about how Tóògùn came to the house and tried to rape her. She is so eloquent that Làágbé believes her, refuses to listen to Tóògùn, and drives Tóògùn out of town.

Tóògùn and his wife go to their farm hut and live as exiles in the bush. One day one of his farm laborers discovers a royal palm nut while working on the farm. Without knowing its value, he puts it under his cap and carries on working. Later he goes to Tóògùn's farm hut to ask for some yam and cold water. "According to Yorùbá custom, when you want to eat you put off your cap." When the farm laborer takes off his cap, the palm nut falls onto the ground. Tóògùn sees it and asks the farm laborer to give it to him, which he does. When the farm laborer gets back to town, he goes to chief Àró (a friend of Làágbé, and one of the kingmakers) to find out when the new Ọba will be installed. Àró tells him that no new Ọba can be installed until they find a royal palm nut. The laborer remembers the palm nut he gave to his employer on the farm and tells Àró how to get there. Àró goes to Làágbé, tells him he is on the trail of a royal palm nut, gets some money from Làágbé, and goes to Tóògùn's farm.

Tóògùn drives Àró away at gunpoint, and he returns shamefaced to Làágbé confessing that he has failed, but telling them exactly where Tóògùn keeps the palm nut. Díẹ̀kọ́lá, the wife ("really a strong woman"), takes over. She goes to a *babaláwo* and gets powerful medicines to enable her to mesmerize Tóògùn. Then she goes to his farm. The medicine works to the extent that Tóògùn welcomes her warmly and shows her every sign of affection. Under cover of the panic caused by an apparition, conjured up by her medicine, she takes the opportunity to slip into the hut and steal what she thinks is the palm nut. However, Tóògùn has had a premonitory dream, and he has taken the precaution of substituting a fake palm nut for the real one. After Díẹ̀kọ́lá leaves, Tóògùn recovers his senses. His wife berates him for his weakness in welcoming his enemy like that, but he reveals to her that the palm nut is still safe. Husband and wife decide to go to town immediately to prevent Díẹ̀kọ́lá from passing the fake palm nut off as a real one.

Làágbé convinces the Àràbà and the chiefs that he has indeed found the royal palm nut and is about to be installed as Ọba when Tóògùn and his wife rush in and halt the proceedings. They expose the fraud, and in return Tóògùn is given the right to bestow the true palm nut on whichever of the two candidates he chooses. Everyone expects him to give it to his bosom friend Làágbé, but at the last moment he switches direction and hands it over to the other candidate, Tòkunbọ̀. Tòkunbọ̀ is recognized as the rightful successor and installed to great acclamation.

The initial setup of this story—the two rival candidates to the throne sent off on a quest—raises expectations of parallel narratives of the fortunes of each, drawing a moral from their contrasting behavior. However, this typical folk-story structure was never followed up by the Adéjọbí Company. From the beginning, the entire narrative focused on Làágbé and his wife and friend, so that the other candidate simply becomes a cipher who represents Làágbé's failure rather than being a character in his own right (he never appears on stage at all between the first scene, when he is sent off on the quest, and the last, where he is made Ọba, and he hardly speaks a word throughout).

What seems to have happened during the life of the play, however, is an increasing emphasis on Díẹ̀kọ́lá, her adultery, and her deceptions. In Adéjọbí's summary of the story, the exposure of Díẹ̀kọ́lá's affair with Aṣaásan is a necessary component in the narrative, for it is the cause of Làágbé's rift with Tóògùn, but it is not given any special prominence. In the performance that I recorded in 1988, however, the adultery scene is enormously elaborated and even embellished with a modular pre-scene of its own. The sequence opens with Aṣaásan's wife giving a long string of orders to her cheeky houseboy Ọkẹ́ (played by Isiaka). She then goes off to the market, and Ọkẹ́ has an extended comic monologue in which he tries to decide which of the tasks to do first, rejecting each of them for ridiculous reasons. Finally he resolves his dilemma by bursting into a solo song-and-dance routine, which he is still doing when Tóògùn walks in asking for Aṣaásan. Ọkẹ́ tells him Aṣaásan has gone to his office, and Tóògùn leaves. Ọkẹ́ takes up his song and dance again, and this time is interrupted by Aṣaásan, who has returned early, bringing Díẹ̀kọ́lá with him. They go into the bedroom, and a moment later Aṣaásan comes out again, half dressed, to tell Ọ̀kẹ́ to say he is out if anyone asks for him. Ọ̀kẹ́ sets up a great din, chanting "My master says he is not at home, anyone who wants to know, my master says he is not at home!" Aṣaásan emerges again, even more undressed, to reprimand him. Ọ̀kẹ́ continues his chant (just practicing, he says), until Tóògùn comes back still looking for Aṣaásan. Ọ̀kẹ́ immediately gives the game away, and then makes exaggerated attempts to cover up his mistake, barring the way to the bedroom and attempting to drive Tóògùn away by force. The next moment Aṣaásan's wife returns from the market and wants to go into her bedroom to put her bag away. To her astonishment, Ọ̀kẹ́ prevents her, saying he is using the room himself. After a prolonged argument she calls in an elder of the neighborhood to help her remove him, but the elder cannot budge Ọ̀kẹ́, and there is deadlock till Aṣaásan himself comes out of the room, yawning and stretching. When he takes in the situation, he tells his wife he came home early because he was feeling unwell and tries to send her out to buy some medicine. She says Ọ̀kẹ́ can go instead, and gives Ọ̀kẹ́ her bag to take into her room. He has no choice but to go in, and he immediately comes out babbling about some "Madam" who has told him not to be cheeky. Aṣaásan's wife begins to get a little suspicious and suggests that they inspect the house to make sure no one broke in during their absence. Aṣaásan insists that she go immediately and buy medicine, but she takes no notice and goes into her room, where she discovers Díẹ̀kọ́lá. Uproar ensues, with accusations and insults flying in all directions, and in the middle of this Tóògùn returns and is immediately told exactly what has happened. He reprimands Aṣaásan for carrying on with the wife of the Ọba-to-be and says he can no longer give him any role in the campaign for Làágbé's selection since he has shown himself untrustworthy. He leaves in anger, and the scene ends with Aṣaásan and his wife fighting.

This scene, then, is complicated, and gives big roles to two characters who thereafter have no further part in the story, Aṣaásan's wife and the houseboy Ọ̀kẹ́. It is set up to extract the maximum amusement and dramatic suspense from the adultery. The entire action is focused on the door to the bedroom and on the question of who will come through it, in which direction, and at what moment. The comic sequence between Aṣaásan's wife and Ọ̀kẹ́ is a long, self-contained turn like a music-hall sketch—a modular addition which is not even mentioned in Mr. Adéjọbí's summary of the story.

But other elements in Mr. Adéjọbí's story, far from being extended and elaborated, were not shown at all in the version I recorded. These included the episode of the farm laborer finding the royal palm nut in the farm; the episode when he goes to eat yams and drink water at Tóògùn's hut and gives the palm nut to Tóògùn; the episode where he goes back to town and tells Chief Àró about it; the episode where Díẹ̀kọ́lá goes to a *babaláwo* to get medicine to mesmerize Tóògùn; and Tóògùn's account of his dream, which prompts his precautionary measures to protect the palm nut. Thus, in the version I saw, there is no explanation of how Tóògùn came to be in possession of the palm nut or how Làágbé's supporters came to know about it; nor is it made clear how Díẹ̀kọ́lá managed to overcome Tóògùn's implacable resistance and hostility—earlier demonstrated when Chief Àró was driven away at gunpoint—the moment she entered his farm; nor why Tóògùn had changed the hiding place of the palm nut. I asked Mr. Adéjọbí why these components had been cut out. He replied that when they first started performing the play, they put everything on stage, including the farm laborer and how Díẹ̀kọ́lá went to the *babaláwo*. But after some time, "we could see that the play would be running to over three hours and we had to cut out that part of the farm laborer, because we considered it less important than others."

What seems to have happened, then, is that one part of the story expanded under the influence of audience approbation until the play got too long to handle, upon which Adéjọbí and Alhaji cut it down to size by removing parts which were less interesting to the audience. Although the components they removed seem to be structurally more important to the narrative's coherence than some of the parts that were expanded, this did not really matter. The play was an old one; the story could be assumed to be familiar to many people in the audience, so that they could easily fill in the missing bits for themselves.

Indeed, Adéjọbí saw the gradual transformation of the plays as an attraction.

> I believe no play is perfect. I've had that belief for quite a long time. . . . We continue renovating our plays all the time. People will like to watch it another time because they know we may have added some part that formerly was not included. (English.)

These changes, though continual, were not undisciplined. Alhaji oversaw them and clearly retained a sharply focused image of how he wanted each play to be. Once, in conversation with him after a grueling trip and performance, he almost told me how he conceived of dramatic excellence. The play was *External Appearances*, which I was seeing for the first time, and he asked me what I thought of it. I said I enjoyed it more than *Besotted Bridegroom*, because it had more verbal wit and less physical horseplay. Alhaji was outraged. "Better than *Besotted Bridegroom*? No! It was bad. *Kò dùn rárá* [it was not sweet at all]." "What makes you say so?" "You see we are professionals, we know how to make a play click. One thing has to lead to another, one give rise to the next, everything has to click together. But tonight it was a mess. Fẹ́mi was just standing there, not interacting at all with Uncle Táyọ̀. He didn't react at all. He missed so many of his lines, it

didn't work at all. A play has to be tight—let me give you an example . . . "
I was hanging on his words. At that moment, the manager of the Ọlálọmí Company of Ọ̀fà came up and sat down next to Alhaji and started a long discussion with him. Meanwhile John came and wanted to be photographed in his Wòlíì costume, and then Ìyá Adé came to discuss the evening's takings with Alhaji. I never got a chance to hear the rest of Alhaji's ideas about what makes a play click.

But some performances of some plays that I had seen—*Articulated Lorry, Taking Care of Kúnlé, The Heir, Láníyọnu*—did seem to fit his description. In these performances, a perfect balance seemed to be achieved between effervescence and control, between expansive improvisation and "scripted" narrative coherence, and between individual self-exploitation and interactive meshing. One thing led to another; the actors filled out their spaces or slots in such a way that each "clicked" into the next one.

At every level, the drama was conceptualized and composed as the activation of potential. In creating a character the actor drew on potential laid down in him or her by social experience; the characters occupied slots or dramatic spaces whose potential the actors could exploit through expansion and elaboration; and the modular structure was suited to mobilizing the potential of all personnel as they became available. The entire drama responded continually to its climate of reception, each element having the potential to expand and become elaborated at the expense of others if audience reactions were favorable, leading to long-term change in the architecture of the plays. In the performances which "clicked," an assemblage of potentials was activated harmoniously and to just the right degree.

6 Filling Out a Play

Actors occupied and expanded the spaces which were allocated to them within the design of the play by means of improvisation which became more self-directed as they became more experienced. But the blanket concept of "improvisation" does not tell us precisely what they did on stage or how they did it. This chapter takes up the ways in which actors concretized the potentialities inherent in a field of performance resources which they shared, to a greater or lesser extent, with each other and with the audiences.

In these plays, the most important element, in the view of both the actors and the audiences, was the dialogue. The plays were led by language, and improvisation was first and foremost a matter of generating speech. It goes without saying that speech did not exist in a vacuum: it was embodied, delivered by means of fluid gestures and eloquent facial expressions, sometimes borne on music and sometimes counterpointed with drumming or exuberant horseplay. The visual dimension of staging—for example the demarcation of space and the choreography of the microphones—was vital to the entire project of the theater, as will be seen in the next chapter. But to understand how plays grew in interaction with their audiences, the only viable starting point is language.

The speech in the plays was extremely extensive, fluent, colloquial, and elaborated. Variations from one performance to the next went far beyond the odd grace note or cadenza—they were so pervasive that hardly a single speech was said the same way twice. Yet it was curiously difficult to pin down these fluctuations and mutations. Only by listening over and over to successive renditions of the same play—from the auditorium, the stage, and the wings—by comparing recordings and transcriptions of recordings, and by reflecting on my own experience of playing a role in it, was I eventually able to get a sense of the growing points of a text, its areas of density and diffuseness, the principles of its repeated emergence.

FIRST IMPRESSIONS

"All in all, an unpleasant play," I wrote after I had seen *Besotted Bridegroom* twice. It was an opinion I didn't come to modify when I had seen it another five times, recorded it four times, acted in it several times, studied the transcribed texts, and talked to lots of people about it. It seemed to me to lack the verbal ingenuity and comic flair that made most of their other plays—at their best—so enjoyable. *Besotted Bridegroom* was neither witty nor polished. It relied a lot on horseplay and crude physical humor arising from blindness, lameness, and even madness. Instead of carefully orchestrated dialogues—like those described in the last chapter—the actors seemed to be awash in an undistinguished mud flat of chaotic, turbulent speech. The play's moral lesson, as encapsulated in the final song, was "Beware of treacherous women." This lesson in itself was no surprise—*Articulated Lorry* and *Taking Care of Kúnlé* said the same thing—but the way *Besotted Bridegroom* did it was uncompromising, bitter, and extreme. The audience thought so too, as we will see in the next chapter.

It was unfortunate that this—the only play in their repertoire that I disliked—was the one I saw most often, documented in most detail, performed my most significant part in, and discussed most with members of the audience. To trace the continuous small increments in the text, to suggest how the drama springs from key lines, and to establish how audience reactions feed its growth, I really have no choice but to use *Besotted Bridegroom* as my example. Fortunately, though, even this play turns out to reward close study and does yield insights into how the theater company generated drama.

I first saw it on March 18, 1983, when it was still a very new play. This was how I described the trip to Ìgbajà, where I saw it:

> I drove to Ìgbajà, in Kwara beyond Àjàṣẹ́ along a dirt road, through towns with extraordinary, colourful architecture, notably a gigantic Mosque like a green iced cake, and a long, low, shuttered house with an old-fashioned brooding look.
>
> I found my way to the ECWA church ("ECWA" was the only direction I'd had from Adéjọbí) and penetrated to the seminary, where a smiling resident told me the play must be scheduled for performance in the secondary school, not the seminary. I went on to the secondary school, to be told by non-smiling residents that the company "will no more perform. They are driven out." But the cryptic addition "Ṣèyí," repeated vehemently, allowed me to deduce that the play would now be performed in the Ṣèyí Restaurant, for which I'd seen a big sign as I entered the town. So I went back to where the sign was, only to discover that it was just an advertisement, not a sign-board. I asked another inhabi-

tant, who directed me back to ECWA, where I should "ask anybody." By this time I was beginning to feel sure that the Adéjọbís had given up after the ECWA rebuff and gone home. But eventually, I found my way to the "Sèyí Restaurant Annex" with its "Model Cinema," and there was the dark blue Peugeot 504 and there, inside a concrete walled yard, were Adéjọbí, Màmá Adé, Emily, Yẹmisí, all installed behind the already erected set. So—another open air performance. Adéjọbí told, with wonder and pity for mankind's foolishness, the story of how they had reached the ECWA school only to be told that the Social Master had failed to inform the Principal of the theatre visit, and that the Principal was so angry that he banned the performance. The Social Master had made a mistake; but the Principal ought eventually to have accepted their combined begging. The Vice-Principal, who was also the owner of the Sèyí Hotel, came to the rescue with his "Model Cinema," a rectangular yard with school benches. The Vice-Principal was doubtful about the prospects. The play had hardly been advertised, since the plan had been to do it in a school where intruders from town would have been unwelcome. I saw only two posters during my search for the Hotel. Although the lorry had been round on "parade" (I didn't see it, though, all the time I was driving around) the Vice-Principal felt that there were not many people in town yet. Awo was coming on a campaign trip on Monday, so on Saturday and Sunday the town would be full of people from Lagos. But today was Friday . . . Adéjọbí also seemed to have decided to cut his losses, announcing in his opening speech that he had reduced the gate fee to N1 to show his affection for the Ìgbajà people. The Vice Principal complained later that the company had paid him only N30 for the use of the premises. (The V-P also helped a lot with fixing up the lighting.)

In the event, though, the yard was packed—mostly with secondary school kids—so full that the back rows were standing on the benches and some were clinging onto the hotel roof which formed one of the side walls. The play started at about nine.

According to Adéjọbí, there are two lessons to be learnt from *Besotted Bridegroom*. The first is that a husband should not go against Yorùbá custom by putting a junior wife over a senior. The second is that it is wrong to abuse a person who is handicapped. But I could see that there was another and more emphatic message: a familiar misogyny—"Don't trust women. Don't let women get control."

Scene 1: The play opens with Tàfá Olóyèdé, played by John, rudely waking up his senior wife, played by Grace, who is asleep in the parlor. He doesn't want the place cluttered up when "Mọ́mì" ["Mummy"—a term of deep affectionate respect for an older woman] comes in. Mọ́mì, played by Emily, is his new wife Mosún, a cash madam (i.e., a super-rich woman), swathed in lace, carrying a large handbag. Tàfá berates the senior wife, Ìyáa Ṣeun, and demonstrates his complete subservience to the junior one. Tàfá is anxious to impress upon Ìyáa Ṣeun that she must not on any account offend Mọ́mì, because Mọ́mì is the person who rescued them from their debts and who is feeding, supporting, and clothing them. The senior wife doesn't care and doesn't want to be supported by Mọ́mì. She causes Tàfá anguish by loudly saying so just as Mọ́mì comes in.

Mosún says that she wants to build a new house and that she is planning to go to her mother's compound and claim her share of her mother's family land so that she can build there. She leaves, and Tàfá and Ìyáa Ṣeun continue their altercation, which closes with Ìyáa Ṣeun taunting Tàfá with "*ọkọ ìyàwó!*" [lit. bridegroom, but suggesting an excessively doting and subservient husband].

Scene 2: The scene changes to Mosún's mother's compound, where the Baálé (the head of the family, played by Adéjọbí) is ensconced. Mosún arrives. At first the Baálé doesn't know her, but she explains that her late mother was his younger sister. She explains that she is a trader who builds houses wherever she goes: she has built one for her father and another for her husband. The Baálé is much impressed and calls in his wife (played by Yẹmisí) to behold a shining example—a woman who built a house for her husband! Mosún goes on to say that now she wants to build a seven-story mansion on the land belonging to her mother's section of the family. The Baálé seems bemused, but when Mosún slips him N50—which he accepts with feigned reluctance—he tells her it will be possible. He sends for the elders of the family to get their co-operation, but only one, Bùárí (played by Alhaji), is available. Bùárí is a senior and respected figure in the compound, but he is also one-eyed, lame, and disfigured.

Bùárí opposes the notion flatly. He explains in detail that all the land has already been divided up between the male heads of the six branches of the family. Most of the land has already been built on, and the rest has been surveyed for buildings planned by members of the family. Where will they find another portion? Mosún says "You are saying that what a man can do, a woman can't?" but Bùárí does not take up the question of women's rights or lack of rights to land inheritance. He simply repeats that there is no land: it has all been allocated. Mosún insists that the Baálé has promised her what is her right, and that Bùárí is just being obstructive. Bùárí is very angry with the Baálé for misleading Mosún and with Mosún for insulting him. He leaves in a fury. The Baálé deplores the turn events have taken, saying "Now things have got very difficult," but advises Mosún to come back the next morning and discuss it again when all the elders are present.

Scene 3: Mosún goes home and tells Tàfá what happened, and he agrees to go back with her to try to make them change their minds. He warns her that he is short-tempered and likely to fly off the handle; Mosún says all the better—the "madman" who is obstructing her deserves to be told off. Ìyáa Ṣeun is alarmed and begs Tàfá not to be disrespectful to his in-laws. Tàfá drives her out, telling her it is none of her business.

Scene 4: At the family meeting the next day, some of the elders have been bought off by the Baálé, while others support Bùárí. Both Mosún and Tàfá behave arrogantly. Tàfá is provocative from the start, and instead of begging a favor he begins to abuse those who stand in his way. The scene develops into a verbal duel—degenerating frequently into a physical scuffle—between him and Bùárí, egged on by Mosún, in which Tàfá gives vent to a long string of *èèbú ara:* insults drawing attention to physical defects. At the end of Tàfá's tour de force, Bùárí is weeping with rage and humiliation. He demands to know Tàfá's full name, and warns him "*Tàfá Olóyèdé, o fenu ko*" [Tàfá Olóyèdé, your mouth has got you into trouble]. The Baálé is unable to restore order, and Mosún and Tàfá leave with Mosún threatening to bring a caterpillar tractor the next day to clear a space for her building and the elders begging her not to do so.

Scene 5: Bùárí visits Tàfá's house on a reconnaissance trip to prepare his revenge. He meets only Ìyáa Ṣeun there. She is humble and polite, and when he reveals that he is planning to do harm to her family, she begs him so wholeheartedly that he relents. He says that as long as Tàfá himself comes to beg his pardon equally humbly, he will not carry out his plan. Just then, Mosún and Tàfá arrive back from the meeting and immediately begin to abuse Bùárí all over again, explicitly confirming that Tàfá meant every word of what he said and takes nothing back. Ìyáa Ṣeun desperately tries to intervene and is chased away by Tàfá. The scene ends in a melee, with Mosún and Tàfá screaming abuse, Bùárí threatening vengeance, and Ìyáa Ṣeun shrieking in horror and dismay.

Scene 6: In his own house, Bùárí lights a pot-torch and in its light he calls Tàfá's full name, and utters *ọfọ̀* [incantations] which will turn his victim blind when he blows it out. He says that if Tàfá comes to apologize, he will re-light the lamp, restoring Tàfá's sight. But if he does not come, he will throw the lamp into the river. He blows out the lamp.

Scene 7: Tàfá is at home when the curse takes effect. There is a lot of comedy as he goes blind. Both wives rush to comfort and assist him, and he keeps pushing the senior one away and asking for the attentions of the junior one. He is in agony. Eventually they decide to take him to the *babaláwo*. Mosún leads him there: he walks taking huge steps and threatening to fall over or bump into something at every step.

Scene 8: The *babaláwo* sits chanting Ifá verses as Mosún and Tàfá arrive. Mosún tells him the blindness was caused by Ìyáa Ṣeun, who bathed his eyes in water used to wash peppers. The *babaláwo* does a routine cure which just makes Tàfá's agony worse. The *babaláwo* realizes there is malign agency behind this, does divination, and tells Tàfá that he has offended someone. The story of the visit to Mosún's mother's compound comes out, and the *babaláwo* tells him that if he doesn't go and beg Bùárí, his blindness will become permanent.

Scene 9: Mosún leads him to Bùárí's house. But as soon as they arrive, Mosún begins to abuse Bùárí, beginning with the announcement "Wicked man, we have come to beg you" and going on from there. Tàfá hardly gets a word in. Bùárí warns him that his wife will be his undoing. The scene ends in a fight, with Tàfá trying to get hold of Bùárí and repeatedly tripping over and running into walls, etc.

Scene 10: They go back to the *babaláwo*, who chants Ifá and then does a comedy turn of assuring Tàfá that his eyes will *là peregede* [open wide] while informing Mosún, with facial gestures, that Tàfá will never see again. As soon as Mosún is sure of this, she creeps off without saying anything to Tàfá. Ìyáa Ṣeun turns up in search of him. The *babaláwo* explains that Mosún has gone, and Ìyáa Ṣeun says Mọ́mì has packed her luggage. The *babaláwo* tells Ìyáa Ṣeun to take Tàfá home at once. Much to Tàfá's disgruntlement, he is forced to accept her guidance home. They leave, Tàfá complaining at every step of her roughness, comparing it with Mọ́mì's gentler handling.

Scene 11: When they get home, Tàfá continues to berate Ìyáa Ṣeun and calls pathetically for Mómì. A neighbor (Ìyá Ìjèṣà) reports that she saw Mómì leaving town lock, stock, and barrel. Tàfá realizes that she has abandoned him. "Mómì, you saw that I was blind in both eyes, and you cast me off, you ran away and left me." A song rises from behind the scenes:

> When things have got to their worst
> You are left on your own
> The world is hard
> When things have got to their worst
> You are left on your own
> The world!
> Please, consider this example
> When things have got to their worst
> You are left on your own.

Tàfá, however, still has Ìyáa Ṣeun. Stricken, he realizes his mistake, and prostrates himself before her, begging her forgiveness. She tells him there is nothing to forgive. A relative of Bùárí's, who was present at the family meeting, comes in to say that he has been to Bùárí's house to beg him on Tàfá's behalf, but that Bùárí has already thrown the lamp into the river. The relative goes on to point out that Tàfá brought it on himself by letting a woman dictate to him. He quotes several of the insults Tàfá heaped on Bùárí. Tàfá stands, staring sightlessly and foolishly, while the cast come on to sing the closing moral song:

> Women cause one's downfall
> Listen, people of the world
> A woman's plans should not be followed,
> You people
> She can cause her husband to go astray
> She can cause her husband to misbehave
> But a wise man
> Will be very careful.
>
> Beware of the world
> Beware of people
> Beware of treacherous women
> Who mislead their husbands
> But a wise man
> Will be very careful.

The actors bowed at the end—very untypically—but there was no applause and Alhaji brought things to a close with an announcement that this was in fact the end.

Adéjọbí said they thought up the story for themselves—they had no written source. Emily said the play *kò ìtíì kún* [isn't yet full]. After doing it for a while, it would get "fuller."

Some teenage girls in the audience told me that the bit they liked best was where Tàfá was abusing the one-eyed man. The next morning, a boy at the hotel who had watched the play said he liked the *ofọ̀* best.

FILLING OUT

Over the next few months, I was able to see both the big structural changes that Alhaji and Adéjọbí planned and introduced and the continual small-scale increments and adaptations—some strategic and thought out, others the temporary by-product of a particular audience's responses—which occurred in every performance.

Two months after the performance just described, I saw the play again at the Ọ̀ọ̀ni Girls' High School at Ifẹ̀. The ending, which in the Ìgbajà performance had left the audience unsure whether the play was over, had been radically changed. Now there was a whole extra scene. Instead of closing with Tàfá's remorse after learning of Mosún's departure, there was a new sequence in which Tàfá ritually curses Mosún, followed by a scene in which he and Ìyáa Ṣeun go back to the Baálé to ask for his help. In this new closing scene, the Baálé supports Tàfá in his desperate attempt to persuade Bùárí to revoke the curse. Bùárí says that he is no longer angry, but the curse can't be revoked: he has thrown the lamp into the river. Ìyá Ìjẹ̀ṣà arrives to say that Mọ́mì is on her way. There is a commotion, and Mosún charges in, dressed in a man's trousers, one leg rolled up and the other hanging down, stark staring mad as a result of Tàfá's curse. Tàfá too has thrown away the charm by which he cursed her, so she will remain mad forever. The Baálé makes a brief speech pointing out the moral—don't abuse your elders—and the relative adds a specific condemnation of *èèbú ara*, repeating some of the insults Tàfá used against Bùárí. The play closes with the song "Women cause one's downfall."

This new ending altered the tone of the play. In the first version, the pivotal issue was Tàfá's unfair treatment of his senior wife and the resolution was the moment when he realized that she, unlike the younger wife he was so besotted with, was loyal and true to him. In the new version, the moment when Tàfá realizes that Mosún has abandoned him is still made much of; but now the play barely pauses over Tàfá's newfound esteem for Ìyáa Ṣeun, passing rapidly on to the sequence in which he curses Mosún. The incantations by which he issues the curse are dramatic, producing a climax which overshadows the earlier moment of repentance.

The new ending has the effect of emphasizing the bleak irreversibility of the punishment meted out to both Tàfá and Mosún. A space is provided in which hope might have been entertained. One might expect that at this formal family meeting involving all the key characters, the matter would finally be resolved, the offenders forgiven, and harmony restored. But the opposite happens. Bùárí laconically informs them the catastrophe is irretrievable, and the main function of the scene is to provide a spectacular punishment for Mosún. Her fate is far worse than Tàfá's. Tàfá has become, as he says himself, a person "who wears clothes without knowing what he's put on, who is given food but doesn't know what he's eating, who is reduced to asking everyone, 'Who are you?'" But Mosún has become something else, a being no longer recognized as fully human. The play's moral center of gravity seems to have shifted, and the emphasis is now heavily on Mosún's bad character and the savage punishment she receives.

What was interesting was the way this shift of emphasis, organized through the large structural change of the additional scene, came to be echoed in many smaller new touches all the way through. The structural change seemed to send ripples throughout the text. For example, in the crucial scene where they go to beg Bùárí and end up insulting him all over again, Tàfá's and Mosún's behavior is now much more sharply differentiated. Instead of simply being dragged along in Mosún's wake, Tàfá now makes a determined effort to apologize to Bùárí, abasing himself and meekly accepting Bùárí's reprimands. He seems to be on the verge of getting the curse lifted when Bùárí adds a further condition: "That abominable wife of yours: drive her out." Tàfá is unable or unwilling to speak, Mosún surges in with a torrent of abuse and defiance, and Bùárí withdraws from the negotiations with the warning "Tàfá Olóyèdé! Your eyes are going into the river!" Thus, in this version, Tàfá comes within an inch of escaping the curse when ọ̀rọ̀ obìnrin [women's matter] once again wrecks his chances. It was left indeterminate whether it was Tàfá's silence or Mosún's ferocious response that was more to blame for finally alienating Bùárí irretrievably. Was Tàfá's downfall caused by the direct agency of the monstrous woman or by his own subservience and weakness? The audience, as we will see in Chapter 7, was divided on this question. But in either case, the effect of the readjustment of this scene was to sharpen the contrast between Tàfá's malleability and Mosún's intransigence.

The atmosphere in this version of the play was more violent. This was partly a response to the extremely rowdy school audience, who became almost hysterical with delight at every physical gag. Mosún's behavior throughout was rougher: she assaulted Bùárí physically, for example pushing him over repeatedly instead of just insulting him. Tàfá's stumbling walk and his collisions with walls, doors, and other people were exaggerated for this audience's benefit. The actors even introduced innovations in the staging to highlight the humor derived from Tàfá's blindness and Bùárí's lameness. At one point Tàfá walks right off the stage—a drop of about three feet—breaching the normally strong division between stage and auditorium to emphasize the physical comedy.

But though some of these effects were a temporary response to this particular audience, the generally increased emphasis on violence and aggression persisted in later performances. The incantations were built up, and the scene when Bùárí curses Tàfá now involved an actual confrontation. Tàfá is "summoned" by Bùárí's utterance of his name, and leaps onto the stage, magical horn in hand. He challenges Bùárí ("What will you do?" "I'll do a lot!") and is physically present to receive the impact of Bùárí's incantations. He then leaves without speaking. In later performances, this opportunity was expanded further: Tàfá was given a sequence of *ofọ* of his own in retaliation, and there developed a war of incantations (always popular with theater and film audiences in Nigeria), which Bùárí wins. In the next scene, Tàfá is shown returning from his mystical journey and explaining to Mosún what happened, concluding "But how on earth I got home again I don't know, it's a mystery!" Bùárí's incantation then takes effect and he is struck blind.

In the Ọòni Girls' High School performance, Mosún's monstrous aggression was given an inexplicable and emblematic quality by one small change, which persisted into all the subsequent performances that I saw. It concerned a caterpillar tractor. In the earliest version I saw—at Ìgbajà—Mosún appears to accept that every scrap of family land has already been distributed, but she suggests that the compound is in need of modernization. There are derelict buildings which she could bulldoze so as to build a new house in their place—"You see according to present-day notions, everybody is building up-to-date houses, they don't want those old tumble down mud houses any more. Look, what's smart is smart, there are standards after all." Bùárí points out that the only "derelict buildings" on compound land are in fact his own house, in response to which she grandly offers to allocate rooms in the new building to him, his wife, and his children. Though Mosún is overbearing, callous, and contemptuous of Bùárí's poverty, her talk of bulldozing the compound is at least part of a reasoned project, a plan to build something new. Only at the end of the increasingly angry dialogue does Bùárí suggest that Mosún's use of the caterpillar tractor will be wholly destructive and that she is coming to knock their house down as an act of aggression.

The change that was made in the performance at the Ọòni Girls High School was simple. Mosún drops all the proposals about building a modern house in place of the dilapidated old compound and distributing rooms to the family. Instead, she loses her temper the moment Bùárí opposes her demand for land, and insults him as an old *alátakò* [obstructive person]. Now when Bùárí challenges her "We'll be expecting the caterpillar you're bringing to knock our whole house down," the caterpillar appears out of the blue. Instead of arising from the previous discussion of building plans, it simply irrupts into the dialogue like an attribute or objectification of Mosún's bullying power.

In subsequent performances, the caterpillar took on a life of its own. Later that year, in October, at a performance at Ẹgbè, it became associated with a new character, the contractor, played by me. The introduction of this character also revealed the way in which a new element could provoke numerous minor adjustments and adaptations, which the actors generated spontaneously.

The first time I played this part, not much thought had gone into its potential function, and my main memory is of standing there not knowing how to live up to the expectations which the other actors were ingeniously generating. Mosún takes the contractor with her on both visits to her mother's family. On the first visit, Mosún introduces the contractor as the person who will be in charge of the building work once Mosún has been given the land she has come to ask for. The Baálé asks Mosún to greet the Òyìnbó [European] and to explain to her that he is the head of the household and the elder brother of Mosún's mother. The contractor tells him that she understands "language"—that is, Yorùbá—and that she will be supervising the building work once the family has resolved the matter of the land. "And if you have any work you want doing yourself, I am at your disposal." Mosún, the Baálé, and Bùárí then play up the theme of the foreign contractor who speaks Yorùbá, Bùárí raising a laugh by attempting to greet her in English. Thereafter, the contractor becomes the representative of the caterpillar tractor and thus an additional emblem of Mosún's clout. When Bùárí says flatly that it is impossible—there is no land left—Mosún replies that she will order her contractor to bring in a caterpillar tractor the very next morning. Bùárí says "We'll be expecting it! You, contractor, you are going to use a caterpillar to knock down our house tomorrow. You, let me speak to you. You bring a caterpillar." Mosún intervenes: "If you abuse her, she'll abuse you back." On this occasion, however, the contractor does not do so, and the scene ends with Bùárí, Mosún, and the contractor hurling challenges at each other ("Is it tomorrow you want me to bring the caterpillar?" "Tomorrow." "Bring it! You with white mouth like new yam. Just bring your caterpillar!").

References to the caterpillar began to crop up throughout the play, as the actors recognized a potential catchphrase and instantly capitalized on it. In Scene 3, immediately after the one just described, Mosún tells Tàfá that the contractor, as well as herself, was insulted by Bùárí and that the contractor is planning to bring her caterpillar to clear a plot whether the family likes it or not. In Scene 4, when Tàfá accompanies Mosún to the second meeting in her mother's family house, the contractor goes with them and sits with them. Bùárí abuses the contractor as well as Tàfá. The contractor says that the caterpillar is already outside. The Baálé, in deep consternation, says "Don't bring it!" and Mosún responds "It's already here." And in the last scene, when Mosún appears, crazy and disheveled, she shouts as she cavorts "*Kòǹtírákitọ̀, wá ńbí, kíákíá, wá ńbí! Kàtàpílà!*" [Contractor, come here, quick quick, come here! Caterpillar!].

The presence of the contractor also suggested to the actors that Mosún had been away in Britain before she returned to her native town. References to Britain began to crop up. For example, Mosún herself now tells Bùárí that she doesn't care whether he removes the curse or not, because she is going to take Tàfá to Britain and get him cured there (an idea which everyone in the audience knew was futile: only the person who laid the curse can remove it, and in any case European doctors know nothing about *jùjú*). Bùárí also remembers this reference to taking Tàfá to Britain and reminds them of it in the last scene.

What was most striking was the rapidity with which all these adjustments were made. Alhaji did not tell me about the part of the contractor until a few minutes before the play began. As noted in Chapter 4, I barely had time to outline to Adéjọbí what Alhaji had told me to do (this was "rehearsing with Papa") before he was due on stage to sing the opening glee. Nevertheless, in Scene 2, I noted that "he made the most of elaborately addressing the contractor through Mosún, gesturing to her to sit down as if she couldn't understand 'Jókòó' and expressing great astonishment at her presence. Yẹ́misí, as Sẹlia, the Baálé's wife, also rose to the occasion, giving the contractor an amazed look and greeting her with trepidation."

The next time I was in the play, at the KS Motel in Ìbàdàn a few days later, the potential dramatic function of the contractor was more fully realized. I asked Alhaji if I could have a very strong insult to retaliate with when Bùárí abuses the contractor for the second time, in Scene 4. He agreed, and said he would think about it. Sometime later I found him sitting in an anteroom behind the stage, in deepest contemplation wrapt. He did not look up as I approached. "Alhaji, is anything wrong?" "I have been thinking of your line," he said. He then suggested that I say "*O ò gbọdọ̀ bú mi, ìwọ afọ́jú àjànàkú*" [Don't insult me, you blind beast]. He explained that a blind *àjànàkú* becomes a rogue, enraged and violent but unable to find its victim. He discussed the meaning of *àjànàkú* with me (I said "*Ṣe bí erin ni?*" [I thought it was an elephant?]), and with Ìyá Adé (she said "*Ekùn kọ́ ni?*" [Isn't it a leopard?]). In the end he decided that it meant a huge and dangerous animal—*erin* [elephant], *efọ̀n* [buffalo], or *ẹkùn* [leopard]. Then, after more thought, he suggested that I say "*Kí ni mo fi ṣe ìwọ bàbá yìí, tó o ń fi ń bú mi, ìwọ afọ́jú àjànàkú*" [What have I done to you, old man, that you should abuse me?—you blind beast!]. Finally, he came up with "*O ò gbọdọ̀ dí mi lọ́wọ́ nínú iṣẹ́ẹ̀ mi, ìwọ afọ́jú àjànàkú*" [Don't hinder me in my work, you blind beast]. "*Ìyẹn bẹ́tà*" [That's better], he said, and the matter was settled. Later in the afternoon I went to check with him about the line, to make sure I'd got the right version. After some discussion I found he had restructured this little episode to increase its comic impact and its power to surprise. I was to say the line not at the close of Scene 4, where the action breaks down into a melee of abuse and counter-abuse between Tàfá and

Bùárí, with Mosún egging Tàfá on, but at the point in Scene 2 where Bùárí first insults the contractor. In this new version of the scene, the contractor was to sit silently beside Mosún, and all the comments about how she understood Yorùbá and taught Yorùbá at the university were to be dropped. She would simply be introduced to the Baálé and to Bùárí as a contractor and would not say a word until Bùárí insulted her. Then she would rise to her feet, look him in his one eye, and deliver the deadly riposte in a loud voice.

This scene went as planned. The contractor's cue was Bùárí's insult, "You with the white mouth like new yam." She rose to her feet and said "*Ìwọ — má dí mi lọ́wọ́ nínú iṣẹ́ẹ̀ mi, ìwọ afọ́jú àjànàkú.*" This brought the house down. The audience was shrieking, howling, and falling out of their chairs with mirth. The uproar went on for what seemed like hours. It became the cue for a blackout and quick exit.

Adéjọbí, Alhaji, and other members of the company were delighted with this new addition. A week later, when I went to Òṣogbo to catch up on the news, they were still laughing about it. As I entered the parlor where Alhaji, Adédùn, Ìyá Adé, and two of the younger children were sitting, Alhaji said "*Àjíké, mo bínú . . . O ò bèèrè ìdí rẹ̀ tí mo fi bínú?*" [Àjíké, I'm annoyed. Aren't you going to ask the reason why I'm annoyed?] "*Ó dáa, kí ni ìdí ẹ̀?*" [All right, what's the reason?] "*Torí pé o bú mi, tó o pè mí ní afọ́jú àjànàkú.*" [Because you abused me, you called me a blind beast.] Everybody fell about laughing.

As well as the carefully planned revision of the contractor's role, there were other changes to the performance in the KS Motel, instigated by the association that had sponsored the show. The representative of the Muslim Graduates' Association (University of Ìbàdàn Branch) had been to Òṣogbo to discuss the choice of play with Adéjọbí about two months earlier. Alhaji had suggested *Besotted Bridegroom* because it had never been shown in Ìbàdàn before. The representative watched a run-through of the play and liked it, but requested some alterations because he disapproved of the moral. He thought Bùárí too unforgiving. He maintained that although Islam does enjoin that you punish people who offend you, it should not be on the first offense, but only after you have forgiven them many times. Bùárí is too implacable: he should accept the begging in the last scene and revoke the curse.[1] The company did their best to accommodate this point of view. In Scene 6, just as Bùárí has lit his pot of fire in order to pronounce the curse, Fẹ́mi—playing the male relative who intervenes at other points too—comes in and asks what he is doing. Bùárí says he is going to make Tàfá blind. Fẹ́mi pleads with him not to do this. He urges Bùárí to have patience and to forgive the person who has done him wrong. Bùárí reluctantly agrees. But the minute Fẹ́mi leaves the stage Bùárí goes back to his burning pot and proceeds to utter the incantation! In Scene 12, the Baálé expands his closing moral disquisition to include the statement that the unfortunate outcome of the story was caused by the fact that neither Bùárí nor Tàfá was sufficiently God-fearing. If Tàfá and Mosún had feared God, they would not have abused an old cripple. If Bùárí had feared God, he would have been more merciful.

The play was still undergoing additions and changes in the next three performances I saw in November and December 1983. The Baálé, for example, was made more explicitly culpable. In the earliest versions he was rather vague about whether or not there was any land available; he expressed doubts and gave Mosún only tentative promises. It was only Bùárí who stated categorically that the land was finished. In the later versions, it is made clear that the Baálé knows full well there is no land. It is only when Mosún slips him an enormous bribe of fifty naira that he changes his story, adding for good measure "What you are asking for, it's your inalienable right to have it." This exaggeration emphasizes the Baálé's volte-face and its cause, which is greed. His culpability was now so strongly highlighted that one commentator who had seen a late performance said that the play needed a different title. "*Àgbà tí ò mẹtọ́*" [The elder who didn't know what's right] or "*Owó ń bayé jẹ́*" [Money is spoiling the world] would "bite" more than "*Ọkọ Ìyàwó*."

Another small shift in the moral weighting occurs when Bùárí is given a stronger reason for desisting from taking his revenge. In the latest versions of the play, when he goes to Tàfá's house and meets Ìyáa Ṣeun there, he learns during his conversation with her that Ìyáa Ṣeun is the niece of a man called Ràúfù Ekì, who once did Bùárí a good turn. He recalls emotionally how he and Ràúfù Ekì once went together to the market at Èjìnrìn to sell cloth. They were waylaid by highway robbers and Ràúfù saved both Bùárí and his property. "I can never forget what he did for me that day. It's said that 'If you throw a stone in the market, it might hit a member of your own household.' If I afflict your family with convulsions, won't Ràúfù ask 'Didn't you know who she was?'"

Thus, Bùárí is no longer deflected from his purpose merely by Ìyáa Ṣeun's gentle and humble demeanor: he is given a much stronger reason—the bonds of male friendship and gratitude. While this intensifies the sense of Bùárí's rage and hate—he eventually curses Tàfá *in spite of* his great gratitude to Ràúfù—it also diffuses the earlier focus on Ìyáa Ṣeun's redeeming mildness. This seems to reinforce the change we noted earlier in the play's life history, when they started glossing over Tàfá's remorse for his behavior toward Ìyáa Ṣeun, in order to get on to his revenge on Mosún.

Finally, there were some little embellishments, which amplified the play without altering its moral emphasis. For example, in a performance in Òṣogbo on December 7th, the *babaláwo* acquired a *kékeré awo*—an apprentice—allowing him to expand his scene by including a sequence in which he instructs the apprentice in a famous Ifá verse. The *babaláwo* recites the passage, the *kékeré awo* repeats it stumblingly, the *babaláwo* corrects him irritably, then the *kékeré awo* says a few lines unaided. "Go on, go on" says Babaláwo testily. "*Bẹ́ ẹ se kọ́ mi dé nìyẹn*" [That's as far as you taught me], says the *kékeré awo*, raising a laugh. Other embellishments included a little song that Adéjọbí introduced into his first appearance, before the arrival of Mosún: he is calling his wife to hurry up and bring his food, and he sings

Kìí sọ̀rẹ́ ara
Má febi pa mí
Ebi o ò, ebi
Kì í sọ̀rẹ́ ara

It's no friend of the human frame
Don't make me suffer hunger
Hunger, oh hunger
Is no friend of the human frame.

In successive performances of this play over a period of 10 months, then, continual, multiple changes could be seen occurring at different levels and with different cumulative effects. At the most visible and conscious level were the deliberate structural changes introduced by Alhaji and Adéjọbí, such as the additional episodes emphasizing the irrevocability of the curse and the horror of Mosún's fate. In keeping with these structural changes there were a number of smaller additions and adjustments which had the cumulative effect of sharpening the moral definition of the play: making Mosún more monstrous, the Baálé more culpable, and Bùárí more implacable. These included the introduction of the contractor, the exaggeration of the Baálé's reaction to the bribe, the insertion of references to Bùárí's friendship with Ìyáa Ṣeun's uncle, and the intensification and expansion of Bùárí's and Tàfá's incantation sequences. Counteracting this trend were temporary alterations such as the moral comments introduced at the request of the Muslim Graduates' Association, which were just enough to satisfy the clients but did not have any permanent effect on the play. Then there were additions which could be seen as embellishments rather than as shifts in moral or thematic emphasis, such as the *kékeré awo* and the Baálé's little song. And finally there were pervasive, tiny adaptations and echoes which flowed from, and into, the larger structural changes and which added up to a sea change in the moral texture of the whole play. New elements, such as the insertion of the contractor figure, could precipitate small but thematically apposite adaptations from end to end of the drama.

The process by which a play became "full" was thus the outcome of deliberate experimentation combined with continuous, small, spontaneous adaptations and increments. The performers did different things each time, departing in a sometimes quite surprising way from their habitual format: as when they lined up and bowed to the audience at the end, or when they broke out of the confines of the platform stage and invaded the auditorium. When a play was at an early stage of its consolidation, and especially when the management was not satisfied with it, quite radical experiments could be tried. The overall changes in *Besotted Bridegroom* led, cumulatively, to a modification of the play's moral shape and definition.

But "filling out" was not a unidirectional process of development; it was more like a continuous ebb and flow in which some things were washed up on shore and others carried away by the tide. Sometimes a new improvisation would lose beautiful elements that had formerly been present. For example, in the Ìgbajà performance, Ìyáa Ṣeun has a wonderful line which does not reappear in any of my later recordings. When she brings Tàfá home from the *babaláwo*'s house, just before he realizes that Mosún has abandoned him, Tàfá treats her with callous ingratitude. "I know that nothing I can do will please you," she says, and then quotes a saying: "*Èérí là á wẹ mọ́; ẹnikan kì í wẹ ìrira mọ́.*" This means "One can wash dirt clean, but no one can ever wash hatred clean," playing on the similarity of the nouns *èérí* [an elided form of *èrírí*, dirt] and *ìrira* [hatred]. In the immediate context, Ìyáa Ṣeun is commenting—bitterly enough, though also philosophically—that after the advent of the new wife, Tàfá has taken an irrational dislike to her which she fears she has little hope of ameliorating. But it also supplies a fitting comment on the theme of the play as a whole. Bùárí's hatred of Tàfá proves to be implacable. Furthermore, this is, as a Yorùbá scholar told me, "not ordinary Yorùbá: it is a rare expression, very special."[2] Nonetheless, it was at least temporarily dropped, along with many other lines. Thus, not all the inspired, hilarious, or significant bits get kept, and "filling out" is not always necessarily progress. Rather, successive performances may seize upon different portions or sequences to develop, leaving other parts relatively inert. There is such a surplus of potential—so many points which could be expanded and elaborated—that a play can never be conceived of as completely "filled out": each performance inevitably retains, elaborates, and expands some elements at the expense of others.

An interesting effect of this ebb and flow is that the actors often drop lines but continue to refer, later in the play, to their content as if they had actually been said. It is as if they were working with the whole field of possibilities rather than with the single concretization currently in hand. And the audiences, being well versed in this mode of dramaturgy, seem able to take this in their stride. Sometimes omissions generate new dramatic effects, as in the omission of Mosún's practical rationale for wanting to bring in a caterpillar tractor. Often, though, it is more as if the narrative and linguistic medium in which they are working is so thoroughly understood

188 THE GENERATION OF PLAYS

by the audience that they can supply whatever happens to be missing in any particular performance. As they watch the actual play, they can scan the wider field of potentialities. This in turn suggests that nothing is ever definitively jettisoned. Even if a line or a sequence does not occur in a particular performance, it remains in the repertory and can be pulled out again in a future performance—perhaps by a different character or even in a different play.

Underlying and making possible the changes at all other levels is the fact that at every point in the unfolding of the drama in performance there are multiple alternative and equivalent options—an indefinitely large number of routes through the overall map of the play established by Alhaji. Many things in the play are substitutable, which is to say that at each point in the action the performer may seize on one alternative rather than another without derailing the narrative or diluting the thematic texture. The options selected might be influenced by the responses of the audience, by the atmosphere in the hall, the lateness of the hour, by something another actor has done, or just by the spur-of-the-moment inspiration or forgetfulness of the performer. This continuous, ground-level proliferation of alternatives underlies and makes possible the processes of "filling out" and the smooth incorporation of and adaptation to larger structural alterations.

SEEDS OF SPEECH

In the discussion that took place at Adéjọbí's house the week after the sensational success of the contractor's part in the KS Motel performance, Alhaji made some comments that helped me understand how the plays were improvised. They were discussing the impact of the line about the blind beast:

> "It was great. The whole Ìbàdàn was talking about it." "Well, Alhaji, it was you who thought it up and taught me to say it." "No, that's not it. The credit was yours because you remembered the line and said it at the right time, and in the right way." Alhaji went on to say "Some of these actors can't do that. You tell them what to say and when they get on stage they say something different. As if, for instance, you had gone up there and said *'Ìwọ afójú adìẹ'* [You blind chicken]. That wouldn't have been good at all. But some of these actors don't have the ability to master something as you do." "Even I," said Ìyá Adé, "sometimes I don't say what I'm supposed to." "It really pains me," said Alhaji. "After I've thought up something really good. You remember how long it took us to find the *'afójú àjànàkú.'* We thought of this, we thought of that, we really sat and thought about it before we came up with it. Now imagine you do all that and then the actor gets on the stage and says something

completely different! It pains me." "Alhaji," I asked, "is it every sentence that you teach the actors like that, or just some selected ones?" "Thank you," said Alhaji, warming to his exposition. "You see some lines are more important than others. There are key sentences here and there that I really don't want them to lose. The rest, they can do it as they like."

In this discussion, Alhaji illuminated for me the whole process by which the play-text is generated and reproduced. The "key sentences," which Alhaji "really didn't want them to lose," can be seen to operate as germs of longer sequences of monologue or dialogue. They were positioned strategically to initiate a new sequence or serve as its culmination. They were usually compact, carefully devised single sentences or expressions. As we have seen, the contractor's insult to Bùárí was the outcome of deep thought on Alhaji's part. He chose an expression which would cap Bùárí's insult to the contractor ("you with the white mouth like new yam") by being even more personal and more hurtful. It was also chosen because it was idiomatic, referring to local popular knowledge about the environment (blind elephants become rogues, much more dangerous than fully sighted ones) and thus maximized the surprise produced by the obvious foreigner standing up and speaking Yorùbá. The phrase referring to the "caterpillar" was even more strategically inserted than the one about the blind elephant, for, as we have seen, it became a motif which several characters wove into their speeches at different points through the play.

There were other moments when I witnessed the deliberate insertion of new key phrases. Before the Odùduwà Hall performance, Grace told me gleefully that she had some new lines in Scene 1. There was a passage where Tàfá asserted that Mọ́mì was the savior of both of them and Ìyáa Ṣeun strenuously rejected this assertion. In the earlier performances she had always said "*Mi ò tọrọ oúnjẹ, mi ò tọrọ aṣọ*" [I never asked (her) for food, I never asked (her) for clothes], a formulaic-sounding statement she made several times. Now she was going to say "*Ọkọ ìyàwó! Ẹlẹ́sẹ̀ adìẹ! Olórí màálúù!*" [Bridegroom! Chicken-legged! Cow-headed!] John was then going to look at his feet in a comical way and say "*Ṣé ẹsẹ̀ adìẹ lèyí?*" [Are these chicken's legs?] According to Grace, this was to make it funnier: it was Alhaji's idea, and he had shown them how to do it. When it came to the point, both Grace and John carried out Alhaji's instructions perfectly, and even threw in a few extra embellishments. This is what I recorded:

ÌYÁA ṢEUN: Ìyàwó elétíi màálúù. Ọkọ ìyàwó olórí màálúù.
TÀFÁ: Jọ́rí ẹ ó pé o. Ṣémi lolórí màálúù?
ÌYÁA ṢEUN: Ọkọ ìyàwó . . . ẹlẹ́sẹ̀ pẹ́pẹ́yẹ.
TÀFÁ: Yéè, ẹlẹ́sẹ̀ pẹ́pẹ́yẹ! Èmi lelẹ́sẹ̀ pẹ́pẹ́yẹ, Orí ẹ ń ṣe ọ́. Jọ̀wọ́ọ̀ mi ó tẹ̀ ọ́, n ó pa ọ́, n ó sì paraà mi sínú ilé yìí.

ÌYÁA ṢEUN: O ó para e. Ọkọọ Síkírá eṅwo.
TÀFÁ: Ṣémi lọkọọ Síkírá eṅwo? Èmi lọkọọ màálúù.
ÌYÁA ṢEUN: Hèéé! ọkọ ìyàwó wọlé, ojú tì í o. Olórí olóṅgbò. Olórìí màálúù.

ÌYÁA ṢEUN: A wife with cow ears. A husband with a cow's head.
TÀFÁ: Have some sense. Am I the one with a cow's head?
ÌYÁA ṢEUN: Bridegroom . . . one with duck's feet.
TÀFÁ: What, with duck's feet! Me, a person with duck's feet! You must be mad. Just let me catch you, I'll kill you and then kill myself in this house.
ÌYÁA ṢEUN: You'll kill yourself. Husband of "Síkírá with horns" [i.e., a cow].
TÀFÁ: Am I the husband of Síkírá with horns? Me, the husband of a cow?
ÌYÁA ṢEUN: Hey, the bridegroom came home, and was ashamed. Person with the head of a cat. Person with the head of a cow.

When I listened to the four separate recordings I made at different stages of the play's life history, I began to hear sentences and phrases emerging that I felt sure had been planted there by Alhaji. Let me look at some stretches of dialogue in Scene 1 to diagnose the function and mode of operation of these key sentences.

At the opening of the scene, Tàfá and Mosún enter to find Ìyáa Ṣeun asleep on the floor in the parlor. Prompted by Mosún, Tàfá delivers himself of an extensive diatribe against the sleeping woman. In the Odùduwà Hall recording:

Óóòò, ìwọ obìnrin yìí, ìwọ obìnrin yìí, o sá mọ̀ pé o ní yàrá tìẹ àbó ọ mọ̀? Tó jé pé ọ̀rọ̀ tá a bá sọ fún ọ lónìí, là á sọ fún ọ lóla. Bó di lótunla, ọ̀rọ̀ kannáà là á sọ fún ọ. O ní yàrá tìẹ, o ò sùn ní yàrá tìẹ. Pálọ̀ tèmi wáá dilé obìnrin, bééyàn bá tìẹ sun pálọ̀, a tìẹ sì jí nídàájí a gbálẹ̀ a kọrí yàráa rẹ̀. Ta ní ó mọ̀ pé pálọ̀ ló sùn? Àlejò gidi tìẹ jí wá káàyàn mólé wọn a bá a bó ṣe sùn ńlẹ̀ báyìí. Eni bá gbọ́ pé mò ń sọ̀rọ̀ báyìí, wọn ò ní í sọ pé mò ń yàn án jẹ? Ńgbà èèyàn ní yàrá tìẹ, pálọ̀ tèmi wáá dilé oorun? Bééyàn bá sì sun pálọ̀, a jí ń dàájí, láàárò, a lọọ wẹ . . . ní kinní alágídí yììi o, ní kinní tó sun-unrun tí ò ní í jí ó wáyé ńjọ mìíìn mọ́. O ó pó ò gbóhùn mi kọ́, alágídí? O ó pó ò gbóhùn mi kọ́?

Oooh, you, woman, you, woman, do you know that you have your own room, or don't you? If I tell you something today, I have to tell you again tomorrow. The day after tomorrow, I'll still be telling you the same thing. You have your own room, you don't sleep in your own room. My parlor becomes a women's bedroom. If anyone wants to sleep in the parlor, they should get up at dawn and sweep the place out, and go back to their own room. Then who would know that they had slept in the parlor? If [not], an important visitor who came early to catch one at home would come across the person stretched out on the floor! If people heard me speaking like this they would scarcely be able to believe their ears. When someone has her own room and my parlor becomes a bedroom! And if someone does decide to sleep in the parlor, she should get up at dawn, go and wash ... but this obstinate thing, this thing sleeping like a log ... You'll say you don't hear me, won't you, obstinate thing? You'll say you don't hear me, won't you?

In all the recordings, John, playing Tàfá, generates a version of this speech from two core statements: (1) If I tell you something today, I have to tell you again tomorrow and the day after tomorrow; (2) You have your own room, but you turn my parlor into a bedroom. He amplifies these two statements in somewhat different ways each time. In Ìgbajà, he supported the reproach in (1) with exhortations: "For God's sake, woman, woman, for goodness' sake"; "Who would believe this?"; "You bring this abuse down on yourself with your behavior"; "I'm going to force you to listen to every word"; "It's you I'm talking to." At the Oòni Girls' High School it came out a bit different, with "Who would believe this?"; "You're pretending not to hear, I'll make you hear, you stubborn creature, even if you sleep the sleep of the dead, even if you just keep on sleeping"; "Have you got ears or haven't you?" Sentence (2), however, is the more important one, the real key to the whole speech. In some versions, it is initially given to Mosún, in which case it opens the whole play: "Has the parlor become a bedroom?" Tàfá elaborates this sentence greatly. In the above version, he approaches it in stages: in the first sentence he says "Do you know that you have your own room or don't you?" In the fourth sentence he repeats this but extends it to complete the idea, "You have your own room, you don't sleep in your own room," and this leads on to the statement "My parlor becomes a women's bedroom." Later in the speech this whole progression is recapitulated in condensed form: "When someone has her own room and my parlor becomes a women's bedroom!" He elaborates with the assertion that if you *must* sleep in the parlor you should at least get up early and vacate the place. This too is repeated, with variations: "Get up at dawn and sweep the place out," "Get up at dawn and go and wash." At the Oòni Girls' High School and at Ẹgbè the key sentence was brought out in one go: "When you have your own room, you don't sleep in your own room, my parlor becomes your bedroom." In all the recordings, John generates a set piece— an extensive monologue in which he holds the stage for as long as he keeps going—by building upon and varying these two basic constituents. The effect in all cases was of a looping, recapitulatory movement in which the key sentence was repeated several times in several different guises.

Ìyáa Ṣeun protests that she slept in the parlor because her bedroom was so hot and that her bedroom was hot because Tàfá has not bought a fan for her as he has for himself and Mọ́mì. Tàfá then announces the next sequence of dialogue by informing her "*Iṣéè̩ re̩ tó o ọ̀ọ̀ maa ṣe láàárò̩, láàárò̩, yóò di dòbùrù láàárò̩ ìí*" [The work which you do every morning will be doubled this morning]. He goes on to explain that Mọ́mì is going somewhere important and that Ìyáa Ṣeun will have to take over Mọ́mì's duties in addition to her own. Ìyáa Ṣeun makes a long speech in reply, saying essentially that she won't do the work her junior wife is supposed to do. The junior wife is supposed to serve the senior—and "even if she were taller than she is, she met me here in this house." Tàfá tries to buttress his position with a proverb: *Wọ́n ní bórogún iyá e̩ni, tó ba ju iyá e̩ni lo̩, iyá làá pè é* [It's said that if your mother's co-wife surpasses your mother, you'll call *her* mother, that is, a wealthy or powerful person is de facto senior]. Ìyáa Ṣeun rejects this argument with contempt, and Tàfá then moves on to the next key phrase which heralds another, variable, spate of dialogue. He tells Ìyáa Ṣeun "*Séwo̩ ò mò̩ pé bí mọ́míì ṣe wà nínú ilé un, lolùgbàlà àwa méjèèjì ló jé̩?*" [Don't you know that Mọ́mì's position in this house is as the savior of the two of us?] Ìyáa Ṣeun is outraged by this, and there is much questioning, repetition, and argument. It is a statement that provides Ìyáa Ṣeun with a taking-off point, and she introduces a variety of idiomatic and colorful responses, varying from performance to performance. "*Ará àdúgbò ni yóò gbó̩ yìí o!*" [The neighbors are going to hear about this!] is one. "*Orúi mi, má mò̩ jé̩ni ó gò̩ ó̩ mò̩ gbó̩n o*" [Don't let a stupid person become wise] is another one: a highly colloquial insult meaning "You are stupid, but that's all right by me; if everyone was wise, who would we rip off?" Another is "*opònú sò̩wé orúi rè̩ nù*" [the nitwit lost his tax receipt] another local and graphic idiom describing the depths of idiocy.

But when she denies flatly that Mọ́mì is her savior, this in turn provides Tàfá with a stepping-stone into an extensive monologue in which he invites Ìyáa Ṣeun to compare her present condition with her condition before Mọ́mì came. Within this diatribe, he has other smaller stepping-stones to help him along. In the Odùduwà Hall performance, he opens this speech with a proverb "Let's drive away the fox before we come back to blame the chicken." He then asserts "I'll explain it to you," and elaborates this statement in turn by adding another proverb "A child who doesn't know the difference between *e̩we̩* and *òwè* beans will pick *e̩we̩* with his left hand and *òwè* with his right" (i.e., an ignorant person will get everything mixed up) and then repeats "The things that aren't clear to you, I will explain them to you, and I'll reveal to you now," further adding the exhortation "*Fi gègé lé é*" [put pen to it, i.e., make a note of it]. He then begins his comparison, listing all the things Ìyáa Ṣeun now eats which she couldn't eat before Mọ́mì came ("You're eating an abundance of yam, you're eating so much yam that people are saying I've made a farm; you're eating as much cassava meal as you like, you're eating as much yam flour as you like, you're eating as much rice as you like—and is it us who are paying? You know very well that it was only when Mọ́mì arrived and said that the meager diet we were making do with wouldn't suit her, that she went and bought sacks of yam, sacks of cassava meal, sacks of yam flour, sacks of beans, sacks of rice, that's how she bought everything.") He expands on this at length, listing all the meats that Ìyáa Ṣeun now eats, and concluding "Even the clothes you stand up in, it was Mọ́mì who bought them for you." Ìyáa Ṣeun has a selection of sentences with which she can indicate her disagreement and disapproval and which she can use to attempt to break into the flow of Tàfá's speech.

Her next key sentence is "*Èmi ò tọrọ aṣọ lọ́wọ́ ìyàwó ẹ, me è sì tọrọ oǹjẹ*" [I'm not asking for clothes from your wife, and I'm not asking for food]. She repeats this with variations and additions (e.g., "It's a poor sort of husband who brings a wife to the house and can't buy food for her") until Mọ́mì herself returns, saying she's forgotten her purse. Mọ́mì now takes over the lead in the dialogue, telling both of them off for making a noise and dragging her name into it. Tàfá is so crushed by this that he prostrates himself before Mọ́mì as she leaves. Ìyáa Ṣeun cries shame on him, and he goes back to berating her, threatening to divorce her, swearing to find somewhere else for her to live—and when she is unimpressed by all this, threatening to beat her. Ìyáa Ṣeun introduces another key sentence in response: pointing out that Tàfá was never dissatisfied with her before the advent of Mọ́mì, she tells him "*Bọ́ ọ bá jáwọ́ nínú kọ́ ọ máa gbé ìyàwó lérí ìyáalé, o óò jìyà, o ó ò jewé iyá mọ́ ọn*" [If you don't stop putting the junior wife above the senior, you'll suffer to the highest degree (lit. "You'll eat suffering, and you'll eat the balsam leaf as well," punning on *ìyà*, suffering, and *iyá*, the balsam tree)]. Tàfá reacts indignantly to this, giving her the lead-in to her final key sentences in the scene, her sequence of insults, quoted in full above, which begins with "wife with the ears of a cow, bridegroom with the head of a cow."

Some of these key sentences could be seen to be structurally crucial, as they lead in to a new sequence of monologue or dialogue. The movement forward depends on them. Others are marked and memorable, and useful to the development of the text, without having this pivotal role. They could move around within the text, and in some performances some of them were dropped, but they were clearly part of the repertoire of reference points the actors relied on when they generated their speeches.

All these key sentences were distinctively "heavy," denser and more resonant than the rest of the surrounding speech, either because they were well known and recognizable formulations or because there was something odd and notable about them. Proverbs by definition attract attention, commentary, and repetition (see Barber 1999), but all the other key sentences in this passage are chosen for their ability to do the same thing. "*Iṣẹ́ẹ̀ rẹ di dóbùrù,*" for example, [your work becomes double] was striking because of the use of the English word "double," adapted to Yorùbá phonology, and "*fi gègé lé e*" similarly stood out because "*gègé*" [pen, pencil] is a Hausa word. "*Mọ́mì ni olùgbàlà àwa méjèèjì*" [Mọ́mì is the savior of us both] was memorable because of its semi-blasphemous use of a concept usually associated with the worship of Christ. "*Me è tọrọ aṣọ, me è tọrọ oúnjẹ*" [I'm not asking her for cloth, I'm not asking her for food] was memorable because of its pattern of repetition. It was very striking, listening to audience responses throughout the performances, that the audience was acutely attuned to the appearance of these marked phrases and sentences. Much of their ongoing commentary consisted simply of repetition and quotation of these sentences—sometimes, reminiscently, long after the moment of their utterance had passed. This reinforcement by repetition and quotation was of course echoed in the text itself, as the actors wove and circled around their stable key utterances and often returned to them, either as reference points in the open sea of speech or to capitalize on a moment which had been successful with the audience.

Much of the text, whether solo set pieces or dialogic exchanges, circles around such seminal sentences. It steps skillfully from one to the next and returns to the earlier ones before moving forward again, thus producing a weaving, circling motion of progress and recapitulation. Even when there are no obviously attractive or arresting phrases in a speech or an exchange, the text seems to be generated by the same principle: it works toward an essential, key idea; it varies or elaborates it; it moves on to the next key idea and then, often, reverts to the earlier one for recapitulation or embellishment. The most humdrum speeches are thus constructed by expanding and circling around a few basic elements.

Dialogue is often generated according to the same discursive principle. Some dialogues could be analyzed as set pieces interspersed with commentary from a second character, whether in encouragement or in criticism. Thus, in the following sequence, from the Odùduwà Hall performance, Mosún tells the story of how she came to be looking for land in her mother's compound. Her narrative follows a familiar pattern, consisting of two preliminary episodes (she built a house for her father, then for her husband) and a buildup to the third episode, which concerns her intention to build a house for her mother too. The buildup consists of her account—presumably mendacious—of a dream in which her mother appeared to her giving her urgent instructions to build a house on her family land. The Baálé reacts with astonishment and admiration. It is his comments that produce the repetitious effect characteristic of other set pieces: they are mainly echoes, summaries, or anticipations of what Mosún is saying.

Filling Out a Play

MOSÚN: Mo ní kí n wáá ṣe àlàyé fún yín, ìdálẹ̀ tí mò ń gbé mo ti kó wálé báyìí o. Dídé tí mo wáá dé, ọ̀dọ̀ọ bàáà mi n mo darí sí.
BAÁLÉ: Hòo.
MOSÚN: Ìgbà tí mo wá darí sí ilée wa, ipò tí mo bá bàáà mi ò tẹ́ mi lọ́rùn. Ilé tí mo fi ọn sí látiye ọdún yìí náà ni ọ́n wà. Mo bá súré mú ilẹ̀ kékeré kan, mo bá yáa kọ́ ọ. Mo ri pé bàbáà mi ti wà ńbẹ̀ báyìí.
BAÁLÉ: O kọ́lé fún bàbáà rẹ?
MOSÚN: Ọlọ́un ló kọ́ ọ, bàbá.
BAÁLÉ: Ọmọ ọ́ kọ̀ọ́lé fún ọ. Èmi n mọ sọ bẹ́ẹ̀. Lọ rèé kọ ọ́'lẹ̀.
MOSÚN: Nígbà tí mo wá parí ti bàáà mi, mo wá pe baáléè mi pé, ìwọ baáléè mi o, mo fẹ́ẹ kọ́lé kékeré kan fún ọ.
BAÁLÉ: Wí pé ...
MOSÚN: Mo kọ́ tiẹ̀ náà, ó yanjú gedegbe.
BAÁLÉ: O kọ́lé fún baáléè rẹ?
MOSÚN: Ọlọ́un ló kọ.
BAÁLÉ: O kọ́lé fọ́kọọ̀ rẹ náà?
MOSÚN: Ọlọ́un ló kọ, bàbá. ...

MOSÚN: I thought I should come and explain to you that after living in foreign parts for a long time, I've finally come back home. When I arrived, I went straight to my father's house.
BAÁLÉ: I see.
MOSÚN: When I reached my father's house, I wasn't happy with the situation my father was in. He was still living in the old house I'd left him in years before. So I quickly went and took a little piece of land and built on it. My father is happily established there now.
BAÁLÉ: You built a house for your father?
MOSÚN: It was God who built it, father.
BAÁLÉ: May your children also build a house for you. I mean it. Go and write it down [i.e., take note of what I say].
MOSÚN: When I'd finished my father's, I called my husband and said, You, my husband, I want to build a little house for you.
BAÁLÉ: You mean ...
MOSÚN: I built one for him too, and it came out beautifully.
BAÁLÉ: You built a house for your husband?
MOSÚN: It was God who built it.
BAÁLÉ: So you built a house for your husband as well?
MOSÚN: It was God who built it, father. ...

The interlocutor may have a more active role, while still serving as a prompt or feed for what is essentially a solo narrative. When Mosún goes home after her first, unsuccessful visit to her mother's family, she recounts her experiences to Tàfá. She is too angry to tell the story coherently, and it is left to Tàfá to draw it out of her. Being rather stupid, Tàfá does not follow all her fulminations. His misunderstandings just make her angrier, as well as amuse the audience:

> TÀFÁ: Èé ti rí? Kí ló dé?
> MOSÚN: Dádì, mo mọ̀ lọ, mo mọ̀ bọ̀. Mo mọ̀ bólórí burúkú pàdé níbi tí mo lọ o. Mo mọ̀ bá wèrè ilée yín pàdé o.
> TÀFÁ: Wéré ilée yín?
> MOSÚN: Ṣé ẹ tiẹ̀ jẹ́ kí n ṣàlàyé ẹ tó maa bèèrè wèrè ilée yín. Nígbà tí mo dọ́hùn-ún, bàbá baálé gbà mí ọwọ́ gbà mí ẹsẹ̀, mo bá mọ̀ bá wèrè yìí pàdé o.
> TÀFÁ: Bóo ni ọ́n ṣe lè fi wèrè sọ́dọ̀?
> MOSÚN: Kì í ṣe wèrè. Àbúrò ló jẹ́ fún mi. Olórí ibuú ni.
> TÀFÁ: Ẹ fún un ní ìnagijẹ ni.
> MOSÚN: Dádì, ohun tí mo fẹ́ẹ́ fà lóhùn-ún nǹkan tẹ́ ẹ wí fún mi pé n má fà á o. Mo ṣáà dàárú ṣá lẹ́nu kan. Mo bínú kúò lóhùn-ún ni.
>
> TÀFÁ: What's the matter? What happened?
> MOSÚN: Daddy, I've been and I've returned. And I met an absolute bastard there. I met your family madman there.
> TÀFÁ: Your family madman?
> MOSÚN: Why don't you let me explain before you start asking what "your family madman" means? When I got there, the head of the family welcomed me warmly, and that's when I met this madman.
> TÀFÁ: But how did they come to be looking after an insane person?
> MOSÚN: He wasn't an insane person. He was my younger brother [i.e., my mother's younger brother]. He's a bastard.
> TÀFÁ: Oh, so you just call him that as a kind of nickname?
> MOSÚN: Daddy, I almost did what you'd warned me against doing over there. . . . I blew my top. I left there in a rage.

Again, you can see the weaving and circling movement in Mosún's exposition. Her story lurches forward in stages—she went and she came back, she was warmly welcomed, her mother's younger brother did something that enraged her, she left in fury—each time going back to repeat that she met a "bastard" or a "madman" there. Tàfá amplifies the repetition when he echoes and tries unsuccessfully to interpret the expression "your family madman."

In many dialogues, the second speaker repeats the words of the first speaker to confirm that that is really what he/she meant, to underline its importance or unexpectedness, and to dramatize his or her reaction to it. In these cases, each sentence gets given added prominence, extra space and time in which to establish itself. In other passages, repetition confers on the words a kind of slogan-like quality, allowing the audience to join in. Thus, in Scene 4, after both Tàfá and Mosún have shown disrespect to Bùárí, Bùárí tells Tàfá that they are discussing family business which does not concern him: he should leave. From his command *"jáde"* [leave, get out] springs a three-way contest revolving around this single word, in which Bùárí repeatedly commands Tàfá to leave and Mosún and Tàfá take it in turns to assert that Tàfá will not do so. At the end of this sequence, such a rhythm has been built up that Bùárí is able to lead the audience to chant his final speech with him:

> BÙÁRÍ: Tọ́ ọ bá ti mọ̀ péọ ọ̀ jáde, ọ̀rọ̀ ti fúyẹ́. Ọ̀rọ̀ ìyàwóò rẹ nípa ilẹ̀, kí wá la féẹ́ sọ? O ti gbénu sọ̀rọ̀, o sì ti bà á jẹ́. *Àní ọ jáde. Ọ̀ lọ́ ọ̀ jáde.* Mọ wáá fẹ́ pa á láṣẹ fún ọ, ọ̀rọ̀ tí mọ bá sọ ńbí yìí, ẹni tí ó yi padà ò sí nínú àwọn tó jókòó un.
> ÀGBÀ ILÉ: Kò sí. Kò sí.
> MOSÚN: Àgbààyà.
> BÙÁRÍ: Ẹni tí ó yi padà kò sí. Torí pé àwa ò ní í purọ́, òótọ́ ọ̀rọ̀ làá sọ. *Mo ní ọ jáde. Ọ̀ lọ́ ọ̀ jáde.* Mọ wáá pa á láṣẹ, kò sílẹ̀ mọ́.
> ÀGBÀ ILÉ: Bẹ́ẹ̀ ni.
> BÙÁRÍ: O gbọ́? *Àní ọ jáde. Ọ̀ lọ́ ọ̀ jáde.* Mọ wáá pa á láṣẹ, kò sílẹ̀.
>
> BÙÁRÍ: If you've decided you won't leave, then there's little to be said. What can we say about your wife's request for land? You've had your say and you've spoiled the case. *I told you to leave. You said you wouldn't leave.* So I'm going to pronounce a decree for you. And whatever I say, there's no one here who will countermand it.
> ELDERS: No one.
> MOSÚN: Wretched old man.
> BÙÁRÍ: No one will countermand it. Because I don't tell lies, I tell the truth. *I told you to leave. You said you wouldn't leave. So now I'm laying down the law: there is no land.*
> ELDERS: That's right.
> BÙÁRÍ: Do you hear? *I told you to leave, you said you wouldn't leave. So now I'm laying down the law. There is no land.*

By the time Bùárí says the italicized words for the third time, the audience is chanting the entire statement in unison, ending triumphantly "There is no land." In sequences like this, it is not so much that remarkable, memorable, or dense phrases are selected to provide stepping-stones through a speech or dialogue; it is rather that in the process of constructing the speech or dialogue, certain ordinary expressions get endowed with repeatability. They are *made* memorable by the way they are inserted into a structure of iteration.

There are passages where the constructional principle of key phrases is foregrounded, as it were. In *Besotted Bridegroom,* this is most apparent in the passages where insults are being traded. The plot turns on the misuse of the powers of speech. The point where things begin irrevocably to go downhill is when Tàfá insults Bùárí in the second family meeting. The sequence in which he does so is extensive, elaborated, and highly explosive. He piles the insults up, almost drunk with excess. Their cumulative effect is so devastating that Bùárí weeps in public with rage and humiliation. They have an afterlife in the play. Bùárí reports what Tàfá said when he does his reconnaissance at their house and meets Ìyáa Ṣeun. Later he reminds Tàfá of some of the insults when Tàfá and Mosún come to see him. Fẹ́mi quotes Tàfá's words again when he comes to report his failure to persuade Bùárí to change his mind (in the Ìgbajà version) or in the last scene when Bùárí announces that he has thrown the lamp into the river (in later versions). Bùárí again recapitulates the whole episode of the insults at the end, when he makes his final statement explaining why he cursed Tàfá and why the curse cannot now be revoked. Thus the sentences in which Bùárí is abused appear as highly charged and strongly marked objects of commentary and recall. They are inherently strong and memorable, but they are given an extra charge by their repeated citation in different contexts. They take on a resonance and live on after the evaporation of the context in which they were first uttered.

The unveiling of the insults starts almost as soon as Tàfá and Mosún walk into the family meeting, where the other elders are arguing with Bùárí about the Baálé's decision to give Mosún some land. Tàfá immediately leaps into the fray, telling Bùárí "Go and sit down, and let the real [proper] elders have their say." Bùárí indignantly asks him to confirm what he has said, and Tàfá repeats the expression twice more. After further argument, Bùárí delivers a speech stating that Tàfá is stupid, that in-laws should be treated with religious reverence, that Tàfá obviously has no elders in his family to teach him and no capacity to learn. He concludes by saying this family business is nothing to do with Tàfá anyway, and there follows the passage, quoted above, in which he attempts to expel Tàfá from the meeting. A few moments later, Tàfá begins to unleash a string of insults on Bùárí.

They go as follows: (1) "Old man in rags strutting tattily around the house." Bùárí responds with a run-of-the-mill insult. (2) "You wear lace to swagger among people, real people—lace that you stole." This one leads to a long sequence of denial by Bùárí and restatement, with elaboration, by Tàfá ("You stole it from the riverside . . . Cloth that the washermen/women were washing in the river"). (3) "They told me that your words would be just like your appearance" (i.e., equally deformed). Bùárí asks who told him this, and Tàfá says that it was Mọ́mì, repeating for good measure "She said that you are ugly, and that what you say is also ugly." Mosún confirms this. (4) "It's said that if you call someone a gaping idiot, he'll close his mouth—but in your case, you just open your mouth all the wider." Bùárí merely exclaims "Me!" (5) "You said earlier that there was no one like you in our compound [i.e., an elder]. It's true. There is no one like you in our compound. If there were someone like you in our compound, we would sacrifice him to Ògún." Bùárí denies that he is a dog, which is Ògún's sacrificial animal. Tàfá repeats the insult in more explicit form: "You are a dog. What's the difference between you and a dog?" (6) "They [the family] ought to have sold you to the cattleherders so that you could drive cattle all over the place" (i.e., he should have been sold as a slave to the despised nomadic Fulani). Bùárí responds that it is up to Tàfá to sell him at a bargain price. (7) "They ought to have traded you in barter. The kind of people who buy bowls with beads, they should have taken you to those kind of people and exchanged you for a bowl." Bùárí says Tàfá came to ask for land but will go away with something else. (8) Tàfá now launches into an extended diatribe, first referring back to his earlier insulting remark that Bùárí should let the real elders speak. "You flew into a rage. Your mouth hangs down like a dog's [broken] leg." (9) "You are just like a *kúlúsọ* insect" (the ant lion: a sand-dwelling insect with a hunched back and shuffling motion). (10) "One eye is dead, you have to make do with the other." Bùárí and the other elders react with indignation. (11) "Blind elephant. Blind elephant." (12) "You scuttle like a crab." (13) "A two-eyed man went to war, and couldn't fight, how much less a one-eyed man. When a person who can see with both eyes goes to war and cannot find the battle, what do you expect a one-eyed man to do?" (14) Tàfá sings: "You are crumbling away / You are crumbling away / Fragments of a dilapidated wall fall into the water / You are crumbling away." It is at this point that Bùárí bursts into tears and then begins a sequence of threats and curses, in the course of which he secures Tàfá's full name, asserts his own pedigree as the son of a famous medicine man, and promises that Tàfá will feel the consequences of his behavior.

Some of these insults are highly ingenious and unusual. It is interesting, for example, that to Tàfá, being sacrificed to Ògún is bad (5); being sold as a slave to a nomadic cattle-herding people is apparently worse (6); but worst of all is to be bartered (7), for trading transactions without money are beyond the pale of civilization. Money makes a transaction more prestigious, even for the person being sold (see Barber 1994). His comparisons with animals are also carefully chosen. Bùárí has one eye permanently closed. His mouth is twisted as if after a mild stroke (not that Alhaji kept his face like this all the way through: Tàfá was exaggerating). He is lame in one leg, which gives him a sideways shuffling gait. The comparisons with the hunch-backed ant lion (9), the blind elephant (11: lifted from my part, since I didn't act in the performance from which this transcription was made), and the crab (12) all allude to Bùárí's physical deformities. Tàfá quotes two proverbs and then gives each a new twist to make it apply to Bùárí. One is the saying "If you call someone a gaping idiot, he'll close his mouth": that is, if you point out someone's shortcomings they are likely to respond by improving their behavior. However, according to Tàfá, insults do not have this salutary effect on Bùárí: the more people point out his gaping mouth, the wider it gapes. His defects, then, are beyond remedy. The second is the allusion to the saying that if fully sighted people go to war and fail, what can one expect when a one-eyed person goes? In proper usage, this would be a metaphor applied to another situation: for example, a child who hadn't prepared for their examination could be told, through this proverb "It's hard enough for the candidates who have done the work—how do *you* expect to pass?" Tàfá, however, does not use the proverb metaphorically: he applies it directly to Bùárí's actual handicap.

Èébú ara are the most unforgivable of insults. To vent such a long string of such painful, apt, and amusing ones produces a highly charged and dangerous atmosphere from which catastrophe is almost bound to eventuate. The audience knows that Tàfá has gone much too far, and they greet each new sally with horrified delight. It is important that Tàfá said these words deliberately and in full knowledge of what he was doing. One of the things Bùárí makes a point of asking, when he visits Tàfá's house after the meeting, is whether Tàfá's words "slipped out of your mouth" (i.e., by accident), or whether "you actually said them" (i.e., intentionally). Mosún confirms that Tàfá said the words "*pèlú ifokànbalè*" [calmly and deliberately], and Tàfá, for good measure, repeats some of the actual insults. Speech uttered intentionally is speech that is effectual, whether to wound or to bless.

The string of insults works like the strings of epithets known as *oríkì* ("praise poetry"). First, it is composed of discrete, self-contained verbal formulations whose relationship to each others lies in their common ascription to a single subject. Each insult is autonomous and can be quoted on its own. Each time Bùárí and others quoted Tàfá's insults they quoted a different selection and in a different order, though half a dozen of the expressions were clearly particular favorites with everyone, including the audience. Thus, the sentences become mobile and self-contained, with a vocative rather than constative force. Second, it is charged, effectual speech, speech which changes the person who is addressed. *Oríkì* may move the addressee to tears of gratification and emotional identification with a place of origin. Tàfá's *èébú ara* moved Bùárí to tears of rage and humiliation and activated his implacable vengeance.

When I studied the transcription of the Òdùduwà Hall text, I felt this parallel with *oríkì* very strongly, but thought it was an observation—perhaps an obsession—of my own. But when I went back to listen to the earliest recording, made at Ìgbajà, there it was, completely explicit. At the end of Tàfá's string of insults, Fémi protests at Tàfá's use of *èébú ara,* and Bùárí says

"It's not *èèbú ara*. He was calling me by my name. He was saluting me with my *oríkì*. So what did he do wrong?" This is heavily ironical, but it clearly indicates that the insults are a kind of inverted parallel to praise epithets, standing in a similarly vital relationship to individuals' self-conception and self-realization. Bùárí goes on to ask Tàfá for his full name, "Because you have just called me by my name, you called me by my name and went on to salute me with my *oríkì*. So let me know *your* name. What is your name?" After some prevarication, Mosún and Tàfá tell him. It is clear to everyone that, once in possession of Tàfá's full name, he can invoke it in the incantations that will curse him.

Speech, in this view of utterance, does indeed "require sacrifice" or "demand propitiation," as the *babaláwo*'s song put it. When intentionally uttered, it galvanizes people, translates them, and can mark them physically. In a sense, then, this play's way of embodying its theme is a precipitate of its very mode of generation. The theater company's habitual use of repeated, quoted speech, which positions weighty sentences strategically and weights ordinary ones through its very strategic and generative repetitions, is brought to the surface and made visible thematically—for the play is *about* the use of weighty and strategic speech, about the dangerous power of deliberate utterance, and about the way dangerous speech lives on, remembered and reiterated by all who were party to it. The play's moral narrative is thus echoed in the very processes of its textual generation. As in many other oral traditions, the mode of generation is as it were solidified, rendered opaque in a way which is not exactly reflexive but which does exemplify, or hold up to view, the inner workings of the text.

AUTONOMY AND ATTUNEMENT

When Alhaji said "for the rest, they can do it as they like" he was respecting a fundamental principle by which the autonomy and self-direction of every being is recognized. Even when masters wish to control their employees' every action, they know they cannot do so. Alhaji had no avant-garde esteem for improvisation as a mode of psychic self-exploration; he just knew the limits of his own power to determine what the actors did. But this pervasive autonomy is the lifeblood of the popular theater. From moment to moment, actors and audience knew that what happened next was not fully determined.

Individual generative acts belonged to their originators. Each actor had his or her layout of key lines, established in advance, and a bagful of verbal materials which were used to swaddle the key lines in a circling, recapitulatory web, extending out until the next key line could be reached. In each performance the web would be differently constituted, the result of numerous micro-choices at each point.

On stage, as in everyday conversation, each moment presents numerous alternative paths onward. The speaker assesses the options, which are suggested not only by her or his own previous utterances but also by those of his/her interlocutor; by the presence of other listeners; by the (possibly changing) purpose or intentions of the speakers and other people in undertaking the conversation; and by the situational frame. This continual, split-second process of assessment and creative choice is present in all live discourse, though it may be heavily constricted by specific rhetorical conventions (see, for example, Bloch 1975). Speech is inherently improvisatory. In the Adéjọbís' drama, the improvisation of speech is modified by the genre conventions and mode of theatrical production in such a way that it attains a certain solidity and opacity. In each performance, the actors cross a terrain already covered with tracks. They orient themselves by familiar landmarks and head for fixed staging posts. Their destination is the same, and their general route does not change without previous planning, even though their exact footsteps do. Thus the moment-to-moment alternatives of speech improvisation are in a sense *present* to the performer in a way they would not be in a one-off, never-to-be-repeated real life conversation: present as embodied memory, in the sense that they may already have been taken in previous performances. There is a certain *materialization* of potentiality, options existing as something actually experienced rather than as theoretically available but unexplored paths.

Furthermore, the speakers' mutual attunement, present in all speech improvisation, is intensified on the Yorùbá popular stage. Their procedure, as we have seen, is to take off from one key line and work toward the next, often by a looping and recapitulatory process, amplifying a point in a web of elaboration until it extends to the edge of the next point. But they undertake these operations *for each other,* confirming and stabilizing each other's remarks by pertinent questions and repetitions. Each actor is responsible not only for the generation of his or her own lines but also for the generation of the lines of other people.

More than this, each actor in a sense inhabits the *whole field* of the play's textuality, not just his or her own part. This field includes previous and possible future performances as well as the present one. The performers "know"—in the sense that they could themselves generate—all the dialogue, not just their own lines. They are attuned to what is going on in the farthest corners of the text. This is why it is so easy for actors to take over one another's parts without rehearsal. This is what facilitates the rapid ripple-like dissemination of effects throughout the text, as when the "caterpillar" motif was instantaneously taken up and exploited by numerous characters. It also fosters the retention of elements over time. Even when a line or sequence is dropped in one performance, it remains as potential for a future one—not only for the actor who originally said it, but for all the cast. Thus, when I was not present to say the "blind elephant" line, Alhaji smuggled it into one of his own speeches. And, as we shall see in Chapter 12, it makes possible a remarkable stylistic unanimity. One play may have a distinctly different style from another, sustained across the entire text of each by the multiple, tiny, and possibly unconscious linguistic choices of all the actors, who are attuned to the totality of the textual field and not just to their own part.

The field of materials and its concretization in performance were thus very close together. Each performance was a temporary and provisional conjunction of choices; the potential alternatives were present in the performative memory of the actors and quite possibly in the receptive memory of the audiences.

The play was never completed; it was continually emergent. Rather than a preparatory period in which a performance is worked upon, worked out, and finally established, followed by a definitive moment in which it is exhibited (Schechner 1988, 180–181), there appears to be an unbroken continuum between the first conception and the last performance of a play: if indeed there can be said to be a first conception (since much of the preparation has in fact been done long before a particular play is even thought of) or a last performance (since so many of its components will be recycled).

Despite the closeness of the performance to the repertoire from which it emerges, however, it would be wrong to think of the plays as mere permutations of an underlying set of plot elements, themes, and linguistic forms. This was not a closed tradition endlessly ringing the changes on a few basic themes. Rather, the theater company pressed their materials to make them speak of what was new in their experience. And though their innovations were encouraged or inhibited by audience response, the dramatists were not the mere mouthpiece of a popular consensus either: for sometimes, as we shall see, they overstepped the audiences' limits and failed to please them.

7 Audiences

The audience plays a constitutive role in the generation of plays, not only feeding the actors with their responses as a performance is actually in progress but also taking it upon themselves to extract a significant "lesson" which they can recount, contextualize, and reapply afterward. But the theater company, at the same time, constitutes the audience—by its use of time and space and by its mode of address—as a particular type of modern collectivity. The interaction between these mutually constitutive processes is the focus of this chapter.

SOCIAL COMPOSITION OF THE THEATER AUDIENCES

The Yorùbá popular theater was capable of attracting audiences from across the full socio-economic spectrum. They could fill university theaters as well as village halls. And a few exceptional companies—Hubert Ògúnǹdé's, Dúró Ládiípò̩'s, Kó̩lá Ògúnmó̩lá's—were highly esteemed as cultural assets by the educated classes. Ògúnǹdé, indeed, was regarded as a kind of cultural ambassador and toward the end of his career was given an official role as director of a government-sponsored pan-Nigerian dance troupe. But most popular theaters were not so fortunate: they were regarded by the social elite as vulgar entertainers and by the intelligentsia as reactionary populists.

The actors had constantly to contend with a low public image even among their most enthusiastic fans. But lower-class audiences, while they were ambivalent or openly disparaging about the plays' creators, were unanimous about the value of the plays themselves and the moral lessons they taught. These audiences were the mainstay of the popular theater. As we have seen, about half the Adéjọbí Company's performances were for "town" audiences, drawn from the community at large in whatever town or village they were playing in. It was very noticeable that these audiences were predominantly youthful and male. Judging by their clothes, they were not

A "town" audience in the small town of Ìgbájọ. ©Elio Montanari

usually wealthy. With their faded cotton trousers and flimsy shirts, they exuded an aura of the motor-park tout or of the hawkers who sell singlets in traffic jams. Among them, however, were more prosperous young men in occupations such as accounting, teaching, banking, the civil service, and trade, and it was usually these individuals who confidently volunteered to meet me to discuss their responses to the plays the following day. It was possible, but unusual, to see "big men" and "big women" there: wealthy, older, well-dressed people, often with a number of younger people to escort them. Because Oyin Adéjọbí was personally respected and esteemed by a wide circle of acquaintances, and because he had many friends in the church and in educational institutions dating back to the period when the theater was an elite Christian pastime, it was always possible that some eminent personality—a college principal, even an Ọba's wife—might appear in the audience.

The social atmosphere at sponsored shows could be quite different. The audience for *Besotted Bridegroom* at the KS Motel in Ìbàdàn for the Muslim Graduates Association, for example, contained a large proportion of well-to-do middle-aged women with towering head-ties and shiny handbags. It was an afternoon performance, which added to the atmosphere of respectability. They listened attentively and applauded at the end of each scene—something the university audiences also did, but which ordinary "town" audiences never did. But other sponsoring audiences—like the one for *Kúyẹ̀* in the Wesleyan Hall, Ìjẹ̀bú-Òde—were indistinguishable from ordinary town audiences.

The disposition of the audience could make a great difference to the quality of the performance. The first time I saw *Taking Care of Kúnlé*, in the National Theatre in Lagos, it seemed like a polished, scintillating farce; the second time, in Ìwó, it seemed a crude pantomime (see Chapter 4). The coarseness of the second performance was only partly attributable to the fact that Alhaji, the master pacemaker of every production, was missing, his part taken over by John with his much blunter, more bludgeoning style. An equally important factor, it seemed to me as I watched it, was the audience response. The Ìwó audience was small, youthful, predominantly male, and very rowdy, responding with roars of appreciation to the obvious jokes and especially to the horseplay. The noise was so great that the actors had no space in which to display their perfect timing and sharply choreographed, interlocking exchanges. They just had to get through it, blasting out the broad, obvious effects and dropping the finer points.

School and college students, who supplied about half the company's audiences, were among the noisiest and most undiscriminating of publics. When I asked Alhaji whether he felt the audience differed greatly from one place to another, he replied:

> Yeah. When you perform to a school audience, they make much noise and they make much noise than when you perform for a gentle man and other stage. Let's say when you come for where an intelligent people like Europeans, big men, watching the play you don't hear any noise, but after the play they just clap, unlike the children who will start to make noise, even noise that will disturb the actors at times. (English.)

I asked if it altered their way of acting. He said "At times you want to say something and you want them to listen, and they insult you. You have to stop, meanwhile. And that disturbs your action. . . . At times, you know, the students, at times even some [town] audience, they come to laugh, they are not ready to look for the story or the lesson that that play is teaching them, they just laugh. You ask them what they learnt, nothing."

John Adéwuni said that there were some schools where the pupils' behavior was acceptable, but others where "they behave like hardened thugs" and where instead of paying for their tickets they crowd outside and try to peer in over the wall. "This happens in town venues as well," he added, "but not nearly as much." But he saw a future benefit stored up in school audiences. As an elite in embryo, school children and students were worth cultivating:

The reason we like to perform for school pupils is that we know that if they watch us at school, then . . . when they are working, they'll know. . . . Maybe they will belong to a club, because some of them will . . . will be members of clubs and will invite us to come and perform for them for a specific occasion, and will sponsor us. That's why we like to perform for school pupils. It's not because the money we make from them is anything much, but because we want them to be able to pass on the word, after they've left school, that "at such and such a time, in such and such a school, Oyin Adéjobí did a certain play, let's invite them": that's why we like to perform for school pupils.

The school audience, then, is a means to secure future invitations from elite associations to give sponsored shows. As in most of the discussions I had with members of the company about their craft, business considerations in Alhaji's and John's answers are inseparable from artistic concerns. The sponsoring club is more rewarding to perform for both financially and artistically. The company makes more money and is able to give a better performance. Indeed, it would probably be accurate to say that profit vouches for art. This relationship is mirrored in the audience, where the big man's wealth is a sign of his "intelligence" and ability to appreciate the play; while his "intelligence" is an attribute of his social standing, that is, his wealth. The parallel is made explicit: the theater company always attributes its success to its knowledge of its audiences and their desires, but by this is meant a putative "gentlemanly" audience, culturally knowledgeable and with aspirations to self-betterment. Some audiences do force the company to simplify and coarsen their performance; but others rise to the occasion. In deferring to "what our public wants," then, the Adéjobí Company is not seeking the lowest common denominator of popular taste but is crediting the audience with enlightenment, discernment, and the ability to interpret complex linguistic texts.

AUDIENCE RESPONSE

No matter what their social composition, audiences react constantly during the performance of a play. Laughter of many sorts accompanies the unrolling plot: laughter suggesting amusement at particular words or phrases; laughter of indignation, protest, or outrage; laughter at the comic demeanor or physical stunts of characters; hilarious storms of laughter when the narrative discharges a built-up joke. Let me discuss some examples from one performance—the Lagos one—of *Taking Care of Kúnlé*. In this performance, the most prolonged and wholehearted hilarity—lasting for more than five minutes, and fed by the actors' extension of the comic business in hand—occurred when the elders escort Wúràọlá back to her home after she has been rescued from drowning. Her husband Ọ̀ṣọ́ has in the meantime been bewitched by Wúràọlá's best friend Àṣàbí and, acting in the belief that Wúràọlá is dead, has set up house with Àṣàbí as his new wife. Àṣàbí has taken to wearing Wúràọlá's clothes and bullying Wúràọlá's son Kúnlé. Ọ̀ṣọ́ is so besotted that he takes her side whatever she does and defies the family disapproval of such a hasty remarriage. A sense of outrage and indignation at Àṣàbí's triumph over Ọ̀ṣọ́ has thus been building up throughout the play. Great mirth has already been occasioned by the scene where Ọ̀ṣọ́ succumbs to Àṣàbí's *jùjú* and becomes foolishly amorous, feeding her spoonfuls of rice and being fed by her in turn as they sit side by side on a settee in the parlor. Further amusement was caused when the two elders Adéwálé and Owólabí come to remonstrate with him and are beaten up by an enraged Ọ̀ṣọ́, ending up entangled in their own robes as they flee the house. But the denouement was the discovery of the guilty couple by the returned wife, who arrives complete with escort of drummers, elders, and hangers-on. As they arrive, Ọ̀ṣọ́ and Àṣàbí are dancing to the popular highlife tune "Angẹlina"—the epitome of romance. This lasts some minutes and causes continuous bursts of laughter from the audience. Adéwálé and Owólabí then arrive, ahead of the others, and watch the dancing for some time, commenting on it and hinting that Wúràọlá might suddenly return to earth at any moment. Ọ̀ṣọ́ becomes annoyed and asks "Did a dead person ever come back in your family before?" His deadpan manner and the dramatic irony provoke a huge burst of delighted laughter in the audience. On Wúràọlá's arrival, Àṣàbí runs and hides in the bedroom. As Ọ̀ṣọ́ tries to divert Wúràọlá, saying they must go immediately to see the Baálé and do the rituals of propitiation customary in their family for people who have returned from the dead, the excitement builds up. Wúràọlá says she must get her *pọtilẹ́dà* (portmanteau) from her room; as she goes in, there are prolonged shrieks of excitement. Àṣàbí is dragged out and Wúràọlá demands the return of her clothes, which Àṣàbí is wearing. Ọ̀ṣọ́ is transfixed with shame, and the elders begin taunting him, singing snatches of "Angẹlina" and imitating the couple's dancing. Throughout this sequence there is a continual high level of excitement from the audience. Finally, Ọ̀ṣọ́ is given the choice: either he must tell Àṣàbí to stay and Wúràọlá to go or he must tell Wúràọlá to stay and Àṣàbí to go. The audience grasps the formula immediately and joins in:

> ADÉWÁLÉ: Ọ̀ṣọ́, Wúràọlá ní 'ó bóóde ni, kí Àṣàbí ó jókòó, àbÁṣàbí ní 'ó bóóde kí Wúràọlá ó jókòó?
> OWÓLABÍ: Hééè. Mọ gbọ́hun tó wí o. Ó ní kí Àṣàbí jókòó. Wúràọlá bóóde. Àṣàbí—

OLÙWÒRAN: "Jókòó!"
OWÓLABÍ: Wúràọlá—
OLÙWÒRAN: "Bóóde!"
ADÉWÁLÉ: Hanìn, Òṣó, ẹnu n mo fi bi ọ́ léèrè, ẹnu ni o sì fi dá mi lóhùn oo. Wúràọlá ní 'ó bóóde ni, kí Àṣàbí ó jókòó, àbí kÁṣàbí ó bóóde kí Wúràọlá ó jókòó?
WÚRÀ: Kí lẹ̀ ń bi léèrèé fún?
AYỌ́RUNBỌ̀: Ọ́ féẹ́ sòrò o.
OWÓLABÍ: Ó ní "Wúràọlá, jókòó—"
OLÙWÒRAN: "Àṣàbí, bóóde!"
ADÉWÁLÉ: Òṣó, is Wúràọlá to go and Àṣàbí to stay, or is Àṣàbí to go and Wúràọlá to stay?
OWÓLABÍ (TO TORMENT ÒṢÓ): Oh, I heard what he said. He said Àṣàbí should stay, and Wúràọlá should go. Àṣàbí—
AUDIENCE: "Stay!"
OWÓLABÍ: Wúràọlá—
AUDIENCE: "Go!"
ADÉWÁLÉ: Er, Òṣó, I asked you in so many words, and you've got to answer in the same way: is Wúràọlá to go and Àṣàbí to stay, or is Àṣàbí to go and Wúràọlá to stay?
WÚRÀỌLÁ: What are you asking him for?
AYỌ́RUNBỌ̀: He wants to speak.
OWÓLABÍ: He says "Wúràọlá, stay—"
AUDIENCE: "Àṣàbí, go!"

This was the climax of the play, which closed immediately afterward with Adéwálé drawing out the lesson, and a final chorus singing "The hawk above / Does not know that people on the ground are watching it." In some performances, the catchphrase "Wúràọlá, jókòó, Àṣàbí, bóóde!" caught the audience's fancy so much that they went on repeating it even after the end of the show.

Both the actors and the audience members spoke disparagingly of those people who went to plays "just to laugh" rather than to extract a valuable message. But laughter was the lifeblood of the actor-audience rapport. Through the constant ebb and flow of hilarity, audiences showed that they were following the narrative and appreciating the wit. The aesthetic of this theater tended toward the generation of a succession of explosions of maximum impact when the dramatic explosion on stage—often signaled by an intensification of volume, as several characters began to shout at once—was matched by the explosion of the audience response.

The audience's keen attention to the words that were being spoken on stage was demonstrated in several other ways besides laughter. Catching on

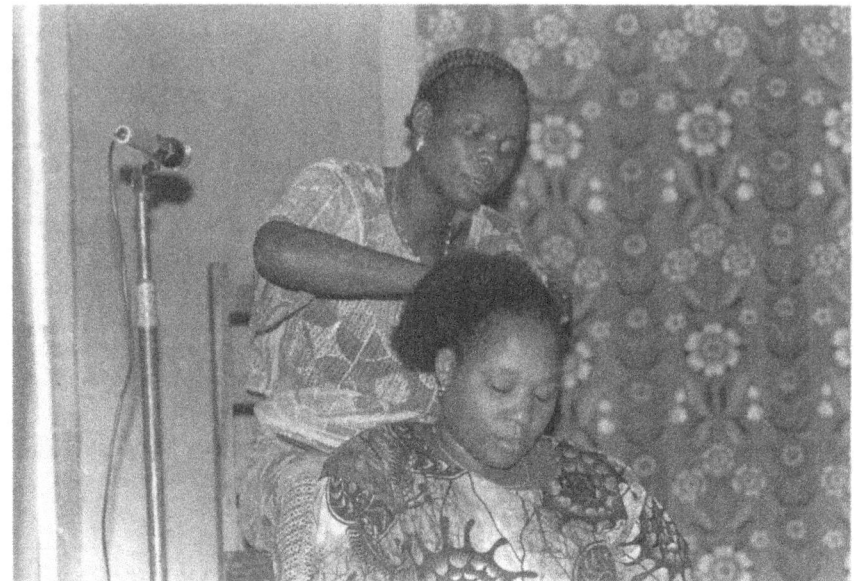

Àṣàbí (Margaret Adéjobí) plaits the hair of a customer (Emily) in the opening scene of *Taking Care of Kúnlé*. ©Elio Montanari

to a formula like "Wúràolá jókòó, Àṣàbí bóóde" was one of the simpler forms of linguistic response and commentary. Whenever an unusual or interesting word was brought into the dialogue, people in the audience would pick it out and repeat it to each other. English loan words, common slang, archaisms, and "deep Yorùbá"—all the "seeds of speech," discussed in Chapter 6, from which dialogue was generated—were keenly noted and assessed by the audience. Àṣàbí explains her presence in Òṣó's house by claiming to be *òrẹ́ aláìsí* [the friend of the deceased/departed]. This idiomatic expression drew the comment from one member of the audience "*Yorùbáa rẹ̀ẹ́ ga!*" [Her Yorùbá is really something!] When proverbs are quoted on stage, audience members often join in the second half.[1]

Audience members would also pick up a formula from one part of the play and quote it in another part with ironical intent or simply to establish the cross-reference. It is a sign of the shared idiomatic repertoire of performers and audience that those phrases most carefully planted are the ones the audience most unerringly picks out for future reference. Near the beginning of *Taking Care of Kúnlé*, news of Wúràolá's supposed death is first broken to the family head and the elders by a character called Ayórunbọ̀, who rushes in with the dramatic announcement "*Èmí sòfò!*" [Lives have been lost!] When asked what has happened, he repeats "*Èmí sòfò.*" When pressed, he launches into a long narrative set piece in which he describes

Morádéké as Wúrà in the Ìjàn-Òtún performance of *Taking Care of Kúnlé*. ©Elio Montanari

in great detail the boat journey in which Wúràolá apparently lost her life. The boatman, a known gin-drinker, was already completely drunk before the journey began. "And then he started to swish the paddle like this. He swished the paddle like this. And we started going *ikẹ̀ẹ́, ikẹ̀ẹ́, ikẹ̀ẹ́, ikẹ̀ẹ́* ... Ha! *Lives were lost!* Father, after a bit the boat reached a whirlpool. It couldn't go forward, it couldn't go back. The boat spun round and round. It went *ikẹ̀ẹ́, ikẹ̀ẹ́, ikẹ̀ẹ́, ikẹ̀ẹ́*. Ha! *Lives were lost!*" The elders continue to prompt Ayọ́runbọ̀, who recounts how a huge wave caused the boat to capsize. The shipwrecked passengers "began to thrash around. They went *ipàṣà, ipuṣu, ipàṣà, ipùṣù, ipàṣà, ipùṣù*. Ha, *lives were lost!*" Ayọ́runbọ̀ himself began to swim, and as he was swimming along, somebody grabbed his leg. The elders assume this was "a troublemaker" and ask "why didn't you shake him off?" But when Ayọ́runbọ̀ looked, he saw it was Wúràolá. "What! What!" say the elders, "which Wúràolá?" Ayọ́runbọ̀ explains that it was their kinsman Ọ̀ṣọ́'s wife. She clung to his leg, and they were swimming along: "Ha, *lives were lost!* ... As we were swimming along, God knows whether I can call it a

The elders hear the news of Wúrà's death in *Taking Care of Kúnlé*. ©Elio Montanari

creeper.... Or whether it was a root, she got caught on it, and she lost her grip on my leg." "Where is Wúràọlá?" asks one of the elders anxiously. Ayọ́runbọ̀ replies "After the boatmen had pulled me out, I looked and looked, but I couldn't see Wúràọlá. Wúràọlá has drowned.... You'd better find a way to break the news to Ọ̀sọ́. Ha, *lives were lost!*"

The positioning of *ẹ̀mí ṣòfò!* [lives were lost!] throughout this narrative is skilful. It simultaneously delays the forward movement of Ayọ́runbọ̀'s narrative, teasing the audience with postponement of the dreadful revelation, and foreshadows the climax toward which his tale is moving. Each time the listeners begin to relax, thinking the story must have a happy ending after all, Ayọ́runbọ̀ revives their apprehensions with this mysteriously impersonal and unspecific announcement. There is nothing especially memorable about the words themselves, but their deployment in this way gives them a resonance which attaches both to the character who utters them (so that *Ẹ̀mí ṣòfò!* almost becomes his nickname) and to the situation (breaking the news of a death).

The audience relished and remembered the phrase. In the next scene, when Adéwálé and Owólabí go to break the news to Ọ̀sọ́, members of the audience quote it out loud at appropriate moments. For example, when Adéwálé tries to sidle up to the crux of the matter by praying *Ọlọ́un máà jẹ́ á sọ̀fò* [May God not let us suffer losses: the passage is given in Chapter 5], several people pick up the echo (*sọ̀fò:* to be lost, to suffer losses) and respond not with the expected "Amen," but with *Ẹ̀mí sọfò!*—thus breaking the news before Adéwálé gets round to it. From then on, each time Adéwálé repeats the prayer, members of the audience repeat the announcement.

Toward the end of the play, it is the same Ayọ́runbọ̀ who arrives at the family head's house to announce that Wúràọlá is alive after all. He tells the tale in exactly the same fashion as before. He begins with a non-specific announcement of joyful news: "Greetings for having survived danger! Blessings! I rejoice with you, congratulations on your good fortune." Instead of going straight to the point, Ayọ́runbọ̀ again launches into a long and detailed narrative concerning a trip to the farm market, again postponing revelation by non-specific answers to the elders' mystified questions: "I'm just saying 'Congratulations on your good fortune.'" He tells how he went on the same boat again (the elders are incredulous) and, on reaching the farm market safely, began to pursue his occupation, which was the collection of contributions for a rotary savings association. As he was doing so, he came face to face with someone. "Blessings. I rejoice with you. Congratulations on your good fortune."

At this point (and at no other in this scene)—a moment before he reveals that the person he encountered was Wúràọlá—someone in the audience said loudly "*Ẹ̀mí sọfò!*" This person seems to have made the link between the two stories: for while the strategic postponement in the first story was achieved through "*Ẹ̀mí sọfò,*" its counterpart in the second story was "*Ẹ kú orí ire*" [Congratulations on your good fortune]. By responding to "*Ẹ kú orí ire*" with "*Ẹ̀mí sọfò,*" this participant suggested that he had sensed the structural parallel. The audience interventions, then, seemed to have been far from random. They showed, on the contrary, a keen ear for pattern in the dialogue.

But audience responses were not confined to laughing at, repeating, or quoting what was said on stage. People would also talk directly to the characters in the play. Thus, when Àsàbí complains about Ọ̀sọ́'s lack of response—"I winked and winked, I dropped every kind of hint, none of it got through to Father of Kúnlé. You see, you men, you never realize when a woman likes you"—a man in the audience called out "What about you women? What about you women?" Sometimes a member of the audience would agree out loud with something a character in the play had said. When Ọ̀sọ́ tells the story of "Mista Wúù" and his unfortunate accident with the machine tool, a member of the audience agreed warmly with Ọ̀sọ́'s statement that "if they put [the limb] back in place immediately, it could fuse back on." At other times the endorsement could be more ironical, as for instance when Ọ̀sọ́ responds to Àsàbí's first advances by telling her "This requires thought, and I'll think about it." A man in the audience said

"Yes. Definitely. He says he'll think about it." The sarcastic tone in which he said it showed that he interpreted Ọṣọ́'s response as a rejection of Àṣàbí's advances. Occasionally the audience would offer the characters advice or warnings, either in a friendly or sarcastic mode. When Àṣàbí is putting the love potion into the food she later administers to Ọṣọ́, the audience begins by commenting impartially "She's doctoring it. That's medicine. She's putting it in [to the food]," but goes on to warn Àṣàbí "Someone's coming! Someone's coming!," so that she will be able to conceal her medicine in time. When Àṣàbí takes the doctored food to Ọṣọ́ and he seems to be about to reject it on the grounds that he has already eaten, they advise her "Put it down" [so that it will be available for him to eat]; but they tell Ọṣọ́, a few minutes later, "Don't eat it. Don't put it in your mouth!" When he is on the point of succumbing, a woman asks "What do you think you are eating?" Sometimes, rather than speaking directly to a character in the play, members of the audience would comment on the action as if it were a contest, on the model of a sports commentator. Àṣàbí's determination to get Ọṣọ́ to eat her doctored food and Ọṣọ́'s reluctance to do so were interpreted as such a contest. When Àṣàbí urges him to take some meat even if he doesn't feel like eating a whole meal, Ọṣọ́ responds disdainfully "I'm not a cat, to be taking morsels of meat out of the pot." The audience sees this as a victory for Ọṣọ́: "Hey! Knock-out!" "Knock-out!" "He says he's not a cat!"

But the responses that revealed most clearly the audience's attentiveness and attunement to what was being said on stage were their acts of anticipation. Several times in this performance of *Taking Care of Kúnlé* they supplied a character's line in advance and then expressed approval when the character actually said the words they had predicted. Thus, when the two elders come to question Ọṣọ́ about his hasty remarriage, Àṣàbí becomes suspicious immediately. As soon as the elders have taken Ọṣọ́ aside to ask him whether or not it is true that he has married Àṣàbí, she calls him: "Er, Bàbáa Kúnlé—" A member of the audience supplies "*Èyin dà?*" [Where are you? i.e., I want to speak to you]. Àṣàbí says "*Èyin dà?*" and the audience member says in satisfaction "That's right!" Later, Owólabí is reporting what happened as a result of his and Adéwálé's attempts to intervene with Ọṣọ́: "I ate something today—" "Suffering!" anticipates a member of the audience. "Suffering!" says Adéwálé. "Yes!" says the member of the audience. Later still, when Wúràọlá is assessing Àṣàbí's guilt after the exposure of Ọṣọ́ and Àṣàbí in the last scene, she states that Ọṣọ́'s remarriage does not surprise her: "Few people will keep on loving you once you are gone . . . " "But dog and goat—" suggests an audience member. "But dog and goat—" says Wúràọlá. "That's correct," says the audience member. "—will love you to your face," concludes Wúràọlá. ("Dog and goat" here have roughly the same meaning as "man and beast" in English idiom, i.e., every Tom, Dick and Harry.)

In addition to these public comments—addressed aloud either to the

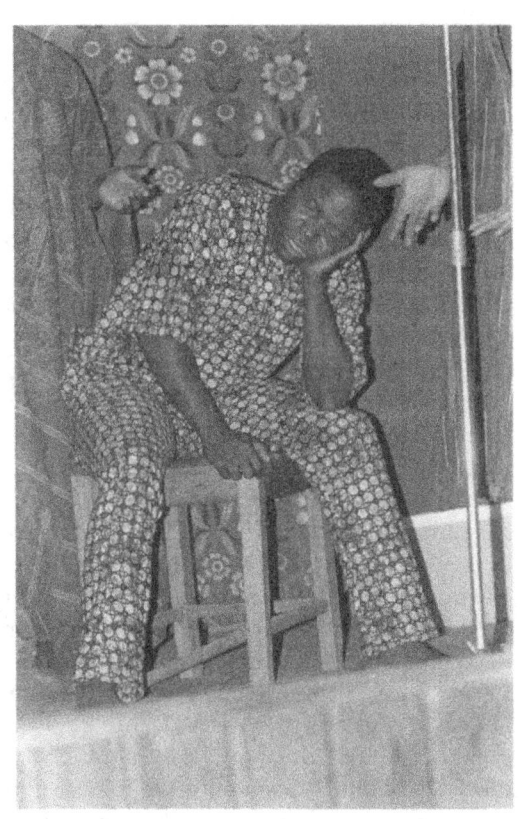

Ọ̀ṣọ́ (Alhaji) in mourning in
Taking Care of Kúnlé.
©Elio Montanari

Family and neighbors join to mock Àṣàbí's downfall. Dayọ̀ and Grace in
Taking Care of Kúnlé. ©Elio Montanari

characters or to the rest of the audience—people kept up a constant stream of private commentary among themselves. Only a few of these commentaries, of course, were audible to me from where I was sitting, and often they were drowned by the voices from the stage. But I could hear enough to form the impression that the comments were often analytical, explicatory, and evaluative. When Àṣàbí's first approach to Ọṣọ́ fails, a man in the audience comments and predicts "Kò bọ́ sí i . . . another style" (It hasn't worked . . . another style [is needed/is going to be tried]). As the elders beat around the bush in the breaking of the news to Ọṣọ́, a woman in the audience explains to her neighbor "He doesn't want to come out with it, in case [Ọṣọ́] goes into shock, he doesn't want him to be injured." When Ọṣọ́ asks Àṣàbí "What about your husband?," an audience member is quick to explain "Kò **mean** . . . Ó ti kú" [That's of no concern . . . he's dead]—an interpretation that is immediately confirmed. When Àṣàbí insists that it is her duty to help Ọṣọ́ bring up Kúnlé, for purely altruistic motives, a woman in the audience says "It's God's responsibility to bring him up, though she's claiming it's hers!" When Àṣàbí protests to Ọṣọ́ that she is truly well disposed toward him, a man in the audience interprets this as the height of deception, commenting succinctly "Yorùbá!" When she offers to move into Ọṣọ́'s house in order to cook for Kúnlé more conveniently, a woman in the audience observes "*Ilée Bàbáa Wándé ni yóò sebẹ̀. Ó ti fẹ́ẹ́ tójú ẹ náà ni*" [She's going to do the cooking in Bàbáa Wándé's house. She really does want to take care of him!]. Someone else points out the relevance of the play's title: "*Ìtọ́júu Kúnlé ni . . . yóò sì maa tójúu rẹ̀ náà ni*" [It's "the care of Kúnlé" . . . and she's going to care for him all right]. When Àṣàbí has got Ọṣọ́ in her power, she begins to dictate to him—for example, she tells him what to say to the elders when they come to investigate. A member of the audience refers to a motif right outside this particular play, saying "*Áà! Mọ́mì! Mọ́mì ló rán an ńṣẹ́!*" [Ah! Mummy! Mummy is the one sending him on errands!] Either this is an allusion to *Besotted Bridegroom*, where, as we have seen, much hilarity is caused by the subservient husband's respect for the woman he calls "Mummy," his rich junior wife; or it could be a wider popular idiom on which *Besotted Bridegroom* itself drew. Finally, when Àṣàbí has finally been driven out, her luggage on her head, an unsympathetic member of the audience comments ironically "She's going to her husband's house" (i.e., getting married—because, like a bride, she is taking her luggage and leaving her place of residence). These comments suggest how continuously the audience would analyze what they saw and heard, and how quick on the uptake they were.

"PICKING A LESSON"

The actors all affirmed that the value of their plays was the "lessons" that they taught, and they all staked out a position as "preachers" and "teachers" from which to impart those lessons. This was intended to counteract the contempt in which the public held the acting profession by claiming a position of social and moral superiority from which to deliver advice and warnings. It was a claim to *ọlajú*, or "enlightenment," which, as J. D. Y. Peel has observed, "tends to be used relationally rather than absolutely: people are considered to display it in relation to others who have less of it" (1978, 153). But the audiences did not oblige by granting the actors the superior degree of enlightenment their self-accorded speaking position claimed. They did almost always say that it was the moral lesson they went for— Alhaji Adédigba, a motorcycle mechanic from Igbó-Ọrà, said "The most enjoyable thing in this play, the real enjoyment that I got out of it, was the lesson that it taught us, that's what made it enjoyable"; Reuben Òjó, a cement trader from Oǹdó State, said "The thing I enjoyed most in yesterday's play was that it teaches one wisdom." But the *ẹ̀kọ́* (lesson) or *ọgbọ́n* (wisdom) was not considered to be easily accessible on the surface of the play, and people felt that it was they, as spectators, who could claim credit for quarrying it out. Several audience members clearly prided themselves on their superior ability to profit from the play: as Gabriel Bámiṣilẹ̀, a *jùjú* musician, said, "The play we watched last night was a play from which people could learn wisdom. Some people, when there's a play like that on, they'll just be laughing, they won't extract any wisdom from it." The suggestion was that the audience must take responsibility for their own edification and actively seek the wisdom that might be embedded in the show.

They were interested, moreover, in finding a lesson that applied specifically to them. Thus, almost all the men I talked to about *Besotted Bridegroom* began their exposition of the moral by saying "This play had a lesson for us men. . . ." Rasheed Balógun, who worked in Koletex Nigeria Ltd in Òṣogbo, for example, observed that "this play teaches a lesson, especially to men about the need for us to be very careful about the women we associate with in this day and age." Moses Dágilọlá, a young man employed as an accountant, said that although the blindness visited upon Tàfá was a harsh punishment, "it taught all young men not to say things they shouldn't, not to say insulting things to people who are physically handicapped in some way." He clearly saw this lesson as applying especially to his own age group. Reuben Òjó was even more specific: "That play was **so interesting** especially for us men, and for me **particularly** . . . for us men who have already got one wife at home, and who go and marry a second one without knowing what kind of behavior she's capable of, just because she has got some money." The only woman who came forward to discuss *Besotted Bridegroom*— Ruth, a married woman from Ẹdẹ—talked exclusively of the lesson the play held for women, specifically for junior wives:

> The lesson it taught us women was that, if we are two in a man's household, it teaches us the lesson that we shouldn't handle the situation in a spirit of greed or a spirit of pride toward our senior

wife in the house. If one has a senior wife and she says "This is how it is," it's up to us who come after her to accept it. Furthermore, if one is giving one's husband advice, one shouldn't do so in a way that inflames his emotions. If you stir up his passions, he won't be able to take care of the senior wife sufficiently for all of us to live together harmoniously. But if the junior wife is arrogant, and if the man likes the junior more than the senior, the suffering that he at first visits on the senior wife will come back to land on the junior wife's head.

Thus, people looked for the lesson in the character whose position in life most closely approximated to their own: the young man found a lesson in the behavior of a young man (Tàfá) who is rude to an elder (Bùárí); the junior wife found a lesson in the behavior of the junior wife (Mosún) in relation to the senior wife (Ìyáa Ṣeun).[2] In each case, they tended to see this character as the principal agent and architect of the play's narrative. Thus, the men agreed that Tàfá was the most to blame for what happened. Rasheed Balógun stated categorically: "Tàfá forgot the wife of his youth, that's why he suffered the fate he did. It was for no other reason." Wilfred, a schoolboy from Anambra State in the east of Nigeria, but fluent in Yorùbá, said that Tàfá "should have married only one wife" and thus averted the tragic ending. To him, the entire plot unrolled from this initial mistake. Alhaji Adédigba felt that "the guilt lay with Tàfá, because he allowed a woman to take him over" (lit. "he rode the horse of a woman," i.e., became possessed or controlled by her; for a discussion of the idioms of possession, see Matory 1994). When I asked Ruth who she thought was most to blame, however, she said "Mosún's behavior to her senior wife was not good enough. . . . Tàfá took his lead from Mosún's behavior, not from his senior wife's. . . . Tàfá did what Mosún told him." To her, then, the key contrast in the play was between the two wives; Tàfá's behavior was secondary, and his mistake was to follow the lead of the wrong wife. The only character the audience was ambivalent about was Bùárí, who was a model for no one. Perhaps because they did not see Bùárí's situation as analogous to their own, they were able to allow elements of doubt to enter their assessment of his behavior. On the one hand, he had every right to take revenge as he did; on the other hand, it would have been better if he had not done so. (Perhaps, though, if this audience had contained some traditional landowning elders, Bùárí might have provided them with a "lesson" of their own.)

The actors' attitudes toward their own parts mirrored and confirmed this interpretative procedure. Actors tended to feel that their own character was the one that embodied the most useful lesson and that this lesson was specially applicable to the corresponding categories of audience mem-

Interviewing a member of the audience. ©Elio Montanari

bers. Thus, asked what lesson *The Royal Palm-nut* imparted, Emily took the question to mean what moral qualities did her own character, Débòmí, represent, and answered in terms of the lesson this character taught to other women. She replied:

> The lesson I think it teaches a lot of women, which they should follow, is, first of all, it teaches them to have the fortitude to stick by their husbands. The husband you have settled with, and you don't know that he did such and such a thing, but like the woman [Débòmí] you should ask first, "Why did you behave like this?" Instead of being terrified by public opinion and abandoning him at the first hint of trouble, I boldly ventured into the forest for his sake to seek refuge, and lived the life of a farmer for a long time before God exposed the truth. If instead it had been the case that when he did that thing—the thing he didn't actually do, but people said he did—and I as a woman had flown into a rage and left him, then the truth would never have come out. But when the truth did come out, her [i.e., my] husband himself acknowledged that it was my staunch support when I went with him into the forest, and my fortitude, that made it possible for the truth to become known—that she [Díẹ̀kọ́lá] had been telling lies against him. Even though not many women could do it—could bring such patience/

endurance to their marriages, [it's apparent that] she [who does so] will be very happy in future with her husband. And it will teach a lot of women that there's nothing in this world, if people tell lies against her husband about something she didn't witness for herself, she ought to take time to investigate carefully before she believes it.

By contrast, Alhaji, who played her wronged husband Tóògùn, thought that the play's message was embodied in Tóògùn and directed toward men:

People shouldn't follow what a woman says, if the woman is lying against someone—we should make sure we don't go along with it. Or, if there's someone who completely trusts his fellow man, when there are two friends who trust each other, then neither of them should betray the other, as in the story of *The Royal Palm-nut.* Women should not be allowed to throw the world into disarray with their lies; men should take time to investigate matters carefully before they react.

This interpretative procedure, shared by actors and audience—whereby characters in the play were held to embody moral messages specifically for spectators of the same gender or occupying the same social role—seems to have been based on a folk theory of moral example. People can be an example only to others of their own kind, because moral precepts arise from experience and are imparted on the authority of experience. This became clear in the comments of Sàláwù Òkéléye, who worked for the Nigerian Electric Power Authority. He criticized the play for its harshness, arguing that both Tàfá and Mosún ought to have been shown repenting and being forgiven. He went on to say that if Mosún had been forgiven and had repented "she too could have told her mates that this kind of thing isn't good. 'Don't behave like that to your husband, this is the way to behave to a husband.' So her friend could also learn how to behave. And if she had a child, and it was a girl, she would know what kind of lessons to impart to her so that she would know how to behave in her husband's house." He implied that Mosún's experience was wasted because she was prevented from passing on what she had learned to other people in her position: that is, other women, especially other recently married young women, and above all her own replacement or successor, that is, a daughter. It is as if abstract precepts have little weight in comparison with advice coming from personal experience. It is traditional for morals and rules of behavior to be imparted in the same way as skills, from elders to juniors of the same gender. Learning how to prepare hot *èko*, how to keep one's clothes neat, and how to handle husband and co-wife were all part of the same body of practical knowledge passed on to young women by senior female relatives. This contrasts with the moral teaching of the church and mosque, in which a young male preacher is considered competent and authoritative to teach every category of person in his congregation and where the morals are usually presumed to be general laws applicable equally to everyone. Thus, although the theater practitioners always stressed their similarity to "preachers, who take a lesson and make it into a story," the theater audiences seemed to regard them as more akin to members of their family or household, differentially placed to speak authoritatively to different categories of person. This active appropriation of morals from specific characters is fostered by the very nature of the drama. A play is not a sermon, despite the actors' self-comparison with preachers; for a play sends its characters out into public space unaided to establish themselves through their own actions and speech. Each character has its own center of gravity and appears to exist through its own agency, not because a narrator or preacher has decided to mention it. Dramatic characters can thus be thought of as independent beings, each bearing its own moral message for the relevant audience members to capture.

The "lesson" was most valued when it could be applied directly and practically to the audience member's own life. Reuben Ọjó was by far the most enthusiastic commentator on *Besotted Bridegroom*, stating, "That play was so interesting that the next time they show it, even if they charge N10 a ticket, I won't mind paying." He added that he had been traveling that day and had got home tired, but when he heard that the play was on he made the effort to go "because their plays should not be missed." The Adéjọbí Company's plays, he said, were always instructive:

> Their plays usually give people **experience,** so that when you go home afterwards you think about it and **plan** your **life** accordingly. There's no play of theirs I've watched where I haven't got home and called my wife so that we can **plan** together on that basis. Their plays are plays that make people **more experienced.**

Besotted Bridegroom, however, was particularly valuable because it saved him from making a dangerous mistake:

> Before, I was **preparing** to marry a second wife, but that play that I watched yesterday, it made me stop and think, in the night; I thought about it and I decided that it wouldn't work out. **Yes,** because what happened at the end, yesterday, is not something that should happen to any decent person.

Audience members, then, not only seek out the lesson that seems relevant to their own situation in life, but they may actually take action in response to it. The narrative is construed as a form of advice, and the ability to take advice is a virtue. As one elderly audience member pointed out, "If several people tell you the same thing, you ought to . . . acknowledge that those people might be right, and that you've taken a wrong path."

The narrative, then, is construed as a model: a demonstration of the consequences of certain courses of action. In this sense it is not a description or depiction of "how things are" so much as a warning or exhortation, telling the listeners "This is what will happen *if* you behave like that." No category of spectators seems to feel that they are being branded by negative representations, for by implication they are always reprieved by this conditional tense. Even when a play ends with the song "Women are not to be trusted," the women in the audience appear not to be offended, for the play is not taken to be saying that *they* are not to be trusted: rather, it is warning them not to behave in a manner that attracts such condemnation, and at the same time warning men not to be the foolish prey of scheming women. The "lesson" serves both as a prayer and as a prophylactic: affirming that wrongdoing *will* be punished, virtue rewarded; and warding off bad events by laying bare the sequence of actions which would lead up to them.

Criticisms of the play almost all concerned what the audience perceived as distortions or omissions in the model. The diversity of these suggestions reflected the different perspectives from which people "picked the lesson." Moses Dágilọlá had an unusual criticism of Bùárí's actions: he should not have been shown throwing his *jùjú* into the river, because "In Yorùbá traditional custom, however angry a medicine man gets, he never throws his medicine into the forest." He should never unleash his full anger or reveal his full power: he should always keep something in reserve. Bùárí should not have been shown violating this customary reserve, lest he offer a bad example to people in the audience. Gabriel Bámiṣilẹ̀ laid much more emphasis than the other people I talked to on the corrupting effects of money, maintaining that Mosún's bad behavior stemmed from excess of wealth: "When a person is flush with money, there's no stunt he/she won't try to pull." He went on to explain that this tended to happen when the wealth was sudden and acquired without prior suffering. Someone who had worked and suffered before becoming wealthy would value it more and use it more judiciously. This interpretation of the play led him to spot a deficiency in the narrative: "They didn't show how she became rich; they didn't show that. And it ought to have been included. How she became wealthy and the kind of work she did to get hold of all that money. We ought to know. Maybe some man just gave it to her, we don't know what kind of work she did." For the lesson to be effective, therefore, Gabriel felt that the chain of actions that led to Tàfá and Mosún's downfall needed to be traced further back, and more of the links needed to be filled in.

Most of the criticisms, however, concerned the harshness of the ending. Ayọ̀ Béjìdé, a teacher, explained that the play ought to have demonstrated the importance of ẹ̀mí ìdáríjìn, the spirit of forgiveness:

> If a person is angry, and the anger is excessive, he ends up offending God. God himself, who created us, is constantly being offended by us. And if we ask him for forgiveness, he will forgive us. So when they went to beg Bùárí that time, if he'd said all right, he forgives them, and he will restore Tàfá's sight so that he will be whole again . . . [that would have been better]. **For example,** you know the family head, the head of that whole family, he acted in a more godly spirit. He called Bùárí, he pleaded with him to remember God, but Bùárí didn't. Do you understand now? That sort of begging should have been shown [on the part of Tàfá]. So that the spirit of forgiveness would be there, so that we would know that if someone offends you, you ought to forgive him.

Implicit in this is the idea that the play should have copied a greater model, that offered by God himself, who always forgives his creation no matter how seriously they offend against him. The play was defective because it left out a vital component present in the eternal model. The fact that angry old men do not always forgive those who have wronged them is neither here nor there, for Bùárí is not a portrait of an individual but a model of action and its consequences.

In the same conversation, and making the same point, Sàláwù used a proverb to express with great richness the way in which he felt the play's model to be deficient.

> The attitude of the two of them—the man who uttered the curses, and the husband who cursed his wife—neither of them had a forgiving spirit. The addition I would have made would be to let us cleave to the glory of God, I would want them to have added the knowledge of God's will. They could have called them both back, and the two of them could have **balanced** to the point where each knew where he had gone wrong. Our fathers have a proverb which goes "If you remove mucus from your eye, you'll show it to your eye, and the eye will know that what it did wasn't good." But this evening, they removed the mucus from the eye and didn't show it to the eye.

The proverb rather whimsically suggests that after you've picked the sleep from your eye, the reason you look at it is in order to show the eye exactly what a nasty mess it's been making. In the same way, if someone does wrong, he or she should be confronted with the consequences to prevent him or her from doing it again. In the play, wrongdoing had consequences:

Tàfá and Mosún did wrong and were punished with blindness and madness; Bùárí and Tàfá did wrong in uttering irrevocable curses which had the consequence of destroying their victims. But only Tàfá had to come face to face with his wrongdoing, and even then only partially. He asks Ìyáa Ṣeun to forgive him, but this is glossed over and he proceeds immediately to his cruel revenge on Mosún. A true confrontation with their errors, Sàláwù suggests, would have led to repentance, forgiveness, and the restoration of harmony. What Sàláwù is asking for is a demonstration, within the play itself, of the efficacity of learning from experience. It is not enough for the audience to learn from the experience of the characters: the demonstration has to be made doubly effective by showing the characters learning from their own experience first, thus providing the audience with a model of how to profit from example, as well as the example itself.

These lessons are already a norm: they demonstrate a truth already known to the audience (even if they need reminding of it) rather than revealing unknown depths of character or motivation. But the audience normalizes them still further by fitting them into a larger picture of received opinion about the world "nowadays," a picture which corroborates and is corroborated by the events shown in the play. Thus, Mosún's wealth, as Gabriel's comments showed, can be fitted into an extensive folklore in which solid, well-earned wealth is contrasted with the illusory and evanescent kind gained by trickery or magic. Although the play does not pursue the question of how she became wealthy—concentrating instead on the effect her wealth has of making Tàfá subservient and dependent—Gabriel knew what kind of story it would be when he said that it is people who have not sweated for their wealth that misuse it and that "maybe some man just gave it to her, we don't know how she got it." A whole network of stories rises up around this subject—stories about "bottom power," magic money, and so on. Similarly, Sàláwù placed the reasons for Tàfá's mistreatment of his senior wife against a background of received opinion about the casual, non-communal processes by which marriages are contracted "nowadays":

> We don't marry our women from out of their parents' homes any more. We pick up women at places like this play or some social occasion. Very few of us go to the woman's parents' house and get to know the parents. But lots of people just do it up against a wall and the woman gets pregnant. And once she's pregnant, her parents can't say she has to have an abortion. He's married her, in other words. And in due course he'll find another woman who takes his fancy, just as he picked her up against a wall. So, he'll dump the first wife somewhere, and the new wife will get all his attention. That's what's happening nowadays.

Again, none of this is shown or even suggested in *Besotted Bridegroom*. There is no reason to believe that Tàfá married either of his wives unceremoniously without their parents' involvement. But the dramatic situation—a husband who neglects his first wife and favors the second—seems to bring with it a penumbra of other stories indicating a general moral deterioration, which Sàláwù draws on with ease and confidence.

Thus, though all members of the audience that I talked to agreed fervently that the play contained wisdom and taught a lesson, the lessons they picked out covered quite a wide range.

THE AUDIENCE AS "PUBLIC"

The theater's relationship to its audience is constituted through its use of time and space in performance and through its mode of dissemination. From its inception, the modern popular theater deliberately differentiated itself from existing theatrical models provided, for instance, by Gẹ̀lẹ̀dẹ́ masquerade and, more to the point, by the professional traveling *aláriǹjó* masquerade theater. In so doing, it imagined, and constituted, the audience in a new way—as a "public": as a horizon of address composed of anonymous and, in principle, interchangeable individuals, of potentially indefinite extent.

Scholars have emphasized the continuity between *aláriǹjó* and modern popular theater, citing Ògúnǹdé's own childhood interest in the masquerade theater and pointing out formal parallels between the two modes, such as that between the opening glee in the popular theater and the introductory chants of homage that open an *aláriǹjó* show (Clark 1979; Adedeji 1973). But while the popular theater did share some aesthetic principles with older performance arts, and borrowed some materials from them, the relationship is certainly not one of unbroken organic development. The popular theater was at pains to distance itself from older spectacular forms and their pagan associations. Its use of time and space draws the line between traditional performance and modern popular theater with particular sharpness.

Aláriǹjó masquerade shows are performed in an arena constituted in the act of performance itself, through the interaction of the audience and the performers. The troupe takes up a position in an open site such as a marketplace and the audience gathers round, either forming a circle right round the troupe or making up a three-quarter circle with a wall or wide veranda steps as the fourth quarter. Here the Ọba, chiefs, and dignitaries of the town may have chairs placed for them, making highly visible the differentiation of status among the spectators.

The boundaries are established in the act of performance, as spectators press forward and the performers, by their movements, press them back to maintain a wide, clear arena. It is remarkable how smooth and even the curve thus constituted often is. The performers use the entire arena, moving across it and round it in long straight runs and wide looping circles. Some items in the show may take place outside the arena—for example, the leopard who appears on a neighboring rooftop—leading to a regrouping of the audience and a relocation and reshaping of the performance space.

The divide in such spectacles is not between "backstage" and "onstage" but between unseen forces that are invoked to empower the performers and the visible stunts and transformations that are the manifestations of such empowerment (see Gotrick 1984). Rather than "dressing up" offstage in order to perform mimesis on stage, the *aláriǹjó* masqueraders change under wraps, but in the middle of the arena, before the eyes of the spectators. The most impressive and prized parts of their show involve slow but complete transformations. The *fààfáá* (whirling mat) turns inside out without the performer inside being glimpsed. The python emerges from a sack; the "vertical corpse" materializes from within a performer's enveloping costume. What the performer wants the audience to see, according to Drewal, is "an elusive being continually changing form and colour in plain sight of everyone" (Drewal 1992, 95).

Before the spectacle commences, the leading praise singer of the troupe notes, or finds out, the identity and praise epithets of the important people present in the audience. In the course of his opening invocations he may address them directly with their *oríkì,* establishing an intense dyadic interchange which the gratified addressee acknowledges with gifts of money. Approaches to individual members of the audience continue throughout the show. When the *fààfáá* has completed its stunning sequence of runs and swirls, it will glide footlessly over to a selected member of the audience and offer him or her a peep, through the walls of the cylindrical roll, at the masquerader inside who is operating it. Similarly, the *òyìnbó* mask—a comic rendering of the European, with awkward gait, umbrella, and gloves—will strut up to a number of different members of the audience to shake them by the hand and inquire gutturally "How ah *you?*" The socially salient members of the audience are paid special attention. Thus, while the performers and the audience share the same plane in space, the audience is treated as essentially internally differentiated, with its own foci or centers of attention, a fact which the performers deliberately highlight in acknowledging them.

Though *aláriǹjó* troupes differ, in general it could be said that their shows unroll with the tempo of everyday rural life. Long periods of apparent inactivity or slow buildup suddenly crystallize into intense bursts of excitement. The spectacle is made up of a sequence of discrete, self-contained episodes, usually a display by one or two masqueraders at a time. There is little narrative structure even within a single episode and none linking the performance as a whole. Each can thus occupy its own time and space, for characters are not locked into each other in sequences of complex interaction, and there is no larger plot to provide a grid. Structurally, like an *oríkì* chant, an *alárìnjó* performance is additive and infinitely extensible. In practice, of course, troupes have a limited repertoire of episodes, but there is nothing inherent in the structure of the show that produces closure. Just as the arena in which they perform is created contingently, out of the space of daily social interaction, so the time of the performance is open-ended, like lived time, and the termination of the performance is not an end predicted and determined by the very premises of the beginning. Their time is static: the time of ancestors or creation, secreted *within* diurnal time.

The modern popular theater established a quite different dynamic of time and space. The most fundamental difference is also the most obvious one. The plays always take place in an enclosed space, the entrance to which can be controlled. Admission is restricted to those who pay for tickets at the gate: "Something which was never seen before," as Ògúnǹdé himself remarked.[3] The time of the spectacle is also demarcated. Plays are always advertised as beginning at a specified hour—in contrast to the *alárìnjó* theater, which would simply begin at a time everyone knew was appropriate. Although the stage plays do not actually start at the time advertised, the exhortations of the posters ("8.oo p. m. sharp . . . Don't be disappointed"— i.e., by being late) implicitly promise an entertainment which will occupy a time slot of a certain magnitude in exchange for the spectator's two naira.

The dissociation of performances from communal cycles and hierarchies, and their concomitant availability as commodities to anyone who could pay the price of admission, was one of the factors Habermas identified as fostering the emergence of a new kind of public sphere in late eighteenth-century Europe (1991, 39–40). Together with the rise of print, this disembedding and commercialization of cultural forms presumed and projected an audience where differences of rank, family, and personal history were—provisionally—irrelevant. All who paid for admission had access, and all were equivalent to each other. Entertainment was separated from other social rituals and became an end in itself. In some ways, developments in colonial Nigeria were comparable. Entertainments were created which did not participate in the annual cycle of religious festivals, as *egúngún* masquerades did, and were not meshed into local royal or political events, but which moved autonomously from town to town playing throughout the year to anyone who was prepared to pay to see them.

The Adéjọbí Theatre laid down a performance scheme which seemed designed to contrast at every point with the older masquerade theater's use of space and time. It was a scheme which emphasized the divide between the presenters of the entertainment and its consumers and which consistently projected the audience as an anonymous, undifferentiated but regulated mass: a "public," though not a public sphere.[4]

The performance space was not only regulated but fixed in advance, so that audiences and actors occupied positions that had already been marked out for them by stage and seating. The stages on which the Adéjọbí company performed varied greatly, as we have seen; but they always established the same frame, the same parameters for the relationship between spectacle and public. The total space in which the event took place was always rectangular or square, and the performers, whether they had a raised stage or not, always occupied one end of this space and faced forward. The audience always sat in rows facing the stage. Audience and actors confronted each other across a well-defined gap which was hardly ever physically breached. The seating was fixed in advance of the performance, the positions of the audience thus being determined by the structure of the venue rather than the other way round. It is notable that even though the linear format could be blurred—as, for instance, when the seating was insufficient and crowds of small children would assemble on the floor in front of the first row of seats, creating a shapeless and turbulent mass—it was never abolished. Members of the audience never got up onto the stage to give money to the actors, as Ghanaian audiences at concert party shows frequently did. Nor did the star of the Yorùbá drama descend from the stage to interact more freely with individuals at the front of the audience, as Ghanaian concert stars sometimes did.

This facing relationship was heightened by the way the stage space was used by the actors. Even when the stage was in fact deep, the performers set up the lights and scenery in such a way that the acting area was reduced to a narrow strip toward the front of the stage. The back curtain and scenery demarcated the total acting area; in front of this, and parallel to it, the fluorescent tube used for lighting the stage was laid on the floor, further restricting the usable space, for the action tended to take place only behind these lights. In some performances, the glare from them made the space behind them invisible to the audience, and actors would use the even narrower strip of space in front of them for all their important speeches.

The actors' base position in relation to each other was a row. In any scene involving several characters, they would form a front-facing line, whether sitting or standing. Individuals would then move out of this line in order to deliver their speeches, creating an effervescent but ultimately static effect. In *The Royal Palm-nut*, for example, there is a scene of accusations and counter-accusations between Làágbé, his wife Díẹ̀kọ́lá, and his friend Tóògùn which ends in Tóògùn being driven out by all the other characters present. The scene involves physical violence—Díẹ̀kọ́lá, in demonstrating how Tóògùn supposedly raped her, accidentally pushes over an old relative who has come to intervene; in trying to get up, the old relative pulls Làágbé down onto the ground; when Làágbé turns against Tóògùn, he and the old relative join forces to expel him physically, beating at him with their caps. But the core of the scene—Díèkólá's false denunciation of Tóògùn—is conducted with elder, husband, and friend sitting in chairs in a row that faces front as the wife storms up and down winding up her eloquence. Each character stands up to intervene or react and then sits down again. Even when they finally get up to drive Tóògùn out, they do so in a kind of conga, lining up behind him. Thus the audience in rows confronts the actors in rows, in a format reminiscent of the posed group photographs that decorate Yorùbá parlors. Jeyifo confirms that this use of space is typical of *all* Yorùbá popular theater groups and is "so basic that even in non-proscenium stages, the troupes automatically and unfailingly present frontal, linear tableaux" (Jeyifo 1984, 17).

In the Adéjobí Company's use of space, the main entrances and exits in all scenes are front right and front left. Entrances through the center back were rare. In general, it seemed to be a convention that such entrances denoted the interior: the inner rooms of a house—such as the married couple's bedroom in *The Royal Palm-nut* and *Taking Care of Kúnlé*—or the depths of a forest. The front right and left entrances denoted the more publicly accessible parts—the street doors of a house, a road or path through a town or forest, and so on. The rare use of the center back entrance was thus significant, heightening the sense of a special, highly charged or forbidden space. But its rarity also reinforced the tendency to line up along the front of the stage. Characters would always go out the same way they came in. Right and left, however, were interchangeable from one performance to the next. When they did *Articulated Lorry* at Òyán, I noted that "everything was staged the other way round, starting from the opening glee, where the two pairs of women were the same but stood at the other side of Baba from yesterday." The orientation sometimes seemed to be decided in the split second before the play started. In a performance of *The Overreacher* at Ìjèbú Ìjèsà, the performance, seen from behind the scenes, began like this:

> Now the first scene was beginning. John bawling his wives and attendants out. Ìyá Adé [Grace] strolled in, with tantalizing slowness poked among her bundles to get out her wrapper and blouse . . . stopped to discuss something with Bàbá [Adéjobí] sitting there in his great metal chair . . . pulled the blouse over her head, poked about again for the extra waist-cloth, got out her head-tie . . . then someone came with an enquiry about the tickets. She had been at the gate. She stopped to give the person change for N10, taking each note separately out and smoothing it flat before handing it over, changing a dirty one for a clean one. . . . Just as our cue was

spoken by the Ọba, she tied her head-tie and we moved forward together to dance in. Fẹmi rushed from the other side, where he must have thought we would enter from, to join us.

But once the orientation was established, the performers maintained their positions in relation to each other with great consistency. In an earlier performance of *The Overreacher*, at Olúbàdàn Stadium, I fled from the Ọba's wrath in the wrong direction, so that I ended up on the opposite side of the Ọba from the other chiefs. John did not like this deviation from the usual staging, and as part of his thunderous attack on the chiefs he yelled "*Gbogbo yín papọ̀ sójú kannáà, hahàá, àbí kí ló ń ṣe yín?!*" [All of you get together in one spot—ha!—what's the matter with you?!]

The bicameral, front-facing, linear mode of performance is further heightened by the use of microphones. The drama is literally broadcast to listeners who are *out there* and who cannot be reached except by artificial amplification. The Adéjọbí company had two standing mikes which they placed in a line along the front of the acting strip. They would be in place before the curtain was drawn back. Just as the chairs and benches established the formation of the audience in advance, so the standing mikes established the channels and parameters of communication before the actors took the stage.

The microphones promoted a choreography of front-facing presentational turn-taking. The actor, behind the mike, would speak not directly to his or her interlocutor on stage nor directly to the audience, but obliquely, through the mike, to a space accessible to both, an intermediate space constituted by the coherent world of the play, on the one hand, and the anonymous but responsive world of the spectators on the other. The microphone was a kind of sounding board as well as a channel of communication. Thus, in *Besotted Bridegroom* at the Ọ̀ọ̀ni Girls' School, I noted that "When Tàfá is abusing Ìyáa Ṣeun in Scene 1, he stands at the left mike and faces the audience, not the sleeping woman who is behind the [fluorescent] footlights." Although the words of the character Tàfá were intended for Ìyáa Ṣeun— and were highly personal and vehement—the performer John was beaming his performance outward. Without addressing the spectators directly, he was bouncing his speech via his microphone over to them.

The microphone stands were rarely moved, but the microphones were on long cords and could be lifted off the stand and held by hand. Most of the action was a counterpoint between the two stands or the two hand-held mikes. Characters used the hand-held mikes freely and casually, gesturing with them to drive a point home. They were relaxed about providing each other with access to a mike, and very little of the dialogue was done without one. (But when, as often happened, a mike blew, they would just put it down and carry on regardless.) In a performance of *External Appearances* at Irèé, I noted that the Aládùúrà preacher, played by John, had possession of a hand-held mike throughout all his scenes. This character epitomized fluidity—dancing, shaking, praying, twitching, kneeling, receiving visions—and he hung onto his mike like a projection of his own character, waving it about and dancing with it.

But though the choreography around the hand-held mikes was fluid, it still participated in the distinct dramatic style which emphasized turn-taking and the authority (or lack of it) to speak. In an episode involving the preacher, the old pagan, and his son (see Chapter 10), only John, as the preacher, had a hand-held mike. He used it to dominate the exchanges, and held it firmly to the old man's mouth when it was his turn to speak. In the same scene, the preacher has a discussion with an old woman played by Grace. Again, they used John's hand-held mike jointly, but this time John, after finishing his speech, moved his chair closer to Grace and handed her the mike, quite overtly conferring on her the authority to speak. Soon afterward, Emily, who had just left the stage, returned in order to provide Grace with her own mike. John and Grace now angled themselves obliquely toward each other, half facing the audience and talking not to each other's faces but to their own mikes. This absence of prolonged eye contact gave even the more fluid dialogues a feeling of being a string of set pieces, an impression heightened by the formal handing over and taking up of the microphones. At the end of every scene, mikes that had been held by hand were returned to the stands. When the curtain re-opened, the channels of communication were once more in place, awaiting a fresh beginning.

The interface of this spectacle is between onstage and backstage. It is a show whose mechanisms of production are concealed behind, and not within, the performing space. The necessity of a screen, separating the actors in preparation from the characters on stage, was made clear in the very first play I participated in, *The Overreacher*, at Olúbàdàn Stadium, Ìbàdàn:

> It is a smallish stadium, more like a field really. A small platform stage had been erected—planks on a metal scaffold—in front of the stadium seats. The company, supervised by Alhaji, was fixing posts at either side to hang the front curtain from. On the first attempt the posts weren't tall enough; extensions were added, one of these slewed over and had to be nailed straight. Eventually the blue cotton curtain was strung up and a set of flats [folding screens] was put in place, with another curtain at the back.... The Church Youth Association [the sponsors] had hired the stadium and hired the stage, which they had brought from Liberty Stadium where it belonged. (Liberty Stadium cost too much to hire.) ...

They had parked the lorry off to stage right and rigged up another curtain between the stage and the lorry; behind this the drummers were to sit and the cast were to wait for their entrances.

Even when there wasn't a "backstage," then, one was ingeniously created. The spectacle was rigorously separated from the spectators, and its mechanisms of production were kept hidden. Stage costumes were kept separate from everyday clothes and actors were careful not to show them in the auditorium—if they were arranging chairs or selling tickets—because this would "spoil the surprise." The "surprise" of the spectacle depended on the pre-givenness of the spatial format. The auditorium, with its laid-out rows of chairs, the stage set with scenery and lights, and the curtain marking the division between the two, preceded any action or interaction.

The curtain which marked the division between audience and performers also marked temporal divisions. The drawing of the curtain signals "inception" and its final re-drawing signals "closure"; between these two signals, there is a stretch of complex, interlocked, and coherent narrative in which the chain of links between action and consequence is uncovered. This demarcated, sequential, narrative time is modeled on the temporal intervals of real life, never uses flashbacks, and rarely even introduces long between-scenes lapses (as in "20 years later . . ."). Action and consequence are tightly bound together, the latter following uninterruptedly from the former. This linear, forward-moving time is very different from the static, transcendent time of the ancestral masquerades. It is the medium through which the play's "lesson" is expounded. Both characters and actions occupy a determinate place in a larger spatio-temporal grid—consciously underlined in Alhaji's aesthetic of "clicking."

This use of time and space hailed the audience as a gathering of anonymous and equivalent members. Anonymity was a fact, for it was difficult to discern individuals in the auditorium, even when particular people were known to be there. The shows usually took place after dark and were lit by stage lights, while the auditorium remained dim. From the stage, what you could see was rows of faces and the occasional glint of a pair of spectacles, a sea of unidentifiable people generating huge roars of laughter. The principle of equivalence was signaled by the regular rows of standard chairs—often metal stackable chairs borrowed from a school hall. (The audience in the Baptist Hall, Irèè, had to sit at rows of desks already set up for a WAEC examination—an extreme manifestation of the principle of a collectivity made up of autonomous and interchangeable elements!) The performers never approached or played up to individual members of the audience: everything they did was projected out to all and sundry without distinction.

At sponsored shows, the officials of the sponsoring association often did make themselves prominent during the course of the evening. They would be greeted in general terms in Adéjobí's opening address, but later on they might interrupt the play to make their own speeches, receive donations from prominent members—who would come up on stage for the purpose—and even stage supplementary entertainments. For example, in a performance of *Láníyọnu* sponsored by the Inner Circle Club of Àgbámú, the chairman of the organization took the stage after the curtain had closed on the sixth scene to make an elaborate speech, in the course of which he honored prominent individuals present at the show and then asked permission to entertain the assembled company with a little performance of *ewì* (the quasi-traditional, quasi-oral style of poetic chant made popular by Láńrewájú Adépòjù and Túnbòsún Ọládàpọ̀). He proceeded to give an extensive rendition of a composition of his own, in the course of which he expressed his gratitude to God and his good wishes for Christmas; praised and thanked Oyin Adéjọbí; and went on to salute one by one all the dignitaries of the Inner Circle Club, with their names, titles, positions in the community, nicknames, short personal *oríkì*, and prayers for a good future. At the end of this, another official took the stage to announce the names of prominent donors to the Inner Circle Club and the amounts they had donated. Applause for their generosity was solicited before the play continued.

This interlude showed that as far as the Inner Circle Club was concerned, the whole point of the evening was to display prominent personalities, using the occasion to honor them and solicit their patronage. *Oríkì* salute what is distinctive, memorable, and recognizable about an individual as well as attributing to him or her an illustrious lineage and ancestry. However, the Oyin Adéjọbí company itself did not shift into this dyadic and individualizing mode of address. The play was in a separate compartment. As soon as the interlude was over, the play continued exactly as before, addressing the audience as an undifferentiated, and in principle unknown, "public."

This did not indicate indifference or lack of recognition by the theater company of the personalities involved in sponsoring organizations. Before and after the play, great warmth and appreciation were expressed by both sides. In some sponsored shows, the sponsors worked alongside the company's "boys" to erect the scenery and lights. In others, they hosted a meal or provided accommodation. But the drama itself was projected out as if to a "public" rather than a personally known audience, and this style of address was not modified even when prominent patrons were known to be present.

The theater company's uses of space and time, then, made a definitive break with the masquerade theater. The enclosed hall, the allocation of a definite (even if notional) time slot for the performance, the predetermined marking out of stage and auditorium space, the front-facing acting style projected out to an anonymous, undifferentiated public: all these features established the popular theater as a spectacle of a distinctive kind.

INFLECTIONS OF MODERNITY

In using the disciplines of space and time to constitute its audience as a public, the theater announced its modernity. Publics (in the sense of assemblages of individuals convened by an address that treats them as, in principle, anonymous, interchangeable, and indefinitely extensible) were a product of social developments in Europe from the late eighteenth century onward. The industrial revolution and the massive urbanization that accompanied it produced the possibility of conceiving of collectivities united not by the multiple filaments of kinship, co-residence, or cooperation, but by the sheer fact of human interchangeability. If workers, severed from ownership of the means of production, could be reduced to units of labor power for sale on the open market, then human beings could be imagined as equivalent and duplicable. The use of identical uniforms in armies, the rise of organized team sport based on a rigorous exclusion of all considerations except a specific ability, the gradual democratizing and anonymizing of pews in churches, and the introduction of fixed, rigid rows of seating in schools—as well as the new use of the "simultaneous" method in which a master addressed all the pupils at once instead of engaging in a series of dialogues with individuals or small groups—indicated that principles of uniformity and equivalence were replacing the mixed, variably convened groupings that had prevailed before.

In nineteenth- and twentieth-century West Africa, these same disciplines of time and space were imported by missionaries, employers, and town planners but imposed on a different social reality (see Barber 1997b for a fuller development of this point). In western Nigeria, as in much of West Africa, the rapid urbanization that took place was not primarily industrial but commercial and administrative. Workers were much more often hustlers, petty traders, or brokers in the informal sector than waged employees. They were not usually wholly separated from their traditional means of production—migrant workers and even long-term urban residents kept one foot in their home town and their fathers' farms (see Berry 1985; Guyer 1997). In the shifting unstable domain of the urban informal sector, individual difference, personal relationships, and creative abilities to innovate and mediate were often essential to economic survival.

In post-colonial western Nigeria, it would be difficult to discern the abstract, impersonal institutional systems which Giddens (1990) sees as characteristic of modernity. People do not rely on neutrally efficient banks, legal institutions, and public services to underpin their daily operations.

"Trust" is not vested in impersonal systems but in personally created and maintained networks. Market women, for example, may have very little in the way of formal occupational organization or institutional backing, but they establish and maintain long-term relations of personal trust with suppliers which may extend far outside their own area and even into other ethnic groups (Trager 1976, 262). Making one's way in life is essentially a matter of creating links between people with potential resources and personally orchestrating a variety of skills and activities; the dynamic of local economies can only be understood in terms of individual career-making, not in terms of abstract market rationality (Guyer 1997). Old modes of organization were not superseded by the colonial state and economy, but were co-opted into it, adapted, and in some ways strengthened (Berry 1985, 9–10). The state itself, moreover, lacked the regulatory power either to account for all its citizens or to hold them accountable. Births, marriages, and deaths went unrecorded; censuses were a joke; tax evasion was rampant; the law was unevenly and capriciously enforced; and there was no conscription or other mandatory public service required of all citizens alike. In Habermas's account, the emergence of the public sphere is a dimension of the rise of the European nation-state; and, according to Benedict Anderson (1983), a nation is characterized by having a bounded, finite population of individuals made conscious of themselves—through public media such as the press and the novel—as existing in relations of equivalence and simultaneity to each other. In Nigeria, where the nation's constituent local populations were incorporated so unevenly and where public institutions were so variably accessible, this sense of equivalent and simultaneous accountability did not take hold. On the contrary, the uncertainties spawned by the unpredictable incursions of state authority into people's lives may have served to develop the existing cultural emphasis on the proliferation of individual difference and on personal self-making, rather than changing the mold. Contrary to Giddens's assumption, the field of relations thus constituted is not necessarily a short-lived transitional phase between "tradition" and Western-type modernity; on the contrary, it is a functioning mode which could perpetuate itself indefinitely.

The disciplines of equivalence were thus imported in the forms of church, school, army, and organized sport but were laid upon a population whose inner dynamic was geared toward the production and maintenance of differences rather than equivalence. The alien, objectifying, and repressive intent of such European disciplinary impositions has been brilliantly analyzed in the case of Egypt (Mitchell 1988); but in western Nigeria, what is remarkable is not so much the repressive nature of these uses of time and space as the way in which they were taken up, and radically modified, by innovative Yoruba cultural producers to realize their own projects.

It would not be too far-fetched, I think, to see this as one of the central characteristics of a typically West African modernity: a modernity defined not so much by the full insertion of plastic human activities and bodies into new disciplines of space and time (Giddens 1990) as by a partial and creative modification of these disciplines, which adopts them and yet subjects them to continual attack.

In the plays, the chosen disciplines of space and time are under constant threat of irruption or erasure. The plot is open to ad hoc additions, omissions, embellishments, and excursions. The actors' line formation is constantly ruffled by effervescent eruptions of movement. The audience hurls slogans and comments back over the divide, addressing the actors (or rather their public personae established by their television roles) as often as the characters. The actors' oblique delivery is constantly on a knife-edge between illusionistic depiction of "real life" (as in Ibsen) and presentational entertainment (as in music hall).[5] It always reserves the capacity to veer into one or the other. Thus, direct address to the audience is always an option. The outermost frame of the show as a whole is direct address: during the opening glee, Mr. Adéjobí would always speak to the audience, welcoming them, saying something topical about the occasion or the town, announcing the title of the play—and sometimes even reprimanding them for not turning up in sufficient numbers! At the end, Adéjobí, if he was on stage, or another leading character if he was not, would in many cases sum up the moral, announce the end of the show, and thank the audience for attending. The distinction between dramatic representation and direct address could be deliberately elided at the end of the play. *External Appearances* ends with a final church service in which the "lesson" of the play is spelled out by John Adéwuni, who played the Aládùúrà preacher. He speaks from a position simultaneously in character and out of it, perhaps underlining the actors' conception of themselves as *all* being preachers whatever character they play:

> We give thanks to God, that He helped us to accomplish this much. This is where we hang up the scythe of this event [i.e., bring it to a close]. The play that you've been watching all this time, *External Appearances,* our prayer is that all you members of the audience, may God not let you suffer failure. Let me give you a prayer before you go. Close your eyes, let us pray. In the name of Jesus, may God save us from failure. Greetings for having come to see the play. Thank you. Good-night. May our own deeds not spoil our lives.

The audience replied "*Àmín oo!*" [Amen] and joined in a final rendition of the hymn that had just been part of the last scene. The impersonal "broadcast" of the picture-frame stage was thus intermittently disrupted by lively direct exchanges across the divide between stage and auditorium.

The "public," correspondingly, though conceived as anonymous, is also credited with the potential to coagulate into differentiated, individual, known persons—but in a different way from the personal and individual audiences of *alárìnjó* troupes. Though acting was an unjustly despised profession, the actors also repeatedly affirmed that one of its great advantages was that it made the actors socially visible, "known to many people," and thus better placed to operate the networks of influence and access. At all levels of society, all operations from the most mundane to the most esoteric were facilitated by "helpers," personal contacts who were prepared to smooth one's path: and helpers cluster around the socially salient. The theater company members were clear that "being known" helped them in practical ways. As John Adéwuni put it:

> The benefits are that . . . take me now, as I am now, because people know me through my work, they've seen me on television, they've heard me on the radio, they've seen me in *Atóka*. So, because I'm well known, if I have an important request to make of someone they'll be quick to help. They'll quickly recognize you: "Isn't this the person who entertained us on television?" "This is the person who performs on radio!" "I myself saw you in such and such a show," and they'll be happy to help you. That's why I say that the benefits of this work are many. If you require some assistance of some kind, if you go to someone and say "I want you to help me with such and such a thing," when they recognize you they'll say "Ah! Aren't you Tàfá Olóyèdé that we see on television, ah, aren't you Bàbáa Wándé, aren't you the Ìyá Òsogbo." And they'll quickly solve your problem for you. It's a great benefit, a great benefit.

The "help" that such recognition might bring was not necessarily trivial. In a situation where every routine bureaucratic procedure is an obstacle race, being known could save one's sanity or even one's life. Alhaji explained the benefits of being in the theater as follows:

> I like the profession. The reason is this, why I like the profession. First, many people admire my performance. The way they talk to me, the way they acted to me in the town, the way many people approaches me entice me much, that I cannot leave the profession. Many people says to me "I enjoy my performances." So many people help me whenever I need help. Like say, when I go to any bank in Òsogbo, I can't stay long there. The clerk helps me, they recognize me and help me with my problem. When I go to hospital, the same thing happens. Anywhere I need help in many offices, they recognize me and give me the help immediately. And I know many important big men, big men. (English.)

The benefits of "being known to many people," moreover, went beyond solving practical problems such as getting money from the bank or getting treatment in the hospital. Social salience was both the sign and the source of prestige. To be a big man was to be *recognized* as a big man, and thus to command resources of influence, assistance, and praise. Being visible was the center of the whole process.[6] There is a proverb that says *A wá owó lọ, a pàdé iyì lọ́nà; bá a bá ti rówó, iyì náà kọ́ là á fi rà?* [You go off in search of money, you meet prestige on the way; if you had got the money, surely it's prestige you would have bought with it anyway?] That is, the goal and culmination of the process of self-aggrandizement is social recognition, being attended upon and looked up to by many people. Wealth that is not converted into esteem is pointless. John pointed out that there were people much richer than he who did not enjoy the same degree of public recognition:

> There certainly are rich people who don't have that kind of advantage. There are some people who have money, but no one knows them—they and their money are quite unknown. We, now, are still praying that God will soon open the way for us too to become rich, but even in our present situation, people know us well, and say "Ah, we've seen you on television, we've heard you on the radio, we've seen you in *Atọ́ka*," and they are happy to see you. . . . As we go about, we hear "Tàfá! Tàfá Olóyèdé! Father of Wándé! Lágbénjó the Òṣogbo woman!" and all kinds of things like that.

The women in the company were as positive as the men that performing on stage made them "known to many people" and that this was a social advantage. As Margaret Adéjọbí put it:

> The difficulties of this work are many and outweigh the profit. **But, there is one advantage, and that's that this work makes people know you, do you understand?** Some people watch you **on the telly, so,** you might meet them and they might be a source of help [in the future].

Nobody suggested that fame or public visibility was enough: all, like John, prayed that the theater would become more profitable and that in future they would become rich. But the salience the theater conferred on them was in their view the greatest asset they had.

Thus, although their performance style presumes an essentially anonymous mass of equivalent spectators, their reflections on the theater presume that within that anonymous mass there may always be potential "helpers." Whereas *alárìnjó* performers were anonymous (their human identities concealed beneath the mask) and their audiences known and concretely manifest in all their magnificence, in the theater it was the actors who were known, while the audience remained a shadowy reservoir of admirers who might at some point step forward and announce their intention to help. Being known *by* the audience in a sense dissolved the audience's anonymity, because it potentially led to contacts, interactions, and assistance outside the performance space. What we have here is not a pyramid of "patrons" and "clients" corresponding to a fixed social hierarchy, but a rhizomatic network of interactions in which one's "helper" may be either superior or inferior in status to oneself. A bank clerk, a hospital orderly, an office boy who refrains from "losing" an all-important file is a helper as much as the "many important big men" that Alhaji had come to know through his acting. An audience is unknown, but it is a sea of potential helpers, big and small; by making themselves salient before them, the actors can seek to activate this potentiality.

In addressing their audience as a "public" the theater company was envisaging the widest possible market for its wares. Unhooked from calendrical and social divisions, it stretched, potentially, to the borders of the Yorùbá-speaking zone and beyond. The anonymity of their address announced that anyone and everyone who could afford the price of a ticket had equal access to the show. This address, however, cannot be explained simply as a by-product of an across-the-board "commercialization of culture." The popular theater practitioners *added* a professional, profit-making mode of performance to an existing repertoire which included festival and ritual drama, domestic and civic performances of praise poetry, and amateur fund-raising shows. They did so not only because they saw an opportunity for making a living by producing a type of spectacle for which people were prepared to pay; but also because to address an extensive, undifferentiated public was to lay claim to a particular inflection of modernity—a modernity which was never mere mimicry of forms introduced by missionary and colonial authorities, but which creatively and flexibly exploited those forms to activate potential social and moral assets. The audience, in turn, brought to the regulated, internally undifferentiated space of the popular theater's auditoria their own personal agendas: refusing the theater company's claims to preacherly superiority but actively seeking out do-it-yourself edification. Both actors and audience, then, saw their role as actively instigatory; where their respective creative activities met, plays and publics were simultaneously generated.

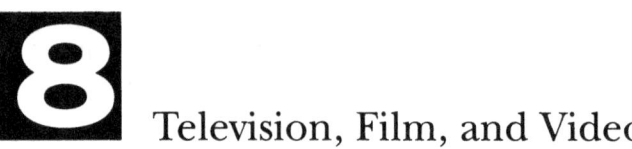# 8 Television, Film, and Video

TELEVISION IN WESTERN NIGERIA

The Western Nigeria Television Service, established in 1959, was the first in sub-Saharan Africa. By 1962 the two other regions of Nigeria had followed suit.

Television throughout Africa is a "mass" medium that is available not to the "masses" but only to those relatively wealthy people who can afford to buy a set. In Nigeria, however, this anomaly appears to be less pronounced than elsewhere. According to the Nigerian Television Authority's own estimates, in the programming year 1983/1984 there were 5 million television sets functioning in Nigeria, distributed among a total population of some 100 million people (Ẹsan 1994). This may have been an exaggeration, for UNESCO's estimate for 1987—5.6 per 1,000 people—was almost ten times lower. But there is no doubt that by the late 1970s, many people in western Nigeria did have at least intermittent access to TV. Communal viewing meant that popular programs might attract audiences up to 20 times greater than the number of television owners in the relevant region. Parlors became small cinemas when a popular program began. Certainly by the early 1980s my impression was that in towns that had an electricity supply most people could get access to a TV set if there was something they really wanted to watch.

There was a proliferation of television stations in Nigeria quite unparalleled elsewhere in Africa. Tensions between the federal center and the regions over the distribution of resources led to repeated subdivisions of political units: after the civil war, state creation proceeded apace, and by 1992 the original three regions—legacy of the Richards and Macpherson constitutions of 1948 and 1952—had become 30 states. Each state required its own parastatal organizations; each aspired to having its own television station as well as its own university. Unresolved issues of power sharing between the federal center and the states, together with the alternation of military and civilian regimes with different attitudes toward centralization, led to a situation where 10 of the states had federal stations as well as their own state-owned stations after 1976. In the crowded southwest of the country, where the population density is high and the states are geographically small, there were towns where it was possible to receive as many as seven or eight different stations.

This proliferation and reduplication of stations quickly exhausted available resources of funding and trained personnel. Even during the height of the oil boom in the 1970s, television stations were run on a shoestring by civil servants not trained in media production. The outcome, anatomized by Louise Bourgault (1995) and Oluyinka Ẹsan (1994), was an inflexible, incompetent management; technicians who were overworked and undervalued; equipment which broke down and was not replaced; and programming which reflected the interests of the political elite, not those of the general public, giving extended sycophantic coverage to the speeches of the military or civilian leaders and little else in the way of "news." Lack of funds did not lead to massive purchases of cheap American serials, contrary to assumptions of the cultural imperialism thesis. Even in the early 1990s, after the Nigerian economy had collapsed and the naira had been devalued to a hundredth of its former exchange value, the federal stations, as a matter of policy, kept foreign imported programs down to about 10 percent of total broadcasting, while the state-owned stations managed 20–30 percent. But lack of funds did mean that more and more airtime was given to unimaginative static discussion programs and speeches by local dignitaries and less and less was given to active investigative reporting and documentary.

Television in Nigeria, then, seems a classic example of imported technology and imported communication genres, adopted for prestige reasons in an atmosphere of regional political competition and individual elite self-aggrandizement, ill-adapted to local needs and conditions. Television was usually boring: "news" which contained no information, "quiz shows" which failed to generate any interest in who won, "talk shows" which put even the talk show host himself to sleep (Bourgault 1995, 50). "It is a nauseating business," one of Ẹsan's illiterate woman respondents told her. "Don't study us. The media don't care for us. It [TV] is not meant for us and we have nothing to say about it" (Ẹsan 1994, 279).

But the hunger of the undernourished media gave western Nigerian television stations—already committed to promoting Yorùbá cultural traditions—an added incentive to invite existing performing groups into their studios. Rather than trying to form new television-oriented cultural groups, they often simply provided air time for popular culture that was already flourishing outside the media. Ẹsan's study—one of the first to deal in depth with media audience responses anywhere in sub-Saharan Africa—shows that audiences outside the educated elite had little interest in imported American and other films. The one genre which unfailingly drew large and raptly attentive television audiences in western Nigeria was the Yorùbá drama. In the household of an elderly woman who was uneducated but well-respected, one of the wives of the Ọba of the town, a crowd "made up of members of different households" was constituted in the parlor when the children announced that a Yorùbá drama was coming up:

> A few people, mainly children and one young mother were the first to report to await a programme which they knew would be coming on. The initial group summoned the other parties who were known to be interested in the viewing.... In doing this, others for whom the summons had not been intended, also overheard and thus became aware of, or were reminded of the programme.... In no time the sitting room was so full that there was not enough space to sit in. The children were made to sit on the carpet.... All the viewers, irrespective of their ages contributed to an on going commentary. (Ibid., 252)

These viewers, who regarded government news and information programs as "lies," and who could not, or did not want to, follow the dialogue of *I Love Lucy* or *Rocky I, II, III, IV,* and *V,* all maintained that the Yorùbá drama was "true" and that it imparted valuable guidelines by which they could steer their own lives. It is said that Jímọ̀ Àlíù's TV drama series *Arélù* was so popular in the mid-1980s that on Tuesdays at 7:30 P.M. you could drive your car from one end of Ìbàdàn to the other without meeting anyone else on the road.

REASONS FOR BEING ON TV

Television was associated with the formal sector, with government, and with educated personnel. It was seen as more respectable than live theater and therefore more suitable for women, well-to-do people, and elderly people. Adédùnmọ́lá, Adéjọbí's eldest daughter, wanted to go to university to study theater arts and then to become a producer in a television station:

> Maybe that's how it will be, because, as a woman.... if I were a man, now, maybe I would be able to do it properly [full-time], by traveling around, performing plays on stage all around.

Adédùnmọ́lá retained a sense that the full-blooded live traveling theater was the real thing, but that for a female graduate, television work was a more appropriate destination. Educated people were not averse to appearing on television, whereas they would not normally consider braving the late-night rowdy audiences in a live stage performance. Adédùnmọ́lá, while working as an untrained teacher in a local school, was approached by another teacher:

> A certain "sewing mistress" told me she had seen me in *Atọ́ka*—those magazines that have pictures in them—she saw me in it, and she was saying she would really like to do some acting work. She said one day when the opportunity arose, if they were performing for the television or for the radio, could I come and call her? I said I would call her if she had the time and the interest to do it.

The sewing mistress knew about Adédùnmọ́lá's participation in the theater through a magazine, not through having seen her on stage; and she specified television and radio as the only two formats she wanted to become involved in. This might partly have been because television and radio were perceived as "one-off" types of performance which would not take her away too much from her regular job; but since one-off participation in stage plays was perfectly possible—indeed easy, as I discovered myself—this cannot have been the whole reason.[1]

Adéjọbí often seemed to be thinking of a television audience when he spoke of the devotion of his "public," and he set store by the fact that such audiences included middle-class professional people:

> After you'd gone yesterday, I had some visitors from Ìlọrin. One was a chief engineer. One was formerly the producer of drama at NTA in Lagos, but he's now joined Philip Morris [tobacco]. That chief engineer was somebody I didn't know at all. I had never met him before. He was a Yorùbá. And he said he thanked God that he had met me face to face today. He said that he had never believed that he would meet me until the day he died. Why all this? His wife and children were devoted fans of our program, *Magistrate's Court*. It meant the world to them.

Implicit in the chief engineer's remarks is the suggestion that Yorùbá television drama is the province of women and children, at least among the elite: it is harmless, respectable family viewing but not sufficiently demanding for the chief engineer himself to admit to watching. In this respect it contrasts strongly with the overwhelmingly male ambience of the live, late-night shows. In small monogamous middle-class families, however, the preferences of the wife and children make more of an impact on the paterfamilias than they might in a lower-class domestic scene: thus the whole elite family is involved, and that is why the chief engineer was dying to meet Adéjọbí.

Television is apparently sufficiently respectable to reconcile angry parents to their children's choice of acting as a career. Isiaka's father was furious when he abandoned his training as a welder and joined Oyin Adéjọbí.

But though he would never go to see live theater, he saw Isiaka on TV and was appeased:

> He's happy that he sometimes comes across me on the television. He'll say "Ha, I greeted you and greeted you" and I'll say that I answered. He'll say "I greeted you and you just didn't answer me." I'll say I answered, and we'll make a big joke of it.

But while television may be a more respectable medium than the stage, the theater company members did not feel themselves to be addressing only the elite when they broadcast their drama through television. On the contrary, they took it for granted that they attracted television audiences of millions, including the kind of people who made up their typical stage audience. Adéjọbí said that he had discovered that it was a mistake to make TV drama out of the same plays that they did on stage, because then the audience would not come to see the live theater. "They'll tell you straight that I can't go again and spend my money, I'll watch the play on television." This assumes that all, or most, of the people who would normally watch live shows also had access to a television; there is no suggestion of a class gap between the stage and television audiences, only a presumption that the television audience was wider, embracing elites as well as the lower classes. Adéjọbí conceived of the TV audience as enormous: speaking of the economic drawbacks of television work in comparison with live theater with paying audiences, he said "One can just think of how many people watch the television, watch your plays, millions of them. Let's say each one of these people pay one naira each, you could imagine how much that would bring to you!"

Television, then, to the theater company was the supreme means of becoming "publicly known." It enhanced their visibility enormously because of its range. In their discussion of the advantages of theater, John, Grace, and Isiaka all cited their media appearances—principally television but also radio and print—as the main vehicles of their public salience. It invested an ordinary appearance with magnetic and memorable qualities. As Grace put it:

> What I see there is that it [theater] gives people public recognition, things we do like television dramas and so forth. Well, when I go out, haggard and shabby as I am, there's nothing but people mobbing me, saying this is "Ìyálóde" going by, this is so-and-so going by. It makes them know you.

Several of the younger members of the company had become interested in theater work not because they had seen the company on stage or because they had participated in school drama but because they had seen the company's plays featured in *Atọ́ka* or watched them on television. And when John Adéwuni ran away from his uncle's house in Ilóbùú to rejoin the Adéjọbí Company, he claimed that no one had the slightest idea where he was. They searched for him everywhere, thinking maybe he'd run away to Lagos, never suspecting that he had come back to the profession he had been earlier dragged away from in Òṣogbo. "It was when they saw me on television that they first knew I had come back here." The suggestion is that his own family, farmers and small-town people, watched television as a matter of course, and that his appearance in a program gave him instant visibility across the Yorùbá-speaking area.

The distance, diffusion, and invisibility of television viewers thus heightened the performers' dual conceptualization of the spectating crowd that was already present, as we have seen, in their relations to their live audiences. Television fostered the idea of the audience as an anonymous and, in principle, infinitely extensive public, at the same time sharpening the performers' sense not only of their own personal distinctiveness and visibility but also their potential to be recognized (and therefore "helped") by individual members of the public.

In itself, television drama was not a particularly good business proposition, because it was not under the company's own control. Television stations had the potential to do the theater companies a lot of good, but both Alhaji and Adéjọbí said that in practice they were a disappointment. They often did not pay the agreed-upon fee on time or in full; sometimes they negotiated a fee and, after the company had invested a lot of time, money, and effort in creating a new production for them, would admit that the station could not afford to pay it:

> An example is what happened recently, when a television station in Lagos approached me for a full-length play. We had earlier agreed on an amount of money, but later on, I got a letter from them. They've agreed to pay that money, we both agreed to the sum. We have even rehearsed the play and I have sent in the particulars. They had even given me the dates, about three or four days in which the play will be recorded by them, from Lagos. Okay, we were all the way expecting them when I got another letter that the station would not be able to pay the money again, so, unless I could agree that a sum of one thousand is taken off. In fact, I have got no time to reply or to react to that station. I am still looking, I don't know what to say because they wasted a lot of my time. We kept at home rehearsing this play. We bought props and costumes, we booked locations and so on and so forth. So the station just disappointed us, that's just it. (English.)

Television stations also repeated and transferred recordings without permission and without paying a repeat fee or royalties. Mr. Adéjọbí gave the example of NTA Àkúrẹ́, which commissioned from him a series of 13 full-length plays and then pulled out after the theater company had already composed, rehearsed, and costumed them, because it had acquired another set of their plays which had already been recorded for NTA Abẹ́òkúta. "Without my permission and without any repeat fee whatsoever! So I lost the money which could have been paid for me if I had recorded the 13 full-length plays for Àkúrẹ́, and I lost the repeat fee which either Abẹ́òkúta or Àkúrẹ́ should have paid to us."

There was not much the theater company could do about this. When I asked him if such maneuvers were not illegal, Mr. Adéjọbí replied philosophically:

> Well, it is illegal, but the television has some funny ways of frustrating one's effort. They would tell you they have no money, or once they have paid you, you are not entitled to anything again. And since the television station belongs to the government, to whom can you go again? Go to anywhere, they direct you to the government. I remember a television station, I wouldn't mention the name, that television station is owing my group some amount of money. When I started pressing for the money the television station was advising me to go to court or anything like that, the authority would then know that they have been punishing the artist. But take the government to court, what do you try to gain there? (English.)

A live stage play, by contrast, was completely under the theater company's control and the payment for each performance was instant. The company was in charge of every aspect of the play's production, advertising, and distribution; they had the tickets printed themselves, sold them at the door, and counted the take on the spot. Adéjọbí and Alhaji were very definite in their assertion that for these reasons the live theater was "better" than television.

Nonetheless, television was a valued outlet. There is no doubt that injections of substantial sums—when the television stations did get round to paying—could help to tide the company over difficult patches. More important, everyone agreed that the television was a valuable form of "advertising." Because of its immense reach, it turned popular actors into household names. It is striking that when the audiences hailed Alhaji, John, Emily, or Grace as they walked onto the stage, it was almost always with the names of characters they played in *Magistrate's Court,* the long-running television serial that Adéjọbí launched in 1967 and which most people in western Nigeria seemed to have watched at one time or another. This kind of recognition, the actors felt, would encourage people to go to the stage plays, which were the real source of income for the company. John thought that "nowadays, people who watch television are beginning to outnumber [those who go to see live plays], and if people get to know us through the television, then when they hear [about a live performance] they'll say 'Oh, so they're going to perform in Òṣogbo today!,' they'll say 'Oh, I'm going to watch the people I saw on television, I'm going to see so-and-so that I often see on TV.'"

In addition to its capacity to promote public recognition, television was valued by members of the company for its associations with "modernity." It involved a technology which was exogenous to their own means of cultural production, and which was costly and prestigious. Adédùnmọ́lá thought more highly of television acting than stage acting because it involved a tougher exposure:

> I prefer television work. The reason is that it gives people more of what the Europeans call "**experience.**" For example if they put a camera in your face, you learn not to be too panic-stricken, and if you can act in front of a camera then you can do anything. Stage performances or anything.

The experience gained from performing in front of a television camera seemed to Adédùnmọ́lá more genuine, and harder won, than the (to me) much more frightening experience of improvising in front of hundreds of roaring teenagers. It was an experience that brought the actors into confrontation with a world of technological expertise normally not under their control; by holding their own, they not only inoculated themselves against the anxieties of one sector of modernity but also at the same time primed themselves for success in all spheres of performance, old and new.

But there were aesthetic reasons too for making television drama. Adéjọbí and Alhaji both saw television as having the edge over the stage because of what it could show. Alhaji was emphatic:

> There are very many things that television can show. You can see, or you can use, a river on television. You can't bring a car on the stage. You can climb an upstair and you hide there on the roof, which cannot occur on the stage. (English.)

Not only did it give them more scope to show a wide range of settings, but it enabled their drama to "look somewhat real," in Adéjọbí's words. "You act in such a location which will look as reality. For instance, if you have any play in which you have a part to be played in the forest or in water, or any other location which could not be easily brought to the stage." On stage, however, "you only go on, make use of only one set throughout." The idea of using a variety of stage sets to create the illusion of different places was dismissed. Scene changes would take too long: "Do you ask your audience to wait until you change over? So, it is not practicable. It is not possible at all."

The effect of "looking somewhat real" extended to performance style.

As we have seen, the influence of television was instrumental in bringing about the gradual shift from sung to spoken text, at first in the plays they did for television but later in their stage plays too. Adéjọbí knew that this transition would marginalize his own great creative gifts as a composer. "Personally," he said, "I was finding it difficult to just abandon music in my play. But I have to ... especially when we started with television, because television wouldn't so much like music, too much music, expressing yourself with music in the play. They feel you will not be able to act to it." Despite personal regrets, he defended the change in the name of modernity. He gave a vivid demonstration of the advantages of spoken dialogue, delivering God's conversation with Adam ("Adam, where are you?" "I hear you, in the garden; I am afraid, because I am naked") first in song and then in naturalistic speech, with humorously appropriate intonation and facial expressions. He asked me which I preferred, and concluded "when you sing, you cannot act with the music. But when you say it in words you'll be able to act to it. That is why the modern way of drama is better than the olden days." This preference for naturalistic representation is symptomatic of the theater's larger conception of personhood, character, and narrative, and I return to it in Chapters 9 and 11.

The television producers' intervention was mildly coercive. They would vet every program, scrutinize the synopses, and watch rehearsals. Their recommendations, Adéjọbí suggests, were always accepted without dispute. "It is their duty to comment on the play and see that the play is suitable for the television.... The reason is that the television wouldn't like any political play or any play which will show some sort of immorality and so on. And after seeing the rehearsal, they make all necessary corrections. For instance, where you hope to sit down to express yourself in the play, they tell you that it is better to stand up, to drive your point home, and many things like that." Their intervention, then, went beyond a general government censorship to detailed advice about staging and performance style. While their interference may have been resented at times, it was also accepted because the media represented modernity. "As time went on, enlightenment increased," as Alhaji said when describing the theater's increasing use of naturalistic dialogue. He associated lifelike dialogue with "enlightenment" because the model for it came from the modern electronic media.

MAKING *HOSPITAL (ILÉ-ÌWÒSÀN)*

This is what I wrote in my diary:

SATURDAY 13 JUNE 1981

> Everyone sat around the big room where goats wander in and thought of the names they would be called in the TV-Àkúrẹ́ Hospital Series. I was drinking my third cup of tea [in Emily's room,

where I had slept], when I heard "Àjíkẹ́ là ń dúró dè" [It's Àjíkẹ́ we're waiting for], so I hastened out. I said I would like to be called Dr. Johnson. They said what about Dr. Àjíkẹ́? The other doctor was Dr. Àlàbí. Ìyá Adé and Ìyá Ají were to be nurses, while Fẹ́mi of Ìlá was the card-man (who handles the patient records and admission to the doctor's surgery). Then we were measured for our costumes. They decided I should have a dark-blue overall with a white cap. "Don't you think a doctor would wear a white coat and no cap?" I asked. "Yes, in real life that's true," explained Alhaji, "but this is for drama—the costumes have to contrast and show up on the screen."

Then we began rehearsing. The story of the episode and my part in it had already been described to me yesterday. The hospital staff were summoned to a meeting by the Doctor Àgbà [senior consultant], played by Adéjọbí, to decide what to do about a letter from the Ministry of Health which says that the people of the town have been bringing complaints and have written to the Ministry accusing the hospital nurses of hostility, lack of sympathy, and rudeness, while the doctors are accused of driving people out of the hospital like goats. Each member of staff is to speak for himself in turn. Adéjọbí recapitulated this scenario and then said "Now let's do it." We all huddled together on a bench while Doctor Àgbà lectured us. Nurse and doctor spoke indiscriminately. The next time round I suggested that the two doctors should sit by themselves and be given precedence: but when we came in one by one, the Doctor Àgbà still told us off like naughty schoolchildren, and we had to make excuses for being late.

After Dr. Àgbà has described the contents of the letter, Dr. Àlàbí speaks. The gist of his speech is that it is true that he drives people out of his ward and that he will continue to drive them! They come rushing in in eights and tens to visit sick relatives, waking up those who should be sleeping, feeding those who shouldn't eat. Then Dr. Àjíkẹ́ intervenes, saying reasonably that all this is quite true but it's not their fault, because they don't know any better. "*Àìmọ̀ ló fà á.*" [It's caused by ignorance.] So we shouldn't drive them out rudely, but try to explain to them. Dr. Àlàbí replies that driving them out is the only thing that will make any impression on them. The stories told by the two nurses and by the card-man seem to confirm that the general attitude is that these dirty, ignorant, superstitious, head-strong louts deserve everything they get. Only the Gateman (Alhaji) is on the side of the townspeople, being one of them (as Alhaji put it himself). He lets the visitors in because he doesn't see why they shouldn't greet their sick relatives. At the end of the scene, he is told off by Doctor Àgbà.

Throughout this episode, Alhaji was telling us what to say— in some cases, word for word (Adéjọbí kept doing something different and with teeth-gritting politeness Alhaji told him again and again exactly what to say, Adéjọbí painstakingly writing it down, because, he said, this TV business has to be right once and for all). In other cases, he organised their material for them—Ìyá Ají had to reorganise her speech so that she started with the story of the Baálé's wife giving the new-born baby tea, which in her first attempt came somewhere in the middle. Ìyá Adé was given lines to remember. We went through it again to time it, because it had to be "more or less half an hour." It was 25 minutes with a few bits repeated.

The second episode continued the general trend of lampooning the townspeople: an anxious husband is getting *àgúnmu* for his wife who is in labour; her friend comes in and persuades him much against his will to go to the hospital because she has been in labour since yesterday morning. They have never been to hospital before. The nurses tell them off (the "lesson" of this episode was that you should attend antenatal clinic regularly), hustle the wife into the labour ward and send the husband off for the list of necessary things, starting with a [razor] blade. The case is serious: things have been left too late; the Gateman overhears Dr Àlàbí saying they'll have to give her blood, and tells the husband to fetch two bottles of it. "Èjè? Kó sáà sọ ó kalè láyò, èjè ò sòro" [Blood? I just want her to give birth safely, getting the blood is not a problem] says the husband and hurries off, coming back with two bottles saying "Mo kókó lọ Sábó, wón ní èjè ti gbẹ ńbè, mo bá loolé mo pa ewúrẹ ìyá ìyàwóò mi, èjè náà rèé" [I tried Sábó (the Hausa section of town where cattle are slaughtered) first, they said the blood had all dried up there, so I went home and killed my mother-in-law's goat, here's the blood]. The nurse (Ìyá Ají) and Dr Àlàbí make fun of the poor man and tell him off. The Gateman is also scolded for interfering.

The husband was Bàbáa Fàtáì, a new member of the company (though apparently known to me as the manager of Ògúndélé's theatre in the past: he seemed to have left after a disagreement, and his c. v. which I caught a glimpse of in Adejọbí's hand showed that he'd been with a different company almost every year for the last twenty years). He wasn't a very good actor and was dictated to by Alhaji without much success.

The third episode however altered the apparent trend of the series' world view. John was a man in terrible pain because of a great weight on his head, it was entering his neck, or his neck was entering him. He gave realistic and frightening jerks and spasms of agony. His friend persuades him to go back to the hospital, though the last time he went the medicine they gave him didn't work for long. Dr Àlàbí looks at him and says he should go and get another X-ray: the first one, which revealed nothing, can't have been right. While they are waiting for the result, the Gateman (to Dr Àlàbí's impatient contempt) discourses on *ayé* and says that this is a clear case if ever there was one, and that if he is given a chance he can cure the man. Dr Àlàbí waves him away. But when Dr Àlàbí goes out, the Gateman seizes the opportunity to teach the man an *ọfọ̀* [incantation], which he repeats after him with *atare* [hot pepper] in his mouth. Instantly he is cured. Dr Àlàbí is flabbergasted; the nurses confirm "Béè ni, ayé ń bẹ" [It's true, witchcraft (lit. "the world") exists].

By now it was after four. . . .

That evening there was a stage performance at the Advanced Teachers College, and the following week there was a trip to Lagos to perform in the National Theatre. The rehearsals for the TV show were resumed the following weekend.

FRIDAY 19 JUNE

I'd promised to be there by 8.30, but didn't leave Ifẹ̀ until then, and got there at 9.30, meeting all the company sitting round for rehearsal, but no television people. "A à rí wọn" [We haven't seen them] was the first thing Adéjọbí said. We rehearsed all day, with a two-hour lunch break in the afternoon, and didn't stop until eight. We set up the whole quarter's ration of episodes—13 altogether. I'd missed 4 and 5, but watched the rehearsal of all the others.

I was to examine Bàbáa Fàtáì, as Bàbáa Tinúkẹ́ (who had taken a herbal infusion with cassava meal instead of corn starch and therefore had terrible stomach-ache) and Adédùn as Tinúkẹ́ (who had taken an overdose of stimulants to get her through her last-minute revision and passed out in the exam). That was episode 6.

Episode 7, according to Adéjọbí, portrayed "Embarrassment at the Hospital." The synopsis as accepted by the TV people was tampered with by Alhaji and would have been tampered with more by a visitor, Elúwolé the manager of Ìṣòlá Ògúnṣolá Theatre, except that Adéjọbí thanked him profusely and adopted none of his elaborate suggestions. It was a story about a widow who owned a beer parlour (originally a young girl who had just left school) who comes to the hospital to have a baby, and after its birth the placenta is claimed by two different boyfriends of hers who each come with a tin to collect it in, and start a fight.

Episode 8 was about a government worker who wants to get sick leave to go to a funeral, so he fakes a high temperature by eating pepper and drinking locally distilled gin. The Doctor Àgbà takes his temperature. They at first thought it would be more impressive to do this with a sphygmomanometer, but since they couldn't get hold of one they decided to make do with the one you put in your mouth. Alhaji taught Doctor Àgbà what to say: "This shouldn't be more than fifty or sixty and it's up to a hundred and seventy! You're on the danger list!" I suggested we could try to make it more realistic: "The temperature ought to be 98.6. If it's very high indeed it might go up to 105 or 106. But not 170! The bloke would be dead!" "Ugh," Alhaji said sarcastically, "not in Africa!" Adéjọbí now started saying "This number, which should be around 98 is now right up to 100! You're on the danger list!" and I regretted my intervention: the numbers were so much less dramatic. Bàbáa Fàtàì was playing this unfortunate man, who is immediately carted off to have an "operation" because his temperature is so high. He found it impossible to say his words right even when Alhaji boiled it down to five simple sentences which he repeated to him in exactly the same form several times. Eventually, he was replaced by John, who did it satisfactorily at the first attempt.

Episode 9 was "Mimipin," a well-worn joke about the Lagos girl who swallows a pin and can't convey to the doctor what the matter is; Dr Àlàbí looks up Mimipin disease in the dictionary and calls in Dr Àjíké as a second opinion. She too is baffled.

Episode 10 is to show that a woman shouldn't be cowardly in labour *(ojora kò dáa)* because she'll wear herself out groaning and won't be able to have the baby under her own power. I was to be the doctor who looked at her and decided "Obìnrin yìí kò lè dá ọmọ bí mọ́, ó ti rè ẹ́. Bá mi gbé e dé ilé iṣẹ́ abẹ" [This woman can no longer give birth unaided, she's exhausted. Take her to the operating theatre].

Episode 11 renews the ambivalent hospital vs. man in the

street attitude. A good Samaritan (Bàbáa Fàtáì again) brings to the hospital a man he found by the wayside knocked down by a hit-and-run driver. The hospital staff detain him until the man revives to tell them that it wasn't Bàbáa Fàtáì who knocked him down but someone else. Bàbáa Fàtáì is angry: "Irú nǹkan báyìí ló ń mú oore ṣú ọ̀pọ̀lọpọ̀ ènìyàn láti ṣe. Tó bá ti kú ńkọ́? Mo dáràn nìyẹn!" [It's this kind of thing that makes a lot of people think twice about helping others. What if he'd died? I'd have been in trouble!] The elder nurse, Ìyá Adé, who has been horrible throughout, especially to women in labour, yells at him that if he doesn't want to do good deeds he needn't bother—and at last gets a ticking-off. Dr Àlàbí, all sweetness and light, explains that they can't help this regulation, they have to have someone at hand to bear witness if the man dies. Bàbáa Fàtáì is appeased.

Episode 12 is a searing indictment of the Card-man, who comes in late, keeps the queuing patents waiting unnecessarily while he reads the paper, is rude and bossy, and finally favours a late-comer who is a pretty woman and related to his family. Violence breaks out, Dr Àlàbí is called in, hears the stories and deduces the truth. The Card-man is told off, but it's obvious that as soon as the doctor goes he's going to relapse into his old ways.

Episode 13 we didn't finish rehearsing before NEPA went. It seemed to be no more than a gruesome representation of a man with cholera whose people neglected to take him to hospital in time—so he dies. Shock horror. Moral (of the whole series): Don't go to *babaláwo* and don't delay going to the hospital.

ITS EDUCATIONAL VALUE

Hospital was explicitly billed as an educational series, not simply in the general sense of providing a useful moral lesson, like all their plays, but in the specific sense of educating the public about modern medicine. Television, associated with the official and formal sectors, was felt to lend itself to the dissemination of messages promoting the values of government institutions. However, it was clear from the beginning that the theater company was not particularly concerned with actual medical advice. They were indifferent to the details of hospital practice, such as the difference in the role and status of doctors and nurses and even the differences between their uniforms. They had little medical knowledge to impart. Alhaji was genuinely incredulous when I pointed out the difference between a thermometer and a sphygmomanometer and was unwilling to change the dialogue in the interests of accuracy. "Operations" of an unspecified nature were recommended with alarming casualness: for a man with a high temperature, for a woman who has been "cowardly" in childbirth. During the rehearsal of the second episode, some of the actors began a discussion of the list of necessities the father-to-be was sent off to fetch. "Is a blade really essential?" one of them asked. "Does it mean a woman can't give birth without a blade?" They discussed this for some time before Alhaji came to the conclusion that women had been giving birth long before razors were imported. The education, then, was not so much in medical knowledge as in a general attitude toward Western medicine. The stories demonstrated over and over again the importance of going to hospital in good time and the dangers in misusing drugs—whether local, such as the *agúnmu* Bàbáa Tinúkẹ́ took with *gaàrí*, or imported, such as the pep pills Tinúkẹ́ took during her exams.

But the structure of the whole series indicates a profound ambivalence about this message. The first episode sets the series up as a conflict between two views of the hospital: that of the hospital staff, who deride the townspeople's ignorance and stupidity, and that of the townspeople, who complain of the hospital staff's callous disregard of their feelings and their convenience. The episodes oscillate between these two views. It is striking that although the hospital staff are played by the core members of the company and are the only characters to recur in every episode, these characters do not have "lives" of their own, unlike in most Euro-American hospital series. There are no doctor-nurse romances, no glimpses into the stress or the drama of a surgeon's day at work. The staff remain as the townspeople must see them: external, authoritarian, unpleasant, autonomous. The "lives" are lived by the townspeople, with their family problems, their friends, their exams, their pregnancies (wanted and unwanted), all only briefly glimpsed for the space of a single episode. But these lives are not, on the whole, portrayed sympathetically. The townspeople are shown as ignorant, foolish, and credulous, even when their indignation against the hospital staff is vindicated. The hospital staff, on the other hand, are not exonerated from blame in the light of the townspeople's idiocy. The card-man is shown up as thoroughly corrupt and lazy. The older nurse is eventually told off for her excessively abusive treatment of the patients. Dr. Àlàbí's Western medical knowledge is shown to be not able to cope with all eventualities.

At the center of this ambivalence is the figure of the Gateman. It is no accident that this literally liminal figure should have been played by the star of the company. The Gateman is a townsman, not a civil servant posted there from elsewhere. He sympathizes with the townspeople and promotes their interests. At the same time he is a member of the hospital staff, subject to hospital regulations. Positioned at the gate, he is responsible for regulating the inflow of townspeople into the hospital. Though a hospital employee, he subverts hospital rules. He lets in far more visitors than he should; he interferes in the doctors' diagnoses and prescriptions. It is he who sends the expectant husband off to fetch two bottles of blood, though it is the husband who is ridiculed in the end. In a later episode, not rehearsed on the days described above, he has a confrontation at the gate with Dr. Àjíkẹ́, in which she tells him "*Màá rí nǹkan ṣe sọ́rọ̀ọ̀ rẹ́*" [I'm going to do something about you]. Dr. Àjíkẹ́ is a kind and sympathetic doctor—the only one in the whole hospital—and her annoyance with the Gateman is supposed to be justified. But the Gateman is not classed with the ignorant townspeople. The episode of *ayé* is crucial. It is the Gateman who correctly diagnoses the cause of the victim's excruciating neck pain, and who—in defiance of Dr. Àlàbí—teaches the man the incantation that removes it. "Traditional" knowledge suddenly rears obstinately up, gaining the endorsement of the nurses ("It's true, *ayé* really exists") and even the bewildered acquiescence of the super-Western Dr. Àlàbí, with his Lagos accent and constant Anglicisms. "Western medicine can't explain everything," says the Gateman, and the hospital employees are forced to admit that this is true.

INVASION OF A MEDIUM

The television people for whom we were anxiously waiting throughout the two weekends described above never came. Mr. Adéjọbí then decided to make the series with a freelance company headed by Mr. Láolú Ògúnníran of Ìbàdàn University. This team came and recorded the first three episodes. The night before they were due to come back to record the rest, a catastrophe occurred. Dayọ̀ Akínpẹ̀lú, who played Dr. Àlàbí in the series, suddenly defected. We heard that he had gone to set up his own theater company. Dr. Àlàbí was crucial to almost every episode. But having waited so long and been disappointed so many times, Mr. Adéjọbí did not want to send the TV people back. Instead, he cancelled the first three episodes and started again, with me as the principal doctor.

We began filming in a hand-to-mouth manner, Alhaji and Mr. Adéjọbí feverishly explaining what I had to do and giving me my key lines immediately before we filmed each episode. The filming was done in a large local house with an open ground-floor reception room–cum–hall and a smaller parlor, which Mr. Adéjọbí had rented for the purpose. The large room was the hospital ward, with a couple of fairly authentic-looking hospital beds, a screen, and a trolley; the smaller room was the doctor's consulting room.

New scenes were invented to take advantage of my new role. One featured a man with swollen testicles. When he was shown into my surgery, he kicked up a great fuss and sulkily refused to be examined by a woman. I was to impart the enlightened message that a doctor is a doctor irrespective of gender and that he should not be so silly as to refuse treatment. Fortunately I was allowed to deliver this wisdom without actually going anywhere near his testicles.

The whole sequence of 13 episodes was filmed in two days. Things did not always happen according to plan. One scene was intended to teach the moral that schoolgirls who become pregnant should not seek abortions. A pregnant girl was to come to my consulting room. I was to confirm the pregnancy, and she was to tell me that she did not want the baby because it would mean dropping out of school. I was to tell her that she should leave school for a year, have the baby, give it to her grandmother to bring up, and return to school. "Don't try to induce an abortion: that's not good. It's against Yorùbá custom." I had more or less mastered this and was sitting at the large table that served as my desk, facing the door, waiting for my patient. The lights were blazing. The camera, placed in the doorway, was looking in with its wicked red eye already winking, when in walked—not a pregnant girl but an enormously fat man.

"What can I do for you?" I asked, trying to conceal my astonishment.

"Well, doctor," he said, "it's my stomach."

"I can see that. But what exactly is the problem?"

"You see, doctor," he explained, "every evening, my stomach swells up like this."

"Every evening?"

"Yes, doctor, every evening without fail. And every morning, it goes down again."

"It goes down again?"

"Yes, doctor."

"Well, that is an unusual problem."

"That's why I've come to see you, doctor."

"Hmmm. Tell me something—what do you normally eat for breakfast?"

"Èbà."

"And for lunch?"

"Èbà."

"And in the evening?"

"Èbà again."

"How many times a day do you eat èbà?"

"Oh, not many times, doctor. Only about five."

"Five times!"

"Five or six."

"In that case, what I recommend is that you reduce the amount of èbà you eat. Don't eat so much èbà—do you hear? Don't eat so much èba. Once a day is enough!"

In this way, another valuable medical lesson was imparted to the public. Later, when I asked what on earth had happened, someone explained airily that the girl had gone off for lunch, so they had had to send in a substitute.

The scenes, then, diverged a great deal from the original synopses and were largely improvised in front of the camera. The timing ("more or less half an hour") must have been very approximate, for we rarely ran through a scene more than once before recording it: there just wasn't time. Nonetheless, the series was purchased by the Ọyọ́ State Television Service and run year after year to great popular satisfaction.

During the next three years, I found out who the most enthusiastic audiences for this kind of television drama were. Girls at supermarket checkouts, clerks in the tax office, motor park touts, gas station attendants, post office workers, bar and restaurant servers—and even bank managers—all recognized me and hailed me as "Doctor! Doctor Àjíké!" My colleagues in the university—whether because they did not watch these programs or because they were too embarrassed at my loss of caste—never said a word about it. I never saw a single episode myself. I could not afford a television on a Lecturer Grade II salary.

Thus, the deference of the theater company, and of Mr. Adéjọbí in particular, to the authority of the television producers was counteracted by a resilient exploitation of all the techniques, repertoires, and skills they had built up in the live theater. Their confidence in their own methods might have been reinforced by memories of their first, much-acclaimed television performance in 1963, when they simply enacted the stage play *Adédigba's Co-wife*—which was in the early stylized, choreographed, and heavily musical format—live in front of the cameras and a studio audience. Though the television managers subsequently encouraged them to shed the songs, submit synopses, and keep to the allotted time, the fact that they started their television careers in full theatrical mode may well have boosted the conviction that they could handle television performance in their own way without needing much guidance. It is true that Mr. Adéjọbí changed the dialogue after I had explained the difference between temperature and blood pressure. I would not have offered any such suggestion if the play had been a stage play; nor would Adéjọbí have welcomed it. It was because I was associated with the formal sector that my role in the television drama was different—both more prominent and more authoritative. But Alhaji was frankly incredulous as well as unwilling to sacrifice a good dramatic effect. Since he was the presiding genius in charge of the whole production process, the theater company cannot have been unduly influenced by the formal sector's interference.

And in any case, it was clear that the television authorities exercised only intermittent and haphazard control. They vetted synopses but accepted programs that did not conform to them; they fixed dates for filming and repeatedly broke them; they commissioned series and canceled them; they bought series that they had not commissioned. Television as a medium was so weak and hungry that the live theater companies could invade it with impunity, importing blatantly populist lampoons of authority even while proclaiming themselves, in all sincerity, as the bearers of formal-sector "enlightenment."

FILM AND VIDEO

In 1988 Alhaji and Adéjọbí began to part company. Both independently began to produce video drama, and in the 1990s Alhaji also started a popular didactic Islamic TV series, *Ìwà Lẹ̀sìn*. The most recent phases of their activity have been almost entirely concentrated on TV, video, and film, to the detriment of the live theater.

After the huge success of Hubert Ògúnǹdé's film *Aiyé*, first shown in 1979, film became the new focus of every theater company's ambitions. Other Yorùbá-language films had been made before this, but *Aiyé* was the first one to enjoy a box office triumph, eclipsing the successes of the live theater. All the theater companies began to search for sponsors and seek out screenplay writers in the hope of making their own films. A surprisingly large number succeeded. In the mid-1980s, cinema began to take over from the live theater as the public's preferred entertainment. Film was prestigious, because it was very expensive to make and because it permitted special effects well beyond the scope of the television programs. Maybe because of that, most theater leaders who managed to raise the capital to make a film began by choosing mythological or supernatural subjects—subjects which had always been regarded as "heavy" and more valuable than contemporary domestic comedies and which lent themselves to extensive use of visual effects. *Aiyé* itself was a graphic portrayal of the nefarious activities of a coven of witches. Mr. Adéjọbí would have made a film of *Ìpadàbọ̀ Odùduwà* [*The Return of Òdùduwà*], his one extant mythological play, if he had been able to persuade the Ọọ̀ni of Ifẹ̀ to commit the capital. Led by the indefatigable Bàbáa Sàlá, however, the film-making groups also mixed in hefty doses of low-life comedy and satire and included among their targets wealthy tycoons whose lives could not easily be represented on the stage but could be suggested on film by the use of shots of splendid mansions, yachts, and limousines.

These films have been dismissed by the major authorities on African cinema (Diawara 1992; Ukadike 1994), and it is true that they have none of the technical sophistication or the stunning visual beauty of the art films being made in Francophone West Africa around the same time; nor do they have the social and political commitment that characterizes many of the Francophone films. They failed to go beyond the live theater on which they were based in terms of ideology, characterization, or conceptualization, while they lacked the essential qualities of linguistic felicity and rapport with a live audience that made the stage plays so brilliant. Nonetheless, they did represent something that was found nowhere else in Africa south of the Sahara: a spontaneous, expanding, and thriving African-language popular cinema which lasted a decade until it was eclipsed by the video boom.

From the point of view of theater companies, there were many advantages in film-making. The prestige of film and the short periods required to rehearse and produce one meant that successful groups could cream off the star actors from several other companies, increasing their box office appeal without committing themselves to a long-term collaboration. Films were seen by the theater companies as far preferable to television drama in every way, above all because the theater company retained control of the product. There was no interference in the production process; they could hire their own experts to write the screenplay, shoot the film, and do the editing. When the film was ready, instead of releasing it to cinemas, they would go on tour with it themselves to all the places where they used to perform their stage plays. Thus they collected the gate money, paid for the hall, and organized the advertising themselves exactly as for a stage play: the only difference was that it was more popular and took much less effort to put on.

Alhaji explained:

Acting on the stage, when you are getting older, it's not easy for an old man to continue acting on the stage. It's not easy, traveling from one town to the other, act today, tomorrow you'll be on the stage.... Next tomorrow you'll just act on the film, you will happy—once—and you'll carry it all over. (English.)

He did not regret the loss of contact with the audience, which he saw entirely in terms of advice the audience could give after the event rather than as the instant oxygen that gave zest and inspiration to the actors' improvisation. He felt that film actually gave better opportunities for gathering feedback than stage plays:

When they [the audience] watch the film—the better—you stay among them, you see their reaction and you listen to their suggestions. (English.)

For many years, Adéjọbí and his company continued to hope that they would find a sponsor. They employed a former member of the company, Sam Babátúndé, who had subsequently taken a film production course in India, to write a screenplay. Meanwhile, individuals in the company, and sometimes the whole core membership, performed in films being put together by other groups. Bàbáa Sàlá's *Moṣebọ́látán*, which was first screened in 1986, starred Alhaji as the protagonist Moṣebọ́látán, and Àlàbí Yellow (who had by then returned to the Adéjọbí Company) as his son; Adéjọbí played the king of the town where Mọṣebọ́látán settles and becomes rich. Bàbáa Sàlá himself was Mọṣebọ́látán's comic, uneducated friend.

However, when sponsorship did not materialize, the Adéjọbí company turned—like many popular theater companies and many new groups formed primarily out of the casts of fairly up-market television serials—to making videos. In the early 1990s there was a video boom. According to Adesanya (1997, 117–18), new videos in the mid-1990s were being turned out at a rate of more than 200 a year, selling between 10 and 60 thousand copies each, which were subsequently extensively re-circulated through illegal dubbing. Swarms of people were competing to get in on the craze:

> In the less than five years of the video rave, close to two thousand new "actors" have emerged and many are ready to hop onto the screen from their other failing vocations. (Jahman Anikulapo, *The Guardian* [Lagos], August 24, 1996, p. 25)

Video was of course far cheaper to make than film, but like film it permitted the construction of supergroups. It also had the extra advantage of allowing expanded narratives running into two or even three two-hour cassettes, creating a captive audience who had to buy Parts 2 and 3 once they had seen Part 1. Instead of touring, the producers sold the videos to the proprietors of the new video rental shops or directly to the VCR-owning consumer in motor-parks, supermarkets and the street. Because pirate dubbing took place on a huge scale, these sales cannot have been very profitable. This has led Jonathan Haynes (1995) and numerous newspaper commentators in Nigeria to condemn the products as junk drama—made at maximum speed, with minimum investment, for a quick turnover. Criticisms include the observations that the producers and technicians are often untrained, the technical equipment is of poor quality, producers do not reinvest their profits in better technology but instead spend it on conspicuous displays of wealth, and the acting style is often not adapted to make use of the possibilities of the screen but instead retains the exaggerated projection and stylization characteristic of the live theater. Production is unregulated; in Anikulapo's words, there is a video market but no video industry:

> For now, what exists is a video market. And like all markets, it welcomes everyone irrespective of wares, method of procuring, displaying and selling such wares; and even origin of the marketer. There can be no industry yet, where in spite of huge investments by a variant of businessmen, there is no control to standard. No regulation to practice. No constant review of progress or regress. No viable critical institutions. And no responsibility to the viewer,

beyond pushing the product no matter how poorly produced and packaged down his throat. . . . Video makers operate more as contractors, reaping and draining the video fortune. (Ibid., p. 25)

The market, though, despite its uncontrolled proliferation, is clearly segmented. Knowledgeable consumers make their choice between English-language, Igbo-language, and Yorùbá-language products. Within the English-language sector, they have a choice between locally made and imported videos. Imported videos—mainly American—include the genres of thrillers, horror, space, adventure, and romance and are regularly denounced by the press as being too often violent or pornographic. Locally made English-language videos are most often set in the affluent urban middle classes and feature marital and family scandals, thwarted romance, social evils including corruption and drug trafficking, and born-again Christianity against the forces of evil. They are criticized in the press either for being too Western—imitating imported video too faithfully and representing only an artificial elite glamour; or for being too indigenous—promoting "magic, witchcraft, and other aspects of local culture that appear better left in the past" (*The Guardian* [Lagos], May 3, 1996, p. 10).

Yorùbá-language videos are usually lumped together in these journalistic critiques as "folk video," and attract little detailed commentary from the critics. However, they constitute a huge segment of the market; one which is again internally segmented and highly diverse. The Yorùbá-language videos range from middle-class stories of professional couples (set in Lagos or Ìbàdàn, revolving around marital discord, monogamy versus polygamy, professional wives, spoiled children, and so on) to stories with uneducated protagonists in rural and small-town settings. There are many dealing with the urban criminal underworld, some in thriller or detective story format. There are even openly political videos.[2] There are dramas which are little more than vehicles for popular music and dancing. There are many melodramas with extraordinarily convoluted plots: several involving children of illicit unions who are unaware of their true parentage and invariably fall in love with their half-sibling; and some representing the corruption of present-day youth, which is blamed on bad upbringing by over-indulgent parents. Dramas reveling in the occult are so common that it is even believed that actors die young because of their constant exposure to *jùjú*, incantations, and supernatural powers.

The relatively profuse and open opportunities offered by video production led to the prominence of a new kind of performer: the young actor who, without belonging to any strongly based theater group, participated in numerous different film and video productions on a freelance basis.

Adéjọbí himself has been responsible for the creation of several video dramas: among them *Adédigba's Co-wife*, a single two-hour drama based on the 1960s stage play which dramatized his own early life; *Ibi Ayé Ń lọ* [*Where the World Is Going*], in two parts; and *Ká Róhun Wí* (*For the Sake of Saying Something:* translated as "No Royal Way to Stardom" on the jacket), also in two parts. All of these are set in provincial towns rather than the capital and deal with a social class lower than the Lagos professional elite. All use many actors who are not part of the Adéjọbí Theater Company, including Lérè Pàímọ́, Bàbáa Sàlá, Mrs. Dúró-Ládiípọ̀, and Kọ́lá Oyèéwọ̀ in *Adédigba's Co-wife;* Kọ́lá Oyèéwọ̀ and Ayox Arísẹkọ́lá in *Where the World Is Going;* and Ayox Arísẹkọ́lá, "Agbako," and "Baba Ijesha" (all popular comedians) in *For the Sake of Saying Something.* Alhaji does not feature in any of these videos. By the time Adéjọbí began making them, Alhaji was writing and co-directing his own videos, including the three-part *Ti Olúwa Nilẹ̀* [*The Land Belongs to God*], one of the few Yorùbá-language video dramas to be praised by the critics. In Wọlé Ògúndélé's words, it is "a very ambitious production . . . unique, very untypical of the usual deluge" (1997, 64). But while Alhaji was not available to perform in Adéjọbí's videos, members of Adéjọbí's company were given parts in Alhaji's videos: notably John Adéwuni and Grace Adéjọbí.

INCORPORATION AND REPRESENTATIONAL EXPANSION

The most obvious reason for the public craze for video drama was insecurity. As Ladi Ladebo, a leading film-maker, put it, "Cinema is dying. . . . The ambience of being in a large dark hall is not possible because there is a lot of crime, life is unsafe. . . . With the boom in satellite communications and home video, people don't go out any more" (*The Guardian* [Lagos], May 18, 1996, p. 33).

But video, because of its association with documentary on the one hand and free-ranging fantasy on the other, and because of its status as a purchasable object of consumption, could also perform certain ideological operations which neither stage plays nor film could. The medium of video is exploited to encompass local aspirations and unease in a way that neither imported "Rambo"-type videos nor the live theater could do. I would suggest that these videos are holding their own against the much glossier and more technically sophisticated imported video dramas because they are better than the imports at importing: that is, they have the capacity to encompass, include, and envision a wider range of disparate experiences, including foreign elements but also including the ever-present sources of pride and unease in modern Nigeria—"tradition," paganism, the occult, the past, and polygamy; and above all, they have the ability—even more than the stage plays did—to bring these disparate elements within one frame, a frame which assures the viewer that the contradictions can be resolved. This, I suggest, is possible because video is simultaneously the me-

Video dramas made by Oyin Adéjọbí and Alhaji Kàrímù Adépọ̀jù.

dium of neutrally documented "reality" and the medium of unlimited fantasy.

The television documentary is not as familiar to Nigerian viewers as it is to British and American ones: it is a genre that is expensive to make well and is generally substituted in Nigerian programming with information or discussion programs made in a studio. Even news programs are hardly documentary in the sense that British television news broadcasts are: there is rarely any footage of actual events outside the capital, and even within the capital such "events" are usually confined to the public appearances of prominent members of government. However, the documentary character of the video camera is well established and recognized. There is a new breed of artist, the young video entrepreneur who records weddings, funerals, and chieftaincy installations on commission; does minimal editing; and sells copies of the resulting tape to the celebrants for distribution to their friends. The requirement is exhaustive coverage, with as many participants as possible being represented and every stage of the ceremony recorded.

The result could be an extremely long, monotonous video with very infrequent awkwardly captured high points. This does not matter, as long as the tape bears witness to actuality—to the fact that the event was held and that the appropriate people were there.

On the other hand, video allows a slow, dream-like unrolling of fantasy, a juxtaposition of images both in sequence (cuts from one glamorous scene to another) and in space (nesting of framed images within the screen or the partitioning of the screen into two or four sections). Music videos carry video fantasy to the greatest lengths. Alhaji Barrister Àyìndé's videos *Fuji Explosion* and *Fuji Extravaganza* drift from yachts in the Marina to dancing girls in gold lamé; from grand walled mansions to plush interiors with velvet sofas, plastic flowers, and prominent sound systems; from sunsets to mosques (see Barber and Waterman 1995). A video is both a consumer good and a meta-consumer good, the encapsulation of all the consumer goods a person aspires to (Lawuyi 1997).

The Adéjọbí Company's videos were made right at the end of its history as a live popular stage company, after their star had left them and their funds were low. Nonetheless, they show the company's continued capacity to adapt itself in response to the thematic opportunities offered by a new medium—and to mutate, extending long arms up into the formerly unreachable world of the middle classes and down into the unacceptable but ineradicable obverse of "enlightenment"—the domain of occult evil. But if the range of sites and scenes they portray has expanded, their morality has, if anything, contracted. In all three videos, the moral lesson is conservative, preaching a return to traditional authority structures and blaming life's deficiencies on "modern times" coupled with the innate weakness or malevolence of women.

9 The World of the Work: Place, Gender, and Politics

> However forcefully the real and the represented world resist fusion, however immutable the presence of that categorical boundary line between them, they are nevertheless indissolubly tied up with each other and find themselves in continual mutual interaction; uninterrupted exchange goes on between them, similar to the uninterrupted exchange of matter between living organisms and the environment that surrounds them. As long as the organism lives, it resists a fusion with the environment, but if it is torn out of its environment, it dies. The work and the world represented in it enter the real world and enrich it, and the real world enters the work and its world as part of the process of its creation, as well as part of its subsequent life, in a continual renewing of the work through the creative perception of listeners and readers.
> —Bakhtin 1981, 254

Uninterrupted exchange goes on between the real world and the world represented in fiction; but Bakhtin's history of the chronotope in the Western novel shows clearly that that "exchange" need not imply resemblance. Early Greek romances were located in an unreal time and a featureless, abstract expanse of space, so detached from real experience that later scholarship was for a long time unable to determine even to which century individual texts belonged (Bakhtin 1981, 91). The plays of the Adéjọbí Company's repertoire, by contrast, were always cut from the cloth of concrete, specific, local, and familiar experience. The world that was acted out on the stage looked and sounded in many respects very much like the world the audience inhabited. But this was not the only option available. Other highly non-realistic models of enactment flourished right beside the popular theater in Nigeria. If Adéjọbí preferred modes of representation that "look somewhat real," this was a deliberate choice. The apparently realist style cannot be taken for granted as "only natural." Its nature needs to be investigated and defined.

In the most obvious sense, the world the Adéjọbí Company represents onstage is created out of real experience by virtue of the theater's mode of dramatic production. The plays are generated by the collective and interactive improvisation of a relatively large number of individuals, each of whom contributes, to a greater or lesser degree, speech drawn from their own reservoir of social competence. They draw on what they have heard people say and what they themselves have found themselves saying in everyday encounters. In a theater tradition with no training schools, no lineage or guild base, and no written texts, the actors see themselves as coming to the theater company already endowed with resources of experience and personality into which they can tap. Moreover, this takes place in a culture in which daily life itself is often experienced and performed as a kind of drama. From childhood, people are taught how to hold their own in street and market by maintaining a pose while calling the bluff of their playmates or their customers. Oyin Adéjọbí said "I personally believe that our life, normally, is drama" and that the endless ongoing dialogues of street and market are themselves artful performances.

It seems likely, too (to borrow a point from Ian Watt's great book *The Rise of the English Novel*), that the Yorùbá popular theater's propensity for lifelike detail was encouraged by the fact that their drama was a new genre, originating in the colonial era and grappling with the unprecedented social situations and experiences that characterized it. They therefore made frequent use of new narratives, often based on "things that are going on today," anecdotes of experience circulating in popular culture rather than narratives drawn from a well-known traditional stock. Because neither the stories nor the mode of representation were canonically established, there was a greater need to place the concrete contents of the situations and experiences they dealt with in front of the audience as fully as possible in order to substantiate them and render them comprehensible.[1]

More fundamentally, though, the plays are embedded in the detail of quotidian real life because they deliver a moral lesson which is presented as the *inevitable* outcome of preceding sequences of moral action. Concretization and specificity, in Bakhtin's view, limit the operations of chance, and the depiction of "the indigenous reality surrounding one" makes such concretization and specificity "absolutely unavoidable" (ibid., 100). The Greek romance plots are ruled by chance, and for this reason they are set in a world whose "degree of specificity and concreteness ... is necessarily very limited" and whose landscapes are abstract, neither local nor exotic, offering no contrast between "home" and "elsewhere." In the Adéjọbí Company's plays, the case is the exact opposite. Chance and coincidence are relegated to the margins. Interventions by extraneous forces (such as spiritual beings) are rare and are always motivated by the larger requirements of justice. In this situation, all concretization—"geographic, economic, sociopolitical, quotidian" (ibid.)—is productive, for it grounds the causal chain, excluding alternative ways of linking the elements of action and consequence.

The idea that the authority of causal sequences of action is firmed up by embedding them in lifelike circumstantial detail is supported by Yorùbá accounts of the generation of moral wisdom. Precepts derive their authority from their origin in actual events. Proverbs are very often simultaneously *explained* and *vouched for* by an account of the circumstances in which they were first uttered (see Bada 1970; Gbadamọsi 1965). Their origin in real experience endows them with authority which carries over into their application to other situations. The circumstantial detail of such accounts can be immense and sometimes improbable to an outside observer; but the more embedded in it the original utterance is, the more authority its subsequent applications seem to bear. Circumstantial detail carries conviction.

Furthermore, members of the audience have to be able to apply what they see onstage to their own life experiences in order fully to appropriate and activate the "lesson." The process of matching was surely assisted by the creation of characters that seemed like real people from everyday well-known spheres of life—with specific and familiar-seeming personalities, pasts, and relationships—placed in a concrete social setting whose form and dynamics would be evoked in innumerable details. The audience, to get its full measure of edification, could not walk into the hall in the closing moments and "pick the lesson" from the summary statement made in the final speech or song. They need to see the axiom *produced*, as the outcome of a chain of events analogous to events experienced in their own lives. It was in this embodying and working out of the narrative, rather than in the bare "lesson," that the originality of the plays resided.

The "actual experience" of the actors and audience, however, already includes narrative and is to some extent apprehended in narrative form. If "our life, normally, is drama," it is also normally narrative. Not only do stories come out of people's lives: it is also in the light of stories that people live their lives. As Dell Hymes and others have suggested, narrative is a fundamental and universal *way of thinking*—a way of explaining things, but more profoundly a way of apprehending and processing experience. Aspects of experience always have the potential to become a narrative by being absorbed into "this invisible, heard-but-not-seen web of order . . . or a potential web available for any experience that could become a story" (Hymes 1996, 118). Stories, correspondingly, provide templates by which people structure their own experience—both retrospectively and as it happens—in the effort to interpret it (Finnegan 1998; Bruner 1991).

In one of the few studies of a Yorùbá community to pay extensive attention to what a number of actual Yorùbá people said (as distinct from what "the Yorùbá believe" or what the Ifá divination corpus announces), Andrea

Cornwall reveals a world in part constituted by the continual telling and retelling of narratives held to be true. People told stories in Adó-Odò not only to describe their experiences and the experiences of others but also to explain situations, justify states of affairs, and put forward their personal philosophy. Thus, for example, in discussing the case of a girl whose married lover denied responsibility for her pregnancy, "the women of the house told me story after story of men who had seen their blood and made amends" (Cornwall 1996, 223). They interpreted the girl's situation in the light of the axiom that fathers always eventually recognize their biological offspring, but this axiom had to be developed and substantiated by "story after story" drawn from experience and hearsay. In the conversation of Adó-Odò people, there seems to be a continuum of storylikeness, at one end the immediate, blurted report, at the other, well-structured narratives in which good is rewarded and evil punished—stories which everyone has heard in one guise or another and which shade into narratives that can be seen onstage, read in a novel, or heard recounted in *ewì*.[2] These stories vouch for each other in an extending web of mutual reference. When members of the audience say that a play's story is "true," "exactly how life is," then, they may mean that it corresponds to other stories which cluster around, and exemplify, the same social and moral point.

What we see in operation is *cycles* of generalization and specification, of formulation and instantiation. On analogy with a word in Voloshinov's analysis, which "only possesses potentiality—the possibility of having a meaning" until it is grounded in a concrete utterance (Voloshinov 1973, 101), one could say that a general axiom ("Treachery is bad") only possesses potential for meaningfulness until it is worked out in a detailed narrative that shows what happens when someone betrays his friend. It is then "picked" by the audience as a "lesson" they can apply to their lives. When they apply it, it becomes re-concretized in a new context. It is the *process* of extracting and re-applying lessons that makes this discourse meaningful. But just as single words carry with them a rich burden of associations from previous uses, so moral axioms in Yorùbá popular culture accrue resonance and authority from their repeated reactivation in fully fledged narratives. The man who saw *Besotted Bridegroom* and decided not to proceed with his second marriage (Chapter 7) would hardly have reacted so decisively to an abstract warning "Polygyny breeds strife" or "Don't put a junior wife before a senior." Rather, his understanding of the axiom was filled out by its embodiment in a concrete lifelike situation which in key respects resembled his own.

The formulas the plays announce as their final outcome might also be available to be "picked" out of a newspaper, an anecdote, or a novel; but each of these genres concretizes and embeds the formula in a different way, using different modes of specification. The theater consolidates its moral credibility in an expansive and demonstrative mode. Characters project themselves through their own words, actions happen before the audience's eyes, and this full, rich embodiment of a hypothetical situation in fact generates a huge surplus, so that what we see goes beyond what the closing homily tells us we have learned.

This chapter will look at the specific ways in which the plays are bedded down in circumstantial detail, drawn from everyday experience of household and town, marital relations, friendships, authority structures, and national politics.

Several important points emerge. First, these "givens" do not present themselves to the dramatists monolithically or automatically. Rather, what the theater company has to work with is a range—a whole field—of alternative scenarios and interpretations, models and examples: different kinds of households, different gender and authority relations, different ways of conceptualizing politics and the state. The dramatists carve out different sections of this field for different plays, so that the "setting" is not a mere backdrop but is always integral to the possibilities and outcomes of a specific narrative. Second, the dramas are shaped not only by the nature of the represented *object*—the dimension of their experience the dramatists are mobilizing—but also by the nature of their representational *means*—the built-in characteristics and relationships of the performers available to play the parts. The representational means may function as a kind of filter, blocking the enactment of some dimensions of common experience while foregrounding others. Third, although the experiences the theater company draws on are familiar to many Yorùbá people—which is the foundation of their popular success—it is also true that the particular social location of the actors and the unusual family and authority structures that arise in a theater company give a distinctive inflection to these common materials. In some cases they may give the theater company a wider range of possible models for family, gender relations, friendship, and politics than would normally be entertained. Getting a sense of the breadth of the ideational field in which they are operating—the extremes of what they can represent—is essential if we are to avoid lumping all of their output together as "conservative" or "stereotyped." And to do this requires looking at a number of different examples of theatrical treatments of the same theme. You will need to be patient as I take you through a range of stories and plot summaries. Finally, the "uninterrupted exchange" between experience and enactment can be both reflexive and subject to huge areas of silence. Reflexivity is seen when the very "embedding" and authenticating properties of circumstantial narrative itself are held up to scrutiny. Silence is heard when the theater fails to comment openly on matters of great contemporary concern—government decrees, coups, and corruption. This silence, I will show, arises not only from fear of censorship but also—and more fundamentally—from the theater company's self-appointed role as "preachers" addressing moral lessons equally to *all* their spectators, so that they can "pick" and apply them to their own lives.

HOUSEHOLDS AND LOCALITIES

In Bakhtin's extraordinarily suggestive discussion, it is the "chronotope"— the way in which time and space interact in the world of the narrative— which offers the essential key to genre. "In the literary artistic chronotope, spatial and temporal indicators are fused into one carefully thought-out, concrete whole. Time, as it were, thickens, takes on flesh, becomes artistically visible; likewise, space becomes charged and responsive to the movements of time, plot and history" (1981, 84).

The space of the Adéjọbí Company's plays was always a definite, specific residential space, ranging from an Ọba's palace to rented rooms in a tenement. It was never selected at random as a mere convenient backdrop. On the contrary, the narrative was imagined in such a way that it could not have unfolded as it did in any other setting. At one end of the spectrum of residential spaces is the great old compound housing an extended patriarchal family; at the other end, mobile, lone individuals renting accommodations in strange towns.

Oyin Adéjọbí had a vividly remembered and often-recounted model of the great old compound at his disposal, for it was in a household of this type that he grew up. As we have seen, he described his childhood home in glowing terms: the wealthy, illustrious father living like an Ọba; his huge household swelled by wives, children, *iwọ̀fà*, and visitors; his daily life enriched by magnificent feasts, drumming, and praise singing. Adéjọbí's own house in Gbáẹ̀mú Street provided another model. It was one of the 1950s-style constructions built when large compounds were being broken up all over Yorùbáland and groups of brothers, formerly co-resident, were spreading out into separate dwellings. The house was occupied by Adéjọbí, his wives, his children, and one or two other young relatives. Though there was no full-blown extended family in residence, the house had an aura of permanence, an air of being connected with others in the town along old lines of kinship.

Apart from Alhaji, most of the other members of the company were not natives of Òṣogbo and did not have a family house in the town. Some, like John and Fẹ́mi Bámidélé, had grown up in small farm villages, others in larger towns. But all had moved around a lot in their youth and stayed with different sets of relatives. In Òṣogbo, some lived in a rented room, or room and parlor; some stayed with senior relatives who were working in Òṣogbo and themselves lived in rented accommodations. Most of them were part of the shifting semi-permanent class of modern urban dwellers who had all kinds of routes and networks within the town they currently inhabited but no permanent home there. This class was particularly well represented in Òṣogbo, with its large population of temporary commercial and administrative immigrants from other Yorùbá towns. And in the case of the youngest of the actors—especially young women—there was always the possibility that powerful relatives would come from outside and forcibly remove them from Òṣogbo. From their own experience, then, the actors were familiar with a whole spectrum of modern urban and rural households.

Besotted Bridegroom is a play that draws on the company's experience of the large, old-fashioned compound. It shows the overweening cash madam, Mosún, going back to her mother's home town and invading her mother's natal compound. The details of this household's setup are essential to the exposition of the story. Each of the six segments of the lineage has inherited a portion of the family land. Though the heads of all the segments are building individual houses on their own portions, it is clear that these are contiguous, forming a complex of buildings. Bùárí's own house is described by Mosún as *àlàpà*, the word used to describe the ruined, rain-eroded remnants of old mud walls—suggesting perhaps that he alone still lives in the remains of the old compound.[3] The family are all within reach of a hasty summons by the Baálé, the head of the compound, and the compound meeting attended by all the male elders functions as the normal and central mechanism for handling family affairs. This choice of household setting allows the theater company to put the greatest possible emphasis on Mosún's disrespectful and destructive greed. The large, close-knit co-residential patrilineage under the authority of a *baálé* contrasts maximally with the autonomous, self-made woman who overrides all customary respect—for age, inheritance, and seniority within her own home. The detailed presentation, by Bùárí, of a family history of regulated traditional land division invites a comparison with the rampant acquisitiveness of a new class of property-owners who purchase plots for building and resale.

Most of the plays, however, focus on smaller, more "modern," households, consisting of a man, his wife, their children, and a network of friends and neighbors—more like Adéjọbí's own household in Gbáèmú Street. In *Taking Care of Kúnlé*, for example, the action circles around Òṣó, his missing wife Wúrà, his son Kúnlé, and Wúrà's false friend Àṣàbí, a widow who appears to live nearby without any evidence of a family in residence. In this play, the townspeople are long-standing residents who all know each other, and the family of Òṣó is subject to the light but uncontested authority of the Baálé, the head of the extended family. The Baálé offers to take Kúnlé in when Òṣó is first "bereaved," and this is treated as the natural, automatic solution, in contrast to Àṣàbí's highly irregular and immoral plan to come and stay in Òṣó's house and look after Kúnlé there. This community, then, appears to be a fairly cohesive small town or village, where old compound authority structures are still residually effective and where everyone knows everyone else—but where people live as small family units and resent too much interference in their affairs. This setting provides a dramatic context in which Ọṣọ́'s affair with Àṣàbí will be observed, commented on, and deplored by the scandalized extended family and townspeople—extracting the maximum effect from the "love" scenes. But they will not put a stop to it, for in this setting the autonomy of the small family unit is too strong for that. The elders of the family can watch, gossip, and offer Ọṣọ́ roundabout advice, but they do not actually dare to interfere in his domestic arrangements.

Further along the continuum is *Articulated Lorry*, where the household is made up of a landlord, his wife, and his tenants, and no family or community life outside the walls of the house really impinges on the action. The landlord has already built a second house to rent to tenants—a practice which has flourished in Òṣogbo since the late colonial period.[4] We know that the landlord has political connections in the town—he has just been made chairman of the local branch of a political party—and that one of the tenants has a shop in town, while another has a mother who comes to visit him from their home town. But all the significant links are between the tenants within the house, none of whom are kin, and none of whom seem to have networks of kin, friends, or business associates outside which are relevant to the plot. Key features of the setup—the autonomy of the members; the property-based authority of the landlord, more provisional and less binding than authority based on kinship—make possible the development of a tight, uncluttered plot revolving around the three central characters, unencumbered by relatives and by the constant surveillance and interference which, in a traditional compound, would have made Ìyá Bùnmi's advances to Àlàbí more or less impossible.

In each of these plays, a specific household setup—the way co-residents are linked, the way kin are distributed in space and related over time—is picked from a spectrum of possibilities. In each case the chosen model is essential to the play's distinctive exposition of its story. In one play, *The Heir*, the relations between place, time, and plot are not only fundamental to the development of the moral theme but also surface into the dialogue in numerous explicit allusions and comments, generating a reflexive commentary on narrative itself. This play shows the conditions of modern life in Yorùbá towns as experienced by the mobile, migrating classes of waged laborers and salaried employees: prolonged residence away from one's natal town, dispersal of families, and separation and loss of contact even among close kin, but combined with an affirmation of extended family membership as an organic bond. These conditions were the ones most central to the experience of many members of the theater company, who were mobile both in their upbringing and in their daily avocation, but were still to varying degrees dependent on, or under the authority of, a wider body of kin. This is one reason, perhaps, why the representation of household, locality, and dispersion in space is more overtly thematized in this play than in any other.

The play opens after the death of Bámgbádé, a businessman who has lived most of his life (and then died) in rented accommodation in a place called Ayédùn ["Life is sweet"] far away from his home town, leaving a young widow. It emerges that Bámgbádé's death was hastened by the disappearance of his only son by his first wife. Brooding on his loss, for "a child is better dead than lost," Bámgbádé was killed by "hypertension." The dead man's good-natured landlord Tàfá takes charge of the funeral and its aftermath and then takes the widow to her late husband's home town. Meanwhile Láńre, a complete rogue who was formerly Bámgbádé's driver, has returned in the guise of a successful entrepreneur. He is first seen cheating a woman cloth-trader by passing off boxes of rags as top-quality lace. Having found out about his former employer's death, he goes straight to Bámgbádé's home town and successfully impersonates the lost son Lásún, inherits the widow, and prizes out of her all Bámgbádé's property. The family elders try in vain to curb him. But then the real Lásún returns to Ayédùn, learns of his father's death, and decides to go to his father's home town to see the family; Tàfá goes with him. By now Láńre's behavior has become intolerably rude and dissolute, and the family elders are delighted when they recognize the real Lásún and realize the other one is an impostor. They set a trap to expose and shame him. They send a message to him that some Europeans have come to buy land to build a steelworks on; will he sell the plot he inherited from Bámgbádé? "It's for sale—all of it" says Láńre at once, and hurries to the compound head's house to close the deal. The elders say that first they have to ask him a question: is he a plant grown from seed, or a transplant? Whose son is he? When Láńre begins to bluster, Tàfá steps forward and identifies him as Láńre, Bámgbádé's thievish driver, and the real heir corroborates this. Láńre tries to run for it; Lásún and Tàfá catch him, beat him, and force him to confess. The head of the compound closes the play with the moral: "May God grant us good children who outlive us," a theme repeated in the final song.

This story, and the moral it delivers, rest on two fundamental presuppositions. First, it is acceptable for a family member to go away to live and work for most of his life in another town. No blame attaches to Bámgbádé for not having seen his natal family for many years. No one criticizes him for building his house in Ayédùn rather than his home town. Nor is the family blamed for failing to take charge of his funeral, even though Bámgbádé is a close relative. It seems to be taken for granted that Bámgbádé's landlord, someone who is not even a relative, should be left to handle that in Ayédùn. "Òkúu Bámgbádé eè ṣeì tá a gbọdọ̀ gbé wálé," says the household head categorically: Bámgbádé's corpse is not one that they are obliged to bring home. Tàfá, conversely, though he does the decent thing by going to

Dayọ̀ as the rogue, Láńre, in *The Heir.* ©Elio Montanari

report the death and escort the widow, makes it clear that he is under no obligation to maintain any link with Bámgbádé's family thereafter. It is this distance—the conviction that people from the two geographically separated households are under no obligation to meet again—which makes possible Láńre's imposture. But, second, there is also the strong presumption that a kin group is a living, organic entity whose corporate rights and obligations are sacred. When the elders of the family learn of Bámgbádé's death, the Baálé laments that their numbers have been depleted: "Alas, we are only three blades [of *eérọn* grass] remaining now." The elders of Bámgbádé's family recognize their obligation, or their right, to take in Bámgbádé's widow; and when Láńre appears as the heir, they hand her over to him as part of the inheritance. The fact that Láńre is prepared to sell land inherited from his father—even if it is legally his to dispose of[5]— proves to the elders that he is a "transplant," not a plant grown from the family seed.

The closing moral couches organic continuity in terms of generational succession from parent to child. This succession is what plugs the gaps in

Dayọ̀ as Lánre and Emily as the widow, Bọ́lánlé in *The Heir*. ©Elio Montanari

The Baálé's sister, Adénínhún (Grace), the widow, Bọ́lánlé (Emily), and the impostor, Lánre (Dayọ̀), in *The Heir*. ©Elio Montanari

The Baálé (Oyin Adéjobí) and his sister, Adénínhún (Grace), in *The Heir*. ©Elio Montanari

Láńre behaves riotously in front of the Baálé in *The Heir*. ©Elio Montanari

the solidary corporate descent group ("My Bámgbádé has come back," exults Bámgbádé's sister when Lásún appears). It was only because of the solidarity of the extended family, which took responsibility for Bámgbádé's inheritance and—eventually—unmasked the impostor, that Bámgbádé's true heir could succeed him. The tension between this collective ethos and the individual's history of isolation and movement is what makes the plot work.

This tension between localized solidarity and geographical dispersion is repeatedly alluded to in flourishes and embellishments of the dialogue. Bámgbádé's extended family in his home town keep drawing attention to the fact that there are idiosyncratic local ways of which Lánre, the stranger, is ignorant: "*Kèè tíì molẹ̀ẹ wa ni*" [He doesn't yet know our land]; "*Kò ì mọ bí ilúu wa ìí ṣe rí*" [He doesn't know what our town is like]; "*Kèè mọbi 'lẹ̀ẹ́ lójú si láàrin ilú wa ìí o*" [He doesn't know the secret pitfalls of this town of ours yet]. The head of the compound warns the impostor "*Kọ́ ọ mọ bọ ṣe maa ṣe nílẹ̀ yìí o*" [You should find out how to behave in this land]; and explains "*Torúi, ilẹ̀ yìí ò jọbi tẹ́ ẹ ti wá*" [Because this land is not like the place you have come from]. The impression is given of a resilient tight-knit local nexus impervious to the ways of strangers, defining itself in contrast to elsewhere.

Conversely, other characters constantly evoke a world outside their own locality, through allusion and comparison. Tàfá, for example, attempts to console the weeping widow by telling her that she should count herself lucky: if she had been bereaved in Lagos, she wouldn't even have had the chance to mourn. "After you'd struggled to collect the body from the hospital, and struggled to get a plot in the cemetery, and struggled to get hold of a coffin, how would you have time to weep?" Lagos, vividly evoked in these words, has no function in the play except as a contrast to Ayédùn.

The comments of Bámgbádé's extended family show that they think of local knowledge as being first-hand, arising from long experience of living in a place, not easily accessible to outsiders. Tàfá's remarks about Lagos show that "elsewhere," by contrast, is apprehended through travelers' tales, hearsay, and anecdote. But right from the opening episode, the play foregrounds the necessity of stories: even within a local community, there are gaps in first-hand knowledge which can only be filled by circumstantially detailed narrative.[6] In the first scene, a woman cloth-seller approaches the lamenting widow to claim some money she says Bámgbádé owed her. She does not know the widow, and though she has seen Tàfá before, she does not know who he is or what his relationship to the dead man was. To substantiate her claim, she therefore has to tell the story of her transaction with Bámgbádé in detail:

Níjẹẹ̀ẹ́dógún àwọn eníbàárà mi ni wọ́n ní kí n gé aṣọ ogún ọ̀pá fáwọn. Ìgbà tí ǹ ń sì ń gbé aṣọ òhún-ún lọ, ni n bá bá bàbá ní ojú-

> òde, n ní ọn bá sì pè mí, wọ́n ní ṣé léèsì funfun wà ńnú aṣọ tí ǹ ń
> kóó lọ un? Mo ní ìgàn kán wà ńbẹ̀. Ni ọ́n bá sì dá ìgàn kan ọ̀hún
> níjọ́ náà. Wọ́n láwọn ọ́ rà á. Mo ní àpò mẹ́ta náírà ni. Ni ọ́n bá lọ́
> dáa o, wọ́n láwọn ọ́ rà á. Ni mọ bá fi gé léèsì ìgàn kan funfun fún
> ọn. Nínú àpò mẹ́ta náírà un, àpò kan náírà n ni wọ́n fún mi níjọ́
> náà. Wọ́n ní tọ́ bá di ọjọ́ mẹ́ẹ̀ẹ́dógún o, wọ́n ní n wáá gba àpò méjì
> náírà tó kù.

> Exactly two weeks ago some customers of mine asked me to cut 20 yards of cloth for them. As I was carrying that cloth [to them], I happened to meet Baba in front of the house, and he called me. He asked me if there was white lace among the cloths that I was carrying. I said there was one piece there. And he bought that one piece that day. He said he would buy it. I told him it was three hundred naira. And then he said it was O.K., he would buy it. And I cut one piece of white lace for him. Out of the 300 naira, he gave me 100 on that day. He said in a fortnight's time, I should come and collect the 200 naira remaining.

Even within the confines of the town, then, trade brings people into relationships with strangers, and narrative has to stand in for personal knowledge. A wealth of circumstantial detail stands in for proof. When people are separated by geographical distance, the scope and need for narrative is greater. Tàfá cannot break the news of Bámgbádé's death to the extended family until he has established his own identity, for he is unknown in their town. And he can only do this by an account of his life:

> Èmi tẹ́ ẹ̀ ń wò yìí, ní ìlú Ayédùn ni wọ́n bí mi sí. Ọmọ ìlú Ayédùn
> gan-an-an ni mí. Ọmọọ'bẹ̀ ni babaà mi. Iṣẹ́ẹ bábà ni mo kọ́. Ọlọ́un
> sì wí péé, kí iṣẹ́ un ọ́ máa lọ dáadáa. Torí tẹ́ ẹ bá dé Ayédùn lónìí,
> bẹ́ ẹ bá lẹ́ ẹ̀ ń bèèrèe Tàfá bábá, èmi tí mọ̀ ń jẹ́ bẹ́ẹ̀ nìín. Ilé mẹ́rin
> n mọ kọ́, òkan nínúu rẹ̀ ni àbúròo yín ń gbé ńbẹ̀, Bámgbádé.

> I, that you see before you here, I was born in the town of Ayédùn. I am a real native of Ayédùn. My father was a son of the town. I learned the barber's trade. And God determined that I would prosper in that trade. Because if you go to Ayédùn today, if you say you want to see Tàfá the barber, well, I am that person. I built four houses, and your younger brother Bámgbádé lived in one of them.

But narratives that stand in for first-hand knowledge are subject to substitution, subterfuge, and fakery. Almost every significant forward shift in the plot takes place through a story recounted by one of the characters. The brilliance of this play lies in its subtle and witty mobilization of plausible but false narratives alongside true ones. Láńre's entire project of deception

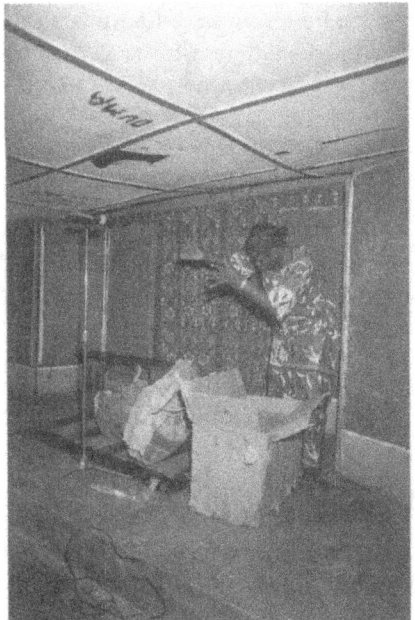 

The cloth-trader (Margaret Adéjọbí) finds she has been cheated.
©Elio Montanari

is carried through by means of elaborately detailed but flimsy circumstantial narratives of elsewhere. On his first appearance, masquerading as a big-time importer, he dazzles the woman cloth-seller with glib references to his business arrangements in Moscow: "They were busy **setting** that lace [when I arrived], and the European who was **in charge** told me to wait, he said I should wait. I said 'I can't hang about in Moscow.' And I **traveled** on to Toronto. That's where I found the kind of lace you asked me for. And I've got it outside."

In the wonderful central episode where he passes himself off to Bámgbádé's family as the heir, he conjures up scene after exotic scene of "elsewhere," overwhelming their doubts with his ever-fertile inventions. He is skating on very thin ice, however, and there are moments when the glib explanations and casual surface detail of his story barely save him. He explains the reasons for his (i.e., Lásún's) earlier disappearance as follows: "On that far-off day," he was on his way home from school when he stopped to steal mangoes. He was captured there by a child-stealer who turned him into a goat and took him by train and boat to Ghana. He was dragged to a dreadful house in the forest where a medicine man turned him back into a human being. The medicine man then cut Lánre's arm and began to suck his blood, but because of its bitter taste he let him go. Lánre left the forest hut and fell into the hands of a party of soldiers, who took him to their barracks and put him in uniform. It was in a town called "Óséowi" that he became a soldier.

The head of the household queries some of this story on grounds of reason (if he was a goat, how could he know that he'd arrived in Ghana?) but is quickly persuaded by Lánre's answer ("You see, Father, I had the soul of a human being, even though all my body from top to toe was the body of a beast"). The household head's sister Adénínhún objects that she knew [mọ̀] Lásún very well as a child and this isn't him: Lásún was dark and did not have protruding eyeballs. Lánre at once explains that on the war front they used a kind of European magical soap, protection against bullets, which turned all the soldiers pale. He adds that there were enormous bomb blasts which made their eyeballs pop out. The family reluctantly accepts this explanation. But one of the elders, Àrólé, has been to Ghana himself. He asks Lánre if he understands "the language of Ghana," and Lánre says that he certainly does.

    ÀRÓLÉ: Jẹ́ n fọ̀ ọ́ sí ọ.
    LÁNRE: E fọ̀ ọ́-ò.
    ÀRÓLÉ: "Àbọ̀ọ̀ sua, wá ń tọ̀tọ̀ sí pápáápá."
    LÁNRE: Yéè, yéè, yéè.
    ÀRÓLÉ: O gbóyiun?
    LÁNRE: Hẹ̀n-ẹ́n-ẹ̀n, èdèe ki ní nìyẹn ... Fámágbẹ. Èdè àwọn Fámágbẹ.
    ÀRÓLÉ: Hàà, Àṣàntí mọ̀ lèyiùn.
    LÁNRE: Háà, Àṣàntí ni. Àṣàntí ni.

    ÀRÓLÉ: Let me speak some to you.
    LÁNRE: Speak it.
    ÀRÓLÉ: "*Àbọ̀ọ̀ sua, wá ń tọ̀tọ̀ sí pápáápá.*"[7]
    LÁNRE: Oh, oh, oh!
    ÀRÓLÉ: Do you understand that?
    LÁNRE: Now let's see, that's that language ... Fámágbẹ, it's the Fámágbẹ people's language!
    ÀRÓLÉ: Ha, no, it's Asante.
    LÁNRE: Asante, yes, it's Asante, definitely.

This seems to satisfy Àrólé—perhaps because his own command of "Asante" is not that good, or perhaps because his motive was more to show off than to test Lánre. In this long, drawn-out, and hilarious sequence, the family's own (defective) knowledge of "elsewhere" is defeated by Lánre's triumphantly confident fictional version; and even their first-hand knowledge—

such as Adénínhún's memory of Lásún as a child—is brushed away with fantastic narratives of things they could not possibly have experienced for themselves—zoomorphosis, European magic, blasts on the battlefield. It is only because families have become stretched and dispersed and because trade, the lifeblood of the community, depends on travel, that narrative impostures like this can flourish.

A quizzical light is thus shed upon the very operation of narrative as an instantiation of the nature and consequences of moral action. While it is in circumstantial narratives that moral truth is most fully demonstrated, the very power of narrative to substitute for first-hand knowledge makes it a potential risk. *The Heir* affirms that the bonds of a blood relationship are such that they will survive this risk: eventually, the elders of the family "see their blood" and "make amends" to the true heir. But the play's brilliance lies in its demonstration of the power of fake stories to dazzle and mislead and in its shrewd diagnosis of the way contemporary social dispersion opens up new spaces in which such fakery can flourish.

In several of the plays, we find some refraction of this dual perspective: the sense that the characters are rooted in and defined by ordinary concrete households and communities, but at the same time that they are potentially or actually on their own—autonomous, subject to dispersal, ejection, capture, or voluntary departure in a world defined by its horizons.

HUSBANDS, WIVES, AND FRIENDS

In almost all the plays, the core relationships that hold the plot together are those of marriage on the one hand and male friendship on the other. These relationships inhabit a sector of the moral sphere supersaturated with models, commentaries, lessons, and exemplary narratives. This is an area of social experience which is highly "pre-narratized," constituted in the light of narrative models.

"Wayward," headstrong, and unfaithful women—the stereotypes Cornwall met in such abundance in everyday discourses in Adó-Odò—are well represented in a number of the Adéjọbí company's plays. The plot of *Dálé Mosú* as described to me by Alhaji (see Chapter 5) could have come straight from that repertoire. *Articulated Lorry* ends with the warning "*Obìnrin — tótó fún-ùn*" [Beware of women]. The closing song of *Besotted Bridegroom* advises "Women cause one's downfall.... / A woman's plans should not be followed / She can cause her husband to go astray / She can cause her husband to misbehave."

But the theater company had a wider range than this of examples and interpretations of men's and women's roles as husbands, wives, and friends. It seems at least possible that the special circumstances of theater company organization not only colored their use of prevailing stereotypes but also

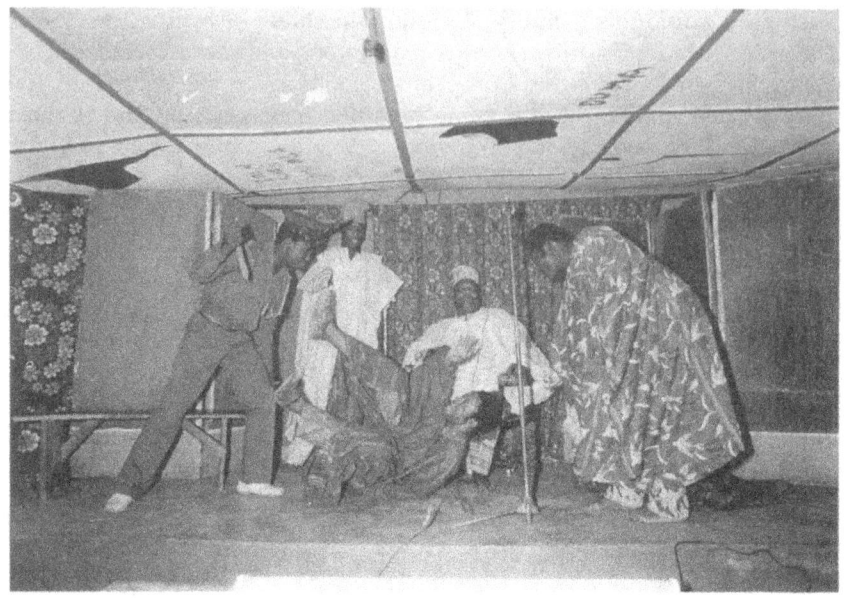

The impostor is brought to justice in *The Heir.* ©Elio Montanari

suggested to them alternative possibilities farther toward the frontiers of their discursive field.

Women in the theater were in an unusual position, giving rise to several specific kinds of gender unease. One source of unease was that women became the special target of the general adverse opinion of actors as loose-living idle riffraff. If it was undesirable for a son to be an actor, it was disastrous for a daughter. In the theater company's ongoing campaign for the moral high ground—claiming the role of preachers, redefining their "plays" as work—women represented the nub of their ideological problem. It was not always possible to convince the public or their own relatives that some of the girls attracted to the theater were leading blameless lives. The core women in the company—Adéjọbí's wives—all seemed pillars of respectability. But there were others: Morádéké, for instance, who had joined the company against her family's will and who lived on her own in a rented room. She had formed a liaison with John Adéwuni, but because of her family's unrelenting opposition she was unable to marry him officially. The family's attitude functioned as a self-fulfilling prophecy: however much Morádéké desired respectability, she had no choice but to occupy the position of "outside wife" or "concubine," deplored in some of the Adéjọbí company's own plays.

As we have seen, theater bosses often bound actresses to the company and gave them a domestic respectability by marrying them themselves. But this resulted in a second kind of unease. The theater came from a church tradition that frowned on polygyny. Even when churches relaxed their rules and allowed it—as many independent churches did, including the Church of the Lord Aládùúrà patronized by Adéjọbí's family—monogamy still represented an ideal of "enlightenment" associated with education, white-collar jobs, and middle-class status. Grace hinted at this when she remarked that Adéjọbí had had to marry several wives because of the difficulty of getting permanent actresses: "It wasn't his wish to marry [lots of] wives, oh no. But if there were no women [in the company], the work would not be able to proceed."

Their attitudes toward polygyny were often ambivalent. Grace, for example, seemed proud of the fact that her father had three wives and many children; but she also blamed polygyny for her mother's long absence in Ghana and her father's inability to pay for her schooling. In Adéjọbí's narratives, this ambiguity was heightened. In the autobiographical story he told me, his father's many wives were associated with wealth, well-being, and status:

> My father was a man of noble status. . . . In accordance with his position . . . as a royal prince, he had a lot of wives, I grew up in a household of many wives in the house of my father who bore me. And by the same token, my father was a very generous man, so that the townspeople would come flocking in and out of his house day and night.

But in the video version of *Adédigba's Co-wife*, Adéjọbí's only autobiographical play, this image was inverted. In a prologue to the main drama, Adéjọbí is interviewed, as himself, by a young researcher, who asks him for the story of his life—just as I did when I recorded the interview from which the above excerpts are taken. Adéjọbí replies ruminatively:

> The story of my life . . . it is extremely long. It's extremely long. A lot of water has flowed under the bridge. Well. The father who bore me came from a house of noble status. Yes. My father was the husband of many wives. He was the husband of many wives.

The idiom is exactly the same as in my own interview with him, but the implications are reversed. Here, many wives spell trouble, jealousy, and witchcraft—dangers associated with "backwardness" and "ignorance" as well as with sheer evil. It is a co-wife who is jealous of his mother that afflicts Adéjọbí with his crippling disablement. Marrying women to supply the company with respectable actresses, then, involved its own self-negation, the slur of "polygamy" associated with backwardness and domestic strife.

A third kind of unease arose from the theater wives' status as employees of their husband. Outside the theater, in normal life, it is accepted that wives should "help" their husbands with certain tasks, but they also have their own occupation which is an independent source of income. The theater company wives are in the unusual situation of working full time for an enterprise owned and run by their husband—so much so that there is generally no scope even for a little independent trade on the side. Margaret's dream was eventually to be set up with a soft drinks stall by Adéjobí, but this did not happen as long as the company remained in operation. Grace had completely abandoned her former occupation of seamstress. When I asked Emily if she had ever wished to train for an additional occupation to supplement her theater work, she replied "There would be no opportunity for that at all, I couldn't get the time off from theater work long enough to learn any other trade. It would interfere with the acting." The wives and children were not paid a salary like the other members of the company. The women had no independent source of income. Even the small commercial activity they engaged in—selling sweets outside the hall before a performance—was part of the company's total economic enterprise, not an independent venture they themselves controlled.

Adéjobí's relations with Grace—the most senior wife—and with Emily, for a long time the most junior one, were notably affectionate. Adéjobí said that he had married all his wives for their own sake and that it was only after the marriage that he had put them on the stage. Nonetheless, he took it for granted that once they were his wives, it was for him to employ them in whatever capacity he wished. When I observed that they all seemed to have had remarkable talent and a love of the theater even before they married him, he replied:

> Even if they didn't have any love of the theater, they had no choice but to develop one. Because, since they had a love for the husband that they married, they had no choice but to join their husband in loving [wanting] what he loved.

The wives, then, were in a sense put into the role of a son or other junior male relative in relation to Adéjobí. On the one hand, this curtailed their natural expansion into their own autonomous business, and this may have caused tensions that were not visible on the surface. On the other hand, it gave them a shortcut to public visibility and even star status. As we saw in Chapter 7, to be the center of public attention and acclaim was to participate in the processes by which "big men" are created. While on the one hand they were subordinated to their husband's enterprise, on the other hand they could become publicly known as active, creative, distinctive individuals and attract all the advantages that public recognition brings.

These specific sources of unease may have given a special inflection to the theater company's reworking of common plots about "wayward women." Though polygamy is still the norm in western Nigeria, the plays rarely show polygamous marriages—except in the case of royalty, where status demands it (as in *Kúyẹ̀* and *The Overreacher*). *Besotted Bridegroom*, the one exception to this pattern, sets out to disclose the dangers within polygamy; it suggested to at least some of the men in the audience that "it is better never to take a second wife." This play, with its quite extreme portrayal of the destructive overbearing wealthy junior wife, was created at a time in the company's history when the frustration of the employee wives and the strains of polygyny were beginning to break out in open quarrels and defections.

But the experience of working in a joint enterprise may also have provided a more liberal model for conjugal relations, allowing the theater to go beyond a narrow core of stereotypes of women. There are hints in some of the plays of a conception of partnership between husband and wife which borrows something from the idea of friendship—normally only thought of as existing between two men.

Normally, men's friendships are spoken of—by men at any rate —as durable and transcendent, more exclusive and more highly valued than their relationships with women or kin. "Two men can hold each other more dear than family; a man will support his friend at the expense of his wife," my colleague Báyọ̀ Ògúndíjọ told me. Men speak of a friendship between two men as being sacred and exclusive. "*Òré ò gbelẹ̀ta; elẹ̀jì lọ́rẹ́ gbà*" says the Ifá verse [Friendship does not admit of threesomes; friendship demands a duo]. Because of its very significance and power, a male friendship can be broken off inexplicably as mysteriously and definitively as it was originally formed. Women (men say) have companions, associates, fellows in trade, gossips. They are expected to have not one lifelong friend, but a network of acquaintances that they can draw on at different times for different things. Women's friendships are expected to be adaptable and episodic.

Adéjọbí placed great value on a few encounters in his career with significant other men. They entered his life with unexpected but predestined reverberations. Consider his account of his first meeting with Kọ́lá Ògúnmọ́lá—one of the moments of greatest narrative intensity in his entire orally told autobiography:

> The way he came [into my life] was like this. There was someone here in Òṣogbo, when I had just founded the theater group, who was called Akínwùmí, Mr. Akínwùmí, Ever-Bright Photographer, that was what he had on his signboard. He was a man who had a great love of the theater. Whenever we held a rehearsal, Mr. Akín-

wùmí would come [to watch]. This Mr. Akínwùmí would keep telling me, **after the practice,** that he had a friend who was just like us who was very talented and interested [in the theater]. One day, he would make sure that we met, and so on, Mr. Akínwùmí would keep telling me this. Then it happened one evening, we were doing a play, we were **rehearsing** that play here, in this very house. When I saw Mr. Akínwùmí come in, I saw a certain **man,** tall, with facial marks, coming in with him. Ha! I guessed [lit. "my heart told me"] that this was the person he had been talking about. Ògúnmọ́lá and I had never met before. So, they arrived in the middle of our rehearsal when I was teaching the actors something, and they were acting it out, and I was **correcting** them, and **putting** them **right,** do you follow me?

So you see, when Ògúnmọ́lá sat down and began to watch ... I suddenly saw him leaping to his feet! He stripped off the gown he was wearing and hung it on a nail in the doorway to Màmá Adé's room, so he was just in his vest, ah! I was wondering "What on earth is this gentleman going to do?" After a while, he said—he went up to that person who was acting, he told him to get up, he told him to watch how he would do it. So he [the actor] sat down, and he [Ògúnmọ́lá] began to do that part, he began to do that part, he began to do it, then he stopped and told the chap to do it like that, he did it like that and we all burst into loud applause! When we got to another bit where they were supposed to dance, he stopped them again, and told them to watch how he moved his feet, ah! And we hadn't even met yet! And we were already in the thick of working together! Mr. Akínwùmí didn't have a chance to **introduce** us to each other. **So,** when we finally finished the **practice** that evening, what happened was that after the **members of the group** had gone, it was only then that Mr. Akínwùmí at last got round to **introducing** us. You see how ... so ... when he had **introduced** us to each other, and we began to talk, our ideas agreed so perfectly that if anyone had heard our conversation, mine and Ògúnmọ́lá's, they would have thought we'd known each other for years.

PAUSE

So you see, when Ògúnmọ́lá and I began to talk, when Ògúnmọ́lá and I began to talk, ah! that very evening, following from what he said, and what I said, that very evening he made the decision to move to Òṣogbo from Adó-Èkìtì. That very evening we became friends.

The epiphanic advent of the male friend—expected but unannounced, mysteriously strange but with the familiarity of a lifelong companionship—had, as its counterpart, the inexplicable rupture. Lásún Ọláíítán was one of the founding members of the company when it went professional in 1963. He had just completed his teacher training, but "theater work didn't interfere with my teaching job at all at that time, and we worked together for a long time." But then a misunderstanding broke out between him and Adéjọbí (whom he referred to as "my boss"). When I asked the cause of this misunderstanding, he replied,

> It was what the Yorùbá call the work of Èṣù, that the Europeans call the **Devil's work.** Because neither of us could ever **account** for the thing that caused it. . . . When people ask the two of us, we can offer all kinds of explanations for what made me leave, but we can't hit upon a single **cogent point** that really explains why I left. But after—a long time afterward, quite a long time afterward, when time had passed on the matter, I began to think about it, when people called us and asked if we had had a quarrel. When they asked me, I would say there had been no quarrel; if they asked my boss, he too would say there was no quarrel. People didn't know whether there was a quarrel or not. So everyone kept quiet and stopped gossiping, saying "In due course they will get back together again." On the evening that I went back to him, I just met him sitting outside the house that day, I said "**Well,** I'm here!" It wasn't long ago, it was less than two months ago. I said "I'm here." And he said "Welcome back."

Male friendship is at the core of several of the company's plays. *The Royal Palm-nut,* though initially set up as a story of two rivals competing for the throne, turns quickly into a drama of two male friends split by the scheming and deceitful wife of one of them. It is because Tóògùn and Làágbé have an unbreakable pact (*ìmùlẹ̀*) to protect each others' interests that Tóògùn feels bound to inform Làágbé when he catches Làágbé's wife Díẹ̀kọ́lá committing adultery. Díẹ̀kọ́lá, however, intercepts Tóògùn and cleverly turns the tables on him by appealing to that very theme of male bonding. She tells Làágbé that Tóògùn came to the house with the intention of raping her, and declares "This man has betrayed your friendship." Làágbé is so shocked at this alleged betrayal that he does not even wait to hear Tóògùn's story before he drives him out of the house and subsequently out of the town. Thus a bond is broken which should have transcended all others and which should have led to Làágbé getting the throne with Tóògùn's help and then sharing his good fortune with him.

What is interesting, though, is that in exile in the bush, a new partnership between Tóògùn and his wife Débòmí gradually emerges; while in town, Làágbé and his wife Díẹ̀kọ́lá plot together to get hold of the palm nut they hear has come into Tóògùn's possession. It is Díẹ̀kọ́lá, acting as Làágbé's agent, who goes to Tóògùn's farm shack to steal the palm nut; and it is Débòmí who points out that even though the palm nut Díẹ̀kọ́lá stole was a fake, the other couple might nonetheless take it to the kingmakers and pass it off as a real one. Débòmí and Tóògùn hurry back to town together and, entering the palace just at the moment when Làágbé is about to be hailed as king by the populace, jointly call a halt to the proceedings. Thus, the partnership of the two male bosom friends has been replaced by the partnership of each man with his wife: Débòmí has become Tóògùn's partner in righteousness, just as Díẹ̀kọ́lá became Làágbé's partner in crime. Though muted, Tóògùn's alliance with his sensible and stalwart wife turns out to be the partnership that endures and finally triumphs.

An even more developed treatment of the theme of conjugal partnership is found in *The Secret Is Out,* adapted from a literary play about an office worker and his educated wife. Here, the wayward character is the husband who has an affair with his secretary, opens negotiations to marry her, and in the process almost loses his staunch, sensible, and loyal wife, the mother of his five children and co-builder of the family house (see Chapter 5). Since my only source for the Adéjọbís' version of this most interesting drama is *Atọ́ka*—and since there is reason to believe that this magazine's rendition owes as much to Dáramọ́lá's published literary text as to the Adéjọbí Company's stage version—it would be rash to draw any strong conclusions. Nonetheless, the very fact that the theater company chose to dramatize this paean to exclusive companionate marriage suggests a range beyond the "beware of women" ambit.

Looking at the corpus of plays in the 1980s repertoire as a field of possibilities, one is struck not only by the repetition of familiar stereotypes—the innocent heroine, the domineering termagant, the sexual predator and adulterer, the garrulous "tough" old woman—but also by the capacity of the theater to encompass new models of behavior, both bad and good. In *Besotted Bridegroom* the company produced an unprecedentedly extreme image of female transgression, requiring extreme punishment. But they also produced, in *The Secret Is Out,* what was probably an unprecedentedly positive and progressive model of companionate marriage, while *The Royal Palm-nut* shows both poles—an aggressive treacherous wife and a sensible one who becomes her husband's partner. My suggestion is that the specific division of labor and the particular problems surrounding male-female relationships within the theater company might have provided materials that went into the expansion of the theater's representational range in both directions.

MOBILE AND PRESIDING POWERS

All the plays in the repertoire of the Oyin Adéjọbí Company showed patterns of power being transformed and reconfigured in the course of the narrative. Even more directly than with the representations of gender relations, the theater company's own internal distribution of authority shaped the way in which power was enacted. Plays could only be constructed out of the materials available, most notably human materials—the actors. But the actors did not come as autonomous individuals; as we have seen, they were part of a tiered, family-like organization in which each had a recognized status and relationship to the others. These relationships, and not just the potential of the actors as individuals, formed part of the material on which the play-makers worked. They filtered the ways in which power was configured on stage. This was particularly noteworthy in the case of the relationships between the two key figures in the company, Oyin Adéjọbí and Alhaji Kàrímù Adépọ̀jù.

Oyin Adéjọbí was the founder, "father," and owner of the theater company. He was the owner of all the company's material components and he also owned the profits, such as they were, once expenses and salaries had been paid. He was the creator of the theater company's earliest nonmaterial patrimony, its songs, and he remained, throughout the theater's life, the only member of the company to sing the opening glee, accompanied by the women. Alhaji was on a salary, and though his role in the management and expenditure of the company's total income was crucial, he disclaimed any rights of ownership. But from the time in the early 1960s when he became the company's manager, he had a central role in the practical business affairs of the company. It was he who took the professional commercial company on tour throughout the decade when Adéjọbí remained tied to his council clerk job, up to 1973. Ten years later Alhaji's importance reasserted itself as Adéjọbí increasingly felt the strains of theater life. Alhaji also had an increasingly important role in the invention and generation of the plays. As spoken dialogue and neatly contrived plots became more important than sung text and lavish casts, so did Alhaji's synoptic vision and precise control of all the components of the performance. His status as the charismatic star actor, recognized and acclaimed by audiences wherever they went, grew throughout the life of the theater company, while Adéjọbí's more mellow self-presentation as a beloved, avuncular figure remained more or less unchanged.

This shifting but always dual structure of power can be seen working itself out in the plays. Adéjọbí always played an authority figure. His characters were of necessity always sedentary, and Oyin Adéjọbí is a large, imposing figure with a wonderfully rich and resonant voice. His authority figures almost always seemed to preside rather than to rule by force. In a number of plays, this presiding power had a counterpart, a more active, migratory, and transformative power, embodied in characters played by Alhaji.

In *Kúyẹ̀*, for example, Adéjọbí played the Ọba of the town where the deaf-mute orphan Kúyẹ̀ (played by Alhaji) innocently joins the wrestling match and defeats the reigning champion. The Ọba's part is the visual and structural center of most of the second half of the play: the wrestling happens at his behest and in his presence; Kúyẹ̀ is taken in at his command to enjoy his hospitality in the palace; when Kúyẹ̀ goes missing, it is the Ọba who convenes his household and sends his messengers out to search for him; and it is to his presence that the miraculously restored Kúyẹ̀ is led. He is a benign figure accorded the greatest respect by his people, but his power is curtailed by the threatening figure of Ṣégẹ̀, the champion wrestler, whose defeat the Ọba is unable to secure. Kúyẹ̀, an ignorant stranger who wanders in out of the bush, is the active and transformative agent. Although he seems a victim, at every stage of the narrative it is his actions that make everything happen. At the end of the play, when Kúyẹ̀ is ennobled, enrobed, married, and a master of the art of Yorùbá rhetoric, a space is made for him beside the Ọba. The Ọba delegates to Kúyẹ̀ the power to judge the debt case of his relatives and to visit on them whatever punishment he sees fit. Kúyẹ̀ raises his own authority to almost sublime heights when he declares that he will forgive them. We end, then, with a bright new power shining under the auspices of the old one.

In two other "folkloric" plays, *The Royal Palm-nut* and *Láníyọnu*, Adéjọbí's presiding authority ends up being replaced by the new power. In both, Adéjọbí is the Àràbà-awo, the head of the divination priests and principal kingmaker, acting as regent in a town which has lost its Ọba and is in the process of trying to appoint a new one. In *The Royal Palm-nut*, he is superseded by Alhaji's character Tóògùn, who takes over as kingmaker at the end; in *Láníyọnu*, the Àràbà's regency—which has lasted 10 years—is blown away by the hero, Láníyọnu (played by Alhaji), who, armed with a magical stave, destroys the monster that is terrorizing the town, subdues the chiefs, and accepts the throne only on condition that they mend their ways.

In the more "modern" domestic moral comedies, the presiding authority is most often a *baálé*, the head of a household or compound. In *Taking Care of Kúnlé* and *Besotted Bridegroom*, Adéjọbí is the head of a compound, in the first case a reasonably wise and benign one, in the second a corrupt one whose greed contributes to the destruction of two people. In *Articulated Lorry* he is the landlord whose rooms the other characters rent. In *The Road to Riches* the figure has been so marginalized—a "big man," rich and patriarchal, who builds a house but is almost irrelevant to the core plot—that though he has all the attributes of a presiding authority he has nothing to preside over. In these plays, Alhaji occupied a much greater variety of roles: in two of them (*Taking Care of Kúnlé* and *Articulated Lorry*) he is a fairly decent man tricked by a predatory woman; in one (*Besotted Bridegroom*) he is a lame and half-blind irascible elder; and in one (*The Road to Riches*) a blameless wealthy man whose success was based on hard work, thrift, and investment. In all these plays, his part is the central character around whom the plot revolves, while the presiding figure played by Adéjọbí at most provides a framework for the action.

Finally, there were two plays in the repertoire in the early 1980s—both relatively new ones—in which there was no role for Adéjọbí at all. In both, the authority figure was instead played by John, and the distribution of power and authority was quite different. In *The Overreacher,* John was in the position of a presiding power—an Ọba of an old-fashioned town—but all the signs were reversed. Instead of presiding, this Ọba bullies; instead of administering the law, he creates senseless new ones. He is a restlessly mobile and destructive power occupying the position of a presiding power. In *External Appearances,* the authority figure at the center of the play is again a non-traditional one: John plays the Aládùúrà preacher to whom Bísí, the modern young woman, comes to seek help in her pursuit of a husband. In this role he is even more mobile than in *The Overreacher:* a whirling, chanting, praying religious enthusiast who keeps his congregation in a constant ferment of activity.

It is apparent, then, that the earlier plays (*Kúyẹ̀, Láníyọnu, The Royal Palm-nut*) assigned bigger roles to Adéjọbí—their importance being enhanced by the fact that in all three cases the presiding authority figure was also in command of all the important sequences of sung text, large chunks of which still survived even 20 years after the transition to spoken dialogue had set in. In the later plays, the presiding authority was less central to the action, and in two of the newest it was absent altogether. It is also apparent that in these early plays, the twin rule of Adéjọbí and Alhaji worked its way into the plays in the form of paired figures (Ọba and hero; Àràbà and hero) in which the new mobile power (Alhaji) either co-existed with, or replaced, the old presiding power (Adéjọbí). But in the later plays, Alhaji usually became the sole magnetic center of the action, assembling the other characters round him through the quiet but irresistible gravitational pull of his deadpan humor, while Adéjọbí's character provided an institutional frame of reference. Finally, in the plays where Adéjọbí did not appear at all, a new pattern emerged where the presiding and the mobile powers were combined into one, in John's character, releasing Alhaji to exploit the subversive and sardonic possibilities of structurally less central figures.

The changing internal structure of the company, then, encouraged or facilitated a mode of representation in the plays that separated power into mobile and presiding forms. The presiding power is usually, though not always, associated with traditional roles such as Ọbaship, regency, or headship of a compound: established roles which predate the holder and which are ascriptive in that they are only open to certain categories of people defined by lineage membership, gender, or seniority. The mobile power in the plays is usually the opposite of ascriptive: attained by an outsider, rendered eligible for the position only by his innate qualities, often against all traditional expectations. The most popular play in the repertoire, *Kúyẹ̀*, is the play where the mobile power—the deaf and dumb orphan—starts out at the greatest possible distance from high office, demonstrating the potential that everyone has for a transformation of social status (see Chapter 11). Láníyọnu, similarly, is converted into a mobile power by being stripped of all his possessions, people, and position, reduced to a quasi-orphan lost in the forest and empowered by a spiritual being whose abode cannot be known by humans. Invited by the chiefs to take the throne of Ayélẹ̀rù, he at first replies "Not me! I'm not a native of this town, for a start. And then I don't come from a lineage that is eligible for the throne. How can I come from a remote place, far far away, to be given a title here?" But his moral qualities are what the town needs for its regeneration, and Láníyọnu is persuaded to stay. The mobile power is thus incorporated into the framework of presiding power, just as it is in *Kúyẹ̀*. In non-folkloric plays, the mobile power may occupy an authority position of its own, but it is likely to be a non-traditional and largely self-created one, such as the Aládùúrà preacher in *External Appearances*.

In all the plays, the office of the presiding power is preserved, but in most of them, assent to the presiding power's authority is partially withheld. The presiding figures are rarely wholly admirable. The lineage head in *Besotted Bridegroom* takes Mosún's bribe and seems prepared to flout lineage land law. As we saw in Chapter 6, some members of the audience saw his venality as the central pivot of the narrative and suggested that the play should be retitled "The Unrighteous Elder" to reflect this. Even so, he retains his status as central moral authority insofar as it is he who pronounces the final lesson. The Aládùúrà preacher in *External Appearances* accepts a huge donation from the heroine's new rich suitor and consequently refrains from discouraging her pursuit of him, even though his spiritual vision has shown clearly that another man, Písí, is the destined one. Nonetheless it is the preacher who lectures Bísí on her greed at the end of the play and leads the audience in pronouncing the verdict on her behavior. The preacher—portrayed with John Adéwuni's usual violent brio—seemed a comic figure with his exaggerated whirling, singing, chanting, and preaching. His sly pocketing of the large bribe from the rich suitor—even while feigning to refuse it—provoked roars of derisive laughter. But when I suggested to Adéjọbí that the play made fun of the preacher, he was shocked.

"Not at all, not at all. Since my own church is an Aládùúrà church, I would not do that at all."

This pervasive ambivalence cannot be explained simply as a case of the familiar distinction between the office (which must be upheld) and the officeholder (who can be criticized)—for many of the venal officeholders continue nonetheless to exercise moral authority rather than being brought to book. Nor can these flips and switches of moral function be fully understood—as they could perhaps be in Ghanaian concert party (Cole 1997; Barber, Collins, and Ricard 1997)—as the product of an opportunistic, loose-jointed presentational aesthetic of "immediate impact," for the style of the Adéjọbí company was much more deliberately coherent, tightly knit, and consistent than that of concert party. It is more as if there was a working agreement to have properly constituted authorities and to respect them and keep them in place, coupled with a permanent skepticism about all power, a permanent reluctance to bow wholly to it.

This interpretation resonates with the strong and widely shared preference in Yorùbáland for individual productive and personal autonomy. To be an independent entrepreneur, with all the risks it involves, is far preferable to "serving" an employer. In the political and social arenas, despite the assiduity with which people cultivate patrons, no one likes to be fully "under" someone else, fully determined by their authority. A fundamental belief in hierarchy as a natural and inevitable feature of social life is fused with a profound reluctance ever to succumb entirely to those set above one by God, fate, or chance. The popular theater company, like other small artisanal businesses, afforded to its practitioners the satisfaction of a relatively high degree of productive autonomy. This may have lent an additional confidence to the theater's representation of power as almost always flawed and to its almost automatic withholding of full assent to any overlord.

POLITICS AND PUBLIC MORALITY

The Adéjọbí Company worked in a public space that was in part defined by the institutions of the Nigerian state. They felt the hand of the government in the daily pursuit of their trade: when officials came to levy an entertainment tax at the very door of the hall where they had just finished performing; when the television studio managers told Adéjọbí that "they didn't want any political play"; and when curfews impeded their late-night return from a performance. They felt the negligence of government, which failed to support them with the public recognition, sponsorship, and permanent civic theater buildings they felt they deserved. In a more general sense, their very conception of themselves and their "public" was founded upon the institutions of state broadcasting, state-run schools, state-sponsored sport, and state-approved public buildings such as community centers and town halls. Though the local self-help ethos permeated all the institutions they worked with, nonetheless the public space in which they operated was at least partially underwritten by the state.

But at the level of explicit comment, the popular theater rarely opened its mouth about politics. The Adéjọbí company was founded in the postwar period of labor unrest and decolonization; it went professional soon after Nigeria's Independence; it lived through the civil war, the coup of 1975, the assassination of Murtala Muhammad in 1976, and the further coups of 1983/1984 and 1985. It operated successfully under civilian and military regimes alike. And it finally began to lose its impetus in the 1990s under the impact of an economic catastrophe resulting from national mismanagement as well as international economic imbalance on a gigantic scale. Yet none of the plays from any point in the company's history seems to have mentioned the state directly. Even the "This Nigeria!" type of commentary—which managed to keep alive in newspaper columns at least up until the advent of Abacha in 1993—was absent.

Only in the opening glees could overt references to Nigeria's political situation and future occasionally be found. One opening glee song is a reworking of the Church of the Lord anthem hailing Africa's spiritual regeneration: "Africa will surely rise / Ah! Plain and patent / Creeping, crawling, she will rise" (Turner 1967, II:312). In the opening glee version, it is Nigeria which is described as "crawling" and for which a glorious future is predicted, and the tone appears patriotic rather than messianic. Another opening glee song, which entered the repertoire in the mid or late 1980s, is a stirring call to citizens to do their utmost for the country: "Nigeria is calling us / Come, and do what is required / Let us work with good will, because / Deeds that are done are recounted." However, songs like this are not only rare, but they are also notable for their uncontentious, vague patriotism. Dark times are alluded to but no blame is laid at anyone's door, and the way forward is through moral reform: hard work, cooperation, cleaving to the truth.

The plays themselves never use the word "Nigeria" and hardly ever mention the government, let alone criticize its policies or leaders. This is in marked contrast with other genres that flourished alongside the theater, such as humorous newspaper columns and topical chanted and printed neo-traditional poetry. The records, cassettes, and publications of artists such as Láńrewájú Adépòjù and Túnbọ̀sún Ọládàpọ̀ continued to broadcast outspoken criticisms of the government—even to the point of naming names—right through the repressive regimes of Buhari and Babangida (1984–1993). In the crisis of the annulled elections of 1993, Láńrewájú put out a cassette which addressed Babangida directly, though in Yorùbá, which the dictator did not understand: "Babangida, get out . . . it's time for you to go."

This makes it implausible to attribute the apparent silence of the popular theater wholly to the fear of censorship. It is true that the live theater—although less subject to routine interference than TV, because outside the operational control of the elite managerial class—was exceptionally visible and would thus have been more vulnerable than other genres to sudden clampdowns if it had stuck its neck out. The bad experiences of Ògúnǹdé, who almost alone among theater leaders had staged overtly political plays, both in the colonial era and after Independence, were well remembered by other theater leaders.[8] Large productions, involving 20 or more actors and a big investment of time and effort (including the huge physical effort of traveling "on tour"), were more exposed than small publications and cheaply produced cassettes which could be run off as required, circulated informally, and easily concealed. Nonetheless, if the theater companies had been burning to discharge explicit criticisms of the government it is probable that they could have found ways to do so—as Zairean popular television troupes did under much heavier surveillance (Mbala Nkanga 1995). The fact is that among the members of the Adéjọbí company, at least, there was little sign that they were practicing self-censorship for fear of government reprisals.

This is borne out by the tone and scope of the one example of explicit comment on national politics that did surface in the 1980s repertoire of the company. In 1979, after 14 years of successive military regimes, there was a return to civilian rule and a general relaxing of constraints. The dominant National Party of Nigeria (NPN) came to power after a massive electoral exercise which had involved months of campaigning, press coverage, and television appearances by the leaders of the five contesting parties. The press loosened up dramatically; there were suddenly floods of reports in partisan papers of the fraud and corruption of members of the other parties. The *Tribune* supported Awólọ́wọ̀ and the Unity Party of Nigeria (UPN); the *Concord* (owned by M. K. O. Abíọ́lá) supported Shagari and the NPN. Politicians were suddenly highly visible, and the news became salacious and often hilarious instead of grimly or blandly uninformative. *Articulated Lorry*, which was created around the time of the elections, participated to some extent in this general talkativeness. At the beginning of the play, when the landlord boasts of his new powers as local chairman of a political party, this incurs his wife's contempt:

> Han-ìn, Bàbá Àkànmú, oyè afinijoyèe baba ẹgbẹ́, ṣé n lẹ wáá sọ di oyè gan-an ni? "Kẹnkẹ Júbílì." Ẹ wò ó, ẹ jémi ó sòótọ́ ọ̀rọ̀ fún yín, gbogbo àwọn tí ń gbé pọtilẹ́dà, ńtorí owó ni. Ẹ rò pé bí wọn ò bá rówó, wọ́n lè máa gbé pọtilẹ́dà ni?

> Er, Bàbá Àkànmú, are you thinking that a mere chairmanship of a

party is a real chieftaincy title? "Jubilee Celebration!" Look, let me tell you the truth. All the people who carry briefcases do so because of money. Do you think they would be carrying briefcases if they didn't get money out of it?

Sèlíá dismisses both the title and the members of the association who bestowed it on him. He is wrong to treat his appointment as a big event, like the old Jubilee of colonial times. "Those who carry briefcases"—the politicians—do so with a view toward lining their own pockets.

The tenants in the landlord's house join in this adverse commentary. They are unanimous in their refusal to have anything to do with the landlord's party. Bàbáa Wàndé, the truck driver, says, "Now, I'm only speaking for myself, but as far as I'm concerned, you can remove my name from any political party. I won't be a member of any political party. I vote for my truck. When I go to Kontagora, and pick up a load of cattle in Kaira and come back via Kano, how could I have time to belong to any political party? I won't have anything to do with it. Cross out my name! Do you understand? Because I won't vote for anyone, and no one will vote for me." His vehemence caused much amusement in the audience, and "I won't vote for anyone, no one will vote for me" was uttered with such succinct emphasis that they picked it up and repeated it afterward. Àlàbí, the young single man whose ambition was to go to university, had a different line of criticism. Rather than rejecting politicians as greedy self-enrichers, as Sèlíá did, or simply declaring himself too busy to be bothered with politics, as Bàbá Wàndé did, Àlàbí criticizes the whole partisan and competitive basis of Nigerian electioneering, its tendency to arouse passions and demand bloc loyalties:

ÀLÀBÍ: Nípa ti òrò Elégbé dé, e jòó sà, mo féé sàlàyé ki ní kan tí ò yé yín . . .
LANDLORD: Èmiiii . . .
ÀLÀBÍ: Béè ni sà.
LANDLORD: Tí ò yé èmi?
ÀLÀBÍ: Béè ni. Hen-en, e wò ó sà, e jé mò wí pé bí a se ń se egbé òsèlú ńléè wa yìí, kò bó sí i rárá.
LANDLORD: Lónà wo?
ÀLÀBÍ: Òdì, òdì, òdì báyìí là ń se é sí.
LANDLORD: Máa ronú nǹkan tó ò ń so o.
ÀLÀBÍ: Hen-èn, oríi won ò sì wáá pé sí i.
LANDLORD: Hèn-én!
ÀLÀBÍ: Béè ni. Bí e bá dé Lóńdònù ní . . .
TENANTS: Lónà wo? Lónà wo?
ÀLÀBÍ: Very good. Lóhùn-ún, bí àwon se ń se egbé òsèlú tiwon, ó

yàtọ̀. Náò, tọkọtìyàwó á wà, wọ́n a maa sisẹ́ ńbìkannáà. wọ́n á
sì maa ṣe ẹgbẹ́ ọ̀tọ̀tọ̀ . . . Tí ọ́n bá dénúulé, wọ́n á gbóńjẹ kalẹ̀,
ìyàwó á maa bi ọkọ wí pé, Baáléè mi, nínú ẹgbẹ́ tó ò ń ṣe, kí ni
ohun tí o rí ńbẹ̀ tí o fi ń ṣe ẹgbẹ́ yìí? Báwo lẹ ṣe ń ṣe ńnú ẹgbẹ́ẹ
yín? Ọkọ náà maa bìyàwó, wí pé, Háhà, ìwọ ìyàwó, báwo lẹ ti ń
ṣe . . . ? Wọ́n á maa fi ọ̀rọ̀ jomitoro ọ̀rọ̀ láàárín araa wọn. Wọ́n
a maa sọ̀rọ̀, inúu wọn á máa dùn. Kò ní síjà, kò ní í sì sásọ̀
láàárín wọn.

SÈLÍÁ: Wọn è é jà rárá?
ÀLÀBÍ: Àtọ́ọ̀l. Àtọ́ọ̀l. Hìn-ín.

ÀLÀBÍ: . . . as far as political parties are concerned, excuse me sir,
I want to explain something that you haven't understood—
LANDLORD: Me!
ÀLÀBÍ: Yes, sir.
LANDLORD: That *I* haven't understood—!
ÀLÀBÍ: Yes. You see, sir, you should know that the way we run political parties in this country is completely hopeless.
LANDLORD: In what way?
ÀLÀBÍ: We've got it all absolutely and completely and hopelessly back to front.
LANDLORD: Think what you're saying.
ÀLÀBÍ: They don't do it in a sensible way.
LANDLORD: What do you mean?
ÀLÀBÍ: It's true. If you go to London, now
TENANTS: How do you mean? How do you mean?
ÀLÀBÍ: **Very good.** There, the way they do their politics is different. **Now,** let's say there's a husband and wife, they're working at the same place but each belongs to a different party. When they get home in the evening, they get their meal ready, and the wife will ask her husband, "Husband, in your party, what is it that you do there that made you join them? How do you do things in your party?" And the husband will also ask the wife, "Ha, you, wife, how do you do things . . . ? " They have amicable discussions with each other in which they compare notes. They'll chat and they'll be content. There won't be any fighting or any quarrel between them.
SÈLÍÁ: Don't they ever fight at all?
ÀLÀBÍ: **At all. At all.**

As usual, the point is not to evoke the utopia of British democracy for its own sake but to use the exaggerated account of other people's ways of doing things as a diagnostic probe for local deficiencies. Àlàbí then goes on to intensify his criticism of Nigerian electioneering:

> Mo fẹ́ kí ẹ ṣàkíèsí ọ̀rọ̀ yìí. Ṣé ẹ wo àwọn tá à ń jìjàdù pé kí wọ́n lè bọ́ sórí àga. Njẹ́ ẹ mọ nǹkan tí ọn ń ṣe? Yẹ̀—yẹ́ ni ọn ń fi wá ṣe. Ẹ wò ó, ńgbà tí ọ́n bá dé Assembly Hall tí ọn tí ń ṣe mítìn, hẹn-èn, èyí tó yẹ kí wọ́n mú sọ nínú ọ̀rọ̀ tó jẹ́ kókó ọ̀rọ̀, wọn ò ní í sọ ọ́. Èyí tí ò yẹ kí wọ́n sọ, òun ni wọ́n ma ma sọ. Wọ́n á wáá wò wá sùn-ùn, wọ́n á bọ́ọ́ta báyìí, wọ́n á yínmú sí wa. Wọ́n á wá kùmọ̀ tó dáa, àdá, kóńdó, wọ́n á fi lé a lọ́wọ́ báyìí, wọ́n á ní ká bẹ̀rẹ̀ síí paraa wa.

> I want you to take note of this. You look at those people on whose behalf we're struggling, in order to get them elected! Do you know what they are doing? They are mocking us. Look when they get to the Assembly Hall where they hold their meetings, they don't say the important things they're supposed to say. They talk about all kinds of things that aren't on the agenda. Then they look at us with contempt, they come out like this and sneer at us. They'll get hold of strong cudgels, cutlasses, clubs, they'll put them in our hands and tell us to start killing each other.

This very outspoken criticism leads to a chorus of arguments and protests against the landlord and his involvement in politics. Bàbá Wándé has the last word: "Look, baba, don't be a 'chairman' any more, be a 'stool man' instead—*I'm* not joining any party!"

This discussion is certainly explicit, despite the discreetly euphemistic name of the landlord's political party—the "Cardboard Box Association." But its upshot is to dismiss party politics as a mug's game. Not only that, but, as we saw in Chapter 5, the sequence is peripheral and expendable in the sense that its topic does not lock into the main narrative and has no consequences for the unfolding of the plot. The theme of the landlord's politics is simply dropped in the remainder of the play. The theme that carries over from Àlàbí's disquisition is the ideal of marital harmony rather than the ideal of rational political participation.[9] Sarcastic and disgusted commentary on politics and politicians, then, is included for its topical appeal, but political activity is not in any way implicated in the moral logic of the plot. And other plays created by the Adéjọbí Company in the brief period of civilian rule (1979–1984) did not take up the option of openly discussing the current political situation at all.

Nonetheless, the theater as a form of modern public address does take up a position such that the government and the nation fall within the purview the theater shared with its audiences. Mr. Adéjọbí clearly felt that the plays successfully addressed the major public issues of the time:

> Theater is so important to the people of our country—specially

Yorùbáland—because I regard the practitioners as practical journalists. If you are a journalist you make the report in the paper. Not many people read the paper, and if they read it they read it for reading's sake. But just imagine putting on the stage the story of an Ọba who misused his position—you see—so there are messages that our people collect from our plays. (English)

One audience member I talked to—a young woman called Rónkẹ́ Abúlúdèé—confirmed that indeed "there are messages" that people "collect" from the plays. *The Royal Palm-nut*, as we have seen, is a play about a competition for chiefly title in which the dishonest candidate almost gets in by cheating but is exposed at the last minute by his uncompromising former friend, making way for the honest candidate to take the title. Rónkẹ́ said, "They did *The Royal Palm-nut* on television at the time of Shagari's elections—it was as if they knew what was going to happen." Shagari's party, the NPN, was widely regarded in western Nigeria as having massively rigged the 1983 elections which gained it a second term of office. Disgust and anger were high until January 1, 1984, when Shagari's government was overthrown by a military coup led by Buhari. What is interesting is that *The Royal Palm-nut* had been in the repertoire since about 1968 and had also been published in *Atọ́ka* under the title *Ayé Ṣòro* [*The World Is Hard*] in 1973. Theater-loving people such as Rónkẹ́ were almost certain to have seen it on stage—or at least to have heard about it—long before the television broadcast. Nonetheless she read this broadcast as a specific commentary on the current political situation—a commentary, moreover, which was even better than journalistic reporting, for in addition to commenting on what had already happened it also foresaw the future!

This goes one step further than the audience's usual practice of extracting a "lesson" from a play and applying it to their own lives. Rónkẹ́ had matched the plot of *The Royal Palm-nut* point by point to a known political situation and concluded that the play was not merely applicable to it (like a proverb) but actually "about" it (like a riddle) and, what is more, was endowed with some curious predictive affinity with it. Perhaps because of the way politics in Nigeria unleashes turbulent, charismatic, and dangerously unpredictable energies, political crises have the power to attract and seize formerly all-purpose free-floating stories, imbuing them with a singular meaning. This means that plays which look bland and general, peddling moral messages reducible to formulas such as "no ruler can succeed unless he takes advice from his subjects," can be read by the audiences as searing indictments of a current, specific malpractice or tyranny.

Such stories, however, are not to be seen as "hidden transcripts" (Scott

1990) encoding the "real," politically subversive message within an apparently innocent tale. Messages about the government, regime, or political party are not uniquely privileged or even especially salient themes. What seems to be important is the larger and more generalizable moral framework which encompasses them. Let me explain this with the example of *The Overreacher*, a new play in the repertoire in 1981 when I joined the company.

The newly installed despotic Ọba in this play proclaims "New water has flowed in, new fish have entered it"—that is, his regime will be different from that of his predecessor. He then announces a string of ridiculous new laws. The sellers of corn-starch loaves in the market will not be allowed to sit next to the sellers of beancakes: anyone who wants to eat ẹko and àkàrà (a standard combination) will have to walk a long way to get it. The customary wedding season is to be abolished, and instead there will be a regulated program of one marriage a day throughout the year. When the supply of new brides runs out, they will have to start re-doing the marriages of those who are already wives. No tailor will be allowed to sew more than one type of garment. "The one who sews a tunic must not also sew the trousers; he who sews trousers must not sew the overshirt." The punishment for breaking any of these new laws will be to drink cassava meal mixed with cement.

The king then interrogates all the town chiefs and dismisses them one by one, rejecting their advice and taking offense at the very idea that they consider it their role to offer it (for an excerpt from this passage, see Chapter 5). He mocks the Ìyálóde, the head of the town's women, saying "You think there are two Ọbas in this town!" When the royal wives sing "It was Ifá who saved this town from war," the Ọba indignantly demands: "Was it really Ifá who saved this town from war, or was it me, the Ọba?"

All these features of the Ọba's behavior are reminiscent of things people were saying about the military government. The deaf ear turned to advisers picks up on constant complaints that the military regimes of 1966–1979 were out of touch with civilian opinion. The Ọba's ridiculous but draconian new laws—laws which attempt to penetrate into people's daily business in their trades and crafts, their eating and drinking, and their family ceremonies—could easily be applied to periodic military government interventions such as the following: price fixing; violent action against "hoarding" by market women; the War Against Indiscipline which forbade, among other things, "rushing onto buses"; the ruthless clearance of Lagos streets of so-called vagrants (including the murder of more than 50 of them in the infamous Black Maria incident); beating of motorists with whips and truncheons by police for traffic offenses; and the barbarity of Bar Beach public executions. Cement itself was, of course, a resonant icon of government folly after the 1975 demurrage scandal, when German importers were able to charge Nigerians huge sums for their delayed access to the overcrowded port as excessive shipments of cement converged on Lagos. And the Ọba's repeated insistence that he alone has power over everything, can change everything, and can take credit for everything is the most salient characteristic of all military governments. The ear-splitting, violent, bullying Ọba repetitiously laying down the law in crude slogans seems to offer a ready-made image of the rulers of Nigeria from 1966 to 1979 and from 1983 to 1999.

The Ọba, however, is not brought down by human opposition but by supernatural sanctions when he tries to force himself on a girl he has seized from another man. He is afflicted with a violent fit of canine howling and barking, and the curse is only lifted when the Ọba (following a diviner's prescription) apologizes humbly to the girl and her betrothed husband. The moral, spoken by the palace messenger Gbajúmọ̀ and reiterated in the closing song, is

> Ipò lo ní ni, má(à) i yanmọnìkejì jẹ. Owó lo ní ni, má(à) e yọmọnì-kejì jẹ. Ọlá lo ní ni, mée yanmọnìkejì jẹ torí wí péé gbogbo nǹkan ipò, ọlá, owó, iyì, ẹni tó ni ín rèé—ỌLỌ́UN. Béèyàn bá lò ó ńlò-kulò, yóò kàbùkùù. Kò sẹ́ni ó ga jàbùkù lọ o. Má(à) hùwààgbéraga o. Kò sẹ́ni ó ga jàbùkù lọ o.

> If you have position, don't use it to exploit your fellow human being. If you have money, don't use it to exploit your fellow human being. If you have high status, don't use it to exploit your fellow human being, because all things—position, money, high status, esteem, the owner of it all is none other than—GOD. If people use these things badly, they will be disgraced. There is no one who is so high he is above disgrace. Don't act arrogantly. There's no one who is so high he is above disgrace.

What is significant in this moral lesson is its insistence that the cure for political ills is common morality, a bedrock of good behavior that is required of all human beings alike. The play does not suggest that the bad leader is a pathological monster who should be eliminated and replaced by a charismatic hero. Rather, it insists that the bad ruler should be reminded of his humanity, his vulnerability, and his inability to escape the common lot. Gbajúmọ̀ underlines this when he explains to the Ọba that if he wants to be restored to normality, he must ask for forgiveness from those he has wronged: "You will humble yourself absolutely. You'll forget that you are the Ọba." If the Ọba refuses to do this, the town chiefs will soon get rid of him: "If after a week or two your mouth hasn't returned to normal and you are still carrying it around like a curved drumstick, it won't be long before they choose a new Ọba." The Ọba has to acknowledge—publicly and formally—his common humanity and his ultimate dependence on the support of his people if he is to retain divine or cosmic sanction.

The call to remember common values regardless of status is, in fact, addressed not just to the Ọba but to the public as a whole, for them to apply to their own lives: if in the future *they* attain honor, status, or money, they should not let it turn them aside from the common and commonsense standard of good behavior. It implies then that *anyone* might in principle expect to be elevated and that *everyone*, no matter how high they rise, should remember they are still just like us. The proverb which Gbajúmọ̀ quotes when remonstrating with the Ọba, "Let us do as has always been done, so that things will be as they have always been," is not so much an appeal to "tradition" per se as an act of *recall*. The Ọba is being called back to the path of established, proper ways of doing things grounded in a presumption of common humanity.

The theater company's apparent reticence about Nigerian political events seems, then, to derive from deep assumptions about the nature of power, action, and character rather than from mere fear of censorship or lack of interest in current affairs. Topical neo-traditional poetry such as that of Túnbọ̀sún and Lánrewájú is, or can be, pure commentary: the individual poet (who thematizes himself in some texts as a special, unusual person as well as a purveyor of received wisdom) sounds off about what he observes and reflects upon. But the plays, as we have seen, are not topical commentaries or expressions of opinion so much as generalizable examples of the consequences of moral action. The moral truths that are excavated and confirmed are seen as inherent in the structure of moral action itself and as universally applicable. These demonstrations, in the theater company's view, did indeed furnish a profound commentary on political affairs. For the theater practitioners did not feel that the really fundamental moral and social issues of life were concentrated in the actions of the state. The state was seen as an irritant, a disappointment, and an outrage. But state institutions, state provision and regulation, and the political regime itself—whether civilian or military, democratic or despotic—were not seen as the key to change that would most beneficially transform people's lives. Deficiencies in the state were seen as a manifestation—almost a by-product—of a more general, shared moral condition, and it was to this condition that the lessons of the plays were directed. Social regeneration would come from general human moral activity and from people's responsibility for the well-being of themselves and their families or communities.

John Adéwuni as the despotic Ọba in *The Overreacher.* ©Elio Montanari

The idea that edification begins at home is pervasive in southern Nigeria and has visible organizational expression. Communal self-betterment—based on the belief that local communities have the organic cohesion and moral will to transform themselves while the state does not—has been a highly dynamic and successful project of "hometown associations" in southern Nigeria since the 1930s (Barkan, McNulty, and Ayeni 1991; Coleman 1960, 213–15, 343–345; Peel 1983, 175–196; Trager 1998). And communal self-betterment in turn is seen as stemming from the active, progressive, public-spirited outlook of individual members of the community.

It is tempting but I think mistaken to read the theater's narratives of adultery, betrayed friendship, and personal greed as *allegories* or *metaphors* for corruption and betrayal by the state—the "private" standing in for the "public." The monstrous, overbearing cash madam in *Besotted Bridegroom* does not seem to me to be a coded or sublimated reference to a monstrous, overbearing, and self-enriching state. Rather, the play is telling its audiences that sudden wealth, no matter where it is concentrated, should not be allowed to overturn the order of things as enshrined in respect for elders and for senior wives, observance of inheritance laws, and collective lineage interests. Common morality, decency, and respect are the only things that can preserve this order. This lesson can be applied very appositely to petro-naira politicians, of course, but only as one example of a more general case.

The continuity between personal, family, community, and state morality is encapsulated in another of the theater company's opening glees. The song asks God to help us regenerate our "own" (our affairs, anything pertaining to us), our "behavior" or moral character, and our "land," in that order:

Èdùmàrè a bẹ̀ ọ́ọ́ọ́
Bá wa tún tiwa ṣeee
Bá wa túnwà wa ṣe
Bá wa túnlẹ̀ wa ṣee
Kógun ó dúróóó
Kọ́tẹ̀ ó parí ooo
Sèrántí pé iṣẹ́ ọwọ́ rẹ
Lọmọ ènìyàn-àn-àn.
Oníṣẹ́ kì í jẹ́ṣẹ́ rẹ̀ ó bàjẹ́
Àààà
Baaba
Bá wa túnlẹ̀ ṣeeee.

Oh Lord we beg you
Mend our affairs for us
Mend our behavior for us
Mend our land for us
So that war will cease
And conspiracy will end
Remember that humankind
Is the work of Your hand.
The maker never allows his works to spoil
Ah
Father
Mend our land for us.

The uninterrupted continuity between people's moral behavior and the state of the country which is subject to war and plotting could hardly be clearer.[10] It is not so much that one level *signifies* another as that all levels are equivalent in being governed by a single, common morality.

The moral address of the plays is thus essentially inclusive. The theater's populist insistence that everyone is at bottom ruled by the same moral exigencies may not spell "subversion" or "resistance"—but it is profoundly leveling all the same. Politics, then, is a subcategory of ordinary morality. This authorizes everyday experience to speak and to proffer its own models of behavior to rulers and those who aspire to be rulers. And it is the concrete detail in which everyday experience is enacted on the stage that endows this morality with the power to convince.

10 Literacy, "Enlightenment," and "Tradition"

The actors, I have suggested, could be described as clerkly artisans: and both halves of this combination were crucial for the formation of the popular theater. In this chapter, I trace the significance of literacy in the practice of the theater and its link with ideas of "enlightenment" and "progress." In the next chapter I look at the significance of artisanal trades and physical labor in relation to conceptions of destiny and self-realization.

SCHOOL

Mission schools were established in Yorùbáland as early as the 1840s. But it was after the entrenchment of colonial rule and the spread of its institutions into the hinterland that a school education came to be widely perceived as the single most potent mechanism for social self-betterment. Literacy and numeracy—and above all the ability to speak and write English— were the passports to the new forms of salaried employment of the colonial era. Schooling not only led to clerical jobs in the civil service and the big commercial houses, it also became the defining feature of the condition of ọlájú—"civilization" or "enlightenment" (Peel 1978, 148)—which enhanced social status. As Ayandele has noted, "To the masses education was the only key that could unlock the mysteries and prosperity of the new world being created" (1966, 289).[1] The rapid expansion of school provision that got under way in the second and third decades of the twentieth century[2] was fueled by demand. The people themselves paid for much of the official educational provision (both government schools and the far more numerous government-assisted mission schools) through school fees and church collections. But this provision was never sufficient to meet their aspirations. They founded their own "private" schools in such large numbers that as early as the 1920s they could cater for four times as many pupils as the government and mission schools combined—to the alarm of the authorities, who tried in vain to curb their expansion.[3] Private unassisted schools remained important and numerous right up to the 1970s (Fafunwa 1974, 127).

Qur'anic schools, which rested on a longer-established tradition of Arabic literacy, were already very numerous by the late nineteenth century, greatly outnumbering both the official and the unofficial Christian schools.[4] But Arabic scholarship, though highly prestigious within Islam, did not provide qualifications for white-collar jobs, nor did it have the associations with "progress" and the acquisition of "development goods" that Western-type schooling did. It is a sign of the immense pulling power of these aspirations that a body of Muslims in Lagos in 1923 set up the Ansar-ud-Deen society precisely to remedy this lack, establishing Western-type schools that taught the same curriculum as the government and mission schools but with an Islamic instead of a Christian ambience.[5] A concerted program of school-building resulted in widespread diffusion of Ansar-ud-Deen and other Islamic primary and secondary schools in the 1950s and 1960s.[6] The Ansar-ud-Deen Society and other associations of the same type were consciously modernizing and reforming, were semi-secular in their endorsement of modernity, and were much influenced by Christian protocol in their services and rituals. The nature of their commitment to literacy and education was probably closer to that of Christian progressives than to that of conservative Muslim reformers such as Al-Hajj Adam Al-Iluri, founder of the Arabic Training Centre, which devoted itself to the production of excellent Arabic scholars, some of whom remained ignorant of English throughout their lives. Nonetheless, the Ansar-ud-Deen schools did not cause Muslim children to lose touch with the older Qur'anic forms of education altogether, and many pupils combined the two. Alhaji, who went to school in the late 1940s and early 1950s, attended first a Qur'anic school and then an Ansar-ud-Deen primary school before he went on to a government modern school. Thus, the project of educational enlightenment was at least partially articulated with an older and very widely diffused Islamic educational tradition. Both traditions, moreover, in different ways were centers of respectful attention and desire.[7]

People sacrificed themselves to get schooling for their children. Even in the depression of the 1930s, the director of education observed that "one of the last economies of Southern Nigerian parents is school fees" (Fafunwa 1974, 131). Everyone of Adéjọbí's generation must have been touched by the extraordinarily active and dynamic search for schooling, involving self-sacrifice, travel, and persistence on the part of the pupils and a do-it-yourself entrepreneurial zeal on the part of the proprietors of the "private venture" educational institutions such as the one Adéjọbí himself attended in Lagos. And when limited self-government through elected regional assemblies was introduced in 1951, one of the principal factors in the Action Group's victory was their promise of Universal Free Primary

Education—a promise they mobilized vast resources to keep, so that by the late 1960s, Fafunwa estimates, 90 percent of primary school–aged children were registered in school (1974, 168).

The Protestant missions which inaugurated "modern," Western-type schooling in the 1840s did so with a view toward the rapid and widespread inculcation of print literacy, so that each individual convert would be able to read the Bible for him or herself and so that mass proselytization could spread, by means of print, farther than the spoken word of the handful of missionaries who worked in the region. For these purposes, basic literacy in Yorùbá, not a literary education in English, was the most efficient tool.[8] From the first establishment of its mission station at Abẹ́òkúta in 1846,[9] the CMS set about producing texts in Yorùbá—grammars, primers, and translations of a number of books of the Bible. In this enterprise the presence of the bilingual and often bicultural Saro catechists and missionaries was surely crucial and helps to account for the early and extensive development of a Yorùbá-language literature unparalleled in West Africa. Not only did the Saro clerical elite greatly facilitate the reduction of Yorùbá to writing and the pioneering creation of a standard written version of Yorùbá grammar and vocabulary (see Ajayi 1960; Awoniyi 1978; Fagbọrun 1994), they also participated in the production of a written Yorùbá discourse of everyday life and events. The *Ìwé-Ìròhìn*, published by the CMS in Abẹ́òkúta between 1859 and 1867, was a newspaper in Yorùbá with English additions; this paved the way for an efflorescence of both secular and religious Yorùbá writing by the Saro elite in Lagos from the 1880s onward, when the rise of cultural nationalism inspired numerous volumes of local history, collections of poetry and proverbs, and works such as E. M. Lijadu's on Ifá divination poetry.

This early concentration on Yorùbá literacy, however, was challenged both by the colonial government (as it gathered the reins of power and began to intervene in educational matters from 1882 onward) and by many Yorùbá people (who wanted an education in English in order to gain access to the growing sphere of salaried employment). A struggle over the status of the "vernacular" in education ensued, both within the Lagos and Abẹ́òkúta elites and between the colonial government and the missions (Awoniyi 1978; see also Zachernuk 1998). The outcome was that though English became firmly installed as the language of prestige and was the sole medium of instruction in secondary schools, Yorùbá-language literacy continued strongly at the lower levels of schooling and was taught as a subject up to the highest level.

The proportion of those who proceeded from primary to secondary school was always tiny. In 1942, when Oyin Adéjọbí was at primary school, less than 3 percent of his cohort could expect to go on to grammar school.[10] Between 1955 and 1965 many more grammar schools were opened, and modern schools were established to provide a shorter and more vocationally oriented post-primary course. But since primary provision was also expanding, the bottleneck was not removed. In 1963, only 8 percent of pupils completing primary school went on to grammar school, while about 30 percent entered modern schools (Muckenhirn 1966, 59). Vast numbers of would-be entrants were turned away from the grammar schools:

> [A]t the time of examinations for secondary school entrance it is not unusual for fifteen hundred to two thousand youth to sit for the examination of a school which is able to enroll only thirty or sixty of the applicants. The stream of parents, brothers, sisters and other relatives coming to the principals' doors to beg places for youthful family members leaves no doubt in the mind of the observer as to the keen interest in education. (Muckenhirn 1966, 105)

Many others were prevented from proceeding by inability to pay the school fees, which in the early 1960s equaled the average annual income in western Nigeria (Muckenhirn 1966, 198; Lloyd 1974, 80, 95).

The result was that the great majority of those who went to school left after primary or modern school, literate in Yorùbá but not—or barely so—in English. By the time I joined the theater company in 1981, the *majority* of Yorùbá people who were 30 (roughly the actors' average age) could probably read Yorùbá and would be familiar with some of the major Yorùbá-language authors, but only a small minority knew more than a smattering of English.

Primary and modern school education did not equip pupils in the 1960s and 1970s to get a white-collar job; but it did make them feel overqualified to continue working on their fathers' farms. Thus, the expansion of education precipitated mass migration to the urban informal sectors—a heterogeneous social zone whose inhabitants had in common a desire to better themselves through their own efforts (Callaway 1960; Otudeko 1977; Lloyd 1974). They shared a willingness to try, in series or in combination, a variety of different trades, crafts, or waged employment, and they often clung to the aspiration to return to school or to acquire additional education by other means. Among them were many of the young men and women who joined the theater company.

The education system, then, created or fed into an urban-oriented, entrepreneurial, predominantly youthful "intermediate class" that was struggling to improve its social and economic prospects and was literate in Yorùbá, though barely so in English. This constituency of Yorùbá-language literates provided a readership (and an authorship) for a rapidly developing and proliferating written Yorùbá culture. In the 1920s there was an explosion of weekly and fortnightly newspapers, Yorùbá or bilingual

Yorùbá-English, founded and edited by enterprising Lagosians (Omu 1978, 58–60; Awoniyi 1978, 75). Out of this came the first Yorùbá novel, originally published in installments in the author's own newspaper.[11] In the late 1930s D. O. Fagunwa began publishing his series of highly acclaimed and much loved moral fantasy tales. There followed a steadily growing output of novels, literary dramas, and poetry which by the 1970s had become a major field on which university courses were taught and theses written (themselves, in some cases, also in Yorùbá).[12] The readership was certainly not confined to schools, although it was in school that the taste for reading Yorùbá was formed. The prescription of books as set texts in the school curriculum provided writers with a ready market, and the availability of books in Yorùbá in turn increased the popularity of Yorùbá as an option in the upper primary and secondary levels of school.[13] The result was a popular literature which was valued by the readership at least partly because of its association with education and self-betterment.

For Yorùbá literature, by virtue of being written, and by virtue of being taught in schools, was associated with the prestigious sphere of "civilization" and "enlightenment." Some of the best-known Yorùbá authors were securely located in this sphere as civil servants, teachers, and broadcasters. But at the same time this literature was accessible to large numbers of people who barely had a foothold in the sphere of privilege. And it was unofficial in the sense that numerous local publishing houses sprang up to print Yorùbá fiction, drama, and poetry with very little, if any, of the editorial selection and regulation characteristic of publishers such as Heinemann, who were the preferred outlets for university-educated, English-language writers in Nigeria. Ease of entry for aspiring writers meant that a huge range and diversity of talents entered print culture, giving rise to all kinds of innovative texts. While sometimes influenced by English and American genres such as crime thrillers and detective novels, most also showed an intimate connection with older oral traditions, either in the form of wholesale borrowing and quotation or in a more pervasive and fundamental preoccupation with the *language* itself, involving continual recreation of the inherited idioms of orature.

The existence of a large and thriving sphere of Yorùbá written literary production meant that in the formative years of the popular theater, the prestigious aura of literacy was not exclusively linked to a culture and language defined and possessed by an alien, dominating and socially impenetrable colonial center. The shared verbal art of everyday life—proverbs, histories, praise epithets, divination poetry—could also enter the sphere of print. When high-status members of the elite "collected" and committed to writing examples of these traditions, the perceived authenticity of these traditions (which gave them their value) was grounded not in the culture of the Saro scholars but in that of the people among whom they were circulated and orally transmitted. Yorùbá authors of popular novels, plays, and poems also tapped into them—often with a freedom born of greater familiarity. The split experienced in many colonial African cultures between traditional-vernacular-oral on the one hand and modern-English-written on the other was thus forestalled. And the division between elite and popular cultural production was not marked by writing itself as much as by language and linguistic register.

Because the stuff of oral creativity was continuous with the matter of printed texts, it was possible for a new sphere of popular cultural production to emerge. In this sphere, Yorùbá oral and written texts deeply interpenetrated, through mutual incorporation, quotation, emulation, and representation. The common people, not the educated elite, had command of it. The popular theater was only one of its products, though an extraordinarily influential one. In this zone, "tradition" simultaneously existed both as a habitus, occupied from day to day by the people concerned, and as "cultural heritage" on which they could consciously draw and from which they could at least partially stand back.

This is the background to the Adéjobí Theater Company's orientation toward schooling. It gave rise to a pervasive duality in the work and lives of the popular theater company: a combination of plenitude and deprivation. Plenitude—a confident and innovative creativity—sprang from three sources. One was the sense that the "traditions" on which the cultural nationalist elite staked their authenticity in a movement that gathered strength throughout the twentieth century were much more within their own ambit than in the ambit of the elite. Though the popular theater distinguished itself sharply from many pagan traditional forms, genres, and practices, it was in living contact with the language. This language was felt to be the repository of the entire culture, and thus it was they and not the elite who were really in touch with the growing points of the culture. Second, the Yorùbá popular theater, though predominantly oral and vernacular in its mode, participated in a sphere of cultural production in which the literate/illiterate distinction had been blurred and in which written Yorùbá texts circulated freely and were frequently assimilated into stage performances. It therefore conceived of itself as not being cut off from the prestigious sphere of written culture but in continuity with it and potentially able to enter further into it. Third, there was a feeling that cultural self-betterment—further penetration into the sphere of civilization and enlightenment—was there for the taking. For *ọlajú* was acquired through education, which people could get for themselves—if necessary by building their own schools—*not* by imitating the behavior of the elites. The uncultured self-made man who betrays his low origins at the bourgeois dinner table was not a specter that haunted the aspiring upwardly mobile intermediate classes of western Nigeria, for the elites did not have a distinct class culture of their own.¹⁴ The intermediate classes, then, could get their "culture" and "civilization" from the same place the elite got it, and by their own efforts.

Deprivation, however, shadowed the enormous cultural confidence of the popular theater. In the precipitously pyramidal education system, those who failed to get into grammar school felt themselves to be thwarted—excluded from salaried employment and from further education at university, the ultimate dream of all. The members of the theater company had all been cut off fairly low down. As we have seen, none made it into grammar school and only a few had been to modern school. Adéjọbí's position as council clerk was the nearest any of them got to a prestigious salaried post in the formal sector. Their buoyant creativity is shot through with strands of envy and a sense of lack, a desire for what they do not have—a lack which is summed up, in their perception, as a defective command of English. As we will see, their relationship with the colonial language, with higher education, with Europeans, and with "overseas" appears in the plays as a potent cocktail of admiration, resentment, and hilarious caricature.

EXCLUSION AND RECUPERATION

Throughout Adéjọbí's life, as throughout the life of his father—one of the earliest Christian converts in Òṣogbo—social existence in western Nigeria was split by proliferating ideological alternatives and contradictions. The field of social and moral authority became ambiguously reduplicated as old, internally sponsored sources of power, wealth, and ideology (big men and Ọbas, local production and trade, local webs of belief) were paralleled and partially co-opted, but not superseded, by new, externally sponsored ones (the colonial government and forces, salaried and waged jobs, missionary religions). People had once been treated as inherently interconnected, at least in certain respects, so that they could be seen as extensions of each other and mutually responsible (Barber 1994); now a view of people was installed—through the law courts, churches, and schools—in which individuals as atomic entities were bearers of rights, duties, and votes. Every institution, relationship, and belief now had an alternative form. "Progress," "enlightenment," and "traditional heritage" became screens behind which processes of radical conceptual ingestion and transformation took place.

The first, and most enduring, form that ideological transformation took was religious conversion. Conversion had begun perhaps in the eighteenth century for Islam and in the mid-nineteenth for Christianity—but it did not take off as a mass phenomenon until well into the twentieth century, coinciding with the period when the proliferation of social and ideological alternatives began to be pervasive and acute because of the increasing entrenchment of colonial institutions. To participate in modernity was to convert; to convert was by definition to exclude and reject some aspects of existing practice and to retain or rehabilitate others. Christianity and Islam constituted a radical break with all previous religious and ideological change in that they put their converts in a position *outside* their former practice, from which they were asked to view it as a whole—as "paganism," "tradition," or "the old ways"—in order to evaluate it and selectively exclude or assimilate elements from within it (see Peel 2000). Cultural nationalism—closely related (though sometimes also antagonistic) to Christianity and obliquely linked to Islam—started from a standpoint made possible by religious conversion when it looked at "traditional culture" as a body of ideas and practices which constituted a coherent whole and which needed to be (selectively) preserved and regenerated.

For religious converts, the lines of exclusion and retention cut through areas of experience that were central to ordinary life—diet, dress, relations between spouses, and recourse to medicine and spiritual powers—and they often involved stark choices which marked the convert out from his or her community or from other denominations and faiths. Nonetheless, the injunctions and prohibitions of the various denominations of the world religions overlapped and were curiously interchangeable. Established mission churches, African and Aládùúrà churches, reformist Muslim groups (of conservative or modernizing orientation), and relaxed "accommodating" Muslims offered their adherents overlapping sets of parameters by which to perform operations of exclusion and selection. Some Aládùúrà churches—including the Cherubim and Seraphim and the Church of the Lord—resembled Muslims in prohibiting pork, alcohol, and the wearing of shoes in the house of worship[15] but had more in common with traditional religion in their stress on spirit possession, dreams, and divination. Most Aládùúrà churches resembled Islam in permitting polygamy, while the Christ Apostolic Church resembled the CMS in prohibiting it (Peel 1968, 184). Most of the Aládùúrà churches resembled strict conservative reformist Islam in prohibiting all recourse to *jùjú*, indigenous medicine, and traditional divination, while the Church of the Lord and Christ Apostolic Church went further and prohibited Western as well as indigenous medicine. The older generation of progressive reformist Muslims, who adopted many forms from Christian worship, included a branch that supported women's emancipation and called for an end to polygamy and female seclusion.[16] Not only this, but divergences occurred within single institutional religious groupings as well as between them. There was a long-term oscillation within the CMS about polygamy, and the Church of the Lord also remained divided and ambivalent on the subject (the founder Ositelu had seven wives, but the other leaders and the disciples were discouraged from following his example). Similarly, in the Church of the Lord, there was a body of opinion stressing the purely domestic role of wives and their subordination in all things to their husbands, but there was also another strand that regarded husband and wife as equal partners in marriage and in their work for the church and assigned women a prominent role in church government.

Conversion, then, asserts a position in relation to the given. It instigates a kind of editing of the habitus from within—but as if from outside. All elements of the habitus were in principle subject to the editorial gaze: when traditional elements were retained, this was as likely to be the outcome of deliberate selection as of sheer persistence. As Turner puts it, "[T]he acute critical activity within the Church of the Lord rules out any simple interpretation in terms of continuity with paganism" (1967, II:137). The overlapping injunctions and prohibitions of the different Christian and Islamic tendencies seem to demonstrate a common will to select and reject *in itself* rather than a demarcation for each of a unique symbolic or confessional space.

Retention of traditional elements, especially in the Christian denominations, often involved acts of translation and re-description. Parallels between Christian and traditional beliefs were sought (Peel 1990)—for example between Ifá (the god of wisdom) and Jesus, between Èṣù (the trickster god) and Satan, between ẹbọ (offerings to gods) and Christ's sacrifice. While Christianity performed such operations of translation and assimilation officially, Islam did it unofficially in the innumerable degrees of "accommodation" practiced by local Muslims and periodically denounced by reformist mallams (Ryan 1978).

The Christian acts of translation and assimilation remained visible and the object of humorous commentary long after their inauguration in the nineteenth century. In *External Appearances,* a new play in the Adéjọbí repertoire in the early 1980s, there is a comical scene set in an Aládùúrà church in which a member of the congregation brings his old pagan father in to have him converted. The preacher and the pagan engage in a long series of misunderstandings revolving around certain key words appropriated from traditional cosmology and given new meanings in Christian discourse. Both characters, from opposite vantage points, turn out to be conducting simultaneous operations of rejection and assimilation. The old pagan keeps assimilating Christian concepts by declaring them "the same as" traditional ones (Jesus and Ọrúnmìlà, hymn-singing in praise of God and *ìjálá*-chanting in praise of Ògún, the heavenly father and his own father now gone to heaven, the preacher as one religious specialist and himself as another, Christian prayers and traditional incantations). But at the same time, when the preacher speaks of "Èṣù"—adopted from traditional cosmology as the Christian word for Satan—the old pagan takes him to be referring to the original, traditional trickster deity. Meanwhile the preacher, though his concepts are drawn from this long history of assimilation of Christian and traditional practices, insists more and more strenuously that lines must be drawn, distinctions made, and pagan notions rejected: he sets light against dark, modern times against the (bad) old days, ẹ̀mí Ọlọ́run (the spirit of God or godliness) against ẹ̀mí-à-ń-jẹbọ (the spirit of eating sacrificial offerings), prayer against incantations, and finally Jesus against Ògún who, at the same time, in a definitive act of ruling out, he says does not exist:

> BÀBÁ ÀGBÀ: Ó ti tó. Mo gbórin un dáadáa. Ohun tí mo bọ́mọọ̀ mi sọ ni pé, ó ní Jéésù tẹ́ ẹ ń wí ìí, Ọ̀rúnmìlà ni. Ó ní nǹkan kannáà ni wọ́n.
> BÀBÁ ÌJỌ: Ẹ wáá gbọ́, wọn èé ṣe nǹkan kannáà. Bí ẹ bá mọ̀ wí pé ẹ fẹ́ẹ́ gba Jésù, ẹ gbọdọ̀ fi Èṣù sílẹ̀.
> BÀBÁ ÀGBÀ: N ò sin Èṣù télẹ̀.
> BÀBÁ ÌJỌ: Ṣé ẹ rí Ọ̀rúnmìlà yẹn, ìránṣẹ́ Èṣù ni. Àwa ń tiwa. Té ẹ ẹ́ẹ̀ bá sin èsìn tia, wọ́n ní ìránṣẹ́ kan kò lè sin baba méjì. Ẹ ẹ́ fi ọkan án 'lẹ̀ sìnkan. Ńnúu kẹ́ ẹ sin Jéésù o, tàbí kẹ́ ẹ sin Ọ̀rúnmìlà tí àwá mọ̀ sí Èṣù. Ẹ ẹ́ fi ọkan án 'lẹ̀ sìnkan.

> FATHER: . . . But what my son said was that this Jesus of yours, and Ọ̀rúnmìlà, they're one and the same.
> PREACHER: Oh, now listen, they're not the same at all. If you decide to follow Jesus, you have to abandon the Devil [Èṣù].
> FATHER: But I never was an Èṣù devotee.
> PREACHER: And you see, that Ọ̀rúnmìlà of yours, he's the devil's messenger. What we say is that if you join our faith, they say one servant cannot serve two masters. You have to leave one in order to serve the other. Either you serve Jesus, or you serve Ọ̀rúnmìlà that we know as Èṣù. You have to leave one in order to serve the other.

Operations in this intellectual zone, then, are characterized by continual efforts of separation and rejection—efforts which in some cases must have cost enormously—and the simultaneous selective recuperation of what appeared to have been expelled, performed by re-describing the entities in question (see Skinner 1978) in such a way as to alter their moral weighting and position.

Yorùbá cultural nationalism, a broad and diffuse tendency which incorporated parts of both Christian and Muslim ideologies, used the same mechanisms to recuperate the expelled, but in the name of "traditional heritage." Traditional spiritual forces and religious practices could be contained, "sanitized," and yet licensed by being re-described as examples of an ancient and glorious cultural heritage. The Christian elite pioneered these acts of cultural rehabilitation, but even the conservative reformers among Yorùbá Muslims, despite their commitment to a supra-ethnic and supra-national Islamic community, also participated in the project of Yorùbá cultural nationalism (see Moraes Farias 1990), and the modernizing reformers went much further.[17] Very often, cultural nationalism sanitized traditional beliefs or practices by highlighting their artistic or philosophical aspects while ignoring or downplaying their implications for action or for social structure.

We have identified two key features so far: first, the very positioning that enabled converts and cultural nationalists to see a whole field of activities and discourses, as it were, from a vantage point outside it—as "paganism" or "tradition"—while still at least partially inhabiting it; and second, the fact that in so conceptualizing this field they continually, and at many levels, performed acts of analysis and reinterpretation upon it, separating the acceptable, recuperable elements from those that they rejected as irredeemably backward. I take these features to be inherently "modern" and indeed to define what "modernity" is, in its coastal West African form. Rather than picturing two discrete repertoires or bodies of ideas, practices, objects, and structures—one called "tradition" (the indigenous, originating in the local pre-colonial world) and the other called "modernity" (the Western, imported and imposed in the colonial and postcolonial eras)—and then proceeding to analyze cultural forms as "hybrids" composed of a synthesis of elements drawn from each repertoire, I will take as "modern" the fact of taking up a quasi-external position from which to edit the existing life-world one inhabits.[18] This life-world has of course long contained exogenous as well as endogenous elements—some novel, some long accepted, some so thoroughly absorbed that they are no longer perceived as imported. Rather than seek to disentangle these elements—as analyses starting from a notion of "creolization" or "hybridity" inevitably do[19]—I propose to ask how the operation of selection and rejection itself works: that is, how the editorial vantage point is established and how the editorial process changed over the 50 years of the theater company's operations.

VIRTUAL LITERACY

Conversion was conversion to religions of the book; writing was installed at the center of the processes of affirmation, self-dedication, and the rejection of all that contravened God's law. "Recite, recite in the name of Thy Lord.... Thy Lord who taught by the pen" proclaims the first *āyāt* of the Qur'an to have been revealed to Muhammad. The elites who pioneered cultural nationalist recuperation, correspondingly, did so by means of writing. Since the late nineteenth century, as we have seen, members of the Christian educated elite invested considerable time and effort in collecting and writing down historical and religious oral traditions and accounts of rituals and "customs." Writing down these things both sanitized them and endowed them with incontrovertibility (once written, they had an authority that could no longer be queried). But it could be argued that in significant respects the intermediate classes—the artisans, petty traders, clerks, and primary-school teachers that made up the bulk both of the Aládùúrà church membership and the new popular culture producers—were even more active than the elites in "editing" tradition and in this sense were the more zealously and creatively "modern" sections of the population. In the case of the popular theater, they did it by means of what we could call "virtual" writing: a writing which, as we saw in Chapter 5, was in the main an orientation rather than an actual written text. For while Africanist literary criticism emphasizes the yearning of written, Europhone literature toward the condition of orality (see Julien 1992), what we have here is the yearning of an orally improvised theater toward the condition of literacy (see Barber 1995a).

The Adéjọbí Company participated—and advertised its participation—in the domain of literacy in several ways. In the first place, it drew on literary sources. The theater's repertoire contained several plays based on written texts—such as *Kúyẹ̀* and *Taking Care of Kúnlé*, both based on novels by J. F. Ọdunjọ; and *The Secret Is Out*, an adaptation of a written literary drama by Olu Daramọla. The theater was also, conversely, itself a source for printed texts, in the shape of the photoplay magazine *Atọ́ka*, which used photographs and bubble captions to give selected plays a permanent written and pictorial form. Adéjọbí was also very interested in my project of recording, transcribing, and publishing some of his play texts (for the result, see Barber and Ogundijọ 1994), and there was no suggestion that there was any incompatibility or incongruity between publishing a volume of plays and improvising them on stage: rather, they were seen as two parallel channels through which the Adéjọbí Company's work could become known.

In the second place, they made much of their bureaucratic uses of literacy in the running of the company—the register of members, the receipts they signed when they were paid, the letter of application. Adéjọbí hoped that these practices would inculcate in his actors an orderly and well-regulated approach to life. Speaking of his method of paying fixed monthly salaries, with annual increments modeled on the pay structure of the civil service, he remarked that even if the sums involved were smaller than a public sector salary, still, it would teach them "how they too should **plan,** so that they make a **budget** [based on the expectation] that 'at the end of the month, I'll get such-and-such an amount,' so that they can feel secure in the knowledge that 'I've got a proper job.'" And he was right in thinking that some of the actors would find this a new and strange discipline. Hamed Akínwálé, one of the drivers, left the company after a few months because "at that time, I wasn't used to monthly paid work, I'd never worked for

The photoplay magazine *Atọ́ka*. This issue serializes *Gbangbá Dẹkùn*, the Adéjọbí Company's adaptation of a literary drama by Olu Daramọla.

monthly pay, I was just used to doing a day's work and getting paid that very day. But then I joined another company, and they paid salaries monthly as well, so little by little I got used to it." Bureaucratic writing not only instilled order and discipline, it also added weight and authority to a communication. You will remember that on December 31st, 1962, when Adéjọbí wanted to announce his momentous decision to convert the theater group into a professional organization, he assembled everyone in his house and then read aloud a prepared written statement to that effect.

Adéjọbí frequently drew public attention to instances of writing that occurred in the process of drama production. For example, when an elite social organization "sponsored" a show, Adéjọbí sometimes showed the letter of invitation during his introductory address in the opening glee, as in this introduction to *Láníyọnu:*

E̩ káàbọ̀ sí orí ètò alẹ́ ìí. Èyí tí àá wáá dárúkọ, òun náà la à mọ̀, s̩ùgbọ́n, fún egbẹ́ tiwa, gbogbo ejò, jíjẹ ni. Eré mẹ́ta, òun ni mo s̩àkíyèsí pé ó wà ní orí ìwé. Ọ̀kan wà nínú *Invitation*, ìwé-ìpè. Ọ̀kan wà nínú *Poster* tí wọ́n lẹ̀ mọ́ta. S̩ùgbọ́n èyí tí wọ́n bá wa sọ, tí àwa ti fẹ́ẹ́ kọ̀, torí pé kí ni o?—ó tóbi púpọ̀ ju méjèèjì yìí lọ, òun náà ni *Ọláníyọnu*.

> Welcome to this evening's entertainment. I don't know what name I ought to give it [i.e., the play], but as far as our theater company is concerned, "all snakes are for eating." I've noticed that three different plays have been publicized [lit. "are on paper"]. One play is mentioned in the letter of invitation. Another is advertised in the public posters. But the one that they [the Inner Circle Club] talked to us about, and which we wanted to refuse to do—why? because it's bigger by far than the other two—that one is *Ọláníyọnu*.

Note, however, that in the act of foregrounding the letter and the posters—announcements that are "on paper" and which involve him in a world of literacy—Adéjọbí shows that these written documents commit the company to very little. The suggestion which was actually effectual was the one that they "talked to us about," that is, discussed orally, face to face. Though the company often talked as if the posters were the most crucial component in the whole business of preparing a new play, there was one occasion when rather than waste a stock of old, surplus posters, they simply changed the title of their current play so that they could use it up. Word of mouth informed the audience what the play would actually be about.[20] Similarly, venues and even dates announced on the posters were sometimes changed if bookings fell through or other problems arose, and it was taken for granted that the would-be audience would easily find out the new venue or date by asking around. Bureaucratic uses of literacy, then, were set aside or circumvented whenever they got in the way of the practical, artisanal business of getting a show on the road. The management's insistence nonetheless on using them and publicly highlighting their use suggests that their adoption went beyond practical utility. Taken together, all these apparently peripheral uses of writing constituted a regime associated with orderly "civilized" life and signaled the theater company's participation in this life.

Third, and most important, was the way in which the plays were produced and the way the actors thought about the production process. As we saw in Chapter 5, Adéjọbí always spoke of writing his plays and laid great emphasis on the solitary acts of inscription and revision. What he wrote was usually a synopsis of a narrative, which he then referred to as he told the story to the assembled theater company. Alhaji, whose task was then to "turn the story into a play," spoke of how he would sometimes walk around until he had "collected" the ideas he needed to form a complete and coherent plan of a play, which he seemed thereafter to carry in his head like a script without ever writing it down. All the actors spoke as if there were a script which Alhaji would "teach" them until they were "perfect," even though in practice the more experienced actors would generate much of the text from their own imaginative resources. When they described rehearsals, they used the language of old-fashioned schoolroom instruction and correction—as if Alhaji had the entire text under his view and strove to impart it to them—but they also knew that the play depended on the resources they carried inside themselves and tapped into in the generation of their parts. They were thus describing an oral process which probably would not have happened in the same way outside the ambience of literacy. Even though they made little actual use of writing in the course of generating a play, the *idea* of the script was an organizing principle to all of them.

The symbolic associations of writing were thus invoked without any submission to its binding and fixing properties. The carefully cultivated association of different dimensions of their practice with literacy strengthened their self-appointed stance as "editors" of the inhabited cultural given. But while furnishing this vantage point from which to conduct acts of discrimination, legitimization, and sanitation, the virtual literacy of the theater company was enormously more inclusive and accommodating than the written texts of the elite. It was a mode of incorporation which never fully subjugated what was encompassed by acts of "writing."

And more broadly still, it could be argued that the very act of staging is a parallel and equivalent operation to the act of writing. The format of the production—spatially and temporally demarcated, set apart both from everyday life and from older performance modes such as masquerade theater—projects a rectangular, front-facing, two-dimensional aspect, like a group photograph with everyone sitting in rows (see Chapter 7). This homology with colonial photography suggests the theater's function of *framing*: assembling and incorporating narrative and performative elements which are simultaneously authorized and tamed by being fixed in this space.

Over its 50-year history, the ideological ground of the theater company shifted. The elements that were subjected to the operations of exclusion and recuperation changed, the mode in which exclusion and recuperation was carried out changed, and the very evaluation of "enlightenment" itself changed. What we see is a pre-history (1948–1962), the days of the native air opera when the group was an all-Christian, amateur, elite body; a great era of efflorescence (1963–1988), when the company was a commercial professional traveling theater jointly run by a Christian and a Muslim that attempted to appeal to the widest possible audience; and an aftermath (1988 onward) when Alhaji was no longer with the group, and when both he and Adéjọbí turned independently to making video drama rather than operating a live traveling theater. I will look at representative texts from each era.

EXCLUSION AND RECUPERATION IN NATIVE AIR OPERA (1948–1962)

The Gospel Fruit in Oshogbo was staged for the Anglican (CMS) church All Saints', Ọṣogbo in 1961, "In Commemoration of The Dedication of The New Church Building," as the program puts it. The performers were all church members or pupils at the church school, and the program opened with a prayer and closed with a benediction, with donations and hymns in the interval. The subject matter was the arrival of the first Christian missionary in Ọṣogbo in 1900 and the conversion of the first generation of Christians. It is hardly surprising, then, that the moral field is presented in stark and categorical pairs of oppositions. They could be summarized as the oppositions between darkness and light, paganism and Christianity, the past and the new age, illiteracy and literacy, ignorance and enlightenment, backwardness and progress, *jùjú* and the Psalms, *òrìṣà* and Jesus Christ. The CMS missionary Mackay tells the chiefs of Ọ̀sogbo, who are refusing to send their children to school:

> I appeal to you all! keep calm!
> Know ye that education brings civilization
> This age of darkness will soon pass away
> Give your children! I appeal to you!
> Give your children for education
> And leave not the coming generation
> In darkness of illiteracy and ignorance!

The *òrìṣà* are vigorously excluded and rejected. One of the first converts, Adéjọbí senior, sings:

Anankasi! onisegun /2 ce
Bowo mi ba te Psalmu; Anankasi onisegun . . .
. . . Ifa o le gbani la! oya o le gba ni la!
Sango o le gbani la! Erinle o le gbani la!
A fi Jesu Kristi nikan, Eni to ku nitori wa.[21]

All in vain! the medicine man
Once I seize hold of the Psalms; all in vain, the medicine man . . .
. . . Ifa cannot save you! Oya cannot save you!
Sango cannot save you! Erinle cannot save you!
Only Jesus Christ alone [can save you], he who died for our sake.

The positively charged sides of these pairs—education, literacy, civilization, light, Christianity—are strongly linked, to the point where they are almost synonyms. Conversion and literacy, for example, are represented as inseparable in this charming scene, in which an Erinlè worshipper, short of cash, goes to ask for a job in construction work on the new mission buildings. (The layout is as in the original program.)

OGBIFO:	Kini iwo fe se lodo Master?	
ODEGBARO:	Emi nwa ise ni. Emi fe sise!	
	Emi nwa se ni: emi fe sise!!!!	
MACKAY:	Iwo o sise ni? (o si rerin!)	
	Kini oruko re?	IDAHUN: Odegbaro!
	O-d-e-b-a-ro!	
	Kini iwo nsin?	Oisa E'nle l'emi sin o!
	Malo! ma lo!! ma lo!	
	Awa ko gba aborisa si ise	
	Onigbagbo ni awa nfe o-ma lo!!	
ODEGBARO:	Ah! Emi yio se gbagbo! Emi yio se gbagbo o	
	Emi ko sin E'nle mo o—emi yio se gbagbo o	
MACKAY:	Nje iwo lagbara?	IDAHUN: Mo lagba a!
	Iwo le reru bi?	Mo le reru.
	Awa yio fun o ni ise	Mo dupe o
	Ogunjide!	Master!
	Take him with you to Ìbàdàn	
	He'll get a copy of ABD	
INTERPRETER:	What do you want with the Master?	
ODEGBARO:	I'm looking for work. I want to work!	
	I'm looking for work: I want to work!!!	
MACKAY:	You're going to work? (he laughs)	
	What's your name?	REPLY: Odegbaro!
	O-d-e-ba-ro!	
MACKAY:	What do you worship?	I worship the òrìsà Erinlè.
	Go away! Go away!! Go away!	

	We don't employ pagans here.	
	We only want Christians—be off with you!!	
ỌDẸGBARO:	Ah! I'll become a Christian! I'll become a Christian I won't worship Erinlẹ̀ any more—I'll become a Christian.	
MACKAY:	Are you strong?	REPLY: I'm strong!
	Can you carry loads?	I can carry loads.
	We'll give you work	Thank you
	Ogunjide!	Master!
	Take him with you to Ìbàdàn.	
	He'll get a copy of ABD.	

Clearly the ABD primer (there is no letter C in the Yorùbá alphabet) was seen as a prerequisite for conversion, just as much as conversion was a prerequisite for waged labor in the service of the mission. Similarly, Christianity is seen as automatically conferring the benefits of "civilization," which is conceived in material as well as moral or spiritual terms. Civilization explicitly includes "development goods"; for example, amenities visible in Ìbàdàn which have yet to reach Òṣogbo. Soon after his conversion, Ọdẹgbaro exhorts his fellow citizens:

> Imọle ti de o—ẹyin ara Oshogbo—ẹ pada lẹhin ẹṣu!
> Ele'nlẹ ni mi nile Aado!
> Mo fi eyi silẹ nitori ko si Igbala ninu rẹ
> Wo o! o ri! ẹni ba de 'Badan
> Yio ri ilaju ati ohunrere ti 'gbagbọ mu wọ bẹ
> Ẹ jẹka gba Jesu gbọ—yio si gba wa la!

> The light has come—citizens of Òṣogbo—cease to follow Satan!
> I was an Erinlẹ̀ worshipper in Aado compound!
> I gave that up because there is no salvation in it
> Look! see! anyone who goes to Ìbàdàn
> Will see the civilization and good things that Christianity has introduced there
> Let us believe in Jesus—and he will save us!

But the dichotomies are not watertight. "Tradition" is recuperated lavishly into this scheme of things—in three ways. First, by displays of dancing, praise singing, and other festivities at the Òṣun festival, which is being held when Mackay makes his first appearance in Òṣogbo. The *oríkì* of the pagan Ọba are performed as he presides over the Òṣun festival, and his ancestors are invoked to support the celebration. After Mackay has paid his visit and gone, the stage directions tell us that "The Òṣun worshippers apply themselves vigorously to the *gbèdu* drum [a large ceremonial drum usually played for royalty]! The Atáoja dances the dance of Òṣun. The chiefs rejoice." Though one cannot be sure exactly how this scene would have been handled, there is certainly a strong suggestion of a full-blown court scene with the Òṣun cult displaying its special songs, dances, and other performance arts. You will remember that Grace Adéjọbí felt that Dúró Ládiípọ̀ had more or less stolen the idea for *Ọba Kò So* from this play, *Ọba Kò So* being probably the most purely pro-traditional of all the plays staged by any Yorùbá popular theater and the one most completely composed of traditional oral genres such as *oríkì*, songs, and *ọfọ̀*. Grace also stressed that before they could stage the play they had to undertake research *(ìwádìí)* in Òṣogbo, and "they [i.e., Adéjọbí] went to every single *òrìṣà*-worshipping compound to make enquiries"—an approach highly reminiscent of cultural nationalism setting out to celebrate "tradition." Second, the grandeur of the pagan ceremonials is referred to with open admiration in order to underline the point that Christianity must be truly great to induce devotees of the *òrìṣà* to leave all that. An *òrìṣà*-worshipper points out to his fellow pagans that several of the leading converts were formerly great *òrìṣà* devotees, famous for the magnificence of their festivals. Adéjọbí senior was of an illustrious Òṣun-worshipping lineage; when Ọdẹgbaro celebrated his Erinlẹ̀ festival "the whole of Òṣogbo knew about it."

> Ẹ si tun wo akatakiti ọkunrin
> Ọla Ile Arinyanyọ—nijo ni ni, Ọla nṣ'ọdun oriṣa ogiyan
> Ta jẹ jẹ jẹ—ta mu mu mu—ta jo jo jo
> T'on na si nj'ijo bata a jo tapa—o fi i lẹ o!
> ... Tabi Gade Ile Layiokun t'ojude rẹ i gbẹsẹ lọjọ ṣango
> Ti nwọn si wa fi gbogbo eyun un lẹ!
> Ẹ ba ma jẹ a gbọ ti wọn o! toh!!

> And then look at that formidable man
> Ọlá of Aríyanyó Compound—remember the day when Ọlá was
>   holding his Òrìṣà Ògìyán festival
> And we ate and ate, drank and drank, danced and danced
> And he too danced *bàtá* with high-kicking zest—he's given it up!
> ... Or Gádé of Láyíókun's compound whose forecourt could
>   never accommodate all his visitors on the day of his Ṣàngó
>   celebration
> To think that they gave all of that up!
> We ought to listen to what they have to say! That's my opinion.

The splendor of the traditional ways is held up as proof of the even greater value of the new ones which have the power to displace them. That this celebration of the great festivities of the old *òrìṣà* worshippers had an enduring resonance for Oyin Adéjọbí is apparent from the way he began his autobiographical narrative. As we have seen, he evoked Adéjọbí senior's greatness by describing how he would not only offer lavish hospitality in his own house, but would also go out—almost in state, like an Ọba—to visit prominent òrìṣà worshippers when they were holding their festivals; and he specifically mentions Láyíókun and his Ṣàngó festival as one of the most magnificent.

Third, the bedrock of òrìṣà traditions is indirectly and partially salvaged by singling out specific abuses for criticism—suggesting that once such abuses have been eliminated, the rest of the traditional beliefs and practices will be rendered more or less acceptable. Thus Mackay is shown persuading the Ṣàngó worshippers to give up their custom of ransacking and razing to the ground any house struck by lightning, in exchange for certain standardized gifts.[22] Mackay's popular victory consisted not in disestablishing Ṣàngó altogether, but only in getting one of the cult's unpopular practices modified. The claims of Ṣàngó were thus at least partially "saved," and the categorical absolutes of the missionary perspective were faintly colored by the continued recognition of something else.

If the play allows the partial recuperation of traditional worship through these mechanisms, it also represents the pre-conversion citizens speaking in a language that has already been infused with a Christian moral vocabulary. Thus, the categorical dichotomy is undermined again from the other side—the pagans seem always already to have been keen on "progress," and the argument is only about how best to achieve that goal. Thus, when Mackay arrives and requests, through the interpreter, that the Ọba grant him a plot of land to build his mission, the Atáọja consults his assembled chiefs who immediately and unanimously declare that

Iwọ l'a ri ki o ku alejo yi o
A r'ohun ajeji
Igba rẹ yi dun mọ wa o
Bo ba jẹ pe t'ile kikọ
Ilọsiwaju ni f'Oshogbo . . .
. . . A yọnda e-e-e a yọnda.

You deserve congratulations for having such a visitor
We are seeing something extraordinary
We are very pleased with this reign of yours
If it's a matter of house building
That means progress for Òṣogbo . . .
. . . We release [the land] gladly, we release it.

And when the chiefs and elders resist the call to send their children to school, they do so on moral grounds which are fully compatible with the work ethic of the mission. They object that school makes the children physically lazy and takes them away from farm work. The Christians' parallel commitment to the virtues of hard work and physical labor is demonstrated in the last scene, when the converts are building the first church and one woman laborer sits preening until the overseer throws mud in her face, whereupon "the woman rinsed her face and got on with her work," while the other workers sing "Take up your hoes, it's time to work." The chiefs and elders, then, share the Christians' general perspective on both hard work and progress, it is just that they are ignorant of the correct way to attain these goals; once Mackay has explained it to them, they align themselves easily with his mission. The presumption is the rationalist and progressivist one that any disagreement is simply a result of misunderstanding or lack of knowledge. Even though the darkness of ignorance and the light of understanding are so categorically opposed, the transition between them is a short step.

The drama enjoys playing with ideas of linguistic and cultural translation. If the Ọba reacts to Mackay's first announcement of "good tidings of Christ [Kristi] the Savior" by exclaiming "'*Kiiti*'! *Tani jẹ Kiiti!*" ['Kiiti'! Who is Kiiti?], and goes on to ask Mackay to "greet Him for me," Mackay himself never succeeds in mastering the "gb" sound in Yorùbá. But such failures can be shown in the full confidence that everyone in the play—missionary, converts, and yet-to-be converted traditionalists—all share a basic faith in progress and in the power of reason to guide people toward it.

ECUMENICAL "EDITING" IN THE COMPANY'S HEYDAY (1963–1988)

Over the period of its greatest florescence, the dividing lines in the theater's intellectual and moral zone shifted as it moved away from the church, as Alhaji's influence increased, and as the audience they sought to appeal to became wider and more heterogeneous. Alhaji's presence helped to shape the inclusive, deeply moralistic philosophy that the theater company now evolved. It was a philosophy that was aimed at, and found ready acceptance in, a popular audience which had expanded both geographically, as the theater began to travel to towns and villages in all the regions of Yorùbáland and beyond, and socially, as it began to embrace school pupils and common town audiences as well as remnants of its former elite constituency. This audience contained many Muslims as well as Christians, western Nigeria's population being divided more or less evenly between the two, with a small residue of "traditional worshippers." Moreover, until the late 1980s Christians and Muslims lived amicably together, sometimes in the same family (see Gbadamọsi 1978, 146–147; Laitin 1986, 140–141), and shared many of the same social aspirations. Although pure Islam did not espouse "progress" in quite the same open-ended, future-oriented, and materially minded way as Christianity did, in practice both Muslims and Christians in the southwest of Nigeria were open to change and pinned their hopes of positive individual and collective transformation on education and self-discipline (Laitin 1986, 77–80). This convergence was made easier by the fact that Muslims had long shared some of the imagery characteristically used to formulate the concept of "enlightenment."[23]

Alhaji and Adéjọbí worked together without any sign of friction to generate moral messages which separated the acceptable from the unacceptable and which recuperated tradition in the name of modernity—but without any reference to a specific faith. After 1963, plays as overtly and categorically tendentious as *The Gospel Fruit* were no longer created (though some of the existing Biblical repertoire continued to be revived on demand at least till the end of the 1960s). Instead, the early secular plays exhibit a modified "folklorized" mode in which Christian/Islamic prohibitions coexist with a much more overt recuperation of traditional values and institutions.

That the exercise of exclusion and recuperation sometimes threw up insoluble ideological problems is evident from plays such as *Láníyọnu*, which was first staged in about 1967, six years after *The Gospel Fruit*. Láníyọnu, driven out of his town by faithless friends, is wandering through the forest when he comes upon an Ọba's daughter tied to a tree. She has been offered in sacrifice by the chiefs of a nearby town to appease a man-eating spirit. He rescues her and escorts her back to her town, where he lectures the flabbergasted chiefs: "When you want to make a sacrifice, can't you find some domestic animal and sacrifice that, instead of taking this beautiful girl?" Sacrifice is one of the concepts most heavily translated and edited by Christian and Muslim thinkers; the exhortation would be familiar to the audience from many sources, including one of D. O. Fagunwa's most popular novels (see Fagunwa 1950 [1938], 58–59). But what makes the exhortation awkwardly resistant to assimilation in the play is the fact that Ifá, the divination system which initially prescribed the sacrifice—much against the will of the chiefs—is also the authority for Láníyọnu's selection as the new Ọba. As he himself points out, he is an outsider who does not even belong to a royal lineage. But Ifá has rejected every local candidate to the throne and announced that the new Ọba will be a strange "hunter" who arrives from the forest. It is this that legitimizes and indeed makes possible the satisfying denouement. One of the chiefs, urging Láníyọnu to accept the title, makes the paradox clear: "We're following Ifá. We'll do whatever Ifá says—that's why we sacrificed the girl." Ifá's authority is apparently right when it comes to Láníyọnu's ascent to the throne and wrong when it comes to the prescription of human sacrifice which is essential for the plot to unfold. The contradiction is not resolved.

The move toward an ecumenical common moral ground became fully established and completely characteristic of the company in the 1970s and early 1980s. Characters who appeal to providence and to destiny (Orí), who thank or plead with God, who preach against the use of *jùjú* without denying its powers, who denounce treachery and adultery, and who affirm the value of literacy are not marked either as Christian or as Muslim, and "paganism" is rarely represented as such. The bedrock of the theater group's collective philosophy was the belief that wrongdoing is eventually punished. As Alhaji put it:

> It [the theater] teaches moral. Good manner. How to behave well, that, if you watch the play you will see somebody who did bad to his neighbor, and what God repays him back. To do evil is not good. It will be punished. You will see somebody who does evil and what is the punishment he receives. (English)

When I asked about the numerous Nigerian evildoers who appear to get away with it, he replied

> If they are not punished, then one day they will get their punishment. In this world, or—you know there is life after death. God will pay everybody what he is owed. I believe. I believe. (English)

Divine punishment in this life or the hereafter belongs to the Judeo-Islamic-Christian tradition as a whole, not to any one strand of it. And it is not necessarily incompatible with the idea of wrongdoing bringing its own consequences upon itself (or attracting the wrath of gods and ancestors), which is the mainspring of innumerable narratives deriving from an indigenous pagan or "traditional" worldview.[24] In the plays of the 1970s and 1980s, the religious content of the "moral" was rarely more specific than this.

The role of the actors as "preachers," on which they so strongly insisted (see Chapter 7), preserved for them a space from which to "edit" the habitus. But it was a non-denominational space. In their exposition of the theme of their preacherly function, they used vocabulary which applied equally to Christian and Muslim preachers, and sometimes they even spelled out the fact that they meant both. John Adéwuni, for example, said "The value of drama is that we, in our capacity as actors, are just like the *wòlíì*, the *àlùfáà*, as they preach their sermons. Because they teach people the way of the Lord, warning people that if they do such-and-such then God will be angry. In exactly the same way, the Muslims preach sermons— our messages are like sermons."[25] In this period, then, their purpose in claiming the preacherly space was not to try to convert anyone to a particular religious faith, but to *position* themselves so that they could survey the mistakes and wrongdoing of their fellow human beings from a moral vantage point partially removed from the scene of action while still very much in it and of it.

In the plays current in this period, the characters all shared one point of reference, Ọlọ́run, "God." Except in *External Appearances*, much of whose action is set in an Aládùúrà Church, the name of Christ is never mentioned in these plays, nor is that of Muhammad. In all the plays, whether they are set in a modern urban tenement or in a traditional royal court, the terms "Ọlọ́run," "Elédùmarè" (a dialect form of Olódùmarè) and "Ẹlẹ́dàáà mi" (My Creator) are used alike by all the characters, from Ifá diviners to fast young city women, and the concept merges seamlessly into the old but still indispensable concept of Orí (Head, or personal destiny). There is never anything to associate these terms with a particular form of religious faith. The theme of religious affiliations as a dimension of social life surfaces only casually and intermittently in the characterization. Only occasionally does a passing reference reveal what faith the actor might be imagining his or her character to belong to. In *The Royal Palm-nut*, for example, the hero Tóògùn, played by Alhaji, first appears, yawning and complaining that he has overslept: "*Irú oorun wo ni mo 'á sùn títí? Àsùbáà ni mo pé n ó lọọlé ọ̀rẹ́ẹ̀ mi kí n bèèrè bọ́rọ̀ ti rí*" [How could I have slept so late? I was intending to get up at the First Prayer and go to my friend's house to ask him how matters stood]. This passing reference to the Islamic daily cycle of devotions is the only thing in the play that would make you identify him as a Muslim. Later, his friend's adulterous wife Díẹ̀kọ́lá (played by Maggie, a Christian) uses the same idiom: "*Tí wọ́n bá ti pe ìrun alákòọ́kọ́ lèmi í jí*" [I get up when they sound the call for the first prayers]. Apart from one or two such details, there is no reference that could be identified as distinguishing Islamic from Christian practices or beliefs. The distinction is utterly insignificant and not commented on in any way by the characters or by the actors talking about their characters.[26]

It was only in the opening glee, which remained Mr. Adéjọbí's exclusive preserve, that echoes of the Biblical phase of the theater company's work persisted. Several of the songs either quoted word for word from the Bible, for example "*Ìrètí pípẹ́ / Ó ń mú ọkàn ṣaìsàn*" [Hope deferred / Maketh the heart sick],[27] or echoed Biblical phrases: "*Ṣe bíwọ ló sẹ́ ọrun / Nígbààníì / O fi kẹkẹ́ ogun jónááà*" [Was it not you who broke the bows / In olden times / You burnt the chariots of war].[28] At least one may allude to the text of a famous early sermon by the founder of the Church of the Lord, Ositelu.[29] Others echo hymns (perhaps specifically Church of the Lord hymns) in their stress on prayer: "*Kò sóhun tó kojá àdúrà / Ká gbóhùn sókè aráááà / Ká má sinmi ààwẹ̀ / Olúwa á gbọ́*" [There is nothing that surpasses prayer / Let us raise our voices, people / Let us not cease from fasting / God will hear]. But these songs are juxtaposed in the opening glee with others that draw on the concepts and phraseology of Ifá divination poetry or appeal to the very widely shared and longstanding belief in *Kádàrá* (Destiny). And the most numerous are those that articulate moral values such as loyalty between friends ("Treacherous friends are bad"), faithfulness on the part of wives ("Don't let me get mixed up with a wife who gossips about her husband and betrays him"), and wealth in people ("People are my cloth")—values which have no specific religious content but can easily be combined with Christian or Islamic precepts.

By the time the company staged *Articulated Lorry*, which was being advertised as a new play when I started traveling with them in 1981, God was scarcely mentioned. The contrast between enlightenment and dark ignorance remained as a fundamental structure of ideas, but independent of any confessional faith. In this play it becomes apparent that by now "enlightenment" was apprehended not so much an achieved state as an aspirational orientation—and one, moreover, that was not as fervently or wholeheartedly endorsed as formerly.[30]

The central figure around whom images of "enlightenment" cohere is Àlàbí, referred to and addressed throughout the play as *akọ̀wé* (clerk). Dayọ̀ Akínpẹ̀lú made a pale, willowy *akọ̀wé*, constantly resorting to English and unable to eat pepper or *òkèlè* (the heavy mass of carbohydrate that constitutes the main component of a Yorùbá meal—whether it's pounded yam, cassava-meal paste or yam-flour paste). He is maximally contrasted with Bàbáa Wándé, nicknamed "Àjàgbé Ejò" (the popular praise epithet for an articulated lorry), a heavy-drinking, forthright, illiterate lorry driver. Mediating this contrast—and causing havoc in the process—is Bàbáa Wándé's wife, Ìyáa Bùnmi, who is better educated than her husband, but less so than Àlàbí. She is frustrated by Bàbáa Wándé's frequent absences on long-distance trips, but she is also anxious to have another child and is sexually rapacious, which propels her into shameful advances to Àlàbí behind her husband's back.

Àlàbí's defining feature is his education. He has been to school long enough to speak English and to secure an office job. His ambition is to proceed to university, perhaps "overseas," and he is prepared to postpone all other social goals until this has been achieved. Clustering around this central feature are numerous other markers of the enlightened way of life. One is an emphasis on cleanliness and hygiene.[31] The Landlord feels that his rise into social prominence must be accompanied by changes in lifestyle. One of his new rules is that his tenants must no longer use wood fires for cooking, lest the smoke should annoy the party secretary who will be using the new house he has lent the party across the way. Àlàbí immediately points out that he uses a paraffin stove, while Bàbáa Wándé darkly observes that "we who use wood know who we are" and explains that he cannot yet afford a stove, thus signaling it as a marker of upward mobility. Another rule is that tenants must sweep up their plantain skins, their yam peels, and the leaves used for wrapping *ẹ̀kọ* and *ẹ̀bà*, and they are forbidden to wipe their greasy hands on the walls after eating. Since it later emerges that Àlàbí prefers to eat bread and "Geisha" (tinned mackerel), it is clear that he is not one of the culprits. It was a common prejudice of the elite that the uneducated people were dirty: in Odunjo's novel *Ọmọ Òkú Ọ̀run,* from which the plot of *Taking Care of Kúnlé* was drawn, the female interloper who takes over her friend's husband when the wife is wrongly presumed dead is portrayed as uneducated, domineering, and a slob in the kitchen, three characteristics which appear to go together as far as the novelist is concerned. The Adéjọbí theater company, characteristically, refrains from taking such a hard line; the dirtiness is blamed on Ìyáa Bùnmi, who is a slob by nature, not because of her lack of education. Nonetheless, Àlàbí's extreme fastidiousness is certainly meant to be a mark of his educational and social superiority.

The action of the play revolves around enlightenment in the form of self-discipline in matters of marriage and sex. Ìyáa Bùnmi behaves badly because she is uncontrolled and greedy. Àlàbí, by contrast, is represented as being commendably abstemious. His mother comes from their home town to tell him she has found a wife for him: her friend the beancake-seller's daughter. Àlàbí objects that he is not yet ready to shoulder the burden of a wife: he wants to pursue his studies first. His mother replies that the marriage will cost him nothing: she will pay for everything, and all that remains is for him and Wúlè to live together and have children. Àlàbí holds his ground, and his determination to remain single provokes Ìyáa Bùnmi to try to seduce him. But again he politely refuses her advances, whereupon she falsely accuses him of attempting to use *jùjú* on her husband. At the end, Àlàbí is vindicated and the Landlord, in summing up the story, commends his self control:

> Mo ro ọ̀rọ̀ náà síwá, mo rò ó sẹ́hìn, ǹjó o mọ̀ pọ́kàn-àn mi ò gbàgbọ́ toríi pé kí ni, hówù, ọdọ́mọkùnrin bí irúù rẹ báyìí, tó o wá sọ wí pé irú ìyàwóo Bàbáa Wándé ń ń wá nǹkan pèlú ẹ, tó o wáá bẹ̀rẹ̀ sí í bínú, ẹlòmíìn tí ò tiẹ̀ tó o páàpáà, ó lè wà ní ìwé kẹta bí tẸ̀ẹbó ni, bí ti Yoòbá ni, yóò maa ṣe bí obúkọ tẹlé obìnrin lẹ́hìn. Hẹ̀n-ẹ́n! O sì wáá lè mú sùúrù báyẹn. Ọlọ́un 'óò jẹ́ ó dáa fún ọ.

> I thought about the matter from every angle and I couldn't bring myself to believe it [i.e., Àlàbí's story], you know why? Well, a young chap like you to say that someone like Bàbáa Wándé's wife had tried to seduce you and that you had turned her down! Other young men, even those who are younger than you, like someone in the third form, whether in the English or the Yorùbá system, they would be running after women like rams. Yes! But *you* were able to restrain yourself. May God reward you.

The enlightened young man expects to make his own choice in marriage, not to have his ignorant mother fix up a betrothal to a beancake-seller's daughter for him. (She even suggests that his "ten years of schooling" might qualify him to become a "bread-seller's clerk"—an ambition that, needless to say, falls far short of Àlàbí's own plans.) He has an ideal of harmonious rational monogamous married life which he evokes in his account of how couples discuss politics in England. Remember his idea that even if the husband and wife belong to different political parties, when they get home in the evening they will get their meal ready and politely ask each other about their respective parties' activities: "They have amicable discussions with each other in which they compare notes. They'll chat and they'll be content. There won't be any fighting or any quarrel between them."

Slovenliness and sexual incontinence are linked with the use of occult powers. When Ìyáa Bùnmi lays out a *jùjú* charm on the floor in order falsely to incriminate Àlàbí, Àlàbí flees in terror, both from the charm and from the accusation, protesting again and again "I don't know anything about medicine." The other characters confirm that an educated person would not be expected to have anything to do with *jùjú;* they believe in Àlàbí's guilt but are surprised at it, Bàbáa Fàtái commenting with coarse sarcasm "So, you clerks also deal in medicines after all!" By contrast, it is taken for granted that Ìyáa Bùnmi would know enough about *jùjú* to frame Àlàbí, while Bàbáa Wándé and Bàbáa Fàtái both utter traditional incantations against him. In this play, the "pagan" worldview is represented only by this reference to malevolent magic (Ifá, òrìṣà, and witches, the stock in trade of the more "folkloric" plays, make no appearance), which has now become representative of social inferiority as much as religious benightedness.

If the uneducated characters know about *jùjú,* Àlàbí knows about Western medicine. One of Ìyáa Bùnmi's ploys is to pretend to have a headache and to come to Àlàbí's room to ask him to help her treat it. He tells her to go away and take some medicine. She returns a few minutes later to ask him to tell her which package to use—what she wants is "Phensic Elérin" (Phensic with the elephant). Àlàbí laughs at her and tells her there's no such thing—the aspirin with the elephant logo is APC. His mockery adds to the bitterness of her rejection.

So far, the moral weighting seems all to be on Àlàbí's side: he is educated, peace-loving, rational, fastidious, disciplined, self-denying, far-sighted; the other characters are to varying degrees ill-educated, ignorant, quarrelsome, dirty, superstitious, greedy, credulous, and impetuous. But, as might be expected, there is more to it than this. Àlàbí is a bit feeble. He can't eat proper food (Ìyáa Bùnmi, by contrast, despises shop-bought processed food and tells him that too much bread causes tonsillitis). When he is falsely accused of *jùjú*-mongering, he responds with distraught denials and even tears ("Now you're dripping at the eyes like the *ebòlò* plant," jeers Bàbáa Fàtái). "*Èrò ilú òyìnbó*" [visitor from Europe] is what Ìyáa Bùnmi calls him after she has trapped him with her false accusation, suggesting someone unable to cope with local realities. Àlàbí's Lagosian accent is affected, and his constant interpolation of English words—the ultimate symbol of enlightened status—is portrayed as rather ridiculous.

Indeed, Àlàbí's apparent inability to express himself in straight Yorùbá is eventually his undoing. When Àlàbí tries to inform Bàbáa Wándé of Ìyáa Bùnmi's misconduct, she pre-empts him with her false counter-accusation: while Bàbáa Wándé was away, Àlàbí abused him with all kinds of insults. Àlàbí begins to protest (as elsewhere, in the translation, phrases in bold show that Àlàbí is speaking in English):

ÀLÀBÍ: **Let me explain myself.**
ÌYÁA BÙNMI: Yéééééé èèèèè.
BÀBÁA WÁNDÉ: Kí ló wí?
ÌYÁA BÙNMI: Ó lóun ò mọ pé lọ́dọ̀ọ yín lòún ti jogún-ùnran werè.
BÀBÁA WÁNDÉ: Akọ̀wé... Akọ̀wé... N ò sí ńlé, o bú mi. Lójúù mi báyìí, o tún bẹ̀rẹ̀ sí í sọ... Jáde níhìín.
ÀLÀBÍ: Mi ò bú yín.
BÀBÁA WÁNDÉ: Mo ní kó o jáde.
ÀLÀBÍ: **Let me explain myself.**
ÌYÁA BÙNMI: Yéééééèèèè!
BÀBÁA WÁNDÉ: Kí ló wí?
ÌYÁA BÙNMI: Ó ní bẹ́ ẹ ti ń sọ̀rọ̀ lẹnuu yín ń rùn, pẹ́ ẹ ẹ̀ẹ̀ ti mugbó àtògógóró tán.
BÀBÁA WÁNDÉ: Èmí mugbó! Èmí mugbó! Akọ̀wé!!
ÌYÁA BÙNMI: Bàbáa Wándé ò mọ sìgáá mu.
BÀBÁA WÁNDÉ: Jáde. Èmí mugbó! Èmí mugbó!! Gbogbohun tó o ní ńkọ́?
ÀLÀBÍ: Mi ò bú yín ìn. Bàbáa Wándé, **please. Let me explain myself.**
BÀBÁA WÁNDÉ: Kí ló wí?
ÌYÁA BÙNMI: Ó ní àbájọ, ó ní èpè tẹ́ ẹ gbà lẹ́nu ọ̀gáa yín, tẹ́sẹ̀ẹ yín kan fi gùn jùkan lọ.
BÀBÁA WÁNDÉ: Témi ò bá tiẹ̀ mọ̀wé, témi ò bá tiẹ̀ mọ̀wéé, ìyàwóò mí mọ̀wé.
ÀLÀBÍ: Iró ni ìn.
BÀBÁA WÁNDÉ: Gbogbohun tó o ní, wò ó, bó o bá sọ̀rọ̀ lo óò tó lọ níbí yìí lónìí o. Ò lémìí gbèpè...
ÀLÀBÍ: Iróọ̀ọ̀.
BÀBÁA WÁNDÉ: Lẹsẹ̀ kan e jùkan lọ. Ẹsẹ̀ẹ̀ mi tó juraa wọn lọ, é e hàn mí o. Èí tó bá juraa wọn lọọ, o óò fi hàn mí o.
ÀLÀBÍ: N ò jẹ́ bú yín.
BÀBÁA WÁNDÉ: Fẹsẹ̀ hàn mí o. Mo ní o fẹsẹ̀ hàn mí o.
ÀLÀBÍ: Óóóóòòòò. **Leave me or otherwise I kick you off.**
ÌYÁA BÙNMI: Áàà. Ó léyin, Àjàgbé Ejò, bójúu yín ti rí "wàì wàì."
ÀLÀBÍ: Óóóóòòòò. Kò burú.

BÀBÁA WÁNDÉ: Ṣéé torí pé ń ń wakọ̀ gúngùn ni mo dÀjàgbé Ejò sí? Ó dáa. Kò burú. Bẹ́ ẹ ṣeé bẹ̀rẹ̀ nù-un.

ÀLÀBÍ: **Let me explain myself.**
ÌYÁA BÙNMI: Yeee. . . . oooh!
BÀBÁA WÁNDÉ: What did he say?
ÌYÁA BÙNMI: He said that he hadn't realized that he would have to put up with the consequences of inherited insanity in your house!
BÀBÁA WÁNDÉ: Clerk . . . clerk . . . I'm not at home, you abuse me. To my face, you begin to say. . . . Get out of here.
ÀLÀBÍ: I didn't abuse you.
BÀBÁA WÁNDÉ: I told you to get out.
ÀLÀBÍ: **Let me explain myself.**
ÌYÁA BÙNMI: Yeee . . . ooh!!
BÀBÁA WÁNDÉ: What did he say?
ÌYÁA BÙNMI: He said when you talk your breath stinks because you've been smoking pot and drinking illicit gin!
BÀBÁA WÁNDÉ: Me, smoke pot! Me, smoke pot!! Clerk!
ÌYÁA BÙNMI (TO ÀLÀBÍ, REASONABLY): Bàbáa Wándé doesn't even smoke ordinary cigarettes.
BÀBÁA WÁNDÉ: Get out. Me, smoke pot! Me, smoke pot! What about all the [other] things you said about me?
ÀLÀBÍ: I didn't abuse you. **Bàbáa Wándé, please! Let me explain myself.**
BÀBÁA WÁNDÉ: What did he say?
ÌYÁA BÙNMI: He said it's no wonder—he said it's the curses you got from your boss that made one of your legs shorter than the other!
BÀBÁA WÁNDÉ: Even if I'm not educated, even if I'm not educated, my wife is educated.
ÀLÀBÍ: It's not true.
BÀBÁA WÁNDÉ: Everything you said, look, you're going to confess it before you leave here today. You said I got curses . . .
ÀLÀBÍ: It's not true!
BÀBÁA WÁNDÉ: . . . and that's why one of my legs is shorter than the other. Well, the leg that's shorter than the other, you're going to show it to me today. The one that's shorter than the other, you're going to show it to me.
ÀLÀBÍ: I could never abuse you.
BÀBÁA WÁNDÉ: Show me the leg! I said show me the leg!
ÀLÀBÍ: Oh! (To Ìyáa Bùnmi): **Leave me, otherwise I kick you off.**

ÌYÁÁ BÙNMI: Ha! He said that you, Àjàgbé Ejò, have eyes that flash like the indicators of a car!
ÀLÀBÍ: Oh! Very well.
BÀBÁA WÁNDÉ: Is it because I drive an articulated lorry that I've now become "Àjàgbé Ejò" as well? OK, all right. That's how you've begun.

Here, Àlàbí's excessive Anglicization is a handicap—he cannot help lapsing into English, giving Ìyáa Bùnmi the chance to play the false interpreter. Bàbáa Wándé's complete ignorance of English is equally a handicap, for he has to rely on Ìyáa Bùnmi to tell him what Àlàbí is saying. Ìyáa Bùnmi, who knows a little English and, more important, is believed by her husband to know a lot ("Even if I'm not educated, my wife is educated"), is thus in a position to set the two of them at loggerheads and triumph over both. A command of English—the passport to white-collar employment and symbol of social superiority—is shrewdly assessed here. Hilarity and sympathy seem to be directed equally at the blundering ignorant lorry driver and the over-refined "clerk"; only the figure who exploits their respective vulnerable points is condemned.

The condition of enlightenment that Àlàbí represents is not fully realized in the play. He is uncontaminated, but also uninoculated, by the plotting, jealousy, greed, and mendacity of everyday life; this makes him like the Ministry of Agriculture chicken—glossy and beautiful, but not tough enough to withstand local conditions. He is vulnerable to the simple and crude ploys of Ìyáa Bùnmi and is unable to defend himself. He depends on the protection of well-wishers such as the Landlord, who is in the end responsible for discovering the truth and rescuing Àlàbí from his plight. It is hard to think that Àlàbí's refined and somewhat unreal character is being recommended as a role model for young people. Rather, he provides a reference point by which to evaluate—and cast a remorseful gaze upon—"our" behavior, that is, the rough, everyday-life kind of behavior which threatens the survival of people like Àlàbí. Like "Mr. Wúù" the expatriate sawmill manager they talk about so admiringly in *Taking Care of Kúnlé* (see Chapter 5), Àlàbí is an ideal projection out of common reality, an inversion of all the everyday deficiencies the moralizing playwrights want to criticize. To this extent, he seems to be an embodiment of the intermediate-class sense of *lack*, the educational deprivation that, I have suggested, runs like a seam through the buoyant self-confidence of their creative output.

INCLUSIVENESS AND DISAGGREGATION IN VIDEO DRAMA (1988–)

In the late 1980s and early 1990s schooling ceased to be the passport to salaried employment (Adepegba 1995; Cornwall 1996; Lawuyi 1997), and salaried employment itself ceased to be a guarantee of prosperity and social status. In the economic collapse that began in the 1980s, fixed salaries had no hope of beating runaway inflation. The most lucrative occupations were smuggling or drug running, and any form of commerce was better than a civil service job. Massive increases in the numbers of school leavers, combined with a lowering of educational standards, further reduced the prestige even of a university degree. In these circumstances, the negative side of "enlightenment"—always present, from the first introduction of the concept by the missionaries in the mid-nineteenth century—came to the fore. And the mechanisms by which the "editing" of culture was carried out underwent extreme change. The video drama *Ibi Ayé Ń lọ* [*Where the World Is Going*], made in 1990, goes beyond the stage dramas both in its capacity for "virtual writing" as a mechanism for selective recuperation and in its ambivalence about enlightenment.

If the live theater was highly incorporative and used its association with literacy and the framing devices of staging as mechanisms for editing and sanitizing elements of "tradition," video had the advantage of a yet more flexible, more authoritative, and less obtrusive framing device. Video has far greater representational reach, and thus can aspire to more and encompass more. When the stage plays mounted battles of incantations and the interventions of spiritual beings, they had to be captured in the dominant theatrical dynamic of the stage. This dynamic, because of its orientation toward progress and modernity, was—as we saw in Chapter 7—deliberately differentiated from traditional theatrical and spectacular forms in its use of time and space. It would have been difficult to incorporate other styles of theater which breached these carefully maintained parameters. Video drama, by contrast, is endowed with the presumption that video is just the outcome of *recording* whatever happens to be in front of the camera, rather than staging or mounting a representation of something according to definite theatrical conventions. Thus, in all of Adéjọbí's live theatrical repertoire, there is no case of a masquerade appearing on stage. *Egúngún* have their own theatrical dynamics, so strong that they would disrupt the forms of time and space established by the stage. Indeed, masquerade theater is the performance genre from which the Adéjọbí theater most clearly differentiated itself, as we saw in Chapter 7. In video this distancing is not necessary, because video *as a medium* is both already incontrovertibly modern and infinitely inclusive.

In *Where the World Is Going*, the opening scene shows the Ọba of a town, his townspeople, and his special visitors sitting down to watch an *egúngún aláriǹjó* show. The masqueraders perform several numbers with only intermittent commentary from the visitors to show that the scene has some (albeit minimal) function within the larger narrative. This subsequently develops into a story of a successful university-educated couple who fail to discipline their children, until the mother's indulgence in particular ends up in the boys turning to crime. The long masquerade episode appears, retrospectively, to stand for old communal values, wholesome participatory entertainment, and respect for elders and ancestors. It is contrasted (in an ironical moment of reflexivity, again made possible by the unlimited encompassing capacities of video) with another form of entertainment— Yorùbá video drama itself—which the loutish truant youths lie around all day watching when they should be at school. The over-indulgent mother even recommends Oyin Adéjọbí's own videos to the delinquent boys! The potentially disruptive aesthetic of masquerade—which is associated with all that is pagan, illiterate, and backward—is disarmed by the bland neutrality of video and appears as a domesticated entertainment in which the townspeople can take pride. Indeed, the performance is shown explicitly as an object of cultural appropriation, for in the video other cameras are shown, members of the "audience" making their own photographic and video recordings. The very first shot looks into the lens of someone else's camera: that of Málọmọ́'s African American wife (consistently addressed as "òyìnbó," i.e., European), a benign, relatively wealthy, and educated visitor who is interested in traditional culture. Another, local, video artist is seen throughout the opening sequence recording the performance. Thus, the video audience is provided with a model of how to take traditions such as *egúngún alárìnjó* as "cultural heritage" suitable for consumption by tourists and visitors. The representation of "traditional" performances continues in a later scene, the funeral of the protagonist Babárìndé's father, where a funeral dirge is sung and a praise singer salutes all the celebrants, who perform a dignified dance outside the compound where the deceased has just been buried. This scene lasts 10 minutes 10 seconds—very long in film time. It cuts immediately to another style of music—"Fuji Explosion," Barrister Àyìndé's latest popular album—as Babárìndé, his wife Láídé, and their two sons sit at table, eating with knives and forks and being served water by a servant. This is also a long sequence, with lingering shots of the table, the glasses, and the fridge, as the nuclear family consumes its meal in silence.

The *egúngún* masquerade and the funeral ceremony, then, evoke community, solidarity, dignity, and tradition. The ancestors are besought to protect their living descendants and the living are exhorted to take care of their own offspring, so that they in turn may receive a fitting burial. The lunchtime scene suggests the good life of *ọlajú* but also hints that the luxury and indulgence of the boys' upbringing is already beginning to spoil them. It is wrong for little boys to sit tight and be served by adults while listening to fashionable pop music. The order of respect between elders and youth has been reversed, and it is implied that these descendants will be unlikely to bury their parents in the proper manner when the time comes.

The contrast in this drama, then, is precisely that between two things which it is difficult for the stage plays adequately to portray: indigenous "traditional" performance on the one hand and the culture of the well-to-do middle classes on the other. Babárìndé comes of a poor family in a small town. It is only because he is adopted and sponsored by Málọmọ́, the wealthy returnee from America, and Mercy, Málọmọ́'s African American wife, that he is able to complete his high school education and go on to university. His university career and his romance with fellow student Láídé is briefly but effectively suggested by a few shots, to music, of the campus, the bar in Odùduwà Hall, and so on. There is no dialogue and no attempt to reveal student life from within: it is rather a gesture at a life beyond the theater company's experience which is nonetheless enough to suggest a whole world of freedom, friendship, and glamour. This is made possible partly because the enlarged group recruited to make the video included Kọ́lá Oyèéwọ̀ as Babárìndé—for Oyèéwọ̀, though not himself a graduate, had worked for many years in the University of Ifẹ̀ Theater, spoke good English, and knew the life of the campus well. The returnee Málọmọ́ was also played by a University of Ifẹ̀ actor, Peter Fátómilọ́lá, and Mercy was played by Arianne, a real African American visitor. But more important is the fact that video vouches for its own authenticity, for it can pretend to be not a metaphorical representation of one thing (university life) by another (a performance on stage), but rather a metonymic allusion to a scene (university life) by mounting excerpts from its own actuality.

So, if video can encompass "traditional" performances, rituals, and arts more comprehensively than the stage theater, it can also reach further into "modernity." The videos reveal how far this modernity is seen as a local concern. It would have been well within the scope of a video drama—unlike stage drama—to show convincing scenes of the "been-to" arriving in London or New York, American cityscapes or campuses, Western shopping centers or pop concerts. But they do not choose to do so, nor do they choose to show Igbo or Hausa towns, and it is rare for any language but Yorùbá to be spoken. There is nothing to suggest that people's gaze is turned beyond the borders of their own country or indeed their own region within the country. And in the video it also becomes more strongly apparent that the term *ọlajú* is locally defined in an ambiguous if not openly ironical fashion.

Though videos are represented within the narrative as the objects of consumption by the youth, the video *Where the World Is Going* affirms the values of the elders. Wives should respect and serve their husbands, even when they are both university graduates. It is Láídé's headstrong and bad-tempered refusal to listen to Babárìndé that ultimately causes the ruin of the two boys. Láídé will not even cook for Babárìndé any more, pointing out that they have a housegirl to do that. "*Kí ni mo wáá níyàwó fún?*" [So what do I have a wife for?] retorts Babárìndé in exasperation. The boys are outrageously disrespectful of their father. As the opening song puts it:

> Níbo ló ti bẹ̀rẹ̀, níbo ló gbé dúró
> Níbo ló ń lọ
> Ẹ wáá wobi ayé ń re o.
> Ayé dayé ọ̀lajú o
> Aya ló ń pàṣe fún ọkọ wọn
> ... Ìyàwó ò fẹ́ẹ́ gbọ́ tọkọ mọ́
> Ọmọ ò fẹ́ẹ́ gbọ́ ti baba
> Ayé ò rí bí a ṣe ń wò

> Where did it begin, where will it end
> Where is it going
> Come and see where the world is tending.
> The world has become the world of enlightenment
> Wives are giving orders to their husbands
> Wives don't want to obey their husbands any more
> Children don't want to obey their fathers
> The world is not as it used to be.

Here enlightenment reveals its own underside and means the corruption and degradation that follows from the abandonment of indigenous traditions. The unresolved double meaning suggests how precarious and provisional is any perspective on the field of contemporary issues, a field marked by disjunction, contradiction, and incompatibility which people daily traverse in their everyday lives. Perhaps one reason for the popularity of video is its ability to enclose wide stretches of this field within its transparent integument, putting opposites into play together with a deceptively untroubled neutrality.

However, not all the videos produced by Adéjọbí or by Alhaji (after his departure from the company) portrayed traditional practices and attitudes positively as objects of cultural value. Alhaji's departure from the company in 1988 took place at a time of increasing religious polarization in western Nigeria. Aggressive fundamentalist Christian sects had begun a propaganda war which made extensive use of print and electronic media. Starved television stations became platforms for the promulgation of born-again evangelism. The video boom provided an outlet which had the advantage over printed tracts of being able to represent vivid and highly dramatic confrontations between good and evil forces through the enthusiastic use of an array of special effects (see Oha 1997). Islamic groups hastened to produce counter-propaganda in the fear that the Christian fundamentalists would colonize the entire public airspace. They faced each other across the public domain, engaged in violent but often well-informed dialogue and contestation, tract for tract, poster for poster, video for video. The field of Yorùbá video drama was expanded by an invasion of amateur but often well-funded religious performance groups. "Tradition" in this atmosphere was subjected to radical but unstable and often mutually incompatible reinterpretations.[32]

Adéjọbí's video films seem to separate out into two different approaches to "tradition." Some, like *Where the World Is Going*, show it as an embodiment of old and uncorrupted ways, before ọlajú spoilt the world. Others combine this interpretation with a more frankly touristic approach new to the theater's range. *Ká Róhun Wí* [*For the Sake of Saying Something*], one theme of which is an exposé of corruption introduced into local politics by a wealthy outsider, opens with a 20-minute sequence of the Òṣogbo Òṣun festival, perhaps the only real tourist attraction in western Nigeria. Others, again, tap into the unsavory side of "tradition." The video version of *Adédigba's Co-wife*, as we will see in Chapter 11, ventured deep into the domain of witchcraft, magic, and the occult—territory the Adéjọbí Company generally skirted around in its stage plays—suggesting a world powered entirely by "pagan" spiritual forces, most of them malevolent.

Alhaji's output, similarly, seems to have split into incompatible strands. Today, he is the director and star of a brilliant but uncompromising Islamic television series, which is dedicated to re-educating "accommodating" Muslims and teaching them to reject everything that is not pure Islam. But in *Ti Olúwa Nilẹ̀* [*The Land Belongs to God*], one of his best video productions to date, he appears to reaffirm the powers of traditional spiritual beings. *Inú Re* [*Generosity*], though sponsored by the Grand Council for Islamic Affairs, is an apparently secular, realistic, and subtle discussion of the problems caused to her family by an over-generous grandmother that has no religious or supernatural overtones until the final scenes. Then, the impatient white-collar son is recalled to a sense of duty toward his mother by means of an eschatological dream in which he sees a vision of hell and is warned by the voice of God, after which his pious uncle expounds the relevant passage from the Qur'an (a page of which is shown on screen, exactly as in the TV series *Ìwà Lẹ̀sìn*). A disaggregation of the theater company's amalgam of ecumenical enlightenment was thus accompanied by a separation of the various strands within the work of each of its two former directors.

The generalization and relaxation of recuperative mechanisms thus allowed vast swathes of formerly excluded elements to be reincorporated: sometimes as "cultural heritage," now seen more as a tourist attraction than as the foundation of ethnic-national revitalization, and sometimes as a lurid field of occult evil. Recuperation became more contradictory and uncontrolled as, on all sides, fundamentalist exclusions and oppositions carved up the theater's audience into smaller and smaller fragments.

In retrospect, the heyday of the theater company can be seen to have coincided with the period when the collaboration of these two artists, Christian and Muslim, was made possible—even encouraged—by the presence of a broad multi-faith public more interested in common morality and self-edification than in partisan proselytization, a public still prepared to believe that personal decency, uprightness, and order, as opposed to the disorderly manipulation of occult forces, are the path to self-realization. At the time, that comfortable but aspirational common ground was taken for granted. Looking back, one can see not only what a great achievement it was in itself but also how it made possible a truly remarkable popular culture.

ORAL GENRES AND THE FOUNDATION OF THEATRICAL ART

The themes of the plays show how the operation of editing, the mechanism of virtual literacy by which editing was performed, and the evaluation of "enlightenment" itself all changed with shifts in audience and theater company constitution and larger changes in the social scene. But we need to look also at a level beneath the thematic site of conscious editorial activity at the mode of theatrical constitution itself. Here we see a profound attunement to older, oral modes of creative generation.

Virtual literacy is more encompassing than actual literacy. But what it incorporates it only semi-subjugates. In this it participates in the mode of oral genres. Yorùbá oral genres are characterized by extensive mutual borrowing and incorporation: *oríkì* incorporate proverbs and fragments of Ifá verses; Ifá verses swallow folktales and have slots into which *oríkì* and proverbs can be fitted; proverbs can expand into lengthy narratives studded with songs and *oríkì* (Barber 1999). There are well-established signatures and formats by which the incorporated material is inflected to serve the purpose of the host genre. When a proverb is incorporated into *oríkì*, it functions as a name; when a folktale is incorporated into Ifá, it is fitted with a narrative mechanism that makes it serve as evidence of Ifá's incontrovertible veracity (Barber 1990). But the incorporated materials retain their identity—they are recognizable still as *other* genres—and still have the potential to reconstitute themselves.

The Adéjọbí theater strove to control and contain the passages of *oríkì*, traditional songs, *dùndún* drumming, incantations, and Ifá verses that it incorporated. Seeing itself as essentially discursive and expository, its linear action unfolding in a framed, almost two-dimensional space, the theater attempted to offer its audiences evidence of the consequences of action, formulated as a theorem. For this project, coherence rather than the fragmentation characteristic of older oral genres, demonstration rather than invocation, were required. By its "virtual writing," the theater sought to subordinate the electrifying, fragmented, vocative mode of old oral genres such as *oríkì* to the dominant mode of the plays, which was linear narrative.

Even in the days when the texts of the plays were wholly sung, they did not participate in the vocative mode of *oríkì*. The song texts were long coherent statements. They were often more explanatory and expository than expressive of characters' emotions or thoughts. The tunes were not based on any of the many modes of *oríkì* chanting, all of which involve an acoustically intense exaggeration of speech intonation rather than a melody; but neither did they mimic the usually short-cycle melodic patterns of Yorùbá traditional songs. They had absorbed certain features of Christian hymns—especially in their lyrics—but could not be seen as being based on the hymn form. They must be seen as a new style of sung text invented by the popular theater to carry out its own discursive project. The shedding of the music over the years, then, did not mean the abandonment of a "traditional" mode of expression in favor of a "modern" one: from the beginning, the mode of expression was adapted to a project of enlightenment. In their own view, the more recent speech-only style was more enlightened than the older sung style, because more naturalistic; but this should not lead us to conclude that the theater somehow "emerged" out of a musical matrix that was traditional and oral. The earliest sung texts were written compositions, and the verbal and musical mode was consciously and selectively forged to suit the theater's own didactic and expository purposes from its inception.

From the earliest plays, the older non-discursive modes of chanted poetry were rigorously quarantined. Even while speaking warmly of the Yorùbá traditional heritage, Adéjọbí made only sparing use of actual traditional performance genres. Incantations are uttered in several plays: but it is always the same token incantation. Ifá verses are chanted when a *babaláwo* appears, but only for long enough to establish that he is doing divination. And when traditional genres are quoted at greater length on stage, they are almost always used to make a definite dramatic point, so that their internal meaning and dynamics are firmly subordinated to the design of the dramatic narrative.

Almost all the instances of *oríkì* chanting were quoted in a way that drew critical or at least ambivalent attention to them, thus limiting the diffusion of their reverberations through the rest of the text (but see Chapter 12 for a partial exception). In *The Royal Palm-nut*, the adulterous wife Díẹ̀kọ́lá chants a snatch of *oríkì* in praise of her husband as he sets off on his quest for the palm nut; since she is in the middle of betraying and manipulating him, this can only be taken as highly ironical. In *Articulated Lorry*, the educated young man's illiterate and strong-willed mother bursts into his family *oríkì* when she comes on a visit: here, the performance represents something valuable which Àlàbí nevertheless distances himself from in his quest for self-betterment, highlighting the fundamental thematic opposition in the play. In all the plays, the *oríkì* are only sparingly quoted, and it is rare for a dramatic situation to be used as an excuse to incorporate extensive outbursts of *oríkì* chanting, as in some other theater companies. We have seen one case where Adéjọbí appeared to respond to the public's liking for excellent renditions of "traditional" genres by providing a slot for a visiting expert—when the part of the old pagan was created for Mr. Láìítán in *External Appearances*. But even here, the old pagan's *ìjálá* chanting is not set up in a free space but is locked into a grid of absolute doctrinal oppositions. Though the treatment is ambivalent, the Aládùúrà preacher does end up with the play's moral authority on his side. The old man's chanting ends up being fenced in by the preacher's classification of it as an example of a pagan art, an out-of-date form that must be abandoned in the name of both modernity and salvation. And the performance is surprisingly brief, considering how highly Adéjọbí valued his old friend's talent.

Oríkì, then—sparingly quoted and often put into the mouths of characters whose actions the play does not endorse—are not the mode in which the playtext moves. In this, the theater of Oyin Adéjọbí followed the lead of Hubert Ògúnǹdé rather than Dúró Ládiípọ̀, his great rival in Òṣogbo. *Ọba Kò So* and *Ẹ̀dá*, Ládiípọ̀'s two best-known plays, are both bathed in a constant flow of *oríkì*, and indeed the whole mode of these two dramas, their ways of striking an intense and evocative chord, is *oríkì*-like (see Ogundele 1997, 53–55).[33] If Adéjọbí did not use *oríkì* in this way, it was by choice, not for lack of example.

But the disciplines by which incorporated genres were subordinated to the discursive project of enlightenment were constantly subverted at the level of theatrical generation. There was a tension between the coherent design of the plays and a proliferating effusion of elaborations and additions; between exposition and invocation. The lesson-giving enlightened theater company attempted not only to control but also to foment—simultaneously to foment and control—the vocative, intense, segmented, high-impact dialogic rapport with audiences which traditional arts enjoyed.

Oyin Adéjọbí saw song as the basis of theatricality in life as in art—the mode that gives drama on stage and in society its power to embody and drive home meaning. And the key examples of "song" that he gave in his exposition of this theme were chanted poetry in the fragmented vocative *oríkì* mode:

> When two men vie for the throne of the town, each of them will have their drummers and their praise singers, so through the drumming and the praise singing they will be telling you that you are certainly going to ascend the throne of your fathers, no matter who might like to oppose you. You yourself will get inspired, . . . So, another example is masquerade, *egúngún*. It's drumming, incantations, and songs that give inspiration. In fact, all shrines in

Yorùbáland are with their own respective songs. So I believe that Yorùbá theater is not complete without songs. (English.)

In these examples, music (song, chanting, and drumming) constitutes a moment of highly charged intensity in the field of social relations: a moment where social processes are focused, heightened, and displayed. When two big men compete for a chieftaincy title, it is the drummers and chanters of *oríkì* who blazon their reputations to the world and fuel their rivalrous displays of magnificence and munificence. It is the chanters of *oríkì* whose direct and intense address to the owners of the praise epithets—the big men themselves—open up channels through which "inspiration" flows. This word, which Adéjọbí used several times when explaining things in English, always betokened a social, not a purely private and individual, experience. It is the acclaim of others that can give you "inspiration." The effect is seen in an even more intense form in addresses to spiritual beings such as the *egúngún* which Adéjọbí goes on to cite. It is the drumming and chanting of *oríkì* and *ọfọ̀* (incantations) that activate the *egúngún*, empower it and instigate its movements, both frightening and benign, around the town. The flow of power unleashed by the fierce vocative address of these forms of utterance is extremely striking. It is not an accident that Adéjọbí's discussion of "song" points first to this central, crucial, and galvanizing form of chanting which, by channeling attention and recognition toward the protagonists, actually plays a significant part in the activation of their potential (see Barber 1991).

This deeply rooted and ancient theatricality, however, is clearly associated with forms of life which are either "pagan" or at the very least lack the identifying marks of the "enlightened" and the "progressive." Competition for chieftaincy titles through public display, though very much a part of contemporary life, has overtones of an old style of social self-realization. It has to do with command over resources of people and occult powers, unlike the "enlightened" style of self-realization involving externally authorized status such as salaried government posts and a patronage based on "helpfulness" rather than might (see Barber 1991). And these forms are associated closely in Adéjọbí's exposition with even more pervasive and intense forms of social song belonging to *egúngún* and *òrìṣà*. So the model of creativity, of intense and persuasive utterance, to which he can refer his own theatrical art, belongs to a world which his church—with varying degrees of sternness—has proscribed. The church stands at the center of a scene of modernity, whose signs are literacy, cleanliness, and the orderly planning and regulation of one's life. It is this scene which the theater aspires to evoke and recommend, even while its very existence as a creative form springs from other soil outside the borders of the world of enlightenment.

For, like these older oral sung and chanted genres, the theater's deepest impulse underlying its discursive mode is to attain a highly charged intensity of impact. This finds its immediate counterpart in the seething, barely containable excitement of the audience. Intensity is generated dialogically. In the opening glee—where song is concentrated—Adéjọbí addresses the audience directly and receives responses to his greetings. Sometimes, after his initial speech of welcome, he makes further short speeches to heighten the impact of particular songs. In the Ọọ̀ni Girls High School performance of *Besotted Bridegroom* described in Chapter 6, one of the songs he decided to include in the opening glee was "Rómọké," a graphic moral narrative of a schoolgirl who lets her boyfriend go too far and ends up dying of a bungled abortion. He paused before beginning this song, in order to explain to the already highly excited young audience:

> In the song we're going to sing now, someone's name will be mentioned. I want to make clear that we don't know the name of anyone here tonight, whether male or female. We want to sing the song as a story of something that happened, which we think could be a lesson to us all, including us teachers whose job is to impart (moral) lessons. So, if you know anyone whose name resembles the one in the song, I don't want you to make fun of him/her. If I hear of any such thing, I'll take the person to court!

This was greeted with cheers and applause. The kids listened closely to the first solo verse, which did not mention anyone's name:

> Ṣe mí bó o ti bá mi
> Ṣe mí bó o ti bá mi
> Tó ò bá ṣe mí bó o ti bá mi
> Rárá o, o ò níí lọ o.
>
> "Leave me as you found me
> Leave me as you found me
> If you can't leave me as you found me
> Then I won't let you go."

But then the chorus came in with

> Róómọkéẹ́ẹ́
> Róómọkéẹ́ẹ́
> Rómọké òò
> Ìyáà reẹ́ wá ẹ oo
> Bàbáà reẹ́ pè ẹ́ o
>
> Rómọké
> Rómọké

> Rómọkẹ́ oh
> Your mother's searching for you
> Your father's calling you

and they exploded into roars of laughter, shrieks of excitement, and prolonged wild applause and general hullabaloo. Adéjọbí, then, used his dialogue with the audience on this occasion to stoke their excitement to fever pitch under the guise of counseling restraint.

Genres based on *oríkì* achieve intensity of effect by repetition combined with the juxtaposition of contrastive autonomous fragments. In the theater, the opening glee to some extent shares this mode, offering a "variety show" format of (mildly) contrastive and self-contained items—speeches, a succession of discrete and bounded songs, and sometimes a sequence of suggestive dancing by the chorus as well. No doubt one reason why the variety show format was so popular and influential with performing groups of the colonial period (see Chapter 2) was that it captured something of the "segmented" character of many of the older Yorùbá arts (see Drewal and Drewal 1983). But in the play proper, the overriding necessity for narrative coherence struggles with the impulse (constantly recrudescing) toward segmentation and maximal contrast of self-contained items. We see set pieces expanding and sometimes gaining a permanent place in a play even when they are irrelevant to the main lines of the logic of the plot; and we see odd little intrusions, where an irrelevant character or even comment pops up and causes laughter.

The requirement of order always prevails, and these outbursts are contained within the overall architecture of the play, vigilantly kept in place under Alhaji's supervision. But the orderly framework does not suppress the intense, expansive, and explosive potential of the performance so much as hold it within an overall boundary. Peaks of intensity of effect and rapport with the audience, comparable with the effects of *oríkì*, are achieved within this boundary, always retaining the potential to take over. Intensity of impact is achieved not through the juxtaposition of contrasting autonomous fragments (as in *oríkì*), but through the generation of coherent sequences culminating in maximal excitement. These are carefully engineered to release the audience's mounting ebullience in periodic outbursts where the noise on stage and the audience noise coalesce. In *Taking Care of Kúnlé*, we have seen how carefully the sequence leading up to the breaking of the news to Ọ̀sọ́ was orchestrated. Postponements, repetitions, and a slow edging toward the news of Wúrà's death built up an almost unbearable excitement, released when Ọ̀sọ́, finally enlightened, lets out a howl of anguish and leaps in the air, where he is caught and held by the two elders. Smaller sequences can be seen to generate smaller buildups and discharges of noise. In *Besotted Bridegroom*, examined at length in Chapter 6, we saw how the insults and abuse—directed mainly by Tàfá and his rich wife against the old lame man Bùárí—built up to a violent, noisy crescendo involving repeated physical assault; a movement that was then recapitulated over and over again in subsequent scenes. Very exciting buildups often ended in a general melee—with all characters present shouting, fighting, and rushing around the stage until the curtain was drawn. To me, these scene endings always looked messy and crude. But they were deliberately engineered and matched the audience's own desire to participate in enormous outbursts of hilarity, derision, and excitement. Audience members several times pointed to sequences of this kind ("when Tàfá abuses Bùárí"; "when Díẹ̀kọ́lá causes Tóògùn to be driven out") as the part they liked best in the play. The mode of the theater, then, was repeatedly to unleash turbulent forces, signaled by high-impact noise on stage and howls of laughter in the auditorium. Repetition—especially of slogans and set phrases—harnessed the audience's receptivity into a rhythm as they began to join in and even anticipate (see Chapter 7).

As with the *oríkì* performances alluded to by Adéjọbí, it is the electrifying rapport between speaker and hearer that is "inspiring" in the repeated buildup and discharge of theatrical energy. In this respect, the theater retained the capacity inherent in older Yorùbá oral genres to incorporate elements without fully subjugating them to their project. At a fundamental level, the drama was constituted in a theatrical mode that retained the potential to burst the boundaries of coherent expository discourse.

And this extraordinary deep-seated tension can be seen surfacing also at the level of the "message." Even though the dramatists strove to generate unified, univocal, moral, message-bearing statements, again and again one comes across formulations that look like contradictions, ambivalences, or paradoxes in the plays, and which I would suggest can better be understood as being a continued endorsement of potentiality. That is, the improvised popular theater could incorporate and hold within one purview very diverse, even incompatible, sources of vision because "virtual" writing retained the open-weave potential-preserving accommodatingness of Yorùbá orature while drawing on the potent legitimating insignia of literacy. This gave the theater a certain freedom of action, and a certain scope for subtlety, as it charted the waters of contemporary ideology, riven with overlapping and contested alternative absolutes.

11 Work, Destiny, and Self-Making

What is it to be a person? And what does it mean to step onto a stage? There is a link, though never a self-evident one, between being in society and characterization in drama or fiction. The way the actors constructed character and imagined social self-realization tapped into a changeable, contradictory, yet fundamentally conservative popular repertoire of shared notions about work, right behavior, destiny, "helpers," and "enemies." It was given its distinctive articulation in the plays, though, by the backgrounds of the actors as artisans and their continued use of artisanal practices in the theater itself in the generation of plays. For just as the theater's self-understanding and actual practice was permeated with a sense of the importance of literacy, so it was also, and equally, galvanized by a practical sense of how to make things work and a corresponding belief that social self-realization is ultimately the work of one's own hands.

ACTORS AS ARTISANS

Most of the members of the company, in common with a large proportion of their fellow pupils across the region, had been apprenticed to a master to learn a manual skill after leaving primary or modern school. The goal of an artisan was to become his own master, and every aspect of artisanship rested on individual self-reliance and initiative.

As a mode of instruction, apprenticeship placed more emphasis on the apprentice's ability to learn than on the master's ability to teach. Active, keen, responsible apprentices could try their hands at a variety of operations and assemble an all-round competence much more quickly than slow or apathetic ones. Apprenticeship provided primary-school leavers with a skill which, with luck and good judgment, could provide them with a respectable and independent livelihood. But this was not guaranteed: masters tended to take on more apprentices than could subsequently be supported by the market, so that many apprentices found it hard to set up on their own after they had freed. They had to be prepared to take the initiative in traveling to other towns to find a niche and in innovating and diversifying in order to secure a fraction of an overcrowded market.

To a greater extent than farming, artisanal trades were considered to be entrepreneurial as well as productive. It was the combination of skill at making something and skill at operating in the market that made these trades satisfying and conducive to self-esteem. Artisans mastered the art of acquiring raw materials at a low price, advertising the product through social networks and attractive salesmanship, building up a clientele, haggling over the sale price, and, often, trading on their own account in the goods associated with their craft (Lloyd 1974, 112). Láníyọnu—probably the character that invites the most unequivocal sympathy and admiration in the whole Adéjọbí repertoire—ascribes his success in life to the combination of hard physical work and astute commercial dealing. He tells his two impoverished (and treacherous) friends:

> A jọ kọ́ iṣẹ́ bíríkìlà ni. Mo rò wí pé, èmi sì kọ́sẹ́ bíríkìlà, èyin lỌlọ́run kọ́ọ́ sọ wí pé kẹ́ ẹ kọ́kọ́ fíríì ṣáájú mi. Nígbẹ̀hìn-gbẹ́hìn, lèmi tóó fíríì. Gbà tí mo fíríì tán, ni mo lọ sí ìdálẹ̀. Mo rí i wí pé, bí oókan bá kún eéjì, ẹẹ́ta ní í jẹ́. Mo fi òwò kún iṣẹ́ bíríkílà tí mo ń ṣe. Bẹ́ẹ̀ bá sì ṣàkíyèsí, ẹ ẹ́ẹ̀ rí wí pé ó sí pẹ́ẹ́lí díẹ̀ ju tiyín lọ.

> We learned the trade of bricklaying together. And I remember that while I trained as a bricklayer, it was you that God determined should complete the training first, before me. I finished last of all. When I finished, I went away on a journey. I realized that if you add one to two, it makes three. I added trade to bricklaying. And you may have noticed that my course of action was a bit more profitable than yours.

Láníyọnu is thus stalwart in the face of setbacks (such as finishing last in the apprenticeship—no doubt because of his master's unwillingness to release him) as well as shrewd and far-sighted in business. He is the paragon of successful men: modest, generous, God-fearing, and determined to raise his useless companions to his own level by helping them establish their own productive self-supporting businesses instead of sponging off him forever. The association of this character with bricklaying is revealing. Bricklaying—like the trades the members of the Adéjọbí Company learned, which included tailoring, goldsmithing, and metal trunk making—is one of the longer-established "new" crafts. It combines extremes of sweat and commercial savvy. It is heavy physical labor, but it also can lead into the most profitable of modern entrepreneurial lines, that of the building contractor.[1] In the oil years, government and big business embarked on extensive building projects, while private property-owners rushed to build houses to rent out to tenants in the congested and expanding urban centers.² The resulting construction boom floated a new class of wealthy building contractors. For the progressive conservatism of the theater company, no more appropriate trade could have been chosen for Láníyonu.

The Adéjobí company members always stressed that what they did was *work*, not play: strenuous work that combined physical endurance and skill with intellectual and artistic effort. Like artisans, the actors were organized around a boss who combined the roles of proprietor and teacher, they learned on the job by doing rather than listening to explanations, they traveled to find their markets, and they constantly innovated while continuing to produce a package that was sufficiently standardized to assure customers that they had got what they paid for. They competed with other theater companies by diversifying and by building up their own clientele of fans and followers through means that were social as well as commercial and that involved the self-projection of a successful persona (see Adam 1995, 80–83 for a discussion of these operations in artisanal trades).

In the actual generation of plays, too, their mode of production shared many features with artisanal trades. Susanna Adam speaks of the way in which tailors and carpenters would construct quite complex garments and furniture without using a separate and antecedent pattern or plan: "Many of them demonstrate an uncanny ability to comprehend and visualize new designs from descriptions or pictures but without the help of preliminary sketches" (ibid., 66). Builders, likewise, "had to coordinate the activities of their labourers with each other and with the drying time of various types of cement and mortar but they did so more with the sense of a choreographer than the analyses of an engineer" (ibid., 132). Similarly, Alhaji, as we saw in Chapter 4, seemed to have a total grasp of the complex sequences of each play, which he referred to as if to a script, without ever writing anything down in advance. He was able to marshal actors and compose scenes without any foreknowledge of the dimensions or shape of the stages on which the play would be performed, without being certain who would actually be available to perform, and without being able to foresee what inspired additions and variations the actors would introduce.

Artisans did not work to a uniform industrial standard: they produced artifacts that were good enough to satisfy their customers' expectations rather than conforming to an abstract ideal of regularity and consistency. When an especially wealthy and demanding customer appeared, or when the materials involved were very costly, all efforts would be made to produce a superior piece of work. Similarly, in the theater we have seen how performances varied. An elite audience (the kind of people Alhaji referred to as "a gentle man . . . intelligent people like Europeans, big men") elicited a polished, brilliant style of performance which the unruly town crowds did not. And in all performances, as long as the play worked, no one was concerned that there was chaos behind the scenes or that characters came on from different sides of the stage from one performance to the next. What struck me at the beginning as alarmingly casual behavior (see Chapters 4 and 7) did not matter as long as the characters got themselves on stage on time and were able to establish spatial relationships to each other which allowed the plot to unfold. In the National Theatre they used the excellent lighting facilities, and the show (to my mind) looked better; but when I asked Alhaji why he did not buy more powerful stage lights for their town and school performances, he said "It is not needed, and our public would not like it." Like car mechanics who excel at keeping vehicles on the road in almost any circumstances, the theater company could get a show up and running no matter what, and it was always good enough to satisfy the kind of customers who had paid to see it. Each show met its own requirements.

Artisanal entrepreneurs have to balance numerous variables when calculating their outlay, re-investment, and prices. Some of these variables are not subject to rational planning, for at any moment massive unforeseen expenses in the form of bribes to the police or unincurred electricity bills may crop up, while supply of materials, demand for products, and availability of labor also fluctuate unpredictably. This means that to succeed, the artisanal masters must become expert at rapid, improvisatory, intuitive calculations, responding to challenges as they arise. Although their skill provides them with a more secure income than is available to daily-paid or short-term waged workers, their position is never fully secure: it requires constant strategic shoring up by procedures not subject to conscious ratiocination. This leads the artisanal entrepreneurs to ascribe their success to forces outside their own individual conscious efforts ("to divine intervention and their trust in God": Adam 1995, 138), even while, as independent operators, they live out from day to day the drama of self-reliance and individual decision making. This is not, of course, peculiar to artisans; indeed, Adam sees it as "basic to the whole of Nigerian society" (ibid.), and Jane Guyer has shown the complexity and flexibility of farmers' continual responses to changing conditions and opportunities (Guyer 1997). But unlike a farmer or a paid employee, an artisan is committed to establishing a solo enterprise where *all* the factors of production must be assembled from scratch and orchestrated by himself. It seems likely that in these circumstances the fine balance between individual autonomy and factors beyond the individual's control is peculiarly central, salient, and permanent.

Artisans, then, thrive by inspired improvisation grounded in the habituation of experience. From this perspective we can see that the theater company's whole mode of production was artisanal: their way of generating action and dialogue on stage was of a piece with their way of assembling a company and organizing a tour. In the face of similar uncertainties, they constantly had to make the same kind of intuitive experience-based calculations that other artisans did. And this worked its way into the worlds of their plays, where individual self-making and divine providence provided two poles, between which the narrative constantly oscillated. Sometimes one pole, sometimes the other was emphasized, as we shall see later in this chapter; but the ontologies of all the plays were founded on the relationship between self-help and reliance on forces beyond the individual's control. Láníyọnu, the artisanal entrepreneur, improves his situation by shrewd investment in trade and counsels hard work and foresight: but at the same time he modestly disowns his own role in his success: "It was God who did it, not I," he tells his friends repeatedly. The structure of the play as a whole, as we shall see, dramatizes this polarity.

REALISM AND THE "EMERGENCE OF THE SELF"

The "self" suspended between self-activation and providential direction in these plays is represented in a way that was new in the colonial era. The Adéjọbí Theatre (and the Yorùbá popular theater more generally) had a mode of imagining and presenting character which had no precedent in pre-colonial genres. It projected persons into an imagined space from where they authorized themselves by their own speech. And the persons thus authorized were usually idiosyncratic, individual, lifelike human beings from the everyday world who functioned as the bearers of a coherent narrative of action and its consequences. The Yorùbá genres which predated the popular theater did not do this. Folk tales, though often dramatic, never left it to the characters to present themselves entirely through their own speech. Masquerade was largely non-narrative, often vehicular rather than representational, and, insofar as it was representational, highly schematic and selective (see Gotrick 1984).

Yorùbá popular theater participated in a general representational shift which took place across Africa. New genres emerged everywhere in the colonial era which represented ordinary life and people in their own terms and which used apparently "realist" modes of representation to do so.[3] But the Yorùbá popular theater's move in this direction went farther than other, parallel, popular colonial theatrical genres elsewhere in Africa. Ghanaian concert party, for example, is more presentational than illusionistic. The characters talk directly to the audience, announcing their names, occupations, habits, and problems in a succinct introductory speech. The Jaguar Jokers' play *Orphan Do Not Glance* begins with two "high-time girls" introducing themselves thus:

> **Abena Dansowa:** Hello, everybody. I'm the oldest in the family and my younger brother is called King Sam. My parents really tried for me so

I managed to reach Form One. However, since I finished, me and my girlfriend Selena have started roaming for men.

Selena: Good evening. I'm the daughter of the popular Appiah Nana and my house name is Akosua, but my Christian name is REAL SELENA (Barber, Collins, and Ricard 1997, 94).

Armed from the outset with all the information it needs to decipher the moral, the audience can then be relied on to accommodate the ensuing sequence of slapstick, pathos, and buffoonery, the jumps in time, slides in space, and switches in the function and moral weighting of characters (see Barber, Collins, and Ricard 1997; Cole 1997). Thus, the world of the play is inaugurated the moment *after* the characters are set in place.

Kúyè, one of the Adéjobís' oldest and most enduringly popular plays, opens in a quite different manner. The curtain is drawn onto an empty stage. An old woman enters, already talking as she walks on, followed at a little distance by a young man. What she says is:

Págà orí mi o, bóo nì ǹ ó ti wá ṣe tèmi ìí sí o? Ohun tí mo ní ǹ óò gbé wá ńnúunlé, mo tún gbàgbé rè ńnúunlé. Hanìn, Kúyè, wá bá n relé o wá rèé bá n gbéhun tí mo gbàgbé wá. Tó o bá débè ò ó rásoòhún ńbè. Wò ó, Kúyè . . . Kúyè o . . . Kúyè, má gbálè mó . . . má gbálè mó, ilè tó o gbá ó ti tó. N ó rán o ńṣé, ò ó rèé bá n gbe nǹkan wá. Wò ó, wá, wá, ǹ ó rán o ńlé. Níbi tá a ti wá, nìisìíín, o óò loolé. Mo gbagbe nǹkan. Mo di aṣo, mo gbé e 'énuònà yàrá ńlé. Wò ó, èmi n óò rán o ńlé. N óò rán o nínúunlé . . . nínúunlé. Wò ó, nínúunlé tá a ti gbégbá ìí wá, o óò loolé. . . .

What a bloody fool I am, what on earth am I thinking of? I've gone and forgotten the very thing I was supposed to be bringing along with me. Look, Kúyè, you run back home and fetch it for me. When you get there you'll see those clothes there. Look, Kúyè . . . Kúyè! Kúyè, stop sweeping, you've done enough. I'm sending you home now to fetch something for me. Look, come here, come here, I want to send you home. The place we've just come from, you're to go back there. I forgot something. I packed some clothes and put them in the doorway of the bedroom. Look, I'm sending you back home. I'm sending you back to the house . . . the house. Look, the house where we've just brought this calabash from, you're to go back there. . . .

This opening conveys the unmistakable sense of a life that was already in existence before the curtain was opened: the speaker is in midstream as

Kúyẹ̀'s aunt (Grace) sells off his father's clothes. ©Elio Montanari

the scene begins. The audience is required to work out for itself who this voluble woman is, why she is addressing the young man in that peculiarly insistent and repetitive manner, and why she wants the clothes that she says she has left in the house. The drama seems to be representing character not as something adventitious and ad hoc, springing into life for the sake of the viewers and to carry forward the plot, but rather as something complex and flowing into which the drama can tap to generate a particular narrative. It gradually emerges—not in direct statements but through asides, manners of address, and implications—that the woman is Kúyẹ̀'s aunt, that his parents are dead, that she is a lowly pepper seller, and that she is about to sell his late father's clothes to a peddler. There are also other details that are not essential to the plot but which suggest that the characters have pasts, sometimes only fleetingly alluded to, and relationships with people who have no role in the story—as when the aunt, in the full flood of her diatribe against Kúyẹ̀, says "*Mo bímọ tèmi, ọmọ tèmi ò dá mi ń gbèsè*" [I have my own children, *my* children never plunged me into debt]. Characters, then, are presented in a way that implies that to be a person is to have memory and to be suspended in a fine mesh of particular relationships.

That this is an intentional and conscious dramatic technique is demonstrated by the fact that there are sequences which comically highlight this style of introducing character and situation. If the opening of *Kúyẹ̀* plunges the audience in medias res, the invitation to work out what is going on is made almost into a joke with the irruption of another character halfway through the scene: a furiously angry man who announces again and again "I'll use Ṣàngó to find it. I'll use Ṣàngó to find it." "What's happened?" asks Kúyẹ̀'s aunt, the Pepper Seller, and the scene continues:

> ÀLÀBÍ: Àǹtí mi, tẹ́ ẹ bá gbọ́ pé ọmọ ékeé kú, àgbàlagbà kú ńnúunlé wa, èmi tí mo ṣe é rèé.
> ÌYÁ ALÁTA: Héèè!
> ÀLÀBÍ: Ṣàngó ni ń ó sì fi wá a.
> ÌYÁ ALÁTA: Háà, ọkọ iyá mi, yóò dáa fún ọ o. Ìran wa è é sapààyàn o.
> ÀLÀBÍ: Èmi ó fi tèmi dá a álẹ̀.
> ÌYÁ ALÁTA: Háà!
> ÀLÀBÍ: Èmi ó fi tèmi dá a álẹ̀.
> ÌYÁ ALÁTA: Hái, má jẹ́ n gbọ́rú rẹ lẹ́nu rẹ mọ́.
> ÀLÀBÍ: Kò burú.
> ÌYÁ ALÁTA: Àwa è é sapààyàn ńlé wa.
> ÀLÀBÍ: Ṣàngó, Ṣàngó ni n fi wá a. Èmi ni mo sọ bẹ́ẹ̀.
> ÌYÁ ALÁTA: Àlémi ló ṣelẹ̀, àbí èé ti rí?
> ÀLÀBÍ: Wọ́n ní ńbi a bá fi nǹkan ẹni sí, níbẹ̀ làá bá a.
> ÌYÁ ALÁTA: Emi ló dé?
> ÀLÀBÍ: Àní ṣé, aṣọ tẹ́ ẹ gbé sí n lọ́dọ̀, mo dénúunlé, mo toko dé, n ò bápòtí aṣọ ńbi tí mo kó o sí mọ́. Ṣàngó ni n óò sì fi wá a. Ṣàngó.

> ÀLÀBÍ: Auntie, if you hear of deaths in our family—children dying, elders dying—it's me who did it!
> PEPPER SELLER: What?
> ÀLÀBÍ: And I'll use Ṣàngó to search for it!
> PEPPER SELLER: Ha, my mother's husband, the Lord preserve you. There have never been murderers in our family.
> ÀLÀBÍ: So I'll be the first.
> PEPPER SELLER: What!
> ÀLÀBÍ: I'll be the first.
> PEPPER SELLER: Hey, don't let me hear another word of that kind of talk from you.
> ÀLÀBÍ: OK.
> PEPPER SELLER: We're not murderers in our family.
> ÀLÀBÍ: Ṣàngó—I'll use Ṣàngó to find it. I'm telling you!
> PEPPER SELLER: Just tell me what's happened, can't you?
> ÀLÀBÍ: There's a saying that you find a thing where you left it.
> PEPPER Seller: What's happened?

ÀLÀBÍ: This is what's happened—you know those clothes you left with me, well, I got home, I got back from the farm, and I didn't find the box of clothes where I left it! I'll use Ṣàngó to find it! Ṣàngó!

Here, with a technique of circling and postponement familiar from other plays we have discussed (see Chapters 5 and 6), the actors play with mystification and gradual revelation. In the end, the Pepper Seller, having finally found out what Àlàbí is angry about, tells him that it was she herself who went to his house and took the clothes. The little episode is blown up like a bubble. A Ghanaian concert party actor might have walked onto the stage and said "Twenty years ago my brother died and left all his clothes for me to keep for his deaf and dumb son Kúyè. But now I am short of money I have decided to sell them. Here they are—I went to my nephew's house and fetched them when he was out." Instead, the Adéjọbí Company creates a little mini-drama that issues from a conundrum: something significant had happened before Àlàbí first appeared on stage—had impelled him into the scene in a state of near apoplexy—but neither the audience nor the other characters know what it is, and as his fury makes him loop and zigzag around the subject instead of getting to the point, the revelation is comically deferred. Recognizing the existence of an anterior life is the whole point of this sequence; it highlights, with hilarious exaggeration, the theatrical mode of the play as a whole.

So the characters are imagined as being fully enmeshed in time and grounded in space, as having relationships, pasts, and memories that they bring with them when they step onto the stage. Their mode of self-establishment as characters is to float these details out in a constant flow of lifelike talk.

I suggested in Chapter 9 that the "lifelikeness" of the plays, their setting in the recognizable ordinary world, were ways of restricting the scope of chance, of forging unbreakable links between specific sequences of moral action and their consequences which popular audiences could appropriate and apply to their own real lives. But we need to ask what the implications of this lifelikeness were for the inner conception of the person. Was this the same kind of "realism" as that which emerged in the eighteenth and nineteenth centuries in Europe? Did it imply similar shifts in the conception of the self?

There are many things about the Adéjọbí Theatre's mode of representation that do bear a striking resemblance to the features identified as characteristic of European realism. The fundamental theatrical setup (the relations between space, time, and theatrical action discussed in Chapter 7), involves the following: the presentation of action like a picture to an audience placed in a fixed position before it; the unrolling of narrative events without interventions from a master of ceremonies or narrator; the resulting establishment of an illusionistic dramatic "world" which, as long as it lasts, is not disrupted by the exposure of the theater's mechanisms of fabrication; and the dominance of rationally explicable causal narrative chains over "spectacular" effects, supernatural interventions, and bizarre coincidences. Time is "dialectic" rather than "iconic" (Beckerman 1990, 61): that is, it is a forward-moving, unidirectional time in which the present is a consequence of the past and a cause of the future rather than being a circular or static evocation of being, as in some religious dramatic modes. All these are among the key characteristics of European realism (Abercrombie, Lash, and Longhurst 1996).

The evocation of places and people within the plays, discussed in Chapter 9, likewise seems to have affinities with the English realist novel and drama. The investment in particularity and specificity of place and person set the Yorùbá popular theater apart from most folktales and from masquerade theater, just as it set the early English novel apart from fantastic tales, romances, and burlesques (see Watt 1963, 331). Individuals in the Adéjọbí theater have ordinary everyday neutral names—Tàfá Olóyèdé, Bàbáa Wándé, Ìyáa Ṣeun—rather than labels indicating a type or an allegorical figure. They inhabit ordinary, recognizable kinds of towns, villages, and households. They are differentiated by being endowed, as we have just seen, with personal webs of memory and relationships. The linguistic style is governed not so much by rules of generic decorum or the requirement to produce a highly wrought artifact as by the requirement that it sound like real people speaking—an effect deliberately achieved over the theater company's history by the progressive shedding of sung text and stylized choruses. Above all, the texture of the plays is characterized by its wealth of detail. The characters talk a lot (about three times as much as their counterparts in Ghanaian concert party: see Barber, Collins, and Ricard 1997); in the constant flow of variable, improvised speech innumerable idiosyncratic details are introduced, constantly replenishing the sense that what these people are and what they say cannot be wholly predicted from the plot or reduced to a formula. Each character seems to hint at a potential reservoir of past experiences, attitudes, and relationships that could at some point be drawn upon in the course of the drama.

But European realism expressed and articulated a historically specific and localized conception of self, which, in Taylor's magisterial account, took shape in an unbroken succession of ideological shifts from Plato to the Enlightenment (Taylor 1989). This emergent self, conceived of as unified, autonomous, and rational, is described as having increasingly become characterized by a certain sense of "inwardness" that rested on a distinction between the inner domain of thought, feelings, ideas, capacities, potentialities, and the outer public and objective world of things and people, onto which the inner properties are brought to bear. In the late eighteenth century, novels began to represent the quality of inner experience for its own sake. There was an increasingly intimate exploration of the "private"—both in the sense of the domestic and in the sense of the mental and emotional (Watt 1963; Habermas 1991). The meaning of life began to be seen as inhering in, and emerging from, the particular lived experience of unique individuals, and ordinary social production and reproduction became the object of the novelist's and painter's attention. Drama underwent a parallel transmutation. Instead of character being the bearer of action, action now emanated from and served to express unique, whole, inner characters. Acting became a kind of portraiture, and actors began both to introspect and to study the behavior of other real people as models. Audiences began to see their task as one of "identifying" with the characters: by "imaginatively occupying their subject position . . . experiencing . . . what it is to *be* Lady Macbeth or Hamlet as subjects, that is, as we experience ourselves" (Burns 1990, 14).[4]

In various accounts of the history of the emergence or construction of the modern Western self and the concomitant rise of realism, a number of distinct notions are conjoined and treated as historically fused even if analytically separable. Concepts of individualism (as opposed to submersion in a group); concepts of autonomous rational action (as opposed to subservience to authority and tradition); concepts of subjective experience (the idea that different people experience the world in different ways) and interiority (the idea that people have an inner life of emotions and ideas which they can access through introspection) are depicted as intermeshed and stimulated by a common historical context of new forms of civil society, bourgeois commerce, companionate marriage, inner-life Protestantism, and other factors.[5]

This history of transition from communalism to subjective individualism—insofar as it happened at all—is charted in detail for Western Europe but is then often transferred wholesale to the rest of the world, on the assumption that it is a universal and repeatable consequence of social change, of transition to "modernity" in its broadest sense. It rests, like most accounts of modernity, on a fundamentally binary sense of "before" and "after"—"before" being the ancient, the medieval, the communal, feudal, and traditional worlds, about which many generalizing assumptions are made, and "after" being all the things which belong to our present condition, or can be assimilated to it, whether as "anticipations" or as steps in an inevitable march forward. But the experience of western Nigeria—and of other parts of Africa[6]—does not match this model. The pre-colonial "before" is not a traditional submersion in collectivity; and the post-colonial "after" does not emerge from it into an Enlightenment-style fusion of subjective experience, interiority, autonomy, individuality, and agency.[7] The bundles of characteristics used to define both the "pre-modern" and the "modern" self have to be disaggregated before the "realism" of the Oyin Adéjọbí company can be understood.

AUTONOMY AND INTERIORITY IN YORÙBÁ GENRES

In older Yorùbá texts with putative roots in the pre-colonial world, we see the imprint of a powerfully conceived notion of personal autonomy, agency, and individuality. Individuality is hailed and enhanced in *oríkì* [praise poetry]. The channel of communication is a hotline between two personalities, the praiser and the praisee, and the *oríkì* expand the space occupied by the praisee's personality by seizing on its idiosyncratic and distinctive features. Of course there is much more to it than that—the *oríkì* also hail the individual in terms of his "people," as a son, grandson, and member of a descent group, and there is a dialectical tension between subsuming his "people" into his reputation and subsuming his reputation into that of a larger collectivity. Nonetheless, it would be absurd to argue that individuality is not valued, or that the identity of individuals is submerged within the collectivity. Individual big men are praised for their autonomy, their difference from other people, even their ability to transgress collective norms and get away with it; profusion of alternatives and of differences is valued and fostered at every level, and there is a strong positive evaluation of the idea of personal choice (Barber 1991).

Ideas of autonomous individual action and the distinctiveness of each person are supported by an ethic of "self-making" that seems to go back at least to the late nineteenth century (see Barber 1994). Even the slave has the potential to redeem himself; everyone, however humble, is thought to be a site of possible transformation. And the transformation is one's own responsibility, the work of one's own hands: one invests in oneself by accruing people, money, and material goods to expand the social space one is able to occupy.

But this focus on autonomy and individuality is not accompanied by any exploration of interiority or subjective experience. There is intense interest in the idea of what is "inside" the individual. However, this is not thought of in terms of inner experience so much as of secret intentions toward others. Other people's "insides" are unknowable; one's own thoughts are best kept to oneself. The *oríkì* of one nineteenth-century big man included the lines:

Àkàndé the father has something to rise and worship
He says you worship Ifá
And you worship Òṣun
But problems arising from other people have nothing to do with the
  òrìṣà

> The person who worships his own inside is the wise one, Ṣónibáṛẹ.
> (Barber 1991, 209)

This man is remembered for proclaiming that there is no point in relying on the gods to solve one's problems: only by attending to one's own *inú*—one's "inside," one's secrets, one's own counsel—can one deal with the hostile and devious actions of other people. You protect your autonomy from the encroachments of others by keeping your thoughts and plans locked up within. *Bánú sọ, má(à) bániyàn sọ,* another common proverbial formulation, means "Speak to your inside, don't speak to people": thus, dialogue is pictured as moving inward and occurring between the prudent person and his/her own interior. But this emphasis on the inside arises precisely because speech is recognized as inherently shared and exteriorizing; the wise person must short-circuit the normal exchange, pen it up within, to protect him/herself. The speech one has with one's inside is not different in kind from public speech.[8]

This conception of individual autonomy and agency *without* a corresponding emphasis on interiority and subjectivity is still very much in circulation, reiterated in poetic performances, popular songs, and other contemporary Yorùbá genres. But other ways of thinking about the person have also been filtering into the discursive field since the mid-nineteenth century, producing new amalgams which cannot be mapped onto the European before-and-after history of the self any more easily than the older ideas of individuality, self-making, and secrecy. Evangelical missionaries laid great stress on sincerity, on a "warm," "lively" faith that sprang from inner emotional assent and intellectual conviction (Peel 2000). Converts were induced to undertake private study of the Bible and to search their consciences. While the older philosophy stressed resignedly that "though the skin of the stomach is thin, you can never know what is inside another person," the missionaries urged that the sincerity of the convert's beliefs should shine through his/her every action.

The missionaries appear to have been somewhat despondent about the prospects for this view taking root (Peel 2000). But the colonial period did see the emergence of new representations of personhood, though perhaps of a somewhat different nature from what the missionaries were aiming at. Two major new cultural forms in the Yorùbá-speaking area, the novel and the narrative drama, developed the notion of the autonomous individual in a new way. They both made the autonomy and individuality of the protagonist synonymous with *moral responsibility*, situated in and arising from the individual's personal experience. And personal experience was represented through the detailed depiction of the individual's life or career.

In several of the landmark Yorùbá novels, the autonomy and solitude of the narrative agent is made almost absolute (see Barber 1997a). In the

Adéjọbí repertoire, as we saw in Chapter 9, the protagonists are often represented as surprisingly free of family or community constraints on their action. The frequent choice of urban settings featuring tenants or migrants (as in *Articulated Lorry, External Appearances, The Heir*) parallels the novel's preference for orphans and runaways: the individual is projected into a scene of moral action in a manner that attracts the maximum attention to his or her own responsibility for what happens.

In the novels, the story of the solo protagonist is often narrated in the first person, evoking for the first time in an extended artistic form a localized, unified center of consciousness which undergoes experiences and subsequently retails them, so that the experience itself—"what I went through"—is foregrounded, melodramatically (as in *Ìtàn Ìgbésí Aiyé Èmi Sẹ̀gilọlá*) or satirically (as in *Olówólaiyémọ̀*). The first-person testimony vouches for the authenticity of the experience.[9] In the popular theatre, equivalent effects are achieved by launching lifelike individuals into a narrative space to establish themselves through their own speech. Each character speaks as if from within the matrix of his or her own personal experience, and innumerable quotidian and idiosyncratic details testify to its reality. In both the novels and the drama, the principal characters are not only held responsible for their own actions (rather than acting collectively, under compulsion or in obedience to tradition), but are always held to be capable of understanding what they have done and why it had those consequences. And the point of these demonstrations is that the individual should experience and reflect upon the consequences of moral action.

In both the novels and the plays, then, consciousness and lived experience are central and are evoked in a way that was new in the colonial period. But this does not mean that the novel and the drama are dedicated either to the celebration of the richness of ordinary life for its own sake, or to the exploration of subjectivity and interiority as a privileged site of representation. When the Pepper Seller walks onto the stage saying "What a bloody fool I am, what on earth am I thinking of?" she is not directly addressing the audience, as in concert party, but neither is she talking intensely to herself and being "overheard" by us, as in European realism. Rather, she is projecting her being into the world—a world which includes the audience but is not limited to it. It is the nature of that projection—that launching of free-standing persons into a new moral space—that we need to explore.

CHARACTER AND CONSCIOUSNESS

The Adéjọbí repertoire exhibits not a single, unified perspective on questions of agency, interiority, and intention, but a spectrum of contrasting positions. *External Appearances*, of all the plays I recorded, has the greatest interest in a character's state of mind, her interior life, her moral responsibility, and the possibility of change in her moral disposition; *Adédigba's Co-*

wife, in the 1990s video version, most consistently represents human action in terms of non-human (or not wholly human) but morally charged agencies—*òrìṣà*, witchcraft, medicines, *ṣìgìdì*—operating simultaneously in, through, and outside their human victims and operants. Charting these two extremes in the repertoire's range will suggest certain underlying shared presuppositions. It will also help to dismantle any unilinear and unidirectional history of the self in Yorùbáland: for the more recent (video) drama is the one that seems to rely most heavily on older ideas about agency and consciousness.

External Appearances is the story of a beautiful, mature woman in search of an advantageous marriage. The milieu is urban and contemporary, and Bísí, a salaried worker, is living alone in rented rooms and making her own decisions. She knows all the important big men in town, and is besieged by suitors ("They would queue up like people in a clinic.... As one was leaving, another would be arriving!"), but seems unable to bring any of them to the point of marriage. "They would use me like rainwater and go." To find a solution, she joins the congregation of an Aládùúrà church where a prophet-like preacher prescribes a course of praying and fasting for her. She adheres rigidly to the program. Gradually the flood of admirers dwindles to a trickle, and eventually the last two to remain become serious about marriage. Bísí takes their names to the preacher and he divines, through a vision inspired by the Holy Spirit, that it is Pírí, the younger and poorer of the two, who is her destined husband. What follows is the consequence of her inability to settle for this deal. While prevaricating with the infatuated Pírí, she hesitates to break completely with the other candidate, Kúnlé. She also has a third suitor in tow: "Uncle Táyọ̀"—an older, much richer, boastful big man, a car dealer who offers her the car of her choice and lavishes gifts of money on her. She eventually breaks with Kúnlé but tries to keep both Uncle Táyọ̀ and Pírí on the boil, and even takes Uncle Táyọ̀ to the preacher to find out by prayer "whether God could join him and me." Despite a generous gift from Uncle Táyọ̀, the preacher's vision is inconclusive, and Bísí continues to procrastinate while keeping both suitors dangling. Inevitably, it all comes out: Uncle Táyọ̀ turns up one day and surprises Bísí with Pírí. Both Uncle Táyọ̀ and Pírí break it off with her, Uncle Táyọ̀ first wresting the car keys back from her by force, and Pírí demanding the return of one of his gifts.

The framework of assumptions in which this drama is set, therefore, takes it for granted that Bísí's marriage and indeed her whole life course are her own responsibility. Her desire for autonomy, privacy, and self-determination is underlined as she calculates what she will sacrifice by placing herself under the headship of a husband—not to mention the domination of an interfering mother-in-law. She suspects Pírí of meanness about money and is afraid that he will neglect and even beat her once they are married. She makes him promise not to run after other girls but is not convinced he will keep his promise. Although the audience laughed derisively at her excessive demands (particularly when she asked him to go and withdraw everything in his bank account for her), no alternative to self-generated action is recommended by the play. There is no family to arrange a marriage for her and no suggestion that her fault lay in making her own decisions. This acceptance by the play of her autonomy and freedom of action, however, is coupled with a strong complementary emphasis on the individual's need to make personal and whole-hearted efforts to *stay on track* in his or her life course. "Destiny," Divine providence, or a more diffuse sense of what is appropriate to people at each stage of their lives, provide a pattern to which the individual must strive to conform.

At first sight, the Aládùúrà church context in which this story is presented does not suggest a focus on inner states of mind and spirit so much as an instrumental this-worldly orientation to human action. The preacher prays on behalf of his clients for practical benefits, and his prescriptions of fasts and prayer seem instrumental and quasi-magical. His language seems almost wholly devoid of missionary notions of the inner life: when divining the right husband for Bísí, he asks her to put the piece of paper bearing their names to her own forehead, explaining, "It's the Orí ["Head" or personal destiny] that chooses a good *ìpín* [lot in life] for people, each individual's destination in this world is where his/her Orí will escort him/her to."

However, Bísí is endowed with an inner consciousness which is central to the play's moral. As she is still digesting the shock of losing both lovers in one fell swoop, her younger cousin from the village arrives with her teenage son to ask Bísí to use her important connections to find a job for him in the city. Bísí agrees, but takes the opportunity to give Àdùké, the cousin, a bit of extra advice. Àdùké has already had seven children and is pregnant again. Bísí says she should do something about it. "*Èmí ò láàrò*" [The breath of life cannot be replaced]. She should not wear herself out having children. "*Omo beere, òsì beere*" [Many children, much poverty]. For her children's sake as well as her own, she should concentrate on looking after the ones she already has rather than continue having more. Àdùké replies respectfully that she has understood what Bísí is telling her. But she goes on to produce her own piece of proverbial wisdom: "People should do their childbearing early in life [lit. 'do the trade of children in the morning'], so that in the evening they can rest. So, I too will enjoy life when the time comes." With this, she leaves, and Bísí remains on stage to deliver a speech, poised between soliloquy and sermon, that seems to come straight from her inner consciousness:

A à tíì kó Ifá ńlè, tí Ifá fi ń se. Èmi n mo sì toro òrò lówó omo yìí o. Tí ń bá so pé kó ronú ara è wò ni, kò níí bùn mi lórò tó so. Araà mi sì sọ́ọ̀kì. Lóòótọ́ ọ̀rọ̀ tó sọ yìíì, ó jẹ́ ẹ̀gún láraà mi, sùgbọ́n ó yẹ kí n fi ro oríì mi dáadáa. Torí pé ká fàárọ̀ sòwò ọmọ. Ẹ wò ó, nígbà tó ń torí ọmọ yìí jìyà, ọmọ ló ti di tiẹ̀ yìíì. Èmi wá ń mámùúbọ́ ní gbogboògbà. Mo mọlée Máníjà báǹkì. Mo mọ ti Bípíeè, mo mọ ti "One hundred." Kí wáá làǹfààní ẹ̀? Ọ̀rọ̀ mi ń fádùúà o. N ń padà dé ọ̀dọ̀ Alàgbà. Torí bí ìì báá ṣe Alàgbà ni tẹ́lẹ̀tẹ́lẹ̀, èmi ti lémi ò fẹ́ olósì Pírí. Èmi ti lémi ò fẹ́ olósì Pírí . . . Èmi ti lémi ò fẹ́ . . .

Before we even get out the divining instruments, Ifá's words come to pass. And I brought it upon myself that this girl should reprimand me. If I hadn't said she should reconsider her own situation in life, she would never have bestowed on me the words she did. I was gob-smacked [lit. "My body shocked (sọ́ọ̀kì)"]. It's true that what she said is like a thorn in my flesh, but I ought to use it to assess my own life course thoroughly. Because we should have children early in life. Look, all the time she was suffering in the struggle to bring up this child, the child was becoming hers [i.e., a support for her later on]. And I keep on failing over and over again. I know the house of the bank manager. I know that of B. P., I know that of "One Hundred." But what's the benefit? My situation needs prayer. I'll go back to Alàgbà ["Senior Man," i.e., the preacher]. Because if it wasn't for Alàgbà before, I would have said I wasn't marrying that wretched [or poverty-stricken] Pírí. I would have said I wouldn't marry that wretched Pírí. . . . I would have said I wouldn't marry . . . (she bursts into tears and rushes off).

The movement of Bísí's thought here is very rapid, from regretting that her own ill-judged advice gave Àdùkẹ́, a younger woman, the occasion to reprimand her; to describing or giving vent to the immediate feeling of consternation and dismay this reprimand of Àdùkẹ́'s caused her; to deciding all the same to take Àdùkẹ́'s advice seriously and apply it to her own situation in order to reassess the direction of her life course; to amplifying Àdùkẹ́'s brief message (Àdùkẹ́ suffered in the early days but now has big children to support her) and gazing in disillusionment at her own achievements (what benefit is there in knowing all the big men if you have no husband and no children?); to her conclusion "My situation needs prayer." Her wrong turning in life, then, she now understands to be the result of wrong desires, wrong goals: she has pursued wealth and social influence instead of following the homespun precepts of her less-educated and less-urbanized kin. In the last scene, the preacher explicitly confirms that the locus of her problem is internal, to do with her moral disposition or orientation to the world:

A kúkú ní o gbàdúà, ò ń gbàdúà. Bá a yan ààwẹ̀ fún ọ, o óò gbàawẹ̀ 'bi tééyàn án gbà á dé. Ṣùgbọ́n ojú kòkòrò, kòkòrò tí ń bẹ lójúù rẹ, ní ń jẹ́ o mámùúbọ́-ọ̀. Kí la tún ní o dà? Bá a ní o gbàdúà, o òò gbàdúà. Bá a ní o sun ilé Ọlọ́un títí ọdún é e parí, o òò sunbẹ̀. Ṣùgbọ́n ojú kòkòrò ní ń jẹ́ o mámùúbọ́. Tó ò bá sì jáwọ́ ńnú ojú kòkòrò, bó o ti máa mámùúbọ́ náà nù un.

> When I told you to pray, you prayed. When I prescribed fasts for you, you would fast to the limit of human capacity. But greed, the greed that infests you, is what's causing you to fail. What else can we tell you to do? If we tell you to pray, you'll pray. If we tell you to sleep in the church till the end of the year, you'll sleep there. But your greed is causing you to fail. And if you don't put an end to that greed, you'll just keep on failing.

What the preacher is criticizing is those fervent members of the congregation who perform all the exterior acts of devotion but fail to reform their inner motives or desires. The play is interested in Bísí's interior state because it is her moral disposition (her "greed" or desire to strike the most advantageous possible marital bargain) that prevents her from wholeheartedly conforming to the proper rhythms of life. And the correct interior state, conversely, would be the one that prompted her to choose sincerely and in good faith to move on to the appropriate stage.

In this picture, the inner self is not something that demands creative expression, nor is it *generative* in the sense of being able to produce social or ideological change. What is inside is not in this sense a source. Rather, it is a potential spanner in the works, something which if it is not properly in harmony with life's moral requirements may derail a person's "destiny" or life course. The fasting was working; the suitors were shaping up; Bísí's destined husband was identified through the operations of *èmí*, a spiritual entity both inside her and continuous with the divine spirit that inspired the preacher. All this was reduced to *àmúbọ́*—failure—because of something wrong inside: her lack of sincerity and her excessive desire for wealth.

In the video drama *Adédigba's Co-wife*, by contrast, the central figure is the *elénìní*—the enemy who unknown to others is destroying their lives. She is evil personified, and it is axiomatic that one cannot know the inner thoughts or intentions of such people. All one can see is their effects on those around them.

The play—in its video version at least[10]—postulates a world of agency in which the church, Jesus Christ, the efficacy of prayer, and the importance of faith are hardly mentioned. Events are placed in a universe framed by destiny, disrupted by human malevolence, and righted by divine retribution through the intervention of *òrìṣà* and other "pagan" entities. Agency is construed almost entirely in terms of spiritual forces crystallized in humanlike forms operating both within and outside of the somatic human envelope.

The opening scene shows Àwẹlé, the youngest wife of the wealthy trader Bàbáa Jíire, materializing like a ghost in a co-wife's bedroom, knocking her out with a powder blown into her face, and then carrying off her child—to be buried alive in the forest by a male accomplice. Bàbáa Jíire's reaction to the lamentations which follow shows that he is quite used to family trouble. It quickly becomes apparent that Àwèlé and her female associates are full-blown, night-traveling, child-eating witches. The family elders, not knowing who is causing their endless misfortunes, summon the household to drink from a ritual bowl of water and swear that they have not killed fellow household members. We see Àwèlé being compelled to swallow two mouthfuls.

Àwèlé goes on to attack her other co-wives one by one. When Bàbáa Jíire begins to court Adédigba, the radiantly beautiful young daughter of one of his customers, Àwèlé marshals a whole range of supernatural forces to attack her and her unborn child. However, Adédigba has an unsolicited protector in the shape of a beneficent white-clad figure who appears to her in a dream, seated amidst the rocks of the river Òṣun—either the deity Òṣun herself or a powerful spiritual priestess. Under her protection, Adédigba gives birth to a healthy son. The boy, Adéjàre, seems destined for a prosperous and successful life until Àwèlé enlists the help of the most powerful witch of all, her own mother. This character's first attempt on Adéjàre's life is again thwarted by the Òṣun figure, who intercepts the dwarfish spirit familiar sent to attack the boy in his sleep. But the second attempt, involving a potent medicine administered to Adéjàre in a stew, is partially successful. The next day, when he wakes and tries to stand up, his legs crumple under him. The family *babaláwo* can do nothing. The leg suppurates. In the end, Adédigba takes Adéjàre on a great journey to another town where a renowned herbalist resides. Here, the boy's wounds are eventually healed and he becomes a "person who walks with a staff," a boy wise beyond his years who promises his unhappy mother "Though my leg is destroyed my brain is not. If my father's family can send me to school, I'll use my brain to teach the world a lesson." In the last scene, Àwèlé appears, a mad, bedraggled mendicant; a flashback shows her drinking the ritual oath water. The power by which they swore has exacted retribution.

Witchcraft as a system was held by classical anthropology to be a system of explanation—a way of accounting for the otherwise inexplicable, imposing order on an otherwise irrational and disorderly world. Though witchcraft as a whole cannot be eradicated, particular witches can be, clearing up a trouble spot, resolving a knot of tension in the social fabric, and thus simultaneously explaining misfortune and putting a stop to it. But Yorùbá witchcraft belongs to the type where witches are rarely exposed and eliminated (see Forge 1970): instead, suspicions may multiply and fester without ever being definitively resolved, and individuals may even gain power from a reputation for witchcraft. Instead of imposing intellectual order, the

Adédigba's dream of a riverside meeting with the goddess Òṣun, in the video version of *Adédigba's Co-wife*. The viewpoint is facing Adédigba from behind Òṣun's shoulder. Note also the superimposed image of Adédigba's head.

forces evoked in this Yorùbá drama seem to foster a mad proliferation of agencies. Each one gives rise to others. Àwèlé recruits and activates accomplices who in turn activate other forces: familiars, assistants, a coven of witches, a wicked medicine man, a dwarfish *sìgìdì* armed with a huge club, magic banknotes that turn her co-wife's trading capital into a tortoise that crawls away, and a whole array of powerful magical powders and potions. Adédigba also activates powers in her support, not through her own volition but because she is innocent, beautiful, and destined to be the mother of an important man: the benevolent Òṣun figure, who can detect and repel the hand of evil; the family *babaláwo*, who in turn activates Ifá, whose long view encompasses the boy's eventual survival of the forces ranged against him, though it seems unable to do much for him in the short term; the great herbalist of Òyán who uses incantations and potions on the boy's behalf. Other spiritual agencies intervene on the side of justice, such as a mysterious naked boy who appears in the Òṣun waterfall and calls to the most senior wife, when she goes to draw water, to warn her that "those who break an oath/betray a trust will perish."

Ọ̀ṣun defeats the ṣìgìdì sent by Àwèlé to destroy Adédigba and her son as they sleep. From the video version of *Adédigba's Co-wife*. The poor image reflects the video quality.

This multiplication and reduplication of powers and agencies seems not to explain anything so much as to complicate the explicandum. The more powers step onto the stage, the wider the tangled web of malevolence becomes. There is no explanation of how and why some people become malevolent witches and others do not: the presumption is just that *Báyé ṣe rí nìyẹn* [that is how the world is]. And *ayé*, the "world," is also the word for "witches," people who are ill disposed toward oneself or toward other humans in general. This crazy excess, this non-explanatory multiplication, may have been intensified by the speeding up, the fragmentation, the multiplication characteristic of colonial and post-colonial modernity (see Berman 1982), and recent African ethnography does suggest that far from being superseded, witchcraft beliefs proliferate under the stresses of modernity. But it is also surely the case that the Yorùbá domain of witchcraft beliefs antedated the colonial era and never was one of the closed, "rational" intellectual systems that Evans-Pritchard postulated. Rather, it was the site where human beings realize that problems cannot in fact be solved but can only spawn more problems—just as one rumor spawns others and every conflict retains the potential to re-erupt years or even generations later.

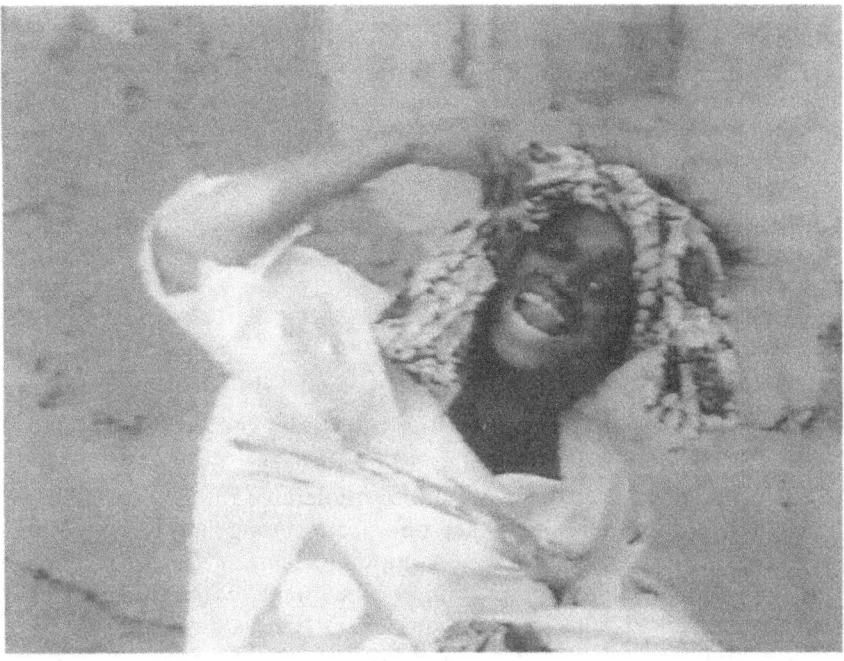

Retribution is visited upon Àwẹ̀lé, who goes mad in the marketplace. From the video version of *Adédigba's Co-wife*.

In the moral universe of *Adédigba's Co-wife*, the agencies and powers that swarm around the innocent victims and guilty evil-doers are messy and entangled at every point with the human. They are activated by humans and may even live inside humans. That is one meaning of the proverb "Though the skin of the stomach is thin, you can never know another person's inside." The secretive, unknowable, unfathomable interior is continuous with exterior, enveloping, or ingressive beings and forces. What is in Àwẹ̀lé's interior? Witchcraft. It may even fly out and leave her physical body sleeping, to hold meetings with other witches and devour the victims of their rage. "What does it feel like to be a witch—what tormented, violent thoughts and feelings boil within?" is not considered a relevant question. The thought moves the other way, and asks: "Why is she doing things that would only be done by people with tormented, violent feelings boiling within? Because she is a witch."

People choose their own Orí (Destiny) in heaven before they come to earth. It is natural therefore to assume that they would have chosen a good one. This leaves people without a transcendent explanation of why things are turning out badly for them nonetheless. Evildoers therefore must be credited not only with rampant and proliferating evil, but also with the power to change an innocent person's self-chosen good destiny. The opening song addresses Àwèlé with the words:

> Orogún ìyáà mi
> O mà ṣebi púpọ̀ o
> Torí pó o ti ríràwọ̀ọ̀ọ̀
> O mà tún mi dá ooo!
>
> My mother's co-wife
> You really did great evil
> Because you saw [my] star
> You re-created me.

That is, jealous of the boy's predicted good destiny, she changed what had been built in to his very creation as a human being. To live in the midst of such powerful malevolence would be intolerable without an infallible mechanism for stopping the wicked ones from getting away with it. In the face of powers like this, God's most important and indeed virtually only role is to guarantee ultimate retribution. The theme of *èsan* (vengeance) is repeatedly invoked. The opening song urges "Let us do no evil deeds / Vengeance is God's." Àwèlé's own last words are "Vengeance is God's, He will repay." Even the Òṣun figure herself reassures Adédigba in the language of the Bible: "They think that Almighty God doesn't see them ... but he will repay every one of them according to their deeds." The afflicted don't pray to God for the strength to endure their suffering, or take comfort in God's love for them: they affirm that God will eventually strike down the person who did them harm.

The possibilities offered by video as a medium for suggesting inner states of mind are not exploited. There are no character's-eye-view shots. Even when characters are "remembering" a previous event, it is not seen from their point of view, but from the spectator's. Flashbacks are not intended to invoke a character's consciousness so much as to remind the viewer of an earlier curse, warning, or prediction which is now coming true—or to compare a character's earlier happy state with her present woe. Dreams and visions are not inner states of consciousness but visitations by spiritual beings. Everything that happens—whether material or spiritual, sleeping or waking—is treated alike as an objectively existing event, not as a subjectively varying experience.

So while *External Appearances* is interested in the moral dispositions of individuals and how these affect their attempts to chart their way toward a good life-situation, the video version of *Adédigba's Co-wife* is interested in the way other people's malevolence can push an individual off course and even alter his/her good destiny—variously referred to as *Orí* ("Head" or destiny), *kádàrá* (fate), *àyànmọ́* (chosen destiny), *ìpín* (lot), and *ìràwọ̀* (star) —by malign interference. In *External Appearances*, there is a notion of conscience and self-examination—at least to the extent that Bísí comes to re-evaluate her own attitudes as a result of her cousin's criticism, not purely as a result of an externally-administered retribution. In *Adédigba's Co-wife,* the interior of the human being is seen almost entirely as the site of secrets, unknowable to others. The coexistence of these two recent plays in the same theatre company's repertoire makes it impossible to claim *either* that Western notions of the modern autonomous interior self have swept away older conceptions of the person, *or* that recrudescent witchcraft beliefs have become a uniquely privileged site for the interrogation of African modernity. Bísí's conscience-stricken self-examination co-exists with Àwẹlẹ́'s apparently motiveless incorporation of an inhuman evil into her interior. Between them they sketch out a range of possible constructions of what it is to be a person. The real question is what these representations of persons are *for:* that is, how these notions are operationalized—in tandem or as alternatives—to further the arguments the theatre company wants to make. What the two plays have in common is a way of mobilizing character to make it serve the purposes of a moral lesson.

In both plays, the conventions of the genre would make possible an intimate divulging of inner feelings and thoughts, if this were what the dramatists wanted. The fine-grained surface naturalism of the style, its sheer verbal extensivity and suppleness, the poise which we noted earlier between illusionistic and presentational acting, all would have made possible a self-revelatory mode of characterization through speech. The video medium could have offered further ways of representing subjectivity. Neither of these plays sought to do this. There is in fact no play in the repertoire to which the appropriate response would be for the audience to "imaginatively occupy their [the characters'] subject position," experiencing what it is to *be* them as we experience ourselves. This is not because the theater company cannot experience or imagine interiority; it is rather that interiority and subjective experience are only relevant insofar as they help to concretize and authenticate an appropriable moral lesson.

For characters function as examples, and examples are always concrete. The lavish lifelike detail with which the characters are portrayed is not a depiction of experience or consciousness for their own sake but the provision of exceptionally efficacious examples. The theater only expresses the thoughts and feelings of characters when these thoughts and feelings themselves become part of the example. Bísí's rapid self-examination is sustained just long enough to establish the point that one's moral disposition is more important than exterior manifestations of devoutness. Bísí has to introspect because the theater of example shows rather than just telling—but the point of her introspection is to offer a model which the audience can incorporate and translate into their own experience—for when people "follow" an example, they re-work it in their own terms. The audience is not invited to enter into Bísí's subjective world and experience it as if from within: rather, it is offered a mechanism by which to evaluate and reshape its own and other people's moral behavior. Experience, including inner subjective experience, is thus the material out of which usable examples can be fashioned.

POTENTIALITY AND SELF-REALIZATION

The plays may not be interested in interior, subjective experience for its own sake. But they are very interested in practices and processes of self-making. The "self" projected by the plays into public space is the focus of a recurrent inquiry into the nature and sources of self-realization. Several of the Adéjọbís' plays trace the route by which protagonists achieve, or fail to achieve, social success and fulfillment. At their heart is a view of human potentiality. They ask not so much what a person *is*, as what it takes to *become* one.

Kúyẹ̀ (c. 1964), *Láníyọnu* (c. 1967), and *The Road to Riches* (c. 1981) span nearly 20 years of the theater company's history, and I have argued elsewhere that changing social and economic conditions—notably the advent of oil wealth in the 1970s—are visible in the changing answers the plays give to the question of the sources of self-realization (Barber and Ogundijọ 1994). But all three plays remained in the repertoire up to the mid-1980s and could be performed on successive nights in the course of one tour. Thus, unlike the chronologically discrete examples discussed in the last chapter, these three could be regarded as co-existing. People did not regard plays as "period pieces" but always as contemporaneous with their own concerns, so we must assume that all three continued to offer a lesson which audiences could apply to their own lives. Though contrastive, the lessons were in some sense allotropes of each other. The dramatists kept returning to the same question and recombining the same range of plot elements, situations, and characters to propose radically different—yet oddly congruent—answers. These three texts are worth analyzing closely, as the reader has access to them in Yorùbá transcription and English translation (Barber and Ogundijọ 1994), making the interpretation less of a one-way exercise than is usually the case with studies of African popular culture—where the presentation of the material is all too often selective and fused with the interpretation.

Each of the plays has a male hero whose fortunes are the focus of the play's inquiry into the sources of self-realization. Kúyẹ̀ starts from a position of maximum disadvantage—a deaf and dumb orphan—and achieves the most resplendent wealth and status. Láníyọnu starts in prosperity and social esteem, loses everything, and then attains a different, more traditional high status. Tàfá in *The Road to Riches* begins poor and ends poor, while his friend Láòṣebìkan begins and ends rich. Each scenario is played out in the ideational force field that we have suggested is especially well-developed in the artisanal experience: a field stretched between the two explanatory poles of hard work and rational calculation on the one hand and destiny, beyond the knowledge or control of human beings, on the other. *The Road to Riches*, the most recent play, gravitates toward the pole of hard work: Tàfá remains poor because of his laziness, improvidence, and folly, and for no other reason. *Kúyẹ̀*, the oldest one, gravitates toward the pole of destiny: Kúyẹ̀ is propelled into wealth and status through a series of apparent chances, later revealed to be providential. *Láníyọnu*, the intermediate play in terms of chronology, also occupies a philosophical position midway between the other two: it is made of two separate parts, one of which is constituted around the idea of hard work, the other around the idea of destiny, the two being reconciled in a way that tells us something about the nature of this polarity.

The opposed philosophical poles of *Kúyẹ̀* and *The Road to Riches* are at their most apparent in the songs. *Kúyẹ̀* affirms the mysterious justice of providence, which works itself out through the actions of human beings without their knowledge. Only in retrospect can one see the path one has been following and how it led to one's present destination. A song in *Kúyẹ̀* says:

> Olórun ọba ní í gbé nií ga
> Bí a ṣe ṣe ṣe dogún ọdún
> Àbáà rìn rìn rìn
> Gbogbòn oṣù
> Kìtàkìtà kò mólà
> Ká ṣiṣẹ́ bí ẹrú
> Kò da nǹkan
> Ará mi ẹ yé ẹ gbọ́
> Àyànmọ́ lọlá
> Ìwà loyè
> Ìwà ní í gbe ẹ̀dá
> Ìwà rẹ ló gbé ọ gòkè o
> Àdìó
> Ìwà rẹ ló gbé ọ gòkè o.

> It's the good Lord that raises one up
> If you strive for twenty years
> If you march
> For thirty months
> Strenuous effort is not what brings wealth.
> You may work like a slave

It means nothing.
My people, please listen
Honor is a matter of destiny [àyànmọ́].
Title goes with character [ìwà]
Character is what brings prosperity to mankind
It is your character that has raised you high
Àdìó
It is your character that has raised you high.

What counts here is *àyànmọ́*, the destiny one chooses in heaven, and *ìwà*, character or, by implication, "virtue" (as opposed to self-interested action). Both *àyànmọ́* and *ìwà* operate within the ambit of, or at any rate in harmony with, the will of *Olọ́run ọba* (the name for God in all religions). The last word in *The Road to Riches*, by contrast, is an uncompromising endorsement of the work ethic, in which God comes in only as a guarantee that hard work *will* eventually be rewarded:

Sisẹ́ o lówó
Dákun má sọlẹ o.
Arísẹ́-má-sẹ
Lòtá owó.
Isẹ́ pèlú owó nìmùlẹ̀ o o o . . .
. . . Bó o bá rí olówó
Má se ìlara
Àsìkò ló tó o o o
Má gbàgbé wí pé Elẹ́dàá tiẹ
Kò gbàgbé rẹ.

Work to have money
Please don't be lazy.
One who has work but doesn't do it
Is the enemy of money.
Work and money are best friends. . . .
. . . If you see a rich man
Don't be jealous
It's his turn
Don't forget that your Creator
Has not forgotten you.

In this philosophy there are no unexpected bonuses from fortune. Success is defined in terms of wealth, and wealth is obtained in proportion to the investment of effort. If you are poor, you have only yourself to blame.

Kúyẹ̀ was probably the most enduringly popular play in the Adéjọbí's entire repertoire. Of all those extant when I worked with the company, it had had the longest history of adaptation and updating, and there were many obvious differences between the performances of the early 1980s and the version recorded in *Atọ́ka* in 1969. Nonetheless it retained a strong aura of the period of its origin. The folkloric plot, the retention of many of the original songs, and the big set piece scenes in the royal court, which required a large cast and rich costumes, were all reminiscent of the earlier, more lavish style of theatricality of the operatic phase.

It was based on a Yorùbá novel of the same name by J. F. Odúnjọ, but in the play the plot is greatly simplified and key themes are much more strongly articulated. This was clearly the outcome of a long process. The *Atọ́ka* version of 1969 shows a much more complicated plot than the one I saw in 1981. Characters whose roles were parallel or re-duplicated in the *Atọ́ka* version were subsequently streamlined and amalgamated: two princesses became one; the jealous suitor was amalgamated with the dangerous champion wrestler. Several characters that complicated the story of Kúyẹ̀'s upbringing were eliminated altogether. Some of these changes may have been made to reduce the size of the cast and make the play quicker to perform. But the overall effect was to throw a stronger light on the central theme. Odúnjọ's novel is a picaresque adventure novel; the Adéjọbís' play, increasingly, was a reflection on language and destiny. A comparison shows how the play's perspective, though certainly not peculiar to the theater company, was not just a "reflection" of a common ideology: rather, it was deliberately created out of materials which originally were quite differently conceived.

In Odúnjọ's novel, Kúyẹ̀, the deaf and dumb orphan, runs away from the last and most cruel of a succession of unkind guardians. He ends up in the forest where he lives for several months, eating the sacrifices left at a forest shrine by the credulous women from a nearby village. Eventually he goes into a nearby town, wins a ceremonial wrestling match, and gains the love of the king's daughter. But doubts about marrying the princess and a nostalgia for the life under the greenwood tree send him back into the forest, where he joins a robber gang. One day when the robbers are out on an expedition, he sees a troupe of sick animals coming to a certain tree and consuming the bark, which has a miraculous curative effect on them. Kúyẹ̀ takes some of the bark himself, tastes it, and finds that he is immediately in full possession of speech and hearing. However, he conceals this from the gang until he has had an opportunity to test his linguistic powers on a villager. Once satisfied that his speech is perfect, he breaks it to the gang and returns to the village, where he marries the princess in a scene of unbelievable splendor. The unkind relatives, along with the rest of the district, turn up of their own accord as wedding guests and are suitably impressed and amazed when they realize who Kúyẹ̀ is.

The theater company altered this plot in three major ways. First, they made Kúyẹ̀'s movements involuntary. Instead of running away from his guardians, he is expelled from his natal village when he attempts to inform his uncle Àlàbí that his aunt is receiving a clandestine lover. Instead of choosing to leave the palace after he has won the wrestling match, he is driven out with a magic spell by his defeated rival, the former champion wrestler who is also in love with the princess. Instead of planning his own return to the palace, he is sought by two chiefs sent by the Ọba and taken back by them. Similarly, the unkind relatives, instead of coming voluntarily to the town where Kúyẹ̀ achieves greatness, are hauled there against their will because of an unpaid debt. Thus, in the play, the theme of the working out of destiny is much more powerful, because rather than being the outcome of people's plans and wishes, it works in spite of them.

Second, the theater company made the forest a liminal site of transformation, not a playground for boyish adventures. In the play, Kúyẹ̀ only goes there once, completely against his will, and he is terrified of the place. It is a site full of spiritual forces; he is shown the cure by spirits, not animals, and these spirits are real and frightening. This change took some time to complete. In the *Atọ́ka* version of 1969, though Kúyẹ̀ does not go voluntarily into the forest, he does spend some time there, eating food from the shrine and frightening a party of devotees before he sees the spirits that reveal the powers of the curative leaves. There is a suggestion—though less strongly than in the novel—that the devotees are credulous and superstitious people and that Kúyẹ̀ finds them amusing. In the 1981 version, all that has been eliminated: Kúyẹ̀ enters the forest in exhaustion and fear, is assailed by chattering spirits, sees one of them cure itself, and naively copies it. He begins to speak and to hear; immediately afterward, he is found by the search party and they leave forthwith. Thus the theme of personal transformation is dramatized through the powerful and resonant image of the liminal forest, installing it in a much more central position than in the novel.

Third, the play, unlike the novel, is very interested in language and the nature of speech acquisition. Kúyẹ̀'s transformation is conceived as a linguistic miracle. The first half of the play is about communication without speech as the deaf and dumb boy tries to make his feelings known through mime, gesture, howls, and grunts; the second half is about the process of acquiring speech followed by the triumphant demonstration of full eloquence. The theater company—unlike the novelist—imagined what it would be like to hear language for the first time. They imagined the comical effects that would be produced if one person simply copied another person's utterances. Recapitulating the sequence of events afterward, the Ọba recalls that at first he did not believe reports that Kúyẹ̀ could speak, "But when he arrived in person . . . 'My Balógun' [I said], he said I was also his Balógun!" "Yes," confirms the senior wife, "whatever we said . . . [he repeated]." The Ọba goes on "[I said] 'How do you come to be speaking?'

He said 'How did I come to be speaking? Ha!'" And in the last scene, Kúyẹ̀'s full attainment of social self-realization is demonstrated almost wholly through his eloquence: so rounded, so pithy and proverbial, and delivered with such magisterial aplomb the spectators audibly sighed with pleasure to hear it.

The play, then, sets out to demonstrate the most extreme possible transformation in the human condition. At the beginning, Kúyẹ̀ is addressed and referred to almost as a beast or an inanimate object. He utters inarticulate sounds in a desperate desire to communicate, accompanied by gestures and occasional frenzied physical attacks on his tormentors. To his guardians he is a dead terminal, unable to transmit the current of communicative electricity that sustains social life. His first guardian, the Pepper Seller, unleashes on him torrents of repetitive, insistent, abusive speech, alternately speaking *to* him—as if to batter through the wall of deafness—and *about* him, as if in disgust at her failure to do so: "You're a worthless wretch. You're a worthless wretch. You're a worthless wretch. I took him in when he was no bigger than this. Even if he were a piece of cloth himself and I took him and sold him, what could he say against it? God will reject you, you useless child, with your huge mouth." The insults his guardians heap on him show that what enrages them is the fact that although he is a big, strong, handsome young man, he is not just an object but a useless object. He is described as "staring about like the *gúre* weeds that grow on the burial ground"—plants that have grown on a gravesite can never be used in cooking, even though these are the ones that will grow the lushest, tallest and greenest. "Staring like the *gúre* weeds," "useless child, with your huge mouth": his relatives make continual reference to Kúyẹ̀'s eyes and mouth. They repeatedly describe him with variations of a single insulting phrase: "you staring-eyed brute, you"; "this thing with his huge round eyes"; "[look at] his big round mouth, the tell-tale." This insistence on the unnatural size of his eyes and mouth suggests that since they are useless for communication, their mere presence is an exaggeration, a redundancy. Like the *gúre* weeds on the burial site, and like Kúyẹ̀ himself, their full development is thrown into ironical relief by their uselessness.

Kúyẹ̀'s uselessness consists—to put it in the most general terms—of his inability to play a part in social reproduction and in the constitution of social being. He cannot work, he cannot marry, and he cannot engage in the continuous social dialogue by which self and other are recognized and confirmed. According to the Pepper Seller and Àlàbí, he is old enough to marry "if it weren't for his handicap": but this, in his relatives' view, is such as to prevent him ever attaining the full social adulthood conferred only by having children of one's own. When his uncle Àlàbí takes him in, one of the first questions Àlàbí's wife Sẹ̀gi asks is what work he will do, "because no one with thick strong arms and legs like that should be sitting around all day doing nothing." There follows a classic Adéjọbí set piece, in which Sẹ̀gi proposes professions for Kúyẹ̀ and Àlàbí finds fault with her proposals: Kúyẹ̀ cannot be a tailor, because he wouldn't be able to understand his customers' orders; he cannot be a driver, because he wouldn't hear the warning cry "Stop there!" when reversing and would reverse right into a huge pothole. In the end they conclude that there is no work Kúyẹ̀ could learn to do: as Àlàbí puts it, "He is going to sit at home, and you are going to feed him." His big mouth can only consume, it cannot produce. He cannot participate in the social exchanges that maintain identity. This is vividly demonstrated on his first arrival in Àlàbí's house. Àlàbí insists on formally introducing Kúyẹ̀ to Sẹ̀gi, and tries not only to teach Kúyẹ̀ how to prostrate to her but also to explain to him how he and Sẹ̀gi are related to each other. It is only when Kúyẹ̀ can acknowledge their social roles in relation to himself and each other that Àlàbí feels able to leave them in the house in order to go to his farm. But the explanation takes an enormous amount of time and effort, and it is never certain just how much Kúyẹ̀ has grasped. Hence his relatives' exasperation: he is not just useless, he is a potential denial or negation of all the complex crisscrossing webs of relationship in which social beings are enmeshed and supported, and to which the characters continually allude.

And yet, right from the beginning, there are signs of Kúyẹ̀'s potential for self-realization. "*Àǹfààní orógbó dà?*" says the Pepper Seller. "*A pa á, kò láwẹ́, a jẹ ẹ́, ó tún korò*" [What's the use of bitter kola? You break it, it has no segments, you eat it and it's bitter]. If it had segments, like ordinary kolas, it could be split in order to share it with others or to throw it in divination (both being forms of communication). If it had the sweetish aftertaste characteristic of ordinary kolas, it would be worth chewing. This proverb seems to write off the bitter kola—and by implication Kúyẹ̀—completely. However, it is one of those ironical sayings that harbors a lurking inversion of itself. Everyone knows that bitter kola does have uses. It is favored by the great *òrìṣà* Ṣàngó, and in the context of his cult, is associated with his royalty and power. The proverb covertly implies that one should beware of dismissing something or someone out of hand just because it, he, or she does not fit with immediate mundane requirements.

Indeed, Kúyẹ̀'s potential is signaled consistently in the opening scenes by the ironical fact that in spite of everything, he *does* communicate—and this is his downfall. He is rejected by the Pepper Seller because he correctly grasps that she is intending to sell his father's clothes and registers his protest through howls and physical attacks on her, Àlàbí, and the peddler (all of whom reciprocate with interest). He is rejected by Sẹ̀gi because he correctly grasps that she is entertaining a lover and "tells" Àlàbí about it with mime and gesture on his return from the farm. It is only because she is quick-witted and in full command of language that Sẹ̀gi is able to substitute

Àlàbí (John) and Ṣẹ̀gi (Deborah) try to think of work for Kúyẹ̀ (Alhaji) to do. ©Elio Montanari

a false story for Kúyẹ̀'s true one and get Àlàbí to believe it and expel him. Kúyẹ̀ is the truth-bearer who cannot speak to his own advantage: without ulterior motives, he is the witness who makes others uneasy.

How then does the play account for Kúyẹ̀'s transformation, leading to his ultimate full and resplendent self-realization as a social being? Two things come into play. The first is Kúyẹ̀'s stubborn righteousness and his sheer agency. He is not a passive character: he acts vigorously even when he does not understand what is going on. It is his righteousness that gets him moved on from the Pepper Seller's household to that of Àlàbí and Ṣẹ̀gi and then out into the bush. It is his sheer propensity to act that propels him into the wrestling match and which causes him to copy the spirit in the forest when it plucks and applies the curative leaf. The second is a conception of destiny or providence which is retrospectively shown to have been at work throughout, so that every adverse event turns out to have contributed to his eventual success. This mode of narrative articulation is disclosed and commented upon in the final scene. On attaining the full power of eloquent speech, the first thing Kúyẹ̀ does is to thank those who were instrumental in his recovery, starting with God and moving on to the Ọba and the doctor-herbalist who assisted in the full recovery of his voice.

Ṣègi gives Kúyè a job to do.
©Elio Montanari

Kúyè outside Ṣègi's bedroom door. ©Elio Montanari

Kúyè attacks Ṣẹ̀gi's lover. ©Elio Montanari

Kúyè uses mime to tell Àlàbí what he has seen. ©Elio Montanari

Ṣègi lies her way out of a tight spot. ©Elio Montanari

But having offered his thanks to these positive agents of change in his life, Kúyẹ̀ goes on to demonstrate that even those people who seemed most hostile and malign were actually also unwitting agents of his transformation. In the course of the last scene he retraces, three times over, the steps by which he finally arrived at his present felicity. On the second occasion, when his relatives are brought before the court for judgment and Kúyẹ̀ recognizes them, he tells the whole story of the Pepper Seller's callousness, Ṣègi's treachery and deception, his expulsion, the wrestling match, how he was driven into the forest, his encounter with the spirits, and his recovery. The Ọba sees the surprising revelation as evidence of God's hand, which has delivered the relatives over to their former victim for punishment: "There's one thing I want you to accept, and that's that the money they owe is very little. If it were not God's plan that their dark secret should be exposed, and that they should go to prison, they wouldn't have failed to find the sum they needed. God wanted what they have done to be exposed. So Àrólé, it's up to you to visit whatever punishment you like upon them." Kúyẹ̀, however, takes a more comprehensive view of the nature of the working out of events. Having confounded everyone by setting his relatives free, he explains, in the third narrative recapitulation of the events that led up to the present situation, why he does not want to exact revenge (for the Yorùbá text see Barber and Ògúndíjọ 1994, 254):

KÚYÈ: I want you to know that I have no relatives closer to me than these. If I exact my revenge on them, if I punish them in any way, it's as if I'd be showing ingratitude to God. Because I could never have foretold that I would attain the position that I am in today. Neither did they ever imagine they could end up kneeling in front of me. For them to kneel in front of me like this, and for me to be in authority over them—that's punishment in itself as far as they're concerned.

SENIOR WIFE: That's true.

KÚYÈ: Something they never thought could happen, that's the first thing. The second thing I thought about was this: God dispenses good fortune in sequences.

SENIOR WIFE: That's true.

KÚYÈ: If that old woman hadn't sold my father's robes, making me leave her in anger, I'd have stayed with her till the day of my death, saddled with my handicap. But just so that I could reach my true destination, she turned me out.

SENIOR WIFE: That's right.

KÚYÈ: My journey wasn't ended, because I passed into this man's hands. But so that I could make further progress—you see—I got into trouble again there and they turned me out again. Then when I found myself in the forest, I met a certain spirit. Don't you know that if the Pepper Seller hadn't turned me out, and Àlàbí hadn't taken me in . . .

SENIOR WIFE: Yes.

KÚYÈ: And his wife hadn't driven me out again, so that I met the spirit, I would never have regained my speech.

SENIOR WIFE: Never!

KÚYÈ: And if I hadn't regained my speech, I wouldn't have attained the position I'm in now. So I believe that they all behaved to me as they did so that I could arrive at my true destination.

In the last scene of the play, then, Kúyè and his interlocutors retrace the course of the plot three times. The *point* of the sequence of events is precisely its sequentiality. At the time that they were happening, one event seemed to follow another in a haphazard succession of misfortunes; but retrospectively, when the sequence is told and retold, it can be seen to have been in some sense intended, purposive, or meaningful. The sequence led Kúyè to his "destination" of great good fortune and in that sense can be seen to have been inevitable. Motive is displaced from the individual agent and relocated in the larger scheme of things: "just so that I could reach my destination," his relatives mistreated him—the purpose was neither Kúyè's nor his relatives', but that of a higher dispensation.

The wrestling match at the royal court of Ẹgbéjọdá. Ṣégè, the champion (Dayọ̀), challenges all comers. ©Elio Montanari

Ṣégè defeats his first opponent. ©Elio Montanari

This narrative structure is common in folk tales. There are many stories with a double plot in which an apparently haphazard sequence of chances is retrospectively shown to have been determined, its outcome the result of the protagonist's moral nature. For example, the innocent younger daughter might, after a sequence of unforeseen events, unsuspectingly do a good turn to a stranger and be richly rewarded; her bad older sister might set out, motivated by envy and greed, to retrace the younger one's steps—but after failing to do the good turn, she is punished to the same extent that her sister was rewarded (for an example see Walker and Walker 1961, 50–54). The first girl's adventures appear at first as pure chance, but when the second girl recapitulates the same events exactly, it becomes clear that the succession is a sequence with a logic. The different outcomes of the two sequences are explained solely by the characters and motives of the two girls: the first is innocently un-selfseeking, the second purposefully and selfishly acquisitive. The inverted parallel structure has the clarity of an experimental proof: good fortune is the reward for not seeking it.[11] These stories are not just affirming the possibility of marvelous reversals in ordinary people's lives. They are also implying that purposive, self-interested action cannot lead to the great reward: it is the unknowing character, expecting nothing, and often destitute, who is blessed.

In *Kúyẹ̀*, the retrospective review of his story serves the same purpose as the parallel inverse plot. Kúyẹ̀ is as innocent, unknowing, and unpurposive as it is possible to be: he stumbles on his good fortune rather than seeking it out. The lesson to be drawn from this is neither fatalistic resignation nor the optimistic expectation of unsought wealth. Rather, the play counsels us to recognize the perpetual potentiality of other people, however low their situation. Kúyẹ̀ says to the court, "One day I would like to tell you the whole story of my life, because 'The slave has a father, it's just that he's far away.'" Even the slave, who has been stripped of many of the attributes of humanity (property, control of his own labor, possession of his own people, even recognition of his own name) retains the potential to be reconstituted as a full social being when he eventually rejoins his progenitor—the source of his social identity. It may take longer than for other people, but it can still happen. The final song, where the play's lesson is encapsulated, affirms that you can never know what another person's potential is, and therefore you should never "think their end," that is, assume that they have no future:

Ẹ̀dá kan ò láròpin ò ééé
Ohun tÓlú ṣe la ò mọ̀
Ká má ṣe rònìyàn pin
Àwá sọ féníyàn
Tílẹ̀ bá ti mọ́ ká tójú . . .
Ọ̀jó lè rọ̀ lówurọ̀
Oòru á mú lálẹ́

The sick spirit approaches the curative tree. ©Elio Montanari

The spirit is cured. ©Elio Montanari

Kúyè copies the spirit and tries the same leaves. ©Elio Montanari

Kúyè is found in the forest by the Ọba's emissaries and begins to speak to them. ©Elio Montanari

Ojú tó ti kú lè padà
Wáá dilẹ̀ ayọ̀ láyé o
Ohun tÓlú ṣe a ò mọ̀
Ká má ṣe rònìyàn pin.

No one's career can be written off
We cannot know what God has planned
So don't let us write people off,
We say to people—
"As soon as day breaks, let us start work"
It might rain in the morning
It might be too hot at night.
Land which has become barren may change
And become fertile again in its lifetime.
What God has planned we cannot know
So don't let us write people off.

Kúyẹ̀, reminiscing about the day when he unknowingly attempted to wrestle with the Ọba, says "I want us all to say amen to this prayer I'm going to say: 'May God not take away from any single one of us the faculties that make us into people' [lit. "by which we are people"]." The play shows speech and hearing to be the most central of those faculties. The word *èèyàn* (people) in the phrase "*tá a fi ń jéèyàn*" (by which we are people) could be understood to mean human beings in general; or it could be understood to mean people who are somebody: important, prosperous or successful people. The very fact that the word has this double acceptation suggests how fundamental the idea of potentiality is. To be a human is to have the potential to become somebody.

The Road to Riches, the most recent of the three plays, is at the opposite pole from *Kúyẹ̀*. It is the simplest of the three plays and is uncompromisingly rational and univocal. Sudden great fortune—overnight transformation—is associated here only with baseless wealth acquired by magical means. And *The Road to Riches* not only denounces the pursuit of such wealth—as did many plays before and after—but actually denies its existence. The *only* way to become wealthy is to work hard. Those who believe in magic money are credulous fools. The play was a failure with the public, suggesting that people were not ready to have their world disenchanted to such an extent.

In this play, there is no transformation. Tàfá and Ọláòṣebìkan are friends. Ọláòṣebìkan, the rich man, is a paragon of all the virtues. Like Láníyọnu, he was a builder who became rich by hard work; at the start of the play he is a big building contractor. Though rich, he remains modest and wise. Even in the midst of his own lavish birthday party (a very elite and perhaps slightly ridiculous way of displaying wealth), he dresses simply

Kúyẹ̀ and the princess (Emily) are betrothed. ©Elio Montanari

and uses the celebration as an opportunity to deliver a wise message to the guests. Instead of distributing expensive gifts to them, as was the custom during the oil boom, he gives out symbolic tokens which embody prayers for their happiness and prosperity: "As I stand here I can tell you that I have the money to buy cows and give them out to you. But these wooden dolls that I've given you instead are a form of prayer I want to make on your behalf. It's said that wooden dolls never die, and all of us, we'll not die an accidental death. Our children will survive us. The dolls are a prayer for you, that however long we last, God will allow our children to bury us."

His friend Tàfá is poor, an uncouth "bushman" who is under the thumb of his dominating termagant of a wife, Ìyáa Ṣèyí. Incited by Ìyáa Ṣèyí, he pesters Ọláòṣebìkan for the secret of his wealth. Ọláòṣebìkan tells him repeatedly that the secret is simply hard work, but Tàfá and Ìyáa Ṣèyí refuse to believe this. Ọláòṣebìkan explains how he makes his own money through the building trade and offers Tàfá a share in any job which comes up. Tàfá is not interested. Eventually Ọláòṣebìkan gets so annoyed that he decides to teach them a lesson. He pretends to have money magic after all and agrees to initiate Tàfá into its use. Since Tàfá is unable to keep anything from his wife, she is included in the fake initiation too. Ọláòṣebìkan informs Tàfá that the "old man" who is going to do the medicine for them must be paid two hundred naira. Tàfá is dismayed and immediately asks

Oláòsebìkan to lend it to him, but Oláòsebìkan explains that this money must be worked for. The "spirits" who make the magic must see the sweat of his brow, since it is the last time he will ever have to sweat. Oláòsebìkan therefore sub-contracts part of a building job to Tàfá and makes sure that Tàfá exerts himself alongside the hired laborers. Tàfá works hard, quickly makes much more than N200, puts away his work clothes, and gleefully looks forward to a life of ease.

The nocturnal "initiation" devised for them by Oláòsebìkan is both painful and humiliating. Tàfá has to carry water from one container to another in mouthfuls while Ìyáa Sèyí stands on one leg holding up a lamp. Then she has to pound nail clippings to a powder in a mortar, sitting on Tàfá's back. Finally, they have to whip each other till the canes are in shreds. All this time, Oláòsebìkan says, the "spirits" are watching them and taking their photographs. They try to cheat, of course, but eventually Oláòsebìkan pronounces their tasks completed. It is time for the spirits to bring what they will "use for the rest of their lives." In the darkness, two calabashes are brought in and Tàfá and Ìyáa Sèyí eagerly and fearfully open them. In the first one is a piece of cloth with the message "The world rejects truth." In the second, there is another piece of cloth with the message "Work to have money." Oláòsebìkan returns to the bewildered couple and delivers a moral lecture to them:

> Wón ní: AYÉ KÒÓTÓ. Eni ó bá wáró ní í ríróó rà. AYÉ KÒÓTÓ. Òtító korò. Eni á bá so fún, sàasàá eèyàn ní í gbó. AYÉ KÒÓTÓ. Mo ní kó o wáá mò wí pé béèyàn bá sisé, òun ní í lówó. Wón ní o sisé o lówó. O wáró, mo sì taró fún o. Èmi sisé n mee lówó. Ìwo náà lo reé sisé, kó o lówó. Kò sí nínú eèyàn tí ó máa fé kówó kan ó wá lónà èrú, típaláraa rè è íí wá léhìnola.
>
> It's said that the world rejects truth. Anyone who goes to look for lies will find lies to buy. The world rejects truth. The truth is bitter. However many people you tell the truth to, very few will listen. The world rejects truth. I wanted you to know that it's people who work hard who get rich. It says "Work to have money." You were looking for lies, and I sold lies to you. *I* worked and that's how I became rich. So you go and work too, and you can become rich. It's impossible to try and obtain money by dubious means without suffering terrible repercussions later on.[12]

Oláòsebìkan then points out that if Tàfá had put as much effort into honest labor as he had into the pursuit of baseless wealth, he would by now have become a rich man anyway. As Tàfá and Ìyáa Sèyí stand mortified and disappointed, the cast walk onto the stage for the only song of the play, the

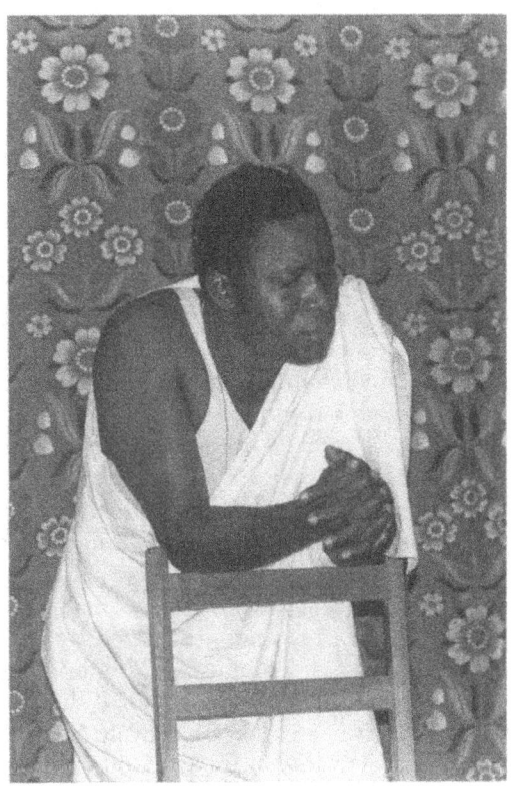

Alhaji as Oláòsebìkan in *The Road to Riches*. ©Elio Montanari

closing moral, which tells them "Work to have money / Please don't be lazy / Work and money are bosom friends."

In the course of the play, the right attitude toward work and money is repeatedly contrasted with the wrong one in a simple series of binary oppositions. Oláòsebìkan tells Tàfá that his problems stem from the fact that he "works like a mouse and eats like an elephant": he should work harder and spend less. Ìyáa Sèyí retorts that it's not a matter of work: you have to have a certain amount of money to start with, or whatever you earn just evaporates. Oláòsebìkan advises Tàfá to work steadily and regularly instead of just working for a few days and then going off to spend what he's earned. Tàfá replies that what he needs is a lucky break, after which he will work hard to capitalize on it. Oláòsebìkan warns Tàfá against doing the pools: "Let me tell you, however hard a man works, if he plays the pools he'll never get on in life." Ìyáa Sèyí takes the opposite view: "Why shouldn't he play the pools—you use money to fetch money!" Oláòsebìkan thinks his intervention in Tàfá's affairs should be limited to helping Tàfá to help himself. Tàfá quotes a proverb: "One helps a lazy person to the utmost: if one makes clothes for the lazy person, one also dyes them in indigo for him." In other words, true help knows no limits. Oláòsebìkan stresses hard physical labor almost as a value in itself; Tàfá can only be induced to do mock labor—the initiation ordeals—by the false expectation that he will never have to work again. Once he has completed the building job that Oláòsebìkan makes him do, he turns down the offer of future jobs, antagonizes his laborers by underpaying them, and takes off his work boots, saying to his wife "Here, put these up in the loft for me. *They've* finished *their* work!"

The view of money and work taken by Tàfá and Ìyáa Sèyí is shown to be embedded in a mass of superstition, irrationality, and envy. He tells his wife that on his way to see the "old man" who is supposed to be making the medicine, he stubbed his right toe three times: this is a lucky portent. Then the old man, whom he'd never met before, gave him a mighty embrace: another good omen. Ìyáa Sèyí remembers that when divination was done for her before marriage, she was told that Tàfá would make an auspicious and prosperous husband. This prediction, she says, is now being borne out. Most entertainingly, she recounts a dream in which she and Tàfá were dressed in the latest and most expensive imported cloth and were meeting on the staircase of a multi-story glass building: a sign that great wealth is at hand (see Chapter 5 for the text of this speech). Tàfá is incapable of assessing his own situation objectively, instead allowing himself to be eaten up by envy of Oláòsebìkan. Even when the written moral messages are delivered to them at the end, Tàfá and Ìyáa Sèyí are so wrong-headed that they misinterpret them: taking "the world rejects truth" to be the name of a bird needed to complete the magic and "work to have money" to be a reference to all the "work" they have just done in the initiation ceremony. It is only when Oláòsebìkan steps forward and spells it all out for them that they finally understand.

The destitute man in this scenario deserves his poverty. He is poor because he is feckless, lazy, and foolish. He is certainly not a candidate for unexplained benevolence from providence, delivered by supernatural agents, as in *Kúyè*. His lack of motive and his failure to plan are serious moral faults, not the twins of innocence and goodness. The final song advises us to accept things as they are and not to become prey to impatience which may lead to rash shortcuts in the pursuit of wealth. Eventually, honest hard work will be rewarded by God. In this play there are hardly any other references to God—or to destiny, *orí*, or the *òrìsà*—and when they occur they are in the form of routine blessings, curses, or oaths, rather than the subject of philosophical inquiry. If God is needed to underwrite the ultimate justice of the system, the immediate practical message seems almost secular and based on the idea that people's fortunes are entirely under their own control. What is needed is not a benevolent providence, supernatural intervention, or even an innocent unselfish moral disposition: but a regular, steady, prudent regime of hard work.

Láníyọnu yokes together the two philosophical poles that organize *Kúyẹ̀* and *The Road to Riches,* with a strikingly mirror-like contraposition of the essential elements of the two plots. In the first half, Láníyọnu is like Ọláòṣebìkan in *The Road to Riches:* a good man who has become wealthy through a shrewd combination of hard work and entrepreneurial skill. He has two friends who started life with him but who through laziness have ended up destitute and dependent on his handouts. Láníyọnu, like Ọláòṣebìkan, is embarrassed by the contrast between their poverty and his wealth and is anxious to help them become self-sufficient. He calls them to his house and proposes to lend them whatever sum of money they think they need to start their own business. Adhering to a central tenet of capitalism, that real wealth is productive wealth, he tells them that handouts are no good because however generous, they have limits and are dead ends: they do not generate further wealth. "Even if I could feed you, could I feed your wives? Even if I could feed your wives, could I feed your children? Even if I fed your children, would I be able to pay all your other expenses? But if you had a business like me—a business you could establish for yourselves—then everything would be all right."

He fails to instill into them an enthusiasm for business, however. The two friends are not interested in the metaphorical fetishism of surplus value but only in the real fetishism of absolutely unfounded wealth, the baseless bounty of forged or magically generated money. Like Tàfá and his wife in *The Road to Riches,* they are convinced that their wealthy friend made his fortune through the use of a money-making medicine or machine, and their proposal is that the three of them should share the proceeds of this contrivance between them. Láníyọnu tries in vain to convince them that he has no machine. "Don't you know that people who believe in something that will produce money for them without the sweat of their brow—they're thieves, highway robbers, cheats, wicked people who think like that." His last exhortation to them, as they leave disgruntled, is "Get down to work." Instead, however, they come back that night, armed, and break into his house to get the machine by force. Láníyọnu's wife is killed and Láníyọnu himself is beaten up and driven out of the house into the bush.

In the second half of the play, Láníyọnu is reborn as a character more like Kúyẹ̀ than Ọláòṣebìkan. Stripped of his wealth and position, he also sheds his big man's graciousness and becomes an endearing comic innocent who acts righteously and without any ulterior motive. He arrives in the liminal space of the forest where, like Kúyẹ̀, he has an encounter with the supernatural. He is attacked and left for dead by a horde of hostile spirits and then revived by a beneficent water deity, who presents him with a magical staff which will kill any enemy he strikes with it. In a mode even more clearly folkloric than *Kúyẹ̀*, Láníyọnu angers the deity by summoning her back on a trivial pretext and accidentally violating her taboo; as a result she says she will never appear to him again (the motif of the unexpected good fortune which a character throws away through folly). However, she does not take back the magic staff, and Láníyọnu sets off to roam the world striking down evildoers wherever he finds them.

Meanwhile, in a nearby town, the chiefs are meeting to discuss two problems: the need to find a new Ọba after the death of the last one and the more urgent need to do something about a monstrous evil spirit, Ọrọ̀-ayé, who lives in the forest outside the town and is devouring their children and animals. Ifá tells them that Ọrọ̀-ayé demands a human sacrifice—the late king's eldest daughter—and after much argument they reluctantly decide to take this girl to the spirit's forest shrine. Láníyọnu, wandering nearby with his magic staff, rescues her, kills the dreadful spirit with the staff, and goes back to the town with the princess. Here he rebukes the chiefs for messing about with human sacrifice (see Chapter 10) and quells their resistance by demonstrating the powers of his magic staff. He is hailed as their new king, and the princess is given to him in marriage. The couple are dressed in splendid clothes, and a new and more honest age is inaugurated in the town.

This is a very strange and curiously attractive story. What is most appealing and provoking about it, perhaps, is the way the sharp oppositions and contradictions seem somehow to be contained or effaced. The contrast between the work-ethic plot and the destiny plot is very sharp—Láníyọnu almost becomes a different person after his expulsion into the forest[13]—yet the opposed poles match and are the measure of each other, between them describing a space in which destiny and individual agency are fused.

Some of the most striking thematic mirror-effects concern the figure of the helper. In the first part, Láníyọnu tries to play the role of benign patron to his destitute friends. He wants to give them the means to become self-sufficient through their own efforts. What the destitute friends want, however, is a magic, gratuitous bestowal of unlimited wealth. They are ungrateful and greedy and terminate Láníyọnu's role in their lives by savagely attacking him. In the second half, it is Láníyọnu who is destitute, and the role of benign patron is taken by the river deity. What she bestows on him is a magic, gratuitous gift of unlimited power. He is innocent and grateful, but—as in the first half—the patron-client relation is abruptly terminated when the client (this time unintentionally) transgresses. But while the ungrateful friends—lacking the magic source of money on which they had foolishly pinned their hopes—rapidly go to the bad, Láníyọnu retains possession of a magical gift he did not solicit or even imagine and goes from strength to strength. He ends up with a reward that he could not possibly have foreseen or aimed for: a crown to which his position as stranger in the town and commoner by birth does not entitle him. What authorizes this elevation is destiny, pronounced through the Ifá divination system, and his own righteousness, bluffly administered through the magical staff.

Láníyọnu is thus both a helper and a helpee—generous patron to his two ungrateful friends, savior of the princess and the town on the one hand, and recipient of blessings from the water deity, who first raises him from the dead and then renders him invincible, on the other. This duality corroborates our observation, made in regard to the actors' view of their audiences (Chapter 7), that the idea of "helpers" as an explanatory principle does not fit neatly into a pyramidal model of patron-client relations. A helper can be anyone, just as an implacable enemy can be anyone; it is not seen as a feature of social structure but as a vector that individuals identify as they make their way through their life courses. Báyọ̀ Ògúndíjọ, in our discussions, stressed the crucial role of the helper—a sponsor, patron, or well-wisher—in every successful person's career. This helper could be a relative but equally well could be a friend or even an unknown person. "*Àjùmọ̀bí kò kan tàánú: ẹni ẹlẹ́ni ní í ṣeni lóore*" [Being related does not guarantee fellow feeling; it's outsiders who do you good turns]. The helper's arrival, then, is essentially mysterious; he/she makes his or her appearance in your life as if gratuitously, without inducement or motivation. He/she is the obverse of *ayé*, the unknowable enemy. "If you have a good destiny, you will have brought your helpers with you from heaven; there is no need to make great efforts to attract them, for they are already there and will appear in due course to promote your interests."[14] The efforts they make on your behalf are also unforeseeable, incalculable, and in excess of normal patterns of reciprocity: your helper "will do everything he can to uplift you." The fated, unpredictable, and gratuitous character of helpers is captured, in both *Kúyẹ̀* and *Láníyọnu*, by their siting in the spirit world.

The injunction not to "write people off"—encapsulated in the narratives of unexpected but deserved good fortune found in both *Kúyẹ̀* and *Láníyọnu*—therefore has a double application. Since wealth is mysterious, you never know which of your impoverished neighbors may "become something" in future. But further, everyone you come across has the potential to be *your* stepping-stone to success. You can never know the limits of another person's potential. You must wait until their behavior reveals what they can become.

In *Láníyọnu*, as in *Kúyẹ̀*, the evocation of a providential order—which reveals one's own potential and the potential of others in the fullness of time—is far from an expression of passive fatalism. In the first half of *Láníyọnu*, God does not bless the lazy faithless friends: activity of the right kind is a prerequisite to blessing. In the second half, although Láníyọnu no longer does any productive work, his rise to kingship is not undeserved either. He earns it by his dogged pursuit of righteousness. He is blessed unexpectedly with a magic instrument, but it is left to him to use it well. It is when the chiefs see that he will use it to set the world to rights that they recognize him as their predestined Ọba. In the closing moments of the play, Láníyọnu, like Kúyẹ̀ though much more briefly, looks back over the sequence of apparent bizarre chances that led to his present good fortune and sees in it the working out of a just providence. His final words deftly fuse the two ethics, encapsulating agency within destiny:

> Mo fẹ́ kẹ́ ẹ kàn kẹ́kòó díẹ̀, nípa ìṣèlẹ̀ tó ṣelẹ̀ sí mi wí pé, ẹnikẹ́ni tó bá dalẹ̀, dandan ni kó bàlẹ̀ lọ. Àwọn ọ̀rẹ́ méjì kan tí mo sọ pé mo fẹ́ẹ́ ràn lọ́wọ́ tí wọ́n sọ mí di èrò àdúgbò yìí lónìí tí wọn ò bá kúú lé mi kúò ńlé, ǹbá wà ńbẹ̀ ni. Ṣùgbọ́n ńgbà wọ́n lé mi kúò ńbẹ̀ un, síbẹ̀síbẹ̀ ńgbà tó ṣe ńkọ́? Mo wáá di ẹni tí a fi jẹ ọba. Ìdí ọ̀rọ̀ọ̀ mi ni pé, ibi tí orí ẹni bá ń lọ, kí ẹsẹ̀ ó máa sìn wá lọ. Kí ẹ fi èyí kọ́gbọ́n.

I want you to learn a lesson from my experiences: that anyone who betrays a trust betrays his own life. The two friends that I told you I tried to help, it was they who turned me into an inhabitant of this town. If they hadn't driven me from home I'd be there now. But when they drove me away from there, after some time, what happened? I became a person chosen to be king. The heart of the matter is this: may our feet lead us along the path our Orí has chosen. Learn from this.

Orí, though usually translated as "Destiny," does not refer to an ineluctible and external Fate. Not only does each individual choose his/her own Orí before birth, but during life there is at least some scope to ameliorate or enhance whatever Orí was chosen. Orí could be understood as a person's individual principle of being, or potential for final self-realization; *ẹsẹ̀* (feet) could be understood as the steps by which a person gets there. On the way, helpers may be needed to smooth one's path; conversely, enemies may throw one off course—even, as in *Adédigba's Co-wife*, destroying one's actual feet and by implication one's ability to follow the path to its destination. Getting there is always fraught with uncertainty, and no one knows for sure what route the path to self-realization takes. One does not know one's *Orí* except in occasional glimpses vouchsafed by diviners, dreams, and other visitations from the spiritual world in which the choice of *Orí* was initially made. Apparent obstructions and deviations may turn out in the end to be the very way forward, as the experience of both Kúyẹ̀ and Láníyọnu attests. Ultimately the only answer is to be upright, do one's best, and not despair or fall prey to jealousy or impatience. But note that getting there is always an active process. You don't simply have a "destiny" which works itself out in spite of you. However backward and unexpected the route may turn out to be, you always have to put your best foot forward and go there under your own steam. Kúyẹ̀ and Láníyọnu, both recipients of lavish and unexpected good fortune at the moment when their lives have reached their lowest ebb, are characterized by dogged activity, stubborn refusal to relinquish agency even in the worst circumstances.

In this sense, *Orí* conjoined with *ẹsẹ̀* may be the concept that actually resolves the artisan's dual view of life: suspended between work, thrift, self-reliance, and entrepreneurial skill on the one hand and providence or destiny on the other as the final explanation of a person's success.

This also is why examples of moral action are held so dear. The lessons taught by the plays are no mere platitudes. Rather they demonstrate possible routes to self-realization, possible fatal deviations from the path, possible consolations for those who are experiencing delay. It is because the route is unknown and the destination unsure that these demonstrations are valued.

And this, I suspect, is partly why *The Road to Riches* failed: for this is the one play in the repertoire in which nothing really happens. Nothing is actually demonstrated from the experience of the characters as they pick their way along their life routes: instead, the whole plot is a fabrication of Ọláòṣèbìkan's, designed to teach Tàfá a lesson. As Báyọ̀ commented, "It is too short. It shows you Tàfá failing to make money by medicine, but it doesn't finish the story. It ought to show how he then takes Ọláòṣèbìkan's advice and makes a lot of money through hard work. Or it could show how Ọláòṣèbìkan himself made *his* money. It's incomplete." The characters do not provide examples of courses of action and their outcome and thus demonstrate the truths to be picked from other people's experience. They tell rather than show. Here also may be the reason why *Kúyẹ̀* succeeded and was one of the most popular plays in the repertoire for over 20 years: for *Kúyẹ̀* shows much more than it tells, a fact which is heightened and emphasized by Kúyẹ̀'s own dumbness. More than the other two plays, it shows with complete clarity that the heart of the matter is human potentiality. Even the most dependent and powerless people may find success. The powerful should take note of this. Since we do not know where someone else's *Orí* may be leading them to, and since we do not know who may turn out to be a helper, in effect everyone has potential. *No one* can be written off. This is not an egalitarian view which enjoins that you treat everyone well *despite* their obviously different stations, powers, and capacities. It is a profoundly inegalitarian view—it is far, far better to be powerful, rich, and gifted than otherwise—which still articulates the popular wish by insisting that the disadvantaged are potentially the advantaged, the apparently useless are potentially the most useful. You never know. Therefore you should treat all humans with respect.

The ideas and practices associated with potentiality, then, that animate the theater company's dramaturgy from the ground up (Chapter 5) are also central to the theater company's conception of dramatic character and to the plays' interpretation of human experience. Characters are enacted in a way that suggests they have a hinterland—of life lived, relationships sustained, and stories to tell—which is not necessarily fully visible or relevant to the narrative at hand. They suggest a potential fullness which is not always evenly activated. If they are nonetheless not "rounded" or endowed with a fully imagined interiority in the manner of European realist texts, that is because instead they have a different kind of potential, a potential for meaning which is only fully realized when they are incorporated and translated by audiences into their own lives. They are projected as examples of behavior and its consequences. And examples have their own kind of potential; they always go beyond themselves and are inherently proliferative. They are intended to be re-enacted, rather than exactly replicated. The audience members undertake to go and work through the implications of what they have seen—in their own way, in the light of their own circumstances. Each application of the example will yield a different, new story. Not only that, but each example suggests other analogous ones in the same field of ideas—for you could hardly have a single example of something. *Kúyẹ̀* suggests *Láníyọnu, Láníyọnu* suggests *The Road to Riches,* and each of these plays calls to mind numerous other written and oral texts offering other examples of the path to self-realization and the obstacles on that path.

Finally, the plays may be *about* human potentiality—in some cases, as we have just seen, quite centrally and explicitly so. The reflections of these plays on what it is to become a fully realized person thus shine a light back onto the question of what it is to be an actor and what it means to stage a play.

12 Language and the Moral Public

We have seen the makeshift improvisatory artisan's mode of production at work in the theater. But something more rose from within the tradesman's art of making do: a genius for language which transcended any limitations of staging, lighting, and style of performance. The linguistic creativity of the actors was collective; it sprang from the life world they shared with the audiences; and it was realized (though to varying degrees) in all performances. This is the final aspect of the theater company's productivity that I want to look at. It arises from a common knowledge of Yorùbá, not from any experience specific to the intermediate classes or to "clerkly artisans." In reaching into it and making it regenerate itself as they do, the actors are operating at a level of inclusiveness which potentially embraces all Yorùbá speakers.

THE CONSCIOUS ART OF LANGUAGE

Language was one of the things people went to the theater for. Younger members of the audience often said they particularly liked certain characters or episodes because of the incantations or curses they gave vent to; adults commented that they appreciated "deep Yorùbá" spoken on stage. As we saw in Chapter 7, audience commentary during a performance mainly took the form of taking up, quoting, and laughing at particularly telling phrases—sometimes long after the moment of their utterance had passed. The theater company was highly conscious of the language they used. Alhaji gave much thought to the significant phrases and sentences he wished the actors to deliver, and all the actors relished their own special lines and rejoiced when they were approved by the audience (Chapter 6).

The plays combined music, spectacle, and horseplay; but their two most significant dimensions, in the eyes both of the theater company and the audience, were the story—in which the consequences of moral action were worked out and demonstrated—and the words. The Adéjọbí plays were essentially a discursive form with very extensive verbal texts. Commentators on the Yorùbá popular theater have tended to ignore or dismiss its verbal output, except in those plays that contain the most substantial borrowings from oral traditions (notably, Dúró Ládiípọ̀'s *Ọba Kò So*). But this is to miss the soul of the Yorùbá popular theater.

Take *Articulated Lorry:* a play that harnesses the considerable talents of the actors to mount a narrative leading up to the all-too-familiar warning "Beware of women." Yet the play is a jewel, a delight from moment to moment as it weaves its sinuously supple course between fresh allusions, recast archival treasures, the familiar, and the slightly peculiar. There is nothing mechanical or predictable about the generation of language in this play.

When Ìyá Àlàbí comes to visit her son in his lodgings, she brings a proposal that he should get married to the daughter of a friend of hers. Àlàbí says no, he wants to further his education before he marries. His mother becomes indignant and raises her voice. Àlàbí's neighbor, Ìyáa Bùnmi, chooses this moment to drop in. She asks "Akọ̀wé [clerk, i.e., someone with book learning], I hope it isn't difficult [i.e., I hope there isn't a problem], because I heard—" Àlàbí's mother breaks in: "There is. There is something difficult." She then elaborates on this, playing on the word *ṣòro* (to be difficult): "*Ó ṣòro. Kódà, ó sàápọ̀n pẹ̀lú. Ó so mọ́ńgòrò.*" *Ó ṣòro* is here wittily re-construed as "Ó so òro": it bore the fruit of the *òro* tree—the Wild Mango tree. "Ó so ààpọ̀n": it bore *ààpọ̀n*, which is the name of the wild mango fruit itself. And then "Ó so mọ́ńgòrò": it bore the cultivated mango fruit, which is bigger than the wild one. So "it's difficult, very difficult, and worse than difficult." Àlàbí, who is probably aware of Ìyáa Bùnmi's potential as a troublemaker, warns his mother "Are you going to spill it all out in front of her?" but his mother is too indignant to be restrained, and asks Ìyáa Bùnmi "This—please, isn't this creature old enough to have a wife? This great staring creature. Is he big enough to have a wife in his house or not?" "Go on," says Ìyáa Bùnmi encouragingly, and Ìyá Àlàbí fulminates "A wife ... huh, he just talks in English! All right, I'll silence the drums for you [i.e., I won't say any more]. All I'm saying is he should have a woman in the house. Ló yarí mọ́ a lọ́ọ́ bíi kòkó àgíríikìí—And he splits his head into branches like 'agric' cocoa ... " *Yarí* means to refuse point blank; but could also be construed as *ya* (split) *orí* (head), suggesting the image of "agric" cocoa, which is never tall but has many branches. Àlàbi protests "What's all this about? I said I want to go to University [*Yunifásìtì*], don't you understand?" Ìyá Àlàbí is not impressed or deterred: "You're not going to *títì* [colloquial loan word for "street," which is what she hears when he says "Yunifásìtì"]. And if you do go to *títì*, you'll have a woman under your roof, before you set foot on the *títì*." Ìyáa Bùnmi keeps on mediating, with a view toward insinuating herself into the confidence of both mother and son: "Please, let's take all this very calmly.... Let me speak to the 'clerk.' 'Clerk'..." Àlàbí responds in English "It can never be possible."

In this brief exchange, the brilliant craftsmanship of the company is fully on display. In the space of four speeches, Ìyá Àlàbí delivers two puns, a withering put-down, a reference to Àlàbí's preference for English (significant later in the plot), a comic misunderstanding of that English, and a reference to a colonial novelty: "agric" cocoa supplied by the Ministry of Agriculture, which—like other colonial novelties—is shrewdly observed and ambivalently evaluated. Yet Ìyá Àlàbí is not just a vehicle for a display of linguistic productivity. Each of these utterances establishes her character as an old-fashioned, forceful, vigorous, uneducated woman, not at all in awe of her educated son but unable at the same time to get the better of him, especially when he takes refuge in an unknown language. Her violent onslaught establishes Àlàbí's unshakable determination to pursue his own course; his use of English, which initially seemed pure affectation, now begins to function as a badge of aloofness and distinction. Ìyáa Bùnmi's soothing and encouraging interventions reveal her duplicity and also grease the wheels of the dialogue: we can already see that she is indecently eager to ingratiate herself with the mother and involve herself in the son's affairs.

This dialogue sounds completely lifelike, vivid, and natural. But it is not simply drawn from the actors' own normal registers of speech. Deborah Adéjobí, who played Ìyá Àlàbí, was a young woman in her thirties when I recorded this performance in 1981. Yet Ìyá Àlàbí's allusions consistently evoke the colonial era, and many of her idioms are distinctly old-fashioned. She says that when she was pleased with her friend, "Mo bun légbaàje" (I gave her *14,000 cowries*, i.e., 3/6d). To express her annoyance with Àlàbí, she says he is "*Bí akódàa ta-npépé*" [like the badge-wearing stinging ant]—a phrase that refers to the court messengers and policemen of the early colonial period who wore sashes as a badge of office and whose interference could irritate townspeople more than the sting of the black ant that infested palm trees. Sèlíá, the landlord's wife, uses similar idioms. "Kenke Júbílì," she mocks the landlord when he is extravagant in his generosity to the political party of which he has been made branch chairman: referring probably to George V's 1935 Jubilee celebration. The younger characters—Àlàbí, the secretary, and Ìyáa Bùnmi—do not use this kind of idiom. It appears to be a deliberate technique for establishing a character, yet it is done with total fluency and ease. The actors appear to have access to several repertoires of idioms and can move in and out of them according to the requirements of their role in an entirely unobtrusive and spontaneous way.

Within a single play subtle changes of linguistic style and density can fulfill a dramatic function. Alhaji, the master builder of the repertoire, had the ability to orchestrate nuance with great precision. In *Lániyonu*, for example, he brought about a delicate but definite shift in verbal style to indicate the hero's change in status. At the beginning of the play, Láníyọnu is a prosperous businessman who is becomingly modest about his success but confident of his wisdom. He lectures his impoverished friends in the orotund rhetoric of the big man:

> LÁNÍYỌNU: Bẹ́ ẹ ṣe wá, ó dùn mọ́ mi ńnú gan-an. Èmi ni mo ránni sí yín. Wọ́n ní, "Otí a máa mọ́rọ̀ gúnlẹ̀," níjọ́ mìíin náà, ońjẹ náà, a máa mú un gúnlẹ̀. N óò kọ́kọ́ fẹ́ kẹ́ ẹ kọ́kọ́ jẹun ná, kí ọ̀rọ̀ tí n óò sọ ó lè baà wọ̀ yín létí. Torí wí pé, wọ́n ní, "Ebi ì í wọnú, kọ́rọ̀ mìíin ó wọ̀ ọ́." Ọ̀rọ̀ mìíin a sì maa wọ̀ ọ́, ọ̀rọ̀ burúkú ni ì í kàn-án wọ̀ ọ́ ni. N óò fẹ́ kẹ́ ẹ jẹun ná. . . . Ké ẹ fi sùúrù jẹun o. Bẹ́ ẹ bá yó, ńgbà náà, ká wáá bẹ̀rẹ̀ nàsíà wa. Mo rò pé ńgbà náà, ọ̀rọ̀ mi óò wáá wọ̀ yín létí.
>
> *(Láníyọnu jáde. Àwọn àlejò bẹ̀rẹ̀ sí í jà sóńjẹ náà.)*
>
> MÁSỌMÍNÙ: O bẹ̀rẹ̀ . . .
>
> ỌTÒLÓRÌN: Kí ni kúnkùn rẹ?
>
> MÁSỌMÍNÙ: Ìwà wọ̀bìà lò ń hù. O bu èkìínní, o bù ú ràgàdù ràgàdù, o tún bu ìkejì, èyíun gba ẹnu rẹ?
>
> LÁNÍYỌNU: I'm very glad that you came. It was I who sent for you. You know there's a saying that "A drink makes the discussion go with a swing," but sometimes food can also make it go with a swing. I want you to have something to eat first, so that the thing I'm going to talk to you about will get a good hearing. Because there's a saying that "If hunger enters a person, nothing else can enter." There is something else that will enter, only bad ones, we hope, will not enter. So I want you to eat first. . . . Take your time. When you're full, then we can begin our discussion. I think that's when my subject will be able to enter your ears.
>
> *(He goes out. They begin to squabble over the food.)*
>
> MÁSỌMÍNÙ: Now you're starting . . .
>
> ỌTÒLÓRÌN: What's your complaint?
>
> MÁSỌMÍNÙ: You're a greedy pig. You take your first handful, you make it a huge one, you take another, hasn't even that filled your mouth?

In this speech, as through all of the first part of the play, Láníyọnu delivers himself of a formal discourse signifying self-esteem, propriety, and modesty. He shows a proper respect for the feelings of his friends. He thanks them warmly for responding to his invitation—though it is to their advantage, not his—and seasons his welcome with prayers for their continued friendship. He quotes several proverbs, showing himself to be an "elder," wise and knowledgeable. He prefaces each with the expression *wọ́n ní*, "it is said/they say that," showing an appropriate deference to his elders and to tradition itself. But he shows his mastery of elders' speech by expounding the proverbs and also deftly adapting them to make his point. His long speeches are developed in a leisurely manner that suggests he is in no danger of being interrupted. This is in sharp contrast with the speech of Másọmínù and Òtòlórìn, who speak roughly and elliptically: "Now you're starting"; "What's your complaint?" and who are unable to summon up the appropriate graciousness even when thanking their benefactor for his generosity.

But after Láníyọnu has been expelled to the forest, left for dead by the ferocious spirits, and revived by Omídiyùn, the beneficent water deity, his style changes. Now it is Omídiyùn who speaks formally, with well-formed oratorical sentences. Láníyọnu responds alternately with brief questions and garrulous explanations, revealing his new character as a sympathetic innocent as well as the state of amazement and confusion he has been thrown into:

> OMÍDIYÙN: Ọmọ ènìyàn, ìwọ kò mọ̀ pé ìwọ ti kú, èmi tí mo jí ọ rèé?
> LÁNÍYỌNU: Pé, mo ti kú!
> OMÍDIYÙN: Béẹ̀ ni.
> LÁNÍYỌNU: Ẹ̀yin le jí mi?
> OMÍDIYÙN: Hùn-ún.
> LÁNÍYỌNU: Àà, ẹ foríjìn mí o. Èmi ò tíì kú o. À, ẹni ó kú a máa sọ̀rọ̀? Ẹ sì ní mo kú! Èmi ò kú o. Kúkú bóo? Èmi ò kú o. Ẹ è gbọ́, èmi ò kú rárá o. Hin-ìn, ìgbà tíí . . . wọ́n lé mi débí ìí, sé è ń gbọ́? Àwọn, àwọn . . . hin ìn, níbi tíí.. àwọn ọ̀rẹ́ méjì . . .
> OMÍDIYÙN: Ọmọ ènìyàn, mo ti rí wàhálà àti hílàhílo rẹ, nítorí náà ni mo ṣe wá láti ràn ọ́ lọ́wọ́.

> OMÍDIYÙN: Child of humans, do you not know that you have died? It was I who brought you back to life.
> LÁNÍYỌNU: I died?
> OMÍDIYÙN: Yes.
> LÁNÍYỌNU: It was you who brought me back to life?
> OMÍDIYÙN: Certainly.
> LÁNÍYỌNU: Ah, excuse me. I haven't died yet. Does a dead person talk? And you say I'm dead! I'm not dead. How do you mean, dead? I didn't die. Listen, I'm not in the least dead. You see, when . . . they drove me here, do you understand? They . . . er . . . they . . . er . . . when . . . where . . . two friends . . .
> OMÍDIYÙN: Child of humans, I observed your trouble and your confusion, that is why I came to help you.

Omídiyùn is speaking not just a formal language but a literary one, associated primarily with the Bible but also with written Yorùbá in general. When she says "*Ọmọ ènìyàn, ìwọ kò mọ̀ pé ìwọ ti kú, èmi tí mo jí ọ rèé*" [Child of humans, do you not know that you have died? It was I who brought you back to life], the use of the emphatic pronoun *ìwọ* and the negative form *kò* with the second person singular is characteristic only of written language; in speech, people would say *o ò mọ̀*, not *ìwọ kò mọ̀*. The absence of elision is also characteristic of written, not spoken, Yorùbá. Láníyọnu's reply, by contrast, is full of colloquialisms. He adds many expressive interjections of "o," untranslatable into English, to add emphasis: "*Àà, ẹ foríjìn mí o. Èmi ò tíì kú o.*" He uses contractions that are typical of informal speech: "*Kúkú bóo?*" for "*Kúkú báwo?*" He repeats himself a great deal in his surprise and indignation. He starts sentences and cannot finish them, and in trying to remember the sequence of events that led to his presence in the forest he becomes thoroughly incoherent, until Omídiyùn silences him with her supernatural authority.

Láníyọnu continues to speak in this amusingly informal manner—which in the scenes with the chiefs has the effect of puncturing their pomposity and self-regard—until he becomes a mouthpiece of moral authority at the end. Then he regains, though not to the same degree as at the beginning, his habit of delivering eloquent well-formed sermons. Láníyọnu's speech thus mirrors his transformations and with comic precision defines his difference from the other beings, human and spiritual, with whom he interacts.

COLLECTIVE CONSISTENCY

While Alhaji was undoubtedly the key to the establishment of a prevailing tone or texture in a play or an episode, the differences between one play and another were too pervasive and fine-grained to have been the product of a single consciousness. It seems rather that the whole theater company, under Alhaji's guidance, became attuned to linguistic style and was able to generate speech within the registers appropriate to different plays. To suggest some of the subtlety and flexibility of this collective control of language, let me compare *The Overreacher* with *External Appearances*. Both plays were new when I first joined the company in 1981, and both of course were performed by the same actors. But their imagery, use of wordplay, and style of humor are systematically different from each other. And in each, the verbal style seemed quite clearly to have an affinity with the play's theme and indeed to add suggestively to its exposition.

The Overreacher is set in a "folkloric" kingdom—not in the sense that it inhabits a fantasy or imaginary realm, but in the sense that all the action of the play revolves around long-standing institutions of kingship, chieftaincy, and traditional marriage customs. As we saw in Chapter 9, the play undoubtedly had a contemporary reference to national abuse of power, but this application was left to the audience to make. The references within the play stayed within the confines of a single town in which government was conducted by an Ọba, his town chiefs, a diviner, and an imam (representing the longer-established of the two world religions)—without any mention of a local government council or a modernizing Christian elite. The Ọba has a traditional household, including a messenger (ẹmẹ̀wà), and when one of the chiefs incurs his displeasure he threatens to put him into palace servitude as one of those who "cut grass for the horses"—suggesting an old royal culture which was fading by the early twentieth century. He retains the traditional royal privilege of first choice among the town's marriageable girls, and his unforgivable transgression is not that he uses this privilege but that he goes beyond it, seizing a girl who was already betrothed to someone else. Underlying all the other outrages perpetrated by the Ọba is his refusal to take counsel from his advisers, thus denying the dialogic constitution of traditional power.

In keeping with this local and old-fashioned setting, the imagery throughout the play draws almost exclusively on everyday domestic, agricultural, and natural life. The new king, played by John Adéwuni, announces his regime with the words "New water has flowed in, new fish have entered it." He abuses his chiefs with strings of homely and unflattering comparisons: "You have eyes like the eyes of a frog," "You who are as pale as the remnants of a new yam," "He's piled his ragged clothes on in layers like the palm frond," "You who are filling the ground like the carcass of a sick beast," "He's as insignificant as the èkùà rodent." Of the imam, who according to Islamic custom neither prostrates nor removes his headdress in the royal presence, he says "He's standing like a frog on the banks of the river ... he's built a sun-shelter on his head ... he's wound a carrying pad on his head." Alhaji, as the ambiguously subversive court messenger, uses a similar idiom to describe the king's reign: "It's like trying to put a live dog into a small pierced pot [in which meat is smoked]"—that is, it's a struggle! After the Ọba has been supernaturally punished for his transgressions—with a strange affliction which causes him first to laugh like a maniac, then to gape and bark like a panting dog, and finally to hoot with his mouth twisted in a lopsided grin—his attendants and chiefs produce strings of common or garden variety similes to comment on this alarming succession of states: "Look at His Majesty's mouth, like a yam-flour sieve," "Whatever has made his mouth into a scoop for serving bean stew," "His mouth is like a rat trap," "His mouth is like the splitting gbúre pod," "His mouth is twisted like a drumstick," "like a water vessel used in Muslim prayer," and so on.

Almost all the characters use proverbs that draw on long-standing traditional relationships and experiences. Some of these sayings are extensive, almost amounting to a parable: the Ìyálóde, caught between conflicting demands, sums up her quandary with the words "Death requests you to do a job for him, your in-laws ask you to do ọ̀wẹ̀ (free communal labor) for them. If you don't respond to Death's demand, he will kill and eat you. If you don't respond to the demand of your in-laws, your in-laws will take their daughter back." Toward the end of the play there is a thickening cluster of aphorisms, as the diviner—earlier banished from the palace along with all the other chiefs—is persuaded to come back and diagnose the Ọba's strange affliction. She looks at his distorted mouth and pronounces "It's said that anyone who does what no one has done before, is bound to suffer what no one . . ." The diviner consults Ifá and reports "Ifá says Kábíyèsí has tried to pick ẹ̀kọ from a basket his arms don't reach into." Her statement that only the Ọba can make the necessary propitiation is glossed by Gbajúmọ̀ with another proverb: "It's said that we use our own hands to repair our behavior," which the diviner caps with a compatible saying, "That's to say that one uses one's own mouth to say 'I won't eat it.'" The crescendo of aphorisms closes with Gbajúmọ̀'s final speech, which piles up a number of related sayings: If you have position, money, or high estate, do not use it to cheat your fellow human beings; the owner of all your worldly assets, including position, money, and high estate, is God; if you use these assets wrongly, you will be disgraced; no one is so high he is above disgrace, so don't be arrogant. The final point is then picked up, restated, and elaborated in the closing song, sung by the whole cast.

There is almost no use of English expressions in this play. Even Dayọ̀ Akínpèlú, whose hallmark was always his affected Anglicisms, kept them to an absolute minimum in the part of the young lover. There are very few references to experiences which would not have been available in a precolonial town. Instead of bringing in loan words, new slang, and allusions to features of modernity, in this play the actors—Alhaji especially—drew on old, almost obsolete vocabulary, such as *ilẹ̀kùn abógundé* (referring to an old type of carved door used in traditional mud-built compounds which began to go out of use in the early twentieth century).

Older verbal arts, especially *oríkì*, are used more freely in this play than in any of the others in the Adéjọbí repertoire of the time. Even here, their use is cautious and ironical, their hyperbole punctuating the Ọba's displays of arrogance with an insistent counterpoint. But as carefully as their reverberations are restricted, the *oríkì* in *The Overreacher*—unlike in the other plays—do find a recurrent echo in the linguistic texture of the spoken dialogue. The strings of similes used by the Ọba to deride his chiefs in the first half of the play, and by the chiefs and attendants to deride the Ọba's affliction in the second half, participate in the vocative, attributive idiom of the *oríkì*. *Oríkì*'s mode is to operate almost entirely through simile and metaphor, often drawing on proverbs as metaphorical vehicles in formulations that are addressed to a subject to enhance his or her aura in an intensive dialogic relationship. The tone is set by the opening lines of the play with the chanted *oríkì*: "The ancestral masquerade discreetly sips his liquor . . ." (an implied metaphor for the Ọba, evoking his secret, sacred, and inherited power); "Weighty and sappy, as if someone were headloading an *ilámọ̀* tree . . . " (a simile comparing the Ọba to a big tree, whose wood is heavy and full of sap); "He is as hard to provoke [with a push in the chest] / As a giant cutting-grass . . . " (a simile hailing the Ọba's invincibility); "The ant does not love the cornstalk from its heart / People's love for one is not sincere" (a saying applied metaphorically to the Ọba to affirm that he is wise and self-reliant enough not to be taken in). As if in tune with this mode, the similes and metaphors which abound in the spoken dialogue are likewise used attributively: that is, to hail or comment on the qualities of a person or other entity, often one present to the speaker, and usually in the vocative case. Most of the Ọba's utterances in the opening sequence are similes that function as novel compositions in the *oríkì* style ("You who are as red as the oil secreted by a crab," "You who are squatting like a chicken coop"). So are most of Gbajúmọ̀'s references to the Ọba's mouth, which could be taken as a kind of anti-*oríkì* or *àkìjà* (see Barber 1991, 13–14).

Metaphors—some so old as to have become clichés, others surprisingly novel—also pepper the text. Chief Jagun salutes his own valor with the well-known metaphor "A cutlass is male!" Gbajúmọ̀ hails the Ọba with a metaphorized proverb: "Your tree cannot make up a forest by itself." When the Ọba is pleased with Gbajúmọ̀, he says "In this palace you have become a mosque that never goes anywhere" (i.e., your position here is secure by my side), and one of Gbajúmọ̀'s allusions to the Ọba's gaping mouth takes the form of a striking metaphor "Just look at His Majesty's town-center of a mouth."

Thus, both halves of the play are full of acts of *salutation,* hyperbolic or comically disparaging. Salutation by *oríkì* is one of the public mechanisms by which the interdependency of power-wielders and power-followers is confirmed. The praiser and the praisee are locked in a mutually constitutive act, in which the follower's role in the creation and maintenance of the leader's position is put on display and put into action. The use of so much comically exaggerated or inverted salutation in *The Overreacher* underlines the fact that what is at issue is the deviant behavior of a figure whose authority should be—but is not—created and maintained by the attentions, the adherence, and approving gaze of others in a dialogic exchange.

There is a current of linguistic wit running through the play that appears to take off from, and counterpoint, the core moral theme of deviation from tradition, summarized in the proverb "Let us do as has always been done, so that things may continue to be as they have always been." Repeatedly, characters in the play take up established conventions of speech or behavior and subject them either to inversion or to a ridiculously literal interpretation. In the Ọba's case, this habit underlines his iconoclastic autocracy. When the chiefs enter singing his praises and attributing the safety of the town to Ifá, he turns on them furiously and says that it is he, not Ifá, who has kept the town safe. When a woman chief explains that her title is "Ìyá Ọba"—"Mother of the King," a traditional ceremonial role held by a senior woman of the palace—he demands to know if his own mother is no longer the one who gave birth to him. He asks the Ìyálóde about her daughter, and the Ìyálóde properly and conventionally replies "Everything I have is yours, Your Majesty. She is your child." But the Ọba rejects this: "A father knows what children he has fathered. And a child knows its father," forcing the Ìyálóde to retract hastily "Oh, I was the one who bore her, it was me."

But Gbajúmọ̀, the trickster-like messenger played by Alhaji, undermines conventions in a sly and subversive vein which takes the wind out of the Ọba's sails and shows up the ridiculousness of his stance. Gbajúmọ̀ establishes this style very simply in the first scene by taking a customary formula literally. The Ọba, offended by Gbajúmọ̀'s attempt to give good advice, issues a summons "*Gbajúmọ̀! Gbajúmọ̀! Gbajúmọ̀! Èèmélòó ni mo pè ọ́?*" [Gbajúmọ̀! Gbajúmọ̀! Gbajúmọ̀! How many times did I call you?]—a standardized formula announcing that an important communication is about to be made to the addressee, to which the conventional reply is "*Èèméta ni*" [Three times]. When Gbajúmọ̀ instead says "*Ó pọ̀!*" [It was a lot (of times)!], the unexpected deviation, as if Gbajúmọ̀ considered the question to be a real request for information but didn't know the exact answer, took the audience by surprise and provoked great hilarity. Later, he plays with the conventions governing the announcement of a birth. He says all the things usually said on such an occasion, and the Ọba and royal wives fall into the trap and supply the appropriate responses, until Gbajúmọ̀ finally reveals the sting in the tail of his announcement:

> GBAJÚMỌ̀: Ẹ kú onílé o.
> OLORÌ: Hòoo.
> GBAJÚMỌ̀: Háá, èé ti jẹ́ Kábíyèsí?
> ỌBA: Ta ló bímọ rí?
> GBAJÚMỌ̀: Háà, mo sáré débí yìí lẹ́ẹ̀kan.
> OLORÌ: Adùn óò kárí.
> GBAJÚMỌ̀: A dúpẹ́ lọ́dọ̀ Ọlọ́un.
> ỌBA: Ta ló bímọ ńnúu wọn?
> GBAJÚMỌ̀: Háà, a dàámú lónìí.
> OLORÌ: Háà. A à sí ńlẹ̀ ni.
> AYABA: Tìẹ náà óò dé.
> GBAJÚMỌ̀: Òkọ̀ọ̀kán tó báyìí.
> ỌBA: Ta ló bímọ rí?
> GBAJÚMỌ̀: Wọ́n sì jọ Kábíyèsí bí ìmumu.
> ỌBA: Ẹ ṣe é. Ta ló bímọ ńnúu wọn rí?

GBAJÚMỌ̀: Han-ìn, mo ní n wáá sọ fún un yín ni o. A dàámú, kó tó di pó bi.
ỌBA: Àní, ta ló bímọ ńnúu wọn?
OLORÌ: Èwo ló bímọ nínú àwọn ìyàwó?
GBAJÚMỌ̀: Hẹn-ìn, ewúrẹ́ dúdú un ló bíbejì.

GBAJÚMỌ̀: Greetings to the owner of the house!
WIFE 1: Thank you.
GBAJÚMỌ̀: Ha, how are you bearing up, Kábíyèsí?
ỌBA: Who is it who's given birth?
GBAJÚMỌ̀: Ha, I rushed here [to tell you] just now.
WIFE 1: May the joy go round everyone.
GBAJÚMỌ̀: We give thanks to God.
ỌBA: Which of them gave birth?
GBAJÚMỌ̀: Ha, we had a lot of trouble today.
WIFE 1: What a pity, we weren't at home.
WIFE 2: Yours [i.e., your own child] will come.
GBAJÚMỌ̀: Each of them was as big as this!
ỌBA: Who gave birth?
GBAJÚMỌ̀: And they're the spitting image of Kábíyèsí.
ỌBA: Thank you. But who was it who gave birth?
GBAJÚMỌ̀: Ha, I was just coming to tell you. We really had a lot of trouble, before she gave birth.
ỌBA: I said which of them gave birth?
WIFE 1: Which of the wives had a baby?
GBAJÚMỌ̀: Why, that black goat had twins.

This jest, while playing with conventional speech sequences, introduces a sly mockery of the Ọba's bestiality (repeated when the Ọba begins to bark like a dog). When the Ọba tells him off with the standard figure of speech "*Wèrè ń bẹ láraà rẹ*" [lit. "There's madness in your body"], Gbajúmọ̀ starts searching his clothes. When the Ọba abuses him "Your head is not complete," Gbajúmọ̀ asks by how many units it is short. When the Ọba cautions him to calm down, using the completely dead metaphor "*Fara balẹ̀*" [lit. "Put your body down / resting on the ground"], Gbajúmọ̀ re-awakens it by suiting the action to the word and lying on the floor.

He also has a flair for producing a proliferation of conceptual categories where normally only one would suffice. The Ọba complains that he has been disgraced that day by the insults heaped on him by the Ìyálóde's daughter. Gbajúmọ̀ first pretends this is a cause for celebration and then inquires which kind of disgrace it was. The Ọba asks how many kinds of disgrace there are, and Gbajúmọ̀ proceeds to generate a set of categories: there is the "little red pepper disgrace," a trivial insult; the "large hot pepper disgrace," an insult so sharp you can't answer back; the "lime fruit disgrace," so large and conspicuous the whole world knows about it; the "thorn disgrace," caused by an insult that is highly appropriate and near the bone. He does the same at the end of the play in an extended jest in which he purports to be saying a prayer for the happy couple, now reunited with the Ọba's blessing. "God who joined you will not sunder you again. If anyone tries to sunder you, he will confess before he does it. After he has confessed, he will begin to bark like a dog.... If anyone tries to sunder you, his mouth will stick out like a Muslim prayer vessel. His mouth will go up and not come down. Anyone who tries to sunder you, anyone who tries to sunder you—God will give him ten children!" (Astonishment is expressed by the other characters.) "Death will kill two of them. Disease will kill two. They'll build houses in the bush for two, because they are lepers. They'll build houses far away from the town for two, that's smallpox. And Ṣọ̀pọ̀nnọ́n will slay the last two." In this final *jeu d'esprit* he uses the form of a blessing (on the happy couple) to issue a curse (on anyone who seeks to divide them), which momentarily resumes the form of a blessing (when he wishes the hypothetical ill-wisher many children to his name), which converts back to a curse (when he pronounces a horrid doom on each of the hypothetical children). Along the way, of course, he takes the opportunity to embed a fairly brazen warning to the reformed Ọba not to revert unless he wants to suffer the same affliction again.

These parodies and inversions of conventional idioms and categories—quite similar to the style of the jester in Elizabethan comedy[1]—are not, in the Adéjọbí repertoire, the prefabricated discourse of a standardized clown figure. They are unique to *The Overreacher,* providing a peculiarly apt commentary on the core theme of the infraction of conventions and traditions. The consistency of the traditional vocabulary; the *oríkì*-like use of vocative, attributive similes and metaphors; and the playful commentary on deviation from the conventions of discourse all work together to generate a linguistic medium that continually reinforces and supplements the exposition of the key themes.

The linguistic medium of *External Appearances* is quite different. This play, as we saw in Chapter 11, is set in an explicitly contemporary urban milieu where most of the characters have been to school and work in businesses or offices. The incidence of English expressions is vastly greater than in *The Overreacher.* While *The Overreacher* opens with the bloodcurdling praise chant of unbridled human power, in *External Appearances* the curtain opens on a hymn exhorting the congregation of an Aládùúrà church to raise the name of the Lord on high. The Preacher then proceeds to address his flock, and in his very first remark produces two striking English borrowings: "*Ẹ gbàdúà. Gbogbo ẹ̀yin ọlọ́mọge tí bọ́í-fureǹdì yín já yín jù ú lẹ̀, bí ìgbà tí típà bá já eèpẹ̀ ẹ́'lẹ̀, ẹ gbàdúà!*" [Pray. All you young girls whose **boyfriends** have chucked you like a **tipper** chucking sand, pray!] In the Preacher's vision which reveals the auspicious choice of husband for Bísí, he tells her he sees a moon on the right and a star on the left, both shining brightly and moving toward each other across the sky. When they have nearly met, both of them put in a burst of speed, "bí ìgbà tí èèyán bá pe **'On your marks'** fún àwọn ọmọ *sùkúù*" [like when they call '**On your marks**' for children at **school**]. All the characters (except the old pagan father who comes to the church to be converted—see Chapter 10) pepper their speech with words like "now," "yes," "what!" and "thank you." They use *láìkì* for "like" (instead of *fẹ́ràn*), *sẹ́ẹ̀tì* for "shirt" (instead of *ẹ̀wù*), *mọ́ọ̀n* for "man" (instead of *ọkùnrin*), *báàgì* for "bag" (instead of *àpò*), *púrọ́búlẹ́ẹ̀mù* for "problem" (instead of *ìṣòro*), *sẹ́ńdì* for "send" (instead of *fi ránṣẹ́*). They use English number words: Uncle Táyọ̀ boasts of being able to spend "millions" where his rivals are spending only "thousands." Bísí calls her first two suitors *Mista* Kúnlé and *Mista* Pírí, and the third one either *Uncle* Táyọ̀ or *Sugar Daddy*. Bísí's friend Bínpé sings a song in English to her husband—"Oh my lover, You must kiss me before you go"—which almost makes him *léètì* for work.

The dosage of English is regulated according to the requirements of characterization. Uncle Táyọ̀ (played by Alhaji) is the character who uses it most. A stupendously wealthy self-proclaimed area boy made good, he stages a display of arrogant big-manship in which lavish expenditure is paralleled by a lavish scattering of English phrases. After coming across Pírí in Bísí's lodgings, for example, he reprimands her in the following egregious mixture of English and Yorùbá:

> Kí ló déé? Kí ló déé? **A man of naira** ló ń bá ẹ ẹ́ sọ̀rọ̀. **Am sorry to see you with those** "ráposíkùlyà." Bísí. Mo wo ìta ńbẹ̀, mo wo ìta ńbẹ̀ yẹn, níbi tí mo **páàk mọ́tòò** mi sí, mo wáá wò ó pé, kí ni **boy** yìí gbé wá! Tó bá tiẹ̀ sonímaasínnì ni **yéèsì. At least,** tí n bá ra **twenty naira petrol** yóò máa roní-**one naira**. Kò tiẹ̀ síhun tó jọ bẹ́ẹ. Só o mọ̀ páriìfín ló jẹ́ sí mi, o ò mọ̀ pó járìfín sí ẹ láti máa wárú ẹ wá? Bísí, ó dùn mí púpọ̀ fún ẹ.

> Why? Why? **A man of naira** is talking to you. **Am sorry to see you with those** rascals [raposikuiya is perhaps an elaborate version of "rascal"—not a Yorùbá word but not a straight loan word either]. Bísí. I looked outside there, I looked outside there, where I **parked my car,** and I looked to see what this **boy** had brought. If he was at least the owner of a **machine** [i.e., motor-cycle], **yes** [that would be OK]. **At least,** when I buy **twenty nairas'** worth of petrol he would buy **one naira**'s worth. But it wasn't so. Don't you know that it's disrespectful to me, don't you know that it's disrespectful to you, for him to come visiting the likes of you? Bísí, I'm very pained for you.

The characters in *External Appearances* use a number of proverbs, similes, and metaphors—though not as many as those in *The Overreacher*. Unlike the figures of speech in *The Overreacher*, those in *External Appearances* are sometimes translated from English sayings (e.g., "All that glitters is not gold"), sometimes drawn from the Yorùbá translation of the Bible ("to bring back the sheep into the fold," "a thorn in my side"), and often capitalize on striking features of colonial or post-colonial life ("they would take **turns** like people in a clinic," "it was like a **tipper** carrying a load the way he would bring money [for me]," "I was babbling, I was talking like someone from Ghana"). In *External Appearances* the figures of speech create a different overall ambience from that of *The Overreacher*, and this is due not only to the range and choice of images but also to the way they are set in the surrounding discourse. In *The Overreacher*, figures of speech are highlighted and often cluster around the key thematic points: no less than three-quarters of the proverbs used in this play have a direct bearing on the central moral of the story. In *External Appearances*, figures of speech more often crop up casually in a rapid and fluent conversation. There are fewer well-known proverbs and more idiomatic and colorful sayings. Instead of standing out as iconic signposts in a moral landscape, they tend to merge into a sea of slang and current idiom. Only at the end is a repeated figure of speech used to encapsulate a key thematic point.

But this more eclectic and heterogeneous verbal mixture works in a subtle and interesting way to generate a commentary on the inner sense of the text. Bísí's fault, as we saw in the last chapter, is diagnosed as greed—her inability to give up the prospect of rich lovers and settle for the ordinary young man who has yet to make his fortune. She comes to realize at the end of the play that she has delayed too long and that she should have settled down and done the "trade of child-bearing" earlier in life. Throughout the play there is a delicate running commentary, carried by the idioms and figures of speech the characters use, which foreshadows this realization and adds nuance to its formulation. This is seen particularly in the constant references to time.

The characters calibrate their lives by calendar and clock time. Bínpé's husband has to get to work on time; Pírí works in an office, where—Bísí fears—he will always be claiming that he has to do "overtime" when he wants to have affairs with other women. Bísí gives her lovers "appointments"; she refuses the drink offered by her friend Bínpé saying "It's still midmorning," and hurries back to her rooms knowing Pírí will be there on time. In the world of business too, fixed dates cannot be flouted. When Bísí takes Uncle Táyọ̀ to the Aládùúrà church to see whether he would make an auspicious husband, the Preacher's vision imparts a bit of extra advice for Uncle Táyọ̀:

> BÀBÁ ÌJỌ: Hanìn, èyiùn kúò. A tún rí mííìn. Wọ́n ní, ńnú ké ẹ máa kọ́lé kan lọ́wọ́, tàbí ké ẹ sẹ̀sẹ̀ féẹ́ bèrè. Wọ́n ní ké ẹ sì dáwọ́ dúó

ná kósù yìí ó fi parí. Kí ilée yín ó má(à) dilé èmì. Njé e mo ohun tí wọn ń pè lémì?

UNCLE TÁYỌ̀: Èmì. Sé e rí, mo féẹ́ dálé-iṣé kan sílẹ̀ ni, mo dẹ̀ ti parí è. A tiè féẹ́ sí i láìpé yìí gan-an. Àwọn Èèbó tó maa bẹ̀rẹ̀ iṣé ńbẹ̀, àwọn ti féèé dé báyìí. Ọjó tá a máa sí i, a ti dá a sónà, a ti máṣọ. A à lè mówó kúò ńbẹ̀ rárá.

BÀBÁ ÌJO: Nbá sọ fún yín pé kí e yẹ̀ é kéṣé, kó rọra kọjá oṣù yìí díẹ̀.

UNCLE TÁYỌ̀: Kò ṣe é ṣe. Àwọn Èèbó ò níí gbà. Kò ṣe é ṣe. Ẹ ménu kúò ńbi èyiùn, kò ṣe é yẹ̀.

PREACHER: I see something else. They're telling me that either you're in the middle of building a house, or you're just about to begin. They say you should hold back until this month is past. Lest your house become that of the migrant rat. Do you know what I mean by a migrant rat?

UNCLE TÁYỌ̀: Migrant rat. The thing is, I want to start a factory, in fact I've finished it, and we want to open it very soon. The Europeans who are going to start work there are about to arrive. We've already fixed the date of the opening, we've ordered our cloth. We can't pull out of those arrangements now.

PREACHER: I'd advise you to postpone it for a little, just till this month is over.

UNCLE TÁYỌ̀: It's impossible. The Europeans won't agree. It's impossible. Let's drop it. It's impossible.

Thus even Uncle Táyọ̀, extravagant and unregulated in his private behavior, is bound to an externally imposed calendar in his business activities.

The church runs its own clock and calendar, which may conflict with the temporality of working life—as in the example just quoted—but which heightens and exaggerates the rigidities of an office timetable. The programs of fasting which the Preacher prescribes to his clients are governed by a strict temporality. One client is an old woman whose goods have been impounded by the customs office. She comes to confess that she can't stand the strain of the three days' fasting he prescribed for her: "On the day that I started, I fasted all day, but at just about four o'clock in the afternoon I began to feel dizzy, and it was only by God's grace that my husband was at home, because it was he who gave me some gruel to drink"; on the second day, at around the same time in the afternoon she began babbling "like a Ghanaian," and after that she gave up. The imposed timetable is impossible for her to sustain—but note that she kept her eye on the clock and knew what time it was when she began to crack. By contrast, Bísí is a model abstainer. She was prescribed 21 days' fast and kept them all. When she comes to report back to the Preacher, he takes her through the program and she is able to confirm that—as he expected—there were definite stages of change: after three days' fasting, the men who flocked to her door "were no longer as numerous, and they no longer used me like rainwater"; after seven days, only two or three men would come each day, and those that came started to propose marriage; by the seventeenth day, she had narrowed it down to the two candidates she has come to consult him about.

The Preacher, then, is at the center of a devotional time in which he assigns and monitors individual programs imposed upon the normal working days of his clients. His role as timekeeper is highlighted by the way he orchestrates his clients in the first scene. He first sees two impoverished young men and then asks them to go and wait in the backyard while he talks to the old woman. Having broached the discussion of her problem he sends her also to wait outside while he talks to Bísí. After a while she comes back in, interrupting at the crucial moment when he has just announced the meaning of his vision to Bísí. The old woman says "My husband will be expecting me" and the Preacher tells her to go home and return the next day. These exits and entrances draw attention to the Preacher's management of his clients' overlapping individual timetables, emphasizing his popularity and the authority that derives from his pivotal position.

This devotional time is enclosed within an epochal temporality which separates the pagan time of darkness from the Christian time of light (revealed when the Preacher tells the old pagan would-be convert that the age of chanting *ijálá*, making sacrifices to the gods, and uttering incantations is over) and which contrasts this-worldly time with heavenly eternity (again brought to the fore when the old pagan interprets "Our Father which art in Heaven" as a reference to his own dead father who, if he is in heaven, will presumably be awaiting reincarnation in the cyclical time of traditional thought). In this larger time frame, all the worshipper can do is "*Dúó de oore Olórun*" [wait for God's blessings] as the Preacher tells Bísí and as she herself confirms when she says she brought the names of the two suitors to the Preacher because she is ready to accept God's will on the matter: "According to the word of the Lord, we should wait until the time that God has appointed."

A third temporality, most essential to the exposition of the theme, runs alongside work time and church time: the traditional temporality of the life cycle and the behavior appropriate to each stage of human maturation. The importance of this temporality is suggested early in the play, when Bísí goes to tell her friend Bínpé that Pírí is the favored suitor and betrays her misgivings: Pírí is neither willing nor able to shower her with gifts like the other suitor, Kúnlé. Bínpé replies that once she is married everything will change: "You'll see that it is different from the time when men would accost us on the street saying 'You, come here' and things like that." This brief and casual statement alludes to traditional conceptions of the nature of the transition from girlhood to wifehood, extensively celebrated in an oral genre known as ẹkún ìyàwó (the bride's lament). One verse of ẹkún ìyàwó makes Bínpé's point more eloquently:

> I've left the stage of "Come in the evening"
> I've left the stage of "Drop in on your way back"
> I've joined the club of mothers of new-born babies
> Mother of a new-born baby that is a boy
> May good luck attend me today. (Barber 1991, 111)

Each stage has its own pleasures and satisfactions, which are quite distinct from each other. The life of carefree friendship, fun, flirtation, and dressing up gives way to the more demanding, but more respected, achievement of motherhood. The marriage ceremony, and the bridal chants that form an important part of it, mark and spell out the completeness of the transition. Bísí, however, is already well into her adult years: she boasts that anyone who saw her in the street without knowing her would think to themselves "This lady must have reached a certain age"—that is, she must be a mature woman ripe for marriage. Nonetheless she does not want to leave behind all the pleasures associated with the girlhood phase during which liaisons are formed and partners selected.

She is revealed as simultaneously too impatient and too sluggish in relation to maturational time. The Preacher has told her that if she marries Pírí she will live long and happily with him, whereas if she marries Kúnlé "things will fall apart before two o'clock," that is before their lives are half done. Yet Bísí is not prepared to marry Pírí and then wait for him to mature and become wealthy: "Do I want to wait around for soup that isn't cooked?" she says to Bínpé. She wants her wealthy man ready-made.[2] But in her own life cycle she is too slow, always postponing the moment when she crosses the line into matrimony and maternity. By the end of the play she realizes that "the morning of life" is long past: it is now high noon and the play suggests that soon it will be too late. In her final visit to the Preacher, he has another vision, in which he sees Bísí with a basket of ripe mangoes, surrounded by little children who are begging for them. "I never said I didn't want to have children" she sobs when the Preacher tells her this. Now the ripeness she had boasted of has begun to seem like over-ripeness.

Throughout the play, the theme of the passing of time is picked up in fleeting but telling allusions. When Pírí and Uncle Táyọ̀ are both waiting for Bísí in her lodgings, they begin a kind of singing contest. While Uncle Táyọ̀ gives vent to a traditional chant that seems to celebrate his own might ("On the day the elephant fell / That was a great day"), Pírí sings love songs that say "Baby, listen to my suit, in good time" and "Don't listen to the malicious people of the world / Tomorrow [i.e., the future] is going to be good." When Uncle Táyọ̀ falls out with Bísí, she accuses him of "turning the clock back"—hindering the progress of their relationship—with his unreasonable anger. Bísí, in fact, is so conscious of the passage of time that when she goes to church after successfully completing her fast, she tells the Preacher "time is getting on, but I made a vow that I would praise God with three songs [once the fast had brought about the desired result]. So as not to waste time, let me just sing one." When Pírí finally breaks off with Bísí, he demands back one of his gifts to her. In view of the pervasiveness of the idiom of time in the play, it seems hardly an accident that that gift is a clock.

The idea of time as something that can be measured, allocated, and controlled is thus interwoven with ideas of time as a process of growth and as a divine dispensation. Bísí succeeded in imposing the strict regularity of a program of fasting on her disorderly life, but the play tells us that her underlying, uncontrolled, and excessive tendencies were untouched by this. The surface regularity must harmonize with a deeper attunement to natural time and to providential time. The orderly and harmonious life that is the obverse of Bísí's would be one in which she accepted Pírí, thus deferring to providential will: she would live on a small income with him, waiting for work and discipline to produce its results in God's time, and mature with him, investing patience in their marriage until in the fullness of time she would be blessed with both children and a wealthy, well-placed husband. In this scenario, providential time, work time, and maturational time would have synchronized, and wealth would have been produced as a counterpart of fruitfulness.

This play is so full of idioms and references to time that it is hard to feel that the discursive style is accidental or insignificant. On the contrary, one can see from the foregoing that every fiber of the text bears out and comments on the theme. The actors thus seem to be able to set up, collectively, a distinctive force field of discourse for each play. Their extraordinary linguistic alertness and mutual attunement enables them to generate language which not only embodies the theme of the play but also comments on it at many levels. I suggested in Chapter 9 that the complex and extended narratives that make up a play are essential in order to produce the moral, which cannot simply be "picked" out of the air but need to be led up to, grounded in a sequence of action of which it is the outcome. But I also suggested that the play may exceed the ostensible moral encapsulated in the closing formulations. In this chapter I have shown how that effect of "surplus" works. Each of the two plays I have looked at offers an assemblage of overlapping, compatible but distinguishable moral suggestions so rich and multiplex that the "lesson" may perhaps better be seen as the play's starting point or trigger, rather than its outcome.

APHORISMS AND PUBLIC CULTURE

This apparently spontaneous, but subtle and regulated, collective linguistic creativity drew from and depended on a wider public responsiveness to language. One of the most striking and engaging aspects of life in western Nigeria in the 1970s and 1980s was the extraordinary vitality of people's relation to Yorùbá. From solemn and intensely gripping expositions of the meaning of *oríkì* to casual chats on inconsequential subjects in taxis or bars, conversations everywhere and at all times revealed people's intense satisfaction in the language, a creative and often humorous awareness of its secrets and its potential. This made daily life—often arduous materially—a sheer pleasure culturally, as one floated from one exhilarating and memorable exchange to another.

While the theater had its creative roots in this broad and enduring linguistic vitality, it was more specifically shaped by its participation in the modern Yorùbá-language public arena constituted around print, the media, church, mosque, and school. All the new popular cultural forms of the colonial era in western Nigeria addressed a pan-Yorùbá public—in principle if not in practice. All used "standard Yorùbá" of sorts most of the time, and all showed a desire to include the full range of local Yorùbá-speaking constituencies in their address. In his 1953 production of *Hannah's Trial and Triumph*, Adéjọbí closes the play with a song saluting, in turn, the Òṣogbo people, the Ẹ̀gbá, the Ìjẹ̀bú, the Ìjẹ̀ṣà, and the Ọ̀yọ́—even though it is unlikely that representatives of all those groups were present at the performance—thus evoking a larger audience of all Yorùbá speakers. For the public is linguistically convened. All popular culture genres in western Nigeria are a love affair with the Yorùbá language, fed by massive intertextuality, intergeneric migration, and continual creative innovation.

The language thus fetishized was harnessed to imparting moral lessons; it revolved around aphorisms. Yorùbás may traditionally have been "in all things . . . religious" (Idowu 1962, 5); but in the modern public arena it would be equally true to say that they are in all things ethical. Regardless of their faith, denomination, language, or place of origin, people were assumed to be united by basic, shared, commonsense principles of fair play, decency, respect, and honesty. Even today, despite the religious polarization and disaggregation discussed in Chapter 10, many Yorùbá-language public texts still stand upon a broad moral platform which is assumed to be shared by participants belonging to other ethnicities and all religious orientations.

The Yorùbá-language fortnightly newspaper *Aláròyé*, for example, is saturated with popular broad-based morality. Politics, features, profiles, commentary, and cultural pieces are all explicitly and loquaciously devoted to the development of moral themes. Even factual news reports become a trigger for extended moralizing—as in the item reporting the accidental decapitation of a schoolteacher by a faulty lawnmower blade, which begins and ends with elaborate reflections on premonitions, prayer, fate, God's will, and personal responsibility.[3] Islamic, Christian and "Yorùbá" (i.e., indigenous-traditional) perspectives are explicitly harmonized and interleaved; when protagonists from other ethnic groups are included they play exactly the same role as the Yorùbá ones, that is, as representatives of moral positions and bearers of moral experiences.[4] Popular Yorùbá songs, novels, and neo-traditional chanted poetry tend to share the newspaper's orientation toward moralizing. So the Yorùbá-language public, though it may be addressed at different times and levels as African, Nigerian, Yorùbá, Ọ̀yọ́, Muslim, Christian, or traditional, is unified by a primary, underlying address as a moral community—as parents, spouses, friends, client-employees, patron-employers. "Moralizing," so tedious to present-day Western ears, is meat and drink to the public spokespeople of the Yorùbá-speaking world (as it is, of course, to Hausa publics—see Furniss 1996—and those of many other contemporary African cultures).

In this moral public arena, language condenses with special density around proverbs, precepts, and aphorisms. Older Yorùbá verbal arts made much of such formulations, too, for they were among the repertoire of compact, "heavy" verbal items (which also included *oríkì* and lines from Ifá divination verses) that constituted the core building blocks of all the great oral literary genres (see Barber 1999). But in the modern public arena there is an overwhelming emphasis on proverbial sayings as vehicles for an explicitly didactic discourse, delivered with a new impetus toward expository clarity. Proverbs are not just cited; great pains are taken to explain them, paraphrase them, and spell out the moral lessons to be learned from them.

All the items in the newspaper *Aláròyé*, whether presented as factual news, philosophical disquisition, or personal narrative, are woven around proverbs and precepts, often stepping associatively from one to another, each being brought forward to corroborate, clarify, expand, or qualify the others. There is a regular feature dedicated to the meaning of proverbs, in which a saying is taken and expounded by embedding it in hypothetical situations but also by wrapping it in layers of analogous or digressive other sayings. Túnbọ̀sún Ọládàpọ̀'s neo-traditional published and broadcast poetry, similarly, recasts older idioms of oral poetry in a clarified, coherent discursive style where didactic points are expounded until they appear perfectly transparent—at least at first glance (for Ọládàpọ̀'s impulse toward clarity is always at war with his desire to excavate obscure and "deep" Yorùbá expressions). And, just in case the reader should get out of her depth, Ọládàpọ̀'s published texts come equipped with explanatory footnotes (Ọládàpọ̀ 1973, 1975). The contrast with traditional *oríkì*—fragmented, deliberately obscure, and extravagantly allusive—is clear.

The new didactic transparency was no doubt suggested by the presence of the school, the church, and the missionary press at the center of the Yorùbá public arena; but it was also fostered by the gradual drying up of deep local pockets of knowledge, on which the allusiveness of genres such as *oríkì* depended. Increasingly throughout the twentieth century, the mobility associated with educational expansion, waged labor, commercial farming, the intensification of trade, and the progressive break-up of large patriarchal compounds led to a dilution of intense, detailed scrutiny and commemoration of the small events of local communities. Correspondingly, the media and modern commercial live popular genres were organized to beam their messages to a wider and shallower knowledge constituency. Their public was addressed on the presumption that it shared a fairly diffuse and widely distributed cultural knowledge that was not tied to specific, local historical references or the secret, specialized secretion of meaning. And the producers of texts in the moral public arena knew that they had to constitute their knowledgeable public in the act of appealing to it: that is, they had to impart and expound, as they adduced, the crystallized, condensed forms of speech that are at the heart of Yorùbá verbal art.

Aphorisms, in this atmosphere supersaturated with moral concerns, had dynamic and generative properties very far removed from the dead clichés which some have seen as typical of the functional, deracinated meaninglessness of Western modernity (see Zijderveld 1979). The narratives of the Adéjọbí plays, as we have just observed, can be seen as existing in order to generate moral lessons; conversely, statements of moral lessons can be seen as the seeds out of which extensive narratives are made to grow. The aphorisms explain what the play is about; the play explains the meaning, or the potential application, of the aphorism. They are the point at which the language and the story—the two things the audiences set most store by—can be seen to intersect: for a proverb is both a scheme for action and a seed of speech.

Aphorisms are felt to gain depth and productivity with repeated activation. Each aphorism recalls and collects around it other analogous or contrasting sayings, stories, and memories. In many of the Adéjọbí plays, as in *Aláròyé* and in neo-traditional poetry, we see a tendency toward aphoristic ramification. Instead of imparting a single moral, the closing moments of the play often produce a flurry of formulations that are linked to each other by resemblance and analogy. We saw in *The Overreacher* that each aphorism gives rise to others, related and complementary. All the proverbs and sayings produced in the course of the final scene converge on the themes of pride, excess, and responsibility. Rather than any single one of them encapsulating the moral of the play, it seems that what we have is an orchestrated clamor in which an extensive, interwoven cluster of sayings comes to the surface, each reinforcing the others, and all suggesting an even greater reservoir of verbal resources that could still be tapped.

Homeric "formulae," according to Michael Nagler (1974), all bring with them an implicit allusion to the whole tradition from which they are drawn, so that apparent gaps and contradictions in the text are made good by the restorative work of the audience's memory. Each element is much more than itself: each evokes a vast yet coherent and organized body of text. The functioning of such a system of reference and suggestion depends, as Nagler points out, on the unity, vitality, and consensuality of the tradition. Now, it is surely a characteristic of contemporary African popular cultures that the integrity of great traditions—if it ever existed—has been fragmented and adulterated. Heterogeneity, rapid and easy incorporation of exogenous elements, and a constitutive instability and ambiguity in the Yorùbá drama are mirrored by a diverse audience, professing different faiths, hailing from different cultural and dialectal "sub-groups," pursuing different occupations. Yet in spite of that, it does seem as if the public addressed in modern Yorùbá texts, seen as a moral community rather than one based exclusively on class, ethnicity, or religion, shares a massive philosophical repertoire, realized in the textuality of aphorism.

This does not mean that there is a single consistent worldview to which all subscribe. Aphorisms can provide staging posts in discursive journeys that take all kinds of routes and arrive at widely different destinations. But it means that there is a recognized, shared *repertoire of materials* out of which to mount moral statements and recognized, approved *forms of argument* in which to present them. Through long usage, materials and modes of association suggest each other, so that any one element brings in its wake a plethora of other possibilities, each aphorism revealing the potential to activate others.

Different genres—popular theater, neo-traditional media poetry, the Yorùbá novel, newspaper commentary—carve different trajectories through the common repertoire of materials and forms of argument. The public is experienced in "reading" and collaboratively reconstituting the specific textual and discursive field surrounding different genres, while recognizing and appreciating the enormous amount of intergeneric borrowing that goes on at all levels. All these genres together address, and in addressing constitute, the same public arena, based in a shared, inclusive, commonplace, but fervently upheld morality.

Thus, though it is very Yorùbá, deeply entranced with the language and culture, the public arena addressed in these texts is also oddly inclusive and non-chauvinist. The Yorùbá are at the center of the world, but as an *example* of humanity in its moral dimension rather than as an exclusive group claiming the *only* humanity. Yorùbá values can be cited to exemplify Nigerian, African, or human values in general (Barber 1997a). When Hubert Ògúnǹdé was appointed to direct a new national dance troupe toward the end of his career, he convened dancers from every region of Nigeria: the stunning Agbor dances from the east and the fabulous Tiv masquerades from the middle belt. And he put them all in a play called *Destiny*, which revolves around the infallible predictions of Ifá, the Yorùbá deity. Ifá here does not represent Yorùbá-ness in contradistinction to Igbo-ness or Tiv-ness (though non-Yorùbá might well have felt that here was another example of Yorùbá cultural imperialism). Ifá represents Nigerianness or Africanity, not by dissolving out its Yorùbá specificity but by serving as an excellent example of a Nigerian and an African cultural entity.[5]

The extraordinary linguistic gifts of the theater company thus took their inspiration from everyday acts of verbal generativity occurring at every level throughout the population—acts which drew their sustenance from a long-term widespread popular passion for the language. But this ardor for *tiwa*—our own thing—also translated into an affirmation of much broader loyalties. In rejoicing in the language, they also simultaneously assumed and created a Yorùbá public which was imagined as transcending ethnic boundaries: a public that was convened through shared language but on the basis of shared morality and was populated with living examples of what it is to be human.

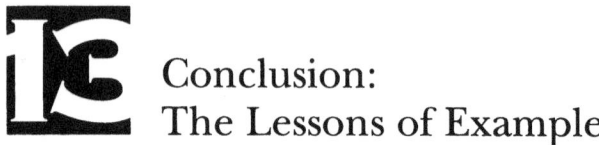 Conclusion: The Lessons of Example

GENERATIVE MATERIALISM

This book has offered an account from the ground up of the generation of plays in a Yorùbá popular theater company. This was the project Lefebvre sketched out: "taking real life as the point of departure in an investigation of how the ideas which express it and the forms of consciousness which reflect it emerge" (Lefebvre 1991, 145).

My starting point was the actors themselves, who are both the conceptualizers of the drama and the material out of which it gets its substance. In the absence of written scripts, training schools, or guild traditions, there is a peculiarly direct and immediate channel between the actors' own social experience and the plays they generate. They embody the text and tap into their experience to produce character and dialogue.

The actors are operating a business within definite practical and material constraints. The necessity of traveling to find audiences (carrying their equipment wherever they go), the necessity of keeping the theater company together without formal contracts, and the sheer unpredictability of life on the road—with variable venues, fluctuating attendance, and missing performers—means that the drama has to be built to be adaptive and flexible. Improvisation, the stock in trade of the artisan, is the foundation not only of the performance mode but also of the entire mode of theatrical production. Plays are assembled in modular form from available textual, linguistic, and human resources; but in their creation, something new is continually emergent. The play "fills out" through the innumerable strategic or spontaneous additions and variations generated by actors and manager; tracing how this happens over a period of nearly a year in the case of a particular play, we come close to sensing the growing points in the process of textual generation.

But this emergent expansion of the text is always done in the presence of an audience, and the responses of the spectators are the oxygen which sustains the growth process. The audiences co-constitute the plays, not only by their continual response of laughter and commentary as the show is in progress—responses which encourage the actors to expand, contract, or adapt their set pieces on the spot—but also because they take it upon themselves to convert the narrative into a moral lesson which they can take away and apply to their own lives. They take responsibility for their own self-edification. In the process, different sections of the audience constitute different, but overlapping and ultimately congruent, interpretations of the play's message.

And if the audience constitutes the play, it is also true that the play constitutes the audience. That is, the performance is directed toward spectators conceptualized in a particular way, as an anonymous, interchangeable and indefinitely extensive mass. The theatrical mode—the way the plays are mounted, the way the actors project themselves out from the stage, the way they use time and space—contributes to the constitution of the spectators as a new kind of public which came into being in the colonial period. The mutuality and dialectical relationship between the constitution of the play by the audience and the constitution of the audience by the play is at the very center of our understanding of the generation of plays.

From the beginning of the theater company's professional existence, the media, and television in particular, played a key role in the constitution of the theater's public. It allowed them to address a vast, unknown, population—potentially stretching to the limits of the Yorùbá-speaking world and beyond. It also brought the theater into interaction with the institutions of the state in a characteristically dialectical mode, for the television instigated changes in the live theater's style but at the same time the theater invaded the medium of the technocrats with its informal, populist, improvised theatrical mode.

What I have gone on to show is how the plays themselves—their narratives, their mode of characterization, and their moral messages—arise from the common experience of the performers and audiences, and at the same time both explore and help to constitute new kinds of social being—new ways of being social.

On the one hand, I have shown that the "givens" of the plays' settings and situations are drawn from common experiences of Yorùbá households, gender relations, and authority structures, inflected and filtered by the specific experience of the theater company members (their histories of extreme mobility, the gender tensions and authority structures internal to the company, and the relationships of the company to the Nigerian state). Their dual formation as "clerks" oriented toward schooling and as "artisans" experienced in the improvisatory techniques of manual trades not only shapes their mode of theatrical production but also colors their selection and interpretation of the central themes of the plays—notably, the exploration of clerkly "enlightenment" and artisanal "self-making." These two sides, however, are not really separate. Rather, enlightenment and self-making converge in the practice of moral edification, for self-making is the making of a moral being.

On the other hand, the theater explored and helped to constitute the public arena from which it arose and which instigated its formation. From its earliest days among the public-spirited coalition of Lagos elite-led associations, the theater grew and adapted in response to audience demand. It was the pressure of eager would-be spectators outside the milieu of the church that prompted Adéjọbí to convert the company to a professional traveling theater in 1963. This in turn led to a remarkable expansion both of subject matter and of inclusivity of address. Themes proliferated and diversified until almost any source could furnish a story. The potential audience—expanded by the increase in waged work, incomes from cash crops, and primary school education—was invited to participate on the shared basis of a pan-Yorùbá identity and a common morality rather than from any specific sub-ethnic or religious standpoint. The efflorescence of a vital, confident pan-Yorùbá popular culture—visible in the explosion of new Yorùbá genres, from novels to media poetry—was, I have suggested, in part made possible by the early establishment of a Yorùbá-language print culture, which rendered porous the boundary between the domains of official prestigious (Anglophone) culture and unofficial low-class (vernacular) culture. The theater contributed hugely to this dynamic inclusive pan-Yorùbá creativity. Its buoyancy is visible in its extraordinary linguistic confidence, which tapped into a widely shared joy in Yorùbá. Its ecumenical inclusivity—addressing a broad constituency of Muslims, Christians, and traditional worshippers as inhabitants of a common moral domain—flourished throughout the company's most productive years, until the end of the 1980s when, simultaneously, religious polarization set in and the audience turned from live theater to video, fragmenting into numerous small publics. In addressing its audience inclusively, the live theater in its heyday helped to foster a commitment to shared concerns which transcended local and denominational allegiances.

In its use of time and space, and in the way it addressed its audience as a public, the theater defined itself as a modern form, deliberately differentiated from older genres such as masquerade theater. But this modernity needs careful specification. The "enlightenment" which the theater espoused and enacted was an unstable and ambiguous category, which increasingly revealed its own underside. Modernity meant not the rejection of the traditional but the possibility of selectively recuperating it—and the editorial operation by which this was accomplished was subject to continual redefinition over the theater company's life span.

The theater put characters on stage who were autonomous and responsible for the consequences of their own actions. The dramatic mode—dispensing with narrators and commentators—required the characters to authorize their own being through their own speech. Concomitantly, they were represented as making their own decisions and acknowledging the consequences of those decisions. The lifelike detail of this style of representation seems to betoken changing ideas of personhood and self-realization. But just as the address to an ostensibly anonymous and indefinitely extensive "public" was always on the brink of dissolution—as audiences hurled repartee across the gap dividing spectacle from spectator, and as actors conceived of the audience as a reservoir of potential "helpers," expected at any moment to make themselves known—so the apparent realism of the theater's style of representation is not after all equivalent to the realism of nineteenth- and twentieth-century Europe. The characters are made to seem like real people not in order to explore actuality in and of itself but to make them more effective as bearers of appropriate moral lessons. They are not unique introspective individuals but walking proverbs. The entire project of the theater is moral. The performers' self-positioning as "preachers" and the audience's endorsement of this in their search for "lessons" gives rise to a form of theater which is neither mimetic nor spectacular, neither realist nor classical; rather, it is the discourse of example. As I shall show in a minute, this is a concept which could productively be applied to other genres of popular culture in Africa.

Thus, the new public arena which gave rise to the modern popular theater, and which the theater in turn helped to constitute, is resistant to assimilation to any universalistic before-and-after account of "the transition to modernity." In Nigeria, impersonal institutions did not supersede reliance on personal networks of patrons and "helpers." There were no national administrative or economic frameworks sufficiently powerful or comprehensive to constitute people as, in principle, equivalent and interchangeable citizens. Activities undertaken for the "public good" were most often self-help initiatives by local communities, churches, and social interest groups rather than the participation by a national bourgeoisie in a common public sphere transcending sectional interests. The public address of the theater was to an unbounded, inclusive, but locally-based constituency which was simply uninterested in the other components of the multi-ethnic nation-state. And, correspondingly, the characters that were evoked and projected from the stage revealed a range of possible constructions of personhood which did not include the "modern self" of universalist paradigms. Yorùbá, and West African, modernity needs to be accounted for in its own terms, not assimilated to a universal (i.e., Western) model. My argument has been that the popular theater is a vital clue to how these processes took place in Yorùbáland and to what kind of modern public arenas and individual selves were constituted. This is because the theater not only participated in their constitution but also reflected upon it in extensive worked-out narrative diagnoses.

I have traced these large themes—of modernity, the public arena, and the representation of the individual—up from the lives and experiences of the performers themselves. It may seem that too much has been made to rest upon too narrow a generative base. It is a basic tenet of modern literary criticism that works, and the ideas they express, cannot be explained or understood by means of an account of their authors' real-life feelings, experiences, or intentions. The work is an independent object to be understood in its own terms. So I may need to point out that this study, though it does indeed trace the generation of texts from the experience of their producers, has at no point been about the individual performers' putative intentions or emotions. It has at all times been a discussion of *repertoires*—of language, verbal genres, social situations, characters, gestures—*available* for incorporation and transformation. And these are shared repertoires rather than personal ones: insofar as elements in them may be personal or colored by personal experience (for instance, Adéjọbí's experience of lameness) they are only mobilized if they can be made to stand for common and exchangeable precepts. Indeed, to the performers and audiences themselves, experience is evaluated for its communicability and its capacity to model shared predicaments. We are not setting out to explain in psychological terms *why* the theater company said a particular thing; rather, we are trying to map out the *range* of things the theater company could say and trace the paths they took at different times through that field of possibilities. Agawu puts it well. The analysis of performance, he suggests, "establishes the conditions of possibility for certain actions, and in so doing maintains a balance between the intended and the fortuitous, the planned and the emergent" (1995, 112).

CONCEPTUAL TOOLS

Looking back over the terrain we have covered, we can trace the path of a number of key concepts which, in their interaction, provide at least a starting point for a possible comparative analysis. For though the local specificities of popular genres are remarkable and abundant, there are also striking commonalities—similar modes of cultural production, similar concerns, similar forms and styles—not to mention rapid and eclectic borrowing, right across sub-Saharan Africa. What is needed is a comparative approach which, rather than bracketing the specificities, makes them the basis of comparison.

Experience, example, and potentiality are three linked concepts which have been pivotal in the preceding chapters. **Experience,** in the accounts of the actors and their audiences, was both something you endure—synonymous with "suffering," the necessary precondition to success—and something you should learn from. An audience member, Reuben Òjó, used the English word almost as if it meant "instruction" or "guidance." He said "Their plays usually give people **experience,** so that when you go home afterward you think about it and **plan** your **life** accordingly. . . . Their plays are plays that make people **more experienced**" (Chapter 7). Experience, then, is not conceived of as an idiosyncratic, subjective, phenomenological state (as in the modernist novel), let alone as a consumer good (as in travel brochures). It is conceived of as the things that happen to people or that people are exposed to—insofar as they lay the groundwork for future success, and insofar as something can be learned from them. If it is good to learn from one's own mistakes, it is even better to learn from those of other people.[1] As the narrator exhorts the reader at the beginning of Jẹbọda's wonderful novel *Olówólaiyémọ̀,* "You my friend, the story I am about to tell is the story of my father's life. Please guard all the lessons you learn from it with the utmost care, because other people's experience is the best source of wisdom." (Jẹbọda 1964, 1). Experience, then, is essentially something that can be transmitted—extracted from the idiosyncratic web of personal circumstances and applied to other situations.

The way that other people's experience is rendered accessible in narrative texts is through **example.** "By various experiments, experience has led to art, example showing the way" as Manilius put it.[2] Exemplification was how the theater company turned "things that happened" into coherent, extensive dramatic pieces from which people could "pick a lesson." Adéjọbí's own life story, which he had told often and reflected much upon, was presented as an example of triumph over adversity (see Chapter 2). He attributed his ability to hold the theater company together—the sine qua non of theatrical success—to the fact that in his own life he presented the actors with a moral example. "If you are devoid of exemplary or inspiring conduct, of good comportment, the group cannot cohere or remain for long," he said (Jeyifo 1984, 90). Above all, the plays themselves offered the audiences examples of moral action and its consequences, and the audiences actively sought to extract these examples in order to profit from them.

The concept of example offers a productive specificity to our approach to genre. It raises a different range of questions, and suggests a different kind of answer, from those raised and suggested by thinking of the plays either as surface manifestations of an underlying mental structure (as in structuralism) or as referentially oriented representations of reality (as in much sociology of literature).

Examples are, first and foremost, irreducibly *concrete.* An approach built around the idea of exemplification dwells upon specificity and seeks to understand its purpose. Thinking of plays as examples draws attention to their "originality," in Jane Guyer's sense of the word (Guyer 1996): the ways in which they are distinctive, elude simple categorization, and work precisely through that distinctiveness.

Through their particularity, examples enable you to seize upon a phenomenon as if intuitively, with the effect of grasping all at once more than you can yet analyze. "Give me an example" I say as I struggle to comprehend your point. You give me an example but I still don't understand, so you give me another example. The second example will be different from the first, and it is in the difference—a fresh angle, a new start—that illumination resides. Though examples always point to something else beyond them—an example is always an example *of* something, usually something more general—the relationship between the exemplified and the example is not the relationship of a law with its instantiation or an underlying mental structure with its surface manifestation. Rather, the general cannot be conceptualized or stated *except* through the example: and its dimensions are never fully known, only partially indicated by a multiplication of illustrations. You work back and forth from examples to what is exemplified, never arriving at a final conclusive statable "model" but rather refreshing your conceptualization of what is being exemplified by every additional example.

Scanning across the whole corpus of plays we have looked at in this book, one can discern a number of big central but rather diffuse themes—themes about loyalty and treachery, truthfulness and deceit, hard work and destiny—which only take on definition and the power to command assent when they are seized upon through concrete cases. Even if you already "know" that treachery between friends is bad, you will go eagerly to see *The Royal Palm-nut*, which shows one friend betraying another and eventually suffering the consequences, for it is only then that the knowledge takes on definite graspable contours. Each new play *adds* to your sense of having understood a truth, rather than merely confirming by repetition the existence of an underlying ideational structure.

Rather than an underlying structure and its surface manifestation, what we are looking at is perhaps more like the relationship between a word in the dictionary and its usages. The *Oxford English Dictionary* supports its definition of a word by giving a range of examples of the word's use. The examples are only useful because they are different from each other and thus suggest a *field of possible meaning*, rather than a single definitive statement.

The relationship between the messages of *Kúyẹ̀*, *Lániyọnu*, and *The Road to Riches* could be understood in this light. All three plays take a stab at answering the same big questions about the relationship between personal effort, destiny, and success; and they all use very similar materials—situations are recycled, character types reappear (Chapter 11). Yet their conclusions are strikingly different: *Kúyẹ̀* places its wager on innate character while *The Road to Riches* emphasizes strenuous activity. Between them, these plays seem to sketch out a field of possible "takes" on the burning question of personal self-realization, related to each other in the same overlapping and contrasting way that the various senses of a word are related.

Yet the concrete specificity of the Adéjọbí plays does not indicate that what they are aiming at is a depiction of actuality or of a state of consciousness for its own sake. They are not "representations" in this sense. When people say the plays are "true," "exactly like life," they are not speaking of fiction's mimetic capacity (Chapter 11) but of its capacity to provide analogies. The point of a story told as an example is not in its own veracity or otherwise, but in the parallel cases it can be made to point to—you tell the story of the boy who cried "Wolf!" not to assert that there was in fact such a boy but as a "way of pointing out the possibility of analogous occurrences" (Walton 1990, 79). What is significant is what the plays *show*—that is, what they show us about *our* lives. This means that "exemplification is never fictive" (Goodman 1981, 126), but it is not factual either; it is demonstrative.

For an example is not only always an example *of* something, it is also always proffered in order to demonstrate something *to* someone. It is directed toward an addressee, who is invited thereby to assess it and extrapolate from it the features relevant to what is being explained. "The rhetorical force of example," as Gelley states, "is to impose on the audience or interlocutor an obligation to judge" (Gelley 1995, 14). This, as we have seen, is an obligation the audiences accept willingly and indeed take it upon themselves to seek out. If, as was suggested in Chapter 10, the characteristic posture of West African "enlightenment" is an editorial stance which selects and modifies existing realities from a quasi-external position, then exemplification is the mode in which it accomplishes this. Exemplification is inherently selective, demonstrative, and assertive: it involves taking up a position in relation to what is being demonstrated.

Looking at the plays as examples, indeed, causes the whole question of the distinction between fiction and fact (and the question of whether it coincides with the distinction between literature and non-literature[3]) to fade into the background. The same thing can be exemplified by a historical figure, a character from fiction, and a personage from mythology. They work equally and equivalently as examples, because they all have the capacity to bear—to bear out—a story which demonstrates something. As Carolyn Heilbrun observes, "Lives do not serve as models; only stories do that" (1988, 37). It is in this sense that the Adéjọbí stories are recognized as "true," whether their source is a novel, as in *Kúyẹ̀*; an oral tale, as in *The Royal Palm-nut;* or something which the playwrights believe actually happened, whether in primordial times, as in *The Return of Odùduwà*, or recently, as in *Adédigba's Co-wife*.

The concept of example supports a view of ideology as a field which you inhabit and through which you find varying routes of argument, in contrast to the structuralist view of ideology as a permanent paradigm or structuring device which inhabits you and which governs all the ephemeral output of your expressive activity. It is a view which lends itself better to understanding how ideas change. Whenever a new historically attested use of the word comes to light, the range of possible meanings indicated in the dictionary must be expanded. Small increments and shifts eventually culminate in a "new" meaning.

This brings us to a third concept which has played a central and organizing role in this study: the concept of **potentiality**. Voloshinov argues that a word, in the sense of its dictionary definition, "means nothing; it only possesses potentiality—the possibility of having a meaning within a concrete theme" (1973, 101). It is in *use*—in actual utterance in specific situations—that words fill out with (thematic) meaning, pinned down by intonation, the identities of and relations between speaker and hearer, the setting to which they refer, their shared "purview" or ideational horizon, and so on. And this meaning is never fixed or stationary, but always a moment in an ongoing interactive exchange. But what is additionally apparent is that the "potential for meaning" Voloshinov speaks of is not *prior* to the concretization of a word: rather, the potential for meaning *arises from* the experience of multiple overlapping and analogous uses of the word in concrete utterance. "Examples" come first; the "definition" of the word comes afterward. With each use, the range of potential meaning may be tested, the limits of previous usage pushed out, new shades of meaning imparted. It is people's experience, then, that generates their sense of the potentiality of things.

Potential is what is as yet undecided. And every chapter of this book will have demonstrated that the actors and audiences of the popular theater understand the whole of experience as imbued with potentiality: everything is continually emergent, continually requiring to be *worked out* afresh in the light of new circumstances. "It's because what tomorrow brings is never the same as today that the *babaláwo* consults Ifá every four days," as the proverb states. Each treatment of a well-worn theme generates something new; each performance of the "same" play re-generates it. People do not regard themselves as being actuated by rules and norms: destiny itself is emergent, only disclosing itself as a result of the individual's self-motivated original activity, his ẹsẹ̀ purposefully taking him along the path where his orí is headed (Chapter 11). "Do not write people off: no one knows what someone may become tomorrow."

The concepts of experience, example, and potential work together to suggest how people continually generate and regenerate their moral environment. They give a handle on characteristic features of performance and discourse in West African popular culture: prime among which are the tendency to multiplication and proliferation; the analogical mode; and the method of composition by assemblage.

The concepts of experience, example, and potential draw attention to the proliferative processes in West African cultural production, bringing us closer to understanding what Jane Guyer has called "the social production of multiplicity among singular people" (Guyer 1996, 2). Examples are inherently multiplicative, suggesting other examples analogically and also asking to be re-enacted in new circumstances by those to whom the lesson is directed ("follow my example"). The point of an example, then, is not so much that it can be repeated as that it can be multiplied. Lessons and examples generate each other in potentially endless analogical chains. Every plot recalls other plots, which is why they can recycle bits of each other; why it is OK to take the title of a defunct play and give it to a new one; why a character can be distinctive and yet in recognizable continuity with another character in another play. It is not because the theater company are short of material or lack powers of invention. To explain that they practice bricolage, making use of what materials come to hand, does not answer the question of why such bricolage is favored when other modes of dramaturgy were well within their ken. Bricolage works for their purposes because all the plays, plots, themes, characters, and elements are different, distinctive, specific, alternative "examples" of the consequences of moral action. They are not interchangeable, because examples, as I have suggested, work aggregatively rather than repetitively, but they are nonetheless related to each other by strong family resemblances, suggesting the presence of larger fields of argument, crisscrossed with tracks and routes left by innumerable passages.

We can see the analogical mode being played out continually in Yorùbá popular texts—in the digressive layering method of exposition in *Aláròyé,* in the piling up of parallel or related observations in neo-traditional poetry and in novels such as *Olówólaiyémọ̀,* in the flurry of proverbs toward the end of *The Overreacher.* In all these cases, an argument is mounted not by exhaustively analyzing a single definitive statement but by building up an argumentative redoubt through multiple, different, analogous, overlapping, and mutually corroborating statements, cases, or illustrations.

This, in turn, sheds light on the process of composition that I have called "assemblage": a process that gives rise to texts or performances governed by an aesthetic principle not of organic unity so much as of effective impact. The multiplicative and analogical modes favor aggregation and "filling out." It might be helpful here to use Peter Munz's version of the idea of "concrete universals": characters and narrative situations that are composed or assembled out of elements drawn from diverse sources but fused to form something that is *recognized* by audiences as *corresponding* or answering to their own experience without exactly matching anything that ever really happened or existed. "It is as though the reflection in the mirror suddenly shows up a central theme or the red thread running through the particular events; without in any way smudging or effacing the manifold detailed features of the particular story" (Munz 1956, 13). What they show us is the *kind* of thing that happens when that kind of person behaves in that kind of way.

This mode of multiplication, analogy and assemblage is, indeed, what makes narratives and characters available for specialized appropriation by sections of the audience—young women appropriating the young woman character from whom to learn a lesson, married men the husband, and so on. The lessons that these categories of participants "pick" are different but analogous. The different categories of spectators enter into the play's dense mat of analogous lessons from different angles and extract those they find appropriate to their own experience and situation. It is the analogical connections that make the enterprise "whole."

Multiplication, analogy, and assemblage evoke potential, each example suggesting others. They suggest the inexhaustible profusion of ways in which moral lessons can be demonstrated and lived out—or avoided. They ask the audience to consider those things that have not yet happened to them. You will have noticed that in many of the Adéjobí plays, as in *Olówólaiyémò*, the examples are negative ones: awful warnings of how *not* to behave, with the injunction to live out one's own experience differently from that of the dramatic protagonists. In these cases, what is good is for the potential to remain precisely that. In others—like *Kúyè* and *Lániyonu*—potential is the potential for self-realization and the play demonstrates that it can be unexpectedly fulfilled. The plays thus continually sit on the frontier between what is and what may—or should, or should not—become.

COMPARATIVE STUDY

The conjunction of these key concepts provides a starting point for a sociology of cultural production which may be useful in other studies of popular culture in Africa and elsewhere.

Yorùbá popular theater draws on a repertoire of techniques found in other small artisanal businesses in the region (Adam 1995), in farming practices (Guyer 1997), and in social networking (Barnes 1986). The same strategies are used in all these domains to compose a working unit through principles of assemblage—recruiting employees, colleagues, clientele, suppliers, complementary specialists, and "helpers" of all kinds. These strategies, in the theater company, apply both to the assemblage of the company and the assemblage of a play, a performance. Business modes and aesthetic preferences converge. The strategy is one of keeping options open, having irons in the fire, and producing a profusion of varieties.

The study of the popular theater's modes of generation, then, can be broadened by situating them comparatively among other parallel institutions and practices within the Yorùbá environment, thus bringing into view a whole social and economic field of operations of which the theater is just one example or one version.

But comparison can also range further afield. The Yorùbá popular theater takes its place in a zone of cultural production which stretches right across the continent. In this "fractal" and "polythetic" field of comparison (Appadurai 1996, 46), recurrent similarities suggest themselves: artisanal modes of cultural production predicated upon individual, entrepreneurial initiative; the presence of a culturally instigatory "intermediate" stratum of the population, active, aspirational but excluded from the elite; the production of new genres of text and performance which are created artisanally and for profit, but which are directed to public edification and which are met halfway by self-improving audiences committed to the active appropriation of moral lessons; the constitution, through this mode of address, of a new kind of "public," in part defined by the commercial accessibility of the new genres (they are detached from ritual and hierarchical occasions and open to anyone who can pay for the ticket), and by new means or modes of communication (public halls and stages, television, radio, recordings, print) enabling the imagining of an audience as anonymous and indefinitely extensive; new modes of representation of the person focusing on the self-activating and self-responsible individual, portrayed in a quasi-realist mode with quotidian detail familiar from the audience's own experience.

The recurrence of these fundamental features throws up remarkable echoes and parallels across the continent. The vitality of the moral public is found everywhere. A key factor, for example, in the "dynamic, expanding, adaptive nature of Hausa culture is . . . the strength of its moral discourse" (Furniss 1996, 214). In Ghana, we learn, TV audiences overwhelmingly assert that they watch in order to benefit from the "lesson," which, as in Yorùbá popular theater, is usually a moral lesson they can apply to their own lives (Ametewee 1993). In Zulu radio drama, audiences engage with the programs in an overwhelmingly active manner (five and a half million letters were sent by listeners to the Bantu Language Services in 1981), and one respondent explained that "It's the *working through* [the narrative] that is important" (Gunner 2000, my italics). The primacy of production and its fusion with consumption—such that "consumers" see themselves as producers of edification, while producers are often in the process consuming and showing people how to consume novel cultural goods—is also evidently ubiquitous. Across the continent, small-scale productive activity mediates people's relations with both the state and the global cultural environment.

Only further empirical studies can establish the extent and significance of the resemblances and divergences between these localized forms. To be fruitful, such comparative study will have to remain firmly planted in the rich soil of distinctive histories, genres, and lives. In the Adéjọbí Company's plays, the concrete specificity of its evocations of place, person, and event are what bed the moral lesson down and render it incontrovertible. This, it seems likely, is also true of other popular genres in Africa and beyond. Their detail, then, is indispensable. If such popular traditions appear to deliver similar messages over and over again with undiminished sincerity and zeal, it is because the stories are continually revitalized by the way they are worked through and worked out, differently specified each time.

What this approach may finally enable us to appreciate about the Yorùbá popular theater—and other African popular genres too—is their excess. They continually do more than is needed to affirm the wisdom they seek to impart. They add a luxuriance of detail, of digressions and embellishments; they create people that the public will not relinquish; and they revitalize the language instead of just tapping into it. Thus in generating a play, the performers regenerate themselves, their audiences and their cultural sphere; in evoking potentiality, they continually promise to go beyond what they have previously done.

APPENDIX 1

SYNOPSES

Hannah's Trial and Triumph (late 1940s)

Elkana has two wives: **Hannah,** the beloved senior wife, who is childless, and **Peninna,** the junior wife, who is blessed with many children. Jealous Peninna never misses an opportunity to taunt Hannah about her barrenness. The family prepares to go on its annual excursion to Silo to make sacrifice to God. Hannah is too grieved to eat and stands apart praying to God for a child until the priest **Eli** sees her and thinks she must be drunk. But no, Hannah sings, that is not the case: "No my lord / I am a woman of sorrowful spirit / I have drunk neither wine nor strong drink / but I poured out my soul before the Lord." Eli then blesses her, and the next scene is a dramatic representation of childbirth, in which the ever-attentive Elkana is thrown into a panic, rushing around calling for medicine. Then the child (**Samuel**) is born and its naming ceremony is held with much rejoicing.

In the second half of the play, the young Samuel, serving the priest Eli, is called three times by God and finally entrusted with a prophecy, that Eli's line will be wiped out because of the arrogance and greed of his sons **Finihasi** and **Hofini**. The Philistines prepare for war, defeat the Israelites once, defeat them again, and take the Ark of the Covenant. The news of Finihasi's and Hofini's death in battle is brought to Eli and he falls down and dies. The last song points out that this was no accident: "The child[ren] you bore caused this to happen to you / . . . 'I have given birth—I have given birth'—that is not a child / To give birth is one thing, to educate the child is another / Educating a child is one thing, the child being wise is another / Anyone who gives birth to a child that is not wise—he has exposed himself to a raging conflagration."

The Gospel Fruit in Oshogbo (1960)

A scene in Heaven, where God calls for a volunteer to go to earth to correct human dereliction, serves as prologue to the arrival of the first Christian missionary in Òsogbo, **Rev. John Mackay,** in 1900. In Òsogbo, we see "the people at worship before the advent of Christianity," engaged in several different òrìsà festivals. Mackay arrives at the **Atáoja's** court in the middle of the Òsun festival. Their cordial encounter is facilitated by an interpreter; their comic mutual misunderstandings do not prevent enlightened co-operation. The next scene shows **Odegbaro,** an Erinlè worshipper, deciding to go to work for Mackay because he urgently needs money; the scene after shows Mackay rejecting him, since he will not employ pagans. Odegbaro immediately volunteers to become a Christian, and Mackay sends him off to Ibàdàn to get an ABD (a child's reading primer). In the next scene the early converts (all named, among them Adéjobí senior) preach to the pagans and secure some instant converts. Another scene depicts Mackay tending the sick. A more confrontational episode then follows, in which Mackay opposes the Sàngó cult's custom of expropriating victims of lightning strikes. When the Ṣàngó worshippers next try it, Mackay and his followers are there to intervene. The Atáọja and eventually the district officer from Ìbàdàn step in to modify the traditional custom in a manner accepted by all. In the next scene Mackay persuades a skeptical population of the value of schooling, so that instead of sending their slaves, all the chiefs right up to the Atáọja himself begin sending their own sons and daughters to Mackay's primary school. There follows a schoolroom scene with all the children chanting the alphabet. Finally, we are shown the building of the first church. Teams of men and women dig and mold the mud. One woman is lazy and prefers to powder her face rather than mold mud. Ọlá, one of the first converts, throws mud in her face to teach her a lesson—and this, apparently, is where the history ends. A final song exhorts the people "*Olọkọ mọkọ, ah! iṣẹ ya . . . kenikeni maṣe ṣọlẹ o*" [Owner of the hoe, take up your hoe, it's time to work . . . let no one be lazy].

Kúyẹ̀ (c. 1964)

Kúyẹ̀ is a deaf and dumb orphan boy who is brought up in a village called Ayétòrò by his aunt, a **Pepper Seller,** until he annoys her by protesting too violently at her attempt to sell off his dead father's valuable clothes. The Pepper Seller then hands Kúyẹ̀ over to her cousin, **Àlàbí,** a well-meaning but credulous farmer under the thumb of his wife **Ṣègi.** Ṣègi is not too pleased to have to take in an extra mouth to feed. She urges Àlàbí to find work for the boy, but they cannot think of any profession he would be able to do.

When Àlàbí goes out to the farm, Kúyẹ̀ witnesses the visit of Ṣègi's lover and tries to use mime to tell Àlàbí about it on his return. However, Ṣègi fobs Àlàbí off with the story that the visitor was a woman friend of hers. She then proceeds to get rid of Kúyẹ̀ by falsely accusing him of stealing her soup and attacking her with a cudgel. Àlàbí drives Kúyẹ̀ out of the village.

Kúyẹ̀ wanders through the bush until he comes to Ẹgbéjọdá, the capital of the district. Here, the **Ọba** is presiding over a wrestling match in the hope of finding someone to defeat **Ṣégè,** the reigning champion and terror of the town. Ṣégè defeats all comers until Kúyẹ̀ innocently wanders in and, without understanding what is going on, enters the arena and throws the champion. The Ọba gives him the title of Balógun, and the Ọba's daughter **Mojísọlá** falls in love with him. Ṣégè, consumed by jealousy, uses magical incantations to bewitch Kúyẹ̀ and drive him out of town into the forest.

In the forest Kúyẹ̀ witnesses a strange scene: a sick spirit enters, goes to a certain bush, plucks the leaves, and rubs itself with the juices. It then recovers its vitality and prances off. Kúyẹ̀ imitates the spirit without knowing why. The juices of the leaves enter his ears and mouth, and he gains the power to hear and speak.

Two chiefs sent out by the Ọba to look for him turn up and are astonished when Kúyẹ̀ copies everything they say. They take him back to the palace, to the joy of the Ọba and Mojísọlá, and he continues to amaze everyone by his attempts at speech. The Ọba betroths him to Mojísọlá.

Meanwhile back in Ayétòrò Àlàbí is planning a party when two debt collectors arrive from Ẹgbéjọdá. Despite Àlàbí's attempts to pull the wool over their eyes, they identify Ṣègi as the debtor and arrest both her and Àlàbí, dragging them away to the capital.

At the palace in Ẹgbéjọdá, Kúyẹ̀—now resplendently dressed and in perfect command of Yorùbá—is recounting the sequence of events that led to his present happy situation. Àlàbí and Ṣègi are dragged in to face charges of debt. Kúyẹ̀ recognizes them, though they do not recognize him. He asks for the Pepper Seller to be brought in too. The Ọba allows Kúyẹ̀ to conduct the case. Kúyẹ̀ reminds them of the deaf and dumb orphan who was recently such a thorn in their flesh; he then reveals his identity to them and magnanimously forgives them their wrongdoing.

Láníyọnu (c. 1967)

Láníyọnu is a wealthy and successful businessman who wishes to help his two impoverished friends, **Másọmínù** and **Òtòlórìn**. He offers to lend them money to set up their own businesses. However, they wrongly suspect that his wealth comes from a machine or magical device, and instead of accepting his offer they break into his house at night, killing his wife and driving Láníyọnu into the forest. They of course do not find a money machine, and are last seen turning to highway robbery.

In the forest Láníyọnu is attacked by a horde of evil spirits and left for dead. He is revived by the beneficent water deity **Omídiyùn,** who presents him with a magical death-dealing staff before disappearing forever back into the river. Láníyọnu sets off on a quest to seek out malefactors and punish them wherever he finds them.

Meanwhile in the nearby town of Ayélẹ̀rù, **Àràbà** (the head of the diviners) and the town chiefs are holding a meeting to discuss two pressing problems: the Ọba has died and a successor has not yet been installed; and the town is being persecuted by a man-eating monster. Àràbà consults Ifá and learns that the only way to appease the monster is to offer it a human sacrifice—the late Ọba's eldest daughter **Adéìfẹ́**. The chiefs are aghast, but Ifá will accept no substitute, and eventually the chiefs call for the princess and tell her that she has been chosen to carry the sacrifice to the monster's forest shrine.

The chiefs escort the princess to the shrine, tie her up, and leave her there. The monster approaches. Adéìfẹ́'s pitiful sobs attract the attention of Láníyọnu, wandering in the forest nearby. On hearing her story, he waits for the monster to return and then kills it with the magical staff. He releases Adéìfẹ́, escorts her back to Ayélẹ̀rù, bursts in upon the astonished chiefs, and rebukes them for their callousness. They at first refuse to believe that the monster is dead, but eventually are convinced and are thoroughly cowed by Láníyọnu's magical staff. They ask him to be their new Ọba, saying that he was the stranger that Ifá had predicted would come from afar to ascend the throne of Ayélẹ̀rù. Láníyọnu at first demurs, but then having warned the chiefs that any misbehavior will be instantly punished by death, accepts both the throne and Adéìfẹ́'s hand in marriage. He is dressed in splendid robes and proclaimed Ọba.

The Royal Palm-nut (Èkùrọ́ Ọlọ́jà) (c. 1968)

The town chiefs and **Àràbà,** the head of the diviners, meet to choose a successor to the throne from among five eligible candidates. Ifá reveals that two of the candidates—**Ayélàágbé** and **Tòkunbọ̀**—are equally favored. The Àràbà reminds the chiefs that at the late Ọba's death, one of the ritual items needed for kingly installation had gone missing—the "royal palm nut," a rare type of palm nut very difficult to find. They decide to kill two birds with one stone by sending the two rival candidates off on a quest: the first to find a royal palm nut will be chosen as Ọba.

Ayélàágbé has a bosom friend, **Tóògùn,** who agrees to help him to organize a search for a royal palm nut. But Ayélàágbé's wife **Dìẹ̀kọ́lá** is having an affair with a neighbor, **Aṣaásan,** and Tóògùn happens to be there when she is caught in flagrante by Aṣaásan's wife. Tóògùn is bound by a pact of friendship to tell Ayélàágbé what he has learned. Realizing that she cannot dissuade him from exposing her, Dìẹ̀kọ́lá launches a pre-emptive strike, telling her husband that Tóògùn came to the house to rape her. Ayélàágbé believes his wife and drives Tóògùn out of the town.

In exile in the bush, Tóògùn and **Débòmí** his wife accidentally come into possession of a royal palm nut. Back in town, Ayélaágbé and Díẹ̀kọ́lá get wind of this find, and send an accomplice, the old chief Àró, to seize it. Àró goes to Tóògùn's farm hut and finds out where he keeps the palm nut, but fails to get hold of it before Tóògùn drives him away at gunpoint. Díẹ̀kọ́lá now undertakes to go herself and steal it. She uses magical preparations to soften Tóògùn's resistance, and he receives her affectionately—much to Débòmí's disgust—but the palm nut she steals is not the real one. Tóògùn had been forewarned by a dream and had substituted an ordinary palm nut; the royal one is safely hidden. Realizing that Díẹ̀kọ́lá and Ayélaágbé might nonetheless try to pass the ordinary one off as a royal palm nut, Tóògùn and Débòmí hurry back to town together and arrive just as the populace is about to acclaim Ayélaágbé as the new Ọba. Tóògùn exposes the fraud and is allowed to choose which of the two candidates he will bestow the genuine palm nut upon. He chooses Tòkunbọ̀, who is installed as Ọba to general rejoicing.

Taking Care of Kúnlé (Ìtọ́júu Kúnlé) (c. 1975)

Wúrà, the mother of Kúnlé and wife of Ọ̀ṣọ́, goes on a trip by boat to a nearby market and is presumed drowned when the boat capsizes. Ọ̀ṣọ́ is devastated when the news is broken to him. Wúrà's friend Àṣàbí, a widow who lives nearby, immediately tries to move in on Ọ̀ṣọ́, on the excuse of helping to look after Kúnlé. Ọ̀ṣọ́ rebuffs her at first, but she offers him some food which she has spiked with a love potion, and soon he is besotted. Àṣàbí proceeds to install herself in Ọ̀ṣọ́'s house, raid Wúrà's wardrobe and mistreat Kúnlé. The elders of Ọ̀ṣọ́'s family observe and criticize but are unable to intervene.

Wúrà, meanwhile, has not drowned, but has been washed up in a neighboring town where she is treated in hospital. When she is discharged, she returns and is taken to the **Baálé** (the head of the compound) by **Ayọ́runbọ̀** (a money collector who travels around on business and who happened to be on the same boat as Wúrà both when she left the village and when she returned). The Baálé warns Wúrà that her husband has married again. She takes this philosophically, but when she is told that the new wife is her best friend Àṣàbí she is outraged by the betrayal and hastens home—accompanied by the family elders—to confront them.

Caught in the middle of a romantic interlude with Àṣàbí, Ọ̀ṣọ́ is deeply mortified. Àṣàbí (dressed in Wúrà's clothes) runs to hide in Wúrà's bedroom, and is dragged out by Wúrà. Ọ̀ṣọ́ is told to choose between the two of them. He chooses Wúrà, and Àṣàbí is driven out with mockery and insult.

Articulated Lorry (Àjàgbé Ejò) (late 1970s)

A wealthy **landlord** has just been made chairman of a local political party, and in keeping with his newfound status decides to introduce new rules of behavior for his tenants. He summons them to a meeting: **Bàbáa Wándé**, a hard-drinking truck driver; his wife **Ìyáa Bùnmi**; a shopkeeper, **Bàbáa Fàtái**; and a young clerk, **Àlàbí**. He announces his political elevation as well as his new rules, and the tenants respond in different ways to both.

Àlàbí's mother arrives to tell Àlàbí that she has found a bride for him; Àlàbí is not interested as he wants to further his education. Ìyáa Bùnmi insinuates herself into the conversation and promises Àlàbí's mother that she will take Àlàbí in hand.

When Bàbáa Wándé next goes on a trip, Ìyáa Bùnmi visits Àlàbí's room under various pretexts, and tries to seduce him. He rebuffs her, and when Bàbáa Wándé returns he tries to tell him about it. Ìyáa Bùnmi gets her story in first, accusing Àlàbí of insulting Bàbáa Wándé as soon as his back was turned. She goes on to frame Àlàbí, accusing him of laying down a charm to kill Bàbáa Wándé. All the other tenants believe her and predict dire consequences for Àlàbí, but the landlord decides to set a test. On his advice, Bàbáa Wándé pretends to leave on another trip, and Àlàbí pretends to seek Ìyáa Bùnmi's favor with heartfelt apologies and romantic invitations. Ìyáa Bùnmi falls into the trap. She agrees to visit Àlàbí in his room at four o'clock. When she keeps this assignment, Bàbáa Wándé and Bàbáa Fàtái are watching through the window. Her guilt is exposed and Àlàbí is fully exonerated.

External Appearances (Mo Ráwọ̀) (late 1970s)

Bísí is a beautiful, youngish woman with many admirers and many influential contacts in the city where she works and lives in rented accommodations. She has become anxious, however, because none of her lovers seems interested in marriage. She goes to an Aládùúrà church and is prescribed a program of fasts and vigils by the **preacher.** She keeps faithfully to this program, and by the end of it the flood of admirers has narrowed down to two men, both of whom are seriously proposing marriage. She goes back to the preacher to ask him to determine through a vision which of the two she should marry. But when the preacher names **Pírí,** the younger and poorer of the two, Bísí is disappointed. She eventually breaks off with the other suitor, but meanwhile acquires a new one—**Uncle Táyọ̀,** an older and much richer man, a boastful businessman who promises her the car of her choice if she will marry him. She keeps both men dangling while she tries to extract the best possible marital bargain from each. But when the two men meet in her lodgings and discover what she is up to, both of them break with her.

Bísí receives a visit from her rural cousin **Àdùkẹ́,** who has brought her oldest son for Bísí to look after so that he can benefit from her contacts to get a job in the city. However, when Bísí advises Àdùkẹ́ to limit her childbearing—for Àdùkẹ́, though younger than Bísí, is heavily pregnant with her seventh child—Àdùkẹ́ in turn tells Bísí that women should do their childbearing early in life so that they will be secure later on. Bísí realizes that she has postponed marriage too long. She goes back to the preacher and tearfully blurts out that she is back to square one. The preacher tells her that no matter how many fasts she keeps, she will go on failing unless she can overcome her "greed."

The Overreacher (Fọlájiyọ̀)[1] (late 1970s)

A newly installed **Ọba,** accompanied by praise-singing royal wives, announces that his regime will be different from that of his predecessors: he has introduced new laws governing the market, crafts, and marriage customs. Although the new laws are ridiculous, the townspeople make no protest. The Ọba then calls upon his chiefs one by one and proceeds to interrogate, insult, and finally dismiss them, announcing that he will rule without their advice. His messenger, **Gbajúmọ̀,** warns him against this, but when the Ọba threatens him with death (by drinking a mixture of cassava meal and cement), Gbajúmọ̀ quickly changes his tune.

The Ọba announces that he wants to marry the daughter of the **Ìyálóde**—the women's chief he has just dismissed—and Gbajúmọ̀ is sent to fetch the Ìyálóde back so that the Ọba can tell her to prepare the girl for marriage. The Ìyálóde protests that her daughter is already engaged to be married to someone else, but the Ọba does not care, and threatens the Ìyálóde with death unless she complies at once.

The Ìyálóde returns home and tells her daughter, **Rẹ̀mínikẹ́ẹ́,** the bad news. Rẹ̀mínikẹ́ẹ́ refuses point blank to have anything to do with the Ọba. The Ìyálóde goes out declaring that her daughter will be the death of her. Rẹ̀mínikẹ́ẹ́ sings a song declaring her love for her betrothed husband, **Olútìmíléyìn.** Gbajúmọ̀ arrives and propositions her, extracting a promise that she will visit him in his apartments by the palace. Gbajúmọ̀ leaves; Olútìmíléyìn arrives, and Rẹ̀mínikẹ́ẹ́ tells him about the Ọba's demand. The Ìyálóde tells him it is all over and offers to give him the bride price back. Olútìmíléyìn seems undecided, but Rèmíníkèé stands firm. Gbajúmọ̀ returns, picks a fight with Olútìmíléyìn, and is thoroughly beaten. Just then the Ọba arrives in person with his entourage. Olútìmíléyìn hides in a sack. Rèmíníkèé defies the Ọba. The Ọba seizes the sack—thinking it is yams—and departs.

Back at the palace, Gbajúmọ̀ devises a scheme to capture the girl by the false accusation that he has spent money on her (by way of engagement) and that she now denies it. The Ìyálóde and Rèmíníkèé come to the palace to answer the charge, and Rèmíníkèé is seized. At night, Rèmíníkèé and Olútìmíléyìn find they are locked up in the same room; as they discover each other, the Ọba enters but is prevented from raping Rèmíníkèé by the intervention of a spirit. The spirit also visits a strange affliction upon the Ọba: he is now unable to speak and barks like a dog.

The **Ìyá Awo** (divination priestess) is consulted and reveals that the Ọba must ask the young couple's forgiveness before he can be restored to normal. He does so. The lovers are united and the chastened Ọba begins to reign in a more accountable manner.

Besotted Bridegroom (Ọkọ Ìyàwó) (early 1980s)

Tàfá has two wives: **Ìyáa Ṣeun,** the senior, is long-suffering and devoted; **Mosún,** the younger, is wealthy and domineering. Mosún plans to build a house on her late mother's family land. She bribes the **Baálé** (head of the family) to agree to make a plot of family land available, but runs into opposition from one of the elders, **Bùárí,** who explains that all the land has already been divided up. Mosún quarrels with Bùárí, and then goes home and tells Tàfá about it. Tàfá agrees to accompany her on a second visit to her mother's family. Bùárí stands by his assertion that there is no land, Mosún threatens to bring in her **contractor** to bulldoze the old compound buildings, and a full-blown slanging match develops, in the course of which Tàfá insults Bùárí unforgivably and Bùárí obtains Tàfá's full name (a necessary prerequisite to cursing someone). Bùárí goes to Tàfá's house to confirm his intentions; he meets Ìyáa Ṣeun, whose gentle demeanor and heartfelt pleas serve to dissuade him from cursing Tàfá. But then Tàfá and Mosún return and repeat their insults; Bùárí leaves threatening vengeance. Bùárí uses a firepot and incantations to curse Tàfá. Tàfá is struck blind. The wives take him to a *babaláwo*, who divines that he has offended someone and must "beg" that person before his sight can be restored. Tàfá and Mosún go to Bùárí, but instead of begging him, Mosún insults him all over again. Bùárí, on the point of being placated, now throws the firepot into the river, making the curse irrevocable. Mosún, learning from the diviner that Tàfá's blindness is now permanent, packs her property and leaves. Tàfá curses Mosún. He goes to Mosún's family compound again to beg Bùárí to reverse the curse. Bùárí reveals that it is now too late. Mosún bursts in, completely mad as a result of Tàfá's curse.

The Heir (Àkọ́bí Olóògbé) (early 1980s)

Bámgbádé has died, leaving a young widow, **Bọ́lánlé,** in Ayédùn, the town where he has lived for many years in rented accommodations. His landlord, **Tàfá,** takes responsibility for the funeral arrangements and then escorts Bọ́lánlé to Bámgbádé's home town to break the news of his death.

Meanwhile Bámgbádé's former driver, **Lánre**—a highly successful con man—returns to Ayédùn and learns that not only is Bámgbádé dead but that Bámgbádé's only son Lásún is missing, presumed dead. Lánre loses no time in going to Bámgbádé's home town and impersonating Lásún, claiming all Bámgbádé's property, including his widow. His dissolute and arrogant behavior quickly makes him unpopular with Bámgbádé's family, but it is only when the real **Lásún** returns that they realize the truth and are able to unmask him.

The Road to Riches (Ọ̀nà Ọlà) (early 1980s)

Ọláòṣebìkan, a rich and virtuous businessman, is celebrating his birthday in lavish style when one of the guests is dragged away in fury by his wife. This guest turns out to be **Tàfá,** Ọláòṣebìkan's bosom friend, who is as poor as Ọláòṣebìkan is rich. Tàfá's wife, **Ìyáa Ṣèyí,** angrily nags him to extract from Ọláòṣebìkan the secret of his wealth. Ọláòṣebìkan insists that the secret is hard work, but Tàfá and Ìyáa Ṣèyí refuse to believe this. Eventually Ọláòṣebìkan decides to teach them a lesson. He makes Tàfá work on a building site to raise the money needed to make the "medicine" that will make him rich; he then invents a nocturnal ceremony involving three painful ordeals for the couple, after which he presents them with two closed calabashes containing the secret of wealth. One contains the message "The world rejects truth," the other the message "Work to have money." The couple do not understand until Ọláòṣebìkan explains that it is a lie that money can be gained by magic; the only secret is to work hard and wait for God's blessing.

The Secret Is Out (Gbangbá DẸkùn): from *Atọ́ka* (vol. 86, nos. 1–5, 1981)

Bàbáa Wándé is an office worker who has been passed over for promotion for many years and who has sunk into gloom and despair as a result. His more resilient wife, **Adéṣọ́dún,** urges him to keep hoping. She also has a job, and independently makes arrangements to put down the deposit on a plot of land so that they can begin to build their own house. While Bàbáa Wándé complains that they have no money to build, she thinks up ways to economize (e.g., by juggling the children's education) so that the building can begin.

Soon afterward, Bàbáa Wándé receives a big promotion and the building goes forward more rapidly. He becomes the target of seductive advances from his gold-digging secretary, **Bísí,** and quickly succumbs. They conduct an affair in the unfinished house, and relations with Adéṣọ́dún and the children at home deteriorate. So does Bàbáa Wándé's work at the office, exacerbated by the interventions of Bísí's former friends, her fellow office workers who disapprove of the affair. When Bàbáa Wándé becomes involved in a minor car accident, Bísí has an excuse to come to the house and tend his injury. Adéṣọ́dún realizes that rumors about his affair are true.

Soon Bísí has pushed him into promising to marry her, and he secretly opens negotiations with his family elders in his home town. These old men are all in favor of Bàbáa Wándé taking a second wife and show little sympathy for Adéṣọ́dún, despite the fact that she has always treated them with courtesy and generosity. They collaborate to push through the engagement ceremony behind Adéṣọ́dún's back. When Adéṣọ́dún finally realizes what has been going on, she refuses point blank to accept Bísí as junior wife, accusing her of wanting to enjoy the good years of her husband's career without having suffered with him through the bad years. Bísí storms off in a temper. Bàbáa Wándé declares that if he has to choose, he will choose Bísí. But when he goes after her, he finds her by the roadside deep in a flirtatious conversation with another lover. The scales fall from his eyes. He rejects her, reclaims his property from the flat he has rented and furnished for her use, and returns to Adéṣọ́dún.

Adédigba's Co-wife (Orogún Adédigba): video (early 1990s)

Bàbáa Jíire, a wealthy trader in Òṣogbo, has three wives, the youngest of whom, **Àwèlé,** is a witch. Àwèlé is first seen seizing and destroying the child of the second wife; then she follows the first wife to the market and wipes out her newly acquired trading capital by magical means. When Bàbáa Jíire begins courting a fourth wife, **Adédigba,** Àwèlé does everything in her power to thwart them. She attacks the unborn child in Adédigba's womb but fails to destroy it: protected by Ọ̀sun, the guardian deity of Òṣogbo, **Adéjàre** is born and thrives for a number of years. Àwẹ̀lé, however, has not given up. She enlists the help of her mother, an even more powerful witch, and when Adéjàre is four years old they finally succeed—not in killing him, as intended, but in crippling him. Adédigba fails to find a cure among the local medicine men, so she takes Adéjàre on a journey to Ọ̀yán, where a renowned herbalist takes care of the boy and eventually cures the suppurating wound. Adéjàre is now able to walk with the help of a staff.

Bàbáa Jíire dies, begging his friends to take care of the unfortunate boy. Adéjàre's wise words to his distraught mother show that he is destined for a great future. Àwẹ̀lé is finally seen dragging herself around the streets, bedraggled and deranged: a sacred oath that she swore years before, after killing her co-wife's baby, has finally caught up with her and divine retribution has been exacted.

Where the World Is Going (Ibi Ayé Ń lọ), part 1: video (1992).

The **Oba** of a small town, surrounded by his people, presides over a performance of *egúngún alárìnjó*. Among the guests are **Málọmọ́**, a son of the town who has been absent in the U.S. for many years, and his American wife, **Mercy**. After the performance, Málọmọ́ and Mercy chat to Málọmọ́'s old friend **Bàbáa Babárìndé** and his wife; they are interrupted when **Babárìndé,** the schoolboy son, arrives in tears to break the news that his uncle, with whom he had been staying in the north, has been killed in a riot. His own parents have no money to continue his education. Mercy offers to take him in, and Babárìndé goes with them to Lagos, where Málọmọ́ now works.

Babárìndé grows up and goes to university; we see him at the University of Ifẹ̀ library, with his girlfriend **Láídé**. They graduate together and get married. Babárìndé's father dies, and the young couple do all the traditional duties of the bereaved. Babárìndé becomes a successful businessman, wearing a suit and running a city office. The couple live in a modern bungalow with their two young sons. But Láídé becomes headstrong and lazy and encourages her sons to go the same way. Babárìndé attempts to remonstrate with her, but she ignores him, egged on by her woman friend. One of the sons is accused of raping a local schoolgirl; Láídé takes his side and throws her weight about at the police station to get him off. Babárìndé makes a final attempt to make Láídé see sense, waking her up in the night to talk seriously to her; she shrugs him off bad-temperedly and goes back to sleep.

Meanwhile, in the dead of night, the boys slip out of the house and go to the headquarters of a criminal gang. The criminal boss is holding court with his pot-smoking thugs and low-life floozies. It becomes apparent that the two boys have been accepted into the gang, and are about to go out on their first raid. . . . Part 1 of the video ends with "To Be Continued . . . "

APPENDIX 2

YORÙBÁ TEXT OF SCENE FROM *TAKING CARE OF KÚNLÉ* (CHAPTER 5)

Kúnlé: Hèé... hèé... hèé.... Mo gé e. Hèé... hèé... hèé... hèé... Mo gé e. Mo gé e. É gòóò! Hèé... hèé... hèé...
Òṣó: Hàn-án, èyí jẹ́ bí i Násánná Stapiim? Ọ dáràn lónìí. Ǹlẹ́ o, ọdẹ. O ti fọpọ́n tíyẹẹ ní o fọ̀?
Kúnlé: N ń tiì loò.
Òṣó: Yóò fẹ́ẹ́ lù ọ́ pa tọ́ bá dé lónìí. Ìwọ burúkú yìí. Pápáa bọ́ọ̀lù wà ńlẹ̀, kò ní í gbá a. Abẹsẹ̀ wọ́rọ́kọ́.
Adéwálé: Ẹ ńlẹ́ eńlé oooo.
Òṣó: Ta ni o?
Owólabí: Ẹ ńlẹ́ eńlé oooo. Ọ̀ṣọ́ọ̀ mi. Han-ìn, Adéálé o, Adéálé o.
Adéwálé: Ha èè, Òṣó, Oṣò.
Òṣó: Ẹ sá maa wolẹ̀ o. Ẹ jókòó báyìí. 'Bo lẹ ti í ń bọ̀? Kúnléé! Kúnlé!
(Kúnlé wọlé.)
Kúnlé: Sá.
Òṣó: Emi ní ó da?
Owólabí: Hééèèè. Hàn-ín.
Òṣó: A à yóó po tiì fún ọn?
Owólabí: Haà, a à ní í lè jẹ nǹkankan.
Adéwálé: A à ní í lè jẹ nǹkankan. A à ní í lè jẹ nǹkankan.
Òṣó: Wá lọ bá ọn ra kókótirókó wá.
Owólabí: Hààà, ńgbà tá à í sàlejò.
Òṣó: Nǹkan múmu ńkọ́?
Adéwálé: A à ní í mu nǹkankan.
Òṣó: Ṣé ò sí nǹkan tí mo fi rí yín báyìí o?
Owólabí àti Adéwálé: Kò sí nǹkan. Kò sí-ì. Kò sí nǹkankan.
Adéwálé: Oólabí lóun fẹ́ẹ́ rí ọ.
Owólabí: Han-ìn, kò sí-ì. Han-ìn, o ò ri. Han-ìn, Òṣó, ọkọ́ ọba ò ní í sá ọ lẹ́sẹ̀ o.
Òṣó: Àmín.
Owólabí: Gíga gíga là á bókè. Gíga gíga là á bósù. Iwájú lọ̀pá èbìtìì rẹ ọ́ maa ré sí o.
Òṣó: Àmín.
Owólabí: Han-ìn, àbúròò mi kan ló tÒkè Òkun dé, nisẹ́ wáá bọ́ lọ́ọ́ rè. Mọ bá ní toò, o ò ní í jókòó lásán, ọ óọ́ maa wá nǹkan ṣe ni. Òṣó, ọ dákun bá n fi í 'bi-sée yín.
Òṣó: Ọ kà tówèé mélòó?
Owólabí: Ó pọ̀ o. Ìwéé rẹ̀ẹ́ pọ̀ o. Háááà, iwéé rẹ̀ẹ́ pọ̀ o.
Òṣó: Mélòó ló kà?
Owólabí: Ó kàwé gan-an. Ó kàwé méwàá, méwàá Èèbó, ogún-un ti Yoòbá.
Òṣó: Só níwèè èrí? Só níwèé èrí?

Owólabí: Sé èyíi sábúkètì?
Òṣó: Hain.
Owólabí: Ó ní-ìn. Ó ní.
Òṣó: Han-àn, bàbá, irú àwọn èèyàn tọ́ bá níwèé èrí báun làwa ń fẹ́ ńbi-iṣẹ́ẹ wa. Sùgbọ́n kinní kan ṣẹlẹ̀ ńbi-iṣẹ́ẹ wa láìpẹ́ yìí, ọ̀la nì bá pé ẹ mú un wá, kọ́ kọ̀wé, wọn ìbá sì gbà á lọ́la.
Adéwálé: Sé ì í sabúrú o?
Òṣó: Aburú ni.
Owólabí: Háìì.
Òṣó: Aburú ni o. Èèbóo wa Misaa Wúù, ni nǹkan ṣẹlẹ̀ sí o.
Adéwálé: Ìyáa rẹ̀ẹ́ kú kọ́ un?
Òṣó: Rárá-à. Sẹ́ ẹ mọ̀ níbi tí ọn tí ń fi ẹ́njìnnì gé irin. Ká má fọ̀rọ̀ gùn o, ináa NẸ́PÀ ni ẹ́njìnnì ń lò. Bẹ́njìnnì ti bẹ̀rẹ̀ẹsẹ́ láàáròòjẹrin o, ká má fọ̀rọ̀ gùn, ni ọ́n bá múná lọ. Èèbóo wá sì ní ináa tiọn. Bí NẸ́PÀ bá mú tiọn lọ, àọn náà a sì fa kinní kan báyìí niná ó bàá bẹ̀rẹ̀, sọ́rọ̀ọ̀ mí yé e yín? Sẹ́ ẹ wáá rí i, ẹ́njìn tí ń gérin lọ́wọ́ . . . Èèbó wáá fẹ́ẹ kojá ńbẹ̀. Njẹ́ kọ́ kojá ńbi irin báyìí nàọn NẸ́PÀ bá múná wá. Ríróólù téẹ́ǹjìn ó ròólù báyìí, ẹni tí óò gbérin 'ókè apá ẹ̀ ló ṣe, àfi hẹ̀ẹ́ẹ.
Adéwálé àti Owólabí: Hòóò . . . háìì!
Òṣó: Ẹnìkan bá ń sáréé bọ̀, ló gbá apá un mú ńbi tí tí ń fò ó ká . . . Sọ́rọ̀ọ̀ mí yé e yín . . . ló bá pé kọ́ sọ ọ́ mọ́ ọn, àsé bí wọn bá sọ nǹkan-án gbóná mọ́ apá un, ó le jọ́ọ́nù, bí ọn ṣe pa á pọ̀ báyìí, ni ọ́n bá mú bébà, wọ́n bá fokùn dì í, ni ọ́n fokùn dì í, pé kí ọn ó máa gbé e lọ sí ọsibítù tààrà o. Ká má fọ̀rọ̀ gùn, àsé ìwàǹwára lẹni ó kọ́ fi bọ̀ ọ́, ìgbà tí óò mú ọwọ́ tí e kò ó báyìí, òdì ló wàà! Lẹ́nu kan, ni ọ́n bá fà á yọ, ni ọ́n wá ṣẹ́ẹ tún fapá un si. Lẹ́nu kan, wọ́n ti gbé lọọ́lúu wọn báyìí o, apá ọ́ jọ́ọnù ni o, kò jọ́ọ̀nù ni o, a à le sọ báyìí o. Ẹni wọ́n wáá gbe sáàyèe rẹ̀, a è réléyun. N tí ó ní í jé n sọ pé kọ́ wá bẹ̀rẹ̀ẹsẹ́ nù-un.
Adéwálé: Háàà, jànbá ò nílé. Ọlọ́un má jẹ̀ẹ́ a sòfòò.
Òṣó, Owólabí: Àmín, àmín.
Adéwálé: Olódùmarè ọ́ má ji a sòfòò.
Òṣó, Owólabí: Àmín, àmín, àmín.
Adéwálé: Háààà! Èèbó tó siṣé siṣé tí mańsín-ǹnì gé e lápá, Olódùmarè ọ́ má jẹ a sòfòò. Èèbó tó jí ń-jíí-ǹjí orí ẹnii rè, tó kí ọmọọ rè, tó kíyàwóo rè, "Ó dàbọ̀ oo," òun ń lọọbi-iṣé oúnjẹ òòjọ́ òun o, níbi tókèlè òun ó ti pọ́n o, tọ́ wáá pàdé ohun tí ọ́ jẹ ẹ́ lọ́nà! Olódùmarè ọ́ má jẹ a sòfòò.
Òṣó àti Owólabí: Àmín-ín.
Adéwálé: Hẹẹ, ẹ wáá wò ó o, ńbi-iṣé àwọn Èèbó wà nu-un o, bÉèbó ọ́ bàá siṣé, tọkàntara lÈèbó fi siṣé . . .
Owólabí: Ká kí wọn ọ́ pò.
Adéwálé: Wọ́n ọ́ bọ ṣòkòtò pénpé, ẹ̀wù pénpé, wọ́n ọ́ wàá máa mu sìgá . . .
Òṣó: . . . Tùù.
Adéwálé: . . . bí ọn tí ń forí ṣe, wọ́n ọ́ máa fọrùn ṣéé. Ẹ ẹ̀ ráwa ènìyàn dúdú . . .
Òṣó: Má sòrọ̀ọ wa mọ́.
Adéwálé: . . . a bàjẹ́ pọ̀ọ̀. Èyí iṣẹ́ tí ọn fún a, a à ní í se é . . .
Owólabí: A lá a bàjẹ́.
Adéwálé: Owó tí ọn bá kó fún a, áá maa fi ka ọkọ̀ jọ bí ẹní ka èkọ . . .
Òṣó: Má sọ ọ́ mọ́. Má sọ ọ́ mọ́.
Adéwálé: Àwọn tá a bá gbà sísé tọ́ yẹ ká fún ọn lówó, a à ní í fún ọn lówó, imú la á tùn-ún máa fi sọ̀rọ̀ sí ọn. Sán-an ti ṣéé? Ṣáan ti yọrí è?
Owólabí: A bàjẹ́ pọ̀ọ̀.
Adéwálé: Èèbó ló siṣé siṣé tí mansín-ǹnì ge lápá un. Olódùmarè ọ́ má jẹ a sòfòò.
Òṣó, Owólabí: Àmín-ìn.
Adéwálé: Ọlọ́un má je a ràrìn-fẹsè-sí o.

Owólabí: Àmín. Han-ìn, ǹlẹ́ Òṣó, han-ìn Kúnlé ńkọ́?
Òṣó: Kúnlé!
Kúnlé: Saa.
Òṣó: Wá wá wá. Àọn bàbá ń kí ọ. Yọ síhìn-ín. Yọ síhìn-ín.
Owólabí: Hanìn, Kúnlé, Olọ́un ó wò ọ́ ọ̀.
Òṣó àti Kúnlé: Àmín, àmín.
Owólabí: Olọ́un ó wò ọ́.
Òṣó àti Kúnlé: Àmín, àmín.
Owólabí: Olódùmarè ó wò ọ́.
Òṣó àti Kúnlé: Àmín, àmín.
Adéwálé: Wò ó bó ti jọ babaa rẹ̀ bí ìmumu. Han-ìn, Òṣó, ọ́ dọwọ́ọ̀ rẹ o. Ọ́ dọọ́ọ̀ rẹ o.
Owólabí: Ọ́ dọwọ́ọ̀ rẹ.
Adéwálé: Ọ́ dọwọ́ọ̀ rẹ o. Díńgíì rẹ rèé o. Kò ní í fọ́ mọ́ ọ lójú o.
Òṣó: Àmín, àmín, àmín.
Adéwálé: Fọ́tòò rẹ nìín o, kò ní í fà ya o.
Òṣó: Àmín-ín.
Adéwálé: Pẹ̀lú òfo Olọ́un, owó tó o óò fi rán ọmọ yìí dé ọfasíì, Olọ́un ó pèsèe ẹ̀ fún ọ.
Òṣó: Àmín, àmín.
Adéwálé: Oríìyáa rẹ̀ náà ó máa ràn ọ́ lọ́ọ́.
Òṣó: Àmín.
Adéwálé: Han-ìn, ìyáa rẹ̀ ńkọ́?
Òṣó: Ọ́ lọọjà oko.
Owólabí: Ó lọọjà oko. Heèèè.
Adéwálé: Dáadáa ni ó dèé.
Owólabí: Dáadáa ni ó dèé.
Adéwálé: Olọ́un má jẹ a sòfòo.
Òṣó: Àmín, àmín.
Owólabí: Han-ìn, Òṣó o, Adéálé.
Òṣó: Hùn-ún.
Adéwálé: Heèè.
Owólabí: Heèè, aburúkú ń ṣelẹ̀ ńlée wa yìí tá à fura.
Adéwálé: Kò dáa.
Òṣó: Èwo ló tún dé o?
Owólabí: Òṣóó, méwàá ń ṣelẹ̀ ńlée wa yìí tá à sì fura.
Òṣó: Kí ló ṣe?
Owólabí: Bí àwọn awakọ̀ọ wa yìí náà ni.
Òṣó: Kí ni ón ṣe?
Owólabí: Háàà, iwàkuwà ọ́ pọ̀. Bẹ́ẹ̀ àwọn bàbáa wa ọ̀ dáké o.
Adéwálé: Wọn ọ̀ dáké.
Owólabí: Wọ́n ń péé bó ọ bá mutí ọ má wakọ̀.
Adéwálé: Wọn ò ní í gbọ́ọ́-ọ̀. Háà! Olọ́un má jẹ a sòfòo.
Òṣó: Èwo ló tún ṣelẹ̀?
Owólabí: Lánàá náà ni, èmi Adéálé à ń tii okoo waá bọ̀, bá a ti dé etí ọjà báyìí, wọn tí ń tajà tí ń rajà, wọ́n n bẹ lápátùn-ún; wọ́n ń bẹ lápásì. Ọ ò rí i, ọkọ̀ eléjò kan, ó ru màálúù ... ọ ọ̀ rí i, eré tí ọkọ̀ yìí ń báá bọ̀, kò ṣe é gbé ...
Òṣó: Àwọn kó-ò. Màálúù n táyà mọ́tò è.
Owólabí: Òṣó o, eré tí ọkọ̀ yìí ń báá bọ̀, díẹ̀ ni kó dé àárín àwọn ènyàn tí ń rajà tí ń tajà, èyí béré—béréki tọ́ tẹ̀ ò bá mu mọ́. Lọ́rọ̀ kan, lọkọ̀ yìí bá já lọ sáàrinjà, lọ́ bá pààyàn lọ bí ilẹ̀ bí ẹnííí!
Òṣó: Ọ́ pààyàn!
Owólabí: Ọ́ pààyàn! Ọ́ pààyàn! Ọ́ pààyàn! Èèyàn tọ́ pa lójọ́ náà, wọ́n lé lógóta.

Ọ̀sọ́: Ẹjòò! Èé ti rí?
Adéwálé: Han-ìn, Ọ̀sọ́, ẹ jẹ́ wáá mò wí pé lójọ́ náà lóhùn-ún ńnúu gbogbo àwọn tí ọn kú, tí àwọn èèyàn wọ́n débẹ̀, wọ́n ń sọ pé, "Háà, ẹ má sọkún mọ́-ọ̀. Ẹ jẹ́ a fọ̀rọ̀ wa mỌlọ́un-ùn. Ẹ jẹ́ a fọ̀rọ̀ wa mỌlọ́un-ùn." Kí wọn ọ́ fọ̀rọ̀ wọn mỌlọ́un. Mọ wáá wò ó wí pé adúrú èèyàn tó kú kí wọn ó fọ̀rọ̀ wọn mỌlọ́un? Èmi náà wáá rò ó nígbèìn gbéín wí pé gbogbohun tọ́ bá dé báàyàn láyé yìí, kọ́ fọ̀rọ̀ rẹ̀ mỌlọ́un. Kọ́ gbà fỌ́lọ́un, ṣe ni kọ́ gba kádàráa rẹ̀.
Ọ̀sọ́: Àwọn èèyàn rẹ̀ . . .
Adéwálé: Han-in . . . Kọ́ gba kádàráa rẹ̀. Wọn a ní, han-ìn, omi lọ́ dànù, agbè ọ̀ fọ́.
Ọ̀sọ́: Héèè. Kóòtù wo ní ó ti rò ó? Ohun tí wọn ée fọ̀rọ̀ mỌlọ́un nù-un.
Owólabí: Ọ̀ṣọ́ọ́, je n wáá sọ kinní kan fún ọ. Nínú àwọn tí ọn kú yìí, obìnrin kan ń bẹ ńbẹ̀ . . .
Adéwálé: Obìnrin kan ń bẹ tọ́ jẹ́ wí pé . . . háà . . . háà . . . haà . . .
Ọ̀sọ́: Èé ti rí?
Owólabí: Obìnrin yìí mà sèèyàn o.
Ọ̀sọ́: Ó sèèyàn?
Adéwálé: Ó sèèyàn.
Ọ̀sọ́: Aráa bo lòun?
Owólabí: Aráabàa wa níhìn-ín náà ni-ìn. Nílée Wọ́n-ní-a-wí, a-à-mà-gbé-kalẹ̀ẹ-rẹ̀.
Adéwálé: Haà, Ilé Odòjé. Odòjé n wọ́n ń pè é ńjọ́un, báyìí a à màgbékalẹ̀ẹ rẹ̀ ni.
Owólabí: Háà, wò ó, obìnrin un tọ́ bá yọ báyìí ó sì pọ́n rúbúrúbú.
Adéwálé: Ó dúdú.
Owólabí: Haà, ó dúdú kọ̀ kọlà. Èèyàn dúdú ni.
Adéwálé: Nígbàa délée wọn témi Owólabí délée wọn, la bá bẹ̀rẹ̀ ẹkún. Làwá bá ń sunkún. Wọ́n ní ẹ má sunkún mọ́-ọ̀. Ẹ má sunkún mọ́, ẹ jẹ́ a gba kádàrá-à. Ká gba bỌ́lọ́un ṣe wí-ì. Gbogbohun tọ́ bá ti dé báàyàn láyé yìí, kọ́ gbà bỌ́lọ́un ṣe wí ni. Kọ́ gba kádàráa rẹ̀.
Owólabí: Han-ìn, Ọ̀sọ́ o, dáadáa n Wúràọlá ó dèé o.
Ọ̀sọ́: Àmín.
Adéwálé: Tọ́ bá ti dé, kọ ọ pè é, o ní Wúràọlá, dákun, bọ́ ọ bá ń lọ ọjà oko, má jókòó létí ọkòọ̀.
Ọ̀sọ́: Bàbá, ẹ è jẹ́rìíì mi, bémi ṣeé sọ kó tóó lọ nù-un.
Adéwálé: O ó jèrè. Lálẹ́ àná nì ń báá wí. Lọkọ̀ yìí ń bá ń lọ o . . . Lọkọ̀ yìí bá ń lọ o . . .
Ọ̀sọ́: Ọkọ̀ wo ló tún ń lọ?
Adéwálé: Han-in, Oólabí, bá n paríi rẹ̀ fun.
Owólabí: Lọkọ̀ yìí bá ń lọ o . . . Lọkọ̀ yìí bá ń lọ o . . . Han-ìn, Wálé o, paríi rẹ̀.
Adéwálé: Ó di gẹ̀ẹ́ . . . gẹ̀ẹ́ . . . gẹ̀ẹ́ . . . gẹ̀ẹ́ . . . Ló di gẹ̀ẹ́ . . . gẹ̀ẹ́ . . . gẹ̀ẹ́ . . . Ló di gẹ̀ẹ́ . . . gẹ̀ẹ́ . . . gẹ̀ẹ́ . . . han-ìn, Oólabí, bá n paríi rẹ̀.
Owólabí: Ló di ranin-iiin. Ló di gẹ̀ẹ́ . . . gẹ̀ẹ́ . . . gẹ̀ẹ́. . . . Ó di gẹ̀ẹ́ . . . gẹ̀ẹ́ . . . gẹ̀ẹ́ . . . gẹ̀ẹ́. Ló di wiriiiiii . . . Ààfi wòòòò.
Ọ̀sọ́: Ẹmi lèyíun?
Adéwálé àti Owólabí: Ọọkòọ̀.
Ọ̀sọ́: Ọkọ̀ wo?
Adéwálé àti Owólabí: Ọkọọ Wúrà.
Ọ̀sọ́: Wúrà wo?
Owólabí àti Adéwálé: Ìyàwóò rẹ.
Ọ̀sọ́: Kí ló ṣe?
Adéwálé àti Owólabí: Ó bómi lọ.
Ọ̀sọ́: Mo gbé òòòòò. Yàáyàáyàá.

NOTES

1. INTRODUCTION

1. The troupes which have consistently been singled out for discussion by theater scholars are those of Ògúnǹdé, as founding father and cultural icon; Dúró Ládíípọ̀, as pioneer of a "purist" traditional style making much use of older Yorùbá performance arts; and Kọ́lá Ògúnmọlá, as master of socially relevant satire. See Armstrong (1975); Banham and Wake (1976); Beier (1954, 1967, 1981); Brooks (1989); Clark (1979); Ladipọ (1970, 1972, 1973); Layiwọla (1986); Ogunbiyi (1981); Ogundele (1997); and Ogunmọla (1968). Unlike most other theater companies, these three received support from official government and educational institutions. Ọbafẹmi's study (1996) is unusual in also discussing the work of Bàbáa Sàlá, the great comedian who excelled at sly low-life satire. Jeyifo (1984) is the only study which offers a historical overview of the whole spectrum of popular theater troupes.

2. For Ghanaian concert party, see Cole (1997); Collins (1994); and Barber, Collins, and Ricard (1997). For Togolese concert party, see Ricard (1986); Barber, Collins, and Ricard (1997). For Tanzanian theatrical variety shows and television drama, see Lange (1995). For Zairean popular theater troupes, see Fabian (1990) and Mbala Nkanga (1995). In South Africa, the best documented example of commercial "people's" theater is Gibson Kente (see Kavanagh 1985; Peterson 1994).

3. Although media reception in Africa has not yet been well documented, it is clear that it is not only in western Nigeria that locally produced films and TV programs are far more popular than imported American or European ones. See Ametewee (1993, 44) for Ghana; Berwanger (1988) for a survey of the evidence throughout the Third World.

4. "Political pamphlets, religious tracts, medical records, houses, gardens, fashion, jewellery, maps and privies, for example, are all of equal critical and political interest as cultural products shaped by a particular knowledge or discourse" (Wilson 1995, 8–9).

2. THE HISTORY OF A FOUNDER, A GENRE, AND A PUBLIC

1. Companies founded and run by women did exist, however. In the formative 1940s period in Lagos there was a troupe led by a woman named Àdùnní Olúwọlé (Jeyifo 1984, 52, 64; Clark 1979, 81–82). In 1980 there were at least two troupes led by women: the Lady Fúnmiláyọ̀ Ránkò Theatre based in Ilésà and the Mojísọ́lá Martins Theatre of Lagos (Jeyifo 1984, 68). For an interview with Fúnmiláyọ̀ Ránkò see Jeyifo (ibid., 158–177).

2. The sphere of literary production identified by Bourdieu emerged in nineteenth-century France in the course of a struggle against the commodification of cultural products by the rising industrial bourgeoisie, a struggle in which "art"

was established as a quasi-autonomous field ("art for art's sake"). Constituted out of objective relations between writers, publishers, distributors, readers, and critics, this sphere was the site of competition between writers and schools of writing which generated stylistic change, sponsored by sections of the public. The sphere of literary production, in Bourdieu's analysis, thus supplies the necessary link between the individual work of art and the social formation at large. The field of popular artistic production in twentieth-century Nigeria, by contrast, was never segregated from commerce; indeed, commercial success was held to be an indication of artistic merit. Nonetheless, Bourdieu's intermediary concept is useful in that it blocks the tendency to derive artistic forms *directly* from large-scale socio-economic structures.

3. In the view of the Rev. Mackay, posted to Òṣogbo from 1900 onward, the railway and the consequent opening up of the hinterland to trade was the main factor in the breakdown of "tribal customs" in the area, as "thousands of young farmers have left the land to take up work as labourers on the railway and on road construction, to say nothing of the hundreds in the employ of trading firms" (quoted in Berry 1975, 67).

4. Adéjọbí's phrasing suggested that Adéjọbí senior worked directly for G. B. Ollivant as their agent. This would mean that he was at the top of the pyramid of produce buyers, at the base of which were "pan buyers" who went on foot from farm to farm buying small quantities of cocoa, and at the middle of which were the "scalers" who were licensed to weigh the produce before bulking it and passing it on to the company's agents (Galletti, Baldwin, and Dina 1956, 39–41). See Peel (1983, 132) for an account of this system as it obtained in Iléṣà (which participated in the same trading network as Òṣogbo). According to Sara Berry, "by far the highest incomes in the cocoa economy accrue to produce buyers" (Berry 1975, 191).

5. See Schwab (1952) on this transition specifically in Òṣogbo; Atanda (1970) on indirect rule in western Nigeria more widely.

6. In 1950, 65.4 percent of the total Lagos population was concentrated on Lagos Island. By 1963, 68 percent of the population was on the mainland (Sada and Adefọlalu 1975, 81).

7. See Gbadamọsi (1978, 98); Peel (2000).

8. Advertisements in *West African Pilot* give the following advice: "AST Ideal tonic for expectant mothers against anaemia, weakness and pregnancy mishaps" (January 18, 1948); "For dangerous worms insist on APECS Worm Expeller, from Broadway Chemist, Lagos" (January 28, 1948); "For headache and pains use APECS powders, price 1/-" (January 28, 1948).

9. Lisa Lindsay's study of colonial railway workers and their families in Nigeria quotes a former railway clerk who lived in the Oke-Awo neighborhood of Lagos in the 1940s: "The neighbourhood was full of railway workers . . . especially single men who held debating meetings, met for drinking and socialising, discussed the events in the *West African Pilot*, and sometimes attended church" (Lindsay 1996, 113). The press of the period is full of references to literary and debating societies. For example, in 1940, the Nigerian Literary Association announced its formation, with its headquarters and first active branch in Lagos; in 1941, the Nigerian Literary Circle met and elected officers (*The Comet*, February 15, 1941); and on July 19 of the same year there was a reference in the same paper to the Muslim Literary Circle.

10. *The Comet*, July 4, 1942.
11. *Daily Times*, December 9, 1948.
12. *The Comet*, August 31, 1940.
13. *The Comet*, May 2, 1942.
14. *Daily Times*, January 14, 1946.
15. *The Comet*, February 7, 1942.

16. Hometown Unions, like other regional and ethnic associations, were formed by groups of migrants from a common place of origin who met for social reasons and to promote the development of their home town.

17. *Daily Times*, November 3, 1948.

18. *The Comet*, April 18, 1942. Stage performances by girls did not go uncriticized by Islamic authorities, however: see the heated debate in *The Comet* between Alhaji F. R. Hakeem and Miss Latifat, from January to March 1944, in which Miss Latifat states that the all-girl entertainment denounced by the Alhaji was of a high moral standard, and the Alhaji responds with a denunciation of girls dancing the foxtrot "with half naked legs in the presence of men . . . to earn money with tickets sold at 5d or 1s or 2s etc etc."

19. *Twelfth Night* was staged by the Bright Star Club in 1946 (*Daily Times*, January 28, 1946). *At the Mercy of Tiberius* was performed in May 1935. I am grateful to John Peel for bringing to my attention the program for this show, which contains a detailed synopsis and full cast list.

20. "Sergeant Solis Abereoje impersonated the female parts throughout and certainly deserves his share of praise. He was extremely feminine! Whimpering and coy like any seventeen-year-old-Miss, who, at first, did not quite know the ropes" (*Daily Times*, January 14, 1946).

21. *The Comet*, January 22, 1944.

22. In 1943 the CMS in Abẹ́òkúta staged a "Yoruba church centenary," with a "pageant representing the first arrival of the Rev. Henry Townsend and the reception by Chief Sodẹké." The program shows that the celebration commemorated the exact date of Townsend's arrival (January 4th, 1843) with a "pilgrimage" retracing Townsend's steps to Sodẹké's house, where he first put up. The pageant, held the following day, was to include the exhibition of "IRON BOX used by Rev. Townsend during his travels in Ẹgbaland in 1843." The synopsis of the pageant suggests a great concern with historical accuracy, even at the expense of dramatic effect, and the cast list reveals an exhaustive representation of all the chiefs of Abẹ́òkúta. In Lagos in 1942, the CMS staged "A Short Play depicting the arrival and early work of CMS Missionaries in Nigeria." The program lists eight scenes, apparently a series of vignettes rather than a linear narrative. I am grateful to John Peel for bringing the programs for these events to my attention.

23. This distinction, however, does not seem to have been consistently made. One show entitled "Birth of Samuel" was advertised as a cantata; but this was also a popular theme for shows advertised as Native Air Operas: Onímọlẹ̀ staged one such at Ikoyi Methodist Church in about 1934 (Jeyifo 1981), and both Ògúnǹdé and Adéjọbí later did the same for other churches.

24. *The Comet*, February 12, 1944; October 25, 1941.

25. What he said was "*tó dẹ̀ ń fún èniyàn ní ìwúrí*" [and which gives you a feeling of *ìwúrí*], a concept impossible to fully translate, but which has associations of deep gratification, to the point of emotional or psychic transformation. *Ìwúrí*, literally, means "the swelling of the head."

26. Radio Nigeria began in 1939, and almost all its programming was devoted to relaying the BBC's Empire Service. Subscribers paid 5/- per month for a wired box through which the BBC signals were relayed like a telephone call. In 1948, there were about 8,000 such subscribers receiving the programs in 10 Nigerian cities. However, Radio Nigeria also originated about one hour a day of programming, broadcast from "a small airless room at the top of the Glover Memorial Hall" (Mackay 1964, 20). The broadcasters were, at least, well placed to keep tabs on the latest cultural developments in the city.

27. In the original *Everyman*, it is Death that God sends to the world to call

Man to account for his riotous living and material greed (see A. C. Cawley 1974, 207–209). This is also what happens in Dúró Ládíípọ̀'s Ẹ̀dá. In *The Gospel Fruit in Oshogbo*, it is a messenger who is unnamed but who seems to be Jesus Christ, judging from the words of the other messengers: "We will meet again on the joyful day when you will return to Father's house to rule over the company [of angels] at our Father's right hand." There are "traditional" stories, possibly influenced by the Christian paradigm, in which other beings get sent down. In C. L. Adéoyè's *Ẹ̀dá Ọmọ Oòduà*, Èlà, God's son by his wife Òrìṣàálá, is the one sent to sort out the world when it gets in a mess (Adeoye 1971). In the texts of the church of Ọ̀rúnmìlà, it is Ọ̀rúnmìlà who is sent by Àjàlọ́run (see Barber 1990).

28. See Chapters 7 and 11 for further discussion of the "helper."

29. Again, I owe my knowledge of this text to John Peel, who kindly made a copy available to me after finding it in the CMS archives at Ìbàdàn, along with several others referred to in this chapter.

30. These figures are derived from the Federal Office of Statistics (1989, quoted in Egunjọbi [1995]). They conflict with Schwab's estimate that Ọṣogbo's population at the time of his research in 1950–1951 was either 65,000 (1952, 30) or 70,000 (1952, 12). Schwab does not give his source, and the discrepancy between his two estimates is unexplained.

31. Writing in 1965, Schwab was of the opinion that nearly a third of the adult males in Ọṣogbo were engaged in the "new" artisanal crafts, such as tailoring, goldsmithing, and carpentry (Schwab 1965, 98).

32. One such school concert was reported thus: "The Band of All Saints School under the control of Mr MA Adejuwon (Master in Charge) produced thoroughly Native Airs to good music throughout." *The Comet*, March 23, 1940.

33. Grace said that the group performed in church halls only when specifically invited by church organizations. Otherwise, the Billiard Room was their normal venue ("owned by a European called Father of Twins—he's dead now"). An advertisement at the back of one of their programs announces a play by the Adéjọbí Musical Party entitled *The Hebrew Slave and Destiny*, to take place in the Billiard Room in September 1953.

34. When the first intake of Universal Primary Education students completed Primary 6 in December 1960, there were two and a half times as many school leavers in the Western Region seeking jobs as there had been one year before (Callaway 1960, 60).

35. Success in all spheres of business was often explained as the result of a pioneering innovation: for example, "I was the first person to bring torchlight and batteries to Ibadan" (Otudeko 1977, 92); "she was the first person to sell European drinks in the town" (Barber 1991, 233). For a perceptive discussion of the broader role of innovation in Yorùbá conceptions of economic success, see Guyer (1997).

36. FESTAC was the name given to the International Festival of African Arts and Culture held in Lagos in 1977.

3. THE ACTORS

1. For a detailed discussion of patterns of migration to Ghana from different areas of northern Yorùbáland, see Eades (1993, 20–24).

2. WASC was the West African School Certificate, WAEC the West African Examinations Council. A small minority of modern school pupils did succeed in getting into university by proceeding first to a Grade II Teacher Training College, where they could take the WAEC or WASC exams. Such students, when they finally

got to university, were usually markedly older and poorer than those who came straight from grammar school. See Muckenhirn (1966, 117); Lloyd (1974, 99).

3. When a person becomes a parent, they become known as "mother of . . . " or "father of . . . " their child, usually (though not invariably) their first-born.

4. This is what Oyin Adéjọbí remembered. According to Awoniyi (1978), however, the 1926 Educational Ordinance for the Colony and Southern Provinces had standardized the curriculum as an 8-year program with Infants Classes I and II and then Primary Standards I–VI. This remained in place until 1955, when it was replaced by a 6-year primary school program ending with the Primary 6 Leaving Certificate.

5. There has been a dramatic change in the formal qualifications held by apprentices since the expansion of education in the 1970s and 1980s. In 1969, Koll found that 56.5 percent of the craftsmen he interviewed had no schooling at all; 34.4 percent had primary schooling, and only 8.7 percent had post-primary education—most of these being modern school rather than grammar school or technical college leavers (Koll 1969, 33). In 1979, Oyeneye found that only 11 percent of the apprentices he studied had no schooling at all; over 60 percent had completed Primary 6, while 10 percent and 4 percent had attended modern and grammar schools respectively (Oyeneye 1979, 86). By 1992, according to Susanna Adam, the *average* level of schooling among apprentices was three years of post-primary education. She explains this not only as a result of a general raising of educational levels (at least on paper) but also as the result of parental disillusionment about the prospects of white-collar jobs for their children. Clerkly occupations did not expand in step with available literate school leavers. What the parents did not realize was that by 1992 the market for artisanal trades was also saturated. The result was an army of apprentices with little prospect of becoming autonomous masters (Adam 1995). In the 1980s, however, when I worked with the company, modern school leavers had a good chance of a clerical job, and apprentices were usually primary-school leavers.

6. It was clearly civil service public sector workers John had in mind when he made these remarks; in Òsogbo, however, it must be borne in mind that the thriving commercial and informal manufacturing sector attracted many migrants from other towns who were not public servants but traders and business people observing a different working cycle from the formal sector. Like the public sector employees, these migrants lived in rented accommodations and were regarded as more forward-looking and "modern" than the indigenes (Schwab 1952, 81). See Guyer (1997, 211) on the way in which the formal sector working week has become the norm for all occupations, including farming, in the last 20 years.

5. THE GENERATION OF PLAYS

1. *Mọrèmi* was an early production that was no longer in their repertoire by the time I worked with them. According to Brooks, Adéjọbí was working on it in 1965, at the same time that Dúró Ládiípọ̀ produced his own version of the story, but unlike Ládiípọ̀, Adéjọbí "has no documentation or recording of his *Mọrèmi*" (1989, 118). I saw them do *The Return of Odùduwà* in 1975, however, when they were invited by the Olókukù of Òkukù to give a guest performance in the palace in honor of my parents, who were visiting.

2. My only source for the Adéjọbí version of the play is the photoplay magazine *Atóka* (86, nos. 1–5, 1981). Since the editor would probably have drawn on Daramọ̀-lá's published text more than on his memories of the Adéjọbí Company's live adap-

tation when preparing the bubble captions, it is likely that the stage play made many more changes than those I have been able to identify from the magazine version. But it is clear even from the magazine version that the theater company's adaptation involved fundamental thematic changes.

3. This is the term used by Richard Andrews to describe the expansible, detachable, and substitutable episodes he has identified in Renaissance Italian literary comedy. Though this comedy is scripted, Andrews attributes the modular sequences to the continued use and influence of improvisation in literary drama of the period (Andrews 1993).

4. "I would have said something important ... water in the pot": Ìyáa Ṣèyí is applying this elaborate saying to Tàfá. It turns on a pun on the word rò (both "to narrate" and "to stir/cook"). Instead of "narrating" some worthwhile matter, Tàfá is merely "stirring" vegetable sauce, that is, wasting his time.

5. A "complete": English word used as slang for a man's outfit consisting of tunic, trousers, and gown.

6. Alágbààà Ìjẹ̀sà: literally, the title of the head of the egúngún masquerade cult of Ìjẹ̀sà. The slang meaning is explained in the subsequent dialogue.

7. In such discourses, it is not only foreigners or "Europeans" who are held up as the contrastive case: other Nigerian peoples serve equally effectively. For example, in the popular poet Túnbọ̀sún Ọládàpọ̀'s Yorùbá-language magazine Ọ̀kín Ọlọ́jà, there is a highly amusing and scathing piece asking why the Yorùbás are unable to choose their political leaders in a peaceful and orderly fashion—when the Nupe elect their Etsu with no trouble, the Igbos their Obi, the Edo their Ọba, and the British their crowned monarch! What is wrong with the Yorùbá? The list of "others" here is cited only to focus attention more vividly upon the Yorùbá.

6. FILLING OUT A PLAY

1. This was a view shared by many members of the audience, both Christian and Muslim: see Chapter 7.

2. My thanks to Professor 'Bísí Ògúnṣínà of Ìlọrin University for this observation.

7. AUDIENCES

1. In *The Royal Palm-nut*, Ifá has approved two candidates to the throne, and one of the chiefs gives voice to the general perturbation by quoting "Àgbò méjì—" [two rams—]; the whole audience joins in "kò mumi ní koto" [don't drink from one trough].

2. A similar tendency has been noted by Newell (1998 and 2000) among readers of Nigerian and Ghanaian popular fiction: readers read for a message embodied in the character whose gender and status most closely resembles their own.

3. *Man of the Theatre* documentary program, "The World About Us," 1982.

4. The associational baggage that comes with the concept of "public sphere" is voluminous and too historically specific to be useful in the modern Nigerian context. The idea of "the public," however, is indispensable—and is used by the theater company itself. The concept of the "public arena" (Freitag 1989) is also helpful, as it is more inclusive and less tied to a particular place and moment in European history than "public sphere."

5. Beckerman glosses this traditional distinction as follows: the "presentational" mode is where the performer "acknowledges the presence of the audience"; the "representational" mode (what others, e.g., Jeyifo 1984, have called "illusionis-

tic") is where the performer "acts as though the activity performed has an autonomous existence." He goes on to qualify this distinction by pointing out that all drama, however illusionistic, is in some sense directed toward an audience; and conversely, all drama, however presentational, to some extent involves the establishment of a "world" of action which is exterior to the audience and established through actor-actor (or actor-self or actor-prop) rather than actor-audience interaction. All drama is thus somewhere on a continuum between the two poles, and many forms of drama deliberately mix the two modes to create theatrical effects (Beckerman 1990, 110–111).

6. Compare Habermas (1991, 12–14), where Wilhelm Meister's ambition to go on the stage (in Goethe's novel of that title) is interpreted as a desire to recapture a fading feudal mode of power which inheres in the person of the powerful, and must be displayed, bodied forth, and enacted—rather than being gained and demonstrated by action, as in the bourgeois democratic world that superseded the feudal. "The nobleman was what he represented; the bourgeois, what he produced" (1991, 13). The nobleman's "representative publicness" was, in Habermas's view, incompatible with the new bourgeois "public sphere" in which differences of rank were bracketed and all participants held equivalent. Clearly Yorùbá and other West African societies animated by the self-aggrandizement of "big men" were far from feudal, but there is a parallel in the centrality in both systems of bodily display and sheer personal salience.

8. TELEVISION, FILM, AND VIDEO

1. Not everyone felt that the electronic media made theater groups respectable, however: the point of Adédùnmọ́lá's story was the reaction of another woman teacher who was listening and who told the sewing mistress "What do you want with this theatre business, what do you want to do there? I swear that if a man wanted to marry me and he did this kind of work, I'd refuse him on that account. How can you, who are educated . . . if it was an uneducated person, that would be different."

2. Adio Majester Gbọlahan made one (*419: Gbajuẹ*), against corruption, which was sponsored by the government and another (*June 12 Messiah*), in support of Moshood Abiọla, which he could only show in London for fear of government reprisals.

9. THE WORLD OF THE WORK: PLACE, GENDER, AND POLITICS

1. This raises the question as to why other contemporaneous African popular theaters arising in similar social contexts should have been so much less "lifelike" in style. Ghanaian concert party, for example, quickly established a repertoire which revolved around stylized permutations of a limited range of plot and character elements. In a most interesting paper, Cole (1997) suggests that the presentational style, comic stereotypes, and "roller-coaster" plot development of Ghanaian concert party were a way of coming to grips with modernity (in a mode which I would see as alternative but parallel to the Yorùbá popular theater's): a way which permitted the integration or at any rate inclusion of disparate and fragmented elements of experience, and which allowed the participants to laugh at contemporary novelties while still endorsing them.

2. For an example at the fully fledged end of the continuum, see the story recounted to Cornwall to illustrate the fate of jealous co-wives, in which an ill-intentioned woman attempts to poison her co-wife's child and accidentally poisons her own. Here the neat plot structure corresponds to a common tale type, and

Cornwall remarks that the story was "repeated to me in many different forms, as a moral tale about the risks involved in trusting a co-wife with the care of one's children" (1996, 163).

3. This was a common sight in northern Yorùbáland, where the old compounds were very large, and where modern bungalows and two-storied buildings were often just erected in a gap created by pulling down part of the old wall, leaving the rest standing. As early as 1952, Schwab noted that in Òsogbo individual men and women who had accumulated some wealth would usually proceed to build a "separate European-type dwelling"—often within the confines of the compound—for the use of themselves and their immediate family (Schwab 1952, 93).

4. By the early 1950s, Schwab noted that "Modern European type dwellings constructed within the agbo-ile [compound] have been built to accommodate the demand for lodging near the commercial centers. They consist of two or more stories and although the individual rooms are generally larger than the rooms in traditional buildings, they are always overcrowded and it appears that these buildings are beginning to form a nucleus for tenements" (1952, 87). And in the Foreign Quarter and along Station Road, purpose-built tenements were created: "many of these houses have been created as separate buildings to be let by the room" (ibid., 93).

5. Some form of permanent division of the land had evidently taken place earlier, for Àrólé tells Láńre that "Your father had half that land, the compound has the other half." Thus Bámgbádé's son is legally entitled to sell the land if he wishes, but as it is contiguous with compound land and was once part of it, the elders see the proposed sale as a violation of collective norms. Ownership and sale of farm land was a hot topic at the time I recorded the play, in the wake of the 1978 Land Use Decree, which was regarded as a threat to lineage land ownership. For discussion of its effects in Ìbàràpá area, see Guyer (1997).

6. See Hallen and Sodipo (1986) for a discussion of the strong contrast maintained by Yorùbá speakers between *mọ̀* (to know—based on first-hand experience) and *gbàgbọ́* (to believe—based on hearsay).

7. This sentence has a resemblance to an Akan language, especially *pa paa pa*, which means "very much." But it is a gobbledygook sentence to which Akan speakers I consulted were unable to assign any definite meaning. I am grateful especially to Rose Mensah-Kutin of the University of Legon, Ghana, for help with this.

8. The colonial government had Ògúnńdé briefly arrested in 1946, and the post-Independence Western Region government of Akíntọ́lá banned his theater for two years for supporting Awólọ́wọ̀ in *Yorùbá Ronú*. See Clark (1979) for an informative account of Ògúnńdé's political involvements throughout his career.

9. I owe this point to Stephanie Newell.

10. For a comparable instance in Ghanaian popular romantic fiction, see Priebe 1978.

10. LITERACY, "ENLIGHTENMENT," AND "TRADITION"

1. E. A. Ayandele observes "So high did the prestige of learning become that . . . it was *infra dig.* for a man who knew how to read or write to carry any load of any kind, including Bibles and hymn-books which had to be carried for the Christians" (1966, 289). Ayandele's source for this observation dates back to 1900. But the general tenor of his remarks corroborates Peel's view that it was only with the diffusion of colonial institutions that schooling became securely associated with economic and social advancement. According to Ayandele, it was new employment associated with "the rapid economic development, the establishment of 'Native'

Courts and Councils, Posts and Telegraphs, the introduction of the bicycle and commercial lorries, construction of motor roads and the 'iron horse'" that gave schooling its talismanic properties.

2. The date at which education came to be seen as desirable varied from one part of Yorùbáland to another. In the Lagos area, Gbadamọsi (1978) cites evidence of school hunger, and especially the desire for English, as early as 1904; for the Ìjẹ̀sà case, Peel puts this development in the 1920s (1978, 148). The take-off of school provision—public and private—on average across western Nigeria appears to have gotten under way around 1910, rapid expansion following from then until about 1930 (Fafunwa 1974, 112).

3. According to Fafunwa, in 1912 there were 150 government and government-assisted primary schools (1974, 97); but a further 200 unassisted schools, founded by independent African Churches or by "private venture," were in operation. By 1926, the number of these unassisted unofficial schools had increased to more than 3,000 (1974, 112). There appears, then, to have been a veritable explosion of unassisted schools in the second and third decades of the century, coinciding with the establishment of colonial institutions and the railway in Yorùbáland.

4. Islam entered Yorùbáland earlier than Christianity: it was well established in Old Ọ̀yọ́ by the late eighteenth century, and Ìlọrin and Ìbàdàn both had flourishing and respected Qur'anic schools by the mid-nineteenth century (Ryan 1978, 111; Fafunwa 1974, 58; Gbadamọsi 1967). Islam, like Christianity, gave literacy a central place in the practices of proselytization and worship. The status of a mallam was defined in terms of his degree of learning, and from the great centers of scholarship radiated rings of less learned teachers, who set up schools of their own wherever they could. These schools, already spreading rapidly by the second half of the nineteenth century, have never been regulated by the Ministry of Education. Since the beginning of the twentieth century they have been ubiquitous. Access to at least some degree of instruction was generally available even in small villages, and knowledge of Arabic written texts was widely diffused. Though Arabic literacy had associations quite different from those of the literacy imparted in mission and government schools, it nonetheless promoted a culture in which reverence for scholarship and attainment of book learning was central. Literate people, in both spheres, become gravitational centers toward which the illiterate orient themselves, offering respect and asking for help.

5. Provision of schools by the Young Ansar-ud-Deen Society was preceded by the Lagos government's establishment of three Government Muslim Schools in Lagos and Ìbàdàn in the 1890s. Ansar-ud-Deen, moreover, was only one association among several that undertook to provide schooling. The Ahmadiyya Movement—influential in the formation of the Young Ansar-ud-Deen Society—was also a recognized voluntary agency which established and ran Muslim schools; so was the Nawair-ud-Deen Society, founded in Abẹ́òkúta in 1923, and several other locally based movements. The Ansar-ud-Deen Society became by far the biggest and most influential of these movements, however (Reichmuth 1996).

6. With the introduction of the Universal Primary Education scheme in 1955, the number of primary schools founded by the Young Ansar-un-Deen society rose to 215, and the construction of secondary modern and secondary grammar schools also increased in the late 1950s and early 1960s. By 1967, there were all together 509 educational institutions being run by Muslim voluntary agencies, of which almost half were controlled by the Ansar-ud-Deen (Reichmuth 1996, 383).

7. Writing of the period 1895–1908, Gbadamọsi observes that advanced Muslim scholars in Yorùbáland "were like literary oases, attracting many eager but fam-

ished students. They brought Islamic education almost literally to the very doorsteps of the Yoruba Muslims, for around each one of them grew an ever-expanding circle of local pupils, far exceeding the number that could travel outside Yorubaland to slake their thirst for Islamic education" (1978, 100).

8. Some CMS missionaries expressed a definite preference for less-educated converts. Samuel Ajayi Crowther's favorite agents of proselytization in the Niger Mission were "those who lacked literary pretensions. They were mainly middle-aged shoe-makers, carpenters, farmers, bricklayers, Government messengers and stewards on board ships, people who had no education of any kind or very elementary education for two or three years in a mission school": for these were "unsophisticated folk who took the Bible seriously and treated it with deep, pious reverence" (Ayandele 1966, 286). The Rev. Henry Townsend was of the same opinion (ibid., 287).

9. The first missionary to visit Abẹ́òkúta was Rev. Thomas Birch Freeman, of the Methodist mission, who stayed only 10 days before returning to his station in Badagry. He was followed by Rev. Henry Townsend of the CMS, who made an exploratory visit to the town early in 1843 and returned to establish a permanent mission station there in 1846. See Ajayi (1965, 31–38).

10. According to the Morris report, in this year there were 313,000 boys and girls at primary school in the southern provinces but only 4,500 at grammar school (Fafunwa 1974, 162). Since there were eight primary classes, the final class could be calculated to have contained about 39,000 pupils; and since there were five secondary classes, the first year could be estimated at about 900 (not allowing for attrition in either case). Very roughly, then, about 2.3 percent of the Standard VI pupils could be expected to proceed to Form One of grammar school.

11. I. B. Thomas, *Ìtàn Ìgbésí Aiyé Èmi Ṣẹ̀gilọlá*, 1929–1930, serialized in *Akéde Èkó*.

12. For further details of the Yorùbá-language literary tradition see Isọla (1988, 1992); Falọla (1988); Babalọla (1985); Ogunṣina (1992); Barber (1995b, 1997a).

13. In 1963, 95 percent of secondary school pupils in the Western Region (by then virtually an all-Yorùbá state, after the excision of the midwest) opted to take Yorùbá as a subject (Awoniyi 1978, 143).

14. This is not to say that the elite do not live differently from the rest of the population. They would not be seen as "elite" if they did not have a distinctive lifestyle. The point rather is that the insignia of eliteness are neither inherited nor absorbed through a lifelong immersion in a particular cultural ambience: on the contrary, they are signifiers which can be acquired by going to school and by having money. Smythe and Smythe (1960) argue that the manifestations of elite membership in western Nigeria at the time of their research were primarily material—involving the acquisition of the houses, cars, and consumer goods associated with the outgoing colonial officer class. They were heterogeneous because of their varied ethnic origins and because recruitment to the elite was relatively open (the son of an illiterate farmer could, after 14 years' schooling, attain elite status); the only cultural homogeneity they manifested was a command of English, the adoption of "Western ways," and "a broader outlook" deriving from travel and privilege—all characteristics which could be acquired through education and money (Smythe and Smythe 1960, 93). Lloyd, writing in 1974, perceived an incipient entrenchment of privilege among the elite—the well-educated being in a position to ensure that their children were also well educated—"An open society is rapidly closing" (1974, 3)—but he confirms that it was still the case that the educated elite did not form a residentially segregated or culturally closed class. They bought standard goods (cars, televisions, refrigerators, furnishings) from a limited selection of im-

ports and this was an index of their wealth and status but not of a class-related "taste" or cultural outlook (1974, 117). In other words, cultural capital is there for the taking—very unlike the contemporary French situation analyzed by Bourdieu (1984, 1998) where, despite the great importance of schooling in allocating people to different positions in the social field, what finally distinguishes one position from another is what *cannot* be learned in school—the imponderable nuances of taste, behavior, and speech that can only be absorbed from a circumambient cultural environment and can therefore be seen as inherited or ingrained.

15. In addition, as Turner observes, the emphasis in the Church of the Lord on almsgiving, fasting, and prayer "provide a trio of injunctions that have an Islamic suggestion about them" (1967, 2: 82); see also Fisher (1970).

16. In Lagos, women Muslims were prominent and active in the Young Ansar-ud-Deen Society, campaigning for women's education (Reichmuth 1996, 379–380).

17. The younger generation of the Ansar-ud-Deen Society permitted their members to participate in the Eyọ masquerade and the Òkè-Ìbàdàn festival (Ryan 1978, 211); and some even tolerated Ifá divination (Ryan 1978, 223)—as of course did many Anglican churchmen—because Ifá was seen as the centerpiece of Yorùbá traditional philosophy and literature.

18. According to Giddens, "what is characteristic of modernity is not an embracing of the new for its own sake, but the presumption of wholesale reflexivity," that is, the opening of all ideas to revision in the light of incoming knowledge (1990, 39). In Yorùbáland, however, it was not "incoming empirical knowledge" which caused Èṣù to be "revised" into Satan and which denied the existence of òrìṣà but affirmed (while denouncing) the existence of *jùjú*. What is characteristic of West African modernity is not Popperian evaluation of evidence but an embracing of the principle of moral discrimination between what is to be rejected and what recuperated, in a proliferating welter of stark alternatives. In an illuminating discussion of concert party, the parallel popular theater form in Ghana, Cole argues that the concert party performers take a position close to the one I am describing: "Concert party practitioners define 'modernity' not according to Western Enlightenment axiologies which dichotomise the civilised and the savage, Africa and Europe, modern and traditional cultures. Concert actors use 'modernisation' to describe an integrative process involving conscious choices of inclusion and exclusion" (Cole 1997, 371).

19. For an incisive critique of such analyses, which tend to treat culture as an essence or substance, see Friedman (1995).

20. This was only possible with new and relatively unknown plays, however. Some of their older plays—especially those which had been shown on television—were so famous and so beloved by audiences that they could not possibly have used their titles for other plays without causing disappointment and outrage among their fans.

21. Texts from *The Gospel Fruit in Oshogbo* are reproduced from the church program of 1961, retaining the original orthography and layout.

22. The depredations of the Ṣàngó cult had long been resented by the communities they operated on, especially in central and northern Yorùbáland: see Samuel Johnson (1921); Doortmont (1994); Peel (1990).

23. The symbolic contrast of the light of understanding and the dark of ignorance, for example—central to the early formulation of the concept of *ọlajú*—was used by the greatest conservative Muslim reformer in the history of what is now Nigeria, Usman Dan Fodio, 50 years before it became the stock in trade of the Yorùbá Christian elites. Urging education for women, he wrote: "Alas! How can

they abandon their wives and daughters in the perpetual darkness of ignorance, while they daily impart their knowledge to their students?" (quoted in Fafunwa 1974, 56).

24. As Alhaji's character in *Tẹni n tẹni* says: "*Búburú kìí déédéé sẹlẹ̀ sínyàn, bí ò bá jẹ́ àkoọ́lẹ̀ á jẹ́ àfọwọ́fà ara ẹni*" [Bad things don't happen to people randomly/by chance, if they are not predestined ("written down," i.e., in the book of fate), then they are brought about by people's own hand]. Recorded in *Atọ́ka*, 82, no. 2, June 1980.

25. All the key words in the statement—*wòlíì* (prophet), *alùfáà* (preacher), and *iwàásù* (sermon) are loan words from Arabic, and almost certainly entered Yorùbá with the assistance of Islam. But they are now used as much by Christians as by Muslims, if not more. See Gbadamọsi (1978, 206–208) for a discussion of these and other Arabic loan words and their connection to Islamic conversion. Reichmuth (1988) argues that *alùfáà* and *iwàásù*, along with numerous other words originally associated with Islam, came into Yorùbá via Songhay rather than Hausa, as had usually been previously assumed.

26. An exception is *The Overreacher*, where one of the chiefs mistreated by the despotic Ọba is the Lèmọ́mù (imam) whom the Ọba taunts mercilessly for his turban and his refusal to prostrate (see Chapter 12). However, it is interesting to note that the imam has in effect been assimilated to the ranks of traditional chiefs, and he is just one of a sequence of interchangeable characters occupying a "slot" in the structure of the scene. His religious orientation has no particular significance to the theme, except to demonstrate that the Ọba has offended all sections of his traditional polity.

27. Proverbs 13:12. The rest of the verse is "But when the desire cometh, it is a tree of life." The words in the song are an exact quotation from the Yorùbá Bible.

28. This echo could be alluding to a number of Biblical passages, but seems closest to Psalm 46:9 ("He maketh wars to cease unto the end of the earth; He breaketh the bow, and cutteth the spear in sunder; He burneth the chariots in the fire"). Turner speaks of the "extraordinary popularity of the psalms among the aladura" (1967, I: 72–3).

29. Ọsitelu preached "The Lord of love is calling you. Do not refuse my invitation, says the Lord. . . . God does not want the death of a sinner, save that he repents and be saved. Remember Nineveh, all tribes" (Turner 1967, II: 337). The opening glee addresses God directly: "*Olúayé/Ìwọ ò fẹ́kú ẹlẹ̀sẹ̀ / Kó ronú pìwàdà / Kó sì maa ṣe rere*" (Lord of the Earth / You do not want the death of a sinner / Let him repent / And do good).

30. The ambiguous potential of the concept of *ọlajú* was widespread and of long standing. According to the CMS missionary James White, writing in 1866, the Àró of Odò complained "that when darkness prevailed upon the country they were honoured and respected for they could sell away all offensive persons—but now all is light and one cannot act as he pleases"—a striking adoption of the missionary idiom of light versus darkness but with reversed evaluative markers (quoted in Cornwall 1996, 46). For more recent examples of ambiguous usage see Peel (1978). The theater company's oeuvre shows a definite shift, over its 50-year life span, from positive to negative interpretations. In conversations with actors and audience members in the early 1980s, the concept was used in both positive and negative senses, but more often ambivalently. Indeed, by then it seemed often to mean something closer to "business acumen" or "worldly wisdom" than "civilization based on book learning." For example, when speaking of the early, amateur phase of the theater company's history, Grace observed that "*Ojú ò là dáadáa nígbà náà*" [Enlightenment/civilization was not fully established in those days]—for there were very

few theater companies at the time, and those that existed staged plays out of interest rather than for money. All the same, she said, "I could almost say that it was more gratifying then than now," because the audiences and performers were so dedicated and enthusiastic. In this usage (also attested elsewhere; see Cornwall 1996, 52), ọlajú is inherently ambiguous, encompassing as it does the expansion of commercial activity in modern Nigeria—an expansion that is both admired and blamed for the loss of older values.

31. This strand in the composite concept of enlightenment was early illustrated in the delightful example of the cultural nationalist Adégbóyèga Ẹdun of Abéòkúta, who defended polygamy in the name of hygiene (Pallinder 1990, 28–29).

32. Examples of all these forms of Islamic propaganda are to be found in the archive of the joint research project "The Role of the Media in the Constitution of New Religious Publics in Yorùbáland" conducted by the School of Oriental and African Studies and the Centre of West African Studies, University of Birmingham. Proselytizing drama videos sponsored by Islamic agencies include *Aha!* (sponsored by the Grand Council for Islamic Affairs), *Ìyá Àdínnì* (presented by the Islam First Association of Nigeria), and *Koto ìparun* (distributed by Al-Tawhid Islamic Centre).

33. Ládiípò's distinctive theatrical style, characterized by its affinity with older oral genres, had its heyday in the early 1960s and more or less vanished after his death in 1978. Many other companies, however, did keep open the option of injecting large amounts of *oríki* and incantations into their portrayals of everyday life. The Adéjọbí Company was always at the realist end of the spectrum of styles open to the popular theater.

11. WORK, DESTINY, AND SELF-MAKING

1. According to Adam (1995), the job of bricklayer is regarded as quite separate from that of building contractor, and while building contractors are potentially wealthy and of high status, bricklaying is one of the lowest of manual trades. However, this compartmentalization seems to be erased in the imagined career of Láníyọnu and, it is likely, often also in real life. In *The Road to Riches* (see below), Ọláòṣebìkan is an extremely wealthy building contractor, but his work is continuous with and not distinct from working on site and even getting involved in heavy laboring jobs.

2. The person who built houses one after another "like a nesting ant" was a common figure to indicate extreme wealth in the popular culture of the 1970s and 1980s: see Lérè Pàímọ́'s *Gbangbá DẸkùn* (Barber, Collins, and Ricard 1997); *The Road to Riches* (Barber and Ògúndíjọ 1994).

3. For example, visual art (Vogel 1991), fiction in English (Obiechina 1972), fiction in African languages (Barber 1997a; Ohly 1985), and popular urban folklore (Ṣekoni 1997) all began to seek to represent the world of everyday experience in its own terms, rather than to penetrate or evoke the hidden, secret world of spiritual forces that lies behind it.

4. Note that the period in which this transition is said to have occurred varies widely from scholar to scholar. Harold Bloom sees Shakespeare as the creator of the first modern characters endowed with interior life (Bloom 1999), whereas Burns places the decisive shift in consciousness almost two centuries later.

5. Porter (1997) offers a vivacious summary of what he takes to be the standard popular version of the history of the emergence of the Western self, in order to criticize its tendencies toward teleology, excessive progressivism, male orientation, and its oversimplification of the medieval mind, which Porter and other contributors to his edited volume suggest was more individualistic than standard ac-

counts allow for. For a concise overview of the way notions of hero, protagonist, character, figure, person, self, individual, and soul in literature provided successive and alternative perspectives on the human being, see Rorty (1976).

6. For African concepts of "the person," see Dieterlen (1973); La Fontaine (1985); Riesman (1986); and Jackson and Karp (1990). Drawing on oral texts from a range of African cultures, Lienhardt (1985) shows that a strong sense of individual difference and idiosyncrasy is not incompatible with strong corporate solidarity.

7. In a polite understatement, Taylor acknowledges that "the evidence of non-Western societies is perhaps not yet fully in" (1989, 310). The nature of the changes in concepts of "the person" and "the self" in colonial Africa has been touched on in passing from numerous angles: in literary criticism, in the large body of work on migration and urbanization, in discussions of religious movements and conversion. Some of these discussions—notably those belonging to "modernization theory" in the 1960s and 1970s—propounded a somewhat simplified, binary, prescriptive view of what it took to count as a "modern" personality in Africa: see, for example, *Becoming Modern*, by Inkeles and Smith (1975). Recent, very stimulating discussions are to be found in Piot (1999) relating to Togo and McCaskie (forthcoming) relating to the Gold Coast.

8. Compare Bakhtin's account of ancient Greek ideas about thought. Plato considered thought to be a conversation with oneself: a conversation, moreover, which "did not entail any special relationship to one's self (as distinct from one's relationship to others); conversation with one's own self turns directly into conversation with someone else, without a hint of any necessary boundaries between the two" (Bakhtin 1981, 134). However, Bakhtin's point is that in ancient Greek thought there was no inner/outer distinction at all; everything was public, and "man was completely *on the surface,* in the most literal sense of the word" (ibid., 133). In Yorùbá thought, by contrast, the most significant and dangerous dimensions of individuals are precisely what is hidden and invisible.

9. Ọládèjọ Òkédìjí's novels, especially his most recent one—*Atótó Arére* (1981)—go further than any other Yorùbá novel in rendering streams of consciousness (see Barber 1995b). Even here, though, it is debatable whether Òkédìjí is depicting ordinary life for its own sake; his novels are the bearers of implacable moral lessons, just like the popular theater and most of the other novels.

10. I have not been able to find a copy of the *Atọ́ka* version of *Adédigba's Co-wife* dating from 1969, so I can only guess at the difference between the video version and the early musical stage play. I suspect that the proliferation of spiritual agencies is partly a feature of the medium—video—which, as we saw in Chapters 8 and 10, was seen as a playground for the mounting of ever more extravagant excursions into the supernatural—and partly perhaps an effect of the increasing distance of the professional theater from the church. Maybe it also reflects a general recrudescence of witchcraft explanations even in Christian milieux in the very hard and uncertain conditions of the 1990s (see Chapter 10). The songs in the video version—which I presume are remnants of the old stage play—are distinctly more Christian in tone than the rest of the text. Even then, however, references to God blend smoothly with references to *ayé, kádàrá,* and *orí.*

11. In many of these stories, the humble, unknowing character attains his or her fortune in the most unexpected way—accepting something which appears poor or undesirable, but which miraculously engenders riches. There are variants of the plot in which only one character is involved—the first time innocently, the second time with ulterior motives—and sometimes the second sequence is truncated when the character, now motivated, is denied a second chance (for an example, see LaPin 1977, II: 476–484).

12. This sentence seems to suggest that Ọláòṣebìkan believes that magic money *does* exist, but that it destroys those who use it—a widespread point of view put forward in numerous plays, videos, novels, and newspaper reports. However, no magic money is shown in the play. The whole ritual ordeal, the "old man" who is supposed to provide the magic and the "spirits" who bring in the calabashes are all fabrications of Ọláòṣebìkan. This means that the dangerous properties of magic money (if it exists) are not the issue here: the issue is the *illusoriness* of such wealth and the folly of pinning one's hopes on it.

13. For a discussion of the way Alhaji effected a complete transformation of Lániyọnu's style of speech, see Chapter 12.

14. According to Lloyd, without the helper, "one's efforts are of little avail; and again one's good character is seen as important in attracting their help" (1974, 51).

12. LANGUAGE AND THE MORAL PUBLIC

1. Compare, for instance, with the verbal feats of Feste in *Twelfth Night*.

2. The theme of the young woman who prefers the sugar-daddy option to settling down with a young man of her own age is widespread in West African popular fiction. See Obiechina (1972); Newell (1998, 2000).

3. *Aláròyé*, October 8, 1996.

4. Take the story of Michael Absuhon, the son of an impoverished Agbor shoemaker in the delta region of Nigeria. After a long struggle to put himself through school, he had gotten as far as teacher training college when, working at night as a watchman to support himself, he was attacked and blinded by robbers. This story provides the platform for an extended commentary on the need for patience in the face of adversity, the impossibility of taking worldly wealth along with you when you die, and the unpredictability yet inevitability of destiny: "In this world we have seen an Ọba who became a slave. Here too we have seen a bondsman who became an important person. Elédùmarè knows who is going to attain honor or wealth. Each of us brought our own life-course with us from heaven. The journey we are going on is short, but our digressions are many, and that is why each of us continues to run around." (*Aláròyé*, August 13, 1996). No comment whatsoever is made about the fact that Michael belonged to a minority ethnic group from the other side of Nigeria: it appears to be irrelevant to the author's moral purpose.

5. Gaylon Jules Ferguson points to another instance of this use by Yorùbás of Ifá as a "national" symbol: a cartoon by a Yorùbá artist in which Nigeria is being dismembered by Islam on the one hand and Christianity on the other, while a *babaláwo* looks on with a worried expression. The *babaláwo* presumably represents Nigerian indigenous tradition as a whole. Ferguson notes that "the disjuncture between an *ethnic* nationalist solution—Ifa is after all a pan-*Yorùbá* divination system—to a crisis in the multi-ethnic *national* polity is ... displayed here" (1997, 183). I could add that *all* popular affirmations of "pan-African" or black racial identity in the Yorùbá popular culture genres with which I am acquainted are conspicuously uninterested in other African cultures. Their "pan-Africanism" is not an attempt to build solidarity through dialogue with other African peoples, or by seeking out the cultural elements they have in common. It is rather an affirmation of the capacity of Yorùbá traditions to *stand for* or *exemplify* a larger identity. Ferguson is right to point to the salience of racial and "pan-African" language in the neo-traditionalist Ifá movement; and this idiom is heard in other modern Yorùbá discourses too, for example the Yorùbá novel and neo-traditional oral/print poetry. But though he notes it, he fails fully to take account of the resiliently Yorùbá-centric character of the conceptions of "race" and "Africanity" there deployed.

13. CONCLUSION: THE LESSONS OF EXAMPLE

1. Proverbs attest to the importance of learning for yourself: *Kùkùté kan kì í fọ́ ni lẹ́po lẹ́ẹ̀méjì* [A tree stump does not break one's pot of oil on two occasions] (Delano 1966, 27). Others stress the value of learning from the experience of others: *Ẹni tó jìn sí kòtò kọ́ ara ẹ̀hìn lọ́gbọ́n* [He who falls into a ditch teaches others coming behind to be careful] (Delano 1966, 19); or of profiting from the wisdom of others: *Ọgbọ́n ọlọ́gbọ́n kì í jẹ́ kí a pe àgbàlagbà ní wèrè* [Other people's wisdom does not allow us to call an elder a fool] (Delano 1966, 28).

2. Quoted by Montaigne (1958 [1580], 344). He quotes in Latin; the English version is supplied by Montaigne's translator, J. M. Cohen.

3. Many attempts have been made to mobilize the distinction in a general theory of literature or literariness. For further discussion, see Todorov (1990); Riffaterre (1990); and Iser (1993).

APPENDIX 1: SYNOPSES

1. The title *Folájìyọ̀* comes from the proverb *A kì í fi ọlá jẹ iyọ̀.* [One does not consume salt as a show of one's wealth], which Owómóyèlà explains as follows: "In small quantities salt enhances the taste of foods. In large quantities, however, it ruins the taste and endangers the consumer's health.... The proverb is used to express the view that some things that are good in moderation should not be done to excess. It also advises people against turning their good fortune to disaster by unwise excesses in their enjoying it" (Owómóyèlà 1988, 40).

BIBLIOGRAPHY

Abercrombie, Nicholas, Scott Lash, and Brian Longhurst. 1992. "Popular Representation: Recasting Realism." In *Modernity and Identity*, ed. Scott Lash and Jonathan Friedman, 115–140. Oxford: Basil Blackwell.
Adam, Susanna. 1995. *Competence Utilization and Transfer in Informal Sector Production and Service Trades in Ibadan, Nigeria*. Munster/Hamburg: LIT.
Adedeji, J. A. 1971. "The Church and the Emergence of the Nigerian Theatre, 1866–1914." *Journal of the Historical Society of Nigeria* 6, no. 1: 25–45.
Adedeji, J. A. 1973. "Trends in the Content and Form of the Opening Glee in Yorùbá Drama." *Research in African Literatures* 4, no. 1: 32–47.
Adeoye, C. L. 1971. *Ẹ̀dá Omọ Oòd'uà*. Ibadan: Oxford University Press.
Adepegba, C. O., ed. 1995. *Oṣogbo: Model of Growing African Towns*. Institute of African Studies, University of Ibadan.
Adepoju, Aderanti, ed. 1976. *Internal Migration in Nigeria*. Nigeria: Institute of Population and Manpower Studies, University of Ifẹ.
Aderibigbe, A. B., ed. 1975. *Lagos: The Development of an African City*. Lagos: Longman Nigeria.
Adesanya, Afọlabi. 1997. "From Film to Video." In *Nigerian Video Films*, ed. Jonathan Haynes, 13–20. Jos: Nigerian Film Corporation.
Agawu, Kofi. 1995. *African Rhythm*. Cambridge: Cambridge University Press.
Ajayi, J. F. A. 1960. "How Yoruba Was Reduced to Writing." *Odu* 8.
Ajayi, J. F. A. 1965. *Christian Missions in Nigeria 1841–1891: The Making of a New Elite*. London: Longman.
Aluko, S. A., O. A. Oguntoye, and Y. A. O. Afọnja. 1972. *Small-scale Industries, Western State of Nigeria*. Ifẹ: University of Ifẹ Industrial Research Unit, Nigeria.
Ametewee, Awo Mana. 1993. *Akan Drama on G.B.C. Television as a Tool for the Education of Adults in Selected Parts of the Accra Metropolis*. M. Phil. dissertation, University of Ghana, Legon.
Anderson, Benedict. 1983. *Imagined Communities: Reflections on the Origin and Spread of Nationalism*. London: Verso.
Andrews, Richard. 1993. *Scripts and Scenarios: The Performance of Comedy in Renaissance Italy*. Cambridge: Cambridge University Press.
Appadurai, Arjun. 1996. *Modernity at Large: Cultural Dimensions of Globalization*. Minneapolis: University of Minnesota Press.
Armstrong, R. G. 1975. "*The Palmwine Drinkard:* An Appreciation." In *Yoruba Oral Tradition*, ed. 'Wande Abimbọla, 1071–1093. University of Ifẹ, Department of African Languages and Literatures.
Atanda, J. A. 1970. "Indirect Rule in Yorubaland." *Tarikh* 3, no. 3: 16–28.
Awẹ, Bọlanle, and Ọlawale Albert. 1995. "Historical Development of Osogbo." In *Osogbo: Model of Growing African Towns*, ed. C. O. Adepegba. Ibadan: Institute of African Studies, University of Ibadan.

Awoniyi, T. A. 1978. *Yoruba Language in Education 1846–1974: A Historical Survey.* Ibadan: Oxford University Press.
Ayandele, E. A. 1966. *The Missionary Impact on Modern Nigeria 1842–1914: A Political and Social Analysis.* London: Longman.
Babalọla, Adeboye. 1985. "Yoruba Literature." In *Literatures in African Languages,* ed. B. W. Andrzejewski, 157–189. Cambridge: Cambridge University Press.
Bada, S. O. 1970. *Òwe Yorùbá àti Ìṣẹ̀dálẹ̀ wọn.* Ibadan: University Press Limited.
Baker, Pauline H. 1974. *Urbanization and Political Change: The Politics of Lagos 1917–1967.* Berkeley and Los Angeles: University of California Press.
Bakhtin, M. M. 1981. *The Dialogic Imagination.* Ed. Michael Holquist. Trans. Caryl Emerson and Michael Holquist. Austin: University of Texas Press.
Bamisaiye, 'Rẹmi. 1995. "Sociological Influences of Western Education in Oṣogbo." In *Oṣogbo: Model of Growing African Towns,* ed. C. O. Adepegba, 52–70. Institute of African Studies, University of Ibadan.
Banham, Martin, with Clive Wake. 1976. *African Theatre Today.* London: Longman.
Barber, Karin. 1987. "Popular Arts in Africa." *African Studies Review* 30, no. 3: 1–78, 105–132.
Barber, Karin. 1990. "Discursive Strategies in the Texts of Ifá and in 'Holy Book of Odù' of the African Church of Ọ̀rúnmìlà." In *Self-assertion and Brokerage: Early Cultural Nationalism in West Africa,* ed. P. F. de Moraes Farias and Karin Barber, 196–224. Birmingham University African Studies Series no. 2.
Barber, Karin. 1991. *I Could Speak until Tomorrow: Oríkì, Women and the Past in a Yorùbá Town.* Edinburgh: Edinburgh University Press for the International African Institute.
Barber, Karin. 1994. "Money, Self-Realisation and the Person in Yorùbá Texts." In *Money Matters,* ed. Jane I. Guyer, 205–224. London: Heinemann/James Currey.
Barber, Karin. 1995a. "Literacy, Improvisation and the Public in Yorùbá Popular Theatre." In *The Pressures of the Text: Orality, Texts and the Telling of Tales,* ed. Stewart Brown, 6–27. Birmingham University African Studies Series 4.
Barber, Karin. 1995b. "African-Language Literature and Post-colonial Criticism." *Research in African Literatures* 26, no. 4: 3–30.
Barber, Karin. 1997a. "Time, Space and Writing in Three Colonial Yorùbá Novels." *The Yearbook of English Studies* 27: 108–129.
Barber, Karin. 1997b. "Preliminary Notes on Audiences in Africa." *Africa* 67, no. 3: 347–362.
Barber, Karin. 1997c. "Introduction." In *Readings in African Popular Culture,* ed. Karin Barber, 1–12. James Currey and Indiana University Press for the I.A.I.
Barber, Karin. 1999. "Quotation in the Constitution of Yorùbá Oral Texts." *Research in African Literatures* 30, no. 2: 17–41.
Barber, Karin, and Báyọ̀ Ògúndíjọ. 1994. *Yorùbá Popular Theatre: Three Plays By the Oyin Adéjọbí Company.* African Historical Sources Series no 9. Atlanta: ASA Press.
Barber, Karin, John Collins, and Alain Ricard. 1997. *West African Popular Theatre.* Bloomington: Indiana University Press.
Barber, Karin, and Christopher Waterman. 1995. "Traversing the Global and the Local: *Fújì* Music and Praise Poetry in the Production of Contemporary Yorùbá Popular Culture." In *Worlds Apart,* ed. Daniel Miller, 240–262. London: Routledge.
Barkan, Joel D, Michael L. McNulty, and M. A. O. Ayeni. 1991. "'Hometown' Voluntary Associations, Local Development, and the Emergence of Civil Society in Western Nigeria." *Journal of Modern African Studies* 29, no. 3: 457–480.
Barnes, Sandra T. 1986. *Patrons and Power: Creating a Political Community in Metropolitan Lagos.* Edinburgh: Edinburgh University Press for the I.A.I.

Beckerman, Bernard. 1990. *Theatrical Presentation: Performer, Audience and Art*. London: Routledge.
Beier, Ulli. 1954. "Yoruba Folk Opera." *African Music* 1, no. 1: 32–33.
Beier, Ulli. 1960. "Oshogbo." *Nigeria Magazine* 64 (special issue *Nigeria 1960*): 94–102.
Beier, Ulli. 1967. "Yoruba Theatre." In *Introduction to African Literature*, ed. Ulli Beier, 243–254. London: Longman.
Beier, Ulli. 1981. "E. K. Ogunmọla: A Personal Memoir." In *Drama and Theatre in Nigeria: A Critical Source Book*, ed. Yẹmi Ogunbiyi, 321–331. Lagos: Nigeria Magazine Publications.
Berliner, Paul. 1994. *Thinking in Jazz: The Infinite Art of Improvisation*. Chicago: University of Chicago Press.
Berman, Marshall. 1982. *All That Is Solid Melts into Air: The Experience of Modernity*. New York: Simon and Schuster.
Berry, Sara S. 1975. *Cocoa, Custom and Socio-economic Change in Rural Western Nigeria*. Oxford: Clarendon Press.
Berry, Sara S. 1985. *Fathers Work for Their Sons: Accumulation, Mobility and Class Formation in an Extended Yorùbá Community*. Berkeley: University of California Press.
Berwanger, Dietrich. 1988. *Television in the Third World*. Bonn: Friedrich-Ebert-Stiftung Media and Communication Department.
Bloch, Maurice. 1975. "Introduction." In *Political Language and Oratory in Traditional Society*, ed. Maurice Bloch, 1–28. London, New York, San Francisco: Academic Press.
Bloom, Harold. 1998. *Shakespeare: The Invention of the Human*. London: Fourth Estate.
Bourdieu, Pierre. 1984 [1979]. *Distinction: A Social Critique of the Judgement of Taste*. Trans. Richard Nice. London: Routledge and Kegan Paul.
Bourdieu, Pierre. 1996 [1992]. *The Rules of Art*. Trans. Susan Emanuel. London: Polity Press.
Bourdieu, Pierre. 1998 [1994]. *Practical Reason*. Stanford, Calif.: Stanford University Press.
Bourgault, Louise M. 1995. *Mass Media in Sub-Saharan Africa*. Bloomington: Indiana University Press.
Boyarin, Daniel. 1995. "Take the Bible for Example: Midrash as Literary Theory." In *Unruly Examples: On the Rhetoric of Exemplarity*, ed. Alexander Gelley, 27–47. Stanford, Calif.: Stanford University Press.
Breckenridge, Carol, and Arjun Appadurai. 1988. "Editors' Comments." *Public Culture* 1, no. 1: 1–4.
Brooks, Christopher Anton. 1989. "Duro Ladipọ and the Mọremi Legend: The Socio-Historical Development of the Yoruba Music Drama and Its Political Ramifications." Ph.D. dissertation, University of Texas at Austin.
Bruner, Jerome. 1991. "The Narrative Construction of Reality." *Critical Inquiry* 18: 1–21.
Burns, Edward. 1990. *Character, Acting and Being on the Pre-modern Stage*. London: Macmillan.
Callaway, Archibald C. 1960. "School Leavers and the Developing Economy in Nigeria." Nigerian Institute for Social and Economic Research Conference Proceedings (60–72). Ibadan: Nigerian Institute for Social and Economic Research.
Callaway, Archibald C. 1967. "From Traditional Crafts to Modern Industries." In *The City of Ibadan*, ed. P. C. Lloyd, A. L. Mabogunjẹ, and B. Awẹ, 153–171. Cambridge: Cambridge University Press.
Callaway, Archibald C. 1973. *Nigerian Enterprise and the Employment of Youth: Study of*

225 *Businesses in Ibadan*. Ibadan: Nigerian Institute for Social and Economic Research Monograph Series no. 2.
Carrithers, Michael, Steven Collins, and Steven Lukes, eds. 1985. *The Category of the Person: Anthropology, Philosophy, History.* Cambridge: Cambridge University Press.
Cawley, A. C., ed. 1974. *Everyman and Medieval Miracle Plays.* London: J. M. Dent and Sons.
Certeau, Michel de. 1984. *The Practice of Everyday Life.* Trans. Steven Rendall. Berkeley: University of California Press.
Clark, Ẹbun. 1979. *Hubert Ogunde: The Making of Nigerian Theatre.* Oxford: Oxford University Press.
Cole, Catherine. 1997. "'This Is Actually a Good Interpretation of Modern Civilisation': Popular Theatre and the Social Imaginary in Ghana, 1946–66." *Africa* 67, no. 3: 363–388.
Coleman, J. S. 1960. *Nigeria: Background to Nationalism.* Berkeley and Los Angeles: University of California Press.
Collins, John. 1985. *African Pop Roots.* London: Foulsham.
Collins, John. 1994. *Highlife Time.* Accra: Anansesem Publications.
Collins, Jim. 1989. *Uncommon Cultures: Popular Culture and Post-Modernism.* New York: Routledge.
Cornwall, Andrea Ella. 1996. "For Money, Children and Peace: Everyday Struggles in Changing Times in Ado-Odo, Southwestern Nigeria." Ph.D. dissertation, S.O.A.S., University of London.
Croce, Benedetto. 1992 [1902]. *The Aesthetic as the Science of Expression and of the Linguistic in General.* Trans. Colin Lyas. Cambridge: Cambridge University Press.
Daramọla, Olu. 1970. *Ilé tí a fi itọ́ mọ.* Ibadan: Oníbọn-Òjé Press.
Delanọ, Isaac O. 1966. *Owe l'Ẹsin Ọrọ. Yoruba Proverbs — Their Meaning and Usage.* Ibadan: Oxford University Press.
Desai, Gaurav. 1990. "Theater as Praxis: Discursive Strategies in African Popular Theater." *African Studies Review* 33, no. 1: 65–92.
Diawara, Manthia. 1992. *African Cinema: Politics and Culture.* Bloomington: Indiana University Press.
Dieterlen, G., ed. 1973. *La Notion de la Personne en Afrique Noire.* Paris: Editions du Centre National de la Recherche Scientifique.
Dollimore, Jonathan, and Alan Sinfield, eds. 1985. *Political Shakespeare.* Manchester: Manchester University Press.
Doortmont, Michel R. 1994. "Recapturing the Past: Samuel Johnson and the Construction of Yoruba History." Ph.D. dissertation, Erasmus Universiteit Rotterdam.
Drewal, H. J., and M. T. Drewal. 1983. *Gẹ̀lẹ̀dẹ́: Art and Female Power among the Yoruba.* Bloomington: Indiana University Press.
Drewal, Margaret Thompson. 1992. *Yoruba Ritual: Performers, Play, Agency.* Bloomington: Indiana University Press.
Duchartre, Pierre Louis. 1966 [1929]. *The Italian Comedy.* Trans. Randolph T. Weaver. New York: Dover Publications.
Eades, J. S. 1993. *Strangers and Traders: Yoruba Migrants, Markets and the State in Northern Ghana.* Edinburgh: Edinburgh University Press for the I.A.I.
Echeruo, M. J. C. 1977. *Victorian Lagos.* London: Macmillan.
Egunjọbi, Layi. 1995. "Osogbo: Aspects of Urbanization, Physical Planning and Development." In *Osogbo: Model of Growing African Towns,* ed. C. O. Adepegba, 13–29. Institute of African Studies, University of Ibadan.
Ekwensi, Cyprian. 1961. *Jagua Nana.* London: Heinemann.
Ẹsan, Oluyinka Anuọla. 1994. "Receiving Television Messages: An Ethnographic

Study of Women in a Nigerian Context." Ph.D. dissertation, University of Glasgow.
Etherton, Michael. 1982. *The Development of African Drama*. London: Hutchinson.
Fabian, Johannes. 1978. "Popular Culture in Africa: Findings and Conjectures." *Africa* 48, no. 4: 315–334.
Fabian, Johannes. 1990. *Power and Performance: Ethnographic Explorations through Proverbial Wisdom and Theater in Shaba, Zaire*. Madison: University of Wisconsin Press.
Fabian, Johannes. 1998. *Moments of Freedom: Anthropology and Popular Culture*. Charlottesville and London: University Press of Virginia.
Fafunwa, A. Babs. 1974. *History of Education in Nigeria*. London: George Allen and Unwin.
Fagborun, J. Gbenga. 1994. *The Yoruba Koiné: Its History and Linguistic Innovations*. Munich/Newcastle: Lincom Europa.
Fagunwa, D. O. 1950 [1938]. *Ogboju Ọdẹ Ninu Igbo Irunmalẹ*. Lagos: Thomas Nelson.
Falọla, Toyin. 1988. "Earliest Yoruba Writers." In *Perspectives on Nigerian Literature, 1700 to the Present*, vol. 1, ed. Yẹmi Ogunbiyi, 22–32. Lagos: Guardian Books Nigeria.
Ferguson, Gaylon Jules. 1997. "Writing Tradition: The Ethnographic Construction of Yoruba Traditional Culture." Ph.D. dissertation, Stanford University.
Finnegan, Ruth. 1998. *Tales of the City: A Study of Narrative and Urban Life*. Cambridge: Cambridge University Press.
Fisher, H. J. 1970. "Independence and Islam: The Nigerian Aladuras and Some Muslim Comparisons." *Journal of African History* 11, no. 2: 269–277.
Forge, Anthony. 1970. "Prestige, Influence and Sorcery: A New Guinea Example." In *Witchcraft Confessions and Accusations*, ed. Mary Douglas, 257–275. London: Tavistock Publications.
Fowler, Alastair. 1982. *Kinds of Literature: An Introduction to the Theory of Genres and Modes*. Oxford: Clarendon Press.
Freitag, Sandria B. 1989. *Collective Action and Community: Public Arenas and the Emergence of Communalism in North India*. Berkeley: University of California Press.
Friedman, Jonathan. 1995. "Global System, Globalisation and the Parameters of Modernity: Is Modernity a Cultural System?" In *From Post-traditional to Postmodern? Interpreting the Meaning of Modernity in Third World Urban Societies*, ed. Preben Kaarsholm, 5–30. International Development Studies, Roskilde University: Occasional Paper no. 14.
Furniss, Graham. 1996. *Poetry, Prose and Popular Culture in Hausa*. Edinburgh: Edinburgh University Press for the I.A.I.
Galletti, R., K. S. Baldwin, and I. O. Dina. 1956. *Nigerian Cocoa Farmers*. Westport, Conn.: Greenwood Press.
Gaonkar, Dilip Parameshwar. 1999. "On Alternative Modernities." *Public Culture* 11, no. 1: 1–18.
Garner, Stanton B. 1989. *The Absent Voice: Narrative Comprehension in the Theater*. Urbana and Chicago: University of Illinois Press.
Gbadamọsi, Bakare. 1965. *Orọ Pelu Idi Rẹ*. Oṣogbo: Mbari Mbayo Publications.
Gbadamọsi, [T.] G. O. 1967. "The Establishment of Western Education among Muslims in Nigeria." *Journal of the Historical Society of Nigeria* 4, no. 1: 89–115.
Gbadamọsi, T. G. O. 1978. *The Growth of Islam among the Yoruba 1841–1908*. London: Longman.
Gelley, Alexander. 1995. "Introduction." In *Unruly Examples: On the Rhetoric of Exemplarity*, ed. Alexander Gelley, 1–24. Stanford, Calif.: Stanford University Press.
Giddens, Anthony. 1990. *The Consequences of Modernity*. Cambridge: Polity Press.

Goodman, Nelson. 1981. "Routes of Reference." *Critical Inquiry* 8 (Autumn): 121–132.
Gotrick, Kacke. 1984. *Apidan Theatre and Modern Drama*. Stockholm: Almquist and Wicksell International.
Gunner, Liz. 2000. "Wrestling with the Present, Beckoning to the Past: Contemporary Zulu Radio Drama." *Journal of Southern African Studies* 26, no. 2: 223–237.
Guyer, Jane I. 1996. "Traditions of Invention in Equatorial Africa." *African Studies Review* 39, no. 3: 1–28.
Guyer, Jane I. 1997. *An African Niche Economy: Farming to Feed Ibadan*. Edinburgh: Edinburgh University Press for the I.A.I.
Habermas, Jurgen. 1991 [1962]. *The Structural Transformation of the Public Sphere*. Trans. Thomas Burger and Frederick Lawrence. Cambridge, Mass.: MIT Press.
Hallen, Barry, and J. O. Sodipo. 1986. *Knowledge, Belief and Witchcraft: Analytic Experiments in African Philosophy*. London: Ethnographica.
Hanks, William. 1996. *Language and Communicative Practices*. Boulder, Colo.: Westview Press.
Haynes, Jonathan. 1995. "Nigerian Cinema: Structural Adjustments." *Research in African Literatures* 26, no. 3: 97–119.
Haynes, Jonathan, ed. 1997. *Nigerian Video Films*. Jos: Nigerian Film Corporation.
Heilbrun, Carolyn G. 1988. *Writing a Woman's Life*. New York/London: W. W. Norton.
Hoch-Smith, Judith. 1978. "Radical Yoruba Female Sexuality: The Witch and the Prostitute." In *Women in Ritual and Symbolic Roles*, ed. Judith Hoch-Smith and Anita Spring, 245–267. New York and London: Plenum Press.
Hymes, Dell. 1996. *Ethnography, Linguistics, Narrative Inequality. Toward an Understanding of Voice*. London: Taylor and Francis.
Idowu, E. B. 1962. *Olodumare: God in Yoruba Belief*. London: Longman.
Inkeles, Alex, and David H. Smith. 1975. *Becoming Modern: Individual Change in Six Developing Countries*. London: Heinemann Educational Books.
Iser, Wolfgang. 1993. *The Fictive and the Imaginary: Charting Literary Anthropology*. Baltimore and London: Johns Hopkins University Press.
Isola, Akinwumi. 1988. "Contemporary Yorùbá Literary Tradition." In *Perspectives on Nigerian Literature: 1700 to the Present*, ed. Yemi Ogunbiyi, 73–84. Lagos: Guardian Books.
Isola, Akinwumi. 1992. "The African Writer's Tongue." *Research in African Literatures* 23, no. 1: 17–26.
Jackson, Michael, and Ivan Karp, eds. 1990. *Personhood and Agency: The Experience of Self and Other in African Cultures*. Uppsala: Almqvist and Wiksell.
Jeboda, Femi. 1964. *Olowolaiyemo*. Ibadan: Longman.
Jeyifo, 'Biodun. 1981. *The Yoruba Professional Itinerant Theatre: Oral Documentation*. Lagos: Division of Culture, Federal Ministry of Social Development, Youth, Sports and Culture.
Jeyifo, 'Biodun. 1984. *The Yoruba Popular Travelling Theatre of Nigeria*. Lagos: Nigeria Magazine Publications.
Johnson, Samuel. 1921. *The History of the Yorubas*. London: C.S.S.
Julien, Eileen. 1992. *African Novels and the Question of Orality*. Bloomington: Indiana University Press.
Kant, Immanuel. 1971. "An Answer to the Question: 'What Is Enlightenment?'" In *Kant's Political Writings*, ed. Hans Reiss. Trans. H. R. Nisbet, 54–60. Cambridge: Cambridge University Press.

Kavanagh, Robert Mshengu. 1985. *Theatre and Cultural Struggle in South Africa.* London: Zed Books.
Kaviraj, Sudipta. 1997. "Filth and the Public Sphere: Concepts and Practices about Space in Calcutta." *Public Culture* 10, no. 1: 83–113.
Kerr, David. 1995. *African Popular Theatre.* London: James Currey.
Koll, Michael. 1969. *Crafts and Cooperation in Western Nigeria: A Sociological Contribution to Indigenous Economics.* Bertelsmann Universitatsverlag.
La Fontaine, J. S. 1985. "Person and Individual: Some Anthropological Reflections." In *The Category of the Person,* ed. Michael Carrithers, Steven Collins, and Steven Lukes, 123–140. Cambridge: Cambridge University Press.
Ladipọ, Duro. 1970. *Ẹda.* Transcribed and translated by Val Ọlayẹmi. University of Ibadan: Institute of African Studies, Occasional Publication no. 24.
Ladipọ, Duro. 1972. *Ọba Ko So [The King Did Not Hang].* Transcribed and translated by R. G. Armstrong, Robert L. Awujoọla, and Val Ọlayẹmi. University of Ibadan: Institute of African Studies.
Ladipọ, Duro. 1973. *Moremi.* Translated with Introduction by Joel Yinka Adedeji. School of Drama, University of Ibadan, and Centre Régional de Documentation pour la Tradition Orale, Niamey, Niger.
Laitin, David D. 1986. *Hegemony and Culture: Politics and Religious Change among the Yorùbá.* Chicago/London: University of Chicago Press.
Lange, Siri. 1995. *From Nation-Building to Popular Culture: The Modernization of Performance in Tanzania.* Bergen, Norway: Chr. Michelsen Institute.
LaPin, Deirdre. 1977. "Story, Medium and Masque: The Idea and Art of Yoruba Story-telling." Ph.D. dissertation, University of Wisconsin.
Larkin, Brian. 1997. "Indian Films and Nigerian Lovers: Media and the Creation of Parallel Modernities." *Africa* 67, no. 3: 406–440.
Lawuyi, O. B. 1997. "The Political Economy of Video Marketing in Ogbomọṣọ, Nigeria." *Africa* 67, no. 3: 476–490.
Layiwọla, O. 1986. "Stagecraft in Nigerian Drama." Ph.D. dissertation, University of Leeds.
Lea, K. M. 1962. *Italian Popular Comedy: A Study in the Commedia dell'Arte, 1560–1620, with Special Reference to the English Stage.* 2 vols. New York: Russell and Russell.
Lefebvre, Henri. 1991 [1947]. *Critique of Everyday Life.* Vol. I. Trans. John Moore. London: Verso.
Leonard, Lynn. 1967. "The Growth of Entertainment of Non-African Origin in Lagos from 1866 to 1920." M. A. dissertation, University of Ibadan.
Lienhardt, Godfrey. 1985. "Self: Public, Private. Some African Representations." In *The Category of the Person,* ed. Michael Carrithers, Steven Collins, and Steven Lukes, 141–155. Cambridge: Cambridge University Press.
Lijadu, E. M. 1908 [1898]. *Ifá: Imọlẹ̀ rẹ̀ tí ísẹ Ipilẹ̀ Ìsìn ní ilẹ̀ Yorùbá.* Ado-Ekiti: Ọmọlayọ Standard Press of Nigeria.
Lijadu, E. M. 1972 [1908]. *Ọ̀rúnmlà.* Ado-Ekiti: Ọmọlayọ Standard Press of Nigeria.
Lindsay, Lisa A. 1996. "Putting the Family on Track: Gender and Domestic Life on the Colonial Nigerian Railway." Ph.D. dissertation, University of Michigan.
Lloyd, P. C. 1974. *Power and Independence: Urban Africans' Perception of Social Inequality.* London: Routledge and Kegan Paul.
Mackay, Ian M. 1964. *Broadcasting in Nigeria.* Ibadan, Nigeria: Ibadan University Press.
Matory, J. Lorand. 1994. *Sex and the Empire That Is No More: Gender and the Politics of Metaphor in Oyo Yoruba Religion.* Minneapolis: University of Minnesota Press.
Mbala Nkanga, Dieudonné-Christophe. 1995. "Multivocality and the Hidden Text

in Central African Theatre and Popular Performance: A Study of the Rhetoric of Social and Political Criticism." Ph.D. dissertation, Northwestern University.
McCaskie, T. C. Forthcoming. *Adeɛbeba: the People of an Asante Village 1850–1950*. Edinburgh University Press for the I.A.I.
Mda, Zakes. 1993. *When People Play People: Development Communication through Theatre.* London: Zed Books.
Medvedev, P. N., and M. M. Bakhtin. 1978 [1928]. *The Formal Method in Literary Scholarship: A Critical Introduction to Sociological Poetics.* trans. Albert J. Wehrle. Baltimore: Johns Hopkins University Press.
Mitchell, Timothy. 1988. *Colonising Egypt.* Cambridge: Cambridge University Press.
Mlama, Penina Muhando. 1991. *Culture and Development: The Popular Theatre Approach in Africa.* Uppsala, Sweden: Scandinavian Institute of African Studies.
Montaigne, Michel de. 1958 [1580]. *Essays.* Trans. J. M. Cohen. London: Penguin.
Moraes Farias, P. F. de. 1990. "'Yoruba Origins' Revisited by Muslims: An Interview with the Arókin of Ọ̀yó and a Reading of the Aṣl Qabā'il Yūrubā of Al-Ḥājj Ādam al-Ilūrī." In *Self-assertion and Brokerage: Early Cultural Nationalism in West Africa,* ed. P. F. de Moraes Farias and Karin Barber, 109–147. Birmingham University African Studies Series no. 2.
Muckenhirn, Erma F. 1966. *Secondary Education and Girls in Western Nigeria.* Ann Arbor: University of Michigan Comparative Education Dissertation Series no. 9.
Munz, Peter. 1956. "History and Myth." *Philosophical Quarterly* 6, no. 22: 1–16.
Nagler, Michael N. 1974. *Spontaneity and Tradition: A Study in the Oral Art of Homer.* Berkeley: University of California Press.
Newell, Stephanie. 1997. "Making Up Their Own Minds: Readers, Interpretations and the Difference of View in Ghanaian Popular Narratives." *Africa* 67, no. 3: 389–405.
Newell, Stephanie. 1998. "West African Popular Literatures: Readers, Texts and Gender Perspectives in Local Publications from Ghana and Nigeria." Ph.D. dissertation, University of Birmingham.
Newell, Stephanie. 2000. *Ghanaian Popular Fiction: "Thrilling Discoveries in Conjugal Life" and Other Tales.* London and Athens, Ohio: James Currey Publishers and Ohio University Press.
Ọbafẹmi, Olu. 1996. *Contemporary Nigerian Theatre: Cultural Heritage and Social Vision.* Bayreuth: Bayreuth African Studies 40.
Obiechina, E. N. 1972. *Onitsha Market Literature.* London: Heinemann.
Odunjọ, J. F. 1964. *Kúyẹ̀.* Ibadan: African Universities Press.
Ogunbiyi, Yẹmi, ed. 1981. *Drama and Theatre in Nigeria: a Critical Source Book.* Lagos: Nigeria Magazine Publications.
Ogunbiyi, Yẹmi. 1981. "The Popular Theatre: A Tribute to Duro Ladipọ." In *Drama and Theatre in Nigeria: a Critical Source Book,* ed. Yẹmi Ogunbiyi, 333–353. Lagos: Nigeria Magazine Publications.
Ogundele, Wọle. 1997. "From Folk Opera to Soap Opera: Improvisations and Transformations in Yoruba Popular Theatre." In *Nigerian Video Films,* ed. Jonathan Haynes, 45–70. Jos: Nigerian Film Corporation.
Ogunmọla, Kọla. 1968. *The Palm-wine Drinkard.* Trans. Robert Armstrong, Robert Awujọọla, and Val Ọlayẹmi. University of Ibadan, Institute of African Studies, Occasional Publication no. 12.
Ogunṣina, Bisi. 1992. *The Development of the Yorùbá Novel 1930–1975.* Ibadan: Gospel Faith Mission Press.
Oha, Obododimma. 1997. "The Rhetoric of Nigerian Christian Videos: The War Paradigm of *The Great Mistake.*" In *Nigerian Video Films,* ed. Jonathan Haynes, 93–98. Jos: Nigerian Film Corporation.

Ohly, Rajmund. 1985. "Literature in Swahili." In *Literatures in African Languages*, ed. B. W. Andrzejewski, S. Pilaszewicz, and W. Tyloch, 460–492. Cambridge: Cambridge University Press.
Okediji, Oladejo. 1981. *Atótó Arére*. Ibadan: University Press.
Oladapọ, Ọlatunbọsun. 1973. *Àròyé Akéwì*. Apá Kíínní. Ibadan: Onibọnoje Press.
Oladapọ, Ọlatunbọsun. 1975. *Àròyé Akéwì*. Apá Kejì. Ibadan: Onibọnoje Press.
Omu, Fred I. A. 1978. *Press and Politics in Nigeria, 1880–1937*. Atlantic Highlands, N.J.: Humanities Press.
Otudeko, Adebisi Olusoga. 1977. "Adjustment of Migrants in an African City." Ph.D. dissertation, Stanford University.
Owomoyela, Oyekan. 1988. *A Kì í: Yorùbá Proscriptive and Prescriptive Proverbs*. New York and London: University Press of America.
Oyeneye, O. Y. 1979. "The Apprenticeship System in Southwestern Nigeria: A Case of Human Resource Development." Ph.D. dissertation, Birmingham University.
Pallinder, Agneta. 1990. "Adegboyega Edun: Black Englishman and Yoruba Cultural Patriot." In *Self-assertion and Brokerage: Early Cultural Nationalism in West Africa*, ed. P. F. de Moraes Farias and Karin Barber, 11–34. Birmingham University African Studies Series no. 2.
Peace, Adrian. 1979. *Choice, Class and Conflict: A Study of Southern Nigerian Factory Workers*. Atlantic Highlands, N.J.: Humanities Press.
Peel, J. D. Y. 1968. *Aladura: A Religious Movement among the Yoruba*. London: Oxford University Press for the I.A.I.
Peel, J. D. Y. 1978 "Olaju: A Yoruba Concept of Development." *Journal of Development Studies* 14, no. 2: 139–165.
Peel, J. D. Y. 1983. *Ijeshas and Nigerians: The Incorporation of a Yoruba Kingdom 1890s–1970s*. Cambridge: Cambridge University Press.
Peel, J. D. Y. 1989. "The Cultural Work of Yoruba Ethnogenesis." In *History and Ethnicity*, ed. Elizabeth Tonkin et al., 198–215. London: Routledge.
Peel, J. D. Y. 1990. "The Pastor and the *Babaláwo*: The Interaction of Religions in Nineteenth-Century Yorùbáland." *Africa* 60, no. 3: 338–369.
Peel, J. D. Y. 2000. *Religious Encounter and the Making of the Yoruba*. Bloomington: Indiana University Press.
Peil, Margaret. 1981. *Cities and Suburbs: Urban Life in West Africa*. New York and London: Africana Publishing Company.
Peil, Margaret, Stephen K. Ekpenyong, and Olatunji Y. Oyeneye. 1988. "Going Home: Migration Careers of Southern Nigerians." *International Migration Review* 22, no. 4: 563–585.
Peterson, Bhekizizwe. 1994. "Apartheid and the Political Imagination in Black South African Theatre." In *Politics and Performance: Theatre, Poetry and Song in Southern Africa*, ed. Liz Gunner, 35–54. Johannesburg: Witwatersrand University Press.
Piot, Charles. 1999. *Remotely Global: Village Modernity in West Africa*. Chicago: The University of Chicago Press.
Porter, Roy, ed. 1997. *Rewriting the Self: Histories from the Renaissance to the Present*. London: Routledge.
Priebe, Richard. 1978. "Popular Writing in Ghana: A Sociology and Rhetoric." *Research in African Literatures* 9, no. 3: 395–425.
Reichmuth, Stefan. 1988. "Songhay-Lehnwörter im Yoruba und ihr historischer Kontext." *Sprache und Geschichte in Afrika* 9: 269–299.
Reichmuth, Stefan. 1996. "Education and the Growth of Religious Associations among Yoruba Muslims: The Ansar-ud-Deen Society of Nigeria." *Journal of Religion in Africa* 26, no. 4: 365–405.

Ricard, Alain. 1986. *L'Invention du Théâtre: Le Théâtre et les Comédiens en Afrique Noire.* Lausanne: Editions l'Age d'Homme.
Riesman, Paul. 1986. "The Person and the Life Cycle in African Social Life and Thought." *African Studies Review* 29, no. 2: 71–198.
Riffaterre, Michael. 1990. *Fictional Truth.* Baltimore and London: Johns Hopkins University Press.
Rorty, Amélie Oksenberg. 1976. "A Literary Postscript: Characters, Persons, Selves, Individuals." In *The Identities of Persons,* ed. Amélie Oksenberg Rorty, 301–323. Berkeley: University of California Press.
Ryan, Patrick J. 1978. *Imale: Yoruba Participation in the Muslim Tradition—A Study of Clerical Piety.* Cambridge, Mass.: Scholars Press (Harvard Theological Review/ Harvard Dissertations on Religion, no. 11).
Sada, P.O., and Adefolalu, A. A. 1975. "Urbanisation and Problems of Urban Development." In *Lagos: The Development of an African City,* ed. A. B. Aderibigbe, 79–107. Lagos: Longman Nigeria.
Schechner, Richard. 1988. *Performance Theory.* New York and London: Routledge.
Schwab, William B. 1952. "The Political and Social Organization of an Urban African Community." Ph.D. dissertation, University of Pennsylvania.
Schwab, William B. 1965. "Oshogbo: An Urban Community?" In *Urbanization and Migration in West Africa,* ed. Hilda Kuper, 85–109. Westport, Conn.: Greenwood Press.
Scott, James C. 1990. *Domination and the Arts of Resistance: Hidden Transcripts.* New Haven: Yale University Press.
Sekoni, Ropo. 1997. "Politics and Urban Folklore in Nigeria." In *Readings in African Popular Culture,* ed. Karin Barber, 142–146. London: James Currey.
Skinner, Quentin. 1978. *The Foundations of Modern Political Thought.* 2 vols. Cambridge: Cambridge University Press.
Smythe, H. H., and M. M. Smythe. 1960. *The New Nigerian Elite.* Stanford, Calif.: Stanford University Press.
Taylor, Charles. 1989. *Sources of the Self: The Making of the Modern Identity.* Cambridge, Mass.: Harvard University Press.
Thomas, I. B. 1929 [1930]. *Itan Igbesi Aiye Emi Segilola.* Lagos: CMS Bookshops.
Todorov, Tzvetan. 1990. *Genres in Discourse.* Trans. Catherine Porter. Cambridge: Cambridge University Press.
Trager, Lillian. 1976. "Yoruba Markets and Trade: Analysis of Spatial Structure and Social Organization in the Ijesaland Marketing System." Ph.D. dissertation, University of Washington.
Trager, Lillian. 1998. "Home-Town Linkages and Local Development in Southwestern Nigeria: Whose Agenda? What Impact?" *Africa* 68, no. 3: 360–382.
Turner, H. W. 1967. *History of an African Independent Church.* 2 vols. Oxford: Clarendon Press.
Ukadike, Frank Nwachukwu. 1994. *Black African Cinema.* Berkeley and Los Angeles: University of California Press.
Vogel, Susan, with Ima Ebong. 1991. *Africa Explores.* New York: Center for African Art.
Voloshinov, V. N. 1973 [1929]. *Marxism and the Philosophy of Language.* Trans. Ladislav Matejka and I. R. Titunik. Cambridge, Mass.: Harvard University Press.
Walker, B. K., and W. S. Walker. 1961. *Nigerian Folk Tales.* New Brunswick, N.J.: Rutgers University Press.
Walton, Kendall L. 1990. *Mimesis as Make-Believe: On the Foundations of the Representational Arts.* Cambridge, Mass.: Harvard University Press.

Waterman, Christopher Alan. 1990a. *Jùjú: A Social History and Ethnography of an African Popular Music*. Chicago: University of Chicago Press.
Waterman, Christopher Alan. 1990b. "'Our Tradition Is a Very Modern Tradition': Popular Music and the Construction of Pan-Yorùbá Identity." *Ethnomusicology* 34, no. 3.
Watt, Ian. 1963 [1957]. *The Rise of the Novel*. Harmondsworth: Peregrine Books.
Wilson, Scott. 1995. *Cultural Materialism: Theory and Practice*. Oxford: Blackwell.
Zachernuk, P. S. 1998. "African History and Imperial Culture in Colonial Nigerian Schools." *Africa* 4, no. 68: 484–505.
Zijderveld, Anton C. 1979. *On Clichés: The Supersedure of Meaning by Function in Modernity*. London: Routledge and Kegan Paul.

INDEX

Page numbers in *italics* refer to illustrations.

Abíọ́lá, M. K. O., 295
Abúlúdèé Rónkẹ́ (audience member), 299
acoustics, 99
actors, 3, 36, 62; actresses as polygynous wives, 283–84; apprenticeship and, 85–92, 87, 91, 348–49; as artisans, 306, 348–52, 423–24; audiences as anonymous helpers of, 237–39, 245, 425; autonomy of, 201–203; characterization and, 143–44; education of, 78–84; family-like organization of, 289; favorite parts of, 139, 142; mobility of, 73, 75–78; name recognition of, 143; personal experiences of, 9, 15, 138, 266, 423, 426; public opinion of, 204, 217, 282; recognized in public, 55, 237–38; recruitment of, 62–73; salaries of, 90, 129–30; set pieces and, 153; social formation of, 7; spoken dialogue and, 43–44; writing of plays and, 138–39. *See also individual actors*
Adam, Susanna, 350
Adé, Ìyá. *See* Adéjọbí, Grace
Adédigba, Alhaji (audience member), 217, 218
Adédigba's Co-wife (play), 42, 49, 70, 261–62, 283, 429; agency and interiority in, 361–62, 365–71, *367–69*; autobiographical aspect of, 47–48; synopsis of, 441–42; television performance of, 257; video version, 340, 362, 365, *368*, *369*, 460n10
Adéjọbí, Adédìran (first son of Oyin), 73, *74*
Adéjọbí, Adédùnmọ́lá (daughter of Oyin), 58, 67, 73, *75*, 78; drumming and, 100; on television, 247; television career ambitions of, 242–43
Adéjọbí, Adélékè, 21, 22, 24, 80
Adéjọbí, Gbádébò (child of Oyin), 66
Adéjọbí, Grace (Ìyá Adé) (first wife of Oyin), 38, *43*, 49, 71–72, 114, 171, 183; as actress, 65; in *Besotted Bridegroom*, 175, 189–90; biographical sketch of, 62–63; on early days of theater, 41–42; education of, 79; in *External Appearances*, 231; family of, 75–76; in *The Heir*, 275, *276*; in *Hospital*, 249; in *Kúyẹ̀*, *354*; on *Ọba Kô So*, 324; in *The Overreacher*, 229; on polygyny, 283; relations with other wives, 66; relations with Oyin, 284; in sewing trade, 85–86; on songs, 48; in *Taking Care of Kúnlé*, 215; on television, 244; in video dramas, 262
Adéjọbí, Oyin, 1, 16, 49; as actor, 175, 249, 276, 289–91; additions/revisions to plays and, 166; Association of Theatre Practitioners of Nigeria and, 56; as authority figure, 289–91; as council clerk, 92, 289, 312; education of, 79–80, 307, 308; family of, 324–25; as film actor, 260; film projects and, 112–13; on friendship, 285–86; getting ideas for plays, 131–35; history (biography) of, 18, 20–22, 427; household of, 87, 138, 270; in Lagos, 22–25; on life as drama, 266; opening addresses of, 233; in opening glees, *59*; oral genres and, 342–44; on politics, 298–99; public regard of, 205; recruitment of actors and, 63–73; on road trips, 118, 126, 129; return to Òṣogbo (1953), 36, 38–40; television and, 243, 244, 245–48; video dramas and, 60, 258, 261–62, 321; wives of, 62–63, 65–67, 284; writing of plays and, 135–44, 320
Adéjọbí Musical Party, 47, 63
Adéjọbí Singing Party, 33–38
Adéníjì, Fẹ́mi, 68–70, 75, 77, 116; education of, 79; favorite parts, 142; in *Hospital*, 249; leaves the company, 129; preacting trade of, 85; as specialist, 99
Adénlé I (Ọba), 39

Adéògún Theatre, 70
Adépòjù, Alhaji Kàrímù, 16, 20, 47, 109, 350; as actor, 140–42, 142, 143, 289–91; additions/revisions to plays and, 166; art of language and, 399, 401–402, 404; on audiences, 206; as authority figure, 289–91; biographical sketch of, 63–65; composing of plays and, 136–44, 170–71, 320; departure from the company, 339; early days of Oyin Adéjọbí Theatre and, 62; education of, 75, 79, 307; in *External Appearances*, 411; filling out of plays and, 188; film projects and, 58, 259; getting ideas for plays, 131–35; in *Hospital*, 249; on improvisation, 188–89, 201; in *Kúyẹ̀*, 379–82, 387; on lighting, 99; on morality, 220, 328; as Muslim, 78; in *The Overreacher*, 405, 408; popular name recognition of, 143; in *The Road to Riches*, 391; on road trips, 103, 104, 109–10, 118; in *The Royal Palm-nut*, 329; as stage manager, 47, 90; as tailor, 85; in *Taking Care of Kúnlé*, 160, 162, 215; television and, 49, 247; video dramas and, 60, 258, 262, 321, 340
Adépòjù, Láńrewájú, 83, 84, 233, 294, 302
Adéwuni, John, 67–68, 69, 72, 74, 75; acting style of, 115; on actors' pay, 90; in *Articulated Lorry*, 146–47; on "being known," 237, 238; in *Besotted Bridegroom*, 175, 189–90, 191, 230; education of, 79, 82; in *External Appearances*, 231, 236, 291, 292; family background of, 270; favorite parts, 142; in *Kúyẹ̀*, 379, 381–82; in *The Overreacher*, 229, 291, 303, 405; popular name recognition of, 143; quoted, 88–89; relationship with Morádékẹ́, 282; on seniority, 100–101; in *Taking Care of Kúnlé*, 162, 206–207; television and, 244–45; on traditional culture, 328; in video dramas, 262
advertising, 50, 125
Africa (West Africa), 5, 15, 433; African culture, 3; Francophone, 258; migration in, 22; pan-Africanism, 461n5; television in, 48, 240; urbanization in, 234
African Studies, 9
"Agbako" (popular comedian), 262
agency, 10, 358, 359–61, 379, 396
Aguda (repatriated slaves), 22
Aiyé (film), 57, 125, 258
Àjàgbé Ejò. See *Articulated Lorry* (play)
Ají, Ìyá. *See* Emily (Ìyá Ají) (fourth wife of Oyin)
Àkànmú, Boọ̀dá, 108–109

Akéwì Theatre, 84
Akínpẹ̀lú, Dayọ̀, 67, 69, 72, 114; in *The Heir*, 140, 141, 274, 275, 276; in *Hospital*, 255; in *Kúyẹ̀*, 384; leaving the company, 140; in *The Overreacher*, 406; in *The Road to Riches*, 139; sound system and, 101; as specialist, 99; in *Taking Care of Kúnlé*, 160, 162, 215
Akínwálé, Hamed, 71, 78, 79, 86, 90
Àkọ́bí Olóògbé. See *Heir, The* (play)
Al-Iluri, Al-Hajj Adam, 307
Aládùúrà churches, 26, 29, 30; Adéjọbí and, 36; membership of, 31, 317; polygamy and, 283, 313; theatrical representation of, 57, 292–93, 329, 362, 412
alágbe ("beggars"), 46
alárìnjó masquerade theater, 225–27, 237, 336–37
Aláròyé (newspaper), 417–18, 419, 431
Àlíyù, Jímọ̀, 5, 134, 242
All Saints' Church, 38, 41, 42, 44, 50, 63
All Saints' School (Òṣogbo), 40
amateur performance, 29, 32, 40–44
amplifiers, 93, 95
Anglican churches, 26, 32, 38, 106–107
anonymity: *alárìnjó* masquerade theater and, 238; audiences and, 232, 234, 236, 238–39, 245
Ansar-ud-Deen Society, 29, 32, 64, 82, 307, 455n5
anthropologists, 11, 366
aphorisms, 416–21
apprenticeship, 77, 85–87, 91, 348–49
Arabic language, 28, 307, 455n4
area boys, 26
Arélù (television serial), 5, 134, 242
Arianne (actress), 338
Arísẹkọ́lá, Ayox, 262
"art" theater, 3
Articulated Lorry (play), 105–107, 111, 143, 171; art of language and, 400–401; enlightenment concept in, 330–35; household in, 272; inessential characters and episodes in, 146–48; learning lines for, 138; lesson of, 173, 281; *oríkì* chants in, 342; plot structure of, 145–46; politics in, 295–98; stage space and, 229; synopsis of, 438–39
artisans, 2, 4, 54; actors as, 348–52; apprenticeship and, 86; former slaves as, 22; in Òṣogbo, 39–40
assemblage, 29, 89, 432
Association of Theatre Practitioners of Nigeria, 55–56
Atọ́ka magazine, 16, 57, 71, 133, 318; actors' popularity and, 237, 243; conjugal partnership theme in, 288; as inspiration

for theater careers, 72, 78, 244; *Kúyẹ̀* in, 375, 376; literacy and, 317; title of *The Royal Palm-nut* in, 299; plays serialized in, 50
audiences, 2, 12, 44; actors' name recognition and, 143; adjustment to, 166; as anonymous helpers, 237–39, 245, 425; boisterous, 99; dwindling of, 59; elite, 19, 350; improvisation and, 188; lessons of plays and, 216–25; modernity and, 234–39; "people's" theater and, 4; as producers, 4; as a public, 12, 32, 225–34; reactions of, 9; religion and, 326; repetition of dialogue and, 197; response to, 180–81; responses of, 207–14, 216, 423; rowdy, 180, 206; scouting for, 88; search for, 54, 422; secular, 20; size of, 126–27; slowness of performance and, 49–50; social composition of, 3, 204–207, 243, 244; views of, 15
auditoriums, 122, 232, 234
authority. *See* power
Ayé Ṣòro [*The World Is Hard*]. *See Royal Palm-nut, The* (play)
Àyìndé, Alhaji Barrister, 264, 337
Ayọ̀délé, Gabriel Adébáyọ̀, 50

Baba. *See* Adéjọbí, Oyin
Babangida regime, 294
Babátúndé, Samuel, 89–90, 259
backcloths, 95, 96, 129
backstage, 226, 231, 232
Bakhtin, M. M., 265, 266, 270
Balógun, Rasheed (audience member), 217, 218
Bámidélé, Fẹ́mi, 70–71, 75; in *Articulated Lorry*, 147; costumes and, 101; education of, 78, 79, 81–82; family background of, 270; favorite parts, 142
Bámiṣilẹ̀, Gabriel (audience member), 217, 222
Bantu Language Services radio, 433
Beier, Ulli, 39, 40
Béjìdé, Ayọ̀ (audience member), 223
Besotted Bridegroom (play), 117–18, 120, 123, 125, 170; audience response to, 217–18, 221–25, 268; audiences for, 205–206; building of excitement in, 346–47; first impressions of, 173–79; household in, 271; improvisation of phrases in, 188–201; lessons of, 174, 178, 185, 281; monologue in, 192, 193; plot structure of, 134; politics in, 303; polygamy in, 285; popular idiom and, 216; power in, 292; slot roles in, 150; songs in, 345–46; structural changes in, 179–88; synopsis of, 440
biblical stories, 34–35, 36, 41, 54. *See also* Christianity
Billiard Room (Òṣogbo), 44
"Bishop's Candlesticks," 29
bit-part players, 73
Bourdieu, Pierre, 19, 447(2)n2
Bourgault, Louise, 241
"Brazilians" (repatriated slaves), 22
bricolage, 431
Britain, 183
Buhari regime, 294, 299

cantatas, 30, 31
cash-crop farming, 5, 20, 21
Catholicism, 22
censorship, 269, 302
chance, role of, 266
characterization, 143, 144
chiefs, traditional, 39, 40
children, 38, 102, 206, 270; in audience, 99; seating and, 228; television and, 242
choral singing, 51
Christianity, 19, 20, 21, 24; Aládùúrà churches, 26, 31; Christian actors, 78; Christian elites, 61, 405; Christian relations with Muslims, 326–29, 339–40, 424; conversion to, 312–15, 321–26; elites, 45; fundamentalist, 339; hymns, 342; mission churches, 29; modernity and, 42–43; represented in plays, 38, 149; schools and, 206–208. *See also* biblical stories; missionaries
chronotope, 265, 270
Church of the Lord, 31–32, 38, 67, 313–14
cinema. *See* films
civil society, 19, 358
civilization, 14, 306, 310, 323
closure, 232
"college" venues, 123–24, 126
colloquialisms, 404
colonial era, 401; realist genres during, 352
colonialism, 2, 266, 295; artisanal production under, 39–40; artists in colonial period, 19; culture of, 12; education and, 306, 308, 454n1; Lagos as colonial headquarters, 23; Yorùbá language and, 4
comedies, 2, 51; domestic, 148–50, 258; Elizabethan, 410; "modern comedies," 144–46; physical, 180
Comet, The (newspaper), 28
communalism, 13, 358
Compagnie Française de l'Afrique Occidentale (CFAO), 39

478 Index

conscientization, 3
consciousness, 8, 11, 361–72
consumption, 5
Cornwall, Andrea, 267–68, 281
costumes, 88, 93, 99, 101; for *Hospital*, 249; replacement of, 129; "surprise" of spectacle and, 232
Creppy, Kobina, 23
Critique of Everyday Life, A (Lefebvre), 8
cultural imperialism thesis, 241
cultural materialism, 7
cultural nationalism, 25, 308, 313; pan-Yorùbá consciousness and, 13; traditional culture and, 42, 315–16
curtains, 232

Dágilọlá, Moses (audience member), 217, 222
Dálé Mọṣú (play), 132–33, 134, 281
"Dance of the Guinea Fowls," 29
Daramọ́lá, Olú, 132, 317
David, A. B., 30, 35
Deborah (Ìyáa Jọkẹ́) (third wife of Oyin), 65, *103*, 104; in *Articulated Lorry*, 401; in *Kúyẹ̀*, *379–82*; in opening glees, 106; in *Road to Riches*, 152
Destiny (play), 420–21
development theater, 3
dialogue, spoken, 43, 48, 49, 193, 406; actors' input into writing of, 139; improvisation of, 172; microphones and, 230; from *The Royal Palm-nut*, 53; set pieces, 150, 194–97; writing of plays and, 136–37
Drewal, Margaret Thompson, 10
drumming, 1, 2, 40, 41, 341; acting and, 67–68; actors' abilities at, 100–101; *dùndún*, 73, 341; social relations and, 344

Eagleton, Terry, 7
Ẹ̀dá (Ládiípọ̀), 35
Ẹ̀dá (play), 343
editing, 341
education, 3, 4, 63, 306–12; of actors, 71, 75, 76, 78–84; availability of, 55; commercial opportunities and, 23; concentration of schools, 23; enlightenment and, 25; expansion of audience and, 424; levels attained, 451n5; modern schools, 64; monogamy and, 283; oil wealth and, 19; school leavers, 45, 86, 348; social level and, 89; wisdom and, 38. *See also* schools
Ẹfúnsetán Aníwúrà (poetic drama), 133
ẹgbẹ́ (association), 130, 336–37
egúngún masquerade, 227, 336–37, 344

ẹkún ìyàwó (bride's lament), 415
Èkùrọ́ Ọlọ́já. See *Royal Palm-nut, The* (play)
elites, 38, 39, 45, 315; class culture and, 311–12; insignia of eliteness, 456n14; school audiences and, 206–207; social esteem of theater and, 61; television and, 241, 242, 243; view of popular theater, 204; Yorùbá literacy and, 308
Elúwọlé, 113, 114, 252
Emily (Ìyá Ají) (fourth wife of Oyin), 58, 65–66, 73, *74*, 78; in *Besotted Bridegroom*, 175; education of, 79; family of, 76; on favorite parts, 139; in *The Heir*, 275; in *Hospital*, 249, 250; on learning lines, 137–38; on moral lessons of plays, 219–20; in opening glees, 106; relations with Oyin, 284; in "staff bus," 95; in *Taking Care of Kúnlé*, 210
English language, 2, 31, 64, 182; as colonial/official language, 312, 424; employment prospects and, 306, 308, 330; English loan words in Yorùbá, 410–11; English words/phrases in Yorùbá dialogue, 334, 411; inserted into Yorùbá dialogue, 401; novels in, 84; Saro elite and, 25; theatrical productions in, 3, 28, 33; translation from Yorùbá, 16; video dramas in, 261; words adapted to Yorùbá phonology, 194
enlightenment, 4, 13, 21, 310; in *Articulated Lorry*, 148; as aspiration, 330; as consensus value, 25; contradictions of, 42; education and, 311; elites and, 40; monogamy and, 283; negative side of, 14, 336, 339; occult and, 264; oral genres and, 342; popular conception of, 217; schools and, 306–12; self-making and, 424; television and, 248
epithets, 9
equipment, 93
Esan, Oluyinka, 241
ethnicity, 28, 420–21, 452n7
everyday life, 8, 15, 18
Everyman (medieval morality play), 35, 449n27
ewì chants, 72, 83, 233, 268
example, 15, 224, 304; of behavior, 282–83; characters' functions as, 372, 398; concreteness of, 427–28; drawn from experience, 304, 427; of moral action, 302–303, 427; moral example, 220–21, 223; theatre as discourse of, 425; Yorùbá as example of humanity, 420–21
experience, 10, 12, 361, 426–27; endurance and, 138, 143; moral precepts and, 220; narratives and, 133; proverbs and, 267

External Appearances (play), 57, 119, 125, 170; agency and interiority in, 361, 362–65, 370–71; Christianity in, 314–15; lesson of, 236; linguistic style in, 410–16; oral genres in, 343; plot structure of, 134; power in, 292; religion in, 328–29; slot roles in, 149–50; synopsis of, 439; theme of, 134; use of microphones in, 230–31

fààfáá (whirling mat), 226
Fágbáyìímú, Sunday, 72, 78, 82–84
Fagunwa, D. O., 310, 327
Fákúnlé Hall (Òṣogbo), 66
false consciousness, 8
family life, representation of, 270–74, 274–76, 277–81, 279
farce, 206
farmers, 54, 86
Fàtàí, Bàbáa, 111, 250–51, 252, 253
Fátómilọ́lá, Peter, 338
FESTAC 1977 celebrations, 54
Fìdítù Social Club, 123
films, 6, 57–59, 60, 112–13, 131, 258–60
fire regulations, 97
Foájìyọ̀. See *Overreacher, The* (play)
folding screens, 95
folk dances, 28, 33
folkloric plays, 148, 290, 332, 375, 394
folktales, 132, 144
formalism, 9
Fortunate Arabic and Quran School, 28
friendships, 285–86, 329
Fuji Explosion (video and album), 264, 337
Fuji Extravaganza (video), 264
fújì music, 4, 54
"full-length plays," 126, 128

G. B. Ollivant company, 21, 38, 448n4
Gambia, 21
Gbangbá D'Ẹkùn. See *Secret Is Out, The* (play)
Gẹ̀lẹ̀dẹ́ masquerade, 225
gender, 14, 269, 289, 423; of audiences, 204–205, 206; as ideological problem, 282
generative materialism, 7, 8, 422–26
genius, 9
genres, 4, 7, 11; African American, 29; autonomy/interiority in, 359–61; documentary, 263; *ẹkún ìyàwó* (bride's lament), 415; in formation, 61; history of, 18, 19; imported, 241; limits and possibilities of, 133; migration and, 23; moral lessons and, 268; nationalism and, 26, oral, 16, 341–47; precolonial, 352; production of new genres, 433; public morality and, 420; speech and, 202; verisimilitude and, 13; of video dramas, 261
Ghana, 21, 22, 63; concert parties in, 228, 293, 357, 453(9)n1, 457n18; migration to, 64, 76, 283; references to in plays, 279–80; television audiences in, 433
Glover Memorial Hall (Lagos), 27, 28, 30, 34
Goldmann, Lucien, 7
Gospel Fruit in Oshogbo, The (native air opera), 35, 50, 321–26, 327; enlightenment theme in, 42–43; speech improvisation in, 44; synopsis of, 435–36
"Grand Native and Arabic Entertainment," 28
Guyer, Jane, 351, 428, 431

Habermas, Jürgen, 227, 235
Hannah's Trial and Triumph (play), 35, 41, 42, 44, 417; biblical text and, 36–38; opening glee of, 36–37, 57; synopsis of, 435
Hausa language, 5, 110, 139, 194
Hausa people, 39, 433
Haynes, Jonathan, 260
Heilbrun, Carolyn, 429
Heir, The (play), 99, 140–42, *141*, *142*, 282; actors' name recognition and, 143; balance in, 171; household in, 272–74, 274–76, 277–81, *279*; monologue in, 150; synopsis of, 440
hierarchy, 293
highlife music, 208
highway robbery, 127
Hindi films, 5
Hometown Unions, 27, 28
hotel rooms, 127–28
Hymes, Dell, 267

Ìbàdàn (city), 40, 48, 59, 76, 112; KS Motel, 183, 184, 188; Olúbàdàn Stadium, 102, 231; as setting for video dramas, 261; television viewing in, 242
Ibi Ayé Ń lọ. See *Where the World Is Going* (video drama)
Ibibio States Association, 28
ideology, 7, 8, 11
idioms, 401, 412, 416
Ifá poetry, 26, 308, 341, 418
Ìgbà lódé [*Modern Times*] (television serial), 142
Igbo language, 261
Igbo people, 131, 421
ìjálá chants, 343, 414
"Ijesha, Baba" (popular comedian), 262
Ìlá, Fẹ́mi. See Adéníjì, Fẹ́mi

Ilé-ìwòsàn [Hospital] (television series), 6, 248–55
Ilé tí a fi itọ́ mọ (literary drama), 132, 133
immigrants, 38, 39
improvisation, 9, 10, 14, 17, 50; as foundation of theatrical production, 422; gains and losses from, 187; narrative coherence and, 171; of speech, 19, 44, 172, 202, 357
incantations. *See* ofọ̀ (incantations)
individualism/individuality, 10, 13, 358, 359–61
industrial development/production, 24, 40
Inland Club of Adó-Èkìtì, 47
Inner Circle Club (Agbámú), 233
innovations, 9
intelligentsia, 3, 204
interiority, 359–61
interludes, 233
intermediate ("in-between") social level, 2, 4, 69, 433; acquisition of culture, 311–12; sense of lack and, 335. *See also* middle classes
intertextuality, 134, 417
Inú Re [*Generosity*] (video drama), 340
Ìpadàbọ̀ Odùduwà. *See Return of Odùduwà, The* (play)
irony, 10
Isiaka (actor), 72, 78; conflict with family, 243–44; education of, 79; lighting and, 99; manual trades and, 86
Islam, 20, 22, 25, 38, 405; conversion to, 312–13; modernizing, 26, 28; Muslim actors, 78; Muslim girls and fashion, 63; Muslim relations with Christians, 326–29, 339–40, 424; on punishment and forgiveness, 184; Qur'anic schools, 307, 455n4; television and, 258; tradition and, 314; Yorùbá cultural nationalism and, 316
Islamic Native Air Opera, 27
Ìṣọ̀lá Ògúnṣọlá Theatre, 113, 114, 252
Issele Union, 28
Ìtójúu Kúnlé. *See Taking Care of Kúnlé* (play)
Ìwà Lẹ̀sìn (television series), 258, 340
Ìyá Aládùúrà [*Woman Aládùúrà Preacher*] (play), 134

Jaguar Jokers, 352
Jáiyésinmi (film), 57
Jeyifo, 'Biọdun, 6, 152–53, 229
Joseph, Moses, 72, 79, 85
jùjú (magic), 105, 107, 111, 208; anger and, 222; compared to Western medicine, 332; denunciation of, 457n18; European doctors and, 183; prohibition of, 313; as subject of plays, 327–28, 331, 332; as subject of video dramas, 261
jùjú music, 1, 4, 22, 26, 44, 54

Ká Róhun Wí [*For the Sake of Saying Something*] (video drama), 262, 340
King, Túndé, 26–27
King Solomon (Ògúnǹdé), 35
Kingsley ("short-stay" actor), 74, 139
Kọ́ọ̀tù Aṣípa. *See Magistrate's Court* (television series)
KS Motel (Ìbàdàn), 116, 118, 123, 126; *Besotted Bridegroom* performed at, 183, 184, 188, 205; *External Appearances* performed at, 119
Kúyẹ̀ (play), 56, 127, 145, 317, 428–29; *Atọ́ka* magazine version, 375; audiences for, 206; costumes for, 99; magical theme in, 134; number of roles in, 144; plot structure of, 135; polygamy in, 285; potentiality in, 432; power in, 290, 292; realism and, 353–56, 354; self-realization in, 372, 373–79, 379–82, 382–83, 384, 385, 386–87, 388; songs in, 51, 57; synopsis of, 436–37; television version, 49

labor, division of, 93, 95–97, 99–102, 144
Ládiípọ̀, Dúró, 33, 40, 44, 324, 343; oral traditions and, 400; pre-theater job of, 77; public regard of, 204; reputation of, 64; style of, 55
Ládiípọ̀, Ojó, 110
Lagos (city), 19, 112, 124; cultural production in, 25–33; elite of, 424; family life in, 277; in 1940s, 22–25; as setting for video dramas, 261; theater in, 40. *See also* National Theatre (Lagos)
Lagos Players, 27, 28, 33
Lagos Progressive Literary Society, 27
language(s), 3, 4, 172, 399–421. *See also* specific languages
Lániyọnu (play), 49, 70, 71, 99, 233, 428; art of language in, 401–404; artisanship in, 349–50, 352; balance in, 171; number of roles in, 144; opening glee, 319; plot structure of, 135; potentiality in, 432; power in, 290; self-realization in, 372, 373, 393–97, 398; slot roles in, 148; synopsis of, 437; theme of, 133; traditional culture in, 327–28
Lároò-oyè, 21
Latin America, 3
Látọ̀nà, Grace Ọwọ́adé. *See* Adéjọbí, Grace
Látọ̀nà II (Ọba), 39

Index

laughter, of audiences, 207, 208, 209, 347, 423
Lefebvre, Henri, 8, 11, 422
lessons, moral, 2, 3, 5, 423, 425; audience activity in extracting, 5, 204, 216–19; of *Besotted Bridegroom*, 173, 174; expansion of, 232; of *External Appearances*, 236; in Ghanaian television drama, 433; of *Hospital*, 250, 253, 256; as kernel of plot, 417; of *Kúyẹ̀*, 373, 385, 388; of *Laniyonu*, 373; of *Olówólaiyémọ̀* (novel), 427; of *The Overreacher*, 301–302; range of interpretations of, 221–25; in relation to example, 427; in relation to language, 417; in relation to lifelike detail, 267; of *The Road to Riches*, 373; of *The Royal Palm-nut*, 219–20, 299–300; of video dramas, 264
"Life of Gbajabiamila, The," 27
lighting, 49, 93, 99, *100*, 232, 351
Lijadu, E. M., 308
literacy, 3, 14, 347; in Arabic, 307, 455n4; artisanal approach and, 131; Church of the Lord and, 31–32; employment prospects and, 306; in English, 309; enlightenment and, 25; rates of, 23; theater company's operations and, 89; virtual, 316–17, 319–21, 341; in Yorùbá, 308, 309
literature, sociology of, 7, 427
Love, Adé, 112, 113
Lukács, Georg, 7

Macherey, Pierre, 7
Mackay, Rev. John, 42
Magistrate's Court (television series), 49, 129, 143, 243, 246
Margaret (Ìyáa Gbádébọ̀) (second wife of Oyin), 65, 66, 76, 78, 104; ambitions outside theater, 284; on "being known," 238; on drumming, 100; education of, 79; on favorite parts, 139; in *The Heir*, 279; in opening glees, 106; pride as performer, 143–44; in *Taking Care of Kúnlé*, 210
marriage, 78, 358
Marxism, 7
masquerade theater, 225, 232, 336–37, 352, 424
men: audience response to plays, 217, 218, 220; friendships among, 285–87
metaphors, 406–407, 411
microphones, 99, 118–19, 172, 230–31
middle classes, 243, 261, 264, 338. *See also* intermediate ("in-between") social level

mimesis, 226
mimicry, 144, 239
misogyny, 3, 174
missionaries, 2, 20, 24, 42, 234; literacy and, 308; in native air operas, 321–26; personhood and, 360
Mo Ráwọ̀. See *External Appearances* (play)
modern schools, 64, 67, 75
modernity, 5, 13, 425; Christianity and, 344; fragmentation and, 368; Ghanaian concert parties and, 453(9)n1; inflections of, 234–39; reflexivity and, 457n18; religious conversion and, 312–13, 316; technology and, 61; television and, 247, 248; traditional culture and, 424; video dramas and, 338; witchcraft and, 371
modular composition, 153–62, 169, 171
money, 23, 49; corrupting effects of, 222; counterfeit, 134; proverb concerning, 238; trade without, 199; work and, 389–93, 397
monogamy, 21, 32, 133, 261; as enlightenment value, 283; ideal of, 332; middle class and, 243
monologues, 150–52, 192, 193
Morádékẹ́ (actress), 72, 78, 79; interview with, 76–77; as "outside wife," 282; in *Taking Care of Kúnlé*, 211
morality, 216–25, 266, 420–21, 425; of church and mosque, 221; conservative ideology and, 264; ecumenism and, 341; politics and, 293–305; television shows and, 256
morality plays, 35, 55
Morèmi (play), 11, 451n1
Mosebọ́látán (film), 259–60
Muhammad, Murtala, 294
Munz, Peter, 431
music, 23–24, 26, 30, 344
music hall tradition (English), 25, 236
Muslim Graduates Association, 122–23, 184, 186, 205
mythological plays, 2, 55, 258

Nagler, Michael, 419, 420
naira (Nigerian currency), 59, 241
narratives, 6, 7, 209, 267–68; as advice, 221; biblical, 30; chronotope of, 270; coherence of, 171; contextual, 51; as firsthand knowledge, 277–78; genres of, 16; inessential episodes and, 145; linear, 341; sources of, 131
National Party of Nigeria (NPN), 295
National Theatre (Lagos), 110, 111, 115, 122, 251; capacities of, 96; lighting

facilities of, 351; rise of professional theater and, 54; *Taking Care of Kúnlé* performed at, 206, 207–14, 216
native air operas, 16, 29, 35, 44; churches and, 30–31; traditional culture and, 321–26
Negro spirituals, 27
new historicism, 7
Niger Hotel (Ìlọrin), 119, 126, 127
Nigeria, 1, 13–14, 127, 262; artisanal enterprises in, 88; civil war in, 240; economic collapse (1980s), 59–60, 294, 336; elections in, 116, 120; ethnic groups of, 420–21, 452n7; independence (1960), 45, 294; map of Western, *94;* migration into, 22–23; military coups in, 129, 294; oil boom (1970s), 4, 15, 54, 59, 241, 372, 389; politics and public morality in, 293–305; polygamy in, 285; power of the state, 235, 423; social transformations in, 5, 20, 26; urbanization in, 234; western, 3, 4. *See also* Yorùbáland
"Nigeria Police Concert," 27
Nigerian Council for Culture and the Arts, 110, 122
Nigerian Railway Christmas Concert (1945), 29
nightclubs, 27

Ọba Kò So (play), 33, 324, 343, 400
Ọbá Mọ́rọ̀ (play), 44
Ọdéjìnmí, Abíọ́dún, 71–72, 78; education of, 79; on fellowship, 91; as lorry driver, 86; on mistakes, 137
Odùduwà Hall, 192, 194
Ọdúnjọ, J. F., 132, 317, 375
Ọ̀fà (city), 118, *119,* 126, 127
Ofiok Udino drama, 28
ọfọ̀ (incantations), 5, 6, 55, 149, 177; battles of, 336; in *Besotted Bridegroom,* 177, 179, 181, 184, 201; *egúngún* masquerade and, 344; on *Hospital,* 251; in *Ọba Kò So,* 324; in plot structure, 134; sparing use of, 342; war of, 181
Ògúnbè, Akin, 144
Ògúndélé, Wọlé, 262
Ògúndíjọ, Báyọ̀, 285
Ogunmọ́lá, Kọ́lá, 40, 44, 77; public regard of, 204; relationship with Oyin Adéjọbí, 285–86; in video drama, 338
Ògúnǹdé, Hubert, 3, 27, 29, 54, 227; Adéjọbí's contact with, 35; as director of dance troupe, 420–21; films of, 57, 112–13, 125, 258; as influence on Oyin Adéjọbí, 343; masquerade theater and, 225; native airs and, 30; political

plays and, 295; pre-theater jobs of, 77; as president of Association of Theatre Practitioners of Nigeria, 56; public regard of, 204; traditional dancing and, 33
Ògúnníran, Láolú, 255
Ògúnṣọlá, Ìṣọlá, 113, 114, 133
Òjó, Reuben (audience member), 217, 221, 427
Òkéléyẹ, Sàláwù (audience member), 220, 223, 224, 225
Oko Ìyàwó. See *Besotted Bridegroom* (play)
Ọládàpọ̀, Túnbọ̀sún, 83, 233, 294, 302, 418
Ọláìítán, Lásún, 72–73, 149–50, 287
Ọláìyá, Moses. See Sàlá, Bàbáa
ọlajú. *See* enlightenment
Ọlániyọnu (play). See *Lániyọnu* (play)
Olówólaiyẹ́mọ̀ (novel), 427, 431, 432
Olúbàdàn Stadium (Ìbàdàn), 102, 122, 231
Ọmọ Òkú Ọ̀run (novel), 132, 331
Ọ̀nà Ọlá. See *Road to Riches, The* (play)
Onímọlẹ̀, G. T., 30
Ọ̀ọ̀ni Girls' High School, 181, 191, 230, 345
open-air sets, *98*
opening glees, 33, 55, *58, 59,* 100; of *Besotted Bridegroom,* 345; costumes for, 96, 129; of *The Gospel Fruit in Oshogbo,* 50; of *Hannah's Trial and Triumph,* 37, 38; masquerade theater and, 225; Oyin Adéjọbí singing in, 289; politics in, 294; of *The Royal Palm-nut,* 329; theme of plays and, 57
oral traditions, 61, 317
Òrànmíyàn Theatre, 134
organic unity, 29
oríki chants (praise poetry), 6, 41, 227, 239, 418; audiences and, 226, 233; constitution of theater and, 341–47; cultural nationalism and, 26; in *The Gospel Fruit in Oshogbo,* 323; individuality in, 359–60; local knowledge and, 419; in *The Overreacher,* 406–407
òrìṣà worship, 265, 321, 324–25, 457n18
Orogún Adédigba (Adéjọbí). *See Adédigba's Co-wife* (play)
Òrókí Royal Theatre Party, 41, 42
Orphan Do Not Glance (play), 352–53
Oshogbo Artisan and Workers Union, 40
Oshogbo Progressive Union, 39, 40
Ọ̀ṣọgbo (city), 19, 20–21, 112, 124; actors as natives of, 270; actors from, 78; Adéjọbí's return to, 36, 38–40; *Besotted Bridegroom* performed in, 185; Fákúnlé Hall, 66; missionaries in, 321; population of, 271; rehearsals in, 128
Overreacher, The (play), 70, 108, 139, 142, 230, 231–32; aphorisms in, 419; filling

out of roles in, 162–66; linguistic style and, 404–10, 412; monologue in, 150; number of roles in, 144; politics in, 300–302, *303;* polygamy in, 285; slot roles in, 148; stage space and, 229–30; synopsis of, 439–40
Oyèésíkù, Ayọ̀, 23
Oyèéwọ̀, Kọ́lá, 262
Oyin Adéjọbí Theatre, 32, 56–59, 70; artisan trades and, 349–50; business arrangements of, 121–30; decline of (1988–), 59–61; early members of, 62; ecumenical "editing" and, 326–41; efflorescence of (1963–1988), 45–59; as example of Yorùbá theater, 6; films and, 112–13; foundational phase (1948–1962), 20–44; getting shows on the road, 93–130; history of, 16, 19–20; households and localities of, 270–74, *274–76,* 277–81, *279;* literacy and, 317, 319–21; modern self and, 13; oral genres and, 341; performance scheme of, 227–28; popular taste and, 207; as professional theater, 319, 424; real and represented worlds, 265–66; schooling and, 311; set pieces and, 161; state institutions and, 293–305; video dramas of, 264
Ọ̀yọ́ State Television Service, 257

paganism (traditional beliefs), 22, 43, 262, 311; gods of, 314, 414; masquerade and, 337; moral ecumenism and, 424; religious conversion and, 313, 321–26; representation of, 328
pageants, 29–30, 449n22
Pàimọ́, Lérè, 65, 134, 262
pantomime, 206
parades, 50, *102,* 120, 128, 174
Paradise Lost (Adéjọbí), 35
parlor parties, 26–27
patriarchy, 20, 21, 89, 419
patronage, 20, 26, 31
Peel, J. D. Y., 217
"people's" theater, 3–4
performance, 12, 15, 28, 96, 123–24, 338
persons, emergence of, 12–17
Phillips, Charles (pastor), 77
picture-frame stage, 9, 99
pidgin, 31
platform stages, 122, 231
plays: filling out of, 162–71, 172–203, 422; generation of, 6–12, 14, 131–71, 266; getting ideas for, 131–35; moral lessons of, 204, 216–25; as period pieces, 372; popularity of, 397; production of, 14; quotation from, 16; slots and set pieces, 144–62; synopses of, 435–42; writing out, 135–44. *See also specific titles of plays*
plots, 16, 132–33; double plots in folk tales, 385; narratives and, 51; number of actors and, 144–45; space/time disciplines and, 236; well-structured, 37
poetry, 4, 26, 72, 83, 302. *See also specific styles of poetry*
police, 97, 123, 351, 401
politics, 3, 4, 147–48, 269, 293–305
polygamy (polygyny), 261, 262, 268, 283; Adéjọbí's wives, 65; family tradition of, 21; religion and, 313; as slur, 283
posters (advertisements), 50, 70, 88, 99; cost of, 116, 125; lack of, 174; literacy and, 319; student help with, 123, 126
potentiality, 8–10, 388, 398, 430–31, 434
power, 56, 289–93, 312, 404
praise poetry. *See oríkì* chants
production, 4, 5, 24; actors in production process, 87; artisanal, 6, 7, 39–40, 433; conditions of, 15; costs of, 129; cultural, 25–33, 432; import substitution and, 45; industrial, 24, 40; Marxist analysis of, 7; signification and, 12
professional performance, 29, 32, 54
progress, 14, 42, 57, 148, 312, 325
props, 93, 99
proscenium, 229
proverbs, 9, 26, 200, 210, 310; audience response and, 223; cultural nationalism and, 308; didactic discourse and, 418; in *External Appearances,* 411; in *Kúyẹ̀,* 378; in *Lániyọnu,* 402–403; on money and prestige, 238; moral wisdom and, 267; *oríkì* chants and, 341; in *The Overreacher,* 405–407, 419, 431; in *The Road to Riches,* 392; on the unknowable interior, 369
public: audience as, 294; and cultural knowledge, 419; emergence and constitution of, 12–17, 423; inclusive character of, 341; as linguistic constituency, 417; as moral constituency, 417–19; television audience as, 243–44; theatre audience as, 225–36
public sphere, 227, 228

Qur'anic schools, 307, 455n4

radio, 27, 41, 50, 57, 129, 433
Radio Nigeria, 34, 61, 449n26
ragtime, 27
Reading Circles, 25
realism, 15, 61, 352–59; European, 356–58, 361, 398; television and, 247–48

Recreation Club Garden (Òṣogbo), 44
reflexivity, 269, 337, 457n18
rehearsal, 88, 128, 137; absence of, 150; for television drama, 248, 251
religion. *See* Christianity; Islam; paganism
repertoires, 10–11, 144, 239, 426; aphorisms and, 420; biblical, 327; open tradition and, 203; shared idiom of performers/audiences, 210; treacherous women, 281
repetition, 196–97, 346, 347
representation, mode of, 266
Return of Odùduwà, The (play), 56, 131, 258, 429
Rise of the English Novel, The (Watt), 266
Road to Riches, The (play), 57, 134, 139, 428–29; actors' name recognition and, 143; monologues in, 150–52; plot structure of, 135; power in, 290–91; self-realization in, 372, 373, 388–93, *391*, 397, 398; synopsis of, 441
"Royal Jester, A" (operetta), 27
Royal Palm-nut, The (play), 56, 57, 72, 99, 429; changes in plot of, 166–70; lesson of, 219–20; male friendship in, 287–88; number of roles in, 144; *oríkì* chants in, 342; plot structure of, 134–35; politics in, 299; power in, 290; religion in, 329–30; slot roles in, 148; source of, 132; stage space and, 228–29; sung and spoken text in, 51–54; synopsis of, 437–38; television version, 49; writing of, 135–36
Ruth (audience member), 217–18

sacrifice, theme of, 327, 394, 414
Sàlá, Bàbáa, 54, 55, 112–13, 258; as actor, 260, 262; films of, 259–60
Ṣálánkó. *See* Adéníjì, Fẹ́mi
salaries, 90, 129, 130
Samson Alágbára [*Samson the Strong*] (play), 66
Saro elite, 25–26
Saros (repatriated slaves), 22
scenery, 49, 93, 122, 228; dismantling of, 127; sponsors' help with, 233
schools, 306–12, 335, 455n4. *See also* education
screens, 231
Secret Is Out, The (play), 132, 317, *318;* Aládùúrà preacher in, 134; conjugal partnership theme in, 288; synopsis of, 441
self-realization, 14, 18, 80, 89, 130; changing ideas of, 425; enlightenment and, 344; plot structure and, 135; potentiality and, 372–79, *379–82*, 382–83, *384*, 385, *386–87*, 388–98; self-making and, 348

seniority, 100
set pieces (monologues), 150–59, 161, 194
Seventh-Day Adventists, 69
Sierra Leone, 21, 22
silence, use of, 111
similes, 406–407, 411
slaves, 22
slots, system of, 148–50
social clubs, 2, 47, 54, 122, 123
Société Commerciale de L'Ouest Africain (SCOA), 38–39
songs, 32, 33–34, 48, 289, 324, 342
"Songs from the Plantations," 29
sound equipment, 49
sound system, 97, 99, *101*
specialists, 88, 93, 99
speech: colloquial, 44; improvisation of, 19, 44, 172, 202, 357; seeds of, 188–201, 210
sponsors, 88, 123, 233
spontaneity, 17
stage: backstage, 226, 232; equipment, 95; picture-frame, 9, 99; platform, 122, 231; proscenium, 229; stage space, 228
stage space, 228
"stars," 93
stereotypes, 281, 285, 453(9)n1
storytelling, 2, 136
structuralism, 9, 427, 430
synopses, 43, 44

Taking Care of Kúnlé (play), 110–11, 113, 142, *160, 162,* 317; actors' input into, 138; audience response to, 207–14, 210, 211, 212, 215, 216; audiences for, 206; balance in, 171; building of excitement in, 346; clinic scene, *149;* costumes in, 99; household in, 271–72; lesson of, 173; modular composition in, 153–59; monologue in, 150; opening scene, 210; slot roles in, 148–49; source of, 132; synopsis of, 438; Yorùbá text from, 443–46
technology, 241, 247, 260
television, 16, 50, 54, 57, 433; communal viewing of, 5–6; documentary, 263; Ìlọrin, 126; as medium of technocrats, 423; new stations, 61; pay for actors and, 129; reasons for being on, 242–48; story synopses for, 136; theater's invasion of, 255–58; theatrical drama on, 48–50, 128; in western Nigeria, 48, 240–42
texts, 7, 12, 15
textuality, 202, 420
theater(s): amateur, 40–44; "clerkly" model of organization, 87, 89, 91; decline of, 59–61; fellowship and, 90–91; manag-

ers of, 40; oral genres and founding of, 341–47; professional, 45–56; road trips, 102–30; school leavers and, 19; television and, 245, 246–47; traveling, 12–13. *See also specific theaters*
thrillers, 55
Ti Olúwa Nilẹ̀ [*The Land Belongs to God*] (video drama), 262, 340
tickets, 123–24, 129, 227
timing, 111
touring/traveling, 93–130, 422
"town" audiences, 122, 124, 204–205, *205*, *206*
"tribal" dances, 27, 28, 29
"tribal" unions, 26

unions, 40
United Africa Company, 38
Unity Party of Nigeria (UPN), 295
universities, 3
urbanization, 5, 234

variety shows, 29, 36, 346
vehicles, 93, 129
video dramas, 6, 16, 33, 258, *263*; ideology and, 262–64; inclusiveness and disaggregation in, 60, 335–41; inner state of mind in, 370; market in, 260–62; replacement of live drama with, 15, 424
Voloshinov, V. N., 420–21, 653–54

Watt, Ian, 266
wealth, 134, 312, 392; acquisition of, 56, 224; mysteriousness of, 395; productive, 393; social standing and, 207. *See also* money
Wesleyan Hall (Ìjẹ̀bú-Òde), 206
Western Nigeria Television Service, 48, 240
Where the World Is Going (video drama), 262, 336–40, 442
witches, 366, 367, 369
wives, 174, 270; conjugal partnership and, 287–88; faithfulness of, 329; junior and senior, 192, 193, 217–18, 268, 284; of Oyin Adéjọbí, 282, 283

women, 26, 38, 41, 282–83; actresses, 45, 65, 75–76, 78; as audience members, 217–18, 222; brides, 415; emancipation of, 313–14; female stage roles, 36, 133; insubordinate, 56; market women, 235; marriage and, 132; moral lessons of plays and, 219–20; stereotypes of, 285; theater companies run by, 447(2)n1; treacherous, 173, 178, 222, 264, 281
workers, 54, 86, 234

Yẹmisí (fifth wife of Oyin), 65, 66–67, 76; education of, 79, 81; on learning parts, 144; letter of application to theater, 89
Yorùbá language, 2, 4, 13, 182; alphabet, 323; aphorisms and, 416–21; churches and, 26; conscious art of language, 399–404; creative control of, 14; English loan words in, 210, 410–11; English words in phonology of, 194; films and videos in, 57–59, 258, 261, 338; in Hausa accent, 139; literacy in, 308, 309; literature (novels) in, 7, 54, 84, 132, 310, 360–61, 375, 424; mixed with English, 31; music in, 30; poetry in, 310, 424; rare expression in, 187; television programming in, 5–6, 48, 243, 245; text in, 16
Yorùbá people, 22, 131–32, 267–68, 420–21, 461n5
Yorùbá theater: audiences of, 204; colonial era origins of, 266; generation of plays, 6–12; history of, 6; masquerade, 225–27; popular production, 1–6; stage space and, 229
Yorùbáland, 14, 64, 70; autonomy as value in, 293; history of the self in, 362; landscape of, 117; mission schools in, 306; religion in, 455n4; tours of, 124. *See also* Nigeria
Young Ansar-ud-Deen Society, 27, 28
youth, appeal to, 55

Zamratul Islamiyyah Education Fund, 27
Zulu people, 433

Karin Barber teaches at the Centre of West African Studies at the University of Birmingham, England. She is editor of *Readings in African Popular Culture* and co-author (with John Collins and Alain Ricard) of *West African Popular Theatre*.